A HISTORY OF
NEW ZEALAND
WOMEN

Whenua/Wahine/Whenua (Land/Women/Land), 1989, by Kura Te Waru Rewiri (Ngāti Kahu, Ngāti Rangi)
Auckland Art Gallery Toi o Tāmaki, purchased 1989

A HISTORY OF NEW ZEALAND WOMEN

BARBARA BROOKES

BRIDGET WILLIAMS BOOKS

In memory of my sister, Deirdre Wilson, 12.2.1944 – 24.9.2015

A History of New Zealand Women: first published in 2016 by Bridget Williams Books Ltd,
PO Box 12474, Wellington 6144, New Zealand. Reprinted 2016.
www.bwb.co.nz.

ISBN 9780908321452 (Paperback), ISBN 9780908321469 (EPUB)
ISBN 9780908321476 (KINDLE), ISBN 9780908321483 (PDF)
ISTC A0220130000061A1
DOI http://dx.doi.org/10.7810/9780908321452

Acknowledgements: The support of the BWB Publishing Trust is integral to all books produced
by BWB, and the publishers gratefully acknowledge this support. The publication of *A History of
New Zealand Women* has been enabled by grants from the Humanities Division of the University
of Otago, by the New Zealand History Research Trust at the Ministry for Culture and Heritage,
by the Stout Trust (with the Friends of the Turnbull Library), and by Creative New Zealand.
This support is also gratefully acknowledged. The author would like to acknowledge the value of
the Hodge Fellowship in freeing her time for research and writing.

ARTS COUNCIL OF NEW ZEALAND TOI AOTEAROA

Images: The images included in this book have been reproduced with permission from the
individuals and organisations credited in the captions. No further reproduction or copies may
be made of these images without prior written permission of the owners or copyright holders
credited. Further information is provided in the Editorial Note.

Front cover: *Early Spring*, 2004, by Star Gossage. Chandra Family Trust, Auckland. With
permission of the artist.

A catalogue record for this book is available from the National Library of New Zealand.
Kei te pātengi raraunga o Te Puna Mātauranga o Aotearoa te whakarārangi o tēnei pukapuka.

Edited by Jane Parkin
Cover and internal design by Neil Pardington at Base Two
Typesetting by Tina Delceg
Printed by Midas, China

Contents

A reflective self-portrait by mid-twentieth-century artist Olivia Spencer Bower. *Christchurch Art Gallery Te Puna o Waiwhetu, purchased 1999, reproduced courtesy of the trustees of the Olivia Spencer Bower Foundation*

Introduction

In 1951, a thirty-five-year-old mother of three, named Hannah, heavily pregnant with her fourth child, embarked on a life-changing voyage with her husband and family. In coming to New Zealand to settle, Hannah hoped that her children would have a better, more secure future, far from the sectarianism of her native Ireland. Her first view of the seaside village that was to become her home was from high on the Port Hills, on the road over from Lyttelton Harbour. Once settled in Sumner, she never looked back.

My mother's life was very different from mine. She did not have the opportunity for a tertiary education, but had to leave school to go to work to help with the family economy. First she worked in a photographic studio in Dublin, colouring photographs; later she worked in the accounts department of Nichols department store. Soon the metal cylinders that whizzed along bringing cash and receipts to the accounts department began to carry notes from a young man who worked in the store's drapery department. That young man shared her Christian commitment, and my mother and he were married in 1939, when she was twenty-two. She had her first child two years later, at the age of twenty-four. When, a decade or so later, my father, Ernest, was offered the opportunity to come to New Zealand to work for his uncle, he left the decision to my mother. Her decision meant that I was destined to be born in New Zealand.

My mother had three sons and two daughters, and devoted herself to home and family. Once married, she never again had paid employment. Yet she was always busy. The church was at the centre of her social life, and she was engaged in a variety of church and community endeavours that she found immensely satisfying. I have three university degrees and three sons, and have been in continual paid employment since obtaining my first academic job in 1982. My commitment to work as an academic historian has shaped my life in such important ways that I cannot conceive of a life without it.

How do we understand such dramatic changes in women's lives over a generation? In the 1950s, my mother believed that the best thing for her was to be at home with her children, and my father's earnings, at a time of full employment and an ideal of a breadwinner's wage, enabled them to support the family of five children on one income. Born in 1955, I benefited from educational opportunities that eventually took me to university on a teaching studentship. Long-term factors – such as state initiatives in education and the erosion of the breadwinner wage – underpinned a raft of new ideas generated by feminism in the 1970s that encouraged me to be independent and academically ambitious. Effective contraception, in the form of the contraceptive pill, meant that I believed I could plan to have children at a time that suited me. That time came after I had completed my PhD and secured an academic job. I married at the age of thirty in 1986 and had my first child at thirty-three. The University of Otago Childcare Association made it possible for me to combine work and motherhood in a way unavailable to, and unimagined by, my mother.

Being born female or male has, for most of our history, determined life's trajectory. What that has meant has varied greatly over time. How, then, does it shift our angle of vision if we put women fully at the centre of the history of Aotearoa/New Zealand? In this book I suggest that beliefs about gender were central to both Māori and Pākehā worlds – but in very different ways – at their point of first encounter in the late eighteenth century. Those beliefs came into collision as Pākehā exploration, trade and settlement increased, reshaping both societies. Whereas Māori traced their descent from both their female and male ancestors, Europeans introduced a system in which women were defined in relation to men: as daughters, wives or mothers. Concepts of home, marriage and family brought by settlers were integral to the settler state, and impacted on the lives of Māori, sometimes violently. New patterns of imperial authority attempted to diminish the role of Māori women. At the same time, learned European men argued that the position of women within a society acted as an index of civilisation.

Each generation of women enacted remarkable change, shaping the creation of hapū, the settler colony, the imperial Dominion and the independent nation. Ana Hamu, a leading member of Ngāpuhi at Paihia, signed the Treaty of Waitangi on 6 February 1840. She had witnessed the arrival of the Church Missionary Society and gifted the land for the mission to be established at Paihia.[1] Less than a year earlier, Mary Bumby, accompanying her missionary brother to the Wesleyan Mission Station at Mangungu in March 1839, brought two hives of honey bees from Sydney, ensuring that the mission would be self-reliant in a resource that otherwise would have to be imported.[2] Through their actions, these women set in train significant social and ecological change. There were countless others like them; through text and images this book tells many of their stories to highlight the diversity of women's experience over time.

Raiha Kenehuru Meurant, for example, was well known to contemporaries in the mid-nineteenth century as arguments raged about the way her legal marriage to a European had deprived her of land rights which, if she had merely lived in concubinage with him, would have been preserved. Her story, recounted in the newspapers now accessible on *Paperspast*, and in government reports, has recently been highlighted by Angela Wanhalla in her history of interracial marriage in New Zealand.[3] Other women who provided vital roles within their local communities are less well known. Frances Haselden, who never married, put her considerable energies into running the Kauaeranga Girls' School in Thames for two decades. Her work, and that of other women in that community, has been recovered by Rosemary Killip in her study of women of the Thames goldfield, in a publication made possible by the 1993 Suffrage Centennial Trust.[4]

Actions were important in recasting society, but so too were ideas. By the 1870s, the position of women was up for debate in settler society. In the pages of the Auckland newspapers and in theatres, Mary Colclough, or 'Polly Plum', a 'firm and earnest woman's advocate', argued for the education of girls, equality of women and men before the law, and women's right to have guardianship of their children.[5] 'Polly Plum' outlined her view of the seemingly age-old problem of 'What Women Want'. She claimed that women should not be deterred from claiming their rights because of the novelty of their demand; there must be, she argued, 'a day of discovery for everything'.[6] Colclough pointed to the past: slavery, for example, had been discovered to be evil and done away with. A 'day of discovery', then, was one that shifted points of view: soon men would see that it was wrong to deny women the rights they had obtained for themselves.

Mary Colclough's prediction proved prescient. An all-male New Zealand Parliament finally 'discovered' that it was wrong to deny women the right to vote and, in consequence, enfranchised women on 19 September 1893. But enfranchisement did not lead to equality and, at various times over the twentieth century and into the twenty-first century, the rights of women had to be reconsidered. Did married women have the right to work during the Great Depression of the 1930s? When they worked, did women, whether married or single, have a right to equal pay? By 1960, the answer was yes in public-sector employment; it remained no in the private sector until 1972. Did women, when faced with an unplanned pregnancy, have a right to abortion? The 1970s answer was no. Was it possible for a husband to rape his wife? The 1985 answer was yes. Could a woman lead the country? Jenny Shipley and Helen Clark proved they could. What prevented women from serving in combat roles in the army? Nothing was the answer by 2007. In 2015, however, women are still routinely paid less than men, and the right to pay equity for female-dominated occupations is once again on the political agenda.

The rights of men, in contrast, were taken for granted. The dichotomy rested, for much of our history, on the intimate association between women and children. In the mid-nineteenth century, European wives and children were assumed to be under the protection of the husband or father: an assumption not shared by Māori, though increasingly foisted upon them by the introduced legal system. Fathers automatically assumed guardianship of their children, and a married woman's legal personhood was subsumed under that of her husband. Each step towards legal and financial independence for married women was subject to debate, since it apparently threatened the family – regarded as the key integrative institution of society. And in that family, women's role was primarily to tend to children and domestic matters. When parental leave was first introduced into the public sector in 1948, for example, it was entitled 'maternity leave'; only in 1987 did such leave become gender neutral.

That intimacy between women and children is well conveyed in Tahu Pōtiki, the wharenui at Te Rau Aroha Marae Bluff (opened in 2003), where remarkable, towering female ancestors hold close their offspring. Women dominate the space. Specific tūpuna were chosen by the local people to link the remembered past with the present. These ancestors are, according to the locals, 'the women who anchored the men': the embodiment of the ties of whānau.[7]

As the meeting house suggests, the history of women is at once large – a story of social transformation and settlement – and intimate – a story of personal relationships, affection, births and generational ties. Social transformations were recorded by Māori in oral traditions, and through the written word by early European explorers. Here Anne Salmond's work on Cook's expeditions has been essential. I draw on such sources in the opening chapter of the book to consider how expectations of women shaped social experience. This theme of transformation brought about by the gendered ideas of Europeans, gradually introduced into Māori society, continues throughout the book. Conventional signposts of New Zealand history, such as the Treaty of Waitangi, the World Wars, and the creation and dismantling of the welfare state, are used to orient the reader in the shifting political context in which women made choices about their futures. My aim has been to highlight the stories of individuals to reveal the texture of women's lives. I am greatly indebted to the biographies of women collected in five volumes of *The Dictionary of New Zealand Biography* and to those recorded in *The Book of New Zealand Women: Ko Kui Ma Te Kaupapa* (1991).[8]

Early chapters discuss the ways in which settler women saw great prospects for their children in a new country that offered possibilities of land ownership denied them in their places of origin. Many of them saw New Zealand as an unsettled land and were oblivious to the harm done to Māori by land sales. Wars in the North Island saw Māori women participating in the campaigns, whereas Europeans attempted to move women and children to safety. The discovery of gold in the South Island saw whānau engaged in exploiting this resource so coveted by Europeans, while the European gold-seeking communities were dominated by men, many of whom had left their families to seek their fortune. Essential sources for this period are Frances Porter and Charlotte Macdonald's *'My Hand Will Write What My Heart Dictates': The Unsettled Lives of Women in Nineteenth-century New Zealand as Revealed to Sisters, Family and Friends* (1996) and Angela Ballara's *Iwi: The Dynamics of Māori Tribal Organisation from c. 1769 to c. 1945.*[9]

Māori women saw their whānau shrink as the ravages of introduced diseases struck communities hard. The status of Māori women as landowners, however, was held up as an exemplar of a more advanced society by advocates of women's rights who welcomed the enactment of the Married Women's Property Act in 1884. This success encouraged a wider campaign for citizenship, fuelled in Pākehā communities by the temperance campaign. The enfranchisement of Māori men in effect disenfranchised Māori women, who had been active participants in their communities. Patricia Grimshaw's *Women's Suffrage in New Zealand* (1972), Tania Rei's *Maori Women and the Vote* (1993), Margaret Lovell-Smith's *The Woman Question: Writings by the Women Who Won the Vote* (1992) and Dorothy Page's *The Suffragists: Women Who Worked for the Vote* (1993) have been key texts analysing the suffrage campaign.[10] With the advent of women's suffrage in 1893, 'New Women' sought to set an agenda for a new century. Expectations of unity among women, however, were shattered by the advent of the First World War.

I have paid particular attention to competing trends in the interwar years – an emphasis on motherhood and the advent of the 'modern woman' – devoting two chapters to that era. A nation which experienced heavy losses in war saw fit to extol and promote Pākehā motherhood in a variety of ways, and government sources pointed to concerns about motherhood and the 'health' of the population, however that was interpreted. Māori mothers, in fact, had much larger families, giving rise to optimism about the future. Essential to gaining insight into the lives of Māori women are Michael King's *Whina: A Biography of Whina Cooper* (1983) and *Te Puea* (1987). Judith Binney and Gillian Chaplin's *Ngā Mōrehu: The Survivors* (1986) contains invaluable oral histories of Ringatū women.[11] An oral history of Pākehā women I have often revisited is the Society for Research on Women's *In Those Days: A Study of Older Women in Wellington* (1982).

'Modern women' – those who had greater education than their mothers and who expected to work in a variety of fields beyond the domestic – expressed new aspirations from the 1920s. Those aspirations were once again interrupted and reshaped by wartime experiences. Nancy Taylor's two-volume history, *The Home Front: New Zealand in the Second World War* (1986), and Deborah Montgomerie's *The Women's War: New Zealand Women 1939–45* (2001) are major sources for this period, supplemented by Eve Ebbett's popular survey *When the Boys were Away* (1984) and Lauris Edmond's oral history collection *Women in Wartime* (1986).[12] In the experience of war lay the seeds of important postwar campaigns, such as that for public service equal pay, charted by Margaret Corner's *No Easy Victory*.[13] A longer overview of the decline in the male breadwinner ideal can be found in Melanie Nolan's *Breadwinning: New Zealand Women and the State* (2000).

In contrast to the upheaval of war, the social stability experienced in the 1950s might appear bland, but the suburbs were alive with the boisterous children of the postwar baby boom whose needs challenged women to find creative solutions. Women's reproductive labour, I argue, has shaped New Zealand's demographic history and fashioned the lives of Māori and Pākehā women in particular ways. In her 2015 book *Panguru and the City: Kāinga Tahi, Kāinga Rua*, Melissa Williams charts the movement of Te Rarawa people to and from Auckland and their role in building new city institutions. Great voluntary labour was poured into households, into churches, and into new organisations such as Playcentre and Parents' Centre, founded in 1952. Helen May's *Minding Children, Managing Men* (1992) captures well some of the ambivalences of this period from a variety of perspectives, while Lauris Edmond's autobiography *Bonfires in the Rain* charts these family-centred years through the eyes of a talented writer.

I have titled the period 1967 to 1977 'Decade of Discovery'. This was when a new women's movement, often referred to as 'second wave' feminism, arose. With that movement's rediscovery of the wrongs done to women came a whole new language to describe them: sex-role stereotyping, sexism and sexual harassment became terms soon understood in everyday conversation. New heroines emerged, quite unlike Kate Sheppard: Australian Germaine Greer was one. Whina Cooper, who took centre stage nationally when in 1975 she led the Māori land march from the far north to Wellington, represented a very different type of heroine, and one who challenged Pākehā feminists to rethink their priorities. New fields of study such as Women's Studies and Māori Studies raised new questions about the intersections between sexism and racism. *Broadsheet* provides an important barometer for feminist issues, while the surveys carried out under the auspices of the Society for Research on Women and papers presented at the Women's Studies Association conferences explored women's everyday lives. The title of Christine Dann's exploration of women's liberation in New Zealand between 1970 and 1985, *Up from Under* (1985), suggests the trajectory feminists were aiming for.[14]

This trajectory of continual improvement in women's position came up against a faltering economy in the 1980s, just as women began to play larger roles in the 'corridors of power', the theme of Chapter 12. Janet McCallum's biographical sketches of politicians entitled *Women in the House* (1993) makes it possible to track the move of women into the political arena.[15] In a new era of government stringency, a Ministry of Women's Affairs sought innovative ways to make women's voices heard. The Ministry's reports provide a fascinating insight into the delicate balances required of working inside a system that many feminists wanted to change. Labour MP Fran Wilde demonstrated that significant change was possible in the political area by her success in shepherding through the decriminalisation of homosexuality in 1986.

Outside of government, feminist activists Sandra Coney and Phillida Bunkle raised important questions about women's rights under the health-care system – questions that eventually led to new code of patient rights. By the beginning of the 1990s, the Ministry of Women's Affairs was focused on celebrating a century since women's suffrage, planned for 1993. That year saw support for a number of publications which have been important sources for this history, most notably Anne Else's *Women Together: A History of Women's Organisations in New Zealand* and Sandra Coney's *Standing in the Sunshine: A History of New Zealand Women Since they Won the Vote*.[16] If enfranchisement in the late nineteenth century represented one dramatic break with the past, the movement of women into the workforce and children into daycare in the late twentieth century remade not only relationships but also New Zealand.

That remaking took on new forms in the 2000s as new possibilities and old problems arose in the digital world. My concluding chapter can only be speculative. The family, once seen as the bedrock of New Zealand society, has been rethought. It is no longer a heterosexual institution and is likely to be 'blended', whether through stepchildren or different ethnicities or both. Women make up an increasing proportion of the elderly – and women significantly outnumber men amongst those who care for them. The association between women and caring (and its consequent low pay) led to court action by rest home workers, and is now subject to a government inquiry. Once more the 'rights' of women – in this case, to be paid properly for important work – are subject to inquiry and debate.

The importance of caring work came home to me forcefully this year as I witnessed my sister being nursed with a critical illness. She regretted that she would not live to read this history. Her care and concern for me, and that of my immediate family, Paul, Jesse, Liam and Benedict, kept the meaning of the present in focus while being preoccupied with the past. Their support and the enthusiasm of numerous colleagues and friends has made this book possible. I want to thank all who have championed the enterprise of making women visible. Charlotte Macdonald and Margaret Tennant (with whom I edited two books on New Zealand women's history in 1986 and 2000) have been steadfast and invaluable companions on the journey of discovery. Their own work has provided constant inspiration. Dorothy Page and I jointly taught a fourth year Women's History paper in 1984, with the support of our Otago History colleagues. Charlotte Paul, Annabel Cooper, Bronwyn Dalley and Jane Malthus have always provided sounding boards for ideas.

Erik Olssen supervised my first research foray into the disreputable subject of abortion in 1976, and I have him and Andrée Lévesque to thank for encouraging me to go to the United States to pursue what was then the fledgling field of women's history. The work of scholars there, and in the London Feminist History Group, made the journey incredibly exciting. Closer to home, scholars in Australia, Patricia Grimshaw, Joy Damousi and Marilyn Lake, have provided generous feedback. Within New Zealand, I have profited from the flourishing of work in women's history evident in the plethora of theses and books referenced in the text. Some of that is by my colleague Angela Wanhalla, but others at Otago, Mark Seymour, Tony Ballantyne, John Stenhouse, Tom Brooking and Michael Stevens, have stimulated my ideas.

Most of all I have learned from the students who chose to pursue topics that grappled with aspects of women's past. This book is for them. Their lives will be very different from those of their parents. What it means to be a woman (or a man) in 2015 is very different from what it was in 1975, 1915 or 1815. Understanding patterns of experience, and why and how they evolved, may help illuminate profound changes in our society that are ongoing today.

Barbara Brookes
Dunedin, 2016

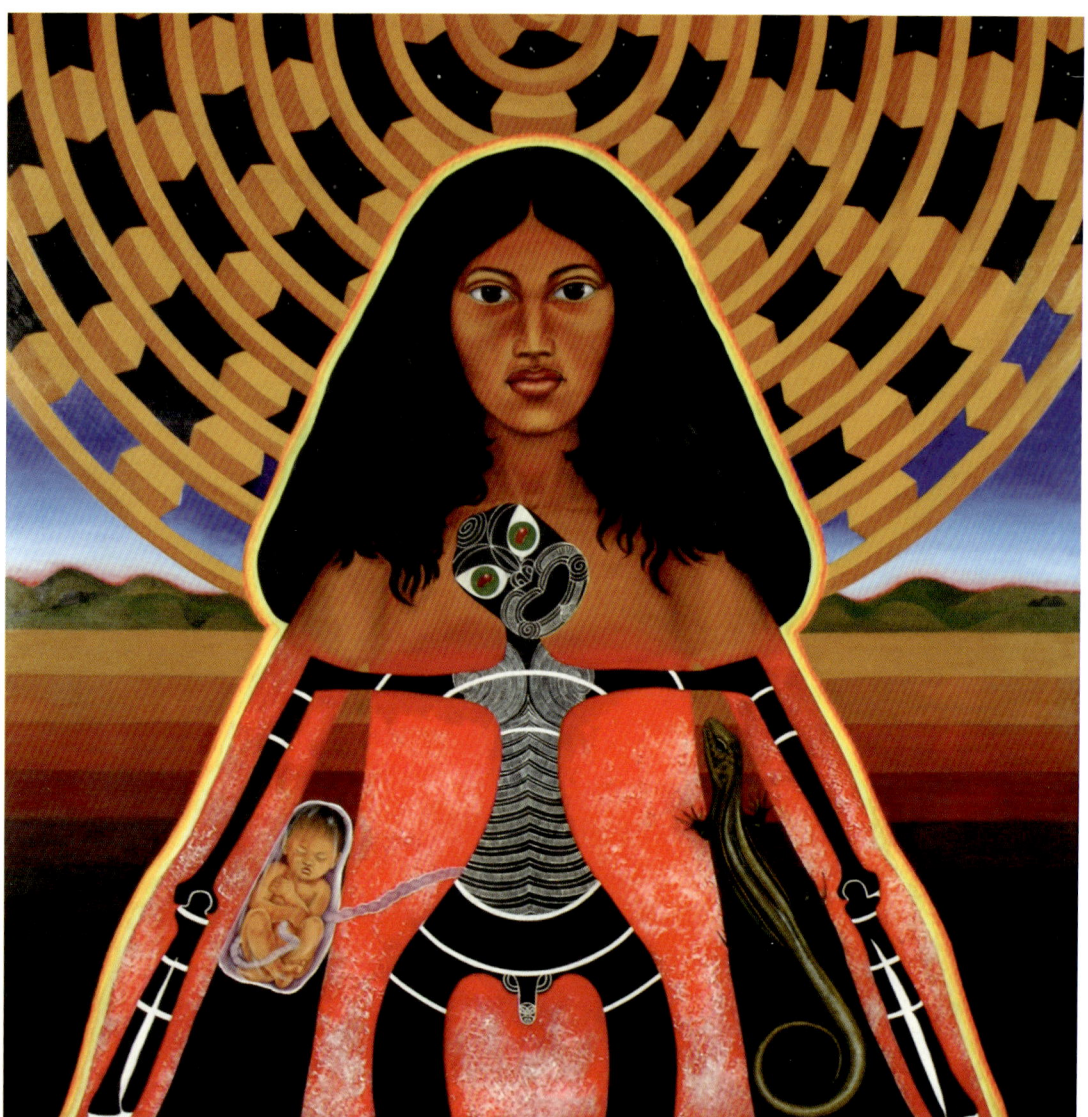

Hinetitama (1980) is one of eight works in the *Wahine Toa* series by Robyn Kahukiwa (Ngāti Porou), who sought to reinstate the centrality of women in Māori traditions. Hinetitama, daughter of Tane and Hineahuone, was the first human to be born of a woman. She became Hinenuitepo, the Goddess of Death, after discovering that her husband was also her father. The painting shows Hinetitama as she changes from a human to a goddess. *By Robyn Kahukiwa, collection of Te Manawa Art Society Inc., reproduced courtesy of Te Manawa Museums Trust*

Chapter One

Origins, Traditions and 'Civilisation'

New Zealand, tradition has it, was first named by a woman. Hineteaparangi, wife of Kupe, sighted land from the canoe *Matahorua* and cried out, 'He ao! He ao!' ('A cloud! A cloud!'). The Polynesian voyagers henceforth called the land Aotea (White Cloud), later lengthened to Aotearoa.[1] Hineteaparangi had in this way called into existence a country hitherto unknown – a place that would become home to successive generations of people.

The Polynesian settlers who came to the islands they named Te Ika-a-Māui (The Fish of Maui) and Te Waipounamu (The Waters of Greenstone) brought old stories into the new context of this place, stories that sustained the people's sense of the past, helped structure relations in the present and set codes of behaviour for the future. Just as in the naming tradition it was a woman who sighted Aotearoa, women conveyed history in composing, among other things, orori (lullabies) that taught children the particular history of their whānau and iwi.[2] Integral to these stories was a belief in the complementarity of woman and man, and how this shaped relations within the group.

The way cultures understood the origins of the world influenced their expectations of women and men. In one Māori creation story, woman is the first human created by the gods; in the Bible's book of Genesis, woman is an afterthought, created from Adam's rib. Stories like these provide perspectives from which to view the lives of women on the ground. Māori women of different hapū contributed to the material well-being and social significance of their communities in which whakapapa (genealogy), rather than gender, determined influence. In eighteenth-century Britain, by contrast, rule by inherited birth-right was breaking down with rapid economic change and the assertion of democratic rights of propertied men – which specifically excluded women. At the same time as their rights in the public sphere were being diminished, women's part in the creation of home and family was elevated above all other roles.

European explorers, whose initial interest in the uncharted lands of the South Pacific was scientific, took ideas about gender with them on their journeys to New Zealand and elsewhere. The treatment of women was one measure they used to determine the extent of the 'civilisation' of the societies they encountered. 'Savage' societies, from the European point of view, were thought to treat their women badly, while 'civilised' societies did not. Other groups of men who visited New Zealand, such as whalers and sealers, were less likely to be concerned with notions of civilisation than with seeking secure footholds in an alien land, whether through marriage or trade. Māori controlled the terms of engagement and Māori women, in particular, worked to integrate the newcomers into their ways.

Māori creation stories

In one version of a Māori creation story told by Nepia Pohuhu, a tohunga from the East Coast, the Earth Mother, Papa, laboured for eons to bring forth her offspring.[3] In time, two of her sons, Uepoto and Tane, escaped from the embrace of Papa and Rangi, the Sky Father, to the outside world, where it was dark and bitterly cold. Tane eventually persuaded his brothers to assist him in separating his parents so that light might come into the world, and this they achieved by brutally severing their parents' arms.[4] The birth of the offspring of Rangi and Papa was followed by the creation of vegetation and animals: first, minor vegetation, followed by trees of every kind, then reptiles and insects, higher animals, birds, the moon, sun and stars. Finally Tane's brother Uru asked: 'How are we to generate offspring to occupy the World of Light? Let us seek the female element that we may beget a race of beings to assume our forms, and so people the enduring world of light around us.'[5] After a long and unsuccessful search:

> Tane and his brethren then gathered at Kurawaka, which is the puke (mons veneris) of the earth Mother, and there formed an image composed of earth, a portion of the body of Papa, their mother. They made the figure so as to resemble themselves; the skeleton, head, body and limbs, all were similar, save the aroaro [genitals], which was adorned by the eye of Tiwhaia, plucked out for the purpose. Punaweko (personified form of birds) provided the hair as an adornment. It was then left for Tane to instil the breath of life into the nostrils, mouth, and ears of the lifeless figure. Then the human airlike breath came forth, the eyelids opened, the eyes gazed, the mouth gasped, a sneeze broke from the nostrils – a sneeze of life, of a living soul in this world, of a person, a female. Woman had entered the world![6]

The gods had created woman: the first human to exist on Earth. She was named Hineahuone.[7] With Tane, Hineahuone began the human race. Tane, in turn, mated with their first daughter, Hinetitama, and together they had a number of daughters. They lived happily until one day it became known to Hinetitama that her husband was also her father. Hinetitama fled in shame to become the goddess of death in the underworld, where she was renamed Hinenuitepo. She became the guardian of the souls of the dead, ensuring that the wairua or soul would not perish.[8]

The demi-god Maui, learning that man must die, declared that he would vanquish death so that man would be immortal. Maui decided that he would enter the body of

Hinenuitepo and destroy her by eating her heart. He turned himself into a type of grub and entered the womb of the sleeping goddess. But his bird companions, on seeing 'the parts of Hinenuitepo opened out', could not refrain from laughing. Hinenuitepo was roused 'and, feeling the squirming of the worm within her, she closed her parts, and strangled the neck of Maui, who was thus killed'.[9] Man remained mortal; woman, who had begun the new race, now denied it immortality.

Such stories of creation and death shaped the way different iwi understood the world, and the place of women and men within it. Language was infused with understandings of gender. 'Te whenua' related both to the land, which nourished the people, and the lining of the womb and the placenta, which nourished the foetus.[10] Descent groups were named in terms of the processes of childbirth. Hence, whānau, meaning birth, was also 'extended family', and hapū, meaning pregnant, was also the clan into which one was born.[11] Iwi, meaning bones and ancestors, was the connection to the wider and genealogically older social group, or tribe. Matua (parent), matua tāne (father) and whaea (mother) were not terms denoting specific individuals but rather relatives of a particular generation. Similarly, tama (son) and tamāhine (daughter) applied to relatives of the same generation.[12] Such conflation of the individual with the group suggests the importance given to communal relations. The whānau, hapū and iwi structures could take precedence over the individual. In a status society, mana, or authority, shaped all. Mana derived from proximity to high-ranking ancestors, and from personal conduct, and women as well as men could use their whakapapa to assert their authority.[13]

Women's tapu (sacredness) was said to exist because women provided 'the channel between the realm of the divine forces and the human realm'; the vagina was both the pathway to life and the source of death.[14] Manuka Henare interprets tapu as a state of being derived from the gods, whereas noa works as its opposite, to limit the spread of tapu: '[Women] are agents to whakanoa – to make noa. This is their tapu, and they are tohunga [expert practitioners] because of their own specific areas of activity.'[15] Menstrual blood was considered to be a particularly potent tapu substance – 'the unfinished stuff of which people are made' – so that women had to take particular care with their activities during menstruation.[16]

Women might be considered closely attuned to the supernatural world.[17] In this cosmology, the female element held 'dread powers of destruction' but also the virtue of nurturance.[18] Rangimarie Rose Pere suggests that women's association with noa is 'usually associated with warm, benevolent, life-giving, constructive influences including ceremonial purification'.[19] Hineahuone was shaped out of the soil of the Earth Mother who represented 'the receptive and passive element', while Tane, deliverer of the breath of life, represented 'the active, fertilising, creative male element'.[20] Both elements were essential to the creation of human life and the continuance of human society.

Māori creation stories presented models of powerful women: of a female element to be reckoned with. And women actively transmitted such stories through composing waiata (songs) that in turn carried traditions down the generations. Such histories informed the structuring of daily life in which whānaungatanga, or interrelationships and a sense of the connection of all living things through shared experiences, shaped actions in the past and continues to shape actions in the present.[21]

Women in Māori society

Before the Europeans came, Māori lived in a society shaped by status, where descent from high-ranking ancestors determined ritual authority. Such mana, however, did not automatically apply to leadership, where personal qualities of authority and courage were important. According to Maharaia Winiata, rangatira or leaders were usually male, although Elsdon Best noted that the word tapairu referred to high-ranking women and that Ngāti Kahungunu had the word māreikura for such women.[22] Concepts of mana derived from wisdom and skill could cut across ideas about gender, and served to mould social life. Winiata gives the example of the kuia, wife of the highest-ranking male member of the whānau, who could exert 'the real leadership and influence'.[23]

Women of spirit, independence and great beauty populate the iwi traditions passed down through generations and recorded later by Pākehā ethnographers. Those writers were themselves steeped in heroic narratives which provided the filter through which they heard Māori oral traditions. George Grey, for example, drew heavily on the narratives recounted by Ngāti Rangiwewehi scholar Wiremu Maihi Te Rangikaheke for his *Polynesian Mythology*, first published in 1855. The text records, among others, the story of Kahureremoa, who refused to marry the man her father chose, and instead undertook a long and hazardous journey from Hauraki to Tauranga to track down the chief of her choice, Takakopiri. From this marriage sprang the descent line of Ngāti Paoa rangatira. Grey also recorded the story of Hinemoa, 'a maiden of rare beauty, as well as high rank', who swam across Lake Rotorua to join her beloved Tutanekai on the island of Mokoia – thus outwitting her people in the village of Ōwhata, who had beached all the canoes in an effort to prevent her leaving.[24]

In a society dominated by competition among kin groups for resources, women, as prospective wives, could prevent loss of mana. Marriage offered a means of settling disputes with honour and of restricting bloodshed. Grey's account of Ngāti Awa's siege of the pā of the chief Rangirarunga serves as an example. Rangirarunga was the father of the renowned beauty Raumahora. Takarangi, the son of the invading Ngāti Awa chief, took pity on the besieged and ill Rangirarunga, thinking: 'That dying old man is the father of Raumahora, of that so lovely maid. Ah, how I should grieve if one so young and innocent should die tormented with the want of water.' As he brought the water, he looked avidly at the young girl, and his admiration was reciprocated. The old man then asked his

Symbolic figures featured in carving throughout Māori history; perhaps unusually, all three of the dancing figures on this pare (door lintel) from Te Āti Awa in Taranaki were female. *Canterbury Museum, 1868.16.1, photograph courtesy of the Auckland War Memorial Museum Tāmaki Paenga Hira*

daughter if she wished to have Takarangi for a husband, to which she replied, 'I like him.' 'Thence was that war brought to an end, and the army of Takarangi dispersed, and they returned each man to his own village, and they came back no more to make war against the tribes of Taranaki – for ever were ended their wars against them.'[25]

Marriage brought important alliances. Daughters of chiefs or women of high rank, known as puhi, were fiercely protected and given special privileges.[26] According to anthropologist Joan Metge, if a girl was betrothed in infancy (taumau), or she was the daughter of a chief, she was placed under tapu and expected to remain a virgin.[27] The marriage ceremony involved the exchange of gifts between the whānau of the couple, and might involve religious ritual to promote fertility. A different emphasis was placed on virginity among those of common birth, and individual preference might be paramount in the formation of relationships. If it was unclear whether elders would accept the preferred partnership, couples could seal their relationship by being found sleeping late together – a public declaration which might result in the woman's family descending upon the man's for muru (plunder). Muru, in effect, sanctioned the marriage by compensating the losers.[28]

Anthropologist Berys Heuer suggests that some types of marriage were rarely countenanced: those between first and second cousins, and between a chiefly woman and a low-born man. Chiefly men might take more than one wife, but the wife of highest rank took precedence, as did her children. Women captured in warfare might become slave-wives. Their low status did not necessarily mean ill-treatment, although they were expected to perform a range of menial, sometimes painful tasks.[29] They might, for example, be made to scrape flax and twist it with their long hair into ropes which were used to carry heavy loads on their backs.[30]

As daughters, wives and mothers, women could create bonds of community. When a high-ranking woman married outside her own hapū, she was bestowed with mana marae in her new dwelling place – 'that is, the authority to dispense hospitality to travellers on her own initiative'.[31] Bountiful hospitality created indebtedness and was an important contribution to the mana of the group.

Women and men often worked together in breaking up the land and planting crops, but the allocation of tasks varied according to tribal area. On the East Coast, for example, women were apparently not permitted to participate in kūmara planting.[32] Among Tūhoe, the privilege of trapping rats was given to women, while the men had rights to the toromiro trees on which birds were snared.[33] Women's labour in producing and preserving food such as rats, birds and fish, however, was essential to the group's survival through the seasons.

In most if not all iwi, weaving was women's particular speciality, and the mana of both the individual and the group was enhanced by skill in that art. A Ngāti Whakaue song goes as follows:

Ma wai e moe tane	Who would marry a man
Mangere ki te mahi kai?	Too lazy to prepare food
He ra to kai ki taua kiri – e!	The sun is food for his fat belly – eh!
Ma wai e moe te wahine	Who would marry the woman
Mangere ki te whatu pueru?	Too weary to do her weaving?
Ko Tongariro te kai ki taua kiri – e!	Tongariro's cloak will cover her – eh![34]

With the exception of the precious kahu kurī (dogskin cloaks), which were made by men, women were largely responsible for making the many kinds of cloaks worn by men and women alike.[35] Cloaks could be highly practical and coarse-woven to ward off rain, or highly symbolic of status, instilled with the mana of the owner.[36] Most prized were the kaitaka or parawai, finely woven flax cloaks with intricate tāniko designs on their borders. Kahu huruhuru, or feathered cloaks, became more valued during the nineteenth century.[37]

Women's land rights could be passed through the female line.[38] Relatives on both the mother's and the father's side were equally important for the transfer of traditional rights and precious goods. For example, stone patu, or pounders for beating flax fibre, were highly valued and handed down from one woman to another. Parents might gift eel weirs, berry trees and cultivations to their daughters. And if women were given use-rights on marriage, those remained their sole property – they did not become the property of their husbands. Any decisions regarding such property remained the woman's, and hers alone.[39]

While strategic marriages could enhance links, women could also be the source of trouble. 'He wahine, he whenua, engaro ai te tangata' ('For women and land are men destroyed'), as a traditional whakataukī puts it. The dangers of marrying outside the hapū were many: the resulting children could claim the land in two areas, which might lead to disputes. Loyalties were likely to be divided.[40] If conflicts did erupt, however, women were less likely to participate in war, and taua (war parties) were usually led by men. Women could play a vital role in securing a lasting peace, as Ngāti Porou elder Tuta Nihoniho explains: peace concluded by men involved 'treachery, deceit, trouble', but if women made the peace it would be 'a firm, durable one'.[41] Preservation of the tribe required that women, particularly during their childbearing years, be protected from death in war or from injury through dangerous tasks.[42] Another whakataukī puts it this way: 'He puta taua ki te tāne, he whānau tamariki ki te wahine' ('As warfare is to men, childbearing is to women').[43]

By the eighteenth century, according to Best, to be born male in Māori society meant to be trained as a warrior. Boy babies were dedicated 'to the service of Tu, the supreme and primal war god of the Maori'. They were taught to handle weapons and to undertake tasks that increased their 'courage, agility and strength'.[44] Men who were conquered and enslaved were excluded from such special tasks and expected to share the work of low-born women.[45] Rank rather than gender, then, may well have been the prime determinant of social roles in tribal society.

Wāhine rangatira, high-born women, debated matters of concern to their people and exercised their power through decisions made on behalf of the group. They could also command respect not only from their own iwi but also from others. Hinematioro, for example, was a leader of Ngāti Porou in Ūawa (Tolaga Bay) around the time of James Cook's visit in 1769. Her leadership was recognised from Poverty Bay to Hicks Bay. The missionary Thomas Kendall described her in 1815 as 'queen of a large district'.[46] When women such as Hinematioro, Tamairangi of Ngāti Ira or Mahinarangi of Ngāti Kahungunu travelled (often carried on a litter), 'villages off the line of march sent parties bearing presents of food supplies to await them on the path being traversed'.[47]

The varied roles of women in Māori society, from wāhine rangatira to slaves, from assisting war parties to making peace, suggest that gender roles were fluid and served the interests of the group above all. A person's place in that group was determined by descent, and rank might be claimed through the female line. Women led communities, they could make decisions about their property, and they could bring about peace. Such authority was not always understood by male observers who came from societies in which social structures served to limit the activities of women.

The Christian creation story

At the time of the Polynesian settlement of Aotearoa, a singular story of human origins dominated western Europe. According to the Christian story told in Genesis, one God created the world and then created man in His own image, and set him in the Garden of Eden. Woman was an afterthought. 'It is not good that man should be alone,' God said, 'I will make a helper fit for him.'[48] So woman was fashioned from the rib of Adam, the first man. Then Eve, succumbing to temptation by the serpent in the Garden, in turn tempted Adam to taste of the fruits of the tree of the knowledge of good and evil. For such disobedience, the couple's nakedness was revealed to them; they tried to hide from God, and were expelled from the Garden of Eden. Eve was the temptress, the seducer. She was the architect of the Fall, and had introduced sin to the world. Her punishment lay in suffering and subordination, in the pain of childbirth and in submission to men. God said to Eve: 'I will greatly multiply your pain in childbearing; in pain you shall bring forth children, yet your desire shall be for your husband, and he shall rule over you.'[49] Adam's punishment was to toil on the land, and both man and woman were made mortal: 'you are dust, and to dust you shall return'.[50]

The Christian story also offered a model of womanhood in the life of the Virgin Mary, the pure woman who gave birth to God's son and thus made possible the redemption of humankind. And this duality – of woman as either the temptress Eve, who served as a warning of women's weakness, or Mary, the embodiment of purity and motherhood – suggested models of behaviour to be rejected or emulated. The biblical stories of Rebekah, Hannah and Ruth served as further exemplars.[51] The beautiful Rebekah was chosen as the bride of Isaac, son of Abraham, after she showed kindness and hospitality to Abraham's servant. Hannah provided an example of a godly mother, who dedicated her first-born, Samuel, to the service of God because He had answered her prayers for a child. She went on to bear three sons and two daughters. Ruth's great love for and loyalty to her dead husband's mother was rewarded by her marriage to the wealthy Boaz.[52] Such stories emphasised the importance of putting service to others before self, and portrayed dedication to a husband and family as the highest achievement of a Christian woman. The Heavenly Father acted as the primary model for male authority, and masculine prerogative was enshrined in law.

Women in eighteenth-century English society

At the time of the departure from England of James Cook and his crew on the *Endeavour* in 1768, the singular biblical Christian story was being followed in a multitude of ways. Religion was no longer equated solely 'with a body of commandments, graven in stone, dispensed through Scripture, accepted on faith and policed by the Church'.[53] Advances in science were raising new questions about Biblical authority. But England was also undergoing an evangelical revival. Religious belief helped shore up the certainties of a nation shaken by the upheavals of the American and French revolutions of 1775 and 1789, respectively. Central to this revival was belief in the idea of the sanctity of the family, a belief deeply rooted in middle-class culture. A quickening of commerce and manufacturing, underpinned by a burgeoning population, heightened middle-class attachment to the moral values of the home, in which men were presumed to be shielded from the excesses of the amoral world of the market.[54] Economic expansion and new commercial developments exposed more individuals to wage labour and drew them from rural areas to the towns. 'Home', wrote John Player in a book-length poem dedicated to the topic, 'is the sacred refuge of our life.'[55] Within this 'sacred refuge', mothers were charged with the responsibility of educating their children.

This focus on the importance of the domestic role for women was signified by Lord Hardwicke's 1753 Marriage Act which, by prohibiting all forms of clandestine marriage, tightened control of the institution in the interests of preserving property. This legislation has since been described as 'a victory of patriarchy and capitalism' that reinforced the dependency of women.[56] In effect, the male line of inheritance had to be secured by ensuring women's fidelity in marriage. Dr Johnson put it bluntly: 'The chastity of women is of all importance, as all property depends on it.'[57] Even more bluntly, the legal existence of women, according to the jurist William Blackstone, was 'suspended during marriage'. Married women had no rights over their children or to matrimonial property.[58] As the Scottish surgeon William Alexander wrote in his two-volume *History of Women*, published in 1779:

> We allow a woman to sway our sceptre but by law and custom we debar her from every other government but that of her own family, as if there were not a public employment between that of superintending the kingdom, and the affairs of her own kitchen, which could be managed by the genius and capacity of women. We neither allow women to officiate at our altars, to debate in our councils, nor to fight for us in the field.[59]

In 1778, the year before Alexander's *History* appeared, and about the time the first European adventurers were exploring New Zealand, women were explicitly barred from listening to the debates in Britain's House of Commons, though they had done so from the gallery or the floor of the House from the early eighteenth century.[60] That same year, seventeen-year-old Mary Wollstonecraft left her unhappy family home in Spitalfields, London, and the tyranny of a violent and improvident father, to take up a post in Bath as a lady's companion to a widow – one of the few occupations open to impecunious lower-middle-class women. Her next, brief venture was to open a school with her sisters in a Dissenting community in London, before she found work as a governess – that overcrowded, poorly paid but genteel occupation for women of limited means – to the daughters of an Anglo-Irish family in Ireland. One year later, she took the radical decision to return to London to try to succeed as an author. In 1792, inspired by the events of the French Revolution, she wrote her most famous and forcefully argued book, *A Vindication of the Rights of Woman*.

Vindication sold around 3,000 copies and made Mary Wollstonecraft a well-known figure.[61] The excitement of women who felt she expressed their frustrations was palpable. 'I have seen Mary Wollstonecraft's book,' wrote one woman in Glasgow, 'which is [so] run after here, that there is no keeping it long enough to read leisurely.'[62] Wollstonecraft deplored the poor education and 'smattering of accomplishments' of women. She argued that women needed a 'moral stake' in civil society if they were to reach their potential. For women's virtues to work for the public good, women 'must have a civil existence in the state, married or single'.[63] 'To render women truly useful members of society,' she

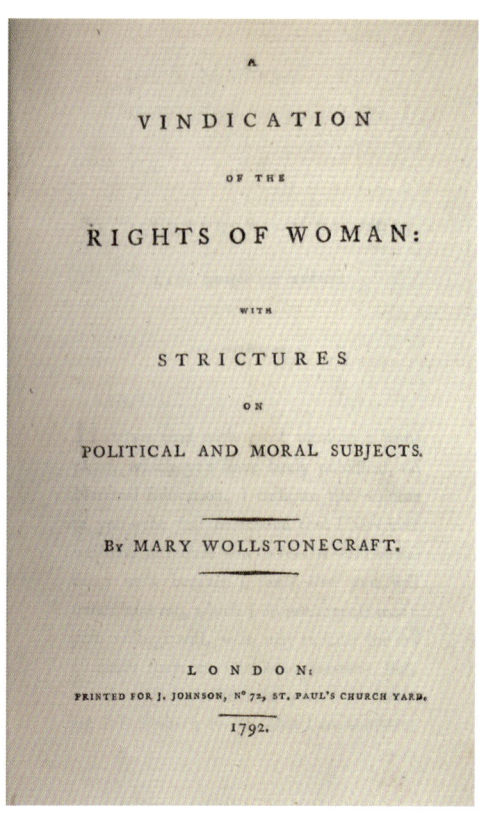

Feminist writer Mary Wollstonecraft was painted by John Opie in 1797. Five years earlier she had written the ground-breaking work *A Vindication of the Rights of Woman* (1792; title page, right), in which she argued that women should have the same rights and opportunities as men. When sitting for her portrait, she was pregnant, with her daughter Mary (later Mary Shelley). The baby's birth later that year cost Wollstonecraft her life. *National Portrait Gallery, London, oil on canvas by John Opie, NPG 1237; Alexander Turnbull Library, Wellington*

went on, it was necessary to have 'their understanding cultivated on a large scale'.[64] A 'revolution in female manners' would restore women's 'lost dignity' and prepare them 'to reform the world'.[65] Wollstonecraft was no longer prepared to take ideas about gender as immutable. Women could reshape themselves in order to reshape social life.

'In the cause of half of the human race she stood forth,' wrote Mary Hays, one of Wollstonecraft's contemporaries, 'deprecating and exposing, in a tone of impassioned eloquence, the various means and arts by which woman had been forcibly subjugated, flattered into imbecility, and invariably held in bondage.'[66] Male critics could be scathing, and Wollstonecraft's book incited parodies such as *A Vindication of the Rights of Brutes*.[67] But opposition failed to quell her exploration of the position of women. 'Was not the world a vast prison, and women born slaves?' she asked in her 1798 novel *Maria: or, The Wrongs of Women*.[68] Men exercised authority in high public office, in the universities, the professions and the church, all of which were closed to women. The advance of science promoted inquiry into the laws of God, man and nature, and inquiry was fostered by literacy. Wollstonecraft protested against the deficiencies of female education, and the fact that women's lives were shaped by the expectation they would marry, and so limit their options for alternative forms of employment. A good education would enable women to find honourable professions, and make them educated equals to their husbands – as well as better mothers of their children.[69]

Wollstonecraft died at the age of thirty-eight as a result of complications in childbirth – a common fate for women of childbearing age. She had achieved her goal of succeeding as a writer, but flouting convention came at great personal cost. She wrote at a time when the ideology of domesticity that she critiqued – private life at home for women, public life for men – was becoming common among the British middle classes.[70] Historian Bridget Hill suggests that over the course of the eighteenth century changes in the organisation of agriculture and the rise of industry meant the range of other occupations open to women narrowed.[71] Tasks became more clearly defined as 'masculine' and 'feminine', and housework, in particular, became 'almost exclusively women's work'.[72] In the words of the Scottish poet James Thomson in 1788:

> Well-ordered Home Man's best delight to make;
> And by submissive wisdom, modest skill,
> With every gentle care-eluding art,
> To raise the virtues, animate the bliss,
> And sweeten all the toils of human life:
> This be the female dignity and praise.[73]

Just as commitment to public life enhanced masculinity, commitment to the home became a hallmark of femininity among the expanding middle classes. To rail against the limitations of woman's sphere, as did Mary Wollstonecraft, was to earn the sobriquet 'a hyena in petticoats' from gothic novelist Horace Walpole.[74] Any blurring of the distinctions between the supposed male qualities of independence and rationality and the complementary female traits of dependence and emotion threatened the basis of the social order.

In the last two decades of the eighteenth century, the nature and scale of Britain's economy were on the brink of dramatic change. The enclosure of common land, previously open to all, went forward apace; this led to more efficient farming, from which individual agriculturalists benefited while smallholders, agricultural labourers and squatters lost out.[75] In towns, industrialising enterprises hummed with new possibilities. The rising population and expanding economic activity fed what has been named 'a golden age of domestic industry' in the cotton trade.[76] And it was women who predominated in the major textile industries. In the 1790s, a kind of embroidery known as tambour work became fashionable, and some young women earned enough from the trade to dress in a 'showy and expensive' manner.[77] A number of women took advantage of the expanding consumer market by setting up their own businesses as shopkeepers, making up over 11 per cent of those in this occupation in the years 1775 to 1787.[78] A woman with education might try to live by the pen, as did Wollstonecraft in the 1790s. Maria Edgeworth, an Irish writer of children's books, published her first novel, *Castle Rackrent*, in 1800. Its immediate success led to her earning between £1,500 and £2,000 for each of her subsequent novels.[79]

Demands for women's work in nascent industries did not offset the adverse effects of both the burgeoning population and the enclosures on women's traditional patterns of work in agriculture, still the main mode of subsistence for one in four families.[80] Opportunities to work on the land decreased while women's employment in domestic service rose as a growing number of middle-class families sought household assistance. In London, the most common occupations for women were domestic service, making and mending clothing, charring or cleaning, laundering and nursing.[81] There was a thin line between making do and impoverishment, especially when women were at their most vulnerable while raising children. Very low wages and uncertain work in volatile new economic ventures could tip a family into destitution.

As their employment and wage rates contracted in the last decades of the eighteenth century, some women without means turned to crime. Housebreaking, a capital felony, was the crime of which Charlotte Badger was convicted at the Worcester assizes in 1796. She was sentenced to seven years' transportation and sent to the old Parramatta Female Factory in New South Wales, Australia. Like many women, Charlotte is difficult to trace in the historical record, but there is a hint she may have arrived in Sydney in 1801, with other female convicts. She is next recorded giving birth to a child in 1806. In April of that year, she and a friend, Catherine Hagerty, were sent to serve out the rest of their sentences as servants in Hobart.[82] They boarded the *Venus* in the company of male convicts to sail to Tasmania and, at Port Dalrymple, joined the other convicts in a mutiny that would see them at last take control of their own destinies.

Accounts differ as to the role Charlotte Badger played in the mutiny. In one version of the story she wore a man's clothing, wielded a pistol, flogged the captain, and raided another vessel for arms and supplies. In another, 'she and Catherine Hagerty are said to have incited the male convicts to rebel'.[83] The *Venus* sailed on to New Zealand, with Charlotte and Catherine working with the men, 'setting sail and steering the brig' on the hazardous voyage across the Tasman.[84] Eventually the ship berthed in Rangihoua Bay, in the Bay of Islands, where the paramount chief, Te Pahi, welcomed Europeans who would facilitate trade with whaling ships.[85] There was great curiosity about Charlotte and Catherine as the first white women in the region; they were declared 'strongly tapu' by the chiefs, and kept in their own quarters.[86] Catherine died shortly afterwards, and Charlotte took up with a local Ngāpuhi chief, raising a child and apparently declining offers of rescue until, after a number of years, she took off once again with a New England whaling captain.[87]

Exile, not exploration, was the imperative behind Charlotte Badger's voyage, though for her and others transportation to a new land might also have offered a new kind of freedom. No women were among the crew of the *Endeavour* when it sailed into New Zealand waters in 1769. While James Cook circumnavigated the globe, his wife Elizabeth Batts Cook maintained his secure roots in England. Aged twenty when she married the thirty-four-year-old James, Elizabeth raised their children and kept the household running in his absences, which stretched into years. The word 'HOME', with its 'blissful associations', wrote the non-conformist clergyman J. A. James, 'even sends its attractions across oceans and continents, drawing to itself the thoughts and wishes of the man that wanders from it at the antipodes; – this, – home – sweet home – is the sphere of the wedded woman's mission'.[88]

The world of middle-class women in England was gradually contracting within four walls even as the nation's horizons were expanding by exploration. In 1832, women's exclusion from the franchise, which was a matter of convention rather than law, became formalised in the Reform Act: in extending the right to vote to propertied 'male persons', it now specifically excluded women from voting. Elizabeth Cook, who was widowed at the age of thirty-seven in February 1779, lived through this era. She outlived her six children, three of whom died in infancy, one from scarlet fever in his teens and two in the service of the Royal Navy. Cherishing James Cook's memory and embroidering his three voyages onto a map of the world, Elizabeth lived on her husband's pension, his grant from the Board of Longitude, 'and the proceeds of his charts and writings' until her death in 1835 aged ninety-three.[89] When the Royal Society struck a medal in memory of Cook, it was presented first to Elizabeth Cook. She acknowledged it thus: 'Be assured, sir, that however unequal I may be to the task of expressing it, I feel as I ought the high honour which the Royal Society has been pleased to do me.'[90]

A marker of civilisation?

When the *Endeavour* arrived in New Zealand in 1769, the groups that encountered each other were markedly different in one respect: communities of men, women and children on shore met an entirely male crew on the ship. For Māori, the absence of women aboard the ships was perplexing, and perhaps reinforced their view that those aboard 'were tupua, strange beings or "goblins"'.[91]

There were, indeed, much broader cultural differences to contend with. Cook and his scientific companions were literate and well read about the field of their investigations; they also had the services of an interpreter, Tupaia, a high chief from Raiatea in the Society Islands. Where Māori had an oral culture and relied on prodigious feats of memory to order their world, Europeans had come to rely on the written word, the printed chart and the navigational instrument.[92] By the eighteenth century, they were dissecting the unity of the natural world by systems of classification. The Swedish botanist Carl Linnaeus

Māori women's weaving encompassed fine cloaks and more functional items such as this early flax kete. Neatly fastened, it was clearly a work basket, containing items such as bundles of dressed flax and mountain daisy leaves, twisted flax thread and red ochre in a pāua shell. *Otago Museum, Dunedin, D24-574*

(one of whose students, Daniel Solander, travelled with Cook on the first voyage) devised a 'global classificatory tree encompassing all life on earth' and divided by 'class, order, genus, species, and variety'.[93] He was the first to mark out humans as primates, and named them *Homo sapiens*.[94] But there were differences and hierarchies within the human species: *Homo monstrous*, for example, included Patagonians and Hottentots.[95]

Later, French and Scottish writers extended such classification to the stages of development of humankind. They theorised that humans began in the natural state of hunter-gatherers, and progressed through pastoral, agricultural and, finally, commercial development. This they laid out as progress from savagery to civilisation and from despotism to the political enlightenment of liberty. The position of women acted as an index of such progress: in primitive societies, women were the slaves of men; in commercial society, women had become the companions of men within marriage.[96] And monogamy within marriage stood for 'a government of consent, moderation, and political liberty'.[97] In this way, political theory upheld a particular gendered form of social organisation as a key to civilisation. Monogamous marriage was essential for political stability, and this key institution structured the reciprocal relations between women and men.[98]

The Pacific island of Tahiti provided French explorers accompanying Louis Antoine de Bougainville in April 1768 with an alternative view: that of the 'savage' inhabiting a world before the Fall, an innocent unconstrained by the restrictions of civilisation, 'the

'A New Zealand warrior and his wife in the dress, etc of that country' is the description of these two people drawn by artist Sydney Parkinson, who accompanied Captain James Cook on his first voyage to New Zealand in 1769. While both wear cloaks that indicate women's weaving skills, the woman is rather more plainly dressed than her husband. This engraving, published in 1784, was based on Parkinson's sketch. *Alexander Turnbull Library, Wellington, PUBL-0037-19*

Utopian inheritor of the biblical Garden of Eden'.[99] Philibert de Commerson, a member of Bougainville's party, wrote of the 'simplicity of [the Tahitians'] moral code', which was marked by '[t]he fairness of their treatment of women, who are in no way oppressed, as is the case with most savages'.[100] The following year, the *Endeavour*'s crew spent three months in Tahiti on their first prolonged stop to observe the transit of Venus, and there they entered into the local domestic and sexual life of the islands. James Cook, of humble origins and a self-made man, rejected what he saw as the fanciful French ideas about the uninhibited society of Tahiti, in favour of seeing in the local society the elements of progress: 'law, marriage, property and rank'.[101]

Observations made of the Polynesian peoples of Tahiti formed the backdrop against which the *Endeavour*'s party assessed the inhabitants of New Zealand. On Cook's first journey, these curious observers were favourably impressed by what they saw. Joseph Banks, the wealthy gentleman and avid naturalist aboard the ship, recorded his observations on the roles of men and women in Māori society:

How the sexes divide labour I do not know but I am inclind to beleive that the Men till the ground, fish in boats and take birds, the Women dig up fern roots, collect shell Fish and lobsters near the beach and dress the victuals and weave cloth, while the men weave netts – thus at least these employments have been distributed when I had an opportunity of Observing them which was very seldom ...[102]

The Christian lens of these observations was evident in Banks's comment that Māori women wore a 'girdle of many platted strings made of the leaves of a very fragrant Grass; into this were tucked the leaves of some sweet scented plant fresh gatherd which like the fig leaf of our first mother served as the ultimate guard of their modesty'.[103]

Dress and adornment were obvious points of difference, as Anne Salmond has noted. Captain Cook noted of the Māori people of East Cape that 'the women may be known by thier voices they paint thier faces red' and that 'the Womens faces are not tattou'd'.[104] Further south, at Kahutara, the *Endeavour*'s men had first sighted Māori women coming out to the ship on a canoe with their menfolk. William Monkhouse, the ship's surgeon, recorded 'the Womens lips were tattoued – one of them was jolly and had large breasts'.[105] In the Bay of Islands, Sydney Parkinson, the Quaker botanical draughtsman with an eye for detail, recorded that people who visited the ship were 'very much tatowed, the men upon their hips and the women on their breasts, necks and bellies'.[106] Women and men were also distinguished by their hairstyles. Unlike men, women rarely wore their hair tied up; they kept it short and did not adorn it with feathers, as the men did.[107] Nor did the visitors observe women wearing fine cloaks, and this led one of the crew to comment: 'The Women contrary to the custom of the Sex in general seemd to affect dress rather less than the men.'[108] It may be, however, that they did not meet high-ranking women.

Superficial differences, according to Joseph Banks, masked an essential similarity with European women. Māori women, although 'rather smaller than European women ... have a peculiar softness of Voice which never fails to distinguish them from the men tho both are dressd exactly alike. They are like those of the fair sex that I have seen in other countries, more lively, airy and laughter-loving than the men and have more volatile spirits, formd by nature to soften the Cares of more serious man who takes upon him the laborious toilsome part as War, tilling the Ground &c.'[109]

After three years of exploration, the *Endeavour* returned to England, docking at the port of Deal on 12 July 1771. One year later, Cook was commissioned by the British government to determine whether there existed a great southern landmass, and embarked on a second voyage aboard HMS *Resolution*, accompanied by HMS *Adventure*. When the ships reached New Zealand, the novelty and appreciation of Māori so evident on Cook's first visit was now tinged with disillusionment.[110] Anthropologist Kathryn Rountree suggests that on Cook's later voyages, when landfall was made in only two locations in the South Island and during bad weather, the crew found the harsh climate a trial compared to that of islands

This finely woven, half-finished cloak was collected by Cook on his third voyage to New Zealand (1776–79), and is one of the earliest examples of Māori garments still in existence. It is the work of a highly skilled weaver. *Museum of New Zealand Te Papa Tongarewa, Wellington, ME007852*

closer to the equator. Compared to Tahiti, for example, the land and the people appeared inhospitable. On these voyages, the crew's judgements on Māori they met conflated the people with the harshness and inhospitality of the environment.[111]

Cook was troubled by the impact of his men on the local population:

[T]his Second visit of ours has not mended the morals of the Natives of either Sex, the Women of this Country I always looked upon to be more chaste than the generality of Indian Women, whatever favours a few of them might have granted the crew of the Endeavour it was generally done in a private manner and without the men seeming to intrest themselves in it, but now we find the men are the chief promoters of this Vice and for a spike nail or nay other thing they value will oblige their Wives and Daughters to prostitute themselves whether they will or no and that not with the privicy decency seems to require, such are the consequences of a commerce with the Europeans and what is more to our Shame civilized Christians, we debauch their Morals already too prone to vice and we interduce among them wants and perhaps diseases which they never before knew and which serves only to disturb that happy tranquility they and their fore Fathers had injoy'd.[112]

For the small group of Māori at Dusky Sound in Fiordland, the all-male European crew of the *Resolution* remained a mystery. One young woman took a liking to two gentlemen and two sailors, thinking they were women. She became particularly fond of a third young sailor until one day she saw him urinating and knew he was a man. 'She soon,' commented an observer, 'was tired of him.'[113]

The appraisal of Māori women by Cook's party had been complimentary during their first visit. This view was revised on the second voyage.[114] Johann Forster, the naturalist, commented that only a few of the women had 'tolerable features' and that the women were 'harshly treated by their husbands, for whom they are obliged to do all the drudgery, as is common in all the barbarous nations'.[115] By the third voyage of 1776 to 1779, Kathryn Rountree has suggested, the men aboard the ships saw Māori women as dominated by their men, 'further down the Chain of Being', and therefore closer to 'savages'.[116]

For those who wished to catalogue the advance of 'civilisation', progress was to be found in the movement from 'the degraded condition of women in the savage state' to women gaining 'the responsibilities of home and the care of children'.[117] It was, they argued, Christianity 'alone which had raised woman to her destined and natural place, neither "tyrannised nor impiously honoured"'.[118] English women were thought to have achieved a remarkable liberty and to stand at the head of a great chain of being, albeit under the shadow of English men.

As 'civilisation' was being delineated through the contrast with the 'uncivilised', so women were marked out by their difference from men. This difference, however, led to the possibility of fusing cultures. One of the crew of the French ship *Mascarin* had recorded in 1772 that the Māori men who boarded the ship 'indicated to the French sailors that their women were pretty, "hoping to attract us by this ploy which is indeed an effective way to unite nations the most disparate in their ways, their manners and their customs"'.[119]

Early alliances

The British and French explorers left some offspring in New Zealand – and probably more venereal disease – as a reminder of their visits, but the official reasons for their forays into the south seas were exploration, not settlement.[120] Other all-male crews who came after them – sealers and whalers – followed the imperative of trade. Whaling and sealing settlements existed in the far south from 1792, and were reliant on Māori goodwill. A number of the men entered into, and benefited from, long-standing liaisons with Māori women.[121] These were alliances on Māori terms, where men's entitlement to land came 'only through their wives and children, and they had no right to alienate the land'.[122] But it was by this means that Pākehā men gained a foothold in New Zealand, and were effectively protected from conflict with local populations.[123] Jack Price, a sealer on the southern coast, was one of these men. His partnership with Hineawhitia, daughter of Pikirauraho and Tahupahi, a chief of Pahia in Murihiku (South Island), secured his well-being.[124]

After 1800, the rise in sperm whaling in the South Pacific led to an increasing number of ships visiting the north-east of New Zealand. American and British ships called at the Bay of Islands, Doubtless Bay and Whangaroa for supplies and repairs.[125] But it was the shore whalers, who plundered the southern right whale for oil and whalebone, who created longer-term settlements in the south. Among these were the whaling stations at Moeraki, Waikouaiti, Ōtākou, Bluff and Aparima, which depended on trade with local Māori.[126]

Māori women sought out liaisons with the incoming men, whether for their own benefit or for the benefit of the group. Patahi, whose story has been told by historian Angela Wanhalla, chose the whaler Edwin Palmer over her whānau's preference that she marry Tuhawaiki, the foremost chief of Ngāi Tahu. Her poignant story, which ended in abandonment and separation from her children, indicates both the independence that women of rank could exercise and the personal cost of cutting oneself off from one's iwi.[127] But abandonment was only one outcome: Wanhalla's work has shown that a number of relationships between Ngāi Tahu women and whalers were long-lasting, and helped contribute to the mixed-descent population that characterises southern New Zealand.[128]

Domestic labour was central to the economy of whaling and sealing, and Māori women were sought for these tasks. Edward Jerningham Wakefield, son of Edward Gibbon Wakefield, the leading proponent of planned colonisation and founder of the New Zealand Company, toured the country from August 1839 into the 1840s. In *Adventure in New Zealand*, the lively record of his travels that he wrote to promote emigration, he noted: 'Regular bargains were struck between the experienced headsman or boat steerer and the relations of the girls selected and in most cases the bargains were adhered to.' The relatives undertook that their kinswoman would:

> get up an hour before daybreak; cook the breakfast and arrange what her lord means to take in the boat … wash and mend his clothes; keep the house in order; and prepare his supper for his return. Then upon her reposes the task of granting hospitality to the traveller while the master of the house is away.[129]

If a woman fell down on her duties of cooking, mending and washing, her relations would recall her and provide a more satisfactory 'helpmate' to fulfil their side of the bargain.

Fanny Weller was the daughter of Māori woman Paparu and English whaler Edward Weller. Born at Ōtākou in the mid-1830s, Fanny was about thirteen years old when this portrait was painted. In it she wears a red blanket as a cloak.
Watercolour by Ralph E. Erskine, Hocken Collections/Te Uare Taoka o Hākena, University of Otago Library, Dunedin, 5,581

The words of one unquiet Māori woman have survived to give an insight into her view of such partnership arrangements. Makariri, daughter of the chief Tohu and his wife Toke, lived with George Willsher, a squatter on the South Otago coast. In overhearing him disparage Māori women, Makariri reminded Willsher of the importance of her labour:

> By and by you go to Otago to Waihora – to Touto. You stay three weeks – you stay five weeks – you stay two moons – you come back – you say Hullo where's the cow? Gone. Where's the bull? Gone! Where the goatee? Gone! Where the chickeni? Gone. The blankety gone the stockeni gone all all gone. You get the Mourie woman, by and by you go to Otago. To Waikawa to toutere – you stay three weeks – you stay five weeks – you stay two moons – you come back you say – Hullo where's the cow? Me say 'All right' You say Where the Bull? all right. You say where the goati – me say all right – You say where the chikini? Me say all right. The blankets all right the stockini all right – all all right – are very good the Mourie woman.[130]

While Pākehā were a small minority on the fringes of the Māori world, such 'marriages', based on Māori customary arrangements, did little to subvert Māori patterns of authority. They were vital, however, in securing peace of mind for the men who wished to profit from their sojourn in an alien land. Ernest Dieffenbach, the New Zealand Company naturalist, noted that in a whaling settlement at Tory Channel the Māori 'wives' did 'all the domestic labour, and excel their European husbands in sobriety and quiet disposition'.[131] Edward Jerningham Wakefield felt certain that the rough conditions in the whaling stations in Otago would have been worse if it had not been for the presence of Māori women, who exerted 'a strong influence over the wild passions' of the men and whose 'habits of order and cleanliness' raised living standards.[132]

The children of short- or long-term liaisons between Māori women and Pākehā men inherited two cultures, but the mother's culture was likely to dominate when men were reliant on her community for support. The absence of English law in New Zealand at this time meant that there was no way of enforcing an Englishman's right to guardianship of his children even if he felt moved to claim it. Those who fathered and then abandoned children in short-term liaisons were later said by Resident Magistrate Francis Dart Fenton, in an official report on Native Affairs in the Waikato district, to have lowered 'the character of the Europeans in general in the eyes of the natives, whose clannish ideas are too apt to convert the sin of the few into the act of the multitude'.[133] To combat such sin, and convert Māori to Christianity, missionaries began arriving in New Zealand from late 1814.

Seventeen-year-old Jane Maria Richmond is pictured at a writing desk in this 1841 sketch by her brother, James Crowe Richmond. The demure image belies her energetic character. Arriving in New Zealand with her family in 1853, she married barrister and solicitor Arthur Samuel Atkinson and raised their children while maintaining a strong interest in feminist and social reform issues. *Alexander Turnbull Library, Wellington, A-245-023*

Chapter Two
A Civilising Mission

'I have entered on a new scene – left the parental roof, and the friends and guides of my youth, to become a wife – forsaken my native land and embarked for a distant barbarous clime as the partner of a Christian missionary.'[1] So wrote Eliza White, the only woman aboard the *Sisters*, headed for the Bay of Islands in 1829. Two years earlier, as the unmarried Eliza Leigh, she had attended a missionary meeting and, fired by the experience, composed the following poem:

> O may my life, my all, be spent
> In telling heathens Thou was sent
> To save their souls from sin and hell,
> That they might in Thy presence dwell.[2]

The much-loved only daughter and youngest child of a prosperous merchant family from the fen district, north of Cambridge, Eliza had long wished to be a missionary. A visit from the Revd William White, a missionary from New Zealand who was eager for a wife, enabled her to fulfil her ambition. The couple married on 30 June 1829.[3] Barely twenty, and with a husband seventeen years older, Eliza was seven months pregnant when their ship arrived in the Bay of Islands. Such was the excitement of local Māori eager to see their missionary's new wife that a great crowd came on board. Eliza wrote: '[I] was completely surrounded by them. Some got in the rigging and examined my countenance and dress with great earnestness.'[4] Transported to Mangungu on a covered sedan chair carried by Māori, Eliza was delighted to be restored to some familiar English female company – Jane Hobbs, wife of missionary John Hobbs, was in residence. The Methodist mission enterprise Eliza joined in the Hokianga had quickly followed the original Anglican mission established in 1814.[5]

The drama of Eliza White's arrival suggests Ngāpuhi were curious to see how a white woman would alter the ways of the mission and the impact she would have on their world. Eliza's clothing, with its unfamiliar fabrics and styles, gave them a novel perspective on what a woman could be. And just as material objects carried by women missionaries provided new reference points, so too did the domestic arrangements of the missionary families. European ideas, and particularly those of Christianity, with its emphasis on one God, challenged iwi conceptions of a world teeming 'with gods and unseen beings',

Left Eliza White came to New Zealand in early 1830 as the wife of Methodist missionary William White. Supporting the work of the mission at Mangungu, Northland, over many years, she later continued her church work in Auckland, starting a night class that was to become the second Young Women's Christian Association in New Zealand. *Right* Dressmaker Eliza Hanham arrived in New Zealand with her first husband, carpenter Richard Palmer, but was widowed young. In 1849 she married German missionary Johann Wohlers, and settled on the remote southern island of Ruapuke. There she taught reading and brought practical skills in nursing, sewing and gardening to the local Ngāi Tahu community. *Auckland Libraries, Sir George Grey Special Collections, 7-A3950; private collection*

possibly disrupting the continuum between the natural and the human world that was an integral part of that view.[6] But Māori took from the newcomers what they wanted. And to the frequent frustration of missionaries, sojourners and settlers alike, Māori also ignored the Europeans' admonitions and questioned their customs when they judged it necessary.

Levels of unrest were high within hapū with the arrival of muskets and as settlers demanded land. Missionaries called for British government intervention to protect Māori from the disorder of whaling settlements and the rampant greed of settlers. The apparent inevitability of colonisation, led by the New Zealand Company, forced the British to take action. The 1840 Treaty of Waitangi delivered a double message in two languages, English and Māori, proclaiming British dominion while apparently reinforcing tribal sovereignty. Even in its signing, the patriarchal implication of British law became clear. British officials sought the signatures of leading men, and gave little or no thought to the mana of leading Māori women. The way was cleared for settlement of European families, in which women's legal interests were subsumed by those of their husbands. Many of the newcomers over the period from 1814 to the 1850s saw in this settling of families a key engine for the transformation of Māori society from a state of 'savagery' to one of 'civilisation'.

The Hokianga Wesleyan Mission Station at Pākanae, with its circular driveway surrounded by gardens, is shown in the early 1840s. Mary Anna Bumby came out to join her missionary brother John at Mangungu Mission Station in 1839, bringing with her the first hives of honey bees. In 1840 she married the Rev Gideon Smailes and they moved to Pākanae, also on the Hokianga. The long harbour provided many opportunities in the timber trade for both Māori and Europeans, and ships had been built at Horeke, or the Deptford dockyard, since the 1820s. But there were few European women in the district, and missionary women often felt their isolation acutely. *Sketch by Richard Taylor, Alexander Turnbull Library, E-296-q-151-2*

Missionary families

Jane Kendall, Hannah King and Dinah Hall, together with their children, had accompanied their lay catechist husbands on the brig *Active* to found the first settlement of the Church Missionary Society (CMS) in December 1814 at Rangihoua in the Bay of Islands. Pregnant with her second child when they arrived on 22 December, Hannah King was placed on a chair to be lowered from the *Active* to a small boat and transported to the shore. Thomas Holloway King's birth, on 21 February 1815, was difficult, and the child died of consumption aged three years and nine months. Hannah went on to have ten more children; her sixth child, Joseph, died aged three years, while her eleventh child, Mary, lived a mere ten days.[7] Of nine CMS families in the Southern District of the North Island in the 1830s and 1840s, seven wives died at an average age of forty-four, while life expectancy for husbands was seventy-three.[8] Infants, too, were frequently at risk: Eliza White's first child was stillborn; her second died at seven months; her third was strangled at birth by the umbilical cord. Of her fourth child, a healthy son, she noted, 'we hold him with a trembling hand lest so sweet a flower should be blighted.'[9]

The mission's hold on life was similarly precarious, and was reflected in its material circumstances. A few days before his son Thomas's birth, John King described the raupō (bulrush) building that was to house all the families:

> our House or Hut is made with flags by the natives it has no Chimney in it it will neither keep wind nor rain out, we have no window in it … This is a very wet Day it has been so for this three days on Sunday last Feb 12 it rained very much the water came through upon our wheat rice bed clothing and the water was half over my shoes in our bedroom from the wetness of the durt floor as our hut is on low flat ground our clothing damp & tho we do all we can to keep them dry we have no fire to dry them when it rains as our fire is out of doors for my own part I am in good health but it is uncomfortable indeed for my wife and Child in the state she is in, it will be a great blessing indeed if it does not make her suffer exceedingly as she has taken a severe cold already.[10]

From the outset of the mission, Hannah not only tended to the needs of her own family but also took in young Māori women, teaching them sewing, housework, reading and writing, the catechism and the Lord's Prayer. Outside the household, she tended to the sick, dressing wounds and giving out medicines.[11] John King described Hannah as a 'willing helper in the work'.[12] But it was the household itself that was supposed to act as an exemplar of the benefits of Christian ways. The great hopes placed in china teacups and writing slates had to be regularly reinforced by prayer in a predominantly Māori environment.

Within Māori society, pressure on resources led to heightened conflict among hapū at the time of the early missionaries' arrival. Battles between tribal groups became more devastating with the introduction of the musket, 'Brown Bess', the weapon most favoured by the British military.[13] The Ngāpuhi leader Hongi Hika saw the advantages of acquiring the muskets initially peddled by European traders, and succeeded in obtaining 300 for his tribe.[14] Thomas Kendall's estimate of 2,000 muskets in the Bay of Islands by 1821 illustrates the depth of desire for this new technology.[15]

Māori women continued to play important roles both in making alliances and in warfare. The high-ranking Ngāti Apa woman Te Pikinga, for example, was married around 1819 to Te Rangihaeata, nephew of the Ngāti Toa chief Te Rauparaha – an alliance that protected her people through a time of great strife.[16] This was a period in which numerous groups invaded the lands of others and great battles took place. Rangi Topeora asserted the supremacy of her people, Ngāti Toa, at the battle of Waiorua on Kapiti Island in 1824. Standing, legs astride, at the gateway of the pā, she forced the enemy to endanger themselves by passing between her legs, thereby replaying Maui's fatal attempt to enter Hinenuitepo. In battle, Rangi Topeora claimed triumph for her hapū.[17]

More European missionaries arrived in the midst of the turmoil that muskets had exacerbated within Māori society. The CMS held out hope for the success of the work of the Revd Henry Williams and his wife, Marianne, sent to establish a mission at Paihia in

Jane Holloway King (later Davis) was born at Rangihoua, Bay of Islands, in 1818, one of eleven children of CMS missionaries Hannah and John King. The detailed sampler she stitched as a child shows what she had learned, both in religious instruction and practical arts such as needlework. It includes the words: 'Remember now thy creator in the days of thy youth, while the evil days come not nor the years draw nigh when thou shalt say I have no pleasure in them. Lay up for yourselves treasure in heaven, where neither moth nor rust doth corrupt and where thieves do not break through nor steal. For where your treasure is there will your heart be also. And there shall be no night there, and they need no candle, neither light of the sun, for the Lord God giveth them light and they shall reign for ever and ever. Jane Holloway King her work, born Feb the 10 1818.' *Auckland War Memorial Museum Tāmaki Paenga Hira, 1965.78.267*

1823. The CMS expressed to the couple its 'best hope that you will exhibit to the Natives the instructive example of a happy Christian family'.[18] 'The native character,' wrote the missionary T. S. Grace, 'requires all that we can give it of the softening and refining influence of the educated Christian woman. The women of this race must be raised, or the Maori will continue to inhabit his whare, with no bed but the cold earth; no door but one that he must enter on his hands and knees ...'[19] While male immigrants were to make the framework of society – the buildings, roads and farms – women were to make the substance, that is, the home.[20]

'No country can be happy or Christian but in proportion as its females become so,' Jane Williams, wife of missionary William Williams, was instructed.[21] In the colonisation project, the 'uncivilised', whether heathen Māori or debauched Pākehā, were to be raised up, and a new world created by the work of European women dedicated to marriage, home and family. '[O]f all the issues in debate in the Maori-missionary encounter,' historian John Owens has written, 'that of the nature of the family unit was the most crucial, for most other issues were influenced by it.'[22] Embedded within the intimacy of those living together in the family lay patterns of power, autonomy, 'dependency, service and protection'.[23]

Missionary women believed they had a special role in educating Māori women, acting both as an example of civilised womanhood and as a conduit of values to do with cleanliness, domesticity and propriety. In marriage they had dedicated themselves to be 'fellow-helper[s] in the work'.[24] Indeed, missionaries without wives felt themselves to be seriously disadvantaged. Johann Wohlers, a German Lutheran missionary on Ruapuke Island, south-east of Bluff, wrote that it was impossible for him 'to carry on the necessary missionary work' and, at the same time, 'produce my own food, cook, wash and preserve cleanliness so that my health might be maintained'.[25] But missionary couples, many of whom were living in similarly isolated communities, were bound not just by duty and the imperatives of hard work. They often had deep ties of faith and affection. On the death of his wife Anne, CMS lay missionary Thomas Chapman wrote: 'My once cheerful home is thus made desolate to me.'[26]

European women's identification with the private space of the home was an alien concept in Māori society, where sleeping was communal, and cooking was performed in separate cooking sheds, or kāuta, away from the tapu interior of their dwellings. Food preparation was the work of low-born women or slaves, and the structure and layout of Māori dwellings reflected the hierarchies within and across genders. Cultural meanings were therefore challenged by the European custom of preparing food indoors. In an early example from the 1830s, Taiwhanga, one of the first converts to Christianity in the Bay of Islands, 'defied custom by cooking inside'.[27] How quickly his example spread is unknown, though one study, based on 'limited archaeological evidence', suggests that the change 'was first made by single men living in conditions similar to single Pakeha male settlers'.[28]

European housing and goods provided Māori with a '"reference group" – the prosperous people who altered the Maori image of themselves. Fernroot was no longer good, when the missionaries dined on flour.'[29] Māori quickly sought the new domestic goods such as nails, iron pots and blankets brought by European ships, and used them for their own ends. New styles of dress were adopted too, sometimes in surprising ways. After Bishop George Selwyn visited Ruataniwha on 15 November 1842, he recorded that:

> when the time came for our departure, [the chief] prepared to accompany us, by dressing himself in a complete English suit of white jean, with white cotton stockings, shoes, neckcloth, and shirt complete. His wife was dressed in a good English bonnet, but without shoes or stockings. The canoe in which we were to cross the lake, being in shoal water, some way from the shore, the dutiful wife saved her husband's shoes and stockings, by carrying him on her back to the boat.[30]

A different sort of duty occupied Selwyn's wife, Sarah, who was expected to keep 'things strait and going forward at home' in Paihia while he toured the country for six months.[31]

Māori women were active participants in the burgeoning trade opportunities that European settlement brought. Riria Ponau (or Poau), a woman of chiefly rank at Whangapoua, controlled timber lands on the Coromandel Peninsula which she and her cousin Te Ngarahu opened up for kauri-cutting contracts in the 1830s.[32] At that time, flax fibre, hand-prepared by Māori women, was likewise in high demand.[33] Enterprising women offered new services. For example, Mata Rawa, of Te Arawa, ran a laundry business, doing washing for local Pākehā and for officers from ships visiting the Paihia mission station. Historian Hazel Petrie notes the importance of women in developing tribal business interests. Ruawahine of Ngāi Te Rangi married John Lees Faulkner and established a trading post at Ōtūmoetai from which they shipped goods north to Auckland and Kororāreka and across to New South Wales.[34]

That Māori women's expectations differed from the priorities of some influential Pākehā is clear in a number of other instances of contact between the two cultures. Mary Ann Martin, wife of William Martin (who served as the first Chief Justice of New Zealand from 1841 to 1857) and a good friend of Sarah Selwyn, recalled how Māori women carried tons of firewood up a steep hill to the Martins' house. She related how her husband 'insisted that no woman should do this'. But Māori resented this 'infringement on the liberty of the subject' and the women, in particular, resented the loss of a job which had been an important 'perquisite'.[35]

Through direct intervention as in this case, more often by example, and increasingly through domestic education, Europeans sought to introduce Māori to new concepts of domesticity. Resistance was strong. A group of Māori women objected vociferously when they found that their daughters, whom they had sent to Mary Ann Martin for an education, were doing housework. They demanded that their daughters return home, and sent the

Anne Catherine Wilson left England in 1832 with her husband, CMS missionary John Alexander Wilson, on the *Camden*, a convict vessel bound for New South Wales. In these pages from her diary, she writes of her work with the 'native girls', of the pain of parting from friends, and of her husband's frequent absence. *Alexander Turnbull Library, Wellington, MSDL-2267*

men to fetch them. Mary Ann remonstrated with the men, asking, '[W]hy do *you men* listen to your wives in this way?'

> One of them, with a droll, sheepish look, caught up a bit of wood, and whittling it to a sharp point, which he prodded against his hand, said, 'Mother, your words are just; but, you see, though women's words are not powerful, they are very sharp, and they go on – on – on.' So we lost our scholars.[36]

While they still retained land and resources, and hence the means of conducting trade and continuing traditional ways of living, Māori were able to be selective about which aspects of the new European culture they wished to adopt – including the pressure to conform to a domestic ideal that centred on the home life of the nuclear family. Nonetheless, missionary wives worked hard to provide models of domesticity, devoting themselves to cooking and cleaning, along with sewing, childcare, teaching and nursing. According to Marianne Williams, they had to 'be housemaid and chambermaid' and the supervisor of whatever Māori help that could be obtained.[37] Shortly after her arrival,

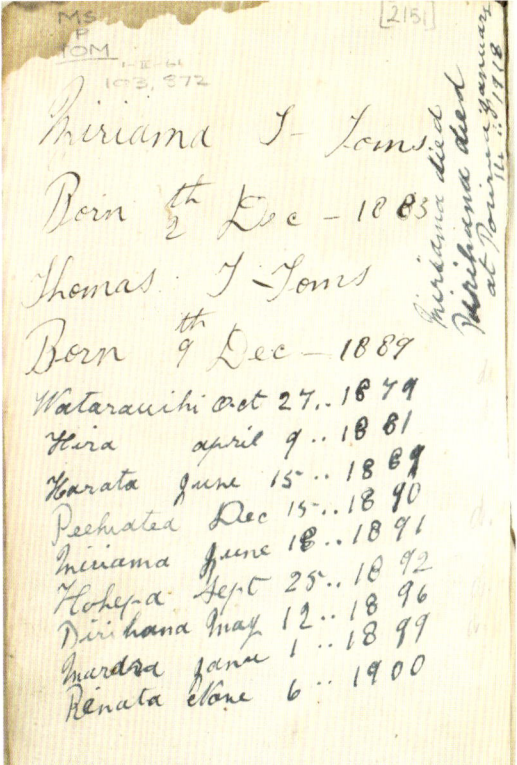

Missionaries taught reading and writing, skills much sought after by Māori. *Left* Details of births, deaths and marriages for the Toms family were recorded in the front of this Bible. *Right* The school slate has been inscribed with a nail, leaving indelible marks – in this instance the words of a waiata whakautu (a song of reply or riposte). In this type of waiata, the woman writer may deny accusations of having taken a lover, complain about disapproval of her chosen man, or protest against her family's demands that she marry another. This one is the first example known to have been written down by the composer. *Alexander Turnbull Library, Wellington, MS-2151; Kerikeri Mission Station, Heritage New Zealand Pouhere Taonga*

Marianne wrote of her 'great pity' for Māori women, believing '[t]heir state is degraded indeed', particularly from the practices of men on ships who had promoted a thriving sex trade.[38] Hope lay in reform and in accepting God's grace. Cleanliness and European clothing were a first step in this process, followed by attempts to inculcate a domestic work ethic. But at times she despaired:

> The very best of them, if not watched, would strain the milk with the duster, wash the tea things with the knife cloth, or wipe the tables with the flannel for scouring the floor. The very best of them will also on a hot day go (just when you are longing for someone to take the baby) and swim, after which she will go to sleep for 2 or 3 hours.[39]

Conversion to Christianity assisted in instilling European ideals of domesticity. Rawiri and Pirihira Waitere, from Cloudy Bay in Marlborough, supported the Christian enterprise, and Rawiri exhorted the Wesleyan Mission to work among his people. Samuel Ironside and his wife Sarah were chosen for this task in 1840. Starting from nothing on a deserted beach near the whaling station of Port Underwood, the Ironsides created their mission station at Ngākuta Bay in the Marlborough Sounds. As soon as a house was completed, Sarah celebrated by painting each of the six rooms a different colour. At the same time she taught the local women reading, writing, sewing and European notions of domestic order. The desire to learn to communicate in writing brought eager scholars, and two Māori women assisted Sarah with teaching her pupils, who were aged between four and seventy.[40]

Literacy was widely sought after by Māori, and by 1845 around half of all adult Māori 'could read or write a little in their own language'.[41] Attitudes to education differed markedly, however. In Māori society, mana could accrue with age, and elders might be revered for their knowledge, while children were expected to make their own way in the world. European society, in which knowledge was seen to lie in the written world, placed more emphasis on the formal education of children. Attitudes to children's discipline were also very different, and Māori thought some European practices to be little short of barbaric.

Just as the Europeans expected wives to defer to their husbands, they also believed children should defer to their parents. When the missionary Nathaniel Turner instructed the chief Te Puhi that children who misbehaved should be beaten, Te Puhi 'appeared quite disgusted and said we were an iwi kino, a bad tribe'.[42] Other missionaries noted the great affection bestowed on Māori children and the absence of punishment. 'Every New Zealand child,' one commented, 'is an indulged child, permitted from its infancy to have its own way in all things, taught to despise the counsel of its parents, yes, even to curse them to their faces.'[43] Despite their misgivings, however, Pākehā were often happy to leave children in the care of Māori. Indeed, Marianne Williams discovered the delights of her infant son only when his Māori nurse ran away, and commented of her Māori helpers: 'For savages I think they do wonders but still they are savages.'[44]

This view of Māori as uncivilised 'savages', like the rejection by Māori of many European ways, ensured a wide distance between the two groups of women, who nevertheless shared the experience of menstruation, childbearing and menopause. A Māori man compared 'in a strain of arch ridicule ... the groans and expressions' of a European woman in labour with 'the hardy resolution of the New Zealand ladies'.[45] Māori often referred to their women as whare tangata or 'houses of the people' – an acknowledgement of their importance to the hapū as a whole.[46] A mother's death was likened 'to an open rent in the bottom of a canoe'.[47] Language reflected the wider community's responsibility for the care of children: the word whaea was used for all the female relatives of one's parents' generation, not just one's birth mother.[48]

Cultures in conflict

To embed Christianity, the missionaries promoted the sacrament of marriage: the relationship in which they believed sensuality should be productively contained.[49] In Māori attitudes to sex, some missionaries saw evidence of 'the depravity of mankind'.[50] Not confined to a marital bed, sexuality 'permeated all aspects' of the Māori world, from symbolism in art to everyday language.[51] For example, carvings on storehouses that represented sex acts and genitalia were a source of embarrassment to missionaries, who were also wary of carvings as 'heathen idols'.[52] Naked bodies, too, disturbed the missionary equilibrium. An early objective of the missionary women was to cover Māori women's bodies with long gowns and to have them cut or bind their hair.[53] Among the supplies ordered for the Mangungu mission were 'cheap but showey prints for Gowns or Frocks'.[54] To the missionaries, discipline in appearance was intended to promote discipline of action, whereas for Māori women the novelty of printed fabric may have encouraged experimentation in dress. Māori women adopted whatever suited them, be it literacy or a 'showey print', inhabiting a far wider world than that of their Christian teachers.[55]

If the missionaries despaired of the waywardness of Māori, Māori were equally puzzled by Pākehā social arrangements. The Wesleyan mission station at Whangaroa consisted of four single men and a married couple, Nathaniel and Ann Turner. On a visit to Te Pere's people, one of the single men, John Hobbs, was asked 'whether I did not live in adultery with Mrs Turner' and whether he 'was not sick with lust'.[56] William White wrote, 'the Danger to which single men are exposed … in this land from Temptation to Native Females is *Great*'.[57] White returned to Britain to seek a wife.[58] But some missionaries were indeed unable to withstand temptation: the married Thomas Kendall, for example, had an affair with Tungaroa, a servant in his household.[59]

It was, however, the whalers, sealers and traders who more readily enjoyed sexual alliances with Māori. The officers on board the colonial schooner *Prince Regent*, anchored near the mouth of the Tāmaki River in August and September 1820, might have declined the offer of women from a canoe sent out, but 'many of the women found husbands among the other inmates of the vessel'.[60] The benefit to the sailors could be more than fleeting, since the presence of Māori women on board ships made them less vulnerable to attack – although the economic importance to Māori of such alliances could lead to intertribal conflict 'over which girls were to have the "privilege" of going on board the visiting ships'.[61] A whaling ship from New Bedford, Massachusetts, dropping anchor in the Bay of Islands in 1838, was immediately surrounded 'with natives and canoes Loaded with potatoes, peaches, melons, grapes, fish, hogs &c &c for traffic also women'. Unusually, the captain of this ship 'sent the women away'.[62] More commonly, Māori wanted the goods the Europeans had to trade, and bartered for them with what the sailors desired.

The missionaries found that they could not compete with the attractions offered by the sailors. Many of their young Māori domestic workers left to go to the ships 'where three weeks on board are much to their satisfaction'. In those three weeks, Edward Markham noted, 'they get from the Sailors as much as they would from the Missionary in a year'.[63] Anne Chapman, married to CMS missionary Thomas Chapman, wrote of the 'large presents' the young women received from the sailors, and noted: 'Fathers and Mothers think nothing of taking their daughters to these horrid places, for the sake of the payments they get.'[64] While the women's earnings might be valued by their kin, the missionaries reproved them for their sexual commerce.[65] Māori men, Thomas Kendall commented, were 'very blameable in allowing their young women to visit our ships', where the women picked up not only bad language but also disease.[66] The uncensored sexual freedom previously exercised by young Māori women became labelled as prostitution, and thus sinful and depraved.[67] The missionaries expected Māori men to exert control over their women, replicating the patterns of authority and deference that structured European families.

The key juncture at which these patterns of authority were cemented was that of marriage. The missionaries strove to promote Christian marriage in Māori society where, although tribal customs differed, an adult union was generally formally sanctioned and, among the lower orders, expected to be permanent and monogamous.[68] Polygamy, however, was enjoyed among men of rank – a practice that had important economic and social implications. According to Samuel Marsden, certain chiefs told him 'that their wives made the best overseers, and that they could not get their grounds cultivated if it were not for the industry of their wives'.[69] But the practice of polygamy was against the missionaries' belief in the nuclear family as the foundation for Christian society. William Williams, of the CMS, recommended that Māori men 'put away the wives they had in excess' so that they could be baptised. He recorded:

> One good natured man sat with a respectable wife on each side. After giving him my advice I asked him what he thought about the matter. When looking very wistfully first upon one wife and then upon the other he replied these women must settle the point.[70]

This man, it seems, paid more heed to the plight of an abandoned wife than did the clergy. There was also the question of the afterlife. 'What was to become of the many wives a man has in this world after they have born him children', one man asked of a missionary, making it clear he did not wish 'to be separated from his relatives at the day of Judgement'.[71] Affection, obviously, and considerations of social and economic ties were important in Māori marriage arrangements, as they were in European ones.

Māori were also aware that the missionaries did not represent the views of all Europeans. If polygamy was wrong, they asked, why then did Pākehā sailors live with Māori women?[72] Moreover, in the face of missionary criticism, Māori could claim superior devotion to their spouses. When the bereaved widow of a chief tried to kill herself, a missionary remonstrated and stated that a white woman would not do such a thing. Another chief, Te Puhi, replied, '[Y]ou white people have no love.'[73]

Māori enthusiasm for Christian marriage increased over time, perhaps kindled less by example and theological argument than by the celebration the ceremony presented. The Māori scholar and linguist Bruce Biggs suggests that traditionally rituals were associated only with the marriages of Māori of rank; most marriages occurred without formal rites.[74] In October 1831, when Matilda Davis, the seventeen-year-old daughter of CMS missionary Richard Davis, was married in the new Waimate mission church, a 'quite regal' scene was created by the bride and bridesmaids, who were carried on armchairs 'draped in white and slung on poles'. Shortly afterwards, some young Māori couples asked also to be married at the church, and 'the chapel was crowded to excess' as local Māori gathered to witness the ceremony in which the bridal couples were dressed 'in neat European style'.[75] Eagerness to participate in the formalities of the marriage ceremony could lead to up to forty couples being married at a time; in one instance, treasured brass curtain rings from the mission household were donated to provide wedding rings.[76]

Participation in the ritual of the wedding did not, however, always translate into an acceptance of the lifelong commitment the missionaries hoped for. At the Wesleyan mission at Ngākuta Bay in Port Underwood, Sarah Ironside was distressed when a young Māori woman, whose marriage to a Māori man had been recently solemnised, was taken aboard a schooner by a European man. The European had formerly lived with the young woman; ignoring entreaties to have her sent ashore, he eventually sailed away with her.[77]

As the number of European settlers increased, marriage between Pākehā and Māori had the potential to undermine traditional notions of authority. The Māori wife of an English settler felt free, for instance, to insult the Ngāpuhi chief Hone Heke by publicly comparing him 'to a side of pork'. The husband was unwilling to offer the compensation regarded as appropriate by Māori, and in revenge his goods were plundered in a bloodless raid, a taua muru.[78]

More often, however, men integrated into the communities into which they married. For example, the Danish whaler Phillip Tapsell married Karuhi, sister of Ngāpuhi chief Wharepoaka, in April 1830. Tapsell enjoyed success as a trader at Maketū in the Bay of Plenty, dealing in, among other things, muskets and gunpowder in exchange for flax. His firearms dealings with Ngāpuhi disturbed the Anglican missionary Henry Williams, but no doubt strengthened his tribal relationships.[79] Some time after Karuhi died, Te Arawa, a rival tribe of Ngāpuhi, sealed their relationship with Tapsell by offering Hineiturama, a high-ranking woman of Ngāti Whakaue of Te Arawa, as his wife; the marriage was later blessed and the children baptised by the Roman Catholic Bishop Pompallier in Whakatāne in 1841. The couple had six children, and the three sons, Retireti, Perepe and Ieni Tapihana (Tapsell), became government officials, playing a central role in Ngāti Whakaue's relationship with the Crown. The eldest daughter, Kataraina, married George Simpkins and together they ran a successful trading enterprise. Ewa, the second daughter, married a government medical officer, a Dr Hooper, who worked among Waikato Māori.

The women in the painting on the left (from about 1850) were identified by the artist, Joseph Jenner Merrett, as Māori and part-Māori – reflecting not only social change in some parts of New Zealand at the time but also his own situation. His wife was Rangitetaea Koa of Ngāti Kōura, and the sketch on the right (from the 1840s) shows her with their baby Ani, who was affectionately known as 'nga mimi', or 'little wet bottom'. *Watercolour by Joseph Jenner Merrett, Auckland Art Gallery Toi o Tāmaki, 1991/18. Sketch by Joseph Jenner Merrett, © The British Library Board, London, Add. MS 19953 p69, plate 197*

The youngest daughter, Tote, married Tamati Hutchinson and lived near Thames.[80] Children of such relationships between newcomers and Māori played an important role as mediators in trader networks and with government.

Māori women found material benefits in relationships with white men, which might include a higher standard of living and, according to the missionary Johann Wohlers, a better chance of raising healthy children.[81] Nonetheless, those children could be seriously disadvantaged in the Māori world, where land claims rarely recognised the needs of the mixed-race population.[82] In 1839, an attempt was made to ensure that their status in the European world was not discounted when the founding of a Victorian Paternal Association for the Offspring of English Fathers by New Zealand Mothers was proposed at Paihia.[83] In England, the authority of fathers as the guardians of their children was guaranteed under the law. No such legislation existed in New Zealand, and there was increasing pressure to introduce a system of authority to regulate the lives of those in the new and

Walking on the roof, a woman removes the tapu on a house that had been made sacred; this ritual was reserved to women. The sketch is also by Joseph Jenner Merrett, whose portraits and drawings offer glimpses of mid-nineteenth century life in northern New Zealand. © *The British Library Board, London, Add 19953, No 258*

growing settlements. The European population had expanded from about 300 in 1830 to approximately 2,000 by 1840.

Among Māori, the benefits brought by increasing European trade had heightened conflict between tribes, who fought to gain control of shipping access at key points and to obtain slaves to produce goods for European needs.[84] Enslaved women were valuable, because they could barter with sex or scrape flax to be traded for muskets. Both outwardly, in terms of adopting features of European dress, and inwardly, in terms of social organisation, those tribes in contact with European settlements were undergoing rapid change and exposure to new kinds of authority.

Not that new kinds of authority were held in awe. James Busby, appointed Resident by the British government and arriving in 1833, made little headway in his mission to establish respect for the Crown. To convince the British government to act, he depicted New Zealand as sliding into anarchy and districts becoming depopulated.[85] The evidence for such depopulation was sketchy, but it was an issue that resonated with those concerned about the fate of aboriginal peoples. Busby called upon the British government to recognise its paternal responsibilities: Māori were, he wrote, children in need of protection.[86] English men stood as the protectors of English women; so too should they assume authority over Māori in order to protect them.

A young woman, seated on the ground in front of a carved whare, is weaving a kaitaka, a flax cloak with a richly patterned tāniko border. Beneath her own cloak she wears a European dress. Tradition is strongly emphasised in this drawing from 1848, but the Māori world was also changing. *Drawing by Charles Heaphy, Alexander Turnbull Library, Wellington, C-025-025*

A system of colonisation

The idea of planned settlement and British colonisation received great impetus from the pen of Edward Gibbon Wakefield, who fantasised about life in Australia while imprisoned and facing possible execution in London for kidnapping an heiress, fifteen-year-old Ellen Turner, and tricking her into a hasty marriage at Gretna Green.[87] In 1829, Wakefield published his plans for organised colonisation in his *Letter from Sydney, together with an Outline of a System of Colonisation*, and the following year he founded a colonisation society. In his *Letter from Sydney* (in fact, from Newgate Prison), Wakefield proposed that young couples were the ideal immigrants: they would relieve Britain of surplus population and ensure the rapid development of the colony.[88] 'A new colony,' he wrote, 'is a bad place for a young *single* man. To be single is contrary to the nature of a new colony where laws of society are labour, peace, domestic life, increase and multiply.'[89] Domestic life was clearly central to his plans to build a new society in a land he imagined was free for the taking, a waste country.[90] New Zealand, he claimed, was 'the fittest in the world for colonisation ... the most beautiful country with the finest climate, and the most productive soil'.[91]

As well as rapidly increasing the population of the new colony, promotion of a domestic life would have other important benefits, which Wakefield articulated in subsequent

This cloak blends old and new. The main fabric is made of muka (processed flax) but its wide tāniko borders incorporate red and black wool, a material adopted by weavers soon after Europeans arrived. *Auckland War Memorial Museum Tāmaki Paenga Hira, 816*

publications. A balance of the sexes would stem the tide of prostitution – a natural consequence, he believed, of men's aggressive sexuality – while a wife halved a man's labour by attending to 'household cares', thus freeing him for productive work. The best immigrants would be true Christian women, for '[a]s respects morals and manners, it is of little importance what colonial fathers are, in comparison with what the mothers are'.[92] As historian Raewyn Dalziel has written, Wakefield 'asserted that a particular configuration of gender relations was the essential precondition to the creation of wealth and the progress of civilisation'.[93] He recognised that the engine of colonial success lay within the private sphere of the family.

Planned settlement became more than an idea when the New Zealand Company hurriedly dispatched the *Tory* to New Zealand in May 1839 to forestall any opposition. The purpose of the expedition, led by Edward's brother William Wakefield, was to buy land to prepare for Company colonists. An Englishman 'who ardently desires the greatest good of his country', Edward Wakefield claimed, would ask 'for the power to increase the territory of Britain according to the wants of the people'.[94] And to be a citizen an Englishman required property for the settlement of his family. Missionaries had already acquired land on which to live, and in this settling of families lay a deeper and transformative idea about property: that men were the property owners, and property owners were entitled to a stake in government.

The British government was forced to consider the question of sovereignty in New Zealand as, by the 1830s, the whaling stations looked likely to become permanent settlements and some settlers had established farming enterprises. Reports reaching Britain from this period onwards painted a dire picture of the sufferings of Māori, thanks to the incursions of whalers, traders and escaped convicts.[95] Māori themselves appealed to the Crown for protection. Thirteen prominent northern chiefs petitioned the King in November 1831 to act as a 'friend and guardian of these islands'. They were anxious to ward off any further forays by the French, who had sent a naval vessel to the area, as well as to control unruly British settlers and to prevent the 'teazing of other tribes'.[96] An increase in French and American whaling and trading activities provided another impetus for action by the British government. Yet, as historian Tony Ballantyne notes, the CMS was opposed to further colonisation, arguing instead for protection offered by the missions and the strengthening of the position of the British Resident in New Zealand, James Busby. Ballantyne cites Dandeson Coates, the secretary of the CMS, who wrote emphatically in 1837 that 'every Instance, as far as my Acquaintance with the History of Colonization goes, has resulted in the most disastrous Consequences to the Aborigines of those countries which they have so colonized'.[97]

At the same time as the New Zealand Company purchased the *Tory*, the Colonial Office in London appointed Captain William Hobson as Consul to New Zealand. When it became clear that the *Tory* was readying for departure with New Zealand Company settlers on board, Hobson was given greater powers as Lieutenant Governor. Colonisation now appeared 'inevitable' and the newly appointed Hobson saw the necessity of 'the protection of British laws'.[98] Hobson, 'so fond of his wife [Eliza] and family and so desirous of having them with him', left Plymouth aboard the *Druid* on 25 August 1839, accompanied by the heavily pregnant Eliza and their three children.[99] Eliza gave birth to their fourth child on 13 December, eleven days before they reached Port Jackson (Sydney), where the family celebrated Christmas before Hobson sailed on to New Zealand on 19 January 1840.[100]

Shortly after his arrival in the Bay of Islands, Hobson issued an invitation for Māori leaders to meet at Waitangi on 5 February. In anticipation, Hobson and Busby drafted a treaty in which the young Queen Victoria was represented as a maternal protector of her distant subjects, 'anxious' to protect the Māori people and to promote good order:

> Her Majesty therefore being desirous to establish a settled form of Civil Government with a view to avert the evil consequences which must result from the absence of the necessary Laws and Institutions alike to the native population and to Her subjects …[101]

The image of a protective Queen failed to make clear the far-reaching implications of Te Tiriti o Waitangi, the Treaty of Waitangi. To the English, the Treaty ceded sovereignty

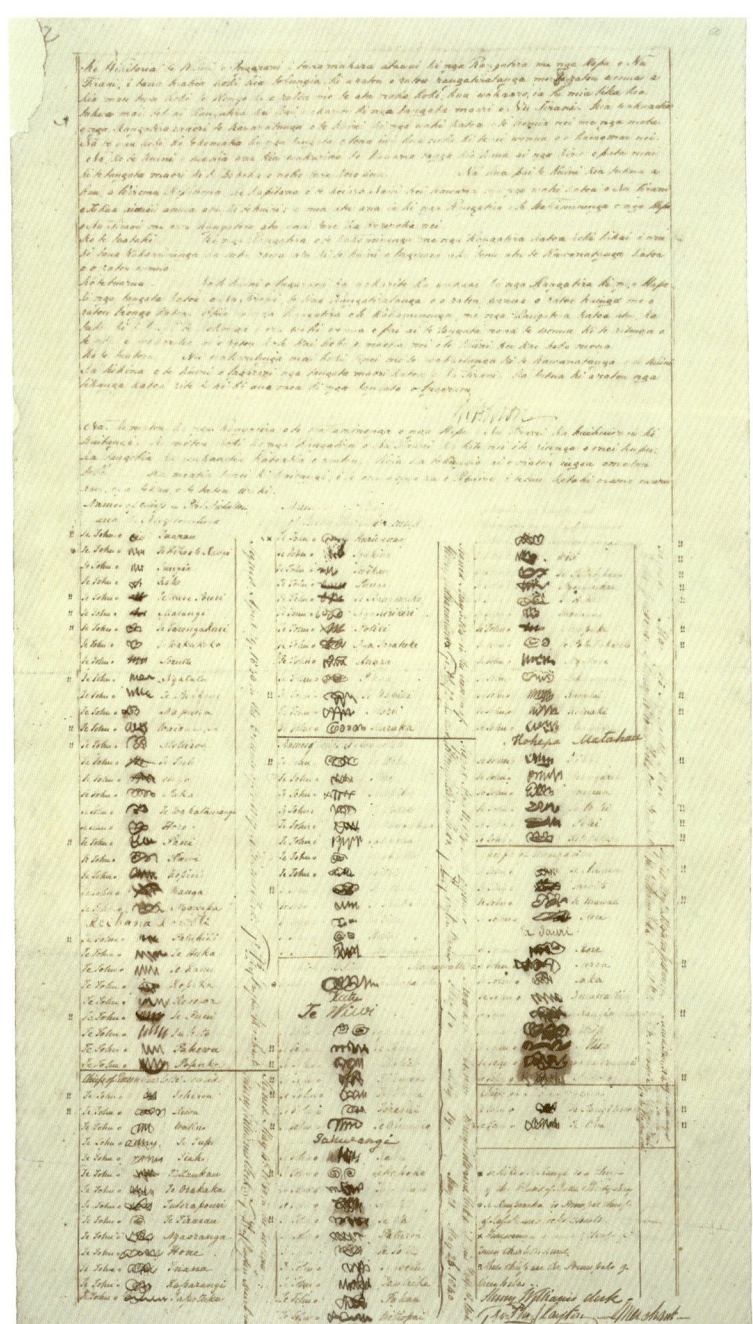

Rangi Topeora of Ngāti Toa, Kahe Te Rau-o-te-rangi of Ngāti Toa, Ngāti Mutunga and Te Āti Awa, and Rere-o-maki of Te Āti Haunui-a-Pāpārangi signed this sheet of the Treaty of Waitangi, which was taken to the Cook Strait area by CMS missionary Henry Williams in mid-1840. Topeora signed below Te Wiwi (Te Whiwhi) in the middle column; Rere-o-maki in the right hand column, above the name Te Tauri; and Kahe Te Rau-o-te-rangi in the fourth line of the left hand column. *Archives New Zealand The Department of Internal Affairs Te Tari Taiwhenua, IA 9/9*

to the Crown. The first article in the English version states that the 'Chiefs … cede to Her Majesty the Queen of England absolutely and without reservation all the rights and powers of Sovereignty'. The Māori version, in contrast, seemed to reinforce the powers of tribal sovereignty. As the Treaty was taken around the country for signing, communities were presented with the Māori version and debated its meanings. Two concepts of authority were set for conflict.

Although ruled by a young Queen, the body politic in England was male, and this was to be the pattern transferred to New Zealand. Eloquent testimony to the gendered pattern of authority was Major Thomas Bunbury's refusal to allow the daughter of Te Pehi, a high-ranking Ngāti Toa woman, to sign the Treaty. Her anger was shared by other women at Kapiti, who 'expressed some disapprobation in not having a more prominent part in the Treaty with Her Majesty'.[102] Rangi Topeora, also of Ngāti Toa, was one of the women who did sign, as did Ana Hamu, the widow of Te Koki who had sponsored the Paihia mission. But the imposition of British rule signalled a diminished role for Māori women in future.

British rule underwent a setback when William Hobson suffered a stroke on 1 March 1840. Twenty-nine-year-old Eliza quickly brought the family from Sydney to join him, and they were delighted to find Hobson recovering in the care of a missionary at Paihia. The family took up residence in Eliza's 'wooden palace', the first Government House at Russell in the Bay of Islands, turning the official presence of British authority into a family affair and a centre of sociability. Under Eliza's guidance, Government House quickly became a focus of civic life, hosting weddings and entertainments at which the townspeople might take 'every opportunity to enjoy themselves'.[103] Her 'kindness, urbanity and hospitality' were toasted by fifty gentlemen at a vice-regal dinner at Auckland's Royal Hotel.[104] Such good fortune was shortlived. William Hobson died on 10 September 1842, leaving Eliza and her five children with bleak prospects. They remained at Government House for a further nine months and Eliza, aware that she could not expect assistance from the British authorities, made some shrewd property investments. In 1843 she returned to Plymouth, and she never again visited New Zealand.[105]

At the time of her husband's death, Eliza Hobson was one of the 597 women resident in the small settlement of Auckland. Mechanics (254) and agricultural labourers (149) predominated in the occupations of the 1,238 male residents. One hundred and four shopkeepers served the needs of the community, as did 98 domestic servants, some of whom would have been women.[106] The first New Zealand Company settlement was under way at Port Nicholson (Wellington), and in February 1842 the first immigrant ships arrived at Nelson. Amid overcrowded and often dirty conditions below deck, ravaged by seasickness and any number of infectious diseases, and at risk of fire and shipwreck, women migrants tended to their children. A number gave birth on board ship – among them, five women on the *Timandra*, which carried 201 free immigrants attracted by the New Zealand Company's promises of prosperity in New Zealand.[107] On one of the ships, the *Lloyds*, the death rate was devastating: 63 children died on the voyage.[108] By mid-1843, the Company had sent 1,052 men, 872 women and 1,348 children (under the age of fourteen) aboard 18 ships. Among the women immigrants there were 59 seamstresses and dressmakers, and 88 domestic and farm servants.[109] On arrival, women and children waited in immigration barracks while their husbands set about the business of building houses from whatever materials they could get.

In the 1840s and 1850s, single women emigrants to New Zealand usually travelled as part of a family group, as did many of the single men. Some of the women who did not marry found alternative family structures. Martha and Maria King arrived in Wellington in December 1840, having travelled to New Zealand with their brother, Samuel Popham King. The two sisters remained unmarried, but lived with their brother and his new wife. They first opened a school in Wanganui and then in New Plymouth, where they all moved in 1847, and quickly became popular members of the community. Martha King found time outside her teaching and household duties to become one of the country's foremost botanical painters. Mary Anne Rymill, a single woman who had been orphaned at an early age, and who came to New Zealand in 1842 to assist an overburdened missionary friend, spent her life as a companion and nurse in church families. When she was unable to rejoin her employers, the Brown family, at the Tauranga mission station during the land wars, she was overcome with loneliness: 'suddenly there was no place' for her.[110] An invitation to join another family, together with an allowance from Alfred Brown, restored her vitality. By the time of her death in 1897, Mary Anne had created a special place for herself in a number of families, including as godmother to five children, and in the broader church community. The Anglican Diocese of Christchurch established a Mary Anne Rymill Memorial Fund in recognition of her services.[111]

To Edward Wakefield's disappointment, the new settlers at Nelson and Wellington failed to show the requisite gratitude, and instead protested that their expectations of work and housing in this new Utopia were not being met. He therefore welcomed the prospect of the religiously cohesive settlements promised at Canterbury with the Anglican Church and at Otago with the Scottish Free Church, under the aegis of the Lay Association.[112] According to historian Erik Olssen, the Free Church, having broken with the power of the state, was keen to inscribe the power of the father as both 'prophet and patriarch of his little state'.[113] After the arrival of the first of the Lay Association settlers in 1848, numbers in Otago began to swell: 12,000 immigrants came in the 1850s. Thirty-seven per cent of the migrants who arrived there between 1848 and 1852 were married, and their children comprised another 40 per cent of that population. The Lay Association 'tried to maintain a balance between single males and females and did not permit unmarried women to migrate unless employed by a family or "under the immediate control of some near married relatives"'.[114]

By the 1850s, migrant families throughout the country were working hard to secure their place in the new settlements by acquiring land and erecting buildings. The Crown

These three portraits were painted by Isaac Coates, who worked mainly in Nelson in the early 1840s. Potie Wright, on the left, was married to hotelier William Wright the 1840s; the couple moved from Wellington to Nelson in 1842. Te Rangiuira (in the middle) was the wife of Ngāti Toa leader Te Rangihaeata (on the right); both wear albatross feathers indicating their chiefly status. Māori–settler tensions erupted in the confrontation at Wairau in Marlborough in 1843; and it was the death of Te Rongo, another wife of Te Rangihaeata, that enflamed the conflict. *Watercolour and gum arabic paintings by Isaac Coates, Alexander Turnbull Library, Wellington, A-286-017; A-286-015; A-286-014*

soon took over the original New Zealand Company policy of reserving one-tenth of purchasable land to be held in trust for Māori, although there was confusion as to how this land should be administered.[115] Such was the disarray that Māori in Motueka, for example, 'undertook, in several instances, to lease and sell parcels of the reserves in that district on their own account'.[116] At the same time, Māori communities – who might have had little say in the selection of reserved land – were pointing out that the reserves were too small.[117] Tension over land was rising.

Settlers, citizens and subjects

Once the Treaty was signed and New Zealand became a British colony, settlements required governance at the local as well as the national level. A lively group of 'burgesses' met in Barrett's Hotel, Wellington, in September 1842 to discuss who might represent the settlement's inhabitants on the town council. Printer and political radical Samuel Revans made an impassioned plea for universal suffrage, claiming 'many a man in England would hug such a privilege'.[118] Anti-slavery advocate and organiser of working men, Rowland Davis, then cross-examined Revans about 'whether he thought it right women should interfere on such occasions'.[119] Davis had apparently heard of two women canvassing 'even on the Sabbath'. Revans replied that 'he had thought and studied much on that point in political economy, but he had never been able to make up his mind decidedly, whether women should, or should not, have a voice in the legislature'.[120] It has been claimed that Alfred Saunders, a Nelson settler and future Provincial Councillor, along with the future Premier, William Fox, advocated for women's suffrage in the following year, 1843.[121] But the truth was that when men throughout the scattered settlements debated

The Greenwood family settled near Nelson in the early 1840s. As a young woman in London, Sarah Greenwood (born Field) had been taught to draw; these portraits of her family were painted for her mother in England. They are (from left): her daughters Jane and Mary, and husband John Danforth Greenwood. While John Greenwood had trained in medicine, in New Zealand the family farmed and traded in flax. Sarah continued to paint, often depicting peaceful landscapes and ordered settlements. *Pencil and watercolour paintings by Sarah Greenwood, Alexander Turnbull Library, Wellington, A-252-025; A-252-022; A-252-021*

the requirements for suffrage, they imagined that public life was, and would remain, a masculine domain.

From the first proposed Municipal Corporations Ordinance for town government in 1842, to the Provincial Councils and the General Assembly created by the Constitution Act passed by the Imperial Parliament in 1852, it was adult males who were to be enfranchised. The Constitution Act replaced the personal rule of governors with representative government. It stated unequivocally that the electorate was to be made up of 'every Man of the Age of Twenty-one Years or upwards' who fulfilled certain property and residence requirements.[122] In theory, Māori men were eligible to vote, but because Māori land was held communally, they were unlikely to meet the property qualification. In 1856, Henry Sewell became first Premier of New Zealand under responsible government, whereby Ministers were required to have the support of a majority of elected members of the House of Representatives. Sewell believed that Māori who had the same leasehold or freehold qualifications as Europeans were similarly entitled to vote. He argued that reserved land was 'vested in the Crown for the benefit of the Natives, just as if they were infants or lunatics, not having legal capacities'.[123] Just as British women were under coverture, submerged in the legal identity of their husbands, so Māori living under customary law lost legal identity in return for the Crown's protection.

In July 1856, Henry Sewell reflected on the first three months of responsible government in New Zealand and concluded:

> In that time we have taken the first real step … to elevate and save the Native by enabling him to obtain an individual title to Land; the first beginning to planting the family, and raising him out of his miserable state of tribal barbarism.[124]

Ellen Valpy (later Jeffreys), who arrived in Otago with her family in 1849, painted this scene of early Dunedin, showing Mr John Barton's house on the corner of Manse Street and Princes Street in 1852. Ellen was born in India where her father worked for the East India Company. She had travelled extensively in Europe, where she received instruction in drawing. *Toitū Otago Settlers Museum, Dunedin, CS/1357*

The patriarchal family form, in which the household had its own political significance, was seen as a vital instrument to transform Māori society. To be a 'householder' was to be a man of property and hence able to participate in political life. To Francis Dart Fenton, resident magistrate in the Waikato, the 'migratory disposition, and indifference to the comforts of life' of Māori meant that they regarded the building of permanent houses as 'a superfluity'. When Māori did erect substantial dwellings on pā sites, ownership 'was claimed by all the members of the family residing in it'.[125] This type of collective ownership was outside the purview of English law and, according to the law officers of the English Crown consulted by New Zealand's General Assembly, was one reason why Māori could not be given the right to vote.[126] In the words of Hugh Carleton, the Assembly's representative for the Bay of Islands, Māori, like English women, had only the right '*to be well governed*'.[127]

If men – and it was assumed they would be white men – were to govern the public (as well as private) life of the colony, white women had a special role to play in providing welfare for those of their community who fell on hard times. The first organised group of white women in New Zealand was the Auckland Ladies Benevolent Society, founded in

1857. By that date Auckland's population had reached more than 10,000, and other Pākehā settlements, including those of the New Zealand Company at Wellington, New Plymouth and Nelson, were growing apace.

Designated as the capital in 1841 and remaining so until 1865, Auckland benefited from public money, and some within the community could afford philanthropy and the luxury of domestic help. The women who formed the Auckland Ladies Benevolent Society were the wives of wealthy and prominent men, and addressed their attention to raising funds for the relief of poverty-stricken women and children in their own community. Fortunes could rise and fall quickly in colonial society: men could lose their ability to earn through accidents, or they might leave in search of work, never to return. Deserted or widowed women might be left without means to feed and clothe their families. It was to the relief of such cases of '*deepest destitution*' that the Ladies Benevolent Society directed its efforts.[128]

The ladies' horizons were limited. The very thing that was enabling some Pākehā to prosper, and to show benevolence towards those in their community who were struggling, was land purchasing. And that was itself a critical means of undermining Māori power to determine their future. Yet Māori continued to practise customary law to assert control over their future in which, they knew, their daughters were of central importance. John Eldon Gorst, a civil commissioner in the Waikato in the early 1860s, noted the power of Ngāti Maniapoto and the iwi's concern with marriage alliances. Gorst recorded how Ngāti Maniapoto, secure in their relatively inaccessible kāinga (settlements) in the upper Waipā, felt free to 'outrage Europeans as they please'. He described a raid on Auckland to reclaim a 'half-caste' woman working in domestic service:

> The tribe having, according to native custom, a voice in the disposal of all the daughters of their women, wished her to come up the country and marry a native. She refused. Upon this, a party of a dozen went down, carried her off in broad daylight from her mistress's house in the neighbourhood of Auckland, and took her in triumph past our police, our soldiers, and our redoubts, to Hangatiki. It is fair to add that, as she still persevered in her refusal, she was not forced into the match.[129]

The battle for authority took place in all arenas as the number of European settlers grew, and in those battles the domestic joined with the political. An undermining of traditions to do with the way daily life was lived – houses, cooking, dress and schooling – challenged the traditional organisation of Māori society. The European missionaries and settlers, who followed in the wake of the early traders and whalers, carried with them particular ideas about the 'civilised' family which, they believed, had reached its fullest development in Europe and was nowhere more clearly displayed than in the treatment of women; this entailed shielding them from the rigours of law and the hurly-burly of politics. Through importing Christianity, education, literacy and the rule of English law, the newcomers acted to transform the lives of Māori women. Resistance, however, was fierce.

Martha King, who arrived in New Zealand with her brother and sister in 1840, produced this exquisite watercolour of a branch of the native New Zealand gloxinia (*Rhabdothamnus solandri*) for the New Zealand Company in 1842. Painting always came second to her work as a schoolteacher, but she is now considered to be one of New Zealand's best nineteenth-century botanical artists. *Alexander Turnbull Library, Wellington, A-005-016*

Chapter Three
Settling Pākehā Families, Unsettling Whānau

'We saw several natives,' Charlotte Godley wrote of the Ngāi Tahu people of Murihiku in 1850, 'but all dressed in coats and trowsers, or else the universal blue shirt, and belt round the waist. The women too had gowns, etc., and only a mat on the top of all; they are not bad looking.'[1] Arriving in Port Cooper (later known as Lyttelton), she observed the local people in a less flattering light. She was puzzled by the way they squatted comfortably on the ground, and by their tattooed lips: 'Some of them, and especially the women, are frightful, but they look very picturesque, sitting about the place with a bright scarlet blanket and a deep black border spread all over them. This is the favourite dress, but costs here about a pound more than a weeks wages for a Maori.'[2] After she met a Māori group in their houses, she wrote: 'To me it was like a dream.'[3]

Charlotte Godley, aged twenty-five, had set sail from Plymouth on 13 December 1849, in the company of her husband, John Robert Godley, lay leader of the Anglican Canterbury Association, and her two-year-old son, Arthur. The Godleys sailed on the *Lady Nugent*, a former convict ship that had been built in 1813 and made over for the transport of colonists in 1843.[4] The journey by sailing ship, lasting more than three months and described by Charlotte as mostly 'nothing but sea, sea and always sea', was one undertaken by successive waves of immigrants from the 1840s to the 1870s.[5] On landfall, many shared Charlotte's fascination with the people to whose land they had come and on whom they were dependent for food supplies and labour.

The settlers soon set about creating households in conditions very different from those in the places they had left. Most of them did so successfully and with remarkable fortitude. Women began their own businesses or assisted their husbands breaking in the land. But there were hazards, too, and casualties. Many settler women married young and had large families; the risks of dying in childbirth were high. Death also stalked Māori communities, as introduced diseases took their toll.

In addition to death and disease, Māori women faced new expectations about their position in society and uncertainties to do with the selling of land. Traditionally thought of as a communal resource to be nurtured, land became recast in European terms as

After the sacking of Kaiapoi and Ōnawe pā by Ngāti Toa leader Te Rauparaha in 1832, the Ngāi Tahu occupants became refugees and did not return home until after 1840, when peace was more secure. They then established villages and set about building new whare and whata (raised storage huts). This village is Rakawakaputa, near Kaiapoi. *Watercolour painting by William Fox, Hocken Collections/Te Uare Taoka o Hākena, University of Otago Library, Dunedin, A432*

'property' subject to individual ownership. In British law, those owners could not be married women. Māori women who wed European men faced the prospect of losing title to their lands, since under British law any property women had, or any money they earned, belonged to their husbands. And the difficulties faced by deserted European wives and widows with no independent property raised demands to reform the law relating to married women's property.

Crossing the ocean and settling in

Caroline Oriental Street took her middle name from the ship on which she was born during its five-and-a-half-month voyage from Plymouth to New Plymouth in 1841. John and Elizabeth Hellier and their seven children were also aboard the *Oriental*, the fourth emigrant ship to sail to the settlement established by the Plymouth Company (which merged with the New Zealand Company in 1841) at New Plymouth in Taranaki.[6] The four girls and three boys of the Hellier family apparently much enjoyed the voyage: the freedom from work compensated for the constant rolling of the ship. Seventeen cabin passengers occupied the main deck while those in steerage were divided into three divisions: 'young men in the bows; young women, aft; and married people with their children adjacent to the young women'.[7] A few 'intermediate' passengers travelled second class, without luxuries such as the stewards who serviced the needs of those on the main deck, but with fewer chores and more comforts than the steerage passengers.[8] Factors such as whether the ship was overcrowded, the weather during the voyage, the health of passengers, and the congeniality or otherwise of fellow emigrants helped shape the ship-board experience.

Whereas first-class passengers might have their own servants, be served their meals, and pay for their washing to be done, women in steerage were kept busy attending to their families' need for meals and clean and mended clothes. Washing in salt water was difficult and hard on fabric, but there was no alternative. Bedding had to be aired and sleeping compartments scrubbed.[9] Historian David Hastings has noted how tasks regarded as women's work on land were regarded differently at sea, since sailors themselves did their own domestic work.[10] Male cooks and stewards made an impression on the migrants, he suggests, and in steerage men hung out the laundry, cooked and washed the dishes. One male passenger noted that 'mothers are all busy washing and we fathers are of course busier nursing. Oh the joys of married life.'[11]

Single women, as the layout of the *Oriental* in 1841 made clear, were to be kept well away from men. An 1864 Queen's order-in-council further stipulated that the rules relating to single women were to thwart 'all immoral or indecent acts or conduct, taking improper liberties or using improper familiarity with the Female Passengers'.[12] Hastings notes the single women were to be 'locked down at night' and when on deck 'restricted to a roped off section of the poop'. Should even the captain or the ship's surgeon wish to visit their quarters, they had to be accompanied by the matron.[13] Jane Findlayson, travelling on the *Oamaru* in 1876, wrote in her diary:

> We had often heard of young women getting acquainted with young men on board ship and afterwards getting married after landing but that sort of work is utterly impossible here, we only see them at a distance, and those who have brothers on board have to get permission from the Doctor to meet half way along the deck and have a chat … we don't see a single man. A girl or two has their beaus here and we are greatly amused at them, they have recourse to letter, the same as on lands, it is capital fun to see it going on.[14]

If some single women found their amusement in observing relationships, other entertainment lay in 'theatricals', deck and board games, lotteries to determine when the ship would cross the equator, and the ceremonies associated with that occasion. Sundays were marked by all aboard donning their best clothes and attending church, and by extra rations.[15] But the greatest excitement came with the sighting of the new land. '*In sight of New Zealand!*' Charlotte Godley enthused on 23 March 1850; then, on arriving in Otago Harbour, 'it is *so beautiful*'.[16]

The Hellier family aboard the *Oriental* arrived at Ngāmotu, which had been renamed New Plymouth by the settlement company to reassure settlers of their continued links with England. Surf boats transported the family to 'a huge whare' built by local Māori; it seemed to them reminiscent of the ship, except without bunks. Scattered clearings in the nascent settlement contained raupō dwellings, built with Māori expertise, and the new arrivals lived in the large whare until they obtained sections of the fertile Te Āti Awa land on which to build.[17]

The quality of housing, be it a tent near a work site, a raupō whare, a cob hut or a gabled weatherboard house, had a direct effect on the nature of women's work experience. Houses in more settled areas were usually built of wood, with brick chimneys that allowed cooking to take place inside. Tents or thatched rush huts were chilly and damp, and the risk of fire meant that all cooking must be done outside. After arriving in New Plymouth in 1853, Jane Maria Richmond spent her first months there 'cooking over an open fire, making bread and butter, washing and mending an accumulation of clothes, and everlastingly sweeping out mud'.[18] A settler in the Karamea district recalled that the women who landed there even as late as 1875 'had never used camp ovens before, and did not know that we should have erected a fly over the fires. No sooner did we get the bread in the ovens than down came the rain and put out our fires.'[19]

The rudimentary conditions of colonial society meant that all immigrant women, of whatever social status, were involved in household tasks.[20] Most were not wealthy enough to employ servants to assist them, but even those with the means to do so found that domestic workers were scarce and wages high. Hard physical labour was part of the daily routine for most. Cast-iron cooking utensils were heavy, water often had to be carried great distances, and the setting and cleaning of fires was a continual task. Food preparation required skill and ingenuity, though some homes had separate, well-sized storerooms for provisions purchased in large quantities when they were available.

Women made jam jars out of beer bottles, kept poultry, manufactured tallow candles and set their own soap. While everyday cooking might be done on the open fire, once a week a separate brick oven was fired up and the day devoted to baking bread, biscuits, cakes and scones, roasting meat and preparing 'trays of apples or quinces or pears'.[21] Women's work was vital to the economy of the family. Butter-churning and cheese-making, when supplies exceeded the family's needs, could provide useful additional income. Washing might be done for others, and looking after the domestic comfort of lodgers provided opportunities to earn additional cash. Women also waged 'constant warfare' against mice and rats in kitchens and storerooms.[22]

Nothing, however, could be done about the dangers inherent in the natural environment. Earthquakes, floods and fires disrupted communities, and reminded settlers of the fragility of their existence. A Wairarapa resident wrote of the massive earthquake of 23 January 1855:

We were sitting round our table with a friend when, at half-past nine o'clock at night, with out the rumbling notice which earthquakes generally give us, the shock commenced; the house waved to and fro, rocked, and jumped, as you might fancy a ship would when she strikes on a rock; the lights were dashed off the table, books, glass, china &c., on the shelves round the room, came down, together with the chimney, part of which fell inside and mixed with the ruins of the furniture, &c.[23]

European structures were particularly badly affected by this earthquake which, at between 8.2 and 8.3 on the Richter scale, remains the most severe to have occurred since the start of colonisation.[24] After her house was destroyed and her family took up residence in their dairy, a Mrs Hume was 'so terrified' that they moved 'to live with the Maoris, upon whose whares the earthquake had no effect'.[25] Aftershocks damaged nearly all the cob cottages in the Awatere district, and chimneys were brought down in Wellington, and in the Wairarapa, where four Māori died after their housing, too, proved vulnerable.[26]

A 'great gale' swept over the country in January 1861, tearing boats from their moorings, blowing down chimneys and outbuildings, and destroying fences.[27] Crops were devastated as well, causing 'irremediable' loss to smallholders.[28] The floods that followed deluged the Hutt Valley, sweeping away bridges, cattle and hay, 'the waters forming one vast sea, miles in extent'.[29] The *Hawke's Bay Herald* foresaw 'an immense amount of suffering and privation' for those settlers whose livelihoods depended on their now-ruined crops.[30]

Danger might always be near at hand, and household work arduous, particularly for those in rural areas, but housework also required creativity, and affection to be bestowed upon those who came within a family's domain. In a country where the servants and goods available in England were scarce, a great many women relished the task of creating households that secured their sense of identity in a foreign land. Charlotte Warburton recalled, 'It was really the women's ability as home makers which settled the land.'[31] In her eyes, Māori land in Manawatū was unsettled. Such a view was shared by others in the European settlements, where solid housing and furniture were regarded as the key accoutrements of civilisation.

'We brought our kitchen furniture, crockery, and plate for our immediate necessities, and we are very sorry we did not bring more; everything like furniture is so dear and bad, and tables, chairs etc., not to be had ready made,' Charlotte Godley wrote in 1850 after her arrival in Wellington, where the family lived for six months. When her pianoforte arrived, she was ecstatic. It was out of tune, but she could 'not resist playing one thing after another all night'.[32] Such items served as reminders of 'Home', and many women saw them as essential to civility – treasured dinner sets and musical instruments provided the means to offer hospitality and to maintain social rituals, from drinking tea to celebrating festive seasons with food, music and dancing. Even those promoting emigration recognised the lasting benefits to women of access to a piano:

Top Betsey Wright Nairn sketched two women making clothing in 1883. One stands at a sewing machine, while the other examines a partially made jacket. *Sketch by Betsey Wright Nairn, Alexander Turnbull Library, Wellington, E-443-q-015*

Bottom Entitled 'A scene in my "office"!!', this sketch of 1846 shows Sophia Bambridge doing the household washing. The artist, her husband William Bambridge (an Anglican missionary), wrote: 'The next sketch represents a little contrivance by my good wife, for the convenience of washing. Would that she did not consider herself compelled to exert and weary her body not only at the wash tub but many other things…' *Alexander Turnbull Library, Wellington, MS-0131-106*

Anna Hunger, a Taranaki settler, made this quilt from pieces of cotton backed with flour and oatmeal bags. She probably began work on the quilt in the 1830s, before she emigrated with her family to New Zealand, but the makeshift backing materials indicate that she finished it in New Zealand. *Puke Ariki, New Plymouth, PA2012.085*

If a lady were hesitating whether to pay the freight for her piano or a chest of drawers, I would decidedly recommend her to prefer the piano. It will afford more gratification and cheerfulness from the associations aroused by its music than can be supplied by more practically useful furniture, for which, after all, it is easy to get a substitute from any skilful colonial carpenter.[33]

Mary Ann Martin, wife of Chief Justice William Martin, was another who took to the task of homemaking with considerable ingenuity. She described how she created domestic comfort out of whatever materials were available. Packing cases and empty boxes were transformed into dressing tables, washstands, ottomans and 'lounges' (couches): 'A little white muslin and pink calico, and chintz cushions stuffed with scraped flax, made a handsome show.'[34] Other women tried to keep alive the memory and comfort of Home in their households in even more immediate ways. Calico screens, extremely useful in draughty wooden houses, were decorated with pictures from the English illustrated papers. Sometimes whole rooms were 'papered with sheets of illustrations from the English Pictorials'.[35] Queen Victoria, William Gladstone and Lord Salisbury might loom large in children's bedrooms as constant reminders of the links of Empire.

Pipitea Pā, established on the shores of Wellington Harbour in the 1820s, was surrounded by the European settlement of Wellington from 1840. This sketch of 1842 shows some occupants of the pā, including a woman who may be cooking food inside the shelter on the right. *Lithograph from sketch by William Mein Smith, Alexander Turnbull Library, Wellington, PUBL-0011-04-1*

The creation of a garden, often with plants and trees that reminded the settlers of Britain, could achieve similar ends. Adela Stewart, who settled at Athenree in the Bay of Plenty in 1878, wrote: 'No one can over-estimate the pleasures of tending flowers. They are the one thing in the world that does not disappoint. They are true friends.'[36] She also accepted that 'gardening must be the woman's department, the men being too busy for anything so purely ornamental as flowers, or unnecessary as vegetables'.[37] For women who moved around the country a great deal, as their husbands' work required, leaving a much-loved garden could be particularly painful. Jane Moorhouse, wife of Canterbury Superintendent William Sefton Moorhouse, was one who grieved at the prospect of leaving her Christchurch house, Merivale, and abandoning the garden where she had seen 'every tree, shrub and flower grow'.[38] It was her tenth move in fifteen years. Gardens, like the other reminders of 'Home', brought joy and a sense of stability in the new country, whatever the uncertainties and upheavals of family life.

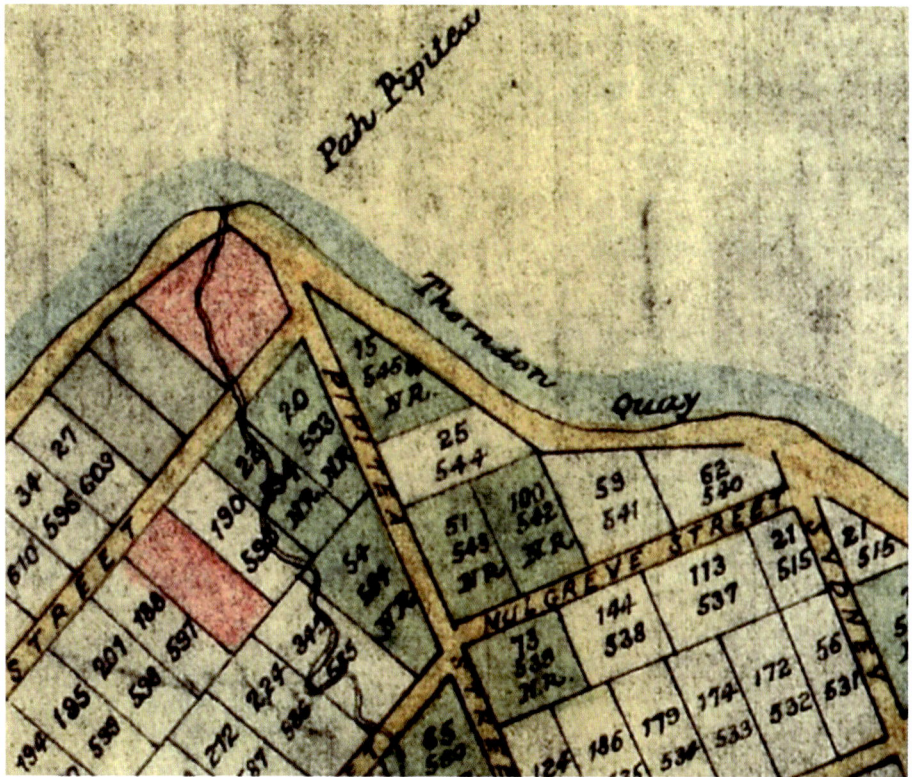

This segment of a survey plan of Wellington, drawn by Captain William Mein Smith in 1840, shows Pipitea Pā (beside Thorndon Quay) hemmed in by sections to be sold to European settlers. European settlers brought new ways of marking out the land and bestowing legal title that worked to undermine Māori customary usages. *Archives New Zealand The Department of Internal Affairs Te Tari Taiwhenua, AATE W4920, Box 79*

Enterprising women

From the start of European colonisation, Māori women were quick to supply newcomers with items for trade, from flax fibre to potatoes, fish and fruit. Flax was highly valued by Māori, who used nearly all parts of the plant in some way – especially the fibre, which was used for clothing and many other items.[39] Europeans sought the flax for rope, and admired the skill of the women who scraped the leaves with shells to produce the fibre, producing half a hundredweight a week.[40] The Sydney traders were said in 1843 to be 'dependent on native women and their shells for the cargoes they obtain'.[41] Māori families drove pigs down from the Manawatū to Wellington to supply the settlers with fresh pork, and in return purchased blankets, tobacco and 'other necessaries'.[42] Women hawked firewood, potatoes, maize and wheat, carrying heavy loads of 50 to 60 pounds in flax kits.[43]

Immigrant women also took to trade, sometimes supplying Māori women with new goods. Susan Waters set up a store soon after her arrival with her family in 1842 and wrote to her sister, '[W]e sell whatever we can buy, anything or everything; and are

In this very early photograph of Wellington, taken around 1860, a group of women and girls stand in the vicinity of Mulgrave Street in Thorndon. By then the people of Pipitea Pā nearby had begun to move away. *Alexander Turnbull Library, Wellington, PA1-f-019-15-5*

getting a tolerable business.' She was quickly engaged in dressmaking, 'mostly for native women'.[44] Dressmakers were in high demand; indeed, sewing was second, in terms of women's employment, only to domestic service. Writing to her sister in 1853, Louisa Rose remarked how she had to wait patiently in Christchurch for an overburdened seamstress to complete work. She suggested that a Mrs Lewis might consider emigrating: '[I]f she is a good dressmaker even merely good plain workwoman she would get plenty of employment here ... Workwomen are as much wanted here as labourers.'[45]

Just as men set up small businesses, so too did women, as historian Catherine Bishop has described. By careful analysis of the records, Bishop has shown how businesses often operating (for legal reasons) under a man's name were in fact run by women. Sarah Masters, for example, ran part of Masters and Perry drapers in Wellington in the 1850s. Another Wellington resident, Jane Levy, married to Solomon Levy, ran a babies' linen warehouse on Lambton Quay in 1866.[46] Millinery, toy and grocery shops were run by women whether married, widowed or single.[47]

The opportunity New Zealand offered for independence greatly appealed to Mary Taylor, an educated middle-class woman who felt stifled by English expectations of female domesticity and the rigidity of class. She noted:

Artist Edith Stanway Halcombe painted this view of the Westoe homestead in Rangitīkei, which she and her husband Arthur leased from the owner William Fox (a relative) soon after their marriage in 1863. Independent and energetic, Edith raised eight children and contributed to various community organisations while continuing to draw and paint.
Alexander Turnbull Library, Wellington, A-188-054

There are no means for a woman to live in England but by teaching, sewing or washing. The last is the best, the best paid the least unhealthy and the most free. But it is not well enough paid to live by. Moreover it is impossible for any one not born to this position to take it up afterwards.[48]

On joining her brother in New Zealand in 1845, Mary found the freedom she was looking for. She taught, bought land, built a house and dealt in cattle. When her cousin Ellen Taylor joined her in 1849, they made plans to open a women's clothing and drapery shop.[49] In 1857, Mary wrote to her friend Ellen Nussey, detailing how the work satisfied her: '[I]t is just the difference between everything being a burden and everything being more or less a pleasure.'[50] She attributed her former 'depression of spirits' to the fact that previously her judgement 'was always at war with my will. There was always plenty to do but never anything that I really felt was worth the labour of doing. My life now is not overburdened with work, and what I do has interest and attraction in it.'[51] Working amicably with her cousin, alternating duties in the shop with housework, Mary operated a thriving business.

Grace Hirst and her daughters also began trading soon after their arrival in Taranaki in the 1850s. Grace's well-off Yorkshire relatives supplied the goods – 'cloth, blankets,

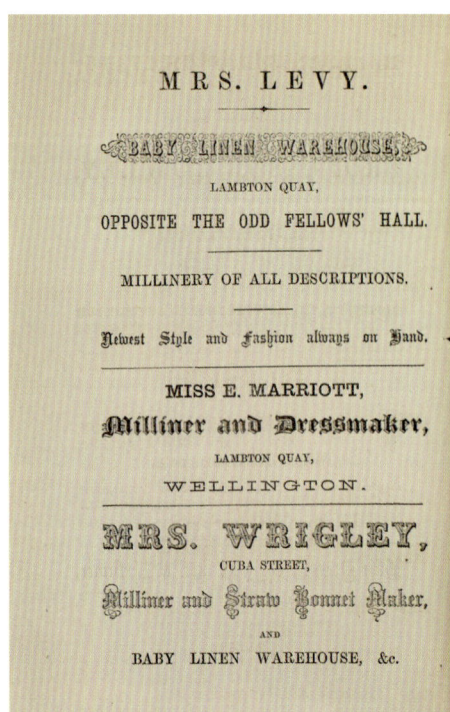

Left Newspaper advertisements reveal that a number of nineteenth-century women were engaged in businesses such as making or selling babies' and women's clothing and hats. *Right* Single women servants were offered free passage when the *Bengal Merchant* sailed from Glasgow to New Zealand in 1839. The women were in demand both for their domestic skills and as potential wives for male settlers. Wellington Almanack and Diary, *Alexander Turnbull Library, Wellington; Copyright People's Palace Museum, Glasgow Green [ca 1981], Alexander Turnbull Library, Wellington, Eph-C-IMMIGRATION-1839-01*

shoes, paper, household appliances' – that helped the family establish themselves in that decade and the next.[52] In Canterbury, products of all types, from 'a flitch of bacon to a pair of boots', were on display in 'a wonderful storehouse of miscellaneous goods' visited by Sarah Amelia Courage in the 1860s. Here she acquired numerous small appliances, from a telescopic toasting fork to a nutmeg grater, to ensure she became 'a model housekeeper'.[53]

A party of men riding around the East Cape in 1866 found themselves short on feed for their horses. An elderly local woman offered to provide them with seven cobs for one shilling, saying that was all she had. After receiving payment, she found some more and charged another shilling. 'By carefully dividing her attentions amongst us, she artfully contrived to raise 5s or 6s out of as much grain as would barely have sufficed for one legitimate feed for the smallest horse belonging to the party.'[54]

Mrs Jane Cross, known for her 'shrewd and sound common sense', ran a shop in Parnell, Auckland, in the 1870s. There she sold, among other things, butter supplied to her weekly by a Mrs Truss. An 'esteemed and steady business woman', she also weighed the oxalic acid needed by a milliner, Mrs Gilbert, for the straw plaiting used in her hats.[55]

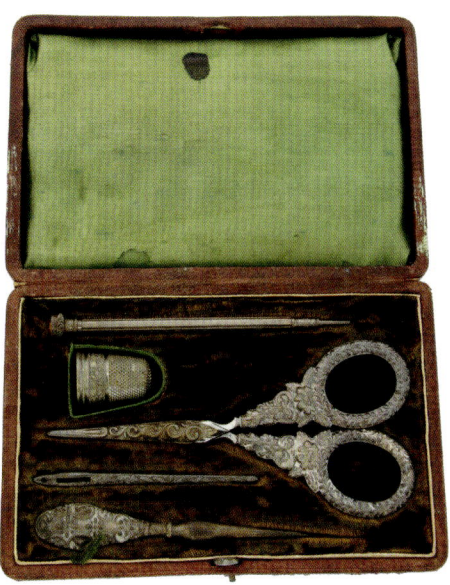

Throughout New Zealand's history, sewing has been a significant part of many women's lives, whether they were making or mending clothes, running a business, or stitching fine embroidery on samplers or household items. The stylised leaves, flower and bird in the top panel belong in the English landscape, where they were sewn probably well before emigration to New Zealand began; the intricately embroidered sewing kit or 'housewife' was made in the early twentieth century; the alphabet stencils, used for embroidery patterns, date from 1900; and the sewing set, with the ornate scissors, thimble and darning needle, are undated. *From top: Museum of New Zealand Te Papa Tongarewa, Wellington, PC000604; GH016432; GH021406; G002145/1-6*

This network of women's business activities – making and selling the butter required by households, making the hats and weighing the chemicals required for their construction – was common in growing towns where confectionery-makers, drapers and dressmakers catered to the needs of their clients.[56] At Mrs Walker's Drapery Establishment on Lambton Quay, Wellington, for example, customers could get '[f]eathers cleaned, dyed, curled, and dressed in the French style in all the fashionable shades (including black)'.[57]

In shops, public houses, hotels, boarding houses, in their own homes and in the homes of others, women worked for independence, to supplement the family economy, and to support themselves when deserted or widowed. While wages for female domestic servants stagnated in rural England, the scarcity of help in New Zealand allowed women to set better terms.[58] The Christchurch labour market report for June 1864 noted the demand for barmaids, who received £2 to £3 per week (comparable to surveyors' men); dressmakers were said to earn £35 to £40 per annum, more than the £25 to £30 per annum a female domestic servant could hope to earn (and less than half the income of a male domestic servant). 'Nurse girls' might hope to earn £20 to £25 per annum, while working girls between the ages of twelve and fifteen could expect to earn £12 10s to £15 per annum – about £1 to £2 less per annum than farm boys of the same age.[59] But active as they were in the paid labour market, women also carried the burden of unpaid domestic labour in their homes.

Creating new families and communities

In the autumn of 1854, a 'Founders Festival' celebrated the fourteen years since the landing of the settlers at Petone, in the Wellington province. Te Āti Awa specially constructed a whare, 240 feet long and 30 feet wide, thatched with nīkau and partially floored for dancing. Of the 300 people who sat down to dinner, including Edward Gibbon Wakefield and his son Edward Jerningham Wakefield, sixty were from the iwi, 'all neatly dressed in European clothing', some of the women wearing 'polkas and veils'.[60] A regimental band played the national anthem, a toast was made to the health of the Queen, and a particular tribute was paid to settler women, 'the tender sex', for their sympathy with Māori. Edward Jerningham Wakefield gave a speech in which he suggested that the emigration of women and men in equal numbers had made for racial harmony unlike any in the colonies chiefly settled by men, which had led to 'cruel extermination of the aboriginal race'. The Te Āti Awa chief Honiana Te Punikokopu replied in te reo, describing his welcome to the first European settlers who, he imagined, would protect him from his Māori foes. He spoke of the friendship between settlers and Te Āti Awa, and his hope that this 'would increase and endure to the end of time'.[61] Much enthusiasm was expressed for the future prosperity of a colony where natives were regarded as 'fellow settlers'.[62]

Writing from Wellington four years earlier, Charlotte Godley had observed a 'curious thing… the almost total absence of *old* people' in the country.[63] While young men had the greatest freedom to venture alone to the furthermost shores of the Empire, and had arrived in numbers as sailors, traders and adventurers, young married couples in their twenties and thirties were, from the outset, the focus of migration policies aimed at creating a stable and productive labour force in New Zealand. To be eligible for a free passage with the New Zealand Company, for example, emigrants had to be under forty, although older couples with adult children were also accepted.[64] The significant exception to this pattern – the recruitment of single women on a large scale in the 1860s – had the ultimate aim of strengthening social stability by providing wives for the abundance of single men, even if the immediate justification for the policy was the need for domestic servants.[65]

The influx of men associated with warfare and gold rushes had a short-lived desta-bilising impact limited to specific regions, Otago being the 'most remarkable'.[66] The demand for domestic service was insatiable as families became established and prosperity increased; and young women from Ireland, Scotland and England responded to the call. The provincial governments offered assisted passages to families from the mid-1850s, and this brought an inflow of people that well exceeded the rate of natural population increase. In total 219,000 new settlers arrived between 1858 and 1874, greatly overshadowing the combined Māori and Pākehā population gain of 96,278 through natural increase.[67]

Emigration and shipboard proximity fuelled the romance between Jane Maria Richmond and Arthur Atkinson, whose families left Gravesend together aboard the *Paget* in December 1853. A nine-year age gap existed between them but – somewhat unusually – Jane Maria was the elder. The reversal of the usual age gap made Maria self-conscious, as she wrote to a dear friend: 'I do not *wish* to be an old fool (not that it is being foolish to love the purest, noblest soul that happens to suit your peculiarities in every particular) but I could not help it.'[68] The families settled at New Plymouth, and Jane Maria and Arthur married in December 1854. The couple took up residence in a one-room cottage near the rest of the growing 'mob' of the two families. Maria greatly enjoyed decorating her new home with 'pale green paper, bright furniture and a scarlet [tablecloth]'.[69] Over subsequent decades, the extended Richmond–Atkinson mob, often sharing houses at close quarters, delighted in each other's company and regretted any distance between the siblings and cousins. Picnics, teas, dinners, balls, cricket and races fostered family links.

Weddings could be particularly important in uniting families, and their anniversaries were as quickly recalled as were the 'anniversaries of their departure [from Britain] and arrival in New Zealand'.[70] Wedding festivities might be shared by the whole community. When Ebenezer Hamlin and Sarah Grace Barriball married on 28 April 1868, the celebrations went late into the evening, during which 'a party of the settlers rode up to Eden Hill, and surprised the company with a feu-de-joie (a celebratory rifle salute) and three cheers'.[71]

The kinship ties that so pleased families like the Richmond-Atkinsons and the Barriballs could, of course, be burdensome to others. Emigration allowed both women and men a way out of family expectations they found to be insupportable. A laundress from

Mary Barker (seated, left) was one of the six children born to Emma and Alfred Barker after their arrival in Canterbury in 1850 (they already had three sons). She was photographed by her father in 1871 with Elizabeth Hewlings. The photograph of her eldest sister Sarah Elizabeth (Lizzy) in evening dress (right) dates from 1868. Their mother died soon after the birth of her last child, in 1858. *Canterbury Museum, Christchurch, 1944.78.191; 1994.78.13*

Sussex, Ann 'Dunn', emigrated to Canterbury to escape from the man with whom she had been living and who 'ill treated' her.[72] John Robertson married Martha Ballantine in Melbourne in 1859, then left her and emigrated to New Zealand where, in 1862, he married Violet Smith. On hearing of his remarriage, Martha Ballantine followed him to New Zealand and sued for maintenance, but was unable to act as a witness because a wife could not, in the case of a felony, appear against her husband. When no witness could be enticed over from Melbourne, Robertson was discharged.[73]

John Robertson clearly liked being married enough to do it twice. In contrast, one swagger claimed that 'an establishment is a nuisance' and a wife 'not so necessary to [his] happiness as other luxuries'.[74] The majority of men, however, wished to marry, even if their numerical dominance in the population denied many of them the chance to do so. 'There are hundreds of worthy and respectable single men who are desirous of getting married and settling down,' wrote 'A Bachelor' in 1870.[75] He was advocating a state 'marriage office' as a solution to the difficulties.

Even as the settler population grew after two decades of organised immigration, loneliness affected both women and men, whether or not they were married or recent migrants. Barely twenty years of age, Sarah Courage wrote of her feelings as a newly arrived settler when travelling through the tussock land outside Christchurch on the way to her new home in the 1860s: 'I felt so terribly alone … the sort of feeling one would imagine of those who were transported for life. The sense of desolation was so great that tears rushed to

Formal balls were held regularly in the larger towns during the 1850s and '60s. This watercolour depicts a ball held at Government House, Auckland, in October 1864. The women, wearing colourful ball gowns, are partnered by soldiers who had recently fought in the Taranaki and Waikato wars. The artist, Colonel Edward Williams, ironically titled the scene 'The horrors of war'. *Alexander Turnbull Library, Wellington, A-284-027*

my eyes.'[76] Such homesickness could be overwhelming, and longlasting. In May 1857, Jane Oates wrote from Taratahi Plains to her family in the English Peak District, saying that she had 'skarse a wink of sleep' thinking of her parents. She wrote, 'I don't know that I dislike hear and we are likely to do very well but I cannot bare thouts of being so far from home.'[77] Many women with family responsibilities on farms and mission stations were unable to make even occasional forays into more populated areas in search of companionship. Mary Ann O'Connor's husband was a road builder, and often away from their rural Canterbury home. If she needed stores, Mary Ann walked the 5 miles to the nearest store at Ashley Bank and back, carrying her produce and her baby. Her elder child was left at home, 'tied to the leg of the bed, to be kept safe while mother was away'.[78]

The little Canterbury town of Oxford grew up around the timber mill serving the Harewood forest. By 1859 there was an accommodation house and a store; a blacksmith's shop followed soon after. By 1862, the number of families established there required a schoolroom, which was also pressed into service as a church, a store and a post office.[79] Connections with those left back in Britain depended on letters, and the post office was a social gathering place in rural communities. So too were churches. Then came the public houses. By 1883 there were four of them in Oxford, and the publicans presented a petition signed by 101 people for an extension of the closing hour from 10 p.m. to 11 p.m. A contrary petition, stating that ten o'clock was 'quite late enough for hotels to be open and that there were already too many licensed houses in the district', was signed by ninety-five residents, forty of them women, 'several of whom were wives of those requesting an extension of time'. The wives lost out and 11 p.m. closing became the norm.[80] At first the town was isolated by the lack of roads and bridges, but links with the wider Canterbury community were secured when the railway came to Oxford in June 1875. Mail, goods and passengers could now be received twice daily, enhancing a feeling of connection with the wider world.[81]

South Island communities like Oxford were able to develop within a relatively stable social environment, far from the conflicts between Māori and colonial forces that took place in the North Island. When settler communities reached a certain size women might band together, as they did in 1869 at Onehunga, near Auckland, to form a Ladies Benevolent Society 'to assist refugees from the Maori wars'.[82] The Hauraki Ladies Benevolent Society was established the same year.[83] Church associations provided the basis for groups offering fellowship for members and aid for the poor. The Knox Church Ladies Association, for example, was formed in Dunedin in 1879 for the purpose of 'rendering aid to widows and orphans and others needing counsel and a helping hand'.[84] Their concern with women and children struggling to survive on their own reflected the overwhelming importance of the family as the central economic unit. Men, women and children were bound together in the endeavour to provide the necessities of life and, if possible, to progress beyond them. If the burden of support became too much, men could – and did – leave families. Women were much less likely to abandon their children, whose needs structured their lives.

The survival of the fittest?

Children abounded in settler society: Pākehā fertility rates were high, and the family was the crucial form of social organisation.[85] Raewyn Dalziel has shown that, in the New Plymouth settlement of 1841–42, daughters married at a younger age than their migrant mothers, and that nearly half those marrying in the settlement were under twenty. They were, therefore, likely to have larger families: an average of 10.4 children, compared to 8.3 in their mothers' generation.[86] Sarah Ann Cripps, accommodation-house keeper, shopkeeper, postmistress and midwife in the Wairarapa in the 1860s and 1870s, was just one who bore ten children.[87] Early marriage, multiple pregnancies and extended lactation meant that menstruation was a rare event for such women. Historian David Thomson suggests that although around 16 per cent of women who married in the 1850s and 1860s had three births or fewer, the average was 7.4 births.[88] In an exceptional case in the south, Sarah Ann Taylor bore twenty-one children, only one of whom died at birth. Married at sixteen to a Southland banker, she ran a highly ordered household. The eight girls had a fresh white frilled apron each day and they, along with their twelve brothers, 'kept splendid health'.[89]

Not all were blessed with such robustness. The risk of dying in childbirth was high. Historian Alison Clarke suggests that, at a conservative estimate, one mother died for every 195 births in the 1870s.[90] Recurrent pregnancies depleted women's physical resources and made them less able to withstand a prolonged labour or septicaemia, both of which were common causes of maternal death.[91] Susan McLean, for example, miscarried in her first pregnancy and died giving birth to her first child – 'a pledge of affection,' her husband wrote, 'which I must not now neglect'.[92] 'My Dear Hannah,' Jane Oates wrote of her nineteen-year-old daughter in 1867, 'was confind on the 16 of July at half past 3 o Clock in the Morning and was Ded at quarter to eleven the same Morning and had left a fine boy and we have got it to nurs and it makes us bisey.'[93]

The health and safety of children was an ongoing preoccupation. Five of Jane Moorhouse's nine children survived, and her journal records not only her delight in their progress but also her constant anxieties about them, particularly when her husband was away.[94] Physical ailments, such as aches and fevers, had to be carefully monitored. Five days of a diphtheria epidemic in 1879 took three of Sarah Ricketts' twelve children.[95] Potential accidents had to be anticipated. The home, with its open fires, water buckets and dangerous substances, was always hazardous. A twenty-one-month-old died after eating phosphorous-tipped matches which her mother had moved in the course of household cleaning.[96] Outdoors, water races, open drains, streams and rivers – all attractive play areas – were just as dangerous. 'The first place to look [for a lost child] was the well.'[97] Older children were expected to look out for the younger ones, and for women absorbed in household work it was often impossible to oversee all their activities. Maria Richmond, pregnant at the time of her infant niece's accidental drowning in a garden pond, expressed in writing what many mothers no doubt felt: 'Until children are given us, it seems as tho' half the possibilities in human life for bringing joy or sorrow remain unrevealed …'[98]

Fire, so necessary for cooking, warmth and light, might also bring tragedy.[99] Jane Crick, a lodger in the house of Margaret Barron, in Wellesley Street, Auckland, apparently ignored her bedroom candle due to her intoxication, with disastrous results. A neighbour rescued the Barron children from the flames but Jane Crick died from severe burns.[100] In Shirley, near Christchurch, four-year-old James Joel Briggs was burned to death when his clothes ignited near the fire burning in an open grate. Mr and Mrs Briggs had left their three children alone in the house. When Mrs Briggs returned after four hours, the house was full of smoke, the four-year-old 'charred almost to a cinder' and the eleven-month-old severely burned on the lower half of his body. The two-year-old was apparently unscathed.[101]

'I cannot help comparing my life to that of a cat with its back constantly stroked backwards,' wrote a discontented Rose Hall from Christchurch to her English sister-in-law Grace. Rose's husband, John Hall, a member of the Canterbury Provincial Council and leading national politician, was 'far too much taken up with public matters to pay attention to the trifles that make up for the happiness of home life'. By 1866, Rose had three living children: Mildred born in 1863, Wilfred born in 1864, and John born in 1865. Their company, in her husband's absence, made her 'thankful indeed for my heart folds closer and closer round them every day; they are very good little things and grow more and more engaging in their ways'.[102]

In this group portrait, taken after the marriage of Edith Clark and William Matthews on 28 September 1909, the bride and groom stand a little to one side of the front row (third and fourth from left) while the centre of the photograph is dominated by other members of the wedding party. The ceremony took place at the Te Kōpuru Church and the reception was held at Whakahara homestead, Northern Wairoa, Northland. *Alexander Turnbull Library, Wellington, PAColl-0036-8-08*

Jane Moorhouse, too, described her young daughter Alice as 'a most pleasant companion'.[103] Julia Wilding, relishing motherhood and the support of her lawyer husband in Ōpawa, Christchurch, carefully recorded her daughter Gladys's development in a 'Life Events' book. When Gladys first went away for a few days, aged five, her mother noted, 'I miss her dreadfully.'[104] Her first-born son had died as an infant, and it was her love of her living children, she wrote, that 'makes the world all bright and radiant'.[105] Jane Williams was beset by a 'great dread' when she thought 'of family ties being broken through and thought nothing of. Our children are much attached to each other as well as to their parents, and it is a feeling we wish to cherish as much as possible.'[106] Jane Maria Atkinson described the brood of young children she cared for as 'an antidote to morbidity'.[107]

As European settler families flourished and grew, whānau appeared to be diminishing: Māori villages were 'deserted', waves of sickness took their toll on adults, and child mortality was high.[108] In 1851, the *Wellington Independent* noted the 'rapid diminution of the natives' – attributing this to an excess of men in the Māori population (approximately 100 men to every 75 to 77 women).[109] Sterility among the women, infanticide of female children in times of war, and the practice of polygamy were some of the other factors that were said by contemporary observers to be causing the decline of the race.[110]

Much more likely was the explanation that Māori offered the missionary William Williams: that new illnesses were 'brought by the ships'.[111] Influenza, measles, tuberculosis and venereal disease played havoc in a previously unexposed population. Māori were said to be 'melting away', with their extinction 'as certain as any thing human can be'.[112] A survey

At this Māori wedding, probably held in the Akaroa area in the 1860s, there are two, possibly three bridal couples who stand together in the centre of the photograph. They and their guests all wear European clothing, and two of the brides appear to be wearing white. *Alexander Turnbull Library, Wellington, E-501-f-072*

of the Port Nicholson, Waikanae, Porirua, Ōtaki, Manawatū, Rangitīkei and Wairarapa districts in 1850 suggested the Māori population was just 4,711, of which children made up a quarter. In contrast, the European population had reached 4,688, nearly half of whom (2,029) were children under fourteen. 'This fact,' the *New Zealander* noted, 'places in a striking light the difference between the two races.'[113] Some settlers hoped that the rapid demise of Māori would take with it 'native questions, native wars, and native policies out of the country'.[114] Māori themselves could only lament the decline of their whānau, debating whether their abandonment of ancestral customs had brought them to this pass.[115]

The future for Māori appeared fragile as white settlers increased their hold on the land. Being born in New Zealand, as half of the non-Māori population was by the mid-1880s, seemed to create a legitimacy of claim to the country. Such a claim appeared divinely and scientifically sanctioned to those who were certain that Māori were a dying race.[116] Herbert Spencer's phrase 'the survival of the fittest' summed up the new ideas in evolutionary theory put forward by Charles Darwin in 1859; this reinforced earlier notions that those on supposedly higher rungs of the ladder of civilisation would oust those below them.

Marriage, property and destitution

The sheer number of Pākehā, as well as the patriarchal and nuclear structure of their families, impacted on Māori. So too did the weight of law. In the late 1840s and early 1850s, 'a question of momentous import' – the rights of 'Anglo-Maories' – was the subject of newspaper reports accusing the government of dishonesty in alienating the lands of Kenehuru Meurant of the Waikato iwi.[117] 'It would appear,' reporters noted, that 'when the native woman married, the land became the property of her husband and, that the Maori title being thus extinguished, and the husband having no Crown Grant, it was liable to be taken as demesne land of the Crown.'[118]

Kenehuru had apparently been gifted land by three chiefs, and this enabled her to bring thirty acres of land in the Waikato to her marriage to Edward Meurant. Twenty acres of this land were subsequently confiscated.[119] 'If a Native woman marry a European subject of the Queen, her land is confiscated to the Crown,' Hugh Carleton argued when Kenehuru's case came before the court in 1854. Carleton maintained that the confiscations were an incitement to immorality, and that Māori women would shun marriage: 'If she merely live in concubinage with a European, all the power in New Zealand cannot touch one acre of that land.'[120]

The English Dower Act of 1833 had put an end to a woman's right to a life-interest in one-third of her husband's estate. English men were free to dispose of their estates at will. Under English law and thus New Zealand law, married women were *femes couvertes*, women covered by the legal identity of their husbands. Marriage, unlike any other contract in which partners set their own terms, was fixed in law, and sexual difference was at its heart. Under its terms, a man and woman freely consented to join together in a monogamous relationship in what was expected to be a lifetime contract.[121]

In the first half of the nineteenth century, marriage negated women's legal personhood. On marrying, women lost their legal, economic and sexual autonomy. Women could retain ownership of 'real' property (usually land), but husbands gained the right to its revenues and could manage it in any way they wished. They could not, however, sell it without their wife's permission or bequeath it in their will. Any other property a woman possessed became her husband's to dispose of. If a woman gave a treasured family brooch to a beloved daughter, for example, it could be sold by her husband but not bequeathed in his will.[122] A married woman had no cash of her own and had to ask her husband for money or for credit in his name to buy goods. Faced with her husband's incredulity that she had pledged his credit, North Canterbury settler Sarah Courage 'reddened with shame ... he looked as black as a thundercloud, and I felt somewhat like a criminal going to be hanged'.[123] In losing her legal personhood on marriage, a woman could not sue or be sued. If a woman committed a crime in the presence of her husband, he was held to be responsible. The only situation in which a woman could testify against a husband in court was when she accused him of assault and battery.

The situation was very different for Māori women of mana, who exercised control of lands through their descent from high-ranking ancestors. 'In a society which recognised the pre-eminent rank and status of *some* women,' Angela Ballara has written, '*all* women could not be regarded as inferior to *all* men.'[124] Hineipaketia, for example, was the 'principal person' in the Heretaunga district from the 1840s to the 1870s, and land sales relied on her endorsement.[125] But English law was bent on undermining Māori communal ownership and inheritance patterns. The 1865 Land Act aimed to abolish matrilineal descent, although some recognition of the customary rights of Māori women was made in the Native Lands Act 1869, clause 22 of which recognised conveyances of property by married Māori women, allowing them the legal capacity of a *feme sole*, a single woman with legal

Left Wearing their best clothes, Mere Whakamairu and her husband Alexander Cowan show off their baby son Peter (Pita) in this photograph of the 1870s. Intermarriage between Māori and Pākehā occurred from the early nineteenth century. *Right* Sarah and William Barnard Rhodes were photographed with their adopted daughter Mary Ann in Wellington in 1858. Sarah, William's first wife, had no children and died in 1862. Mary Ann was William's daughter from a previous relationship; her mother was Māori. *Alexander Turnbull Library, Wellington, PA1-q-131-32-1; PAColl-5601*

standing.[126] Women also continued to give evidence and conduct cases in the Land Court, which recognised their ownership, and they were frequently grantees under the 1865 Act.[127]

Māori women were also quick to take advantage of the English law of equity which, by use of a settlement or trust, allowed the possibility of endowing a woman with separate property that was unable to be touched by her husband. Two sisters of Māori descent, Mary Hardy and Euphemia Arthur, made a settlement 'with the assent of their respective husbands', so that their lands in the Rākaukākā block, near Gisborne, were held in trust. Euphemia received a £100 annuity for as long as she lived, and Mary became a tenant for life, able to receive income from rents for herself and her children.[128]

Most women, however, lacked the protection of a settlement or trust, and had to rely on their husband's ability to provide. Supporting his wife and family was one of an English man's primary responsibilities, but the mobility of colonial society meant that such responsibilities often broke down. As a remedy for the 'excess' number of deserted wives, in 1860 the men in New Zealand's House of Representatives (consisting of the elected Lower House and the unelected Upper House, or Legislative Council) introduced the Married Women's Property Protection Act.[129] This provided that a deserted wife could apply to a magistrate for an order protecting her earnings and that, for as long as she was deserted, she could exercise all the rights of a *feme sole*. In this instance the colony exceeded the protection available in English law, which required a judicial separation before such protection could be enforced.[130] The Act was considered necessary because '[i]t sometimes happened that the property [deserted women] had accumulated by their own industry during the absence of their husbands was taken possession of by the latter on their return, and the wives had no alternative but to submit'.[131] Protection was extended, however, only 'to property accumulated during the period of desertion'.[132] In this light, the legislation might be seen less as a victory for women than as a means of ensuring that destitute persons did not become a charge on the state.[133]

Men died or were injured in accidents, unemployment might strike, or husbands might be required to work far from home. Movement in search of work was the typical male response to poverty, whereas women might be less inclined to move because of children. Martha Bluett, for example, brought up her thirteen children without much assistance from her husband. He worked at a sawmill at Woodside, some distance from their home at Oxford, returning to the family only for Saturday nights and Sundays. His wife refused to move to the mill to live 'because there was no school [there] and she was determined to have the children sent to school'.[134] Female poverty was closely linked to the childbearing years.[135] If other avenues for earning money (including piecework or taking in lodgers) were absent, women might apply for charitable aid. Widows with children were most likely to receive aid; deserted wives were also seen as deserving, while single women with children were 'regarded as authors of their own fate'.[136]

Historian Margaret Tennant has demonstrated the plight of women alone. In October 1872, in Auckland, 35 widows with a total of 149 children applied for 'outdoor' relief – money, food or clothing given to them in their homes (rather than the family being taken into an institution for the destitute) – while 13 deserted wives with 44 children, and 9 wives who had husbands in prison, with 24 children, also applied.[137] Rations were meagre. Tennant notes the case of a family of eight whose daily ration comprised 2 ounces of tea, 3 ounces of sugar and two 2-pound loaves of bread.[138]

That children might be abandoned in such circumstances is perhaps not surprising. The Neglected and Criminal Children Act, passed in 1867, referred to children begging, thieving and associating with prostitutes and habitual drunkards.[139] Twelve boys and eight girls were found to be neglected and abandoned children by the Auckland Police Court in March 1872, at a time when the European population was estimated to be about 75,000.[140] They may well have been the offspring of the women appearing in the court that month: 36 women were charged with being drunk and disorderly, 105 with vagrancy (which included prostitution, keeping of a brothel, and being a 'notorious drunkard, associating

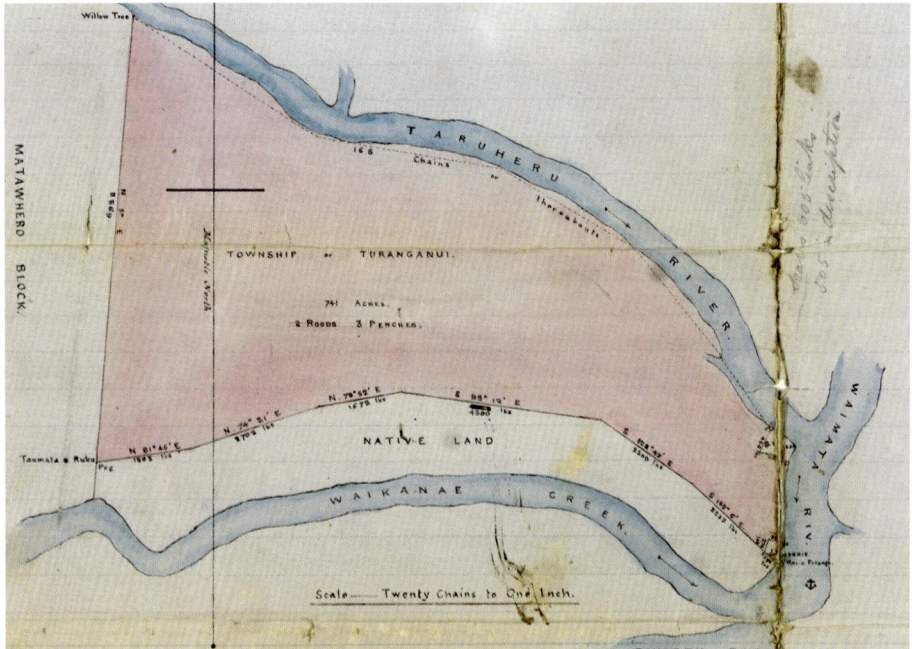

Riperata Kahutia, a Te Aitanga-a-Māhaki woman of mana, was one of the principal owners of the Tūranganui No. 2 block which was sold to the Crown in 1869 to provide land for the township of Gisborne. This map comes from the deed of sale, which she and her half-sister Kateraina signed. Another signatory was Kate Wylie (Keita Waere) of Rongowhakaata. When the sale of Tūranganui was negotiated, Riperata made sure the southern boundary of the town fell short of the Waikanae River so her tribe could continue to access food resources. *Archives New Zealand The Department of Internal Affairs Te Tari Taiwhenua, ABWN W5279 8102 Box 165 AUC 339 (R12 153 923)*

with thieves, and having no lawful means of obtaining a livelihood'). Many of the latter were said to be 'depraved young girls', sixteen to twenty years old, while others were 'old women… who live on the infamous earnings of their daughters'.[141]

In the decades following New Zealand's European settlement, the apparently seamless unity of husband and wife was being torn apart not only by the vicissitudes of the colonial experience but also by British and American advocates of women's rights. News of the agitation over married women's property rights came to the colony from family and friends, and through sought-after newspapers and periodicals.[142] Disputes over property – landed or not – disrupted the internal economy of households. Such disputes had implications for the state, for if married women were left destitute by absconding husbands, to whom could they turn for support? The ready availability of John Stuart Mill's 1869 *On the Subjection of Women* in the year of its publication, and of the feminist Frances Power Cobbe's *Dawning Lights*, both advertised by the Wellington bookseller William Lyon in September 1869, fanned flames in the debate about women's position.[143] Property debates within households, however, were overshadowed in the 1860s by conflicts over land between Māori and Pākehā.

Jane Maria Gray was the daughter of Alexander Gray and Kotero Hinerangi, who married at Paihia on 20 May 1830. In this formal studio photograph in about 1857, Jane posed with her children Frances Sophia Herries (left) and William Frederick Herries; their father was William Stansfield Herries of the 65th Regiment. Jane's sister Sophia Hinerangi became famous as the leading tourist guide at the Pink and White Terraces at Lake Rotomahana. Their half sister, Lucy Takiora Lord, worked alongside the government forces in the wars of the 1860s. *Photograph by Garry Trevor Clark, Alexander Turnbull Library, Wellington, 1/2-137188-F*

Chapter Four
War, Gold and Dispossession

Nineteen-year-old Catherine Carran held her baby in her arms as she boarded a boat to take her down the Waikato River. It was 1861. Leaving the land of her mother's people cannot have been easy for the daughter of Irihapeti McKay, of Waikato and Ngāti Pūkeko descent, and John Horton McKay, a storekeeper. Catherine was travelling to join her husband, a Pākehā stockman called William Carran, who had gone south, lured by the possibility of gold and a desire to escape the probability of warfare in the Waikato region. The year of Catherine and William's marriage, 1860, was an inauspicious one, with the government sending troops to quell Māori opposition to land sales in Taranaki. Lines of loyalty were hardening, and to have allegiances across the boundary of race – indeed, to be connected by blood to both sides – held particular dangers.

When they reached Onehunga, Catherine and her child boarded a sailing ship bound for Dunedin. From there, Catherine wrote to her husband to inform him of her plans, and embarked on the *Star of Dunedin* for Campbelltown (Bluff). No one was there to meet them when the ship arrived. Catherine waited for a week in a hotel in the hope that her husband would come. When he still did not, she put her baby on her back and decided to walk the 25 miles around the wild coast to Waimāhaka station, where William was working. She found shelter for the first night in a shepherd's hut but spent the second night in the sandhills, keeping warm beside a driftwood fire. The following day the local runholder, James Wybrow, took Catherine and the child to his home, restored their spirits with food and rest, and eventually delivered them to William Carran. William had never received his wife's letter.[1]

The dislocation wrought by warfare affected families throughout the country during the 1860s and 1870s, and brought an influx of unattached men as soldiers, unsettling the prospect of planned development. While European women and children were often sent to safety during the wars, many Māori women and children participated in the fighting. The discovery of gold was destabilising in a different way, drawing men to the goldfields from within New Zealand as well as from Australia and California. Many of them left behind wives and children. Some women, however, found new opportunities on the goldfields, profiting from the needs of miners.

Gold strikes offered the allure of instant wealth, but the acquisition of Māori land held

Kate (Kati) Middlemass (left), Sophia Hinerangi, and another tourist guide (right) were photographed outside Hinemihi meeting house, Te Wairoa, south-east of Rotorua, by Elizabeth Pulman in 1881. From the 1870s, bilingual Māori women guided tour parties around the thermal attractions at Whakarewarewa in the central North Island. *Photograph by Elizabeth Pulman, Alexander Turnbull Library, Wellington, 1/2-029217-F*

out more long-term prospects for settler families. The same Parliament that was busy confiscating Māori land also enfranchised Māori men in 1867, solidifying the concept that citizenship was a male affair. The 1860s and 1870s, which saw the entrenchment of British law, undermined the rights of Māori women. Advocates of women's rights took a different view. Inverting earlier ideas about European women being exemplars of civilisation, they looked to Māori women's independence as a model for European society to emulate.

The spread of war in the North Island

The government's success in acquiring about two-thirds of the land in the South Island was not matched in the North where, in 1861, Māori still held approximately three-quarters of the land. In 1858, a number of iwi had given their allegiance to the Ngāti Mahuta chief, Potatau Te Wherowhero, as their King, and applied his veto on land sales. In the formation of the Kīngitanga, or Māori King movement, Māori showed their determination to assert their authority against the settlers, and to live on Māori terms in their own

A few Māori women fought with or assisted Imperial and colonial troops during the wars of the 1860s. Lucy Lord, also known as Takiora, pictured with her sister Mata (left) was a guide for Major Gustavus von Tempsky until his death at the battle of Te Ngutu-o-te-manu in Taranaki in 1868. Another sister, Karaana (or Kararaina/Caroline), posing with weapons, fought with troops in Taranaki until her accidental death. *Alexander Turnbull Library, Wellington, PA2-2830; PA2-2559*

territory, 'the King on his piece; the Queen on her piece, God over both; and Love binding them to each other'.[2] They imagined, as historian Philippa Mein Smith has written, an equal future, 'walking in parallel'.[3] The settlers, however, wanted land, and one system of law and order – and for that to be British.

Māori wished to protect their sovereignty, and fought to retain possession of their lands as the source not only of economic prosperity and physical well-being but also of identity. The traditional saying of the Whanganui people, 'Ko au te awa. Ko te awa ko au' ('I am the river. The river is me'), is just one expression of the centrality of place to hapū or iwi identity. For Te Āti Awa, majestic Mount Taranaki to the south and a long coastline to the north between Ōnukutaipari and Te Rau-o-te-huia, near Motunui, marked their identity and the boundaries of their fertile lands.[4] The New Zealand Company's decision to establish there the settlement that became known as New Plymouth sowed seeds of disruption that led to the first of the major wars of the 1860s. In this instance, a junior chief, Te Teira, offered to sell a 600-acre block of land near the mouth of the Waitara River to the Governor, Thomas Gore Browne. The Governor took up Te Teira's offer in spite of a veto on the sale by the senior chief, Wiremu Kingi. Gore Browne saw this as an assertion of authority, as he noted: 'I must either have purchased this land or recognized a right which would have made William King virtual sovereign of this part of New Zealand.'[5] But his hopes for a short, sharp victory were dashed, and warfare spread from Taranaki into the Waikato.

At the request of the settlers, the British imported thousands of fighting men and organised a military system of supply to sustain them. The small contingents of the Colonial Defence Force and the Forest Rangers were supplemented by militias. Nearly 12,000 men were committed to serve with the Imperial forces, while the total number of men involved in the British forces 'at some time or another' reached 18,000.[6] Warfare, and the consequent influx of soldiers, spread through the North Island, affecting Taranaki in 1860, the Waikato in 1863, then Tauranga, Whanganui and South Taranaki in 1864. Fighting stretched into the 1870s as the government attempted to subdue challenges to its authority from new prophetic movements that gave hope to Māori from different areas. The millenarian Pai Mārire faith, founded by the prophet Te Ua Haumene in 1862, was adopted by Tawhiao, who succeeded Potatau as King, and spread through the King Country. Te Kooti Arikirangi Te Turuki led the Ringatū, or the Upraised Hand, a faith that spread among people in Poverty Bay, East Cape and Te Urewera from 1875.

Communities were thrown into confusion by warfare, and though Māori were over-whelmingly opposed to attempts by Pākehā to dispossess them of their land, there were no straight lines of loyalty. Settlers hungry for land opposed Pākehā such as Sir William Martin, the retired Chief Justice, and the Revd Octavius Hadfield, both of whom advocated for the Māori position. Some Māori fought with the Crown.[7] Pākehā who had been settled in an area for a long time might receive protection from Māori friends, while allegiances among Māori groups shifted with new interpretations of events. Some women were forced to fend for themselves. Lydia Burr, living amongst a large Māori community on a farm at Whirokino, near Te Awahou (Foxton), successfully deterred a raider by suggesting she had encircled her storehouse with gunpowder.[8] Others sought solace together. In March 1860, when the battle of Ōmata broke out, 700 settler women and children waited fearfully in the crowded New Plymouth barracks while their men fought.[9]

For families of mixed race, decisions had to be made about where their allegiance lay. 'The Maori perspective,' Sally McLean has written, 'was that these children [of mixed marriages] belonged to their mother's tribe.'[10] But uncertainty as to whose custom defined the law became heightened in the turbulence of the 1860s when many of those with Pākehā-Māori parentage were claimed for one side or the other.[11] Girls were removed from schools at Ōtāwhao and Waipā 'to bake bread for the taua'.[12] Waikato Māori 'removed all the native women and half-caste children' in the district, reported a Mrs Allen.[13]

Grace Hirst, a general merchant in New Plymouth, made keen observations of the local scene. She wrote of the influx of military settlers onto confiscated land in September 1863: 'such numbers of young men lounging about and so much levity in the appearance of the young ladies'. The following year she wrote to her daughter Grace, in Germany, that

Caroline Abraham (left), Mary Ann Martin (seated) and Sarah Selwyn (right). The wives of a bishop, a judge and a bishop (respectively), they were photographed in the early 1860s, when war was disrupting the missionary efforts of the church. They were unafraid of expressing their views, publishing a pamphlet in London entitled *Extracts of Letters from New Zealand on the War Question*. They thought the government, in forcing land sales on Māori, was acting in bad faith and denying Māori their rights as British subjects. *Alexander Turnbull Library, Wellington, PAColl-10135-3*

'these new people have caused a great change in the place – amongst so many strangers there are sure to be indifferent characters and we seem now to be more afraid of the white men than the Maorie'.[14] Women who came to settle imagined that they would be joining communities made up of families, but war brought bands of unattached men who undermined such expectations of stability.

Attempts were made to keep European women at a distance from the fray. They were not expected (or allowed) to join the fighting, but instead often required to leave the war-torn districts. The 'grateful and laudatory address' delivered by 180 'ladies at Taranaki' to the British men who stormed Waireka Pā in late March 1860 indicates the restraint and supportive role expected of Pākehā women.[15] Maria Atkinson resisted entreaties that she leave New Plymouth for Nelson: 'I can't make up my mind to go away to die by inches of

Gate Pā, a massive fortification, was constructed by Tauranga iwi on Pukehinahina Ridge in 1864. When government troops attacked it on 29 April, they suffered heavy losses. *Alexander Turnbull Library, Wellington, PA1-f-046-13-3*

anxiety for I know when at a distance I shall probably magnify the dangers Arthur [her husband] and all are exposed to.'[16] In the stone cottage in New Plymouth where Maria and her sister-in-law took refuge, having left their beloved rural home at Hurworth, they had '3 riflemen, generally 4, to guard us'.[17] Grace Hirst and her family dug holes in their garden surrounding the house before leaving their farm, Brackenhirst, at the Bell Block, for New Plymouth, and buried any lead, 'spare crockery, and anything that would not spoil'. They feared that if Māori found the lead, they would steal it to make bullets.[18]

Warfare tore many Pākehā families asunder. Anxious husbands bundled their wives and children onto boats at New Plymouth to escape the conflict, so that they became 'fugitives at Nelson and supported by public charity'.[19] In Nelson, those unable to procure accommodation of their own crowded into communal barracks where they anxiously awaited news in the hope they could return to their homes. The barracks operated under a strict regime. Breakfast for 130 was served at 7 a.m. and mothers, anxious to see their children fed, sometimes found no food left for themselves. Residents chafed at the routine, the monotonous diet of 'baked meats, not enough vegetables', the lack of space for children to play, and the presence of rats.[20] Mary King found life in Nelson with her six children, the youngest of whom was still an infant, to be a 'vile separation' from her husband Thomas.[21] The end of the hostilities, whenever that might be, would relieve them both 'of great anxiety'.[22]

Māori women and children played a much more direct role in the hostilities. The initial survey of Waitara that began the 1860 conflict was disrupted by a 'party of old women' who seized the surveyors' tripod and chain.[23] In direct confrontations, women priestesses inspired warriors with strength to meet the enemy. Ana Pene of Te Arawa shouted 'with a mighty voice to urge her men on as they sapped up to an enemy pa'.[24] Women from the Upper Whanganui, widowed after early fighting in Taranaki, 'took revenge by biting savagely at the preserved head of the British soldier Lloyd, carried to their villages by the Pai Marire emissaries'.[25] And when in 1864 the British called on Waikato Māori besieged for three days at Ōrākau to release their women and children, the reply was: 'The women will fight on with the men.'[26]

Māori women took part also in the disputes between iwi. When Kereopa Te Rau

Heni Te Kiri Karamu, also known as Heni Pore (Jane Foley), was a Te Arawa warrior woman and supporter of the Kīngitanga who became famous for an act of compassion towards the enemy at the battle of Gate Pā. At risk to her own life, she gave water to Colonel H. J. P. Booth and several other wounded government soldiers. This was in accordance with a code of conduct drawn up by the Māori defenders of the pā before the battle. She was photographed in old age, probably in the 1920s or '30s, wearing a feather cloak, huia feathers and a hei tiki – all symbols of mana. *Alexander Turnbull Library, Wellington, 1/2-041822-G*

determined to lead a Pai Mārire party to Waikato in May 1865, a Ngāti Manawa group of forty, half of whom were women, joined the Ngāti Rangitihi guard in order to prevent Kereopa and his people crossing their land. Five of the combined forces were killed and ten wounded, but Kereopa's force sustained heavier casualties.[27] At Tokomaru Bay, local people organised to hold off the Pai Mārire forces:

> Each seizing a gun, three of the young women, named Mere Arihi Tipuna (daughter of Arapeta Potae), Te Mangi (Rangi) i paea (daughter of Tamati Waka) and Hine Pahuahua joined the young chief at Hicks Bay ... Hati, the chief, incited the defenders; the old men loaded the guns, and handed them to the women. As the guns were only fowling pieces, loaded with old-fashioned powder, paper and bullet, it was a matter of importance to be ready ... The young women showed great bravery, fearlessly facing the foe, and shooting down each of the assailants as he attempted to scale the cliff.[28]

In the same region, the Church Missionary Society leader William Williams noted the increasing discontent of Māori women, expressed by their return to tā moko, the practice of tattooing the face. The missionaries regarded this as the 'devil's thumbprint', a sign of earlier degenerate days.[29] 'Hirini's wife,' Williams noted, 'has been having her lips done and so has Miki Parani.'[30] By re-adopting long-held traditions, Māori women were signalling their independence from the dictates of the Christian mission.

In 1864, the *Lyttelton Times* noted that the success of Māori in war relied to a great extent on the way whole communities – men, women and children – consolidated into 'a compact fighting force'. Women and children, while not necessarily wielding weapons, assembled the food supplies and carried them, a task for which the colonial troops used horses. The women, the newspaper observed, 'cast bullets, make up ammunition' and, importantly, 'labour at pick and shovel', constructing the complex 'native field works' which gave the British troops 'so much trouble'.[31]

Dispossession and peace

By 1863 the *Taranaki Herald* was able to claim that the wars had made 'the Maori in reality what by a legal fiction they have long been in name, British subjects'. Further steps towards assimilating Māori into British law lay in the Native Land Acts of 1862 and 1865.[32] These Acts ended the Crown's right of pre-emption, under which 'only the Crown could extinguish Maori customary title to their lands', and set up a Native Land Court.[33] The court would determine ownership of Māori land and transform customary title into individual title in conformity with British law.[34] In this, and the New Zealand Settlements Act of 1863, lay the seeds of land alienation on an unprecedented scale.

Dispossessed of land, some groups withdrew from all contact with Pākehā. Te Āti Awa, for example, went to live in the steep hills and dense bush between the Waitara and upper Whanganui rivers.[35] After the defeat of the Kīngitanga forces at Ōrākau, millions of acres of the highly desirable, fertile Waikato land were confiscated. Tawhiao, the second Māori King, retreated with his people to the south, into Ngāti Maniapoto territory beyond the aukati (boundary) where settlers and the government were unwelcome.[36]

The beginning of a waiata tangi thought to be composed by Rangiamoa of Ngāti Apakura, who had fled to Taupō from her homeland in the Waikato, speaks of the effect of such disruption:

E pā tō hau, he wini raro, he hōmai aroha ī
Kia tangi atu au i konei, he aroha ki te iwi
Ka momotu ki tawhiti, ki Paerau. Ko wai e kite atu?
Kei hea aku hoa i mura ra, i te tōnuitanga ī?
Ka hara-mai tēnei, ka tauwehe, ka raungaiti au ī.

The wind blowing softly from the north brings longing,
And I weep. My longing for my people
Gone far off to Paerau. Who can find them there,
Where are my friends of those prosperous times?
It has come to this, we are separated and I am desolate.[37]

After the wars, dispersal and migration gave birth to new communities. Māori travelled to find work, 'shearing, harvesting, fencing, bush-felling, track-cutting, flax-cutting and gum digging'.[38] Work, whether clearing, stumping and fencing land to re-establish farms or trading in the towns, was a communal enterprise in which women and children played a vital part. Gum-digging took people to temporary encampments in the north, creating changes in domestic arrangements. Records from the 1880s noted that: 'Instead of living together in large numbers at their different settlements, and cultivating large areas of food in common, as they used to do, they now separate into families or parties and go away into the hills to dig kauri gum, where they remain for months.'[39]

Population decline, particular economic opportunities, and the desire of hapū to occupy their lands in order to protect their interests in the Land Court may all have contributed to change in Māori communities. Historian Angela Ballara suggests that Ngāti Maru of the Hauraki–Thames area, for example, were buffeted by shifting allegiances and economic change.[40] The discovery of gold in the Firth of Thames brought a rush of miners intent on opening up Ngāti Maru land. In late 1867, Ngāti Maru agreed that land at Manaia could be leased to the Crown for gold mining, in the hope that this would increase their revenue and create a new market for their produce.[41] But the mining population quickly overtook that of Hauraki Māori, and the newcomers displaced Māori in local industries.[42]

In peacetime, Māori men had wider work opportunities than Māori women. The need to earn cash – the new and increasingly important means of exchange – drew some Māori women into the urban economy. While men could seek employment on public works projects and in white collar occupations, Māori women's options were often limited, just as those of Pākehā women were, to trading, domestic work and prostitution.[43] But new avenues of opportunity for women opened up in trading and even in education. In 1875, for example, Mary, wife of the trader Hemi Tautari, opened a boarding school primarily for Māori girls in the Bay of Islands that achieved a 'high reputation' and attracted pupils from afar.[44] There pupils learned 'instrumental music and household duties' so as to become, a visitor noted, 'European-ised as much as possible, and in all respects rendered fit to become the wives of settlers'.[45]

Māori women could also play an active role as claimants in the Land Court: until 1884, their rights as property holders could not be denied as those of Pākehā women were. Riperata Kahutia, who belonged to the Te Whānau-a-Iwi hapū of Te Aitanga-a-Māhaki, was steadfast in her pursuit of land claims in the Poverty Bay area. Often in conflict with other claimants, Riperata's arguments were spirited and compelling. In an 1875 claim, 'She spoke for over an hour without wavering from the subject and with a fervid eloquence that was listened to attentively even by her opponents.'[46] She succeeded in many of her claims, and leased land to Europeans as well as deriving an income from selling timber rights. Rewards were ploughed back into the community as she and her relatives set about establishing a marae. The meeting house Te Poho-o-Materoa, named for a female ancestor, took a central place, while the marae also included a church and 'a substantial European-style house'.[47]

In the wake of the North Island wars, individuals and communities, Pākehā and Māori, had to reorient themselves to new futures. '[T]he problem now to be solved,' wrote Mary Atkin from Tāmaki to her aunt in June 1870, 'is how to repair the mischief that has been done? How to produce union and harmony where all is now discord?, and how best to "gather up the broken fragments" of the Maori people.'[48] The influx of fighting men had disturbed those Pākehā who had expected to live quietly within settled family communities. Māori faced confiscations of their ancestral lands and were forced into increased accommodation with the settler state.

Women of both races were at the forefront of rebuilding communities, whether in settlements that bustled with activity as farms were established or in diminished circumstances on the margins of the economy. Ruta Te Manuahura wrote to the Native Office as one of the latter: 'I have had much land taken from me for no reason whatever, for neither I nor my husband committed any wrong against the Crown.'[49] Pākehā founded new settlements on land long occupied by Māori, creating new opportunities for themselves while displacing, and denying the rights of, the traditional owners.

Women on the goldfields

While many communities in the North Island were fragmented by the disruptions of war, discoveries of gold in the South Island brought a different kind of disorder. Following the promise of gold as a way of securing their futures, men flocked first to Otago in the early

1860s, then to Nelson–Marlborough in 1864 and to the West Coast from 1865, before the North Island's Thames–Hauraki diggings became viable in 1867 and 1868.[50] The predominantly male tent towns of miners caused consternation among those who had hoped for a land of settled families, but others, including women, took advantage as best they could of the chances offered by these new communities.

Settler society was increasingly differentiated by the economic opportunities that attracted rough and respectable men alike, as soldiers, miners, constables and officers. Some prospered; some fell on hard times. Some advocated temperance while others sought solace in the bottle. The Christchurch *Press* feared that the influx of men would 'derange the whole condition of the social system', and called for the importation of women to help right the imbalance.[51] Even more particularly, as the small town of Dunedin was overrun by men from the declining gold diggings of Victoria across the Tasman, the provincial administration quickly instructed its recruiting agents in Edinburgh and London to attract only single women. More than 1,350 young women arrived in Otago over the course of ten months in 1862, to find themselves ill-housed next to the male constabulary who had been imported from Victoria in an effort to keep order among the hundreds of arriving miners.[52]

The great majority of single women from England, Wales, Scotland and Ireland emigrated as general domestic servants. Reduced employment opportunities in agriculture and the rise of industrialisation had led young women across Britain to seek work in cities, and domestic service often provided a place to live as well as a modest income.[53] Emigration was yet one more step on the journey which, for some, began with leaving home at the age of ten or twelve.[54] Historian Charlotte Macdonald has deftly unpacked the journeys of these women and the ways they might decide to seek opportunity on the other side of the world. Hannah Arthy, born in 1835 in an Essex village where her father was a farm labourer, was the sixth of eight children. Before migrating she was employed near to her family as a farm servant, helping with dairy work as well as in the house.[55] Other women had moved to the city before migrating. Catherine Emily Phillips had been employed as a machinist by the Alexander Sewing Machine Company in Great Portland Street, London, until business declined and the firm could no longer employ her. Nineteen-year-old Catherine sailed for Lyttelton six months later. Residing in a London industrial school, twelve-year-old Elizabeth Oliver was one of twenty orphans selected to be sent to Lyttelton. The Canterbury Superintendent, James FitzGerald, who was also the emigration agent for the Canterbury Association, planned that the orphaned girls and young women would be trained for domestic service.[56]

Those who migrated as married women, or single women who married soon after arrival, might find themselves deserted by husbands who sought instant wealth on the goldfields.[57] Advertisement columns of the goldfields' newspapers were sprinkled with urgent notices:

A Māori group in the foreground surveys the town of Dunedin in this painting of the early 1860s. The painting, based on a photograph, records a substantial town and a busy harbour. *Watercolour by Walter Scarlett Hatton, Alexander Turnbull Library, Wellington, B-078-007*

John Warner, come back to your wife at Half Way House, Kapitea Creek. Situation Waiting.

Mark Blight Webster, last heard of at Hamiltons Otago, two years ago … communicate with your wife Ann Webster, Post Office, Hokitika. Information as to his whereabouts will be thankfully received.[58]

If married men did not take responsibility for the welfare of their immediate families, it was unclear who else would do so. When men had rushed from various Canterbury districts to Australia in search of gold in 1852, James FitzGerald wrote in a letter to the *Lyttelton Times* (which he had founded):

[W]ives can, in all cases, prevent their husbands deserting them by applying to the Magistrates: if they do not do so, they must take the consequences, and they have no right to expect any aid from charitable or other sources in case they should be reduced to distress.[59]

The Otago government reportedly sent a woman and her family of eight children off to Hokitika to find their gold-prospecting husband and father.[60] 'Every third person,' wrote young surveyor Gerhard Mueller to his wife, 'seems to have a wife sitting somewhere on the other side of the Island, or in Australia.'[61]

The Thames settlement, developed from 1867 onwards, had a high proportion of married miners and, unusually, most were accompanied by their families. In the Thames–Hauraki goldfields, the work of extracting gold from quartz was expensive and likely to be long-term. Single men were unlikely to strike it rich alone, and a number entered into partnership with others. Women made up nearly half the town's population from

Irish-born Bridget Goodwin, or 'Biddy of the Buller' as she was known, was a gold miner in the Buller Gorge area on the West Coast from the mid-1860s. She worked alongside two male diggers, and like them wore moleskin trousers and boots and smoked a pipe. She outlived her companions, dying at Reefton in 1899. *Nelson Provincial Museum, Tyree Studio Collection, 39942*

1874 onwards, and a number of those who were unmarried chose to remain single.[62] Frances Haselden, for example, was a respected unmarried member of the community who served as head teacher at Kauaeranga Girls School from 1878 to 1898. Her enthusiasm for teaching was such that, as well as her daily duties, she ran evening classes in French for young ladies.[63]

Elsewhere, Māori were much more likely than Pākehā to seek gold in the company of whānau. At the Buller and the Greenstone diggings on the West Coast, Māori prospected in groups, and women and children were as vital to the task as men. According to historian Stevan Eldred-Grigg, the labour of whole families enabled Māori 'to undertake heavy earthworks and waterworks' more readily than the Pākehā prospectors. He notes that thirty Māori women and men were observed 'systematically shovelling and washing a riverbed' at Waikoropupū Springs in the Tākaka Valley.[64] Harry Evison has suggested that 600 Māori men, women and children worked alongside 1,300 Europeans on the Collingwood goldfields in the late 1850s.[65] Māori appeared 'to be pouring in from all quarters from the other island' as well as from the local area, and were said 'to have got the best … of the workable claims of the river'.[66]

But not all Māori shared in the hope that gold would bring prosperity. Others felt strongly that the incursions of the gold-hungry threatened their land. Tribal divisions at Ōhinemuri in the Coromandel came to a head when a block of land was sold in 1867. Mere Kuru Te Kati led a group of 'singing and chanting women' in disrupting the survey, triumphantly confiscating the surveyors' billhooks and threatening to throw the land-seller into the river.[67]

Unlike the cooperative whānau groups, Pākehā women on the goldfields often strug-gled alone, taking in boarders, doing laundry, and providing food along with that most sought-after of commodities – strong drink. Catherine Lucas ran a store in the Central Otago town of Roxburgh in the 1860s, and then built a hotel with a dining hall and a billiard room. Strategically placed on the route between Dunedin and the goldfields, Roxburgh was a good place to do business. Catherine, an English immigrant to Victoria, had married Harry Waigth in Melbourne in 1855 and had one son before her husband's death in 1860. She then accompanied her second husband, C. R. D. Richardson, to Otago in 1864, and settled in Roxburgh. Richardson drowned in 1868, leaving Catherine with two sons and a daughter.[68] In 1871, she married Charles Lucas, but carefully preserved her autonomy by placing her hotel's licence in her son's name.[69]

Jessie McLeod's Lady of the Lake hotel in Queenstown was shut down because of the rowdiness of the patrons. Well known to the police, and described as a 'prostitute of the lowest class', Jessie had earlier left the Dunstan goldfields with debts totalling £24 5s. Not afraid of defending herself, she had caused one man to bring a case against her for using threatening language and 'putting him in bodily fear'. Undeterred by the closure of her hotel, she reopened the Lady of the Lake as a restaurant and continued to sell liquor.[70]

Top Settler women were outnumbered by men, as this photograph of Westport in the 1870s suggests. A group of men, including the proprietor, G. T. Craddock, stand outside the Waterman's Arms, while Craddock's daughter Maria hovers in the doorway. William Phillips and Mrs Pollock stand outside the cottage next door. *Alexander Turnbull Library, Wellington, 1/2-003049-F*

Bottom Men lounge outside the Dillmanstown Hotel while a woman watches over a group of children. Dillmanstown was near Kūmara on the West Coast, and grew rapidly when gold was discovered nearby in the 1870s. *Alexander Turnbull Library, Wellington, F-25542-1/2*

Behaviour such as Jessie's was part of the 'defiled turbid torrent' that Susan Wood, wife of John Nugent Wood, the Otago goldfields warden and later resident magistrate, feared would overtake society in the wake of the gold rushes. Strong in her Christian faith, she believed that women had 'the power of raising the moral and intellectual condition of the land'. In the 1860s and 1870s, Susan Wood's verse, essays and short stories entertained readers in southern New Zealand and exhorted women 'to uplift domestic life for the betterment of society'.[71]

Wood's encouragement meant little to women seeking to earn their living on the West Coast when the rush moved there between 1864 and 1867. West Coast hoteliers recruited 'dancing girls' and paid their passage across the Tasman. The women were contracted to work as barmaids, to dance with anyone who asked them, and 'otherwise make [themselves] generally useful'.[72] They earned high wages – barmaids and servant girls were said to earn as much as or more than government clerks.[73] But prosperity, if it happened at all, was hard won. One sixteen-year-old woman at Kaniere danced every night until 11 p.m. and then was expected to keep entertaining the miners, usually by playing cards, until 6 a.m. When her health collapsed and her sister took her away, the hotel proprietor took her to court for breach of contract. Another woman who had come to the Coast from Victoria attempted suicide. She was deeply in debt, had been living in a brothel, and was reportedly 'sick of her life'.[74] 'Apoplexy brought on by excess drinking' was the reason recorded for the death of a Hokitika woman – occupation 'prostitute'.[75]

Some women prospered by relieving men of their 'roll' during the night's entertainment. 'All our hard earned gold,' complained one miner, 'goes away to pay for bad grog and finery for the soiled doves.'[76] The mix of high wages, riotous dance halls and ill-conceived or speculative ventures gave Pākehā women like these new freedoms, albeit at the expense of their reputations. The woman from Ōkarito who won five-mile horse races riding 'astride a horse just like a man' was adjudged 'disgusting' by the *West Coast Times*.[77]

The goldfields also attracted women entertainers of a slightly more reputable kind: in acting troupes, and as singers and dancers, acrobats and magicians. A Mr and Mrs Woodroffe gave a glassblowing exhibition at the Thames goldfield in September 1870, while at the end of that decade Professor and Madame Alexander, 'the Great Indian Actors', enacted war dances, hunting scenes and 'scalping', all, apparently, 'as natural as life'.[78] The 'English magician and Japanese Impersonator', Blanche Fane (Jennie Anderson), enchanted audiences by producing 'everything from a Union Jack to a flying dove' from the sleeves of her voluminous kimono.[79]

But more mundane tasks occupied the majority of women in Thames and other gold-rush towns. Mud roads made for dirty hems and boots, while the water for washing and cooking had to be carried – a routine and heavy task. Both housing and sanitation were primitive. Sandflies, rain and rats added to the discomfort. And the noise of pumps and stampers was usually continuous. Under these conditions, women cooked for the men and did their best to keep clothes and households clean, and to protect the health of their families. As Elizabeth Holman, who brought her children from Auckland to join her husband in Grahamstown in Thames, later recorded: 'I often look back and wonder how I got through the amount of continual hard work that always seemed ready for me. Nothing but the goodness and love of the Almighty could have possibly sustained me in my constant work.'[80]

Adding to the hardship, the ever-present danger of mining accidents meant that married women were faced with the possibility of having to carry on without their husbands. Three women were instantly widowed when an explosion at the Kuranui battery, near Thames, in 1874, killed Alfred Cook, Richard Watson and Matthew Paul. Watson and Paul between them had seven dependent children.[81] Rock falls, raging rivers and suspect machinery were constant threats. Historian Philip May suggested that accidental deaths on the West Coast goldfields might well have exceeded Pākehā deaths in the North Island wars.[82]

Isolation also took its toll. Ellen Piezzi's Swiss-Italian husband died after river flooding on the West Coast made it impossible for a doctor to attend to his infected hernia. Ellen, widowed with two children and pregnant with a third, felt her isolation deeply. '[P]oor me. I got no one neder of mey one [neither of my own] or Julius but black strangers to spake to god help me.' She struggled on with running their hotel, the Helvetia, at Goldsborough, a rugged journey from either Kūmara or Hokitika, and eventually found some security when she began anew in business with a fourteen-bed boarding house in Rimu, south-east of Hokitika.[83]

Māori futures

The Māori hope for the future of their children was, most urgently, that they should live. Demographer Ian Pool characterises the post-1840 years as 'Decades of Despair', with the most rapid Māori population decline taking place between 1840 and 1878 when colonisation began in earnest, spreading previously unknown diseases among Māori communities.[84] Warfare exacerbated the depredations of disease in the 1860s and early 1870s, no matter which side Māori fought for, and their growing reliance on the money economy for food because of disruptions to agriculture led to hunger. Infant mortality was high. Epidemics of measles, whooping cough, typhoid and influenza ravaged a previously unexposed population. The nineteenth-century scourge, tuberculosis, took hold. 'I do not think the Natives in the Tauranga district are on the increase,' an official commented in 1868, 'comparatively few children are to be found among them.'[85] In the Waikato in 1884, death was reported as having 'been busy amongst the children'.[86] Verses of 'A Song of Sickness', perhaps initially composed by Hine Tangikuku of Ngāti Porou in the face of a scarlet fever epidemic in the 1790s, expressed the desolation of later communities as illness took its toll:

Several notable women were associated with Rongowhakaata military leader and prophet Te Kooti Arikirangi Te Turuki, who evaded capture by government troops during the 1860s and '70s. Makurata Himiona (left), a well-known Tūhoe weaver, helped Te Kooti escape through Te Urewera to sanctuary in the King Country; his wife Makarena Ngarewa (seated, centre) was taken prisoner after Te Kooti and his followers killed settlers and Māori at Matawhero in November 1868; and Heni Kumekume (right), his favourite wife, supported him at the end of his life. *Alexander Turnbull Library, Wellington, 35mm-100276-F; PA2-2586; photograph by Samuel Carnell, PA2-0394*

Tirohia atu koia mo ko Tawera,
Whakakau ana mai ki uta.
Hohoro mai koia, hei hoa moe ake
Moku ra, e tiu nei.
Me he porangi au e keha ana
Me haurangi, kai wipiro;
Me he tahuna rere i te amo hau,
He perehia rere ki tawhiti.

Tiro iho ai au ki ahau,
Rinoi ra e te uaua;
Te koha kore o te kai ki ahau,
Heke rawaho i te kiri ora.
Waio au kia poaha ana,
He rimu puka, kei te ahau.

The morning star swims in the sky
To this shore, where I
Lie washed in a sea of pain.
Writhing like one insane.
Fever-drunk, drifting
Like pollen in a dream, sifting
Like seed, I am not what I seem.

I see myself, twisted sinew,
Wasted flesh; the body I once knew
Has no substance, unsustained,
Is itself the sustenance of pain.
I am dead weed cast upon the shore.[87]

An outbreak of fever (probably typhoid) in the north between 1883 and 1885 caused 'shocking mortality'.[88] A measles epidemic in Wanganui in 1887 led to the deaths of 30 to 40 per cent of its child victims.[89] Poor diet only increased the likelihood that people would succumb to illness.

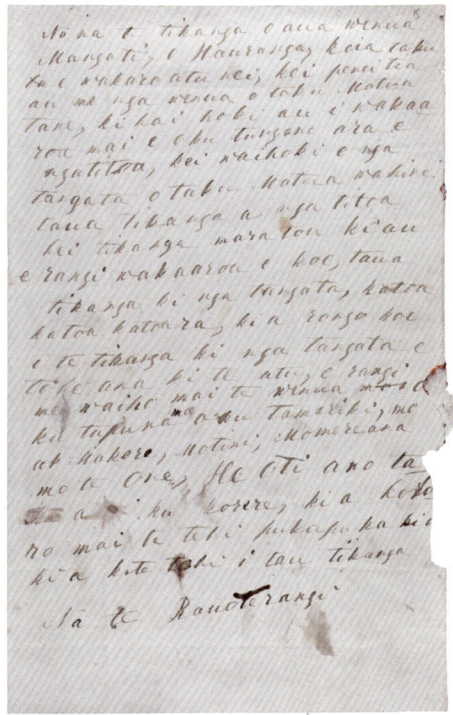

This letter written by Kahe Te Rau-o-te-rangi of Ngāti Toa, Ngāti Mutunga and Te Āti Awa argues that she has a claim to land belonging to her father and states her wish leave it to her descendants. Te Rau-o-te-rangi had an eventful life, taking part in the migrations of Taranaki Māori to the Kapiti area in the 1830s. She settled on Kapiti Island and married English whaler John Nicoll, making journeys with him to trade with Māori in the Marlborough Sounds and Whanganui area. She became known for her seven-mile swim from Kapiti Island to Te Uruhi, with a child strapped on her back, to warn of an impending attack. She was one of a few women who signed the Treaty of Waitangi in 1840. *Alexander Turnbull Library, Wellington, MS-Papers-0032-0702M-15*

Some communities, like those of Tūhoe in Te Urewera, were starving. In 1868, government troops invaded the Urewera lands where the prophet Te Kooti and his people had been sheltering. The object of the campaign was to destroy the food supply – and thus undermine Tūhoe's opposition to land sales. Colonel Whitmore, the troops' commander, described the tactics that ruined the crops. Wild pigs were let into the enclosures that had been carefully fenced for potatoes: 'By next morning in every case the whole of the ground was turned over by the animals, and all the potatoes they did not devour were spoiled by the heavy frosts which occurred every night. A few cattle were found and shot for consumption by the men.'[90]

This was not a new strategy. In July 1865, the *Colonist* reported that 'the all-powerful moving force of utter and absolute starvation' lay behind the willingness of the eastern Waitako Ngāti Hauā leader, Wiremu Tamihana (William Thompson), to negotiate with government troops. Tamihana's people, the paper continued, were 'literally reduced to the extreme of hunger, by the destruction of their agricultural settlements. Emaciated and a prey to disease, they are dying, many of them, from the effects of this physical prostration.'[91]

With their cultivations destroyed in the course of the wars, or land lost through confiscations and sale, Māori were forced into greater reliance on the money economy. But by the 1860s, Angela Ballara argues, Māori had fewer means, apart from land sales, to participate in this economy.[92] Whereas once Māori had kept settlements provisioned,

Photographed at Parihaka in South Taranaki, around 1900, these women wear the raukura – a white albatross feather symbolising peace. The pacifist community was sacked by government troops in 1881; the Parihaka leaders Te Whiti-o-Rongomai and Tohu Kakahi, along with many of their followers, were arrested and imprisoned for their non-violent resistance to Pākehā occupation of their land. The prisoners later returned to rebuild the community. *Photograph by William Andrew Collis, Alexander Turnbull Library, Wellington, 1/1-012053-G*

European farmers were increasingly supplying the settlers' needs. Escalating debt from the purchase of now-necessary goods and from the expense of land surveys led to the sale of yet more land. Meri Matimati wrote to Chief Land Commissioner Donald McLean, requesting food: 'we are very sick, starving for want of food'.[93] In another letter to McLean, Mereana Heremaia of Ngāti Apa in the Manawatū requested settlement of a land sale 'because I am living unprovided for, and it is for you people to have compassion on orphans, widows and the destitute'.[94] Not all those who were impoverished had fought against the government. Ngāti Rāhiri, for example, had fought for the government, yet still had their lands confiscated.[95]

For some Māori communities, an alternative vision of the future was provided by the teachings and example of prophetic leaders who drew on biblical as well as traditional sources of spiritual inspiration. These leaders gave their followers hope that they had the power to shape the future in a country where they had lost much of their land and were now being rapidly outnumbered. Between the 1840s and the 1880s, the Māori population almost halved, from 80,000 to around 45,000, while the European population had reached 500,000 by the early 1880s.[96] In Te Urewera, Te Kooti provided a focal point for Tūhoe resistance to the survey and alienation of land.[97] Taranaki Māori and others who had

After the wars, soldiers were given land in some areas, to settle with their families, and they sometimes also acted as a local garrison. This little group at Pungarehu near Parihaka, photographed in 1886, includes a man in military dress, along with several women and a child. *Photograph by the Burton Brothers, Museum of New Zealand Te Papa Tongarewa, Wellington, C.010274*

suffered dispossession flocked to the settlement at Parihaka, where from the early 1860s to 1881 Te Whiti-o-Rongomai and Tohu Kakahi led peaceful resistance to land occupation through ploughing and protest.[98]

Te Whiti and Tohu's settlement offered a haven for the restoration of order. There no alcohol was allowed, high standards of cleanliness were observed, and food was plentiful; there were many, healthy children. 'The inhabitants are the finest race of men I have ever seen,' reported Taranaki's medical officer in 1871.[99] Te Whiti had proclaimed a 'fighting peace' to ensure no land was sold and no unjustly confiscated land surrendered. But his intransigence and apparent incorruptibility in the face of settler determination to settle the Waimate Plains led to great pressure on the government to act. The gathering at Parihaka of thousands of Māori from different iwi came to be seen as a challenge to British sovereignty.

In October 1881, the government issued a proclamation demanding that the Parihaka people retreat to the reserves offered and 'willingly submit to the law of the Queen'.[100] Enthusiastic settlers cheered on the government and volunteered to join the Armed Constabulary troops to march on the settlement. But on 5 November those itching for combat were met with peace; loud cheers went up from the waiting children of Parihaka, and 500 loaves of bread baked by the women were ready for the invaders.[101] When Te Whiti and Tohu were marched away, their wives, the sisters Wairangi and Hikurangi, followed them.[102] In an effort to disperse the settlement, men from Whanganui were arrested but the Whanganui women refused to identify themselves. There is evidence, according to the Waitangi Tribunal's *Taranaki Report*, that women were 'raped and otherwise molested'.[103] Finally a collaborator was found who identified the women, and they were marched out of Parihaka.[104]

The 1880s also saw prophetic movements led by women. In the Hokianga Ani Kaaro was a visionary Ngāti Hao leader inspired by Te Whiti's teachings. Her rivals for leadership were the sisters Maria Pangari and Remana Hi, descended from an important Ngāti Hao chief, Pangari. Maria abandoned Roman Catholicism and predicted the end of the world. When she died, her sister took over her mantle and claimed to be able to raise the dead to life – an alluring promise in a society ravaged by disease. In her Upper Waihou community, named Mount Zion, followers dressed in white to symbolise their pacifism and ignored the Christian sabbath since, they claimed, every day was the sabbath. These prophets challenged the European church that had so manifestly failed them. 'Who can tell which is the right religion,' Remana Hi's followers told the Revd T. G. Hammond, 'you Pakehas have so many different churches.'[105] Infighting between the followers of Remana Hi and those of Ani Kaaro, and rumours about the practices of Remana's community, led to a police invasion. Five Māori and two constables were wounded in the fighting that ensued, and twenty-three Māori were arrested. Remana Hi was imprisoned for three months.[106]

Through the assaults on the Parihaka and Waihou settlements, the government demonstrated its determination to destroy Māori communities that were standing in the way of settler ambitions. An equally insidious method of undermining Māori claims to the land lay in the Native Land Court. Through its dealings, historian Keith Sorrenson has argued, the Land Court was responsible for the loss of thousands of valuable acres, and the social disintegration and depopulation that followed. Prior to the 1880s, dealing with the Land Court could require claimants to travel hundreds of miles to hearings held in Pākehā settlements. Cultivations at home languished while Native Land Agents offered claimants liquor, food and clothing on credit. Indebtedness grew and alcohol took its toll. Frequently the level of indebtedness was such that Māori had no option other than to sell their land. Robert Cunningham Bruce, Member of the House of Representatives for Rangitikei, was shocked at the consequences of attendance at the Native Land Court at Wanganui for the inland hapū in his Manawatū–Wanganui electorate. Bruce stated in the House:

> I believe we could not find a more ingenious method of destroying the whole of the Maori race than by these Courts. The Natives come from villages in the interior, and have to hang about for months in our centres of population ... They are brought into contact with the lowest classes of society, and are exposed to temptation, and the result is that a great number contract diseases and die ...[107]

When the Land Court sat in Ōhinemutu, Rotorua, Māori women were said to be 'lying about the settlement on the roadside, helplessly drunk', and the bars were crowded with young and old of both sexes.[108] The *New Zealand Herald* ascribed the 'unusual number of deaths' in the area to the poverty and intoxication of the people.[109]

In areas such as the Waikato where Māori refused to sell land, they were more likely to avoid the potential ravages of disease. 'The difference between the Kingites and the Maoris that Europeans are accustomed to see is very marked,' noted a *New Zealand Herald* correspondent on 8 May 1878. He continued:

> The men and women are healthy looking, while the number of children playing about, and of fine stout infants to be seen in the arms of their mothers, is remarkable. It is sad to think that those Natives who have least to do with Europeans are in every respect the best of their race; but so it is.[110]

Women and property

Communities at a remove from settler society could continue to operate under customary law that recognised the rights of Māori women. But in statute law, English custom, under which the legal rights of married women were transferred to their husbands, often took precedence. The Native Lands Act of 1873, for example, required husbands to be party to all deeds signed by married women.[111] Despite Deacon Samuel Williams's protest that Māori women did not consider 'that their husbands had any voice in the matter and the husbands considering that they had no voice to interfere', the clause remained in place until 1881.[112] But the displacement of Māori women was most clearly signalled in the Maori Representation Act 1867, under which Māori men were given the right to elect four members of the House of Representatives, three for the North Island and one for the South. The Act defined a Māori as 'a male aboriginal inhabitant of New Zealand of the age of twenty-one years and upwards and shall include half-castes'.[113]

Pākehā legislators transferred into Māori society their expectations about men as the legal representatives of their wives. Yet voices were raised amongst the settlers about the wrongs this inflicted on married women. Mary Ann Griffiths emigrated to New Zealand in 1850 to escape a cruel husband – a common enough occurrence at a time when divorce was difficult to obtain.[114] Remarried in New Zealand to a widowed doctor named Müller, Mary Ann began contributing articles under the name 'Femina' to the *Nelson Examiner*. She argued for the economic independence of married women and, in 1869, wrote a pamphlet advocating women's right to vote. *An Appeal to the Men of New Zealand* provoked much discussion and was reprinted a number of times. 'Why,' she asked the male law-makers of New Zealand, 'when the broad road of progress is cleared for so many human beings, is the Juggernaut car of prejudice still to be driven on, crushing the crowds of helpless women beneath its wheels?'[115] In the Auckland province, Mary Colclough expressed similar indignation on lecture platforms and in newspaper columns during the early 1870s. Her husband had squandered her earnings 'in ruinous speculations'. In a letter to the *New Zealand Herald* she argued that women's legal subjection was 'a frightful wrong':

> for what is the use of knowing how to act rightly, and guide a family properly, when it may so happen that you may be joined to a man who may choose to nullify all you would gladly accomplish? and who, in the present state of society, can do so, simply because he wills it so, without being obliged to assign any reason for his acts.[116]

Such arguments, in the view of the *Hawke's Bay Herald*, did 'an infinity of mischief', and many agreed with the male correspondent who wrote: 'The vessel of a woman's mind possesses admirable sailing powers, but not sufficient ballast to be safe in a storm without a firm hand at the helm.'[117]

The breadwinner's hands at the helm, however, were often made unsteady through drink, lack of application to the task, or the difficulty of finding work. Influenced by the arguments for reform circulating from England, J.C. Richmond introduced a Married Women's Property Bill in 1870. Richmond was one of the large and lively extended Richmond–Atkinson family who were keenly interested in women's rights, and he had seen his aunt Helen Hursthouse suffer at the hands of a drunken husband.[118] He intended his Bill 'to place all married women in the same position in relation to their property as their husbands, or at least as unmarried women'.[119]

During the debate in the House, Richmond related how he had heard, 'within the last twenty-four hours in this town one of the old cries raised against it … that marriage was in the nature of a religious institution, and that society, in fact, was founded upon the subjection of the woman …' Granting women independent legal rights, according to these critics, would cause society to crumble.[120] Despite these kinds of objections, the Bill was passed in the Lower House, only to be eviscerated in the more conservative Legislative Council, or Upper House, whose members were men of property with much to guard. The final Act enabled protection of women's property by court order only if a woman could prove cruelty, open adultery, habitual drunkenness or failure to provide maintenance without reasonable cause. The onus was, therefore, upon wives to prove that their husbands had defaulted on their marriage contracts. The Act provided for alimony payments and allowed for a resident magistrate or Justice of the Peace to direct exclusive custody of children to the mother, a right they had not previously had.[121]

But while Pākehā women with the resources and knowledge to go to court had made some advances towards independence, in 1881 Māori women lost the right to bequeath their property as they wished. Under the Native Succession Act of that year, those 'validly married according to Māori customs and usages' became subject to New Zealand law with regard to disposing of their property – that is, they were subject to the same restrictions as English women, who could not make a will without their husband's consent, unless they had been widowed.[122] The defects of the Native Succession Act were quickly understood, and an Act to provide 'for certain technical and other defects' was introduced the following year. Under the Native Lands Amendment Act of 1882, deference to 'Native custom' was reintroduced, allowing Māori women testamentary capacity once again.[123]

'Native custom' gave Māori women an independence their Pākehā contemporaries lacked, a point rehearsed in the growing agitation over married women's property. New Zealand appeared not to have kept up with the changes wrought in England by an 1870 Act which gave protection to married women's separate property. The 'inalienable privileges' to which English women were entitled would be lost in coming to New Zealand, unless a woman went through the 'humiliating' and 'degrading' process of gaining redress by applying to a resident magistrate to expose her husband's shortcomings.[124]

To remedy this situation, and to promote 'the social welfare of the people', the Hon. George Waterhouse introduced the 1881 Married Woman's Property Bill to the Legislative Council. Based on a Bill then before the English Parliament, it aimed to 'give a woman the full and free right of protection over her property'. The Hon. P. A. Buckley declared that the Council required time to consider 'a proposal of so startling a nature'.[125] Speaking in favour of the Bill, Waterhouse expressed disquiet that New Zealand was lagging behind England as far as women's rights were concerned. He pointed out that 'even in the colony of New Zealand the principle of the Bill was acknowledged so far … as Maori women were concerned. Every Maori woman held property in her own right, without being in any way subject to her husband.'[126]

This Bill failed, along with similar Bills brought before the House in the following two years. The Hon. Henry Scotland of Taranaki argued that they went 'too far': a change in the status of married women, he said, 'deeply affected the peace and happiness of families'. He suggested that if the 1881 Bill passed, it would soon be necessary to 'bring in a Bill for the better protection of the property of married men'. Women, in his view, were poor business people and, if left to trade on their own account, likely to plunge families into poverty. Women's economic independence would therefore give rise to 'increased discord and separation'.[127]

An advocate of reform, Richard Oliver, representative of the City of Dunedin and member of the Executive Council (made up of Ministers), argued that the status of women in any society was a reflection of 'the advance of that community'. Societies in a savage state, he contended, drawing on the Enlightenment ideas that so inspired the eighteenth-century explorers, generally treated their women little better than slaves or beasts of burden. There was, however, one notable exception near at hand, in a race 'not far advanced in civilisation … the Maori race'. Oliver argued that:

A Maori woman was permitted to hold land, and European interference with Maori custom by the establishment of English law was simply retrograde as far as the Natives were concerned. They were precluded by the establishment of British law from the exercise of those rights which they had held before the advent of British law – a most extraordinary condition of affairs, and one altogether without parallel so far as he was aware.[128]

The loss of property as a consequence of marriage was a factor Māori women were considering by the 1880s. Indeed, Waterhouse reported that some Māori women in Hawke's Bay were refusing to marry European men 'because they would thus be deprived of land held under Crown grant which then became subject to British law'.[129] Marriage, which in Māori society could facilitate the transfer of rank and property transmitted through both the male and female lines, was in danger of being transformed by Pākehā law into a patriarchal institution. Until 1884, it became another of the various legal means by which Māori land could be lost.

In that year, all married women in New Zealand gained the right to own and control their own wages and property. In effect, the Married Women's Property Act 1884 copied the 1881 English legislation which maintained an idea of married women's separate property, rather than giving married women the same property rights as men.[130] This legal recognition of equality, however, did little to eradicate the deeply held expectation that a woman would be economically dependent on her father or spouse – an expectation that shaped European attitudes to women's education, work and wages. Women's work was regarded as short term and usually of a domestic nature – a prelude to marriage. Most Pākehā women did marry (three-quarters of those aged fifteen and over in 1871 were either wives or widows) and those who did not found their lives shaped by expectations of female dependency.[131] Within marriage women strove to furnish households with food, clothing and comforts, and to raise their children. While settler families grew and thrived, many Māori whānau struggled in the face of land confiscation, disease and despondency.

New futures

In resilient communities, Māori were active in promoting their children's interests. In 1867, the government introduced a Native Schools Act to continue the earlier work of mission schools in 'civilising' Māori. The Act laid down that local communities had to request the foundation of a school, provide the land and half the cost of the buildings, and contribute one-quarter of the teacher's salary. These stringent requirements were relaxed somewhat in an 1871 Act that allowed Māori to donate more land instead of money. By 1879, fifty-seven scattered communities had established native schools.[132] At Pāpāwai, in southern Wairarapa, Tamahau Mahupuku and his well-connected wife, Raukura, secured a native school in 1882. By the late 1880s, the school was an important

Jewellery often has strong personal associations. The bracelet engraved with birds (top left) and the gold wedding ring from the early nineteenth century would probably have travelled to New Zealand with their owners. From later in the that century come the brooch containing a portrait (middle right); the greenstone brooch (middle left) which honours an elder, perhaps a grandparent, with the words 'Arohanui kia Taua'; and the mourning brooch (bottom left), with a lock of hair. In the twenty-first century, Victoria McIntosh's brooch (bottom right) pays homage to the domestic labour of women by repurposing an old kitchen grater. *From top, left to right: Museum of New Zealand Te Papa Tongarewa, Wellington, GH002308; GH003426; ME023878; GH004726; GH012036; courtesy of Victoria McIntosh*

centre of Māori community life. In 1889, a great dance 'with the most extensive and elaborate repasts possible to imagine' was planned to raise funds for additions, such as shelter sheds.[133]

The government's ideal was to appoint a married couple to take charge of such schools, since the teachers' task was not just to provide education but 'by their kindness, their diligence, and their probity, [to] exercise a beneficial influence on all the natives in their district'.[134] The Inspector of Native Schools, James Pope, described the example of 'a well-ordered family' as 'one of the greatest benefits' a school could bring to a Māori community.[135] The duties of the married couple were laid out 'to show by their own conduct that it is possible to live a useful and blameless life, and in smaller matters, by their dress, in their houses, and by their manners and habits at home and abroad, to set the Maoris an example that they may advantageously imitate.'[136]

Implicit in this 'civilising mission' was the importance of the family. The teacher's wife or daughter would teach the girls sewing and knitting, and their household would provide an exemplar to counteract supposed Māori carelessness in regard to their houses and gardens.[137] New notions of order and use of time were to be inculcated. Tasks in the classroom were strictly allocated. The timetable was 'to be hung up in a conspicuous position in the school-room' and its direction was 'to be always strictly followed'.[138] The teacher was expected to keep a quarter-acre garden 'constantly in good order, and make it, if possible, the model garden of the village'.[139] Girls had a particular duty to learn to sew, from the basics of threading needles and hemming in Standard One, to making button-holes, darning and knitting stockings by Standard Four. Education had a number of ends, but one of the most ingrained was to transmit, both by example and by instruction, European codes of gendered behaviour. Women teachers taught needlework and hygiene whereas male teachers concentrated on improving boys' carpentry skills.[140] The curriculum attempted to assimilate Māori into new ways of living.

Ripeka Love, of Te Āti Awa, reflected on the year of her birth, 1882:

> I came into the world to find two totally different peoples and cultures endeavouring to live in harmony and striving to obtain a balance of understanding in life and outlook. My generation, still steeped in the order and ritual governing the life and soul of the Maori people, accepted without question the authority of their chiefs and tohungas and also the teachings of the new settlers.[141]

Both peoples had things to learn from each other. Pākehā women could see Māori women participating in warfare, acting as eloquent advocates in court, and exercising unquestioned rights with regard to property. For many Māori, Pākehā education promised skills in literacy and numeracy that would enhance opportunities in the changed world. In fact, the exchange of skills and understandings often occurred in that most intimate of sites, the family, as marriages between (usually) Pākehā men and Māori women took place unhindered. (In many other settler societies, marriage between groups was strictly regulated.)[142]

By the 1880s, the numerical dominance of settlers was assured. But an important demographic change was beginning. From the 1870s, Pākehā began restricting the size of their families, in part to maximise each child's opportunities. And when Kate Milligan Edger become the first woman to graduate from the University of New Zealand in 1877, it became clear that girls' opportunities might even include tertiary education. 'Let us hear no more of the intellectual inferiority of women,' commented the *New Zealand Herald* upon her success.[143]

With the decline in family size, and with the growth of the European population in urban areas, it became possible for middle-class women to expand their horizons beyond the domestic sphere. But a reverse pattern was taking place for Māori, as the precipitous decline in population began to slow and there were signs that a recovery was under way. Rather than family limitation, family expansion was the key to the future of Māori.

As settler society grew and matured, options for Pākehā women's involvement in a range of non-domestic activities increased. Goods once produced in the home could be bought more readily in urban areas, and domestic help was easier to obtain. In growing towns, middle-class women delegated household tasks to Pākehā working-class women and, by doing so, gained time to carve out a role in public life by forming voluntary associations to address apparent problems. They found new ways for women's voices to be heard – ways that allowed the articulation of concerns about the health and welfare of Pākehā women and children to be brought to public notice. In this way, they held forth the possibility of the transformation of settler society. Women whose families were prospering banded together to support the less fortunate and began to learn the political skills to agitate for change. Giving a voice to women, they suggested, would make the world more like home. In particular, the founding of the Women's Christian Temperance Union in 1885 set in place a national organisation that would put women's concerns at the forefront of the national agenda.

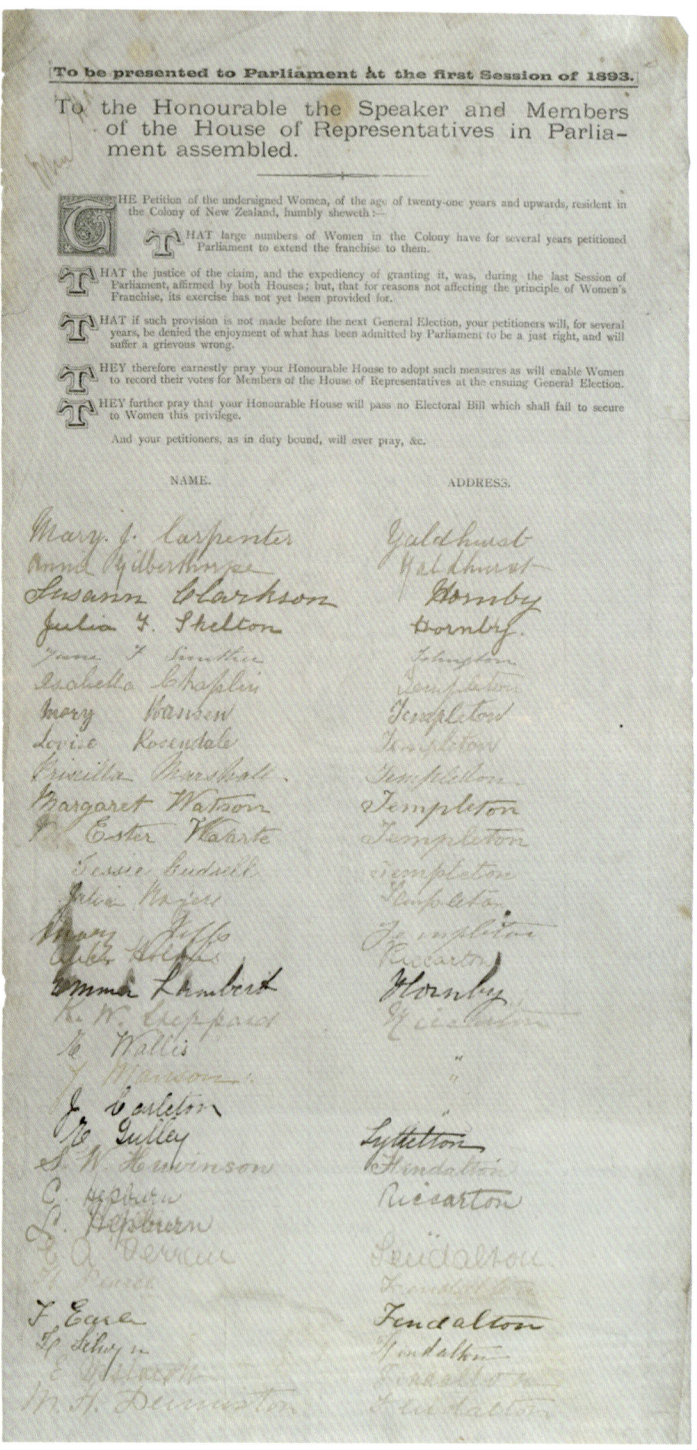

Chapter Five
The Quest for Citizenship

Mary Leavitt, an American envoy for the Woman's Christian Temperance Union, set sail across the Pacific from San Francisco in November 1884, arriving in Auckland in January 1885.[1] The former schoolteacher and divorced mother of three was propelled on her long journey by an idea: that Christian women had a duty to rid the world of the threat that alcohol posed to homes and families. In towns throughout New Zealand, Mary Leavitt spread the news of the American 'Women's Crusade' formed to 'check the tide of demoralisation' wrought by alcohol.[2] She used the example of Wyoming, where women had been enfranchised, to show what women's suffrage could achieve in controlling the liquor trade.[3] Her slogan, 'Do Everything', aimed to encourage women into public and political life.[4] The motto of the WCTU declared its allegiances: 'For God, home and humanity'. The life of Christ provided Christian women with a model for action and held out the prospect of a new kind of society: one in which women were citizens alongside men.

In the same year the WCTU was founded in New Zealand, Maria Pangari's religiously inspired movement attracted a following among Māori in the Hokianga region.[5] In her settlement near Kaikohe, alcohol – that gift of the Europeans that had brought indebtedness and encouraged land alienation – was banned. Maria Pangari promised deliverance from the havoc wrought by Pākehā incursions into Māori society, declaring that the return of Christ held out the possibility of transformation and new life. Poverty and dispossession would disappear with the creation of the kingdom of God on Earth.

The question of who should have a stake in creating the new society was one that had been debated from the earliest time of settlement, but by the last quarter of the nineteenth century the debate over citizenship became intense in both Māori and settler society. Settler women read of the progress of women's rights activists elsewhere, and took up opportunities offered to women ratepayers to vote in local body elections, for school committees, liquor licensing committees, and Hospital and Charitable Aid Boards. Determined that a new society should make the world anew, they joined temperance organisations and petitioned for women's suffrage, succeeding in their claim in 1893. Some

Opposite A huge petition supporting women's suffrage, signed by 'Mary J. Carpenter and 25,519 Others', was submitted to Parliament on 28 July 1893. This is the first page; Kate Sheppard's signature appears about half way down the left column. *Archives New Zealand, The Department of Internal Affairs Te Tari Taiwhenua, LE1, 1893/7a*

This beautifully made cloak makes innovative use of new materials, while maintaining the traditions of fine weaving. Rows of silky angora wool are woven into a muka background, with two deep tāniko borders that use both wool and traditional dyes. The cloak would have been made in the years after the angora goat was introduced to New Zealand in 1860. *Museum of New Zealand Te Papa Tongarewa, Wellington, ME001154*

These Whanganui women and children were photographed in the late nineteenth or early twentieth century. One of the children protectively cuddles a cat, suggesting that they are at home. All the women have moko, and wear Pākehā dress which by then was customary for everyday use. *Whanganui Regional Museum, 2003.1.66c*

Māori women, usually those with Pākehā connections, joined the WCTU and added their names to the suffrage petitions, seeing hope for their communities within the political system.[6] Others, less sanguine about the Pākehā political world, focused on whānau and survival, supported by the spiritual beliefs of their communities. For those disillusioned with the Pākehā state, a separate Māori parliament appeared to be the way forward. Full participation in society, as citizens, required a number of transformations in social life, and activists from both cultures were at the forefront of change.

Pathways to citizenship

Political activity among Māori was intense in the last quarter of the nineteenth century. Māori wanted authority within their own country. Under Article Three of the Treaty of Waitangi, Māori gained 'all the rights and privileges of British Subjects'.[7] The allocation of four Māori parliamentary seats in the House of Representatives in 1867 incorporated Māori men within the Pākehā political system but, while allowing a Māori voice to be heard, ensured that it could always be overwhelmed by the vast majority. Many within Māoridom preferred the notion of separate but equal systems of authority. The Kīngitanga was a key expression of this independence, and in 1884 Tawhiao travelled to England in the hope of meeting Queen Victoria to request the return of Waikato's confiscated lands. The audience was denied and Tawhiao told that the matter was one for the New Zealand government. On his return, Tawhiao nevertheless continued to advocate mana motuhake (political independence).[8]

Settlers had debated the meaning of citizenship since their arrival. Citizens, the *New Zealand Gazette and Wellington Spectator* had announced in 1842, were those 'who have the good of the community sincerely at heart' and therefore should vote in elections. While it was Pākehā men the paper had in mind, the column later noted the political participation of women in England. Over a quarter of a million signatures had been collected by the women of Manchester and surrounding towns in 1842 to request repeal of the Corn Laws.[9]

Women were excluded from the franchise under the New Zealand Constitution Act of 1846, which gave the vote to men over twenty-one who were owners and occupiers of dwellings, and were able to read and write in English. The language requirement, in effect, disenfranchised Māori men literate in their own language.[10] It was abandoned in 1852 when a new Constitution made the electoral franchise almost universal for men, with a minimal property qualification. This latter qualification, however, served to inhibit Māori participation, since their remaining land was not held by individuals but by the community.

For Māori, allegiances were overwhelmingly local – to whānau, hapū and iwi. Customary law remained important, and women and men were equally subject to its dictates. Women of high status could be lawmakers in their communities. Rahera Te Kahuhiapo, for example, was connected to many tribes in the Maketū and Tauranga district, and because of her mana over land and people 'disputes were brought to her for settlement. Her word was regarded as law.'[11] But Māori were forced, through the imposition of English law, to engage with a new type of authority: a growing body of legislation emanating from Wellington (the capital from 1865). Laws made by men in a single location – the 'separate political public space' of the Houses of Parliament – were now to be enforced throughout the country.[12]

Some Māori demanded entry to that public space. '[O]pen the doors of the Parliament to us,' demanded Ringori Te Ao of Te Arawa. 'Let us be ushered in.'[13] The door was opened a little with the Maori Representation Act of 1867, which enfranchised Māori men over twenty-one (including 'half-castes') and allowed them to vote for the four Māori seats created by the Act. Māori with property could also vote in the general electorates where they held property.[14]

Wi Tako Ngatata, a Te Āti Awa leader appointed to the Legislative Council in 1872, commented that the settlers maintained the 'body of the law' while giving Māori 'only the ghost of it'.[15] The Native Land Court, set up in 1865 to translate Māori customary land claims into recognisable English legal land titles, served as just one example to Māori of the way imported legal systems undermined their interests. Tensions between hapū were heightened; necessary seasonal tasks were abandoned because of court hearings; and court decisions could serve to override women's traditional land rights. Some Māori wished to withdraw from cooperation with Pākehā completely and to see the state dismantled. Others, such as the Member for Eastern Maori from 1887, James Carroll, sought to remove all legal distinctions on the basis of race, and to secure equal property and citizenship rights.[16] 'Probably at no time in New Zealand history,' historian Claudia Orange has suggested, 'were the contrasts in Maori society so marked.'[17]

Pākehā women seeking citizenship were kept both informed and inspired by press reports of women's political activities in other countries. In November 1868, the *Tuapeka Times* reported on the 'loud applause' that greeted a paper by Lydia Becker, correspondent of Charles Darwin and initiator of both the first English Women's Suffrage Committee and the *Women's Suffrage Journal*, when she made a rousing address 'in defence of woman's equality with man' to the British Association at Oxford, England.[18] Readers in Otago and on the West Coast could learn about the first annual meeting of the Manchester National Society for Women's Suffrage and the Women's Suffrage Convention in Boston in 1869.[19] A lecture on 'Women's Wrongs' by the famed American Quaker orator Anna Dickinson to an overflowing audience in the San Francisco Metropolitan Theatre was reported widely. Women's choice, Dickinson believed, was between 'destitution or dishonour', since women were 'kept from their proper sphere of usefulness': denied access to honourable work, their only alternative was prostitution.[20] Another, more radical American advocate of equal rights (and free love), Victoria Woodhull, made a plea for 'Constitutional Equality' to an audience in Washington DC that was reported less sympathetically to the readers of the *West Coast Times*.[21] In 1871, Nelson readers were given a long report on John Stuart Mill's address on women's suffrage to a crowded public meeting in Edinburgh. In a cogent argument, Mill claimed that women needed the vote for self-protection, and reminded his audience that there should be no taxation without representation.[22]

Mill's 1869 *The Subjection of Women* had done much to persuade a number of men in the New Zealand Parliament of the unjust denial of women's political rights.[23] Newspaper reports of activities in England may have strengthened their resolve. An 1872 article from London about 'Women's Advocacy of Woman's Suffrage', for example, was full of admiration for the arguments of the English suffragists.[24] *Sixteen Reasons for Women's Suffrage*, a tract which originated in the United Kingdom, circulated in New Zealand in 1874. The thirteenth reason was: 'Because the recent extension of the franchise to a class of men often ignorant as well as poor makes the denial of it more galling to educated and taxpaying women.'[25]

There was great enthusiasm for universal suffrage in New Zealand in the late 1870s. Robert Stout's Electoral Bill, introduced in August 1878, included the radical proposal that women ratepayers should be eligible to vote and stand for election to Parliament – a move that, if successful, would mean 'the first time the doors of Parliament have ever been

Photographer Margaret Matilda White took this striking image of women assistants at the Auckland Mental Hospital in the 1890s. Nursing at such institutions was challenging and demanded particular strength of character. *Photograph by Margaret Matilda White, Auckland War Memorial Museum Tāmaki Paenga Hira, PH-NEG-B3491*

opened to women'.[26] James Wallis, an Auckland medical practitioner and Presbyterian minister, along with former Premier Sir William Fox, put the case for women's rights. 'Women are in many respects equal to men,' argued Fox. '[T]hey are equal to men in their minds, in their influence, more than equal to men in their influence upon wise legislation of any kind, more than men's equal in those sentiments which have most influence in promoting the true welfare of a country.'[27]

Mr Cutten, the new member for Taieri, however, found the proposal absurd:

[I]f women occupied seats in the House one member (female) would probably be engaged in carrying a little Bill through the House, while another one would be carrying one through the bedroom. (Laughter.) While women were occupied in the House of Parliament, men would be occupied in their own houses making the beds.[28]

The provision to allow women to stand for Parliament was removed during the Electoral Bill's committee stage, but the principle of extending suffrage to women ratepayers was upheld by substantial majorities in both Houses of Parliament. Nonetheless, the Bill was discarded because the two Houses could not agree over changes to the Māori franchise, and the issue lapsed until the following year.[29] It met with no more success in 1879 (the year all men aged twenty-one and over were given the right to vote) even though John Ballance, husband of Ellen Ballance, a future vice-president of the Women's Progressive Society, hoped to sway the issue by substituting the word 'person' for

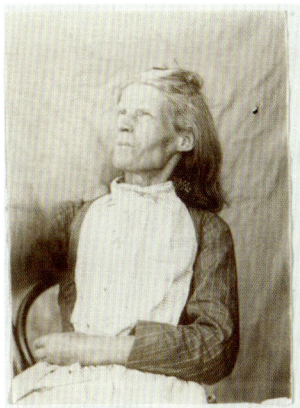

2984

Patient's No.:

Name in full: *Johanna Beckett*

Committed on order of *Robert S. Hawkins. SMW*

At *Gore*

Date of committal: *7th January 1897*

Sex: *Female*

Age: *59 years*

Married, single, or widowed: *Married*

Condition of life or occupation: *Domestic*

Religion:

Previous place of abode: *Waimumu Mataura*

Whether first attack: *No*

Age, first attack: *Not Known*

When and where previously treated: *Sunnyside & Seacliff Asylums*

Duration of existing attack: *Not Known*

Supposed cause: *Unknown*

Whether subject to epilepsy: *No*

If suicidal or dangerous: *No*

Names of relatives and address: *Henry Beckett (husband) Waimumu Mataura*

Johanna Beckett was a patient at Seacliff Asylum north of Dunedin in 1896, one of those women for whom the vicissitudes of life led to multiple breakdowns and consequent institutionalisation. Although the facts recorded here in the casebook are sparse, further asylum paperwork documents her life of hardship and perhaps violence in her marriage to an impoverished miner and biblical literalist in Waimūmū, Southland. The Medical Superintendant of the Seacliff Asylum, Frederic Truby King, found Johanna to be 'smart and often witty'. Henry Beckett divorced Johanna in 1910 on grounds of her lunacy. *Archives New Zealand The Department of Internal Affairs Te Tari Taiwhenua, DAHI 19956 D264 42:2397*

Emily Siedeberg wrote a letter of application to the Otago Medical School in March 1891, and became the first woman to study medicine in April. She was joined by Margaret Cruikshank in 1892. Both women had been encouraged in their ambition by teachers at Otago Girls' High School. More women medical students followed them but remained a small minority until the 1970s. *Hocken Collections/Te Uare Taoka o Hākena, University of Otago Library, Dunedin, MS-1689/001, Item 17b*

'man'. James Wallis reintroduced women's suffrage in 1880 and 1881, and once again failed. One of the obstacles was the ongoing disagreement between those who accepted the enfranchisement of women ratepayers and those who demanded no property qualification.[30] And there were always those who agreed with William Gisborne that:

> Woman's Parliament is her home, and it is within that sphere that her function lies for making laws for our peace, order and good government. I believe that, if you transfer her from that sphere to this, you spoil her for both.[31]

While the national political structures of the country – the elected House of Representatives and the appointed Legislative Council – were reserved for men, women's participation had already been welcomed in local body politics, first in Nelson and Otago in 1867. Women who paid rates could vote in local elections under the Municipal Corporations Act of that year, an Act consolidated following the abolition of the provinces in 1875. They apparently did so with enthusiasm. Whether or not married women were 'householders', and therefore entitled to vote or stand for school committees under the 1877 Education Act, was clarified by the challenge to the validity of the election of a Mrs Tasker to a Wellington school committee. The Wellington Education Board found that the word 'householder' referred to any adult man or woman.[32] The Taranaki Education Board was the first in the country to acquire women's skills when Emma Jane Richmond became a member in 1886.[33] Women became eligible to serve their communities as members of the local liquor licensing committees established in 1881 (application had to be made to these committees to set up a liquor outlet), and as members also of the Hospital and Charitable Aid Boards founded in 1885. And many believed that women's suffrage was the logical next step.

For many of the early supporters of women's rights, the quality of girls' education was a crucial issue, since a good education would enhance their claims to citizenship. Learmonth White Dalrymple, a Scottish immigrant to Otago, led a ladies' committee in a campaign for the foundation of a secondary school for girls to match Otago Boys' High School (established in 1863). This resulted in the opening of Otago Girls' High School in February 1871. Not content with secondary education, Dalrymple and her supporters successfully lobbied for the admission of women to the newly founded University of Otago in August 1871. Access to university would, Dalrymple claimed, enable women to participate fully 'in the educational domestic and social duties of life'.[34]

The first woman graduate from the University of New Zealand, Kate Edger, received her tertiary education courtesy of the headmaster of Auckland College and Grammar School, where she studied, eyes downcast, with the boys in the top class.[35] The school's affiliation with the University of New Zealand allowed her to study for a degree, and on 11 July 1877 she became the first woman in the British Empire to be awarded a Bachelor of Arts. She went on to complete a Master's degree while teaching at Christchurch Girls' High School and was subsequently appointed principal of Nelson College for Girls, which opened in 1883. The prominent Canterbury politician William Rolleston, who worried that higher education might 'unsex women' by encouraging them to enter into competition with men, might have been surprised that Kate Edger married in 1890 at the age of thirty-three, and went on to have three sons and a busy life committed to family, teaching and social service.[36]

To the small and organised group of Pākehā women seeking the right to vote, citizenship held out the possibility of transforming the state to take account of the needs of women and children, not just in respect of education but also, crucially, as the protector of the weak. 'Because women are affected by the prosperity of the Colony, are concerned in the preservation of its liberty and free institutions, and suffer equally with men from all national errors and mistakes', they should be entitled to the suffrage. So ran the third of the WCTU's 1888 *Ten Reasons Why the Women of New Zealand Should Vote*, sent to every member of the House of Representatives.[37] The 1884 Married Women's Property Act had asserted women's stake in the community as property owners. In a speech to arouse support for suffrage in Gore, Marion Hatton, president of the Women's Franchise League in Dunedin, argued in July 1892 that 'as women are now competent to own property, and are in every respect liable to the same privileges and responsibilities as men, we claim for ourselves the same privileges and rights as are enjoyed by them'.[38] As taxpayers, women demanded a voice 'in saying how that tax money is spent'.[39]

Isabel Hodgkins, often overshadowed by her sister Frances, painted this New Zealand lake scene in 1900. Isabel continued to paint after her marriage to William Henry Field in 1893 but, as for many women, her domestic responsibilities left no time for serious study. *Museum of New Zealand Te Papa Tongarewa, Wellington, 1950-0005-2*

Organising for the women's vote

Temperance was the international lightning rod that drew women together for political action and led to an organisational basis from which to argue for the vote. It called upon women to use their moral authority for the betterment of society – to assert their power, but within a context of improved well-being for children and families. Even women who had no desire to enter the male world of politics were attracted by a cause that stressed the importance of 'home protection' from the evils of the drink trade.[40] The internationalism of the WCTU, which became a world organisation with the combination of the American and British arms in 1884, became a model for other women's organisations whose concern with a common humanity overrode a narrow nationalism. 'We are one world of tempted humanity,' wrote Frances Willard, the first president of the World WCTU.[41]

Temperance societies had come to New Zealand with early European colonisation and were usually attached to non-conformist congregations. One of the country's earliest published pamphlets, from Paihia in 1836, was entitled *Report on the Formation and Establishment of the New Zealand Temperance Society*.[42] Women were welcomed into the campaign against drink, and found in the Good Templar Order, in particular, that they were respected and allowed to speak, their position based 'upon a mental equality with the sterner sex'.[43] Founded in America in 1852, when it was clear that women were taking up the temperance pledge more avidly than men, the Templars had spread to England, South Africa, Australia and New Zealand by the early 1870s. The American Templars, according to historian Ian Tyrrell, 'rested their appeal on equality between the sexes'.[44] The Templars

Ellen Cheeseman painted this detailed study of a butterfly in the 1880s. She was the sister of botanist Thomas Frederick Cheeseman, curator of the Auckland Institute and Museum from 1874 to 1923. *Watercolour by Ellen Maud Cheeseman, Auckland War Memorial Museum Tāmaki Paenga Hira, PD-1994-6*

also had some appeal to Māori in the King Country from 1876, although Māori on the East Coast, for example, had successfully instituted their own initiatives to control alcohol.[45]

Alcohol was regarded as inimical to good government. Drunkenness and lawlessness at Kororāreka had hastened British annexation of the country, and paternalistic concern for Māori, who indeed had no tradition of drinking alcohol, led to an 1847 Ordinance to Prohibit the Sale of Spirits to Natives.[46] According to Waikato and Waipā leaders, alcohol was 'the worst thing hitherto brought to New Zealand … we have determined, therefore, not to allow it to be used'. They asserted: 'Let the Maori law … be sacred, namely that the Natives be not allowed to drink spirits'.[47]

'Colonial New Zealand,' writes historian Miles Fairburn, 'was gripped by a particularly severe drinking problem.' High rates of consumption of spirits and beer marked the 1860s and 1870s in particular, decades that also saw high levels of Pākehā male violence.[48] The public house – and there was no shortage of these in Pākehā settlements – could be seen as 'the rival of the domestic hearth', taking money from the home that might have been spent on children's boots, food and clothing 'in abundance for all'.[49]

The temperance crusade was broad enough to unite some Māori and Pākehā women. In 1883, the Salvation Army brought its own 'forthright teetotal stance' into New Zealand.[50] Women were active in its ranks, attracted by temperance and the possibilities for leadership in the organisation. One of these women was Maraea Moana Mahaki, of Ngāi Teremoana, who joined a number of others in spreading the temperance message in Māori communities.[51] Another woman who observed the havoc caused by alcohol was Ngawhakaheke, wife of Heta Tokiriki, from Mōkau on the North Taranaki Bight. She believed that alcohol had played its part in her name being falsely signed on a land lease deed: 'Owing to my being busy and the beer I had drunk, I did not go to the house where the signing was going on, or touch the pen. I drank a good deal of beer that day. I could get as much beer as I liked as long as it lasted.'[52] Alcohol, then, was one more means by which Māori were dispossessed, and some saw in the temperance movement a means of cultural preservation.

Their Pākehā sisters were equally disturbed by 'the evils of intemperance'. On a grey and rainy August day in 1884, a number of Invercargill women met to discuss the issue. They resolved to form New Zealand's first women's Christian temperance organisation to 'unitedly array Christian women against the manufacture, sale and use of intoxicating liquor as a beverage'.[53] The formation of the Women's Christian Temperance Union in New Zealand in 1884 marked a new stage in the development of women's consciousness. The advent of a gender-specific organisation underlined women's belief that by banding together they could exert their interest in matters that were ignored or overlooked by male politicians. The women quickly concluded that temperance laws were needed to reform society, and this meant advocating 'the extension of voting power to women for electing committees and local option under the Licensing Act'. Hence their first order of business was to petition Parliament to create such voting power.[54] Nothing seems to have come of this initiative until the nascent organisation was galvanised the following year by the WCTU's American envoy, Mary Leavitt, who stressed on her six-month tour that alcohol was the 'natural-enemy' of 'woman's kingdom', the home.[55]

When Leavitt's tour ended in June 1885, nine branches of the WCTU were in operation. By the end of the year, fifteen branches had been established throughout the country, thanks in part to the efforts of Anne Ward, the first national president, who had travelled around New Zealand encouraging women in small towns to set up branches.[56] The Wanganui members focused on social reform and the transformation of the individual, rather than national party politics.[57] The national union emphasised how the values of a good home, respect for the aged, protection of the weak and 'concession to the rights of others' were the foundations of good citizenship. The state, WCTU activist Kate Sheppard argued, was 'an enlargement of the family', and women's involvement was vital to both.[58]

Kate Sheppard, born Catherine Malcolm in Liverpool in 1847, had received an excellent education and a deeply religious upbringing before emigrating to New Zealand with her mother and three siblings in 1869. The family settled in Christchurch where Kate, aged twenty-four, married Walter Allen Sheppard in 1871. Already active in the Ladies' Association of Trinity Congregational Church and the Young Women's Christian

Association in Christchurch, Kate responded enthusiastically to Mary Leavitt's proposal to establish a branch of the WCTU. Her first major involvement in temperance was to campaign for the abolition of barmaids, gathering signatures for a petition banning their employment. Signed by 4,800 Christchurch people who believed that the employment of women in bars was a strategy to lure men into vice, the petition was forwarded to the petitions committee of the House of Representatives, merely to be tossed aside with 'no recommendations to make'. This, to Kate Sheppard, was a clear indication of 'women's powerlessness', and she resolved to work for the enfranchisement of women as a means of countering it. Franchise departments were formed by local branches of the WCTU in 1887, and Sheppard took up the post of national head of the franchise and legislative department so that women might have 'the power to repeal bad laws and to make good ones'.[59]

Petitions were an important means by which those without a political voice could bring their concerns to the attention of the government.[60] In 1884, Parliament received more than fifty petitions advocating for the right of women other than ratepayers to vote for local liquor licensing committees.[61] Petitions also served an educative purpose in that their sponsors had to explain their reasoning in the course of soliciting signatures. In this way, too, members of the WCTU who had little experience in political debate honed their skills in the exercise of convincing others that signing a petition to Parliament was worthwhile. Sir John Hall, a former Premier and leading conservative Canterbury politician, was sympathetic, and advised Sheppard that women's suffrage needed a public profile. He recommended 'petitioning, influencing, and representing public opinion'.[62]

The WCTU was a small group of committed women who had large aims. Kate Sheppard ensured that every WCTU branch appointed a member in charge of 'the franchise agitation'. Helen Nicol took this responsibility in Dunedin, Lily Kirk in Wellington, and Amey Daldy in Auckland.[63] The Christchurch branch obtained pamphlets advocating women's suffrage from the American WCTU, and Kate Sheppard distilled them into the succinct *Ten Reasons Why the Women of New Zealand Should Vote*. The pamphlet promoted debate in literary societies and adult education groups, and helped form the basis of newspaper articles on the subject. Resolutions passed at meetings were forwarded to Parliament and its members were canvassed for support. Petitions proved to be another way of publicising the cause, as well as a way of answering the view often expressed, according to the *Thames Star*, that women themselves did not want the vote.[64]

Two petitions to enfranchise women were organised by the Auckland WCTU in 1886 and 1887, the second going to Parliament supported by 300 signatures. In that year, Colonial Treasurer Sir Julius Vogel introduced a Women's Suffrage Bill that would have enfranchised women on the same terms as men and made them eligible to stand for Parliament. Despite having the support of a majority, the Bill was 'shipwrecked in committee' by disagreements over whether only women of property should be enfranchised.[65] Sir John Hall, at that time without office but a member of the House, introduced a motion

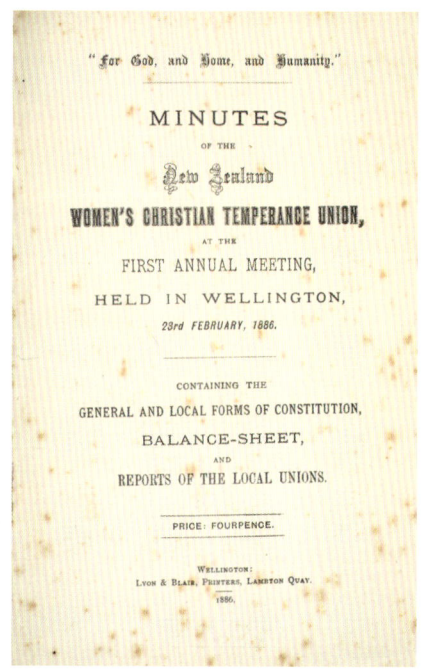

Left Maraea Morete of Te Aitanga-a-Māhaki became an ardent temperance advocate and member of the Salvation Army, an organisation that gave women leadership responsibilities. This 1887 portrait of her in uniform, holding the *Book of Common Prayer*, was first published in the Salvation Army's newspaper, the *War Cry*. *Right* The New Zealand Women's Christian Temperance Union was established as a national body in 1885; these are the minutes from its first annual meeting, held in Wellington in February 1886. *Courtesy of Salvation Army Headquarters, Wellington;* Minutes of the New Zealand Women's Christian Temperance Union, *title page, 1886, Alexander Turnbull Library, Wellington*

in 1890 that 'the right of voting at the election of members of the House of Representatives should be extended to women' – a motion supported by a majority of twenty-six. However, his subsequent Women's Franchise Bill was defeated, in part because opponents still believed there was no strong evidence that women wanted it.[66]

The WCTU realised that it had to demonstrate the extent of public support for its aims and, within five weeks of the defeat of Hall's Bill in the House, began organising a national petition. Volunteers to collect signatures were not, however, immediately forthcoming. Helen Nicol reported that 2,832 inhabitants of Dunedin and Port Chalmers had signed the petition, but commented: 'Our largest suburbs, quite near town, have not been canvassed for want of canvassers, but we are resolved (if necessary) to canvass again on this question. We feel confident that we can easily get 5,000 names.'[67] Harriet Morison, vice-president of the Tailoresses' Union, argued that women wage-earners had 'a right to a voice in those laws that control … competition, and they cannot have a voice or be properly represented, unless they have a ballot in their hands'.[68] 'Mater' (probably Morison) wrote in the *Globe* that working women were met with '[d]isabilities of some kind at every turn'.[69] The vote was women's right, Morison contended, and 'the mind is the standard by which humanity

The Invercargill Lasses Band, pictured here in 1888, helped spread the message of the Salvation Army through music.
Courtesy of the Salvation Army New Zealand, Fiji & Tonga – Heritage Centre & Archives

must be gauged, not the garments worn'.[70] She enlisted the Federated Tailoresses' Union, composed of nearly 2,000 women, to support women's suffrage.

The difficulty of garnering support for the cause at a time of slow transport and uncertain roads was apparent in Christchurch. William Sydney Smith, printer, radical, and close friend of Kate Sheppard, noted that there were good results from inner-city areas 'but the numbers of signatures obtained from the outlying districts was extremely small'.[71] Rose Hall, wife of Sir John Hall, canvassed in Hororata, in rural Canterbury, and outlined the difficulties to Sheppard: 'People live so far apart in this neighbourhood that it takes time to visit all the people.' She suggested holding a public meeting to debate suffrage and gather signatures from among those in attendance. Rose Hall was disappointed that heavy rain kept people away from one such meeting but noted that some had travelled as far as 6 miles. At another 'entertainment' which brought the rural community together, the Halls presented the petition and received a favourable response.[72] The *Lyttelton Times* christened the 9,685 women who signed the 1891 petition across the country 'the Amazon battalion'.[73]

Sir John Hall dramatically unrolled the seventy-four yards of the petition before the House on 14 August, but the extent of support did not convince opponents, who stonewalled until the Bill passed its second reading on 24 August by a majority of twenty-five. Opponents of the Bill, led by Walter Carncross, a friend of the liquor trade, added a clause to allow women voters the right to stand for Parliament, ostensibly because this was a logical corollary but in reality to increase opposition to the Bill. The ploy succeeded, and the Legislative Council, fearing 'mannish women and effeminate men' if women entered political life, defeated the Bill by seventeen votes to fifteen.[74] 'Woman's sphere is not politics. Home is, or should be, where they should rule by love or peace,' announced the Hon. John Thomas Peacock of Canterbury. If women entered Parliament, 'love, possibly, would fly out the door'. He drew a picture of how life might be transformed:

> There may be possibly some of our wives who would be politically inclined, and who might be in the other Chamber. Suppose an honourable gentleman sitting in this Chamber were to retire home as usual at five o'clock p.m. for dinner and find dinner prepared, but his wife not there – she might be dining at Bellamy's; he might retire to his couch and wake up in the morning and find his wife not there. Where has she been? There has been a long sitting of the House until daylight. What a pleasing prospect! How would he like this?[75]

Delay was urged as the best measure, since such a revolutionary change should not, if it was made at all, be made in haste.

'Map out your town into streets, blocks or districts, so that every avenue … may be thoroughly canvassed,' Marion Hattan and Helen Nicol of the Dunedin Women's Franchise League advised the people of Ōamaru who came to a meeting on women's suffrage in May 1892.[76] The response was immediate. Writing to the *North Otago Times*, 'Senex' complained: 'In my opinion this cry or agitation for women's suffrage is just another form of the Prohibition agitation.' This, he believed, was led by 'wild-minded female agitators' bent on 'curtailing the freedom and rights of every British-born male subject'.[77] A 'Young Man' quickly asserted that the liquor trade was a source of poverty and distress, and that 'women have just as much right to vote on questions relating to the government of our country as men have'.[78]

Even the Salvation Army, whose members had worked tirelessly for the temperance cause above all else, weighed in with a view. By 1892, more than half of its 269 full-time commissioned officers were women. Lieutenant Gertrude Gates, an officer member of the 'Lasses Band', wrote in a special number of the *War Cry* edited and written by women:

> I often feel like speaking my mind on the subject of women's rights … God has given us brains, then why should we not use them, particularly when it is for His honour and glory? The Army has broken the orthodox idea that woman's place is at home, and has given us what has long been needed – unrestrained liberty of action and thought.[79]

Constant rejection made the suffragists even more vigilant, and activities reached a new peak, particularly when attempts were made in Dunedin to attract working-class women to their cause.[80] From 1890, canvassing may well have taken place in factories employing large numbers of women, such as the Roslyn Woollen Mills, textile manufacturers Ross and Glendining, and Hallensteins.[81] Maude Hooper, a twenty-three-year-old clerk living in Dunedin's seaside suburb of St Clair, Ellen Hopkinson, a machinist from working-class South Dunedin, and Mary Ellen Burgess, a tailoress from Caversham, were among the working women who supported women's claims to enter the world of political debate. Women in South Dunedin signed the 1893 suffrage petition in far larger numbers (57 per cent signed) than the national average (just under 25 per cent of all women signed). In South Dunedin, strong support came from women members of the Roman Catholic and evangelical Protestant churches, as well as women in the families of skilled working men.[82] Canvassing was clearly very well organised in this part of the country, though not always welcomed in others. One Auckland business displayed a sign warning: 'No canvasser for the WFL [Women's Franchise League] need call in business hours.'[83]

Harriet Morison, the union organiser central to the founding of the Tailoresses' Union, was one of the founders of the Women's Franchise League in Dunedin in April 1892. Unlike the WCTU, the League aimed to attract members regardless of their religious beliefs or views on temperance. Soon there were branches of the league in Gore, Waimate, Tākaka, Feilding, Marton, Ashburton and a number of other towns across the country.[84] Lively debates took place about the respective social roles of women and men. In Gore, a Mrs Smalley was moved to point out that 'it takes infinitely more brains to train children than to rear sheep; and yet are not many of our members of Parliament sheep-farmers?'[85] Nearly 30,000 women throughout New Zealand asserted their right to participate in political decision-making by signing the 1893 petition.

Sir John Hall once again unfurled a suffrage petition on the floor of the House: this time it stretched for some 300 yards. A women's suffrage clause was contained in the 1893 Electoral Bill, introduced by Premier Richard Seddon, which passed through all stages in the House. But Seddon was no supporter of women's suffrage. He had appointed new members of the Legislative Council to facilitate the government's business, but although he had promised in public that they would support women's suffrage, he then denied this, saying that the new members were not required to support every government issue.

The liquor lobby was intent on influencing members, since a new liquor Bill entitled those enrolled in national elections to vote in licensing elections. The Licensed Victuallers feared that if women were enfranchised their votes would reduce the number of licences. They were keenly aware that the temperance advocated by suffragists threatened to limit manly pleasures and, most importantly, undermine the revenue of the drink trade. The 'brewing party' in the Lower House therefore extracted a promise from Seddon that the enactment of the Bill would be delayed until the next election. Seddon did all in his power

Top The National Council of Women was established in 1896, and this photograph was taken at its first meeting in Christchurch that year. From left, standing, are: Mrs A. Ansell (Dunedin), Mrs Henry Smith (Christchurch), Miss A. E. Hookham (Christchurch), Mrs G. Ross (Christchurch), Miss Jessie Mackay (Christchurch), Mrs Isherwood (Christchurch), Mrs Black (Christchurch), Mrs Widdowson (Christchurch), Miss F. Garstin (Christchurch), Mrs Wallis (Christchurch), Mrs Darling (Christchurch), Mrs J. M. Williamson (Wanganui), and Mrs Wilson (Christchurch). Seated are: Mrs G. J. Smith (Christchurch), Mrs A. Daldy (Auckland), Mrs Hatton (Dunedin, vice-president), Lady Anna Stout (Wellington, vice-president), Mrs Kate Sheppard (Christchurch, president), Mrs A. J. Schnackenberg (Auckland, vice-president), Mrs W. Sievwight (Gisborne), Mrs M. A. Tasker (Wellington), and Mrs D. Izett (Christchurch, secretary). Seated on the floor are: Mrs C. M. Alley (Malvern), Mrs A. Wells (Christchurch), and Miss Bain (Christchurch). *Alexander Turnbull Library, Wellington, 1/2-041798-F*

Bottom Women voters head to the polling booth at the Drill Hall in Rutland Street, Auckland, on election day in 1899. *Auckland Libraries, Sir George Grey Special Collections, 7-A12353*

A photograph of 1891 shows delegates to the first conference of the Federated Tailoresses' Union, held in Christchurch. Secretary Harriet Morison is seated to the left of president Mr J. Cleworth. With her encouragement, the union became involved in the suffrage movement. She commented: 'There were many reforms wanted amongst working women, and they would like to have a voice in the return of members to Parliament, who would look faithfully after their interest'.
Hocken Collections/Te Uare Taoka o Hākena, University of Otago Library, Dunedin, S10-062a

to stymie the Bill to satisfy the brewing interests, but in the course of doing so he went too far. When two Opposition members became aware of the extent of Seddon's manipulations, including persuading a member of the Legislative Council to alter his vote, they were 'so incensed' that they switched sides and voted for the Bill.[86] 'Political Tricksters were tricked,' commented Dunedin's *Evening Star*, 'and hoisted up by their own petard.'[87]

A crowd of women watched anxiously from the gallery as on 8 September 1893 the Bill was debated and eventually passed by a majority of two. The Bill still required the Governor's assent, and there were fears that this might be delayed, preventing women from voting in the upcoming election. Some Wellington women opposed to suffrage saw their chance and quickly organised the Anti-Women's Franchise League; they presented all those who had voted against the Bill with a red camellia.[88] The liquor lobby organised anti-suffrage petitions, signed mostly by hotel patrons who were sometimes bribed with free drinks, and these were forwarded to the Governor, Lord Glasgow, from Auckland, Wellington, Christchurch, Dunedin, Southland, Napier, New Plymouth and Hawke's Bay.[89] But the thousands of signatures collected were insufficient – and arrived too late.

The Governor gave his assent on 19 September. 'Womanhood Franchise granted!!!', a joyful Catherine Fulton, former Dominion president of the WCTU, noted in her diary that day.[90] Women throughout the country attended thanksgiving meetings. The Dunedin Women's Franchise League held theirs in the Dunedin YMCA, where women crowded in and 'the proceedings were of a jubilant character'. Jubilation was, however, tempered by 'a feeling of grave responsibility'.[91] Time was short if campaigners were to ensure women put their names on the electoral roll. The suffragists therefore turned their attention to enrolling as many women as possible in the six weeks before the upcoming election.[92]

Early on the morning of 28 November 1893, a Mrs McPherson and a Mrs Benyon ran neck and neck towards the polling booth in Greymouth, competing for the honour of being the first woman to record a vote in the district. Mrs McPherson won, and was followed by a stream of women eager to cast their vote. The *Grey River Argus* reported that the election was 'the quietest' and 'the driest' ever seen in the district.[93] In New Plymouth, the majority of voters were 'of the fair sex', and in Wanganui 'the women played a most prominent part'.[94] Women in Wellington 'voted freely', especially at a booth especially reserved for them at the Skating Rink. They seemed, the *Colonist* recorded, 'thoroughly to enjoy their first appearance in the political arena'.[95] 'Lady canvassers' were said to be 'numerous and zealous', outstripping their male competitors 'in efforts to capture votes'.[96]

No 'vestige of rowdyism or a man worse of liquor' appeared on the streets of Auckland, where the presence of women 'seemed to have an excellent effect'.[97] The Christchurch voters were noted for their 'earnestness': the only difference from previous elections was that 'female prohibitionists were extremely emphatic in insisting on the claims of their candidates' at the polling booth entrances.[98] Women voters in Christchurch were, however, 'slow in exercising their new duties', and people feared that not all would do so before the booths closed. Eventually the women voted in large numbers in the central city and in the suburbs.[99] At the close of the polls, approximately two out of three adult women, including about 4,000 Māori women, had voted.[100]

'The advent of the political woman' in Wellington, the *Otago Witness* reported, 'was today accompanied by perfect weather'. The well-dressed women were said to make no secret of their votes, with 'prohibition women and workers' wives' giving their allegiance 'to the water knight'.[101] That 'knight' was Sir Robert Stout, who was closely allied with the prohibition movement and vying with Richard Seddon for leadership of the Liberal Party by promoting local liquor licensing option polls, which could lead to the abolition of all licences and hence turn localities 'dry'. Seddon bested Stout by coming up with a compromise measure of a triennial poll by which communities could reduce the number of licences in their electorate, but total prohibition in an area would require 50 per cent of the voters to turn out and three-fifths of them to vote to go 'dry'.[102] Seddon thus skilfully divided the prohibitionist support. That both men had to pay attention to this new group of voters underlines the women's contribution to the growing strength of the first political party to dominate in New Zealand politics – a party committed to instituting 'strong central government' to oversee a raft of innovative social and economic experiments.[103]

The *Evening Post* attributed the success of the Liberals in the elections to the women's vote: 'The women worked nobly, and by their energy and intelligence fully vindicated the wisdom of entrusting them with the franchise.'[104]

December 1893 saw Elizabeth Yates elected Mayor of the Auckland borough of Onehunga, the first woman to become a mayor in the British Empire. Kate Sheppard thought this an apt ending to the year, but warned of the difficulties a woman officeholder would face. These were quickly felt: four male councillors resigned, not wanting to serve under 'petticoat government'.[105] The Town Clerk shared the same prejudice and moved on. Elizabeth Yates's election brought international attention but her path was difficult and she was defeated after one year.

Nevertheless, women's electoral participation was welcomed (albeit well after the fact) by Premier Seddon at a large and raucous meeting in the Christchurch Opera House on 6 February 1896. Looking back on the two years or so since the election, Seddon expressed a 'deep debt of gratitude' to 'the ladies' for returning the Liberals with such a large majority. He claimed that his government had been working to retain the confidence of women by protecting wives' property, by legislation protecting family homes and by raising the age of consent.[106] Seddon was signalling the fact that all future governments would have to take the women's vote into consideration.

Māori citizenship and the 'regeneration of the race'

In March 1881, a meeting of 3,000 Māori at Waitangi called for the establishment of a Māori parliament 'with the power of veto over all questions affecting Maori people'.[107] They had little confidence that participation in the Pākehā government, which seemed intent on land alienation, would lead to redress of their grievances. In fact, it would be more than ten years before that Māori parliament convened, but in the meantime men and women took part in direct action against continued European disregard for their interests. In 1885, for example, Māori obstructed the building of the Thames–Rotorua railway by throwing materials into the river and cutting down the Waitoa bridge, near Matamata.[108] The following year the resident magistrate at Hokianga reported that a government survey party at Motukaraka was 'forcibly stopped by a party of women'. The 'ring-leader' was arrested and imprisoned.[109] In 1888, Māori obstructed the contractor at the Ngāwapurua protective works in the Wairarapa, reasoning that the government 'had not yet compensated them for the land already taken for bridge and railway works'.[110]

Māori men had a stake in national government because they could vote, but the four Māori members were heavily outnumbered in the House, and effectively powerless to implement change and reverse the loss of land. Indeed, their fellow parliamentary members were, more often than not, encouraging Māori to break up communal land. John Ballance was Minister of Lands, Defence and Native Affairs in the Stout–Vogel government of 1884–1887. He suggested at a Waipū meeting that by dividing up their land and receiving individual title Māori could vote in the European electorates, as well as for Māori seats, if they were ratepayers or had freehold land to the value of £25 (unlike European voters who were not subject to a property qualification from 1879).[111] Airini Tonore (Mrs Donnelly), a woman who owned and farmed a large estate in Hawke's Bay, was forthright in reply:

> Seeing that the Natives were the owners of the land in New Zealand, she considered that the franchise should be extended to them, without obliging each man to have land worth twenty-five pounds in his own right. The Natives all had a great stake in the colony, and many Europeans voted whose only possessions in the colony were the clothes they wore and what they carried about with them; the only condition was that they should have lived in the colony for six months. These vagrant Europeans were allowed to elect members to Parliament, who go there and make laws which are a burden upon the Natives.[112]

Airini Tonore articulated what many observed: that Europeans with little attachment to the land were given more rights than the indigenous people.

From 1892, those earlier calls from Waitangi for a separate institution that might act decisively in the interests of Māori were met when Te Kotahitanga, the Māori Parliament, convened for the first time – just when the agitation for women's suffrage was at its height. Composed of an Upper House of fifty appointed chiefs and a Lower House of ninety-six elected men, Te Kotahitanga echoed the gender norms of the Pākehā government and aimed for equal status with the New Zealand Parliament. In May 1893, Meri Te Tai Mangakahia of Te Rarawa, supported by Akenehi Tomoana, presented a motion to Te Kotahitanga requesting that Māori women have the right to vote and stand for election to that parliament.[113] She pointed out that many Māori women were landowners and knowledgeable about land management. She ended her plea by asserting that women might be more successful in petitions to the Queen than men had been, because 'the Queen may listen to the petitions if they are presented by her Maori sisters, since she is a woman as well'.[114] While her speech was generally well received, no action on her motion was taken.

Māori women were included in the 1893 Electoral Act that gave all New Zealand women the vote, despite the misgivings of the Hon. Major Wahawaha of the Legislative Council, who had suggested the measure be delayed until Māori women were consulted.[115] Within weeks of the Act's passing, the *Auckland Star* reported that thirteen Māori women had formed a committee to canvass for a candidate in the Hutt, near Wellington.[116] At about the same time, the member for Southern Maori, Tame Parata, reassured a deputation of chiefs who met at Temuka that, while Māori women had the right to vote, they could not vote for the Māori seats if they registered on the general electoral roll.[117]

In 1895, at a meeting at Te Hauke to mourn the passing of the chief Hone Nea Nea of Ngāti Kahungunu, Māori women, still excluded from Te Kotahitanga, held their own parliament, an occasion reported throughout the country.[118] To the *Taranaki Herald*, the

'Wahines Bossing the Men' could only be 'A sign of decadence in the race'.[119] Readers from north to south learned of the women's resolve:

> We find that after many years men's endeavours to carry out our interests have failed, and therefore we women have formed ourselves into a parliament or committee and now we are going to do what we can. Our lands are slipping away from us every day into the hands of the government, and therefore we must protect ourselves. Should we not succeed we will find ourselves like shags on a sandbank spreading our wings to the wind.[120]

The women decided that they should have nothing more to do with the Native Land Court; that they would cease selling lands; that no further surveys should be undertaken; and that there should be no further renting of lands. Anyone breaking these regulations was to be fined. After the novelty of the women's parliament had passed, however, the press lost interest and failed to report whether these resolutions were enforced. Komiti wāhine, however, according to historian Angela Ballara, burgeoned at this time in the lower North Island, where support for Te Kotahitanga was strong. Preventing land sales, the havoc wreaked by the Land Court, and material deprivation were central to their concerns.[121]

By the turn of the century, Māori had a limited resource base, with only about 2 million hectares of land remaining in Māori ownership.[122] Individual women, such as Rahera Muriwai Uru of Ngāi Tahu, Tutimakahu of Ngāti Māmoe, and Tuhuru of Westland were tireless in their campaigns for the redress of grievances.[123] The women's claims made clear the ways Europeans had imposed patriarchal family forms upon Māori. Kataraina Uru, in her evidence to one of the many government commissions examining the title to lands, stated:

> My husband was one of the original grantees. My name was not on the grant. I am one of the women who attended the meeting with Mr Buller [when he] said grants should issue in favour of husbands and wives. When the grants came out they were in favour of husbands only. We demanded from the government inclusion in the titles, but were not included until a number were dead.[124]

The assumptions of the Pākehā culture had overridden Māori communal interests and had dispossessed women in particular.

Without land, Māori women sought to provide for their families by taking whatever work was available: gum-digging in the Hokianga; seasonal labouring on farms; making and selling kete; hawking fish and produce; and guiding at Lake Tarawera. The Tūhourangi people profited from tourism at Lake Tarawera until the 1886 eruption of Mount Tarawera destroyed the lake's world-famous Pink and White Terraces.[125] Some guides, such as Maggie Papakura, became well known as the tourism business subsequently developed in Rotorua.[126]

Women are among those waiting outside the Rotorua Court House to vote for one of the Māori seats in Parliament in the 1890s or early 1900s. *Auckland Libraries, Sir George Grey Special Collections, 7-A14995*

The survival of Māori communities forced into the margins through land loss often lay in 'the compassionate disposition of the natives towards each other' under circumstances of great deprivation.[127] The resident magistrate responsible for the area from Manukau Heads to Port Waikato commented that families there found work 'digging kauri-gum, cutting flax, and a few work in flax and saw-mills'.[128] A drought in the Rotorua district in 1886 meant that potato crops failed, raising fears that 'many of the natives will be short of food during the coming winter and spring'.[129] The developing money economy had, in the view of one Hokianga observer, destroyed 'good old habits of thrift and industry'.[130] But some Māori made that economy work for them. Māori in the Hutt Valley grew strawberries and vegetables to supply the Wellington market; 'as much as £150' was said to have been earned by one entrepreneur from a season's growth of strawberries.[131] In the Southern district, taking in Akaroa, Amuri, Ashley, Ashburton, Selwyn and Cheviot, Ngāi Tahu communities were said to be 'in good circumstances' with 'good houses and gardens'. In those districts, Māori found work with 'good wages' alongside Europeans at harvest, shearing and grass-seeding times.[132]

Government officials monitored the state of Māori settlements, and from the mid-nineteenth century some were predicting that the race was dying out. 'The cruel law of the survival of the fittest is inexorable,' noted an editorial in the *Otago Daily Times* in 1885,

Top left Akenehi Tomoana supported the motion of Meri Te Tai Mangakahia for women to be able to vote and stand for election to Te Kotahitanga, the Māori Parliament, in 1893. Their representations were received well, but did not result in change. *Top right* Airini Tonore (Airini Donnelly), pictured here in the 1870s or '80s, was a Ngāti Kahungunu woman of mana, and, together with her husband, Irishman George Donnelly, fought through the Native Land Court to acquire large tracts of land in Hawke's Bay, while opposing land sales to Pākehā. Her extensive knowledge of tribal history contributed to her success in land claims. *Bottom left* Marata Te Heuheu was photographed probably in the 1880s. She was married to Urupene Puhara of Pakipaki, Hawke's Bay. *Bottom right* This carte de visite photograph of Meretene Panapa was taken at Napier in December 1893. *Alexander Turnbull Library, Wellington, 1/4-022200-G; 1/4-022134-G; photograph by Samuel Carnell, 1/4-022190-G; photograph by Samuel Carnell, 1/4-022201-G*

'and it has long been evident that the extinction of the Maori race is merely a question of time.'[133] In the four northernmost counties, as well as in Te Urewera, the Bay of Plenty, Rotorua and Taupō, East Coast, Whanganui and parts of the King Country, Māori communities were raising children in new and unfamiliar circumstances. Traditional Māori building methods made for waterproof and warm housing, but the upheaval wrought by land confiscation in many areas led to movement from healthy hilltop pā sites to 'squalid conditions in damp river valleys'.[134] In such conditions communities fought the ravages of typhoid, respiratory diseases and tuberculosis.[135] Old patterns of living persisted, following the rules of noa and tapu which involved the separation of cooking and sanitary arrangements from sleeping areas. However, these were continually refashioned as Māori responded to European ideas about housing patterns and 'scientific hygiene'.

Among the most avid promoters of 'scientific' rules of health was a new generation of Māori who were familiar with the Pākehā world and schooled in its ways. Though the overcrowded and damp conditions in which many Māori lived aided the spread of disease, Māori men trained in medicine, like their Pākehā educators, frequently attributed high infant mortality rates from gastroenteritis and diarrhoea to 'maternal ignorance of the principles of diet and hygiene'.[136] Mothers were seen to be both the problem and the solution to poor health. Not all European innovations were to be followed, however. Te Rangi Hiroa (Peter Buck), the first Māori medical graduate, claimed that the custom of bottle-feeding infants had 'slain more than the guns of Hongi'.[137] Like James Carroll, Apirana Ngata and Maui Pomare, Te Rangi Hiroa was a member of the Young Maori Party, the organisation formed by graduates of Te Aute College in Hawke's Bay with the aim of improving Māori health and welfare.

Regular counting of the Māori population took place through censuses, although in many Māori communities such processes were greeted with suspicion: did the government want to take more land or charge more tax?[138] Ineffective counting made total population figures uncertain, but the trend appeared to be downward. By 1896, the Māori population was a mere 39,805. Of those, only 18,260 were female.[139] The Māori proportion of the total population had fallen to 5.5 per cent by 1900.[140] One estimate suggests that by the 1890s, 50 per cent of Māori girls died before the age of seven and just 42 per cent reached adulthood.[141] For women working for the survival of their communities, the future of their children became paramount.

Childbirth itself held terrors, as historian Alison Clarke has documented. Among the stories she relates is that of an unnamed Māori woman whose first ten labours (a not unusual number) were 'easy and short'. Her eleventh child, however, was in a transverse position, causing a protracted labour and eventually requiring medical intervention. The doctor turned the baby in the womb and used forceps to assist delivery, but the mother's uterus had ruptured and the doctor assumed she would die. He left her to her whānau to be made comfortable. To his astonishment, she recovered.[142]

The 1901 Census was the first to document an increase in the Māori population: from its nadir of under 40,000 in 1896, the figure now stood at around 45,000. Gradually, and at varying rates according to tribal location, Māori developed immunity to the introduced acute infectious diseases such as measles, mumps and whooping cough.[143] Natural immunity, and improved living conditions, lay at the heart of the Māori population recovery. Large families and successive births were seen as a sign of a happy marriage and signalled hope for the future.[144] Women began bearing children young, and the support of whānau, along with the fact that most Māori were rurally based, meant children were welcomed and easily absorbed into the community. The tragedy of losing children, as in the accidental drowning of sixteen children from the Ōmāio School in the Bay of Plenty on 5 August 1900, struck deep: people from that small community changed their names to remember the children, and hapū of Te Whānau-a-Apanui were also named to commemorate those who had drowned.[145]

'If the race as a race is to be regenerated,' the Revd Frederick Bennett, of the Anglican Maori Mission, argued in 1901, 'it must be done through the instrumentality of our Maori women.' He suggested that 'the education of our Maori women has been somewhat neglected in the past', and that the Māori girls' schools promoted by the Young Maori Party promised a bright future.[146] In many communities, the native schools, established under the control of the Native Department set up in 1867, became important sites of activity and hope, with the schools themselves seen as 'a mediator between Maori and Pakeha worlds'.[147]

Māori women were taking their own initiatives with regard to education. The *White Ribbon*, the magazine of the WCTU, reported on a meeting of 'Up to date Maori Women' in May 1901. A committee of women from several tribes gathered in a 'certain North Island village' and summoned the young local state school mistress to meet with them. The teacher was informed that the purpose of the committee was 'to ensure the punctual and regular attendance of the scholars'. Any absentees over the age of seven were to be reported by the teacher to the chairwoman of the committee. The chairwoman would then impose an appropriate fine on the parents of the child.[148]

Young Pākehā women teachers played an important role in mediating between the Māori and Pākehā worlds. Agnes Grant, for example, graduated with a Bachelor of Arts from Canterbury University College in 1897. 'Deeply interested' in Māori, she took up a post as head teacher at the newly opened Karioi Native School in the King Country in 1898.[149] When, shortly afterwards, she was forced to close the school because of a measles epidemic, she transferred her attentions to looking after pupils in their homes. She reported:

Last week the epidemic took a much more serious form and several of the children had bad relapses and we were all busy from morning to night nursing them. No less than seven of

Top A Tūhoe whānau working party, including women and children, clear the bush on a Pākehā farm at Te Waimana in 1904. *Photograph by C. and J. Ryan,* Auckland Weekly News, *29 September 1904, p.11*

Bottom Māori women harvest a kūmara crop in the early 1900s. *Alexander Turnbull Library, Wellington, 1/1-006265-G*

A teacher takes an art class at Karioi Native School in 1908; the children, who have been drawing on slates, are showing their artworks to the photographer. Pākehā women who taught in the schools often played an important role in the local communities. *Alexander Turnbull Library, Wellington, 1/2-048102-F*

them had temperatures of 105 & three nearly reached 106. Already fifteen of the children have either had the measles or are ill with it at present & three more are apparently sickening.[150]

Care of this kind brought the teachers into close contact with whānau and assisted the spread of Pākehā healthcare methods, often alongside traditional practices, in Māori communities. One doctor, acting as a locum in Manaia in Taranaki, wrote of his despair that the government took 'fine care to register even its dogs, but did not trouble to register Maori births, deaths or marriages'.[151] He added his voice to the calls by the Young Maori Party for vital registration of births and deaths to better monitor Māori health.[152]

When Young Maori Party activist Maui Pomare, of Ngāti Toa and Ngāti Mutunga descent, returned from his medical training in the United States in 1901, he was appointed the first Maori Health Officer, ranked second to the head of the newly created Public Health Department.[153] In that role he argued that the education of Māori girls was crucial: 'Strike the mothers and you strike the entire rising generation ... The hygiene of the home, personal dress, the science of cookery, the nursing of the sick, the upbringing of babies: these are the essentials that ought to be taught in every Maori school in the country.'[154]

Pomare and his wife Miria Woodbine, of Rongowhakaata and Te Aitanga-a-Māhaki, were representative of the new generation of educated Māori leaders committed to combining elements of Māori and European culture. While her husband was active in national politics, Miria bore three children and worked tirelessly for a diverse range of voluntary organisations, exerting citizenship through social leadership in their 'elegant home', Hiwiroa, in Lower Hutt.[155] Heni Materoa, also known as Te Huinga, was married to prominent East Coast politician James Carroll. Heni's mother, Riperata, had opposed her daughter's desire to marry Carroll, known then as Timi Kara, so the couple had eloped by ship from Gisborne and married in the Wellington registry office in July 1881. Later that year they returned to Gisborne, where Heni became a leader among local Māori. She was a 'generous benefactor' in support of the welfare of women and children, and of women's sport, particularly hockey, golf and bowls. The Kahutia Bowling Club was named for her.[156]

But Māori women sought the regeneration of society in very different ways. Some, like Miria Woodbine and Heni Materoa, worked within the European political structures that others chose to challenge or eschew. Followers of the Taranaki spiritual leader Te Whiti-o-Rongomai, such as the prophetess Ani Kaaro, looked forward to the return of their lands and the day when Pākehā would enter servitude to Māori.[157] The prophecies of Atereta Kawana Ropiha, named Mere Rikiriki by Te Whiti and Tohu, would have great influence in the early twentieth century. Mere, who was born around 1866, was descended from Maata, a medium and a healer, and she developed a faith that blended Māori traditions with Catholicism. She passed on her own faith-healing gifts to her kinsman T. W. Ratana, and prophesied that he would become a leader of people.[158] In the 1920s, the settlement at Rātana Pā, near Wanganui, became a haven for dispossessed Māori, and the Rātana movement would grow into a major political force.

'Throughout the Dominion,' a writer commented in the *White Ribbon*, 'there is a feeling of dissatisfaction amongst the younger members of the Native race; they feel and know life is not given to them to be wasted.'[159] Hope for the future lay in the health of children. Wetekia Ruruku Elkington, who was born and lived on D'Urville Island, married early in the 1890s, and went on to have thirteen children. Her first son was only ten days old when he died of whooping cough. Her second child, a daughter, died aged three. Of the eleven subsequent children, nine lived to adulthood. Along with her own children, Wetekia raised those of her cousin and other whāngai (informally adopted children) for whom she could provide a good start in life. Proud of her Ngāti Koata and Te Āti Awa heritage, and expert in the genealogy of Tainui, Weketia imparted to her children and grandchildren a pride in their Māori past and 'a vision of what can be achieved'.[160]

By ensuring the health of their children, Māori women were shaping the citizens of the future. Enfranchisement, which had meant so much to Pākehā women activists secure in the growth of their population, meant little to Māori if it seemed there were only a few to exercise that right. By the dawn of the twentieth century, there were encouraging signs that communities were reviving. A young population would have their own particular demands – for education and welfare – in the modern world.

Lady Mildred Amelia Tapapa Woodbine Pomare, of Rongowhakaata and Te Aitanga-a-Māhaki descent, sat for this studio portrait around 1910. In 1903 she had married doctor and politician Maui Pomare (later knighted), and while raising three children was heavily involved in community work and patriotic schemes during the First World War. With Lady Liverpool, the Governor's wife, she established a Maori Soldiers Fund in 1915 to provide food and garments for men of the Maori Contingent serving overseas. The Fund continued after the war to provide assistance to returned servicemen. *Alexander Turnbull Library, Wellington, 1/1-014582-G*

Top Women of the Whiting and Vaughan families, camping at Kapiti Island in 1910, cook on a camp fire. *Alexander Turnbull Library, Wellington, 1/2-071079-F*

Bottom Nita Lomba (on horseback) delivers and picks up mail for the Paranui to Mangōnui postal service, Northland, about 1910. Mrs Olive Taylor (right) takes receipt of a letter. *Alexander Turnbull Library, Wellington, 1/2-030466-F*

Chapter Six
New Expectations for a New Century

'You are not a New Woman surely? You don't want to do what men do?' an alarmed friend inquired of Anna Paterson Stout in 1895.[1] Anna, wife of Robert Stout, the former Premier, had firm political views of her own, including that women should have equal rights with men. She had no hesitation in declaring herself to be a 'New Woman', pointing out that such a woman had no desire to claim the vices of men. 'New Women,' she said, 'wish to have the right to be educated physically, mentally and morally, so as to be able to live their own lives and support themselves without the degrading necessity of accepting a home at some man's pleasure'.[2] Keenly aware that the 'eyes of the world' were on New Zealand women and the experiment with women's suffrage, Anna Stout noted that the 'New Woman has set herself the task of improving the conditions of life for women, hoping thereby to improve the conditions for men as well'.[3] The success of the New Woman was contingent on creating the 'New Man'.

Once the vote had been attained, Pākehā women activists looked to the state to guarantee women's independence. From the 'Ladies Gallery', women watched as men debated the issues before the House of Representatives. The women themselves were watched in return: a columnist in the popular pictorial weekly the *Free Lance* noted the amusement of the Māori women in attendance: one even laughed outright at a member's mispronunciation of a Māori name.[4] A number of Māori women were of the view that members of that very House had failed to honour the Treaty of Waitangi and continued to undermine their communal culture. If the state was unlikely to bring redress, they had to look to their own resources to carve out a future for their whānau. Like the woman with the moko dressed in 'a military frock of khaki with scarlet facings' who listened attentively to the politicians, Māori women wished to keep elements of tradition while engaging in the opportunities the twentieth century presented.[5] Unlike those who watched from the gallery, most Māori women lived in rural areas and their concerns were very different from those of urban-based activists in the women's movement.

The suffrage campaign had anticipated 'New Women' who would be educated and economically independent citizens, able to participate in political life. Outside that arena, young women took up new employment opportunities as factory, clerical and shop work increased from the 1880s, and new forms of professional training such as nursing and medicine developed. Māori women, increasingly assured that their families would survive, participated in new ventures and retained older ways. Diversity characterised their communities, shaped by a history of displacement.

The advent of the First World War exposed divisions amongst women that had been papered over during the suffrage campaign. Pacifists opposed patriots, social purity advocates berated the realism of campaigner Ettie Rout in her efforts to prevent venereal disease, and anti-conscriptionists led by Te Puea Herangi in the Waikato angered those Māori who saw in war service a way to uphold their equality as citizens. Wartime demands for labour drew young women into towns and heightened expectations that they could do men's jobs for the duration. Having proved themselves in a variety of fields, activist women expected full citizenship to follow: that is, that women would have the right to stand for Parliament.

Tackling the taboos

Unlike their white counterparts in Australia, who won both the right to vote and the right to stand for Parliament in 1902, New Zealand women were denied the right to stand for Parliament until 1919.[6] New Zealand women, therefore, had to resort to lobbying and public meetings. In their petitions delivered to Parliament, women's groups made connections between legally diverse issues in order to pursue their aim of creating a single moral standard.[7] British feminist Josephine Butler's international campaign against the Contagious Diseases Acts (which allowed the policing of women thought to be prostitutes in order to protect men from venereal disease) acted as a spur to New Zealand activists who opposed such a double standard. An international social purity movement appealed to women of religious convictions who wished to clean up vice.[8] Women, they claimed, should no longer be regarded as the property and playthings of men either within or outside of marriage.

By upholding equality and economic independence within marriage and equal pay outside it, feminists aimed to increase women's options so that their lives were no longer governed by the economic necessity of forming a sexual contract with one man as a wife, or, in the case of prostitutes, with many men. Activists sought to undermine contemporary beliefs in an ungovernable male sexuality that sanctioned unlimited childbearing for wives, as well as prostitution, adultery and seduction. In an age of consent set at twelve for girls, in the differential access women and men had to divorce, in the double standard

Opposite D. K. (Dorothy) Richmond painted this study of a fashionably dressed woman with a poodle, probably in the 1890s or early 1900s. One of the first New Zealand women to receive professional art training overseas, Richmond became a respected artist and art teacher. The daughter of painter and politician J. C. Richmond, she was part of the Richmond–Atkinson clan. *Hocken Collections/Te Uare Taoka o Hākena, University of Otago Library, Dunedin, 18,486 28*

of the Contagious Diseases Act and the absence of any law against incest, feminists saw women's autonomy discounted in the interests of men. By the participation of women in the legal process as lawyers, jurors, police and parliamentarians, they hoped to create a legal system that responded to women's needs.

The double standard, which entitled men to sexual licence while expecting chastity from women, was a key issue for reform. For as long as it was in place, women were understood in terms of their sexuality, whether as 'ideal' or 'fallen' women. The women's movement asserted the sisterhood of all women, pointing out that the existence of the double standard meant that 'somebody's daughter' had to be sacrificed to male lust.[9] In the world they wished to create, the 'New Woman' would be 'she who has discovered herself – not relatively as mother, wife, sister, but absolutely'.[10] This quest to assert women's autonomy was an important part of the campaign to reform male prerogatives by legislative change. The debates over incest, adultery, the age of consent and repeal of the Contagious Diseases Act were essentially attempts to create a chaste 'New Man' as a fitting counterpart for the 'New Woman'.

Curbing men's sexual liberties

'[A]s the divine law allows no liberty to sin, or immunity from punishment, on account of sex,' the Dunedin Women's Franchise League argued in 1895, 'we demand that the statutes of our Colony should be brought into harmony with the law of God.'[11] Women's participation in the political process was the way to ensure that this would happen, although a variety of views existed within the women's movement as to which reforms were the most crucial. Some saw an emphasis on temperance as the route to social harmony, while others wanted to focus on the protection of young women.

A group of Wellington citizens, outraged by working-class girls apparently roaming the streets at night 'soliciting prostitution', organised the first petition on the age of consent in 1888. And in 1889 the Offences Against the Person Act was introduced, making carnal knowledge of a girl over twelve and under fourteen years of age a misdemeanour warranting up to five years' penal servitude. The consent of the girl was to be no defence, but a man's belief that the girl was fourteen or older could be raised in defence. Prosecution had to be undertaken within one month of the offence taking place.[12]

Activists believed the 1889 Act left the age too low, and that the time limit was unrealistically short for prosecution to be successful. The only reason the Dunedin Women's Franchise League could see for making the offence so different from property crimes by imposing a one-month time limit was for 'protecting immorality and making vice safe'. They suggested nothing less than a six-month time limit.[13] In 1894, the Liberal government received nineteen petitions from various women's groups and church associations requesting that the age of consent for girls be raised to sixteen years. Members of the Auckland branch of the WCTU advocated raising the age to eighteen years. Annie

Schnackenberg, a member of the Auckland branch and national president of the WCTU, urged that the age be raised to twenty-one. She argued that the age of consent should be called the 'age of protection … because it ought never to be possible for a girl or woman to consent to her own ruin'.[14] Lucy Smith, editor of the WCTU's page in *The Prohibitionist*, described the causes and consequences of a girl's ruin:

> [T]rustful affection for some professed lover has probably been the occasion of their fall. Disowned and cast aside by inhuman friends, they have been made to feel that their mistake means ruin and disgrace for life; that never again can they be received as happy, honoured members of decent society, – and so they sink into the gulf which yawns beneath them. And their partner in guilt – what of him? Is he banned by society, shunned by the world? Does society refuse to see, hear or speak of him? Not for one moment. He is 'only sowing his wild oats'.[15]

Activists saw raising the age of consent as one means to shift responsibility for sexual behaviour on to men, because it allowed the possibility of a carnal knowledge prosecution in which the fact of a girl's consent would be no defence. The man, instead of the girl, would be publicly disgraced. This was a responsibility that many within the conservative Legislative Council, whose members were appointed rather than elected, were unwilling to accept. Despite Seddon's best efforts as premier, the Council blocked the 1894 Criminal Code Bill which aimed to raise the age of consent to sixteen years but compromised with fifteen, and extended the time limit for prosecutions from one month to within two months of the offence.[16] When the Council debated the Bill, the Hon. James Bonar expressed reservations others clearly felt: 'girls in the colonies of the age of fifteen were very much older than girls at Home, and they were perfectly well able to take care of themselves. He believed that there were very few men who would willingly do wrong to a girl if it was not for her consent.'[17]

Members of the WCTU, however, believed that all girls required protection from male licentiousness. The *White Ribbon* responded:

> Our legislators in the Upper House are of the opinion that fifteen year-old girls should have knowledge and strength of character to protect themselves from impure men of any age. We presume these honourable gentlemen think it necessary that their own daughters should be protected by chaperone or escort till considerably over that age. The fathers in a lower social scale are unable to exercise such care. Have we not a right to demand that the state should step in, and provide protection for those who cannot reasonably be expected to protect themselves?[18]

William James Culver, 'an earnest young Congregationalist', and Henry Wilding, a Justice of the Peace who presided over instances of cruelty and desertion, shared the WCTU's concern about the cases of seduction and cruelty to women and children. They assisted in the founding of a new organisation, the Society for the Protection of Women and Children, in 1893.[19] The society's aim to promote laws for the protection of women

Artist Margaret Stoddart painted the garden of the Godley House, Diamond Harbour, where she lived with her mother and sister from 1907 to 1913 after returning from study in Europe. A student of the Canterbury College School of Art in the 1880s, Stoddart was a founding member of the Palette Club, whose members were interested in plein air (outdoors) painting. *Christchurch Art Gallery Te Puna o Waiwhetu, purchased with assistance from the Olive Stirrat bequest, 90/56*

and children indicated the centrality of the view that the state should protect the weak. At their very first meeting, attended by eight men and seven women, members outlined three aims in addition to legal reform: to prosecute cases 'of alleged "cruelty, seduction, outrage or excessive violence to women and children"; to advise women who had been treated cruelly; and to provide for children whose parents or guardians were found to be unfit to have charge of them'.[20] Branches spread throughout the country. Now active as citizens with voting rights, women such as Anna Stout, who spearheaded the Wellington branch in 1897, sought new laws to protect women and children.

While some Legislative Councillors opposed state intervention in private life, they were happy to support it in the case of the Contagious Diseases Act, which enabled the compulsory medical examination of women thought to be prostitutes. In an 1895 debate on the removal of the 1869 Act, the spectre of 'Mrs Grundy' was raised before the House.

· ꝓURIRI ·
(VITEX LITTORALIS).
NATIVE OF NEW ZEALAND.

Ida Eise produced this study of a branch of the pūriri tree for her Art Class Teachers' Certificate at Elam School of Art, Auckland, in 1912. Interested in the Arts and Crafts movement, she went on to join the more adventurous New Group in the 1940s; she taught at Elam from 1920 to 1956. *Alexander Turnbull Library, Wellington, D-008-023*

This 'terribly proper person … a tall, thin woman, with a long nose, very compressed lips and somewhat flat in the chest', had the killjoy and sexless nature that many members feared would characterise the women who sought entry to Parliament.[21] Only those women 'carrying the big umbrella', they argued, would want to participate in politics.[22] To parliamentarians it was not 'the better class of womanhood' who wanted to be politically active but the 'masculine women' seeking notoriety.[23] Activists in the women's movement, on the other hand, wished to divest women of sexual objectification and so reform the identification of women with men's pleasures.

The Legislative Council refused to support repeal of the Contagious Diseases Act. John Rigg, a Liberal–Labour member from Wellington, stated that: 'it was not the men

In 1909 leading New Zealand feminist Anna Stout travelled with her family to London, where she became involved with the Women's Social and Political Union, the radical wing of the British women's suffrage movement. She led marches with British suffragettes in parades such as this one of 1910 where she is second in the procession. In front of her is fellow New Zealander Dr Alice Burn. *Auckland War Memorial Museum Tāmaki Paenga Hira,* Weekly News *(1910), PH-CNEG-C11446*

who generated these diseases. They were not generated even by the ideal woman, but by the other woman.'[24] He advocated a system of licensed prostitution since the 'evil would always exist until they [New Zealanders] were in a very different form of civilisation from what they had at the present time'.[25]

Activists were outraged by the parliamentarians' rhetoric and intransigence. The *White Ribbon* expressed the view that by 'revealing their own incompetency, these gentlemen intituled "honourable" are seeking to pave the way for lady law-makers'.[26] A quickly convened conference of interested women in Christchurch in 1895 passed resolutions protesting against the Legislative Council's refusal to raise the age of consent and to repeal the Contagious Diseases Act. Those assembled were reminded that 'Women's Societies throughout New Zealand, with the exception of the Women's Liberal League' had petitioned both Houses to attend to these two issues.[27] 'We may no longer condone the sowing of wild oats. We cannot sow evil and reap good,' the conference declared.[28] Eveline Cunnington, a founding member of the Canterbury Women's Institute who was active in a variety of social welfare causes in her province, reported that the two largest maternity homes in Christchurch were populated by girls under the age of eighteen. She pointed out

Three nurses at an Auckland private hospital ride their bicycles in the 1890s. Bicycles gave women new freedom in the later nineteenth century, and were particularly useful for district nurses who had to travel to patients. Photographer Margaret Matilda White worked professionally as a young woman arriving in New Zealand in the 1880s, and continued to document women's lives in a series of remarkable photographs through to her death in 1910. *Photograph by Margaret Matilda White, Auckland War Memorial Museum Tāmaki Paenga Hira, PH-NEG-B3542*

'the irreparable injury inflicted on a girl, physically, mentally, and socially' by an unwanted pregnancy, and the harm to the children. 'By far the lesser evil,' she argued, 'was, perchance for a few innocent men to run the risk of blackmail.'[29]

The *White Ribbon* expressed its disgust at Legislative Councillors who believed 'that prostitution should be licensed by the state; that any girl over fifteen is fair prey for the grey-haired villain; that opportunities for men and women to debase themselves below the beasts of the field by strong drink should not be curtailed'. By its 'ignorant and one-sided legislation', the paper argued, the Legislative Council demonstrated the need for women's intervention in the state.[30] The Dunedin Women's Franchise League went further, and urged the Premier to bring in a Bill to limit the veto power of the Legislative Council 'and enable measures demanded by the people to be passed into law'.[31]

The Bill to Repeal the Contagious Diseases Act returned to the Legislative Council in 1896. George Whitmore expressed his annoyance that 'certain old ladies, who really knew nothing about the question' kept raising the matter. The Act, when in force in Auckland, he said, had proved most successful in checking 'juvenile prostitution'.[32] John Rigg objected to 'the continual discounting of men', arguing:

Young women play a game of tennis while others watch at Nelson Ladies' College in 1889. The first generation of women university graduates passed on their love of learning at the new girls' secondary schools. *Alexander Turnbull Library, Wellington, 10x8-0131-G*

As regarded this question of sex, he looked at it in this light: that a woman who was a proper woman – not one of the new women – but a woman who had the proper feelings of a woman and the finer sentiments, would know her place and keep it. If women of another character did not know their place it was the duty of man, as being the nobler creature, to teach her her place, to put her in it, and to keep her there.[33]

It was precisely this type of arrogant refusal to see men's role in prostitution that incensed women's groups. The Dunedin Women's Franchise League called the Contagious Diseases Act 'a degrading abomination', and suggested that if the power the Act gave to police and other officials 'to offer indignities' to women could be used against men, it 'would not be tolerated anywhere in the world'.[34]

The Legislative Council, however, stood firm and voted against the second reading of the Bill. Further Repeal Bills in 1897, 1899, 1901 and 1903 were similarly dismissed. By 1910, when the WCTU Annual Convention requested repeal, the Attorney-General, J. G. Findlay, wanted to promote discussion of venereal diseases, claiming that 60 per cent of men 'contracted sexual disorders'.[35] There were many who continued to see the issue in terms of diseased prostitutes decoying young lads, but the politicians bowed to the 'very strong movement' of women who regarded the Contagious Diseases Act as 'an insult to their sex', and repealed the Act.[36]

Women activists' emphasis on social purity rather than on sexual pleasure needs

A young woman plays tennis around 1910. Tennis became popular in New Zealand from the 1870s and women soon took it up, but they had to contend with restrictive clothing, and sometimes social disapproval. *Alexander Turnbull Library, Wellington, PAColl-5936-38*

to be understood in the context of the sexual dangers all too apparent at the turn of the century.[37] The very real risk of passing on a range of sexually transmitted diseases to children led Gisborne temperance and suffrage activist Margaret Sievwright to claim that '[w]e women must see to it that none save men of pure life shall become the fathers of our children'.[38] In 1910, the Attorney-General suggested that 'an estimated 35% of all hospital outpatients' suffered as a result of venereal disease.[39] Later estimates of the incidence of venereal diseases in the population ranged from one person in every 32 to one person in every 428, with rates in men about five times higher than those in women.[40] Given the lack of effective and safe treatment for syphilis prior to the invention of Salvarsan in 1911, and the devastating impact of syphilis on foetal development, women were rightly concerned about the effect of this and other venereal diseases on families.

Other insults of a sexual nature required remedy too. Ada Wells, a stalwart of the Canterbury Women's Institute, argued that the enfranchised woman must be concerned with the situation inside homes. The home, the 'Englishman's castle', had to be breached to remedy the circumstances of women 'in servitude, physically and economically'. Homes teaching 'degradation attaching to sex-intercourse' required exposure. It was, she argued, comparatively easy to agree that such things happened among the poor. It was 'not so easy for us to see that, in modified form, they honeycomb society'.[41] And one matter of 'sex degradation', to which many were blind, was incest.

'I have heard of a large number of meetings of ladies being held in various parts of the colony,' Henry Feldwick, former member of the House of Representatives for Invercargill and father of three daughters, told the Legislative Council in September 1900, 'at which they deal with all kinds of subjects – and they apparently have a weakness for dealing with rather strong subjects at times.'[42] The topic under debate was the inclusion of incest in the Criminal Code. When in 1896 Feldwick had introduced a Bill to this effect, he was met with considerable disbelief. Councillors from Wellington and Westland expressed their concern at how such a Bill would reflect on the colony. One of them, Dr Morgan Grace, believed the measure to be 'an insult to the decency of the country', while James Kerr, a newspaper editor and prominent politician on the West Coast, regarded the Bill as 'ridiculous'. It would, he suggested, make people inside and outside the colony 'think those in New Zealand were a community of indecent people'.[43]

Feldwick, however, spoke of the prevalence of incest, noting that convictions could be obtained only 'when the crime was committed upon a child, under the age of consent, or by violence'.[44] When he came to giving examples of cases supplied by the Society for the Protection of Women and Children, it was clear that the crime was one committed by men against women. Not surprisingly, then, when the matter was raised again in 1900, members of the House were told that they must be aware of its importance because of the 'circulars received from ladies' organised societies in different parts of the colony'.[45] Samuel Shrimski, a pillar of the Ōamaru community, and like-minded colleagues opposed the Incest Bill, charging that the cases cited were mere rumour. The troublesome matter arose only because of 'the interference of certain women in these and similar matters [which had] gone on continually since the women got the franchise'.[46]

To the 'interfering women', there was a clear connection between the age of consent, incest and the Contagious Diseases Act. To those who denied the existence of incest, there was no such connection. And by opposing repeal of the Contagious Diseases Act or legislation that raised the age of consent, they were asserting that male sexuality could not be controlled in the face of 'designing women'. But the activists continued to emphasise that women should be safe in the streets and in the home. Indeed, once the incest provision had been adopted into the Criminal Code in 1900, the vulnerability of girls became clear. The first reported criminal cases involved fathers and young daughters.[47] The evidence also indicated that far from being 'simply animals', the men involved could be respected members of their communities. In 1907, *Truth* reported the case of a thirteen-year-old girl pregnant to her grandfather who was a verger at Christchurch Cathedral. The judge, pronouncing it 'the most painful and at the same time the most shameful case' he had dealt with, sentenced the man to ten years' hard labour.[48]

Equality in divorce

The demand for equal access to divorce was high on the agenda of the women's move-ment internationally. John Stuart Mill's famous 1869 essay, *On the Subjection of Women*, co-written with Harriet Taylor, had powerfully equated marriage with slavery for women.[49] In 1888, New Zealand newspapers picked up on the debate sparked by London's popular newspaper the *Daily Telegraph*, which drew 27,000 replies to its question: 'Is Marriage a Failure?' The great majority of responses agreed that it was.[50] The *Wanganui Chronicle* noted the debate's overwhelming conclusion: 'the law of divorce must be enlarged'.[51] Following English law, New Zealand's 1867 Divorce and Matrimonial Causes Act allowed a husband to divorce his wife for adultery, whereas a woman could divorce her husband only for adultery aggravated by bigamy, sodomy, incest, rape, cruelty or desertion for five years.[52]

Some within the Legislative Council opposed equality in divorce. A wife's adultery, George Whitmore argued, created the ominous possibility that 'her illegitimate children may inherit the property of the husband's family'. He opposed the unsuccessful Divorce and Matrimonial Causes Bill of 1894, which proposed adultery on either side, desertion for three years, or habitual drunkenness and neglect to support a wife, as some of the possible grounds for divorce.[53] To Whitmore, the suggested reform meant 'a woman is to be enormously supported as against a man'.[54]

In 1895, the House received seven petitions from WCTU groups, the Auckland Women's Liberal League and the Gisborne Women's Political Association, among others, specifically requesting that a husband and wife be placed on the same footing 'in regard to dissolution of the marriage tie'.[55] Other petitions frequently addressed both equality in divorce and the age of consent; the Canterbury WCTU added the admission of women to Parliament for good measure.[56] Lawyer and self-proclaimed radical Francis Henry Dillon Bell stated that 'there were a great many people of the other sex who had made this a cardinal part of their political programme', while Premier Seddon attributed the divorce agitation to 'women's opinion'.[57] Seddon believed that the Liberals 'had done a great deal for the women of New Zealand', but thought that amending the divorce laws was dangerous to social stability and 'against the interests of the women, the wives and mothers of the colony'.[58]

The heart of the objections to women's claims to equality under the divorce law was laid out by Captain W. R. Russell of Hawke's Bay. The crime of adultery, he argued,

> differed essentially in the two sexes. Man had a strong natural sexual instinct, and the gratification of that instinct was, he might say, almost the most powerful impulse of his existence. With women, on the contrary, the instinct was maternal, and was very materially different to the powerful desire on the part of the man. The two crimes, therefore, differed essentially, inasmuch as in the one it was the application of the sexual instinct natural to man, while the instinct of woman was mostly maternal.[59]

Activists in the women's movement refused to accept the view that male sexuality was uncontrollable. Such a view excused men from paternal responsibility, while women faced either the stigma of raising a child outside marriage or the burden of repeated childbirth within marriage. Male sexuality, they argued, had to be reconstructed as controllable: to admit otherwise was to sanction not only illegitimacy and unlimited childbearing, but also incest, prostitution and rape. Kate Sheppard protested against the gentlemen who 'think, and freely express their opinion, that the question of property should govern the marriage law', while most of the women's organisations in the country had declared 'that there must be no sex distinction in the State's conception of morality'.[60]

In 1898, the divorce law was finally amended to make, among other provisions, simple adultery by either spouse a matrimonial offence. By this time, women's groups could feel encouraged that some of the statutory changes they had sought to defeat the double standard had been put in place, even if it was left to the male arena of the court to determine outcomes. But it was actually liberalisation of the divorce law to include desertion and drunkenness (not the adultery clause) that increased the numbers of women petitioning for divorce. Whereas prior to reform men made up approximately two-thirds of petitioners for divorce, by 1899 women were equally likely to bring petitions.[61]

The centrality of sex to the marriage contract came under scrutiny in the early twentieth century when cases were taken after one or the other partner refused sexual intercourse. In 1906, two cases were heard that came to opposite conclusions. In the first, heard in the Canterbury Supreme Court, Mary Ann Lees had decided she no longer had

This lilac silk dress trimmed with cream lace was worn by Rosa Criscillo at her wedding to Antonio Moleta in Wellington on 5 May 1909. Rosa travelled from Stromboli, Italy, accompanied by her father and brother, to marry Antonio, whom she had never met. *Museum of New Zealand Te Papa Tongarewa, Wellington, GH016409/1-2*

any 'soul affinity' or affection for her husband, although they had had two sons and 'lived amicably' until 1896. Around that time, Mary Ann became involved in a religious group that spent a good deal of time examining the relations between the sexes. As a result she refused her husband intercourse, on the grounds 'that she had no affection for him'. She returned her jewellery and her wedding ring, left briefly for America, then returned to reoccupy the family home. Her husband refused to have her back unless 'the normal relations of man and wife' were resumed. Mr Justice Denniston held that her conduct 'was desertion in law' and thus grounds for divorce.[62] In the other instance, heard in the Wellington Supreme Court, a Mr Pybus cohabited with his wife but occupied a separate bedroom and 'refused to perform his duties to her as a husband'. Mr Justice Stout held it was not desertion.[63] Such opposing judgments suggested a persistence of the view that sex within marriage was a male prerogative.

The question of a husband's sexual access to his wife was fully aired in the Court of Appeal as a result of a question pertaining to the Mental Defectives Act 1911. A man had been accused of carnal knowledge of his wife while she was detained in a 'mental hospital'. The court had to consider whether husbands were included in the section of the Act which prohibited '[e]very person' from having 'carnal knowledge of any female who is detained under the provisions of [the] Act'. Defence counsel argued that the marriage contract 'conferred on the husband an irrevocable right to intercourse' and that the wife, by entering marriage, gave consent to intercourse that could not be withdrawn. In arguing that husbands were not exempt from the 1911 Act, Chief Justice Robert Stout pointed out that 'the status of a married woman [was] very different from what it was even fifty years ago'. Wives had the right to their own property, and husbands could no longer imprison or assault their wives. For a man to have sex with his mentally ill wife was, therefore, 'highly improper, if not abhorrent'. He noted that if husbands were excluded from the provisions of the 1911 Act, 'a husband may rape his mentally defective wife and yet not be guilty of any offence'. Stout doubted that the intention of Parliament was to leave women 'in such a woeful position'. Only one of the five Court of Appeal judges held a dissenting view: that wives could not withdraw their consent from marital intercourse, that the husband in the case 'yielded to a natural desire', and that to prohibit a husband from intercourse in this instance would deprive him 'of the legal rights conferred upon him by the matrimonial contract'.[64]

Debates about appropriate sexual behaviour outside marriage reached a peak when in 1915 the colourful and popular *New Zealand Truth* launched a campaign to fight for the release of Alice Parkinson, imprisoned for life for the murder of her errant lover. Parkinson, a domestic worker in Napier, had become pregnant to a man called Albert West and delivered a stillborn child after a difficult labour. West had promised to marry Parkinson and she had put all her savings into buying furnishings for their home. When West repeatedly failed to fulfil his promise of marriage, Parkinson shot him, then tried to shoot herself. The jury at her trial recommended that she be found guilty of manslaughter and dealt with mercifully, but the judge, Chief Justice Robert Stout, overrode their verdict and found Parkinson guilty of murder. He sentenced her to prison for the term of her natural life.

In the face of such a harsh sentence, the women's section of the Social Democratic Party lobbied other women's groups to call for Parkinson's release. The WCTU asserted that she had 'already been punished by the laws of nature'.[65] The *White Ribbon* shared the view expressed at a campaign meeting by a Mrs Donaldson, who hoped that:

> the day will soon come when women would be upon all juries where women were being tried, and when women would be upon all public bodies including parliament. The lenient sentences inflicted on men guilty of gross offences against little children, compared with the terrible sentence imposed upon Alice Parkinson, were a disgrace to the country.[66]

In response to a petition signed by nearly 70,000 people, Stout defended his verdict, stating that there was no law that allowed a woman to assassinate a man who had seduced her, and that in this instance there was in any case no proof of seduction.[67]

Alice Parkinson's cause served to unite women from across the political spectrum who saw her as a woman who had been 'ruined' by a man, yet had aspired to fulfil the feminine ideal of having a home and family.[68] Many regarded her lover's treatment of her as clear provocation for murder, since she had been robbed of the life to which she aspired. An indignant 'Mother' wrote to *Truth*:

> Poor creature! Just launched into young womanhood, deceived and ruined by a brute who told her she would be his wife. Cast off as an unclean creature; ... Wrecked! No man would want a second-hand polluted article. She knows there was no chance to recover her lost womanhood ...[69]

The Parkinson case was a lightning rod for public indignation at the plight of the woman characterised as 'a mother but no wife'.[70] Women's groups were insistent that men should be responsible for the consequences of their sexual behaviour. But this was a view increasingly at odds with the environment created by the outbreak of the First World War. It was also at odds with the aspirations of other kinds of 'New Women', whether Pākehā or Māori.

Working women

In 1890, one young woman decided to leave her employment in domestic service 'because I was not strong enough'.[71] Her earnings of 7s 6d a week as an under-housemaid failed to compensate for the long hours, heavy labour and expectations of deference. Like many young women, she began looking for opportunities beyond the familial context of domestic service, which absorbed the energies of about one-third of working Pākehā women in the

1890s. Factory work with its defined hours and higher wages was more attractive than domestic service. One young woman, for example, who left domestic service and began work in the Mosgiel woollen mill in 1900, doubled her income from three to six shillings a week.[72] Women working in the boot department of Hallenstein Brothers were paid from seven shillings to 12s 6d per week in the late 1890s, rising to between ten and thirty shillings in the first decade of the twentieth century.[73]

The completely unregulated state of domestic service prompted labour activist Harriet Morison to try to organise a union for domestic servants in 1890. She was unsuccessful, but fresh hope came in the form of a parliamentary attempt at regulation in 1896, with the introduction of a Domestic Servants' Half Holiday Bill that would enable servants to receive the same entitlement as other workers. The Bill, introduced to 'elevate the position of the domestic servant' and thus ease the shortage of domestic help, would have other benefits, according to Thomas Mackenzie, speaking for the Bill in the House. Girls who had gone into domestic service rather than factory work or dressmaking would 'undoubtedly' make the best wives for working men.[74]

Other members of the House, however, were opposed to the Bill's attempt to transform the supposedly familial relationship of employer and servant into a contractual one. Servants, it was asserted, would work to rule and employers would become more exacting. The apparent dangers of this led to heavy-handed humour. John McLachlan, member for Ashburton, proposed that the one blot on the Bill was that it did not include wives. Some members, he suggested, supported the Bill in order that their wives would be taken up with domestic duties while they themselves spent the holiday afternoon with the servant girls.[75] This, said George Russell, member for Riccarton, turned the debate into a burlesque.[76] The Bill languished for lack of support.

Concern for women's assumed future role as mothers had led to limitations on factory work as early as 1873. Industrial work was perceived to be dangerous to women in a way that farm labour or domestic service was not, even though both of these could involve very long hours and backbreaking work. Agnes Dodunska, for example, did the heavy work required on the small farm she and her husband Joseph Fabish purchased on Hursthouse Road, Inglewood, in 1894. Joseph's daytime work in a sawmill kept the couple financially afloat; he used the evening to clear the stumps. Agnes was in charge of milking the cows, chopping wood for the fire, growing vegetables, and feeding and clothing the family, which eventually grew to include fourteen children.[77] Theirs was a collective economy, whereas wages paid to a single individual were more commonly the source of income for families in urban areas. On the land, where a small majority of the population still lived in 1900, couples, extended families and whānau usually worked together to keep the enterprise going, and a barter economy made ready cash less necessary.

Work in the home, no matter how heavy, was regarded as appropriate training for women. The Employment of Females Act 1873 restricted women to eight hours of factory

Artist Frances Hodgkins captured women's domestic work in these watercolours of the family maid Euphemia (Phemie) around 1890. Other paintings in the series trace laundry work from washing through carrying the laundry basket (above) to hanging out the clothes, then ironing them. Another shows Phemie at work in the kitchen. *Alexander Turnbull Library, Wellington, E-425-q-020; E-425-q-010*

work per day, and prohibited them from working between the hours of 6 p.m. and 9 a.m. (later amended to 8 a.m.). Pieceworkers were specifically excluded from the Act and saleswomen ignored. Four days' annual holiday and no work on Saturdays from 2 p.m. were allowed without loss of wages.[78] The hours of women employed in steam laundries, where work was hot and exhausting, were untouched by the Act: there women might work for twelve or more hours a day, including Saturdays.[79] The clothing and textile industries were big employers of women, and they also worked in boot, brush, cardboard box and confectionery factories.[80] From the late 1870s to the mid-1890s, the 'Long Depression', caused by a crisis in British banking and New Zealand's unsustainable levels of borrowing, heightened male fears that the employment of women workers would undercut men's wage rates. Unionising to protect their interests, male workers excluded women from membership.[81]

Women machinists work at Staples and Company boot manufacturers in Wellington, around 1906 or 1907. Although their labour was essential to the production of footwear, the industrial award system of wages (set by the Arbitration Court) kept women firmly in a secondary position to male bootmakers. *Alexander Turnbull Library, Wellington, PA1-o-367-33*

In the 1880s, eighteen young women went to work at the Government Printing Office in Wellington, where they folded, sewed, gathered and collated sheets of paper into books. Sequestered in two rooms away from the male employees, they worked under a forewoman and entered the building by a separate entrance from the men.[82] Other women worked in much less comfortable circumstances. As a consequence of a depressed economy, employers turned to the piecework system wherever possible, paying workers per item rather than for the hours they worked. Unable to make enough during the day, seamstresses took work home at night, sewing late for a miserable sum. In October 1888, Rutherford Waddell, minister of St Andrew's Presbyterian Church in Dunedin and a strong supporter of trade unions, held his congregation riveted by a sermon on the 'Sin of Cheapness'.[83] He criticised those who bought cheap clothing made by underpaid women working as 'sweated labour'. The impact of Waddell's sermon was such that the government set up a royal commission to investigate 'sweating', and appointed Waddell as a member. Due in part to the findings of the royal commission, William Pember Reeves,

Waitresses at the Alexandra Tea Rooms, Gisborne, enjoy a rest and a glass of lemonade in this 1906 photograph. Working in tea rooms, department stores and factories allowed women to enjoy the company of their fellow workers; domestic service was more isolated. *Photograph by William Crawford, Tairawhiti Museum, Te Whare Taonga O Te Tairawhiti*

Minister of Labour in the Liberal government, introduced greater regulation of factory work in Acts passed in 1891 and 1894.[84]

In 1894, seventeen-year-old Ettie Rout enrolled at the 'Christchurch School of Shorthand, Typewriting, Book-Keeping etc', all subjects said to be 'indispensable to a successful business career'.[85] She would go on to become renowned during the First World War for her liberal views on sexuality – antithetical to those of many social purity advocates – but in 1890s Christchurch it was her clerical skills that marked her out. The typewriter, by writing 'three times as fast as the pen', was transforming business practices, and Ettie Rout was at the forefront of the young women learning new business skills.[86] An expert typist and rapid taker of shorthand, she had by 1896 become the breadwinner for her family, cycling across Christchurch to pick up and deliver work.[87] This was highly unusual: from 1901, the New Zealand Census defined only adult males as 'breadwinners'. Women were classed as 'dependants' doing domestic work at home. 'For able-bodied men,' historian Erik Olssen has written, 'a job and a wage sufficient to support a family had become central to their identity as husbands, fathers and heads of households.'[88]

In fact, new opportunities were opening up for young women at the same time as men's commitment to breadwinning was strengthened. More and more young Pākehā women were attracted to jobs in the burgeoning urban service sector as housemaids, cooks and waitresses in restaurants, boarding houses and hotels. These were jobs that required little training.[89] Others like Ettie Rout who had some education increasingly sought clerical positions. Typing and secretarial skills soon became desirable in the eyes of parents who wanted their daughters to escape domestic service.[90] New technology created other openings, too. By 1912, eighty-four women were permanent employees in telephone exchanges.[91] In 1913, the three typists, one clerk/typist, and one library assistant/typist employed by the Dunedin City Council were women.[92]

But men were wary of the competition women clerks brought to the workplace. In 1904, the national conference of the New Zealand Trades' Council passed a resolution brought forward by Canterbury members to ask the government to legislate for the introduction of equal pay for equal work by women and men.[93] An anxious 'Clerk' wrote to the Christchurch *Press*, noting that the poor pay of clerks would be driven down even more by competition from women, that housewifery skills would decline, and that the birth rate was at risk if women stayed in employment.[94]

'New Zealand Born', on the other hand, could not understand how the 'Post Office authorities arrive at the abstract conclusion that £120 a year to an unmarried woman is as good as £200 to a young man'.[95] Self-supporting teacher and journalist Jessie Mackay's 1904 *White Ribbon* article entitled 'Woman: A Fraction' addressed inequalities in employment. Women who worked as Post Office clerks were paid at three-fifths the male rate. Mackay asked: '[I]f woman is financially only three-fifths of a human being, why is the ratio not maintained in all relations? She is an entity when it comes to paying taxes. No merchant charges goods to her at three-fifths of their value.'[96]

In addition to receiving low wages, women were routinely denied advancement. In the civil service, women were excluded from the most important and well-paid positions.[97] When a commission was established to examine efficiency and pay rates in the public service, it reported that there were a number of 'female officers' taking shorthand and working as typists. The commissioners believed 'it would not do' to pay them male wage rates because 'they cannot stand the strain of a rush of pressure of work in the same way that men can'.[98]

Professional aspirations

The educational opportunities presented by the admission of women to tertiary study at Otago in 1871, at Canterbury in 1873, and throughout New Zealand when the University of New Zealand was formed in 1874, attracted a number of high-achieving Pākehā women,

Rosaline (Rose) Frank was one of New Zealand's first female professional photographers. She worked for the Tyree brothers in their Nelson photographic studio from 1886, and bought the business in 1914. While women photographers were relatively unusual, women operated a number of businesses that thrived in urban environments, such as drapery, confectionery and florist shops. *Nelson Provincial Museum, Tyree Studio Collection, 181303*

most of whom chose to go teaching. Through their work in primary and secondary schools, they played a significant part in shaping the aspirations of the next generation of young women. In teaching, however, the 'drudgery of the profession' was left to women teachers but the 'paths of higher responsibility were barred to [their] approach'.[99]

Professional aspirations were limited to women whose families, Pākehā or Māori, could afford to support them during extended periods of training. But women entered teaching – and nursing – in growing numbers at the beginning of the twentieth century. These were seen as occupations that would serve women and their communities well for a short interval between leaving school and marriage – which would, almost inevitably, mean the end of a woman's professional career.[100] In January 1912, the *Hawera & Normanby Star* reported a 'New Departure' by the Wanganui Education Board which had employed the very young Miss Rangi Drummond as a temporary assistant at a new school. Sixteen-year-old Rangi had taught at Turakina Maori Girls' College, where she had also been dux; she was expected to teach more than twenty Māori pupils enrolled in the newly created Te Ara Kura school near Feilding.[101]

The government provided some scholarships for Māori, and a few 'clever children' were given the opportunity to study at the denominational boarding schools so that they might return to be leaders in their communities. These schools, historians Kuni Jenkins and Kay Morris Matthews note, were highly regarded by whānau, even though they took girls away from their local and usually rural communities, and immersed them in a Pākehā environment.[102]

In 1913, Hohepine (Whina) Te Wake took up a trainee teaching post at Pawarenga Native School on Whāngāpē Harbour in the Far North. She had been sent from Te Karaka in the northern Hokianga all the way to Napier to attend the first of the Māori girls' schools, St Joseph's, opened by the Catholic Church in 1867. Native Minister James Carroll assisted the family financially so that Whina could take up this opportunity.[103] The Anglicans also chose Napier as the site for their Māori girls' school, Hukarere, founded in 1875 with the aim of providing girls with an equivalent education to that offered to boys at Te Aute College.[104] The Anglican Queen Victoria School for Māori girls (the counterpart to St Stephen's for boys) opened in Parnell, Auckland, in 1901, followed by the Presbyterian-founded Turakina in 1905 and the Anglican Te Wai Pounamu in Christchurch in 1909. In proposing an Auckland Anglican school for Māori girls, the Revd Taimona Hapimana suggested that the Māori boys educated at St Stephen's returned home and 'married ignorant girls of their own tribes and so became degraded'. Māori girls' schools, he argued, were more 'absolutely necessary for the progress of the race than boys' schools'.[105]

Many agreed with Maui Pomare, who in his capacity as Native Health Officer in 1904 argued: 'Educate the mothers to recognize the efficacy of the bathtub, cleanly warm clothes, plain and wholesome food, and you will regenerate the Maori quicker than by teaching the youth and maidens embroidery, Latin and Euclid …'[106] Another solution to the poor health besetting Māori had been proposed by future Young Maori Party member Hamiora Hei at a conference of the Te Aute College Students Association in 1898. He took the view that Māori nurses would 'strike at the root of many evils', working 'below the surface' to 'increase the numbers of the race'.[107]

The Education Department agreed to make scholarships available to allow pupils from one of the Māori girls' secondary schools to undertake hospital work. Premier Seddon noted that the Europeans were responsible for the introduction of diseases and 'other unfortunate things', and argued that 'if native girls were trained and sent back to the pas, they would prove a saving agent'.[108] Ema Mitchell of Pakipaki began as a day pupil at Napier Hospital in 1898; Sara Burch of Waimā began her training the following year; and Eva Wirepa of Te Kaha trained as a day pupil at Napier Hospital in 1901.[109] In 1909, Akenehi Hei (Whakatōhea and Te Whānau-a-Apanui) and Heni Whangapirita (Ngāti Porou) were the first Māori women to become fully qualified, and both went on to work for the Native Branch of the Health Department. The scheme, however, was greatly hampered by the unwillingness of hospitals to accept Māori women as nurse probationers. 'I don't want Maori nurses,' said the forthright matron of Thames Hospital, expressing the view of many others. 'I have quite enough trouble with the white ones.'[110]

The arduous scientific training medicine demanded was seen to be the preserve of a few Pākehā men and even fewer Māori; only very brave, unusual and ambitious Pākehā women made the attempt. Three cheers greeted the announcement of Emily Siedeberg's graduation in July 1896, 'the first lady who has taken a medical degree in the colony'.[111] Siedeberg herself was absent, having proceeded to the Rotunda Hospital in Dublin to study obstetrics, followed by the study of gynaecology, children's health and skin disease in Berlin. At the end of 1897, with the assistance of her father, she set up a private practice in Dunedin, mainly attending women and children. Her obstetric training came into good use when in 1905 she was appointed medical superintendent of Dunedin's St Helen's Hospital, which provided affordable midwifery services for women unable to meet the fees of private hospitals.[112]

In 1909, the Edinburgh-trained Australian, Dr Agnes Bennett, was appointed medical superintendent of St Helen's in Wellington (where she had been practising). These state-subsidised hospitals became excellent centres of training for midwives, and had an enviably low incidence of maternal mortality. Many of the early women doctors ended up in positions devoted to the health of women and children, including in the School Medical Service established in 1912.[113] Given that scepticism about the abilities of women doctors often impeded their ability to build up a general practice, salaried state appointments provided a welcome boost to their income.[114] The legal profession, thought to require hard-headedness and to involve the cut and thrust of the courtroom, was even more hostile to women, and it was some time before even a few women followed Ethel Benjamin's 1897 entry to the profession. Law and medicine both held out the possibility of equal pay with men, but the realities of practice, where women were denied advancement or access to the most lucrative posts, meant that differentials remained entrenched.

Māori recovery

By the 1926 Census, 95 per cent of the Māori population remained in rural areas, where many traditional practices continued to sustain communities and offer them hope for the future.[115] Old rituals relating to birth continued, and tohunga were consulted for advice. Paati Matene of Te Āti Awa and Anihaka Park of Ngāti Ruanui lost a number of children in infancy. The couple sought the advice of a tohunga who told them their next child should not 'be born on the mainland or in their own district of Petone'.[116] So Ripeka Wharawhara was born on Kapiti Island on 28 June 1882. Ripeka thrived and, when she was fifteen, a marriage was arranged for her with nineteen-year-old Wi Hapi Love. The marriage in December 1917, attended by more than 2,000 people from tribal districts throughout the country, united leading Te Āti Awa families. Hapi Love was a substantial landowner with a large holding at Waiwhetū and, with Ripeka, other blocks of land around Wellington, the Hutt Valley, in Taranaki and the Marlborough Sounds. Inherited wealth meant they could live in style in their large house, Taumata, in Petone, offering great hospitality and providing leadership in the community, particularly in the Anglican Church.[117]

By the time of Hiria Kokoro Tiratahi's second marriage, to Francis George Te Hau Barrett at Temuka in around 1903, the increased natural immunity of Māori to introduced diseases was assisting the revival of the population. Hiria Tiratahi, of Ngāi Tahu and Ngāti Māmoe descent, had three daughters from her earlier marriage to William Gray, a labourer with whom she had eloped to escape an arranged marriage. After Gray's death from pneumonia in 1895, Hiria had spent eight years living with her parents at Arowhenua Pā in Canterbury, learning the traditional skills of whakapapa, karakia (chants or prayers) and waiata, and the appropriate seasonal rituals. She also learned to work harakeke (flax) and ribbonwood for piupiu, cloaks, headbands and sandals. After remarrying she went on to have another nine children (two sons died in infancy), feeding her growing family and trading produce from gardening, gathering and fishing. As well as trading the sought-after kātaha (herring), trout, kōkopu (whitebait), mussels and pipi, Hiria made and sold tea cosies. Income from her business skills helped fund the annual March to June sojourn on Taukihepa, or Big South Cape Island, for the tītī (muttonbird) season. There, housekeeping, cooking and fishing, in addition to catching, plucking and preserving the birds, kept her fully occupied.[118]

Other Māori women farmed and laboured on the land, planting kūmara, digging gum and cutting flax. Not many Māori women worked as domestics or in the manufacturing, service or clerical sectors. Those who did so were likely to be in Auckland, where some found work in laundries, or as waitresses, private nurses and domestics. Historian Charlotte Macdonald has pointed out that because domestic service was typically undertaken between childhood and marriage, it did not fit with the pattern of Māori women's lives, where there was little hiatus between childhood and adulthood. In addition, she suggests, Māori women were largely averse to leaving their communities and taking on work of low status. In 1908 Anna Stout suggested, as had others, that Māori girls be trained as domestic servants. One 'native lady' replied: 'I think myself that this is a difficult subject. Maoris from their infancy have been taught to look down on anything to do with slavery, and they are very proud by nature.'[119]

Few Pākehā living in the cities would have encountered Māori women in their day-to-day activities. In the absence of contact, their view of Māori women's lives would instead have been informed by what they saw in newspapers: as performers in romantic depictions of New Zealand's tourist spots, or in discomforting court reports about the sale of liquor to Māori women (illegal since 1895) or obstruction of Pākehā plans. 'An Evening Scene, Lake Rotorua' in the *Christmas Graphic* for 1904, for example, depicted 'native women and children washing, cooking, gossiping and playing in the hot springs'.[120] The following year, the *Otago Witness* included a photograph entitled 'In Lighter Vein: Maori Women expatiating on the beauty of their respective babies'.[121] In 1906, the *Auckland Star* reported that 40 miles from Rotorua, four women, Morehu, Kiri Whakarau, Naraka Ngapeka and Nepi Nepi, obstructed the survey of the Whāiti block. Each of the women was fined one pound and costs for her actions.[122] The exploits of Māori women might also be used to amuse readers. Under the heading 'The Eternal Feminine', the *Auckland Star* reported the March 1914 case of two 'native belles' who chanced upon the 'costumes, silk blouse, petticoats' and other items of another Māori woman in an Auckland boarding house. Unable to resist the temptation to try them on, the two women wore the clothes 'about the town'. Then, 'in dread of detection', they destroyed the finery.[123]

If Māori women were just as attracted to finery as their Pākehā counterparts – and surviving photographs certainly suggest they were – items such as silk blouses were probably beyond the means of the great majority who were rurally based. Reremoana Koopu, born in 1893, described her upbringing in Ōtūwhare, in the eastern Bay of Plenty. It was typical of the period:

> We had a kauta [external, earth-floor shelter for cooking and eating food], then. It is a big one, though, with a big chimney we cooked in. You have your fire and you would cook all your kai there, with the pieces of iron to hold your pots. We had our kitchen things buried in the chimney – oh, it was nice. We had big pots – whaling pots …[124]

Women washed laundry in the creek and used a stick to beat the clothes. Life was hard, Reremoana recalled, but 'we seemed to be quite happy then, as long as the work is finished, and done, and the kai cooked, and that's all that matters'.[125] Women often worked communally within these rural settlements, harvesting crops and foraging for food such as pūhā and watercress for their growing families. By the 1920s, around 62 per cent of the

People gather at a Native Land Court session at Tokaanu, south of Taupō, in 1914 (above and below). Established to convert indigenous customary title to an approximation of British land title, the Native Land Court soon became known to Māori as 'te kōti tango whenua' – the land-taking court. *Photographs by Arthur Ninnis Breckon, Auckland War Memorial Museum Tāmaki Paenga Hira, PH-NEG-19997; PH-NEG-19999*

This photograph of students of Queen Victoria School, Auckland, was taken in the early 1900s. The Anglican boarding school for Māori girls opened in 1901 and closed in 2001. *Auckland War Memorial Museum Tāmaki Paenga Hira, PH-NEG-B2968*

Māori population was twenty-five or younger. Families also worked together in shearing gangs in Hawke's Bay and on East Coast sheep stations, where women and children worked as shed hands.[126]

In the Far North, Te Urewera, the Bay of Plenty, Rotorua and Taupō, the East Coast, the Whanganui River and parts of the King Country, Māori still predominated, and they sought to continue traditional ways of life as best they could. Diversity characterised these communities, but whatever their prosperity, Māori economic interests were firmly tied to land, and women played their part in trying to preserve it. While her father sought to prevent a local Pākehā farmer from draining mudflats at Whakarapa (Panguru) by pursuing action through Parliament and the courts in 1913, eighteen-year-old Whina Te Wake (later Whina Cooper) took direct action, setting a course for a lifetime's commitment to land rights. The local mudflats provided the Whakarapa community with seafood when wet, and land for horse racing when dry. When farmer Bob Holland began draining the flats to sow grass and graze cattle, Whina and a group of other young people from her community filled in the drains 'as fast as the Hollands dug them'.[127]

A life of action also lay in store for the granddaughter of the Māori King, Tawhiao, although not until she had challenged some of the expectations of her elders. Te Kirihaehae Te Puea Herangi was born in 1883 and raised near the Waikato River at Mangatāwhiri

Women are pictured outside the meeting house Te Whai-a-Te-Motu at Ruatāhuna in 1903. The house was built to honour the leadership of Te Kooti Arikirangi Te Turuki. Its name translates as 'the pursuit through the island', and refers to Te Kooti's travels through Te Urewera while evading government troops in 1869 and the early 1870s. Te Whai-a-Te-Motu was one of many significant meeting houses built as Māori regrouped after the wars and built strong political movements.
Photograph by James McDonald, Museum of New Zealand Te Papa Tongarewa, Wellington, C.1684

Māori joined Pākekā and immigrants in the Northland gumfields in the late nineteenth and early twentieth centuries. As this photograph from 1910 shows, the gum-digging villages were home to whānau, with women and children often sharing the arduous work. *Alexander Turnbull Library, Wellington, 1/1-006280-G*

(Mercer). Te Puea was marked out to be a leader in the Kīngitanga and schooled in tradition by her uncle, Mahuta, who would become the third Māori King. At the age of twelve she was sent to school in Auckland, until recalled in 1898 after the sudden death of her mother. Wracked with tuberculosis, Te Puea believed her life would be cut short and she determined to live it to the full. She was a beautiful young woman, and her relationships with a number of men worried her elders – none more so than her relationship with a European, Roy Clements Seccombe, with whom she lived for a year in Māngere in about 1910. On returning to Mercer for a visit, Te Puea was confronted by her uncle, who accused her of forgoing her responsibilities to her people by taking up with Seccombe. When his argument failed to persuade her, he made as if to lie down on the road to be run over in a final act of despair. Te Puea at last responded – first dragging Mahuta from the road, then breaking her relationship with Seccombe and returning to Mercer.[128]

Te Puea, like many Māori women, worked the land, but she was also the beneficiary of 600 acres that had been gifted to her mother. In another economic venture, undertaken to fund hui and other events of the Kīngitanga, she reinstituted a whitebait tribute from tribes on the lower Waikato. She also initiated a project to bring together Tawhiao's elderly followers to record tribal history and genealogy. Nonetheless, her leadership in the Waikato was at first accepted by only a few, and she had to prove herself to those who doubted her uncle's choice. The first test, given to her by Mahuta, was to garner support for Maui Pomare's attempt to wrest the Western Maori electorate from Henare Kaihau in 1911.[129] Though this was successful, a much greater challenge arrived with the outbreak of the First World War, when Te Puea was called upon to uphold the independence of the Waikato.

Wartime challenges

Te Puea expressed the sense of disenfranchisement felt by many Māori when New Zealand committed its troops to war in 1914. 'They tell us to fight for King and country,' she said. 'Well, that's all right. We've got a king. But we haven't got a country. That's been taken off us. Let them give us back our land and maybe we'll think about it again.'[130] Māori were excluded when conscription was first introduced in 1916, but the constant need for more troops to fight overseas led to an extension of conscription provisions in June 1917. Waikato–Maniapoto remained recalcitrant, but the Minister of Defence made it clear that Māori conscription would apply to the men of those districts alone, since other iwi had supplied their share of volunteers. When Te Puea became the leader of the Waikato anti-conscriptionists, she was continuing the stand against bloodshed taken by her grandfather, Tawhiao, in 1881. He rejected warfare with these words: 'I shall bury my patu in the earth and it shall not rise again… Waikato, lie down. Do not allow blood to flow from this time on. War shall not come to this island. It has been outlawed.'[131] Now Waikato men who refused conscription were arrested and taken to Narrow Neck training camp in Auckland, where they were subjected to severe punishment. Te Puea would travel there to sit outside the camp, within sight of the men, to encourage them in their civil disobedience.[132]

To the Māori members of Parliament, the opportunity for Māori men to serve in the forces meant they would serve the Empire on an equal footing with Pākehā – an equality of opportunity previously denied to so-called 'native peoples'. More than 2,000 Māori men served in the Native Contingent and Pioneer Maori Battalion. Patriotism was not divided on racial lines. The Maori Ladies Committee of Ngongotahā, for example, petitioned Cabinet to deny old-age pensions to anti-conscriptionists of the King Movement.[133]

Miria Woodbine Pomare led the highly patriotic Maori Soldiers' Fund, and coordinated Māori women's committees throughout the country to support the men who served. Proceeds from the sales of Māori craftwork, concert performances and auctions helped fill the coffers. The 1,500 parcels sent monthly to the Māori soldiers, along with the 500 sent to the Cook Islands men serving overseas, contained knitted items as well as 'personalised taniko (ornately woven flax items), and special delicacies such as strings of dried pipi… and preserved muttonbirds'.[134] Miria Pomare's contribution to active citizenship was recognised when in 1918 she became the first New Zealand woman to receive an OBE.[135]

Heni Materoa Carroll, the wife of another prominent Māori politician, became the chairperson of the Ōmāhu branch and member of the central steering committee of the Eastern Maori Patriotic Association founded by Apirana Ngata. She attended and spoke at fundraising hui throughout the East Coast in support of the cause.[136]

At the outbreak of the war, Pākehā women were advised to 'Hold Nothing Back'. According to impeccably bred British suffragist Lady Frances Balfour, women had 'done their duty as citizens' by bearing male children, and they now had to ensure that those sons served the nation 'in time of adversity'. Her message to the women of England was assumed to be equally applicable to the women of New Zealand, who were to send forth their sons 'with the ungrudging sacrifice of all personal feeling'.[137] In the face of overwhelming patriotic fervour, most mothers felt compelled to support the war effort. One young man eager to prove his patriotism begged his mother to drop her opposition to his enlisting. After outlining the various possibilities for his future, which included being wounded 'or blown right out', the young man continued: '[I]f this war lasts there'll come a time when I will not be able to be stopped and then you won't be asked … PS. If you don't let me go I am going to learn to dance and spend my money that way.'[138]

Communities nonetheless recognised the high cost to mothers of their sacrifice. The mother of three sons who all volunteered was presented with a gift at a social event in Kelso, Tuapeka County, in recognition of her contribution. Edna Valentine Trapnell's sentimental poem entitled 'Who Pays?' led the *Maoriland Worker* in 1915:

'Victory stood to our banners, only a handful lost —'
Only! We bore those bodies, and we knows what bodies cost!
(Mothers and wives of the soldiers dead — who better can gauge the cost?) [139]

The government also acknowledged that cost by providing earnings-related pensions for the widows of those who died, and for the wives of the disabled. War pensions were more generous than the civil pensions, and a soldier's illegitimate children (although not those born of a soldier's wife) were provided for if paternity could be proved.[140]

As the war lengthened and uncertainty about the future of their loved ones increased, some sought reassurance in predictions of the future. In October 1917, three Auckland women – Mrs Stewart, May Leon Lees and Alene Arnold – were sentenced to fourteen days in prison for fortune-telling. One had predicted that the war would end in 1925, another that it would be won by the Chinese, the third that it would last another five years and that the Americans would be the victors.[141]

Approximately one in four of the total male population aged over fifteen served in the First World War, leading to fears of labour shortages, particularly in agriculture.[142] The latter were unrealised, in part because farming families worked to keep things going. The *Clutha Leader* reported young women taking over some harvesting tasks and cutting gorse, and one young woman was noted working a six-horse team.[143] In fact, the war accelerated women's work in specific fields, largely as a consequence of two newly established organisations – a National Efficiency Board, which explored the potential of female labour, and the Women's National Reserve, which undertook voluntary registration of women willing to replace male workers.[144] Women filled the ranks of clerical workers, central to the operation of public service departments, and hence kept the business of government going. Women were increasingly employed in banks, in the Post and Telegraph Department, and in post offices. The Wellington branch of the Bank of New Zealand employed no women before the war, but by 1915 had thirty women working in subordinate positions, such as shorthand typists, that did not require them to serve customers – a task reserved for men.[145]

Such was the increase in the employment of women that in 1916 the government decided to permit girls to sit the Public Service Examination, previously restricted to boys. By March 1917, the number of women employed in the public service had more than doubled from 1,826 before the war to 4,153.[146] Numbers of male typists fell, and by the end of the war employers preferred women 'typistes'. Men, however, were still preferred for the higher-paid clerical positions which carried more prospects of advancement. Indeed, many of the posts taken by women were temporary, and it was expected that they would vacate them when the men returned.[147] 'The policy under which women are engaged for the period of the war instead of permanently', noted the Post and Telegraph Department, was 'rendered necessary' by the government undertaking to keep jobs open for men who joined the forces.[148]

Many women who were not in paid employment during the war directed their energies into patriotic societies, writing letters to men in service, doing volunteer work in hospitals, undertaking prodigious feats of knitting and sewing for soldiers' kits, and fundraising for 'Soldiers' Clubs' at home and for the sending of 'comforts' to the men abroad.[149] In 1915, the Otago and Southland Women's Patriotic Association knitted 3,800 balaclavas and 7,400 pairs of socks, and assembled 3,400 sewing kits to send overseas.[150] Many of the fundraising ventures were designed to provide social contact and fun for participants as well. The Otago Queen Carnival – three days of festivities in Dunedin in late August 1915 – culminated in the crowning of the 'Country Queen', a young woman from Roxburgh who represented Tuapeka County. The carnival raised £126,134 for the Wounded Soldiers and Dependents' Fund.[151] By war's end, New Zealand women had raised £4,866,520 to support the war effort.[152]

Voluntary work of this kind was taken up by thousands of New Zealand women, but responses to the war spanned the spectrum from those willing to send white feathers to men they accused of cowardice, to followers of the jingoistic Women's Anti-German League, to advocates of peace involved in the Women's International League. Peace activists argued that 'where militarism flourishes, the democracy is in danger, and women's rights are trampled under foot'.[153] Women, as the bearers of life, could not, they argued, condone the taking of life.[154]

In June 1916, Prime Minister William Massey received a deputation of thirty women opposed to the Military Service Bill which introduced conscription. Mrs Donaldson, described in the press as 'a well-known platform speaker in Wellington', articulated the deputation's concerns:

> As mothers of the nation we protest against bringing lives into the world to be used, when reaching manhood, in the interests of a class which does not represent our interests. The working classes have always fought their battles, paid their debts, and lost their liberties when great wars have been fought.[155]

Mrs Taylor, whose son fought at Gallipoli, believed the Bill insulted those who were already serving. 'Conscription was not wanted to win the war,' she argued, 'but to keep down the workers and get a tighter grip of the worker.'[156] The assembled women bombarded Prime Minister Massey with objections to compulsory military service, which they believed would fall heavily on workers' rather than 'rich men's sons'. Massey bowed out of the meeting after an hour, and the Military Service Act 1916 was passed.

Nevertheless, the great majority of women supported both conscription and the war effort, to the extent that the government was overwhelmed with offers it could not accept. More than 600 women applied to serve abroad as nurses by September 1915, but only a very small number of them were sent overseas.[157] One Auckland woman's offer to serve as either an assistant dispenser in a hospital or an ambulance driver had to be turned down because women were not permitted to enlist.[158] Dr Agnes Bennett found her offers of service fell on deaf ears in New Zealand, so she left the country, intending to serve overseas. Disembarking at Cairo, she was snapped up for duty by the New Zealand Medical Corps, though denied a commission. After a year, she left to join the Scottish Women's Hospital Service where she served with great distinction.[159]

Disquieting developments

Other women used the circumstances of the war to press their cause. One well-qualified woman, applying for the position of 'correspondence clerk' at the Dunedin City Council in 1918, wrote:

> I realise it has been the position of the Council heretofore not to open any of the better positions in the service to women, for reasons which I am quite able to understand, but under present conditions it will perhaps do no harm to tender my application …
>
> There is one point, especially, on which the Council might hesitate to employ a woman in this position and that is that certain night work is entailed. It is a matter of opinion, but I would not mind coming at night as I am used to attending night classes. I may say that I am entirely dependent on my own living and shall be for many years to come.

During the First World War, women contributed to the war effort in many ways, both at home and abroad.

TOP: *Left* The Otago Women's Patriotic Association raised large sums of money for the benefit of soldiers. *Right* Lady Liverpool and Lady Pomare's Maori Soldiers' Fund supported Māori troops. The executive committee is shown here: from left (standing), Mrs W. Waitai, Mrs F. Morrison, Mrs Raukura Tamahau, Mrs W. Ngahana, Lady Pomare, Mrs Kahui Grace, Mrs Te Puni, Mrs Ripeka Love; (sitting) Mrs Raukura Heketa, Mrs W. Uru, Miss Lily Love, Miss Ana Pomare. *Toitū Otago Settlers Museum; Alexander Turnbull Library, Wellington, 1/1-014579-G*

MIDDLE: *Left* The Spinsters' Club in Wellington knitted socks for soldiers during the First World War. From left: Miss Daisy Isaacs, Mrs V. Gray, Miss Dora Levi, Mrs L. M. Hyams, Miss M. Lyons, Miss Eileen Driscoll, Mrs I. McIntyre, Mrs A. McKillop. *Right* Women pack hospital supplies to be sent to Egypt and England at the Nelson Red Cross depot about 1915. *Alexander Turnbull Library, Wellington, 1/2-030986-F; 1/1009356-G*

BOTTOM: *Left* New Zealand nurses in Egypt take a break from their duties in 1915. Matron Bertha Nurse (left) and Sister Ida Willis are on their way to the pyramids by camel. *Right* During the Gallipoli campaign, Ettie Rout (hatless, centre) established the Volunteer Sisterhood to provide catering and hospital services for troops in Egypt. *Alexander Turnbull Library, Wellington, 1/2-148832-F; 1/1-014727-G*

The Dunedin town clerk found that the male applicants were less well qualified, but the job was given to a returned serviceman who lacked shorthand skills but had 'done his bit' during the wartime crisis.[160]

Women employed in domestic service greatly outnumbered those in industry, but the war accelerated the trend away from service. The range of women's wartime work extended to newspaper editing, horse training, motor vehicle driving, and employment in the railways and grocery shops. Women employed in factories worked long hours – the number of overtime hours worked in the predominantly female hat- and cap-making factories, for example, increased by 75 per cent between 1915 and 1916.[161]

The influx of young women into towns to take up employment opportunities led to a desperate need for accommodation. It also introduced widespread concern about a novel situation: young middle-class women moving unchaperoned to urban areas to work. The dangers and pleasures of the city, where lonely servicemen looked for company, threatened to upset fixed moral codes. A representative of the Women's National Reserve believed the shortage of accommodation for women in the cities constituted 'a moral danger to girls'.[162] Fears of young women being entrapped into prostitution, or 'amateur' immorality, became so heightened that in mid-1914 the WCTU distributed nearly 10,000 copies of a pamphlet entitled *To the Men of New Zealand*, outlining the dangers to women of 'white slavery' – that is, enforced prostitution.[163] To protect young women from roving servicemen in the cities, women's groups called upon the government to establish hostels where women could be safely housed.[164]

'The years of the war,' wrote an essayist on the topic of 'Women as Citizens', 'will most certainly mark the dividing line. Women's citizenhood will be established on an entirely new basis, and will, I think, appear to many in a new light of responsibility.' According to the author, 'woman has taken [her] place in public life, and taken it well'.[165] Not all were sure, however, that Ettie Rout, who had circumvented all official opposition and led a body of 'volunteer sisters' to Egypt to nurse New Zealand troops, stood as a respectable model of New Womanhood. This was because of her interest in stemming the incidence of venereal disease among the troops, and providing treatment. 'Miss Rout,' reported the *Auckland Star*, 'discusses the venereal menace to our soldiers with great candour, courageously faces unpleasant facts, and offers bold advice for dealing with the menace from a purely hygienic point of view.'[166] Some others within the press and the forces applauded her work, but women's groups committed to social purity in New Zealand were appalled by her mission to make 'vice' safe, as was Prime Minister Massey.[167]

Inspired by a British example, the WCTU campaigned for the formation of 'women patrols' who would 'work in the neighbourhood of camps of expeditionary forces, for the safeguarding of young people and the prevention of disorderly conduct'.[168] Such women, they believed, could prevent vice, not sanction it. In late 1917, the introduction of a Social Hygiene Act mollified women's groups opposed to any resurrection of the Contagious

Writing was important for many women, and some achieved national or international recognition as authors.

TOP: *Left* Mary Ann Muller arrived in New Zealand in 1850 and began to write articles about women's rights under the pen-name 'Femmina'. In 1869 she published *An Appeal to the Men of New Zealand,* in which she argued that the law should not discriminate against women and that women should have the right to vote. *Right* Katherine Mansfield left New Zealand in 1908, but some of her most famous short stories recall her childhood in Wellington. She earned international recognition as one of the founders of literary modernism. *Alexander Turnbull Library, Wellington, 1/2-021456-F; MNZ-2532-1/2-F*

BOTTOM: *Left* Jessie Mackay is remembered for her poetry, but she was also from the late 1890s a highly influential journalist. Through her articles, she campaigned for causes that included feminism, prison reform and prohibition. *Right* Iris Wilkinson, better known by her pen name Robin Hyde, earned a living as a journalist but also wrote poems and fiction. The highly original novels she wrote in the 1930s reflected her socialist and feminist perspectives. *Alexander Turnbull Library, Wellington, PAColl-6260-2-01; 1/2-043599-F*

Diseases Act by implementing plans for 'female health patrols'. Two women were to be appointed in the four main centres to 'assist in guarding the health and morality of young persons'.[169] Applicants over forty years of age were invited to apply for the posts, and those appointed would receive an annual wage of £156.[170] In the event, the women were not appointed until July 1919, after the war had ended.[171]

The experiences of wartime convinced leaders in the women's movement that women's absence from the legislature meant their concerns could too easily be dismissed by male politicians. In 1916, when a large deputation of women met with Alexander Herdman, Attorney-General and Minister of Police, to advocate for the appointment of women police officers, their request was rebuffed. An earlier request for women on juries for cases involving women and children had also been denied.[172] But by winning places on public bodies and through local elections, women were proving their fitness for public life. Six of the twelve women candidates who stood for the Wellington Hospital and Charitable Aid Board were elected in 1916. Mrs G. A. Smith became the first woman elected to a Chamber of Commerce in New Zealand when she won selection in Waitematā in March 1918.[173] Other openings seemed inevitable, although once again a concerted effort appeared to be necessary to assert women's right to hold public office.

Moves were already afoot to reinstate the National Council of Women, which had been in abeyance since 1906. Reconstituting the council, supporters felt, would 'unite all organised societies of women for mutual counsel and co-operation' that were working for the attainment 'of justice and freedom for women, and for all that makes for the good of humanity'. A second object was to encourage the 'formation of societies of women engaged in trades, professions and in social and political work' who did not have organised unions.[174] The stalwarts of the Christchurch suffrage campaign, Kate Sheppard, Christina Henderson and Jessie Mackay, set up a committee, and in 1917 wrote to prominent women throughout the country proposing that the National Council of Women be reinstated. A preliminary meeting was held in Wellington in April 1918, and from that date the future of the organisation was assured.[175] By uniting the various women's organisations, the council aimed to promote women's civic engagement to ensure the welfare of the community.[176]

Infant Janet Wilkinson (later Paul) is held here by her nurse, Marion Ngapo, Ngāti Porou, from Kennedy Bay,
Coromandel. Janet's mother was ill after she was born in 1919 and the family hired Nurse Ngapo to care for her.
Private collection

Chapter Seven

Motherhood, Morality and a Voice for Women in the Interwar Years

In November 1918, when towns throughout New Zealand were celebrating the Armistice, there was quiet in the tiny village of Whakarapa in the Hokianga. The quiet marked desperate activity and fevered suffering: the village was in the grip of the influenza epidemic that had quickly swept the globe in the wake of the First World War. Whina Gilbert (later Cooper), heavily pregnant with her first child, lay in bed and expected to die. From her window she watched corpses being taken up the hill to be buried. 'There were no coffins, no tangis, no funerals. They were just wrapped up, hauled up the hill and put in a hole. We didn't even mourn them, then. We just said things like, "Oh, our Joey's gone".'[1] About half of the forty inhabitants of Whakarapa died. Whina, to her surprise, recovered, and on Boxing Day she gave birth to a healthy daughter, who was named Carla Te Morehu Gilbert. The name Te Morehu ('the survivor') commemorated the survival of both mother and daughter through the mate urutā, the epidemic.[2]

Deaths occasioned by war and by the flu epidemic raised questions about ways to encourage women to give birth and to reward motherhood. Women were active participants in these debates, as well as in later debates to do with abortion and birth control as the need to limit families was heightened by the Great Depression of the early 1930s. Fears that certain 'desirable' sections of the population were limiting birth led to eugenically charged discussions about just who should be encouraged to marry. Māori leaders engaged with this question with respect to relationships between young Māori women workers and Chinese market gardeners.

Women's voices were primarily heard outside of Parliament, although women were involved in whānau decisions, local body politics and in claiming women's right to relief during the Depression. The development of the political party system worked to limit the impact of women's suffrage by ensuring candidates' loyalty to the party platform rather than to the wider electorate. Despite the efforts of the suffragists to promote the potential value of women sitting in the House, it was 1933 before Labour member

Top During the 1918 influenza epidemic, many people went to public inhalation chambers set up by the Public Health Department, like this one in Christchurch. A dose of zinc sulphate was administered in the throat as a way of restricting the spread of the disease. *Alexander Turnbull Library, Wellington, 1/1-008545-G*

Bottom Typhoid, a disease transmitted through food, milk or water contaminated by faecal matter, was common in the nineteenth century, especially in new towns without adequate sanitation. It persisted in poverty-stricken Māori settlements well into the twentieth century. This typhoid tent camp at Maungapōhatu in the Urewera region was established to treat those suffering from the disease after an outbreak in 1924. *Alexander Turnbull Library, Wellington, 1/2-030884*

Elizabeth McCombs became the first woman to do so. There, she was quick to announce her commitment to improving the lot of women, albeit within the family. In 1935, the First Labour Government came to power, and set about creating a welfare state that would support the nuclear family – just as a new generation of working women were beginning to question the intense focus on motherhood during the interwar years.

Children first

The global forces of war and disease contributed to the reshaping of even the most isolated parts of New Zealand. Some 18,500 New Zealanders lost their lives during or as a result of the war, and the memorials erected in towns throughout the nation in succeeding years testified to what communities had suffered. In less than two months, nearly 8,600 New Zealanders died as a result of the influenza epidemic. Such huge losses in a small country put a premium on new births and heightened concern about the declining Pākehā birth rate. Historian Maureen Hickey has pointed out that monuments to motherhood in the form of Plunket Society rooms, where the health of babies was monitored and mothers received advice and reassurance, were likewise erected throughout the country.[3] And discussion about how to raise healthy children and reward the work of mothers was intense.

'Without the knowledge of [hygiene],' a popular health manual warned in 1920, 'the mother's love too often finds its recompense only in a child's coffin.'[4] Its author, Charles Budden, warned that 'the air is full of germs. Houses, therefore, that are dirty are particularly dangerous.'[5] A small booklet published by Whitcombe & Tombs, *Housewifery for Use in School and Home*, also warned women that in all 'household tasks, such as sweeping, dusting, cleaning, it is well to remember that the foes to combat are not visible'. There followed a catalogue of all the cleaning tasks the good housewife should undertake: boiling clothes, beating rugs and dusting every surface as part of a weekly routine.[6] This was only one of a number of texts which made clear women's responsibility for the health of their families. Yet scrubbing and cleaning had proved to be no protection against the influenza epidemic when it arrived in New Zealand in November 1918.

Men accounted for 63 per cent of all European fatalities, and they were men in the prime of life, between twenty and forty years of age, many of them breadwinners.[7] Female death rates were highest in those between the ages of twenty-five and twenty-nine. If there was any consolation to be found in the pattern of the spread of the disease, it was that children between five and fifteen were most likely to be spared.[8] But that left a great many children without parents, particularly among Māori, whose death rates were four-and-a-half times higher than those of Europeans. In the Waikato, Te Puea Herangi visited all the settlements from Mangatāwhiri (Mercer) to the Waikato Heads, gathering up the more than 100 children left orphaned by the disease. They became the responsibility of her community at Te Paina, near Mangatāwhiri.

The epidemic also exposed needs that had previously gone unnoticed. Much press

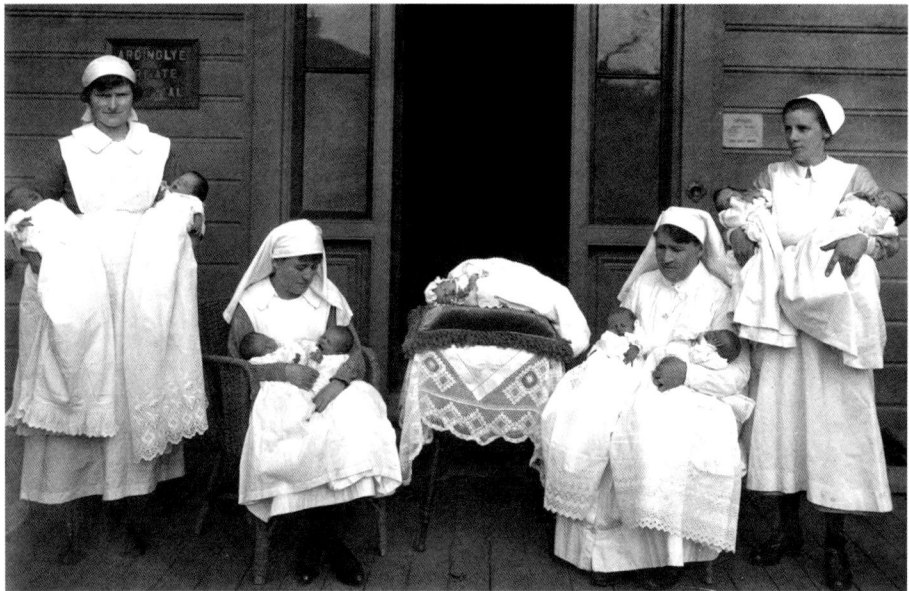

Nurses at the Ardinglye Private Hospital in Masterton show off four sets of twins in 1921. Around that time, Pākehā women were likely to have their babies at home or in small private hospitals such as this. *Masterton District Library and Archive, 01-187/43*

attention was directed towards the case of a young woman found delirious in a room bare of furniture, food or any clothing apart from the fur coat and the one good dress through which she kept up appearances at work.[9] Housing in general came under close scrutiny, especially in Māori communities where people were much more likely to die of influenza. Observers were shocked at the 'hovels' and 'slum shanties' without flush toilets and piped water in these communities – though many rural Pākehā homes also lacked such facilities, as did some of the slum housing in the towns.[10] Some disgruntled Pākehā accused Māori of clinging to substandard housing, and in the early 1920s ratepayers opposed to Te Puea Herangi's new settlement at Ngāruawāhia, which she called Tūrangawaewae, demanded that the Health Department inspect the settlement. The inspector could find nothing wrong, 'and said the standard of cleanliness and hygiene was higher than that in many European homes across the river'.[11] Like Apirana Ngata, the Ngāti Porou MP for Eastern Maori and a prominent advocate for his people, Te Puea understood that the marae was just as important to Māori as individual housing. As writer and historian Ranginui Walker has noted: 'The Marae gave a modicum of stability and cultural continuity in the face of Pakeha dominance and assimilationist pressures.'[12]

The impact of the epidemic was 'sharpest and the most painful' at the level of families and households, whether Māori or Pākehā.[13] In an unprecedented move, the government decided in late 1918 to provide pensions not only for widows but also for widowers with children. The latter provision recognised that men who had lost wives now needed to hire

This Arts and Crafts design was produced by Edith Collier, whose early painting showed great promise. However, when Collier returned from overseas study in 1921, her work was savagely criticised and her father burned most of her female nude studies. She took on family responsibilities, and painted less and less as she got older. *Collier Collection, Sarjeant Gallery, Wanganui, photographed by Richard Wotton*

paid housekeepers to care for their families. In 1919, the pension was paid to 828 widows with 2,323 children, and 89 widowers with 366 children.[14]

A Health Department pamphlet proclaimed the health of children to be of 'the Greatest National Importance' in the interwar years.[15] The decline in the birth rate gave rise to fears that European New Zealanders were dying out and leaving the country open to invasion by more prolific races from Asia. Despite the particularly heavy losses suffered by Māori in the influenza epidemic, some believed that white New Zealanders now also appeared to be losing out to Māori. 'It seems possible,' remarked a British pioneer in the infant welfare movement who was familiar with New Zealand, 'that at some future time what the Maori have lost owing to inferior armament, they might regain by superior fertility.'[16] While the Pākehā

Caring for children is important in the lives of women – as mothers, family members and sometimes paid workers.

TOP: Families travelled together to Land Court sittings: these two women with their babies were photographed amongst the groups waiting outside the Native Land Court in Tokaanu in 1914. *Auckland War Memorial Museum Tāmaki Paenga Hira, photograph by Arthur Ninnis Breckon, PH-NEG-19998; PH-NEG-C470*

MIDDLE: *Left* In Nelson in 1891, Edith Fell was photographed with her children Phyllis (left) and Sylvia; she was in bed recovering from influenza. *Right* Plunket nurses tend babies outside the Karitāne Hospital in Dunedin the early 1900s. In the Plunket guidebook of 1910, Dr Frederic Truby King stated that: 'At the Karitane Hospital the babies live out of doors all day, and a broad stream of pure cold outside air flows through the sleeping rooms all night long; tiny delicate babies, after a week or more of gradual habituation, sleep well, grow and flourish in rooms where the temperature frequently falls as low as freezing.' *Alexander Turnbull Library, Wellington, 1/2-C-06457-F; Hocken Collections/Te Uare Taoka o Hākena, University of Otago Library, Dunedin, S10-062b/AG-007-001/002*

BOTTOM: *Left* Maud Adkin was photographed bathing her first child, Nancy, in a tin tub on the verandah of her Levin home in 1917. *Right* Prize-winners in the baby show pose for their photograph at the 1914 Gala Day at Wainoni Park in Christchurch. *Museum of New Zealand Te Papa Tongarewa, Wellington, photograph by Leslie Adkin, O.002607; Christchurch City Libraries, CCL-PhotoCD18-IMG0019*

Women volunteers in Christchurch did many loads of washing for the Plunket Society during the 1918 influenza epidemic. *Alexander Turnbull Library, Wellington, 1/1-008615-G*

birth rate reached new lows, the Māori birth rate grew rapidly, and in 1930 outstripped the general rate by 68 per cent.[17] In the decade from 1926 to 1936, those of Māori descent increased in number by 34.8 per cent, compared with the non-Māori rate of 10.6 per cent.[18]

Reasons were sought as to why Pākehā women were choosing to limit the size of their families. One of the answers appeared to be that, despite declining rates of infant mortality, the risk of death in childbirth remained high. In 1921, the rate of maternal death for Pākehā was 6.48 for every 1,000 live births; to the shock of many, including the Minister of Health, this was the second highest rate in the western world.[19] The fact that Māori women faced much greater risks was unrecorded in the international comparisons: in 1920, their maternal mortality rate stood at 22.86 per 1,000 live births.[20] In their apparently highly valued role as mothers, women's health needs were clearly not being met. Historian Philippa Mein Smith has described how the experience of birth – a woman's initiation into motherhood – was transformed for Pākehā mothers in the interwar years from a home-based, family event to a medical procedure within hospitals. This dramatic cultural shift signalled new anxieties about childbirth. What was once regarded as a natural and inevitable part of family life became an infrequent occurrence, as family size declined to an average of two or three children.

In 1918, Pākehā women were likely to have their babies at home or in a small facility run by a local nurse or midwife. Giving birth at home meant women could continue to monitor the household, and attending nurses, even in the late 1930s, would do some housework – preparing meals, tidying the woman's bedroom, and 'making things nice'.[21] Those who could afford the services of a private nurse for a fortnight had the luxury of welcoming their child and adjusting to the new relationship in familiar surroundings. By the mid-1930s, the psychological security of home was being abandoned in favour of the promise of a safe delivery made by the advocates of hospitalised birth. Free antenatal clinics, an emphasis on aseptic techniques for midwifery, and the medicalisation of childbirth in upgraded hospitals became important components in the campaign to reduce deaths in childbirth.[22]

Dunedin made 'a record in New Zealand Medical History' in March 1935 when Kathleen Johnson (always referred to in the news reports as Mrs George Johnson) gave birth in Dunedin to healthy quadruplets. A fund was immediately established to allow the public to contribute 'towards the maintenance of the children whose advent has so greatly increased the domestic responsibilities of a working man'.[23] For the first ten months, Mrs Johnson's 'domestic responsibilities' towards the children were taken over by the Plunket Society's Karitāne Hospital in Anderson's Bay. The Johnsons, already the parents of two children aged eight and six, expressed the family's gratitude to the society when the quadruplets came home, and 'particularly noted the expert and loving care given to the children by the matron and her staff'.[24] Respect for Plunket was widespread. Women volunteers nationwide joined the society in the interwar years and raised funds to create an impressive network of urban infant-welfare services. New mothers mostly welcomed the advice of Plunket nurses and took comfort in the support offered.[25] By the late 1930s, there were 131 Plunket nurses, each carrying a caseload of about 160 babies per annum, and 'Plunket' had 'become a household word' in Pākehā communities.[26]

Plunket's reach did not extend to rural areas where most Māori were based. Medical initiatives around birth were also unlikely to reach Māori women who were averse to examinations before childbirth, particularly by male doctors.[27] Most Māori women gave birth at home.[28] Reremoana Koopu's twelve children were all born at home with her husband's help, in traditional Māori practice. She recalled, 'Yes, he's good too. I like him because, when I am like that, I'd rather just have him. Just my husband.'[29] Two medical students engaged in a study of the Rātana settlement in 1940 arrived a few hours after a woman had delivered a child with the help of her mother and husband. They found a cheerful scene: 'the mother sitting up in bed strumming a ukelale [sic], and the baby with a six inch cord roughly tied with string, wrapped in a blanket beside her'.[30]

'Anyone go to hospital – he no come back' was the verdict of two medical students summing up the attitudes of many Māori to hospital care.[31] Yet historian Derek Dow has shown how attitudes varied by region, and that the low rate of hospital admission among Māori perhaps had more to do with non-Māori ratepayers' reluctance to support unrated Māori. Cash-strapped hospital boards sometimes manifest this reluctance. Arguments about responsibility for payments continued until the Social Security Act 1938 introduced free hospital care for all.[32]

Outside of hospitals, many doctors were unwilling to attend to Māori women in their own homes 'on account of the bad sanitary conditions'.[33] Members of the First Labour Government appointed to an inquiry into the adequacy of maternity services throughout the country were shocked by the poor housing conditions they found in the Māori communities they visited: 'homes being no more than iron sheds full of holes, with mud floors and no sanitary conveniences, no water and no washing facilities', where women worked hard to 'keep these places clean and tidy'.[34] Because Māori were poor, it was difficult to recover fees from them – an added disincentive to general practitioners providing maternity care.[35] In 1935, only 16.8 per cent of Māori live births took place in hospital, in contrast to 78 per cent of non-Māori births.[36] Antenatal services were also beyond the reach of most rural-dwelling Māori.

The high maternal mortality rate of the 1920s encouraged an emphasis on the dangers of birth in subsequent decades. Dr Doris Gordon, the outspoken first secretary of the New Zealand Obstetrical Society, claimed 'even the so-called normal case of today is fraught with pain and penalty, that birth and death go hand-in-hand'.[37] In the hospital setting, women could receive pain relief and bed rest, but at the expense of an active role in birth and with the acceptance that giving birth in a public hospital meant they might be viewed as valuable teaching material. Doris Gordon led the successful campaign, supported by women's groups, to endow a chair in Obstetrics at the University of Otago, thereby confirming the importance of medical attendance at birth.

Not everyone shared Gordon's enthusiasm. The strict hospital routine of four-hourly bedpanning and swabbing, separation from babies except at set feeding times, and the presence of students at examinations led one woman to comment: 'I think there is very little difference between hospitals and prisons, because in one you are a case and in the other you are a number.'[38] Hospital practices, and particularly the routine disposal of the umbilical cord (pito) and placenta (whenua), were even more objectionable to Māori women. Traditionally, these organs were returned to the earth.

While many commentators bewailed the 'selfishness of mothers' that was leading to a decline in the Pākehā birth rate, there were few accolades for the unselfish Māori women caring for numerous children. Māori families were likely to have at least six children, in part because Māori women began bearing children at a younger age. Both high maternal mortality rates and the difficulties faced by Māori women with large families concerned health workers such as Ruby Cameron who, after working as a district nurse on the East Coast, was transferred to Rotorua in the early 1930s. Nurse Cameron saw that there was much that Māori women could do for their communities. She persuaded local leaders to support her work in establishing health clinics on local marae to assist mothers with issues of child health and hygiene.[39] Local women responded enthusiastically, and in September 1937 Cameron drew on their support to form a Women's Health League in Ōhinemutu.[40]

Limiting families, rewarding mothers

'Tired of the sentimental references to the "mothers of the race"', which appeared 'to be part of the stock in trade of candidates for public positions', ten Wellington women wrote to the *Evening Post* in November 1920, noting that, while butter producers were financially subsidised by the government, 'the poor mothers of our coming generation, on whom so much depends, far from being subsidized, are being continually harassed by ever rising prices and the unsympathetic treatment of those who are supposed to attend to the affairs of the community'. They asked for practical legislation 'that would assist the much belauded, but otherwise neglected, mothers'. The question was urgent because of the ongoing impact of the First World War and 'the rapid economic strides of the yellow races'.[41]

'Powerful indictments' about the dangers of 'Race Suicide' – that is, the spectre of a declining white population – faced New Zealanders from the war years onwards. American feature films such as *Race Suicide*, 'a present-day story of a woman who postponed the natural result of marriage until it was too late', entertained and instructed New Zealand audiences.[42] The banner headline advertising the 'photo-drama' entitled *I Want My Children*, shown throughout the country, summarised the key concern: 'Should A Wife Shirk Motherhood?'[43] Another film, *Where Are My Children?* – 'not a picture for those of tender years' – starred famous actor Tyrone Power as an attorney who supported birth control but was devastated to find his wife had repeatedly resorted to medically induced abortion to maintain her social life.[44] The film conveyed 'a terrible indictment of medical malpractice as a way of saving selfish women butterflies'.[45]

Some linked the declining non-Māori birth rate with the cost of giving birth. A 'Worker', writing to the *Auckland Star* in 1924 under the heading 'Our Empty Cradles', listed the costs of confinement: the nursing home charged £9 15s (about $860 in 2015 terms) while the doctor's bill was £5 5s.[46] This was a substantial amount for families who might typically live on £4 per week.[47]

In addition to fears about the white races dying out and women shirking both motherhood and its associated duties, commentators expressed concern that procreation was no longer seen as the prime purpose of marriage. In 1929, a New Zealand woman wrote to the English advocate of birth control, Marie Stopes, saying: 'all the books I had read dealing with sex matters held up continace [*sic*] except for procreative purposes, as an ideal to be striven for, impossible though this was admitted to be for many people'.[48] Stopes's 1918 bestseller, *Married Love*, had made it permissible for women to think differently about sex by suggesting that it had as much to do with 'intense physical pleasure' as it did with conceiving children.[49] '[T]o have had a moderate number of orgasms at some time at least,' Stopes claimed, was 'a necessity for the full development of a woman's health and all her powers.'[50] She prescribed strategies to ensure that marriage entailed 'enduring passion' – the title of her 1928 book. Marriage, the *Otago Witness* pronounced in 1927, was now 'made for the love of two people to be perfectly expressed, and only secondarily for the creation of children'.[51]

New Zealand's own Marie Stopes, the freethinking and unconventional Ettie Rout, suggested that marriage could be made 'safe' by the prevention of venereal disease and the use of contraception. She advised that women could use douches, suppositories and pessaries to prevent conception.[52] New Zealanders (unless they were doctors) were, however, denied her wisdom after her book *Safe Marriage* was banned in 1923.[53] Those seeking advice on birth control could nonetheless order, from among a range of catalogues, one of 'intimate necessities': the *Husband and Wife's Handbook,* a treatise on a subject of 'Vital Importance' to all married persons, and guaranteed to be posted in a 'plain wrapper'.[54]

Ettie Rout's and Marie Stopes's lack of reticence on sexual matters, unusual in women of the time, was condemned by many, although the *New Zealand Truth* named 'Sex Education as THE problem of the day' in 1924.[55] In 1929, when an unsuccessful attempt was made to have a bookseller prosecuted for indecency for selling Stopes's *Enduring Passion,* the Director General of Health, T. W. H. Valentine, declared it to be 'a perfectly beastly book'.[56] Valentine's views were supported by others such as 'True Patriot', who regarded birth control as 'medically unsound and ethically harmful'.[57]

Whatever opinion they might express in public, many New Zealanders were using various methods to prevent pregnancy, particularly when they feared that another child might tip the family into poverty. One woman ascribed her success at family limitation 'entirely' to her husband who, she said, 'never dreams of worrying me more than once or perhaps twice a month'.[58] Her experience of sex as a bothersome exercise initiated by the man may well have been common at a time when, despite the efforts of Stopes, many couples were unable to communicate their needs because so much of the language associated with sex was tainted by notions of obscenity.[59] Sex was something 'nice' women did not discuss either among themselves or with their husbands. In addition, some men clung to the idea that their 'conjugal rights' took precedence over their wives' well-being. One of Wellington's first woman solicitors, Hinemoa Richards, successfully sought a divorce on the grounds of sexual cruelty. She stated that her husband had exercised 'his rights' to the detriment of her health. Six days after her child was born, he had tried to enter her bed in the hospital.[60] It was a similar case of a husband asserting his 'marital rights' when his wife was recovering from childbirth that made Doris Gordon a staunch advocate of hospital deliveries and fourteen days' rest for women after giving birth.[61]

Considerable male restraint was required for probably the most common method of fertility control, coitus interruptus or withdrawal. This had the advantage of being free, and a private matter between husband and wife; it was also considered 'natural', unlike barrier methods.[62] Condoms could be bought from a variety of outlets, including barber shops, but they were expensive. By the 1930s, catalogues suggest that a range of condoms was available, from reusable varieties made of thick rubber to the latest latex versions.[63]

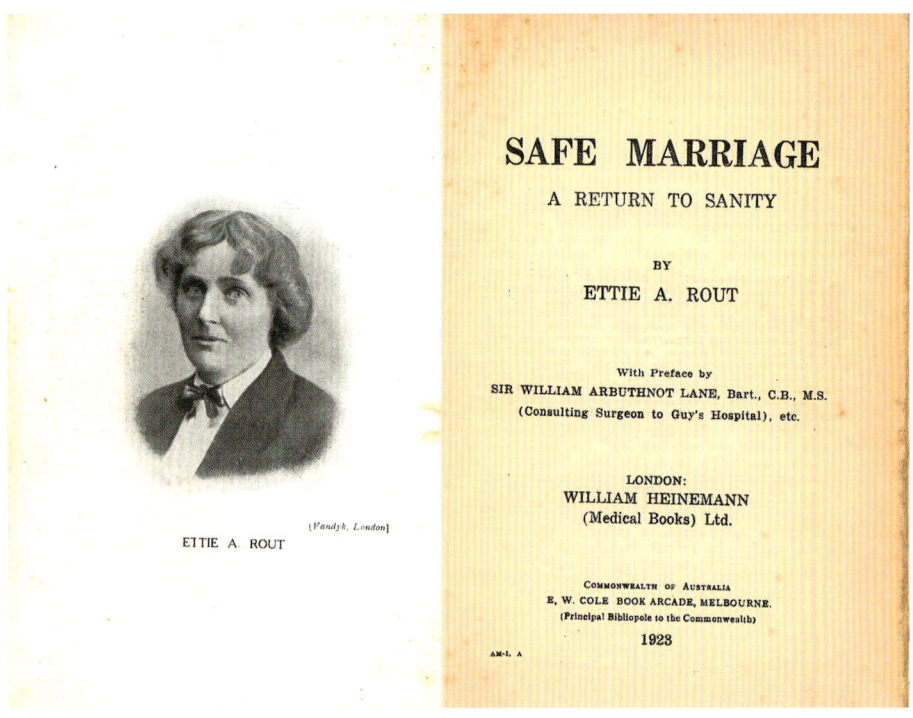

SAFE MARRIAGE

A RETURN TO SANITY

BY

ETTIE A. ROUT

With Preface by
SIR WILLIAM ARBUTHNOT LANE, Bart., C.B., M.S.
(Consulting Surgeon to Guy's Hospital), etc.

LONDON:
WILLIAM HEINEMANN
(Medical Books) Ltd.

COMMONWEALTH OF AUSTRALIA
E. W. COLE BOOK ARCADE, MELBOURNE.
(Principal Bibliopole to the Commonwealth)
1923

ETTIE A. ROUT

Pioneering New Zealand safe-sex campaigner Ettie Rout published a contraception manual for women, *Safe Marriage*, in 1923. It was banned in New Zealand but published in Britain and Australia. Rout had already achieved notoriety for distributing prophylactic kits and organising inspected brothels for New Zealand soldiers serving overseas during the First World War. *Frontispiece to* Safe Marriage *(1923), Waikato University Library*

Women could buy rubber diaphragms over the counter in chemist shops, where the pharmacist might haphazardly guess at the appropriate size, while foaming pessaries were available by mail order.[64] Most doctors believed that motherhood was women's destiny and were opposed to contraception. They had no training in the area, and were unaware of the latest developments, and few male doctors were comfortable with the idea of fitting diaphragms. Their views were summed up by W. H. Symes, a well-known Christchurch practitioner and Chief Health Officer of Canterbury, who argued that birth control led to 'immorality and general deterioration of conduct'.[65]

By the 1930s, Pākehā women were becoming increasingly vocal in their demands for some sort of help in planning their families. In 1931, the Auckland branch of the National Council of Women urged that 'birth control information must be made available to married women through the public health authorities'.[66] Three years later, the Women's Institute forwarded a remit to the National Council of Women, suggesting that 'the Health Department be urged to provide free of charge on application, information on birth control'.[67] In 1935, the Timaru branch of the Labour Party suggested that birth control clinics be established at 'maternity wards of public hospitals and similar institutions'.[68]

In Auckland during the Depression, movie-themed balls were held to raise money for the unemployed, with proceeds going to the Mayor's Metropolitan Unemployment Relief Fund. This programme was for a masked fancy dress ball held at the Dixieland Cabaret on 13 July 1933. *Auckland Libraries, Sir George Grey Special Collections, Eph.MovieMagic*

Even more radical was the formation that year of the Sex Hygiene and Birth Regulation Society in Wellington. Its women members believed parents should be able to plan their families and that 'the bearing and nurture of children are not the aim and end of women's existence'.[69] They were concerned that, '[a]t a conservative estimate, ninety percent of New Zealanders using contraceptives are following methods inefficient, damaging to health or psychologically harmful.'[70] The society's founders were aware of the large number of women having abortions, and saw the obvious solution in promoting ways 'to make it unnecessary for women to risk their lives'.[71]

The illicit trade in backstreet abortion, usually the subject of whispers at work or over the back fence, came dramatically to public attention whenever an abortionist went on trial. Mrs Annie Aves, a tall, striking woman with a penchant for furs, lived in a typical suburban house in Fitzroy Avenue, Hastings, in the 1930s.[72] She was well known to women in the town and throughout Hawke's Bay as an abortionist – a speciality that made her much in demand in the Depression years. In one eighteen-month period when she dealt with 183 women, Annie Aves earned over £2,000 (the equivalent of about $224,500 in 2015). Unlike other abortionists who preferred to operate before the third month of pregnancy, Mrs Aves did not hesitate to perform later abortions. She mostly used the sea-tangle tent which, when inserted into the neck of the uterus, absorbed moisture and so caused dilation and eventual miscarriage or premature labour. In 1936, the police found twenty-two separate collections of fetal remains buried in her garden. As a consequence, Annie Aves was brought to trial four times, but she was not convicted because the all-male juries could never agree on a verdict. Such unwillingness to convict suggests considerable popular sympathy for the plight of women faced with an unwanted pregnancy.

Whatever individuals' private views, concern about the prevalence of abortion led to a formal government investigation in 1936. The Abortion Inquiry recognised that 'women of all classes are demanding the right to decide how many children they will have', but blamed this 'selfish' outlook on women's unwillingness to take responsibility for families, their desire for pleasure and their reluctance to give up paid work. Most commentators agreed with the opinion expressed in Wellington's *Dominion* newspaper, under the heading 'New Zealand's Unborn Citizens', that what was needed was a 're-enthronement of the child in the national esteem … or, more properly, re-enthronement of the larger family'.[73]

A number of women's groups had sought some way of providing recognition, if not recompense, for the work of mothers. The Auckland Women's Branch of the Labour Party, the WCTU and the National Council of Women were among those advocating some form of 'motherhood endowment'. They argued that the existing wage system failed to provide for families, and women in particular.[74] The solution lay in dividing up the husband's wage packet and paying part of it directly to his wife. This would undercut wives' dependency on their husbands and ensure that mothers were able to provide for their children.

Another remedy, in the form of Family Allowances, was advocated in 1922 by a judge of the Arbitration Court who suggested allowances 'as a solution to the sharpening debate between the worker's right to a living wage and the economic conditions affecting trade or industry'.[75] Now fears about the health of children and about the declining Pākehā birth rate added fuel to arguments made by women's groups that motherhood required encouragement.[76] In 1926, the Reform government led by Gordon Coates reluctantly introduced An Act to Make Provision for the Grant of Allowances towards the Maintenance of Children by Parents with Limited Income. Described by historian Elizabeth Hanson as the 'first nation-wide act of its kind in the world', the Family Allowances Act recognised that large families ran the risk of impoverishment. New Zealand's award system, which governed wages through the Arbitration Court, determined men's wages based on a family of four. The Act, therefore, made provision for an allowance of two shillings (equivalent to $10 in 2015) per week for the third and each additional child of families earning less than £4 (about $372) per week.[77] 'Aliens' (defined as those from Asia, and including Lebanese), unmarried mothers, morally disreputable persons and families owning property additional to the family home were disqualified.[78] The Alliance of Labour, a group attempting to unite all trade unions, argued that the allowance of two shillings a week granted under the 1926 Act 'would not keep a well developed fowl let alone a healthy child'.[79]

The Family Allowances Act 1926 recognised that many families with more than two children required assistance. But the importance of the Family Allowance lay less in the meagre amount paid than in the precedent it set for state assistance to families.[80] Significantly, the allowance was paid to the mother upon application by the father, and this allowed women to feel entitled to determine how the money might best be spent. A small resource for individual families, the measure itself was large in conception, because it was the first benefit to seek 'a general social outcome': a higher birth rate.[81]

Māori who were ready to fill out forms detailing family members' weekly income could receive the benefit – as long as they were not disqualified by communal land ownership. Poverty was a reality for many Māori communities, and the benefit of two shillings a week for each child after the second could make a big difference to the finances of struggling couples, most of whom had large families. One analysis suggests that Māori received 'up to one-fifth or more of the pensions granted prior to the Social Security Act 1938, at a time when Maori were less than 5 per cent of the population'.[82]

Yet the terms on which Māori received the benefit could be humiliating. In Te Kao, in Northland, women were denied receipt of their allowances, which were paid instead to the Pākehā storekeeper 'because it was claimed they handed their payments to the Ratana Church instead of using them to maintain their families'.[83] Mrs Ani Rikihana led the women in making a successful complaint to the Minister of Pensions, requesting payment in the same way 'as other women are'.[84]

Top Women picking strawberries at Lower Motueka in the early 1920s take a break from their work. *Alexander Turnbull Library, Wellington, 1/4-023678-F*

Bottom A group of Māori, including children and a woman, cut flax at Lake Ōhia in Northland around 1919. The flax would be sold to a local mill. *Alexander Turnbull Library, Wellington, 1/1-006285-G*

Benefits remained firmly targeted at families. Women's groups and Labour parliamentarians argued in favour of extending the Family Allowance to deserted wives. The United and Coalition governments, however, remained committed to the principle that, to be entitled to a benefit, a family required a male breadwinner; to allow otherwise would be to encourage desertion. Entitlement to benefits, no matter how small, 'endowed a person with a sense of rights', removing the humiliation attached to the receipt of charity.[85]

What kind of population?

At the heart of the concerns about motherhood and children was the question of what kind of society New Zealand should be. 'It has rightly been decided,' noted a government inquiry, 'that this should be not only a "white man's country," but as completely British as possible'.[86] New Zealand should be British with a twist: a European country with a superior indigenous population that enabled good race relations. Māori were incorporated within the definition of 'white' in this 'white man's country'.[87] It should not be 'Asiatic', or populated by 'defectives' supposedly born to those with venereal disease; if possible, children were to be born free of defects.[88]

Three official inquiries in the 1920s serve to illustrate the government's heightened interest in the sexual behaviour of its citizens: an inquiry into venereal disease in 1922; into mental defectives and sexual offenders in 1924; and, in the face of growing concern about the mixing of Māori and Chinese, into the employment of Māori on market gardens in 1929. Influential activists and policymakers believed that unbridled female sexuality had the potential to 'lead to the decadence of the nation'.[89]

'Women from the very fact of their maternal functions', argued Isabel Howlett, a trained teacher of 'backward children', could either revive the race by good motherhood or add to its deterioration by bad motherhood.[90] Howlett was summarising the views of the National Council of Women and the WCTU, two of the numerous voluntary women's associations concerned with a vision of 'race betterment' in the interwar years. Women reformers, historian Angela Wanhalla has argued, engaged in a rhetoric 'of female moral superiority' in which white women emphasised the importance of motherhood and argued for 'political recognition and participation' on this basis.[91]

The National Council of Women and the WCTU attracted women proponents of social reform who enthusiastically adopted the promise of eugenics as a way of promoting a healthy 'race'. By encouraging the socially desirable (that is, mostly middle-class educated people) to reproduce, and discouraging the socially undesirable (mostly working-class poor people) from doing so, the international eugenics movement sought to rescue nations from social degeneration. Its advocates aimed to do this by limiting the freedoms of 'unfit' women, whether sexually promiscuous and therefore at risk of bearing illegitimate children or contracting venereal disease, or mentally defective, 'feeble-minded', socially deviant or simply poor.

Vigorous outdoor activities demanded practical clothing. These three women wear trousers and boots to go tramping in the 1920s. *Alexander Turnbull Library, Wellington, PAColl-4288-01*

Lady Jacobina Luke, wife of the Mayor of Wellington, was one of those seeking greater control over 'mental defectives'.[92] Renowned for her commitment to social services in Wellington during the First World War and the subsequent influenza epidemic, she was typical of middle-class women who had the resources to commit themselves to voluntary work in a number of organisations, including the Young Women's Christian Association (YWCA), the National Council of Women, the Citizen's Day Nursery, the Plunket Society, St John's Ambulance and the Victoria League.[93] At the age of sixty-two, Lady Luke was the only woman appointed to the special committee set up to undertake the 1922 Inquiry into Venereal Diseases in New Zealand. This inquiry took the view that: 'Girls stay less at home and assist less in the work of the home, preferring whenever opportunity offers, to go to the pictures or some other form of entertainment.'[94] The 'sexually suggestive' dress of modern women and 'modern forms of dancing' seemed, moreover, to be undermining earlier values of self-control.[95]

The inquiry found proof of the dissolute behaviour of young people in the fact that between 1913 and 1921 there were 10,841 illegitimate births and 12,235 births that occurred within seven months of marriage. In effect, it suggested, more than 50 per cent of first births 'result from sexual contact prior to marriage'.[96] The willingness of young women to engage in sexual activity was, in the inquiry's view, indicative of promiscuity. Since the police could find only 104 'professional prostitutes' in the country, it was young women 'amateurs' who must be responsible for the spread of venereal disease.

Golf was a popular sport for New Zealand women from the 1890s. Dress remains quite formal for these women taking part in a round in the early 1920s. *Alexander Turnbull Library, Wellington, PAColl-9404*

The *Truth* newspaper put it this way, under one of its lurid banner headlines, 'Society's Scarlet Scourge':

> It is the cash-amateur, or CLANDESTINE PROSTITUTE who provides the great menace to social purity in New Zealand ... The abandonment of the lilies and languors of virtue for the alleged roses and raptures of vice in their case is often done not so much for money, as for 'presents' from their gentlemen friends ... It is the desire for dress and personal adornment, and the impossibility of gratifying that desire on the meager wage of the waitress, shop girl and factory hand that sends these girls to hell.[97]

Reflecting widespread social attitudes, the inquiry divided women into two categories: the sexually active 'amateur' and the 'innocent wife'. Both of them might contract venereal disease. The committee recommended better sex education, the appointment of 'Lady patrols', a requirement that parties intending to marry should sign a document affirming their 'freedom from communicable disease', and that women doctors should attend women's clinics. In their concluding remarks, the committee members noted that 'already there is far too large a proportion of mental and physical defectives reproducing their kind'. They went on to note that 'clear evidence' existed that women of this 'unfortunate class' had 'a tendency to lead dissolute lives'.[98]

These 'dissolute lives' came under even greater scrutiny in the 1924 Inquiry into Mental Defectives and Sexual Offenders in New Zealand. The only woman appointed to this committee was Ada Paterson, a graduate of Otago Medical School and director of the Health Department's Division of School Hygiene, who had a special interest in 'mentally backward' children. Historian Margaret Tennant notes that in the questions Ada Paterson put to those appearing before the committee, she is revealed as a 'woman of her time, sharing contemporary concerns about the threat to society posed by the "feeble-minded"'.[99] The committee regarded 'unrestricted multiplication' of the 'feeble-minded' as 'a most serious menace to the future welfare and happiness of the Dominion'.[100] 'Over-sexed' girls were a particular problem, and the solution lay in institutionalisation and surveillance.[101] The committee recommended that a register be kept of all 'mental defectives', persons with severe epilepsy, 'moral imbeciles', and persons discharged from mental hospitals. Those on the register should not be permitted to marry, and it would be 'an indictable offence' to have sex with any registered person.[102] In the event, few of the recommendations were implemented by Parliament. Provisions for the regulation of marriage and for the sterilisation of sexual offenders were dropped from the Mental Defectives Amendment Act 1928.[103] Parliament legislated instead for a Eugenics Board, ostensibly to keep watch over the gene pool of the nation.

Three women, Ada Paterson, Jean Begg and Janet Fraser, were appointed to the seven-member Eugenics Board, reinforcing the hopes of women's organisations that women's expertise should be brought to bear on this important issue. Ada Paterson represented a new type of single professional woman with an influential role in the public service in the interwar years.[104] Jean Begg was another. She had trained as a Presbyterian missionary and spent the years between 1910 and 1919 on Tutuila, a tiny island of Samoa, before going on to train in social work in New York.[105] She became general secretary of the YWCA in 1926. Janet Fraser, a voluntary worker and mother of one child, had been married twice, the second time happily to Labour politician Peter Fraser. Like many middle-class women, Janet Fraser contributed to the community through her voluntary work as a health visitor, as a member of the Wellington Hospital Board, the League of Mothers, the New Zealand Society for the Protection of Women and Children, the Plunket Society, the Women's Borstal Association of New Zealand, and the Federation of University Women.[106]

The main focus of the Eugenics Board became the coordination of policy in the different government departments dealing with children with mental deficiencies.[107] In fact, the board had a short life, and eugenics receded as a national priority as the economic depression of the 1930s deepened. The Women's Division of the Farmers' Union, however, remained convinced that the problem of unemployment could be attacked at its roots by preventing 'the increase of the unemployable, the children of the unfit mentally and physically'.[108] The Women's Division continued to advocate for the regulation of marriage.

The question of who should marry whom was at the forefront of the 1929 Inquiry into the Employment of Maori on Market Gardens, set in motion by Minister of Native Affairs Sir Apirana Ngata, and carried out by three men representing the Labour, Health and Native departments. The issue of white women working for Chinese employers had been on the agenda of the National Council of Women since July 1927, when an associate member sponsored a League of Nations proposal that the council 'should urge that heavy penalties be imposed upon Chinese who interfere with our girls in New Zealand and that the whole problem needs investigation by experts'. After 'considerable discussion', the members decided not to support the proposal. They did, however, pass a resolution to 'approach the government with a view to legislation being passed to prevent the employment of white girls by Chinese'.[109] At the same time, the National Council of Women worked to ease restrictions on the entry to New Zealand of the wives of Chinese men, and sought to interest Chinese women in joining a branch of the organisation.[110] When the Committee of Inquiry into the Employment of Maori on Market Gardens was announced, the National Council of Women protested that none of its members were women, and requested representation. The request fell on deaf ears.

The inquiry's findings offer valuable insights into the work of Māori women, as well as contemporary concerns about relationships between Māori and Chinese. Their entry to New Zealand subject to a poll tax, a literacy test and a permit system, Chinese men mainly worked as vegetable farmers or as laundrymen. Few women accompanied the men who left China, so the more than 2,000 Chinese men in New Zealand generally lived in male-only communities.[111] The inquiry was charged with ascertaining 'how many female Maoris are living with Chinese or Hindus, whether lawfully married or not', and 'whether it is in the interests of public morality that the employment of Maori girls and women by Chinese and Hindus should be permitted to take place'.[112]

'Public morality' signified concern about racial 'degradation' through miscegenation. Pākehā imagined themselves to be in a relationship of 'equality' with Māori, but not with 'aliens'.[113] Māori and Pākehā could voluntarily enter lifelong unions, and many in the community regarded intermarriage as the way to create true New Zealanders. Te Rangi Hiroa, for example, argued that miscegenation was 'the stepping stone to the evolution of a future type of New-Zealander in which we hope the best features of the Maori race will be perpetuated for ever'.[114] This benevolent view of the workings of intermarriage was questioned by Apirana Ngata, who was firm in his belief that the Māori future relied on 'preservation of unique Maori bloodlines and adhering to the principles of tribal organisation and leadership'.[115] Intermarriage carried with it the danger of biological absorption, through which Māori would become indistinguishable from Pākehā.

Those who had prompted the inquiry feared that Māori women would enter relationships with Chinese men if they worked closely with them. One of the most sought-after occupations was work in Chinese-run laundries, which 'paid very well indeed', but it raised the problem of women 'spending the nights' with the Chinese men – at least in the view of Dr Mildred Staley, a former medical officer who had served in London, India and Fiji, and was a well-known lecturer on social issues in Auckland.[116]

Work on Chinese market gardens was also popular, and William Goffe, a Māori interpreter and land purchase officer, told the inquiry that Māori women were attracted to this work for 'pleasure and dress'. He said that girls were being enticed into the work by a Māori woman who told them that the 'Chinese were far preferable to either their own race or the European, because they were kinder and treated them better than most of them'.[117] Mildred Staley confirmed that the Māori women found the Chinese men in the Ōtaki district to be 'very generous. The girls showed me beautiful rolls of silk that have been given them.'[118] The young women also appreciated the willingness of the Chinese to advance money. One Chinese market gardener reported that women often came to his house on a Saturday 'to get some money for the pictures'.[119] The officer in charge of the Labour Department in Auckland noted: 'The Maori girl is something like her white sister and she has to advance with the times: that is what forces her to work for the Chinese – she is beginning to feel her feet.'[120]

Miriam Soljak, a political activist with the Auckland Women's Branch of the Labour Party, a fluent speaker of Māori and a former teacher in native schools, stressed the economic conditions that forced Māori women into whatever work they could find. She painted a picture of the difficulties Māori women faced in seeking work in the city – 'social ostracism' and the danger of becoming the prey 'of any evil-minded man (European or otherwise) who happens to see her'. She reminded the inquiry that 'Maori girls have equal rights of citizenship with their European sisters' and hence had the right to choose to work where and for whom they pleased.[121]

Soljak suggested that there should be a hostel for Māori women where they could train as domestic workers, in home nursing and child welfare, but she recognised that not all women were temperamentally suited for such work. In her view, Māori women were natural gardeners, so work for the New Zealand Tobacco Company (for example) would be preferable to factory employment. When Soljak reported on her meeting with the inquiry, the Auckland Women's Branch of the Labour Party passed a resolution stating that Māori women faced an economic problem that could be solved only by 'a scheme which will assist these girls to attain their social and economic independence'. Any remedy, they suggested, 'must take into consideration the civic rights of both Maoris and Chinese'.[122]

What the *New Zealand Herald* described as the 'Maori Girl Problem' came to dominate proceedings, for concerns about the economic position of Māori were entwined with questions of sexual commerce.[123] While intimate relationships between Māori and Pākehā were accepted as unremarkable, perhaps inevitable, and even to some desirable as a means of hastening assimilation, Māori men speaking at the inquiry expressed a great deal of concern about relationships between Māori women and Chinese men. George Graham and Mr Rukutai of the Akarana Maori Association, a group instrumental in the establishment of the inquiry, claimed that fifty-five Māori girls were living with Chinese and only two were married. But a Dr Ellison cast these figures in a very different light –

Zilla Raynes painted this scene looking across the Māngere inlet towards Ōtāhuhu in 1930. In the foreground Chinese market gardeners and their Māori workers toil in the potato fields. The previous year the government had held an inquiry into the employment of Māori women and girls by Chinese men. *Auckland Libraries, Footprints 02538, original held by Mangere Bridge Library, MNP: MS 2*

that fifty-three Māori girls were living on the premises of the Chinese, not *with* the Chinese. The women themselves asked the Revd A. J. Seamer, general superintendent of the New Zealand Methodist Home Mission, to refute the allegations of immorality made by the Akarana Maori Association. He duly pointed out that the women worked in the gardens because it was the only employment they could find; they were, he said, hardworking, 'struggling to earn sufficient to purchase the necessities of life for themselves and their dependents'. He also pointed out that there were very few Māori-Chinese children and that most of them had been born within wedlock.[124]

While resisting the pressure to prevent Māori women from working for the Chinese completely, the inquiry recommended that those under the age of twenty-one should be prohibited from working in market gardens 'controlled by Asiatics' without supervision. The inquiry also endorsed a resolution of the Māori members of the Anglican Synod that

This silk cheongsam (long dress) was made in Hong Kong in the 1940s for Chak Man Kong, who brought it with her to New Zealand when she fled the impending Japanese occupation of Hong Kong in 1941. She was able to enter New Zealand with her daughter Mayme Chanwai because her husband and father-in-law were residents. From 1939 the government offered two-year permits to wives and children of Chinese men who were permanent residents, and as war escalated, the permits were extended. After the war women and children were allowed to stay permanently in New Zealand because of political changes in China. *Museum of New Zealand Te Papa Tongarewa, Wellington, GH017196*

called for the repatriation of Ngāpuhi women and girls 'who have drifted into the city and suburban areas and seek employment in market gardens'. These women were said to have 'land interests and remunerative occupations to return to' in the north.[125] The Akarana Maori Association resolved to provide accommodation for girls in town that would prevent them from drifting towards the gardens and counter the town attractions of a 'gay life and gaudy colours' with 'rational amusements'.[126]

The association did not, however, have the last word. In August 1930, Mere Newton, president of the Tamaki Maori Women's Welfare League, wrote to Apirana Ngata.[127] In view of the poverty of the Māori people, she said, her members were against any plan to

Jessie and Dora Wong had their passport photographs taken at William Berry's Wellington photographic studio in 1932. *Museum of New Zealand Te Papa Tongarewa, Wellington, B.046944*

prohibit their work in Chinese gardens. The league suggested monitoring the behaviour of the working women through the appointment of educated Māori women as 'Welfare or Patrol Officers' who would inspect the gardens regularly 'from a Health or Moral point of view'.[128] Its recommendation, in effect, replaced the paternalism of the Akarana Maori Association with maternal surveillance by older, more affluent women.

Representing women's interests

Successive governments, in the interests of preserving New Zealand's population from degeneration and decline through miscegenation and the 'indiscriminate use' of birth control and abortion, endeavoured to uphold the position of women as 'mothers of the race'. In pursuit of that aim, they inquired into sexual behaviour in unprecedented ways. 'Degeneration' through venereal disease, 'mental deficiency', and intimate relations between Māori and Chinese threatened an ideal of a New Zealand society centred on particular notions of home and family that were based on breadwinning fathers and mothers devoted to domestic life. Male Māori leaders expressed concern about the behaviour of Māori women, and wished to reassert elders' control over the young – an increasingly difficult task as new educational and employment opportunities in the urban centres became more attractive. While women might wish to enter the debates about what kind of society New Zealand could become, male politicians imagined that women had a particular preserve in political life: as one expressed it, 'the influence which a good mother brings into the home a good woman will bring to the floor of this House'.[129]

To many of the women who had been active prior to the war in the temperance and women's suffrage campaigns (the so-called first-wave feminists), women's representation within Parliament had seemed to be a crucial precursor to refashioning the state in the interests of women and families, and central to translating family needs into rights. Many Māori were less optimistic, agitating for parallel political institutions rather than relying on the Pākehā Parliament. To at least one Māori member of that Parliament, the question of the representation of women was difficult. 'The Native people of this country will not agree,' Te Heuheu Tukino, chief of Ngāti Tūwharetoa, had said when at last the Women's Parliamentary Rights Bill 1919, seeking to give women the right to stand for Parliament, came before the House. He asserted in the Legislative Council that the Bill, if passed, would lead to a good deal of trouble in the home: 'our women would be here in Parliament and we, the husbands, would be left at home to look after the children'. He was convinced that representation by a woman was 'against the customs of the Maori people'.

> It has been the custom of our people from the time of their ancestors down to the present day that the male should on all occasions and under all conditions be the leader, and be the channel through which the affairs of the people should be cared for; that he should think out what is best for the people and for the protection of the people. The male has always been the mastermind.[130]

Tukino's voice was in the minority, however, and the 1919 Women's Parliamentary Rights Act enabled women to enter New Zealand's Lower House, the House of Representatives, although the Upper House, the Legislative Council, remained closed to them. It was a matter of enormous satisfaction to the tireless campaigners in women's organisations such as the WCTU and the National Council of Women who believed that women required a voice in Parliament to claim their rights.

Ellen Melville, Rosetta Baume and Aileen Cooke put themselves forward for the election held just weeks after the passing of the Act. Ellen Melville was the second New Zealand woman to become a qualified lawyer. As an unmarried professional woman, she remained firm in her belief that women had a duty to serve their communities. Partnership provided the 'best government', she believed, a partnership 'drawing on the talents of both sexes and all classes'.[131] 'We have only ourselves to blame,' she stated, if 'governments and government departments take no interest in women.'[132] Of the three candidates, she was the only one born in New Zealand and the sole female candidate with party backing. She stood for the Reform Party, which had come together in 1909 and promoted the interests of rural conservatives in opposition to the Liberals.

Weaving was an integral part of the lives of Māori women, who continued to develop exceptional skill in this art-form through the changing world of the nineteenth century. Feather cloaks, or kahu huruhuru, were greatly treasured, and worn on ceremonial occasions. While new materials such as wool or peacock feathers were often incorporated, this prestigious cloak was made entirely of orange kākā feathers, woven into a base of muka (processed flax). *Museum of New Zealand Te Papa Tongarewa, Wellington, ME015838*

At the same time as women were granted access to Parliament, the organisation of political parties was strengthening. Like the earlier conservative grouping in the Reform Party, socialist and labour organisations had coalesced into the Labour Party in 1916. Their success in turn prompted organised opposition, and in 1936 the National Party emerged, committed to halting state regulation of the economy.[133] Political parties 'tamed' the impact of the democratic franchise, making candidates more responsible to the party, the leader and national issues rather than to the specific class or gender interests of the electors.[134] Parties were also 'men's clubs'.[135]

Ellen Melville experienced the impact of the men's club at both the national and local political level. Although she polled very well for Reform in her traditionally Labour Grey

Lynn electorate, winning 30.9 per cent of the vote to Labour's 36.5 per cent, the Reform Party replaced her with a male candidate at the next election. To add insult to injury, the new candidate was a former Liberal. 'The only conclusion to be taken,' Melville commented, 'was that they did not want a woman in Parliament. They preferred a Liberal man to a Reform woman.'[136] On the Auckland City Council, Melville was twice passed over for the role of deputy mayor (in 1938 and 1941) at a time when, as Sandra Coney writes, 'she should have won by virtue of her seniority in council and her ability'.[137] One of the ironies lay in the fact that the political 'men's clubs' were underpinned by the work of women who 'washed the dishes, made scones and cakes, served, ran dances and card parties'.[138]

Compelled by her sense of civic duty and her commitment to women's issues, Ellen Melville stood for Parliament, unsuccessfully, seven times. She was one of the three women who stood in the 1922 election and one of the five who contested the 1928 election. That year saw the entry of Elizabeth McCombs to the parliamentary contest, as the first woman to stand for the Labour Party. Like Melville, McCombs played a major role in local government, as a member of the Christchurch City Council and the North Canterbury Hospital Board in 1921, and the Tramway Board from 1927. A committed prohibitionist and Labour Party activist, McCombs stood as the candidate for Kaiapoi in 1928 and for Christchurch North in 1931. She became the first woman to enter Parliament when she won the 1933 by-election called after the death of her husband, James McCombs, who had held the Lyttelton seat since 1913.[139]

Nearly forty years to the day since New Zealand women had won the right to vote, Elizabeth McCombs' election was cause for celebration among women Labour supporters and women around the world. On the night of 13 September 1933, thousands of Christchurch citizens gathered in the wet and rain outside the offices of the *Star* to hear the results of the election.[140] McCombs won by a stunning 2,500 votes over her male opponent – a vast improvement on her husband's 56-vote majority in 1931. Elizabeth McCombs saw the result as a 'step forward in the women's movement'.[141] Many could only agree, since the defeated Independent Labour candidate E. L. Hills had aligned himself with Hitler's view that 'the woman's place is in the home', adding that 'the difficulties of the country are too great for women to grapple with'.[142] Kate Sheppard, who had fought for so long to see women 'sitting side by side with men in the legislative assemblies', lived to see that happen. She died on 13 July 1934.[143]

Awaiting her introduction to the House, McCombs read a congratulatory telegram from Mrs Corbett Ashby, president of the International Women's Suffrage Alliance in London. The Australian Federation of Women voters wrote of their hope that the opening of the door of Parliament 'will allow other women to follow'.[144] But not all were delighted, and a rumour spread that when McCombs first rose to speak, six people from Te Arawa who were in the visitors' gallery rose and left, explaining later 'their belief that it was not woman's role to be involved in politics and public speaking'.[145] The Revd

H. W. Munroe, a member of the Te Arawa party, described the story as 'fantastic' and said that no such discourtesy to Mrs McCombs was intended.[146] Members of the group had simply left at different times when they became bored by the debate. Apirana Ngata suggested that too much had been made of the incident; although one elderly Arawa man had expressed 'his impatience' at a woman being allowed to speak in the House, women in some tribes certainly did have that right and had even spoken on behalf of their people at Waitangi celebrations.[147]

McCombs was forthright in her belief that women's voices should be heard. Mothers had 'a great stake' in the 'good government' of the country, she said, and women had played an important part in building the nation. She committed herself to serving the welfare of all, and used her maiden speech to highlight the plight of unemployed youths and women. As a consequence of her election, the 'No Women Permitted' sign over Bellamy's dining room in Parliament was removed, the wording of the swearing in was altered, and 'members' rather than 'gentlemen' now participated in the House.[148]

McCombs' dedication to the Labour cause was marked on the occasion of her funeral, just fifteen months after she entered Parliament. Three hundred trade union members led the procession, employees of the Tramway Board formed a guard of honour, and thousands of Christchurch citizens lined the streets to pay their respects to their member of Parliament, who had been a 'fearless fighter' for the less fortunate.[149]

Transforming needs into rights

The 1930s Depression exposed the paucity of assistance for those thrown into poverty, and increased pressure on the state to provide a coherent system of relief. Labour activist Margaret Thorn provides an example of the political contribution women could make to planning improved welfare. Thorn was a committed socialist who had founded the Miramar branch of the Labour Party in the 1920s, while at the same time raising three children on a minimal budget and writing for the socialist *Maoriland Worker*. Appalled by the conditions facing women in the early 1930s, and by the injustice of their being ineligible for relief, she and Margaret Semple (married to Labour politician Robert Semple) founded the Wellington-based Unemployed Women Workers Association in 1932. The newly formed Women's Branch of the Unemployed Workers' Movement in Dunedin also decided to 'put their men's inactivity to shame' in the face of miserly relief policies, and marched on the local relief depot on 8 April 1932. The gloved hands of the city's mayoress as she dispensed food made her a particular target of the group's contempt for the rules and regulations surrounding entitlement to relief. The demonstration turned riotous and the crowd attempted to overturn the mayoress's car.[150]

When Margaret Thorn's husband Jim became Labour candidate for the Thames seat in 1935, she canvassed 'every town and hamlet' from Cape Colville to Te Aroha. Everywhere she stopped, 'the miners' wives gave us comfortable beds and delicious meals'.[151] Other

Unemployed workers and union supporters, led by women, take part in a May Day demonstration at Christchurch in 1932, with a large crowd looking on. *Hocken Collections/Te Uare Taoka o Hākena, University of Otago Library, Dunedin, P1998-028/02-002*

women were active too. One woman supporter of Labour's policies stood for Parliament as an Independent in the Northern Māori electorate in 1935. Rehutai Maihi of Ngāpuhi was descended from Hongi Hika on her father's side and from Patuone, elder brother of Tamati Waka Nene, on her mother's side.[152] It was this high lineage, according to one report, that allowed her to 'overcome the aversion' of elders to women going into politics.[153] A prominent tennis player and experienced journalist, Rehutai Maihi made the improved welfare of women and children the 'main plank' of her platform.[154] In the event, she polled only 156 votes against Tau Henare, who was resoundingly returned for the Coalition (which became the National Party the following year).[155] It would be another fourteen years before Iriaka Ratana became the first Māori woman member of Parliament.

Labour's promises to introduce a decent standard of living for all through the redistribution of resources meant that the 1935 election generated great excitement throughout the country. The promise of an income sufficient to provide a man and his family with everything necessary to make a '"home" and "home life" in the best sense of the meaning of those terms' spoke to Labour's commitment to the Pākehā nuclear family.[156] And it was a powerful message that appealed to many voters. The pivotal figure in 'home life' was, of course, the mother. Women and children were classed together as dependants,

Orderly rows of shoes, donated to be given to wives of unemployed men, fill a large room. The photograph was taken in February 1932. *Alexander Turnbull Library, Wellington, PAColl-6304-33*

to be provided for by the male wage earner. Motherhood and the home were an anchor and a refuge, providing a sense of stability in a changing world.[157]

Once in power, Labour set about implementing its vision of a nation of working men supporting their wives and children by ensuring the passage of the 1936 Industrial Conciliation and Arbitration Amendment Act. The Act solidified the informal practice of higher wage rates for men, on the basis that a man's wage would be supporting a couple with three children (as the family norm). Wives, in this calculation, were assumed not to be in paid employment. As a consequence, the Arbitration Court set the minimum rate for women workers at 47 per cent that of male workers. Elizabeth McCombs' son, Terence, who succeeded her in Parliament, justified this disparity during debate on the Act in these terms: 'a living wage has to provide for an average family'.[158] The economic independence of the male breadwinner was supposed to act as a guarantee of the support of his wife and children. Single working women, who were assumed not to have dependants, could therefore be paid less.

The all-male Parliament quickly embarked on a series of economic reforms to underpin its aim of providing more generous levels of entitlement to welfare, free of the taint of charity. Pensions were an immediate target of reform, and the Pension Amendment Act

1936 provided, for the first time, pensions for invalids and deserted wives. A deserted wife was to be treated 'as if she were a widow', although access to the benefit was hedged around with restrictions. Historian Margaret McClure cites one woman recipient of this pension expressing her heartfelt gratitude to the prime minister: 'There are many like myself, refined, sensitive, and too proud to accept charity of any kind, so you can understand why tears of joy came to my eyes when I realized what this pension would mean to me ...'[159]

Catherine Stewart had been an ardent suffragette in Glasgow before emigrating to New Zealand in 1921. In Wellington she threw herself into work for the Labour Party, believing that 'the men needed women to give the women's viewpoint in affairs of state'.[160] In 1938, she received the party's endorsement to run for the newly created seat of Wellington West, focusing her campaign on the far-reaching nature of the social security legislation proposed by Labour. Decent old-age pensions, a medical service that would be free to all, increased accessibility of education and good-quality housing were part of the package promised by Labour.[161] Stewart's win in the 1938 election bucked the trend which saw a reduced majority for the party.

The Social Security Act 1938, introduced just over four weeks after the election, became the occasion for celebration as families realised that superannuation would become universal, the Family Benefit would increase and they would no longer have to pay for doctors' bills. Janet Frame, in her autobiography *To the Is-land*, recalled how her family immediately threw the doctor's bills onto the fire.[162] The Minister of Agriculture, W. Lee Martin, described the Act as 'the greatest piece of humanitarian legislation in the world'.[163]

Labour's stated commitment to equality between Māori and Pākehā did not play out in the implementation of the Social Security Act, however. Section 72(2) allowed discretion in the payment of benefits, meaning that Māori continued to be treated as if they had fewer needs.[164] In other respects, the Act treated Māori the same as Pākehā when they may, in fact, have preferred different services. The state, financed by taxpayers, took over the cost of maternity care and hence accelerated the move from home to hospital births, even though the latter were not widely sought by Māori women. With the provision of free maternity and hospital care, and subsidised visits to the doctor, what were once seen as individual needs became translated into rights. This state commitment to providing care was the culmination of a shift towards increased state concern for the health of children that had begun with government support for the Plunket Society, and been extended with the School Medical Service, which from 1912 monitored the health of school children. Mothers' role as guardians of their families' health was increasingly subject to oversight in the interests of the health of the nation. Because they were predominantly rurally based, Māori were less likely to be subject to state intervention, but they were also less likely to receive state support.

Under the Social Security Act, men and women, Māori and Pākehā, were to be rewarded for their respective labours through universal superannuation. Women became entitled to equal superannuation rights, 'regardless of their own level of tax contributions or whether their life's work had been paid or unpaid, and irrespective of the level of their husband's contributions'.[165] Men were also given a new equality in that their age of entitlement was lowered from sixty-five to sixty, to match the eligibility age of women. Women's right to support in old age, regardless of contribution, was consistent with Labour's commitment to the family and a recognition of women's work in the home.

Single women workers were not forgotten under the Social Security Act, which entitled them to an unemployment benefit. But this was not available to married women workers; instead, unemployed married men received additional sums for their wives and children. The nation needed children to shore up the declining Pākehā birth rate; children needed mothers to care for their health and welfare; and married women's rights were regarded as subsidiary to these needs. Miriam Soljak protested in the pages of *Woman Today* that the legislation showed 'the general disregard of the claims of women to equal consideration in legislation, and the inherent tendency of our legislation of all parties to treat a married woman as an appendage of her husband'.[166] Elsie Andrews, long active in the Women's Teachers' Association, wrote to the *Otago Daily Times* in 1939:

> Man's potential fatherhood does not dominate but remains subordinate to his standing as an individual. The same is true of women's potential motherhood. Primarily she is an individual; secondarily, she may be a mother as well, hence the claim that women teachers, and indeed all women, must be allowed to decide for themselves whether to retire from or continue in gainful occupation after marriage.[167]

The focus on motherhood as the purpose of female existence was increasingly being contested by a new generation of women who experienced independent working lives in the growing towns. As one said, 'All a flapper wanted to do was to have a jolly gay time.' The war was over, the men were back 'and we felt we had no cares'.[168] Rising hemlines and boyish silhouettes provided the external signs of changing aspirations.

Evelyn Page's sensitive portrait of her friend, musician Valmai Moffett, was exhibited several times during the 1930s. Page was known for her love of vibrant colour and painted many memorable portraits during her long artistic career.
Dunedin Public Art Gallery, 11-1966

Chapter Eight

The 'Modern Woman' of the Interwar Years

A full-page photograph of Gladys Sandford – 'Our Pioneer Aviatrix' – clad in her aviator's jacket and helmet, and staring out purposefully, graced the front of the pictorial section of the *New Zealand Free Lance* in December 1925. On the following page was a photograph taken at the women's exhibit at the Dunedin South Seas Exhibition of a much older woman ('great grandmother') dressed in a long gown and a crocheted shawl, concentrating on spinning her raw wool. If the women's exhibit with its display of handicrafts suggested the continuity of women's past roles in their interests in the present, Gladys Sandford represented something fundamentally different: a woman going places never gone before and soaring to new heights through her own determination.[1] The ambitions of young women – wearing shingled hairstyles, smoking cigarettes and pursuing new pastimes – unsettled some of the older generation in the interwar years. Freud was not alone, in 1925, in asking, 'What does woman want?'[2]

The First World War had widened the horizons of a generation of women coming to adulthood in the 1910s. By 1918, young women were no longer chaperoned, nor expected to wear ankle-length skirts, with their long hair tied up signifying their adulthood. But as the relative economic buoyancy of the 1920s gave way to the hard times of the 1930s, the everyday difficulties of earning a living made the aspirational fashions and lifestyles displayed in a new wave of Hollywood movies seem even harder to attain. The feats of glamorous young women on screen and in the air also led to new discontents between the promise of fulfilment in marriage and the loss of independence (gained through work) that marriage and motherhood brought. While Pākehā women might resist large families, Māori families increased in size, and initiatives supported by Apirana Ngata in Parliament and carried to fruition by Te Puea Herangi in communities gave those families new futures.

The Depression helped undermine the expectation that only men were breadwinners, but the employment of married women remained contentious. The reach of the state into the lives of its citizens was extended by the 1935 Labour government's commitment to security from 'the cradle to the grave'. Such state initiatives did not overly intrude on the

Aviator Jean Batten acknowledges the crowds who had gathered to greet her after one of her epic flights in the 1930s. In 1936 she made the first direct flight ever from England to New Zealand. *Auckland War Memorial Museum Tāmaki Paenga Hira, PH-NEG-C45347*

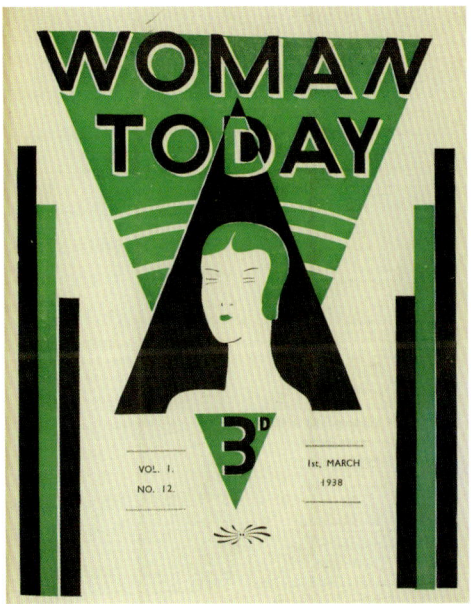

Left Woman Today, published from 1937 to 1939, was founded by a group of women including Elsie Locke. It discussed issues that were controversial at the time, including contraception, abortion, divorce reform, childcare and equal pay. *Right* This 1930 poster for Christchurch department store Ballantynes advertises the latest in women's fashions. Woman Today, *March 1938, Vol 1 No 12, Alexander Turnbull Library, Wellington; Museum of New Zealand Te Papa Tongarewa, Wellington, GH015776*

lives of rural Māori families, although the provision of welfare benefits drew them into a system that required legal marriage and birth certificates. But by 1939, war was on the horizon again. Just what that would mean in women's lives remained uncertain.

Working lives

If the glamorous Jean Batten in her white flying suit represented the height of modernity in a way most could not aspire to, young women found a variety of new opportunities in the workforce in the early decades of the twentieth century. 'The world is changing,' John Vigor Brown from Napier declared in the House of Representatives in 1918:

> Women are carrying out the work of men, and, all things being equal, they should be paid accordingly. In many of the suburban branches of the [Postal and Telegraph] Department women have been in charge during the war, and the fact that they have been retained in their positions is an indication that they have successfully carried out the duties that the men formerly performed.[3]

By 1921, over 50 per cent of young women between the ages of fifteen and twenty-four were in paid employment, compared to about 39 per cent in 1891, and an increasing number of those were in 'white blouse' service occupations, which increased nationally from 7.2 per cent in 1901 to 29.7 per cent in 1936.[4] In contrast, the number of married women in employment, about 6 per cent in 1916 (because of war needs), had dropped to 4 per cent in 1926 and 1936.[5]

Teachers, nurses and social workers were all socially acceptable roles for women, as serving the needs of the young, the sick and the distressed had long been regarded as women's preserve. New professions such as dental nursing – a New Zealand innovation – also called on the idea of women's special skills.[6] Setting up the dental nurse scheme, T. A. Hunter of the Education Department suggested 'as a general rule women were temperamentally better adapted for handling young children'. The nurses would be under the direction of qualified dentists and would work at schools during school hours, relieving male dentists of having to deal with 'tired and fractious' children after school.[7] Any fears that the dental nurses might encroach on male employment were allayed by the Minister of Health's assurance that the women would 'not be able to practice [sic], except under the Education Department'.[8]

Women were increasingly employed by the state as its interest in health broadened under the Health Act 1920. The Act created seven divisions, dealing with hospitals, school hygiene, public hygiene, dental hygiene, child welfare, Māori hygiene, and nursing. The latter, predictably, was the only one to be headed by a woman: Hester Maclean. As Assistant Inspector of Hospitals since 1906, she had encouraged the backblocks district nursing scheme, the training of Māori women as nurses to work in their own communities, the development of the school nursing service and improved midwifery training.[9]

Earlier pioneers of nursing saw their profession as a lifetime vocation, one that involved duty and dedication. They were critical of the 'modern nurse' entering the profession in the interwar years who sought 'the pleasures of life which are so generously offered'. Such young women appeared to be attracted by nursing as a 'means to a livelihood' rather than 'a desire to nurse the sick and help the poor'.[10] To an older generation of nurses, a focus on achievements had displaced an important emphasis on character.[11] The 'modern nurse' of the interwar years was younger, less likely to be motivated by religion, and had a higher standard of education. She was also, perhaps, more likely to chafe at the requirement to live in a nurses' home under supervision, with no late leave while under probation, and thereafter a 10 p.m. curfew six night a week and 11 p.m. once a week.[12] To maintain their social lives, nurses would return at 10 p.m., check in and leave again later via the window. Unlucky enough to get caught, nurse Betty Hunter was dismissed from Dunedin Hospital in 1923 for being out all night with a medical student – an incident that, presumably, had no impact on his career.[13]

Māori women were not always welcomed into nursing training, and those who were might suffer in an environment that paid no heed to their language or their cultural practices. Unlikely to be employed in the hospitals, however, they were invaluable in the Māori health service. Mirika Wehipeihana, of Ngāti Tukorohe and Ngāti Raukawa, trained as a nurse at Waikato Hospital, graduating in 1924. She completed a postgraduate qualification in midwifery at St Helen's Hospital, Wellington, the following year. Her first appointment, in 1926, was as a district nurse for the East Coast area. Supported by Apirana Ngata, she taught Māori women infant and family health care on the marae. In 1934, after taking further training in the prevention and treatment of tuberculosis, she became responsible for monitoring the disease in Waiapu county on the rugged East Coast. In this predominantly Māori area, she piloted a tuberculosis hut scheme as a means of segregating patients without their having to leave their communities – an initiative that was taken up nationally.[14]

For women who dedicated themselves to teaching, some found a lifelong and satisfying career that offered other important social roles as well. Irene Paulger trained as a teacher in Dunedin, qualifying in the early 1920s. Her first appointment was at the Nūhaka Native School in Hawke's Bay. In April 1925, she went deep into the Urewera to develop a government school for the people of Maungapōhatu. In that isolated environment, living with few amenities, she 'became nurse, post-mistress, registrar of births and deaths, and "mother" to several children'.[15] The number of adult women primary teachers had grown during the First World War (to 3,394 in 1919, compared to 1,606 men), but began to decline in the 1920s because an increase in salary for sole-teacher schools attracted men into the profession. In deference to their status as breadwinners and heads of households, men were concentrated in the better-paid head-teacher positions. Women predominated as lowly paid assistant teachers, reflecting the expectation that their work was a temporary interlude before marriage.[16]

Teaching seemed the obvious choice for tertiary-educated young women. Phoebe Norris (later Meikle) recalled that she 'didn't know' why she went to Auckland University College in 1928. But there she found the joys of acting in student productions and 'the pleasures of coffee evenings; of ping-pong, played in a room next door to the men's students' common room and thus an excellent place for meeting young men; and of playing in the B basketball team'.[17] College life with 1,300 students was intimate, but staff were distant, the college run by men, and formalities included the wearing of gowns. Phoebe nonetheless made lifelong friends as she embarked on her training for secondary school teaching.[18]

Young women like Phoebe, whether Māori or Pākehā, saw that they would have very different lives from those of their mothers. Many of the anxieties about the woman's sphere in the interwar years arose from tensions between young women's traditional expectations – that they would make marriage and domesticity their career – and the new opportunities available to them for education, work and mobility. The prewar expectation that young women would remain at home under the control of their parents, helping out with domestic tasks between school and marriage, was largely eroded by the 1920s, although parents might still expect to determine suitable employment for their daughters. Pākehā women worked in factories, offices, hospitals, schools and restaurants, while Māori women were more likely to find agricultural work, whether through choice or necessity.

Dorothy Bogle and Margaret Vincent take a break for a cigarette while working in George Northcroft's cowshed in 1923. Farm work of various kinds, such as milking cows, tending crops, and assisting with shearing, occupied many women, both Māori and Pākehā. *Macmillan Brown Library, University of Canterbury, Christchurch, 18958*

Country gatherings often included sports and competitions – some more lighthearted than others. These women participate in a running race 'for married ladies over 45' in 1931. *Alexander Turnbull Library, Wellington, 1/2-C-016197-F*

Mere Hall, principal of Hukarere School in Napier, noted the limited demand for Māori women as teachers and nurses in 1930: 'It is not easy for a Maori girl to get work even if she wanted it ever so much.'[19]

Domestic service remained a key occupation, but it was less attractive than work that offered shorter hours, more companionship and less constant surveillance. A number of parents no longer wished their daughters to train in domestic subjects, supporting their move into the commercial training in typing and shorthand offered by the technical colleges.[20] But though they had new opportunities, daughters were not necessarily free to do just as they wanted. Thelma McMillan, the first Miss New Zealand in 1926, was offered a Hollywood film test. Her mother 'would not allow it, and Thelma simply went back to work' in the Dunedin department store Arthur Barnett's, where she was 'mortified' at the crowds who came to 'gawk' at her.[21]

Change was afoot in rural areas too. 'Flocks of farm women', according to the *New Zealand Dairy Exporter*, were providing the bulk of the country's eggs but producing them at a loss. The magazine called for women instructors to advise women how to succeed in running profitable poultry businesses, since 'success in keeping poultry mainly depends on attention to detail and real cleanliness, and in these matters women certainly have an advantage'.[22] And if New Zealand followed Britain's lead, the next sensible move would be to appoint women as dairy-herd testers. Such a job 'would be an excellent livelihood for country girls who otherwise would have to seek city occupations'.[23] The Government Seed

Testing Station in Manawatū, the magazine argued, also provided an example of a new kind of employment for young women with 'keen eyesight and deft fingers'. The women applied science to seeds in 'an example of co-ordinated efficiency'.[24]

In most blue-collar occupations, women's ability to compete against men for jobs was severely limited by the Arbitration Court, which set awards determining minimum wages and working conditions. These might include clauses excluding women or limiting the ratio of women to men. Awards that did include women would specify maximum weights they could lift and designated the provision of facilities, such as rest rooms, both of which acted as disincentives to employers.

The 1919 Whakatane Freezing Works Employees' agreement with the East Coast Co-operative Freezing Company specified that no female workers were to be employed in the freezing industry.[25] The Poverty Bay Freezing Works' agreement made an exception, allowing women to work 'in the bag room'.[26] Working with raw meat in freezing works and butcher shops was a masculine preserve (despite women's acknowledged skills in the kitchen), perhaps maintaining older traditions about the dangers of menstruating women around foods in 'certain states of transition'.[27] For some unknown reason, a special provision covered pork butcher shops, allowing women over seventeen years to be employed as shop assistants.[28] By 1930, the New Zealand Refrigeration Company was employing women in the preserving department to shave beef and lambs' tongues and place them in tins, and to perform the finishing stages of trimming meat. The Arbitration Court held that, because 'all the rough work' was performed by men and the women's tasks were 'in no sense heavy', the work was suitable for them.[29]

The exclusion of female labour from various workplaces and from apprenticeships helped to maintain male pay rates, and reinforced the masculinity of certain types of employment. When women were employed for certain processes, such as chain-making by manufacturing jewellers, their tasks were detailed in the relevant award, and they were not to be apprenticed to the trade: the expectation was that their work was temporary and that they themselves were easily expendable.[30] In the boot and shoe industry, women making boots were called 'assistants' rather than apprentices as a way of limiting their participation in the trade and ensuring they could be replaced easily.[31] Some awards, such as that of the South Canterbury Bakers and Pastry Cooks, allowed the employment of women when men were not available, and in Wellington women in the bakery trade were able 'to perform certain skilled operations for which they are particularly suited, at a rate equivalent to two thirds the journeyman's rate'.[32] In other workplaces, women's participation was limited by ratios set in awards. The Northern, Wellington, Canterbury, Otago and Southland General Warehouseman's award stipulated separate pay rates for women, and set a ratio of one woman for every three men employed in a warehouse.[33]

As horse-drawn transport gave way to cars, the question arose as to whether women could be employed in the expanding motor trade as garage attendants. In 1928, the

Top Brought up on farms and later married to a farmer, Elizabeth Lissaman taught herself to make and fire pottery in the 1920s, and produced all kinds of domestic ware including plates, bowls, mugs, jugs, jars, condiment sets and ashtrays. She was one of New Zealand's pioneer potters. *Alexander Turnbull Library, Wellington, PAColl-0785-1-109-006*

Bottom Nell Garrick of Christchurch was an expert in making tapestries. She was photographed at work in February 1938. *Alexander Turnbull Library, Wellington, PAColl-8983-66*

Māori women clean fish in a canning factory north of Auckland, 1930s. *Photograph by Percival Frederick Nash, Auckland War Memorial Museum Tāmaki Paenga Hira, PH-NEG-H404*

Arbitration Court decided that much of the work required in garages was 'unsuitable' for women, so the relevant award was not intended to cover them.[34] In the most masculine of worlds, that of bottlers and brewers, there was little change over time. In 1938, women were still excluded from working in breweries, malthouses and bottle stores.[35]

Māori women in the north might find work in forestry nurseries, for the New Zealand Tobacco Company and, 'to a very limited extent', in local hotels. They were less likely to find work in Auckland hotels 'on account of colour'.[36] A deaconess, Sister Ivy, ran a club for Māori girls under the auspices of the Auckland Methodist Mission, and thirty-seven of the women who attended had jobs: some in hotels, and some as domestic servants in private homes or boarding houses.[37]

Where women were employed in numbers – in textile, clothing and food-processing factories – women factory inspectors noted improved conditions by 1925. Rest rooms, cooking facilities, and provisions for washing and first aid were provided by employers. Nine Auckland 'soft-goods houses' (textile, clothing and bedding factories) took the lead in 1925 by forming an organisation for the health of 'girls', one even going so far as to purchase a large seaside cottage for use by employees as a 'convalescent or rest home'.[38] Maintaining the health of workers was now regarded as a 'paying proposition'.[39] Large firms could afford welfare measures such as hot lunches and libraries, but smaller operations

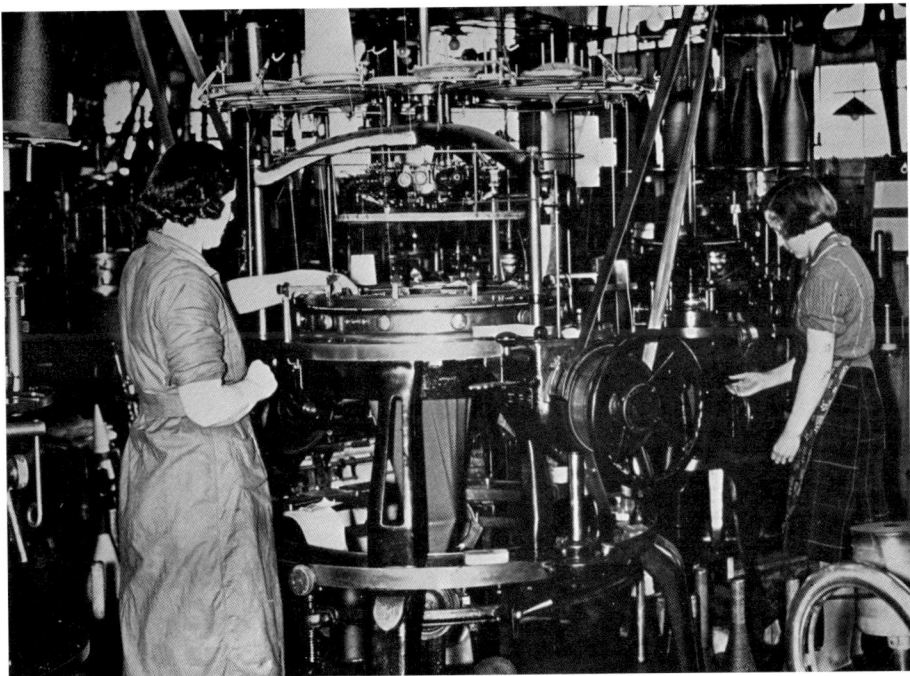

Staff work machinery for making knitted goods at the Manawatu Knitting Mills, Palmerston North, in 1939.
Pātaka Ipurangi – Manawatu Memory Online, Palmerston North City Library, 007N_Bc27_WOR_0079

that employed fewer than 100 workers (such as brush and broom makers, and hosiery, soap, candle and match manufacturers) were less likely to provide a range of amenities.

The movement of young women into the paid workforce both demanded that women look a certain way and gave them the means to pay for that look. Women hairdressers, dressmakers and milliners could earn well from the business of beauty. Between 1921 and 1936, the number of 'lady hairdressers' expanded rapidly, from 100 to 1,500 nationwide. Short-cut or 'bobbed' hair as seen in the world's fashion centres of London, Paris and New York became the rage; it was described as 'hygienic, labour-saving, and attractive'.[40] According to the *Auckland Star*, '[s]uffrage, war [and] new occupations for women' had led to a mannish look and 'a revolution in the status of women' in the 1920s.[41] Part of that revolution was one of style.

Consuming pleasures

The urban experience was, as historian Charlotte Macdonald has argued, 'central to modernity'.[42] A wage packet gave women of the 1920s a new degree of independence and created opportunities for businesses. 'You see young "flapper" girls in this town,' Legislative Councillor William Earnshaw commented of Wellington in 1925, 'receiving good money and dressing lavishly upon it.'[43] Annie, born in 1907, recalled that her first jobs

Young women shop assistants are shown at work in the homeware section of Watchorns Limited, a Palmerston North department store, in the 1930s. *Pātaka Ipurangi – Manawatu Memory Online, Palmerston North City Library, 007N_Bc69_WOR_0083*

after leaving school were minding children and housework. Then she left home. 'A friend and I went round these various places in New Zealand working at hotels, shops, milkbars. We had a lovely time. We did this until we were about 23 [in about 1930].'[44]

While modesty was still regarded as a female virtue, young women were now encouraged to put their bodies forward for assessment. Some young and single women paraded in bathing costumes in beach beauty contests, while others sought their moment of fame in film clips shown to cinema audiences who voted for the woman whose appearance pleased them the most. In 1927, Dale Austen, the reigning Miss New Zealand and former Miss Otago, was awarded a first-class return trip to Los Angeles and a 'studio engagement' with Metro-Goldwyn-Mayer in Hollywood as part of her prize. She played minor roles in several films before achieving prominence as the second female lead in *The Bushranger*, supposedly set in Australia though filmed in California. She decided against an extended contract and returned home, saying later: 'The Hollywood swinging scene was parties, drinking, sex … I didn't drink. I wasn't prepared for the fast life.' Back in New Zealand, Austen appeared in two of pioneer film-maker Rudall Hayward's films, *A Daughter of Dunedin* and *A Bush Cinderella*.[45]

Universal Pictures came knocking at the door of Witarina Harris, of Ngāti Whakaue descent, whom Apirana Ngata had recommended to the film-makers as a possible star

Well-dressed women shoppers stand alongside a display of 'Serenade' beauty creams in a Wellington department store in 1938. *Photograph by Gordon Burt, Alexander Turnbull Library, Wellington, 1/1-015466-F*

for a new New Zealand film. Witarina, an accomplished typist, had been chosen to work for Harold Hamilton at the newly established Maori Arts and Crafts School in Rotorua in 1927. It was there that the American film-makers found her, and after her screen test they decided she was right for their silent film telling a Māori love story in which the young puhi (high-ranking virgin) resists marriage to the man chosen for her by her tribe.[46] The film, advertised as 'New Zealand's First Movietone Triumph', was accompanied by 'Maori Songs and Melodies'.[47]

While *Under the Southern Cross* was a local film, American movies provided an important conduit for new fashions. Nothing distinguished the modern woman more than her dress, and the divide was most obvious between generations. Pearl, born in 1912, valued the independence work brought her, and even on 'low wages I'd managed to keep myself well dressed', as well as saving money and accumulating her trousseau.[48] In rural communities, too, young unmarried Māori women 'generally [tried] to follow fashionable models in their clothing'. One study noted:

> They think of their clothing in terms of sports clothes, afternoon dresses, formal or dance outfits, the sort of distinction that is completely foreign to the older married women or the old women. These younger girls also try to build up a wardrobe of clothes together

with appropriate toiletries and underclothing that the fashionable women's magazines emphasize as being essential to the well-dressed young lady. Or if these girls cannot follow this advice in practice, it is their secret dream to do so. The girls also paint their fingernails, use lipstick, rouge, and silk stockings, and perhaps experiment with exotic hairdressing. Again, none of these things are done by the older married women or old ladies, who are content to remain Maori according to their own fashion. Whereas the younger girls are more or less consciously imitating the middle-class pakeha version of Hollywood fashions.[49]

Sports clothes and uniforms became more common as participation in sport moved beyond the leisured few. Exercise was seen to be essential to women's health, and sports organisations proliferated in the interwar years. Lifesaving teams wore identical bathing suits; gym frocks allowed greater freedom of movement for hockey and basketball players; and the new sport of marching was in part distinguished by its inventive uniforms. Service organisations such as the Girl Guides (1923), the Girls' Brigade (1928) and the YWCA Girl Citizen Movement, founded in 1923 with the aim of increasing knowledge of a citizen's rights and duties, all promoted physical recreation as well as spiritual development.[50] Older prohibitions that prevented menstruating girls from physical activities were gradually rethought as girls stayed longer at school and participated more fully in the curriculum.

Company-sponsored teams allowed young women to carry on the sports they may have begun at school. Cadbury Fry Hudson's Dunedin-based biscuit and confectionery company employed more than 300 young women, some of whom participated in two basketball teams and the 'very keen' B-grade hockey team. Hilda Maher, who worked at Dunedin's Wax Vesta match factory, recalled: 'we had a netball team, we had a marching team, we played tennis'.[51] The marching team's uniforms, based on the colour of the matchboxes – green, red and yellow – had skirts that, daringly, ended well above the knee. What would have been unseemly prior to the First World War became standard as young women took to sporting and other leisure activities with enthusiasm.

Modernity was also signified by the hunger for constant reinvention through fashion.[52] In the main centres, department stores beguiled customers by offering 'ready-to-wear' dresses, the latest fashions in millinery and 'chic Lingerie'.[53] Fashion provided women with 'a sensual and social pleasure'.[54] The mid-afternoon fashion parades – obviously aimed at leisured women – held at stores like Collinson & Cunningham in Palmerston North brought middle-class women together to enjoy live music and view models showing the 'newest gowns for day and evening wear'.[55]

Not all approved of young women's new freedoms, fearing that feminine graces were being lost in the clamour for new boyish fashions and public display. 'Shingled or bobbed,' warned the *New Zealand Free Lance* in 1925, 'the transformation to a race of boys in skirts is complete.'[56] Members of the New Zealand Club – well-off women who grouped together for social and intellectual companionship – were said to 'almost unanimously' disapprove

Elegance in footwear has always been important. Clockwise from top left: black buttoned boots, about 1900; black Cuban heeled shoes, about 1900; cream shoes with buckles, about 1929; green platform shoes, 1940s; brown leather and suede shoes, about 1930; and pink embellished shoes, about 1902. *From top left: Museum of New Zealand Te Papa Tongarewa, Wellington, PC001127; PC000948; PC003404/1; PC004272; PC004013; PC002507*

of bobbed hair.[57] 'Flappers' were seen as 'good-time' girls and as fair game for cartoonists, who delighted in depicting their reckless driving or devising lines such as 'a flapper a day separates a sailor from his pay'.[58] The *Ladies' Mirror* conveyed the anxiety about young women's behaviour by reproducing a London photograph of two young women motorcyclists sharing a light for a cigarette. The caption read: '"Mere Man" is being elbowed out of a sport he once regarded as his exclusive domain by those he once dubbed the "weaker sex". Not only that, but his attire and habits are being sedulously aped.'[59] Climbing hemlines, a slim silhouette and bobbed hair signified a growing generational divide, not only in fashion but, some feared, also in morality: 'youth became a symbol of the modern age'.[60] An *Auckland Star* cartoon of 1929 showed a 'grandmother' inquiring of a 'flapper' what kind of wedding she had been to, and the 'flapper' responding: 'Oh, a pretty binding sort, I should think'. New attitudes were abroad, amongst them the possibility that permanent relationships were not the only option.[61]

Modern marriage

The behaviour of young women living away from traditional communities worried Māori elders. Their concern was not just about the independence that came from earning an individual wage; it was also about the traditional expectations of whānau and male honour. In a rural context, where Māori values prevailed and were understood, the wider community could exercise control. This was much more difficult to assert in urban areas, which offered young women like Witarina Harris, born in Ōhinemutu in 1906, new opportunities.

Witarina's family lived near the busy Papaiōuru Marae, and her mother was a person of mana in the Ngāti Whakaue community. Witarina had been chosen by her grandfather to marry the oldest son of another local family: 'it would have been a binding of our two families, strengthening the mana of both'. But she fell in love with and wished to marry the young man's brother. Witarina's mother wouldn't have it: '[Y]ou turned his older brother down! Now you want to marry the youngest brother. Grow up. Over my dead body. You can't reject the older brother and then ask for the youngest!' So Witarina 'dropped' the younger brother. Soon afterwards, she left Rotorua for Wellington. In 1932, she married a Pākehā without asking her mother's permission. 'I think she was disappointed,' Witarina recalled, 'but she accepted the situation. And she couldn't do enough for us.' Her husband's father, an Englishman who had never met a Māori before, was disapproving, and did not speak to Witarina until her first son was nearly nine months old. 'I won him over,' she recalled, 'but it took a long time.'[62]

Another young Māori woman, Putiputi Onekawa, daughter of the Tūhoe leader and prophet Rua Kenana, was unable to escape the pressure to marry the man selected by her father and other Tūhoe elders, although she ran away a number of times. In May 1928, she finally gave in to family expectations and took up residence with the chosen man, signalling their marriage in the customary Māori fashion. Thirteen years later, and one month after the birth of their seventh child, the couple had a Christian wedding conducted by the Presbyterian missionary the Revd John Laughton.[63]

The continuation of customary marriage created difficulties for Māori in an increasingly bureaucratised state. Te Arahori Potaka, of Ngāti Tūwharetoa, met her husband, from Te Āti Haunui-a-Pāpārangi, in 1922. Te Arahori heard about the Family Benefit as the number of children in her family increased, and went to inquire about whether she would be eligible for it. She was asked for her marriage certificate:

> I said 'Well I haven't got one, but I'll soon get one.' Which I did. My husband was outside and I went out and said, 'Right, we're going down to the registry office. I can't get any family benefit unless we show them a marriage certificate.' We never worried about it [legal marriage] because we looked at the old people – that was their way of life. Once you sleep together, that's it, that's law as far as they're concerned. They say that the certificate is only man-made law.[64]

As the number of state benefits predicated on legal marriage grew, so too did the status of marriage itself.[65] 'I feel that in marriage I will find my greatest happiness,' one woman wrote in 1933:

> I am a young woman who wants to marry. I think that there are a great many girls like me – girls who work in offices and who are steady and intelligent and efficient in their jobs, yet who feel that they will not fulfil themselves until they are wives and mothers.[66]

'Marriage,' another woman recalled, 'was a form of freedom' – a freedom to organise her own house and time in ways that were impossible in the parental home, where the majority of young women resided before marriage.[67] The author of 'Home circle' in the *Maoriland Worker* wrote in 1922:

> Every woman, at the back of her mind, cherishes one dear dream – that some day she will have 'a home of her own'. It doesn't matter a scrap whether we work in a shop, an office, a factory, or in some one else's house, we're all 'sisters under one skin' in this matter of The Big Dream. A 'Home' of some kind is an absolute necessity to the woman who IS a woman.
>
>   So the 'Roomer' piles her cushions and books, hangs her curtains and pictures, and plays 'Let's Pretend'. By and bye, if Fate is kind, she will attain the Reality![68]

But the messages given by parents about how to attain this were not always straightforward. Gwen Alley's father prepared her for relationships with men by advising: 'If a man touches you in a certain place you are done for.' Gwen recalled:

> I did not know where this 'certain place' could be and even became sure I was 'done for' when a male cousin put his arm around my waist … I often lived from month to month in fear because while dancing my partner had squeezed me rather too tightly.[69]

This beautifully crafted mother and child doll was made around 1930 by Bessie Murray of Taihape. She was a widow and sold dolls like this one to help support her family. They were based on her observations of Māori women who used to sit on seats in front of the Taihape bakery shop. *Museum of New Zealand Te Papa Tongarewa, Wellington, PC004224*

Imported women's magazines often contained free sewing patterns for women's garments. Such patterns were essential when home sewing provided the main items in family members' wardrobes. These magazines were imported from the United Kingdom in the late 1920s and 1930s. *Museum of New Zealand Te Papa Tongarewa, Wellington, GH015238; GH015234*

During her study at Christchurch Teachers' College, Gwen became firm friends with Crawford Somerset, a fellow student with whom she exchanged books and ideas. Later, while teaching in Oxford, Canterbury, Gwen recommended Crawford (denied a teaching certificate because of severe osteoarthritis) for a relieving teaching position. Maintained through the years by correspondence, the intellectual companionship blossomed, and the couple became formally engaged in 1928 when Gwen was thirty-four. They married in January 1930.[70] Marrying at thirty-four was older than the norm, but many couples delayed marriage as economic circumstances tightened prior to and during the 1930s Depression. Households needed the income of all members, including adult daughters and sons, and the uncertainty of employment meant that the Pākehā mean age at marriage rose above twenty-six.[71] Long engagements were common, sometimes stretching for years, as young couples saved for a home of their own and young women assembled a trousseau of lingerie, a travelling dress and that most prized item: the wedding dress. When Ethel Rebecca Parker's fiancé broke off their engagement in 1928, she took action for 'Breach of Promise', claiming £75 for the cost of her trousseau and £350 for general damages.[72]

Unlike others who planned for their 'special day', twenty-two-year-old art student Rita Angus married Alfred Cook 'on the spur of the moment' in June 1930 – much to her family's surprise. The four-year marriage apparently was never consummated, but for Rita it may have afforded 'protection', enabling her to pursue her passion for painting and live

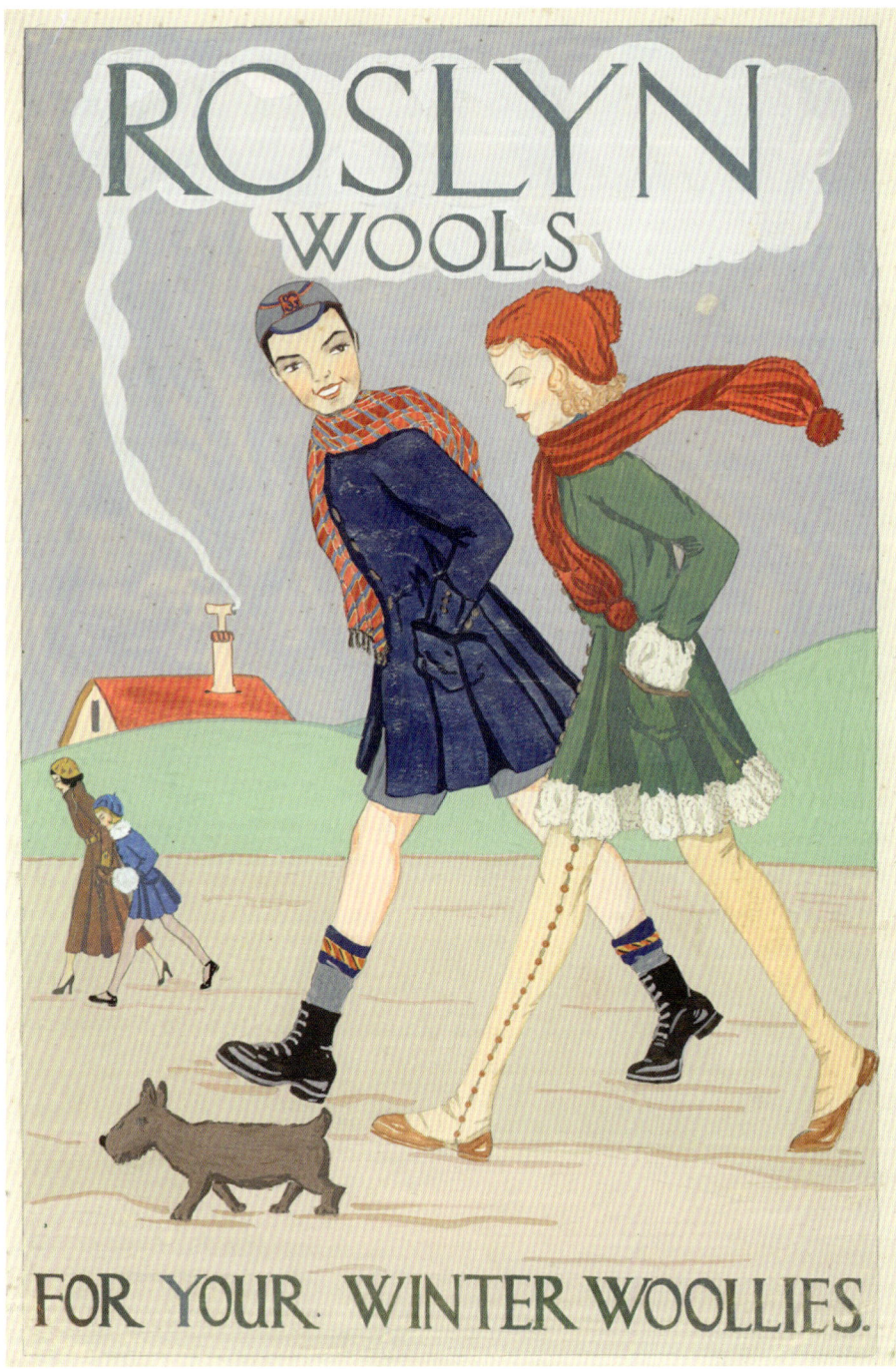

Knitting was a skilled craft practised by many women. This poster, designed by Heather Masters for Roslyn Woollen Mills in the 1930s, advertises knitting wools for winter garments. *Museum of New Zealand Te Papa Tongarewa, Wellington, GH015775*

Two women in fashionable cloche hats enjoy each other's company while one crochets a garment. They were photographed at Hastings in December 1925. *Photograph by Leslie Adkin, Museum of New Zealand Te Papa Tongarewa, Wellington, B.022306*

respectably with someone equally committed to art. In Alfred's company, Rita was able to travel to Auckland and study at the Elam Art School. In Christchurch she had role models in artist-couples such as Rata and Colin Lovell-Smith and Elizabeth and Cecil Kelly. These relationships appeared to allow the women 'to flourish' and sometimes exceed their partners' reputations as painters.[73]

For many other women, marriage provided a base from which to move not only into respectability but also into motherhood, and into increasing commitment to voluntary work as their children grew. Membership of the local Women's Institute could encompass a range of interests and social activities for both town and country women, including participation in plays and drama festivals.[74] At the Alicetown Women's Club's third birthday celebration in July 1936, the packed hall enjoyed the Glee Singers, followed by a song of welcome in te reo Māori. The assembled women admired the skilfully iced birthday cake and were amused by two comic impersonations, followed by solos by a Mrs Burgess and a violin item. A 'delightful and amusing' play by the Taita Women's Institute Drama Circle capped the evening off.[75]

In the midst of family life, women knitted and sewed, sketched and gardened, combining pleasure with their daily routine tasks. Reading and writing were other popular occupations for married women. Some sent in contributions to the *New Zealand Dairy Exporter*'s 'Farm Home Journal' section, which catered to the perceived interests of

Olivia Spencer Bower painted *The Verandah* about 1935, capturing life on the family farm in North Canterbury. The twin daughter of the artist Rosa Spencer Bower, Olivia studied at the Canterbury College School of Art and then the Slade School of Fine Art, London. After her return to New Zealand in 1931, she devoted her life to painting. *Collection of Christchurch Art Gallery Te Puna o Waiwhetu, bequeathed by an anonymous donor, 1968*

women and children, in response to a monthly set essay question. 'Should Mrs. B. leave her husband at home, when she has a holiday off the farm?' was the question for 1 April 1936.[76] The postbag bulged with replies, the editor reported, 'with quite a large proportion of our essayists apparently in favour of leaving Mr. B. to mind the farm while they sampled the joys of town life'.[77] The topics for June and July 1936 were 'The best age of life' and 'How can the women of the world combat the menace of war?' The August topic, 'What would you like to do if you were free to do it', brought responses ranging from the prize-winning desire to create a 'home' to submissions from those who wanted to leave home for 'a charming island', 'fit out a small sailing boat and set sail', or 'pilot an aeroplane'.[78] The latter signalled a feeling of constraint within the home at a time when the glamorous, single and fearless Jean Batten was achieving astonishing feats in the air.

Modern homes

Māori women were unlikely to be beneficiaries of the 'sweeping change' that proceeded apace in the interwar years: the domestic use of electricity. Electrification was announced in *The Young New Zealander incorporating New Zealand Woman and Home* as 'nowadays rapidly taking place in the equipment of houses, a change that makes any house, old or new, into a real *home*'. The article continued:

A row of state houses in Māhoe Street, Lower Hutt, was photographed in the 1930s. After the Labour Party came to power in 1935, thousands of state homes were built for lower and middle income families. *Alexander Turnbull Library, Wellington, MNZ-2154-1/2-F*

Woman's work under the old methods was 'never done,' her position in the home was that of the domestic drudge, and when the day was well advanced she dragged herself to bed, tired out.

Electricity, with its scientific application to cooking, water heating, clothes washing, sweeping, etc., emancipated the housewife from the worst forms of domestic drudgery. A mere turn of a switch abolishes for all time the filth and fumes of the old fashioned fires, of stoves, brooms and washtubs. More leisure hours are provided for mental and social recreation, and a touch of happiness is introduced that has hitherto been lacking.[79]

If electricity failed to introduce happiness, it did at least make some tiresome domestic tasks more bearable. Electric irons were often the first domestic appliances purchased, changing ironing from a process requiring the use of the stove to an independent activity.[80] Electric lights put an end to the constant maintenance of kerosene lamps and gas mantles. Electricity for cooking and water heating obviated the need to constantly maintain a coal range, and electric stoves may well have halved the time involved in cooking and keeping the kitchen clean. A drop in the price of electricity in the 1930s and successful advertising by supply authorities led to increased consumption.[81] The number of electric ranges sold by the Wellington City Corporation, for example, increased from 208 in 1927 to 3,915 in 1936.[82]

In spite of improvements in household technology and the increasing availability of readymade clothing and tinned food, housewives who could afford it still sought assistance with domestic tasks. However, the number of women employed in private domestic work rose only slightly between 1921 and 1936, from 20,621 to 29,262.[83] 'Home life in New Zealand,' the *New Zealand Herald* opined, 'was suffering because of the shortage of domestic help.'[84] The so-called 'surplus women' of Britain appeared to present a ready solution, and single female domestic workers were encouraged, by the offer of free passage, to emigrate to New Zealand. More than 4,500 women aged between eighteen and forty, who were 'bona fide' domestic workers, came between 1920 and 1932, lured by the free third-class passage and a £2 gratuity. Most found work in the main centres, disappointing hopes that women in rural areas would benefit from the increased availability of domestic help.[85]

Two medical students visiting the Ratana settlement thought it 'an excellent idea' to place young Māori women in Pākehā households and give them an opportunity 'to see modern methods of housekeeping'.[86] Several women from Rātana apparently found work as domestic helpers in Marton and surrounding areas. Modelling of Pākehā ways was practised in the childhood home of Vera Morgan, who grew up in the Hokianga. Her mother had not been to school but had worked in Auckland from a young age. Vera recalled the strict standards of behaviour her mother required at the dinner table. 'She went housekeeping for eight years for a Pakeha family and never stopped talking about them and her experience and exposure to another way of life.'[87]

As the Depression deepened in the early 1930s, household work was often seen by both the government and women's groups as a solution to the problems of unemployment, much to Elizabeth McCombs' disgust. 'Is every unemployed woman, whatever her profession,' she inquired acidly in Parliament, 'to be asked to do housework at 2s 6d a week? Has the government no other idea?'[88] In some quarters, domestic training was also seen as a way to solve health problems among Māori. In 1931, the Methodist Women's Missionary Union raised funds for the Kurahuna School of Domestic Service and Hygiene in Onehunga, and most of the Māori girls leaving the school during its early years went into domestic service.[89] Long-term, however, live-in domestic service was declining: in 1936 servants made up 8.6 per cent of the inhabitants of private households; by 1945, they made up only 2.6 per cent.[90]

Instead, married women at home were expected to take responsibility for washing, mending and cooking, and from the 1930s the magazines gave increased professional instruction on aspects of household care.[91] The *New Zealand Woman's Weekly* – a new source of advice – started publishing in 1933, and quickly developed into a national institution. 'A slovenly and untidy woman certainly is a grief to her husband,' the magazine stated, 'but since the cause of it is sheer laziness, there is no cure for it.'[92]

Whatever the comforts of a house, it was the ties amongst its residents that transformed it into a home. A home could contain multiple generations and a diversity of arrangements. Lucy Atareti Winiata, of Ngāti Raukawa, and her husband Harry Jacob lived with her parents after their marriage, and looked after them in their old age.[93] Writer Ruth Dallas's grandmother was an integral part of the family's domestic life, baking, cooking, providing childcare and working in the garden. Only when cancer of the throat took hold in her late seventies did she cease to be a mainstay of the household.[94] Others created different family forms. Nurse Fergusson, who worked in the far north as a district nurse for Māori, was accompanied by a Miss Kidner who received a small assistant's wage from the Health Department. When Miss Fergusson left the service, the two women set up a poultry farm together outside Wanganui.[95] Mary Downie Stewart acted as hostess and companion for her invalid brother throughout his tenure as a member of Parliament.[96] And there were the many youngest daughters who, like Bessie Turnbull, chose not to marry because 'I thought it was my duty to stand by my mother and give her a good ending in life.'[97]

'An assemblage of relations and other adults – boarders, actually, but invariably friends of the sons and daughters of the house, who would be invited to stay if they needed a home', made up Dorothy Butler's household and enriched her happy childhood. Her maternal grandparents' house in Surrey Crescent, Grey Lynn, 'reverberated with good cheer'.[98] Dorothy was born in April 1925, and her childhood seemed like years of 'perpetual sunshine', full of activities like making tin canoes, soap-box trolleys and huts in trees, swimming at the beach and playing on the mudflats.[99] Parents like hers did much to protect their children from the worries of adult life, with mothers devoting themselves to providing 'as happy a childhood as [they] possibly could'.[100]

A happy family life was of course not guaranteed, and the burdens of caring for children could sometimes be extreme, especially when children had physical or intellectual disabilities. The parents of a boy adjudged to be an 'imbecile' kept him in a hut after he failed to develop control over his bodily functions. They were initially charged with failing to provide their son with the necessities of life, but the Supreme Court judge evinced sympathy for the circumstances of the couple and refused to impose any punishment.[101] There was often little understanding of the children's difficulties, and not all families had the information or resources to take advantage of increased state provision for children with disabilities at special schools, such as Otekaieke School (for boys) established in Otago in 1908, and Richmond School (for girls) in Nelson in 1916. For children with serious developmental difficulties, psychopaedic hospitals were established: Stoke Villas in Nelson in 1922 and Templeton in Christchurch in 1929. Down's syndrome children, for example, were often hidden away at Stoke Villas.[102]

Some parents resented what they saw as state surveillance of their children by the School Medical Service, which was created in 1912. The inspection of children by the service's doctors often translated into direct criticism of parents when children were judged to be dirty or undernourished. One mother saw the 'system of espionage' as

At the height of the Depression, women volunteers set up and ran soup kitchens to provide some sustenance for the unemployed. This soup kitchen was located in Wellington around 1932. *Alexander Turnbull Library, Wellington, EP-8645B-1/2-F*

designed to harass poor parents who were simply trying to do their best to keep their families clothed and fed.[103]

The nature of family life was changing for middle-class and urban-based women. As children's physical survival became more assured and family size reduced, mothers were able to focus more attention on fewer children and on their psychological well-being. Advertisers reinforced the message of the school curriculum that domestic science was women's sphere, and that the health of families depended on mothers' cooking and hygiene skills. Family health, however, depended on the breadwinner's income, and as economic conditions worsened that could no longer be taken for granted.

The Depression and the right to work

Men's right to work, or to state support when work was unavailable, was at the forefront of national consciousness as the economic downturn of the 1920s led into the Great Depression of the 1930s. Riots broke out in the main centres in the early part of that decade, highlighting the desperation of men no longer able to fulfil their role as providers. In earlier times the state might have directed married men to move in search of employment, privileging work over family, but by the 1930s a community consensus prevailed that the role of married men was to be at home with their families.

During the Depression of the 1930s many women could not afford to buy clothing and had to recycle materials: the boy's shorts lining (top) is made from a Crown Milling Company flour bag. Flour, oats and oatmeal came in cotton or calico sacks (below) that could be reused for clothing and other items. *From top: Owaka Museum, CT81.1561k; Museum of New Zealand Te Papa Tongarewa, Wellington, GH005293; GH016341; GH005289*

Unemployment on a large scale led to debate about both men's and women's right to work. The United–Reform coalition government formed in September 1931 saw male breadwinners as having first call on relief measures, while the Labour Opposition pointed out the plight of unemployed women.[104] Opinions were strongly divided over the rights of married women, and even of single women, to work. Many blamed women for taking work from men when times were hard. In a debate on unemployment in 1931, Legislative Councillor Robert Masters argued:

> One has only to go through the offices in any of our cities, and particularly in this city, to be convinced of the fact that … the unemployment of men has been brought about by reason of the fact that the positions in these offices, stores and other places have been taken by girls, and if we can induce these girls to go into domestic service, and leave these positions open for men, then it would ease the position considerably.[105]

From 1931, working women (apart from those in private domestic service) were taxed on their wages but had no right to unemployment relief. Single and married women took to the streets to assert their right to be granted this relief. As a result of a clamour from women's organisations – and, more provocatively, the activities of 'screaming women' described by a *Free Lance* reporter as leading 'the onset of wreckers and looters' in the April 1932 Queen Street unemployment riots – the government set up a Women's Advisory Committee to coordinate the work of women's unemployment committees in the four main centres and in some smaller towns.[106] These committees organised employment bureaus and training centres. In Dunedin, for example, the School of Home Science offered to provide teachers of sewing, dressmaking and household skills such as cooking, provided the Women's Unemployment Committee found accommodation for the vocational lessons. This it duly did.[107] Run by middle-class women keen to resolve the servant shortage, the committee in effect encouraged women into domestic work.[108] In the absence of alternatives, the numbers employed in all types of domestic work grew 63 per cent between 1921 and 1936, whereas the growth in other women's occupations was just over 10 per cent.[109]

Resistance to women's financial independence through paid employment heightened as the Depression bit deeper. 'A Worker' expressed a common view that employers should hire 'only those who really need work'. He went on to suggest in a letter to the *Press* in 1931 that all office girls should be dismissed, 'especially those whose parents can employ them at home'.[110] The *White Ribbon* claimed indignantly that there should be 'No Sex in Citizenship'. Girls should not be expected to be dependent on their families, given that the same did not apply to boys, and 'positions should go to the better qualified, male or female'. Until married women had their own incomes (in the form of a motherhood endowment), the paper argued, 'no obstacle should be put in the way of a woman earning her own living'.[111]

Women's organisations stepped in to fill the void created by the lack of government relief. The Society for the Protection of Women and Children, along with the YWCA, registered unemployed women and attempted to find them work. The YWCA set up needlework and handicraft classes, where unemployed women did mending for others at a moderate fee.[112] Such measures, however, did little for those in desperate straits.

The situation of teachers illustrates the impact of the Depression. Women teachers were generally kept at lower salaries than men and denied opportunities for advancement, but when they complained about the matter they were informed that a differentiated salary scale 'was necessary to keep the proportion of men in the service'.[113] Male secondary school principals, for example, earned about £100 per annum more than their female counterparts.[114] Salaries were reduced for all teachers from 1931; teachers' colleges were closed in 1934; the hours of non-permanent staff were cut; and five-year-olds were excluded from school. The difficulties encouraged the New Zealand Women Teachers' Association to speak out, protesting against salary cuts and the privileging of male teachers in appointments and promotions.[115]

In response to hard times, the nine District Education Boards, which exercised discretion in appointments for their respective areas, first asked married women teachers 'to give details of their household and finances' to determine if they needed a job. In the late 1920s, the Canterbury Education Board made it clear 'that it would not appoint a married woman teacher who was not a breadwinner'.[116] As the Depression deepened, members of the public gave voice to the view taken up by the Christchurch Unemployment Committee that no work of any kind should be offered to married women.[117] In 1931, boards were given the legal authority to 'terminate the engagement of any married woman employed as a teacher in the service of the Board' with three months' notice.[118]

The imposition of a marriage bar reflected the widely held belief that married women's place was in the home. The Minister of Education explained it this way: 'Women were employed whose husbands were earning good money and young girls could not secure positions.'[119] The Auckland branch of the Women Teachers' Association responded by taking a challenge to the Supreme Court, and was delighted with the ruling that the legislation (under the Finance Act 1931) applied only to appointments and could not be used to dismiss teachers already in posts.[120]

The vision of husbands earning good incomes was belied by the reality. Nearly one-third of the Canterbury Education Board's married women teachers had no husband at all. They were widowed, separated or deserted. Of those with husbands, few were in a position to rely on their income. The list read: '"Husband Returned Serviceman – incapacitated"; "Husband earning eight pounds per annum"; "Husband invalid"; "Husband unemployed"; "Husband mental patient"; "Husband bankrupt farmer and semi-invalid"; "Husband Returned Serviceman – vacating farm".'[121] Working to support their families and maintain the home, these women were able to retain their positions because of the 'undue hardship' that would be caused through their loss of employment. The bar did, however, reduce the number of married women teachers in the schools.[122]

More pervasive and important than actual regulations governing women's work was the ideology of the male breadwinner. In a debate on the 1932 Amendment to the Industrial Conciliation and Arbitration Act, Robert Semple, Labour member for Wellington East, argued that the master engineers, who advocated for the employment of girls rather than men for light work in factories, would 'degrade the manhood' of the country 'by throwing men out of employment and driving them to charitable-aid institutions and to desperation'. Young girls, hired at lower wages, would drive their fathers and brothers out of work as a consequence of being forced 'into the factories to be sweated by the employers'.[123]

The question of the degradation of manhood preoccupied households too. 'Sarah' wrote to the *Woman's Weekly* agony aunt, Dorothy Dix, in 1936 to say that she was keen to work to supplement her husband's poor wages but refrained from doing so because she had been told that a working wife 'breaks a man's morale and belittles him'. In reply, Dorothy Dix laid out the current orthodoxy. A woman with young children should work outside the home only 'in case of dire necessity'. Other women should decide according to their husband's attitude: 'If she humiliates him by taking a job it will develop an inferiority complex in him that will wreck him because it will break down his belief in his ability to succeed.'[124] While arguing that it was old-fashioned to see a working wife as a poor reflection on a man, Dix endorsed the view that it suggested he was a bad provider: 'If he can't give her what she wants, he doesn't stand in the way of her getting it herself.' A working wife, she concluded, might enable a couple to find their feet financially 'and then they can have the home and children they crave'.[125]

The Pākehā ideal of the non-working wife made little sense in Māori communities where the work of all members was necessary for survival. During the inquiry into the place of Māori women in Chinese market gardens of 1929, for example, Wirepaheta Raka had stated that his wife and daughter worked for the Chinese because he himself was unemployed.[126] Shortly afterwards, the Depression closed off many employment options for Māori. The kauri-gum market was brought to a virtual standstill; timber companies cut work; and from 1931 public works employment on roads and railways was slashed. The Native Minister, Apirana Ngata, pressed ahead with government-sponsored land development schemes that relied on low wages paid to labourers on state work schemes. The 1930 Unemployment Act, which had originally exempted Māori from registration and contribution to the unemployment fund, was amended to allow optional registration because some Māori sought relief work.

Those who did so were primarily employed on Māori development schemes sponsored by Ngata, who obtained state funds to promote effective farming of Māori land under tribal control. By August 1930, 1,045 Māori men were employed on the schemes. Ngata, in accordance with the principles of the Unemployment Board, could not employ women and children, who traditionally would have worked alongside the men. Eruera Tirikatene, member for Southern Maori, highlighted the plight of women and children in 1933, telling Parliament that the only work they could get was casual gardening for sixpence per hour: 'That is what some of our Native women have to do to provide enough for their children. That is the only wage they can get for ten hours a day in gardens weeding and so on.'[127]

At its peak, Māori unemployment is estimated to have reached 8,500. And whereas Pākehā men on a work scheme in May 1931 received 15s a week if single and 25s if married, Māori men received 10s and 15s respectively. Māori also suffered the indignity of having prohibitions placed on their spending power, such as having to use a special savings bank plan or being denied credit at certain stores for particular items.[128]

In the depths of the Depression, when some married men were sent away to relief camps, the strain of making ends meet could become unbearable. In Ōamaru in January 1936, Cecily Fitzmaurice crushed twenty-three Veronal tablets with her rolling pin and distributed them in four portions, three in cups for herself and the two older children, and the fourth in the baby's bottle. The infant died but the other children and their mother survived. She was charged with murder and a jury returned a verdict of not guilty on the grounds of insanity.[129] A neighbour attributed Fitzmaurice's actions to financial worries and her fears for her children's health because she was unable to heat the house. Sending the husband and father to a relief camp had brought the Fitzmaurice family to breaking point.

A large group of married men expressed their resentment at the prospect of separation from their families, at a noisy protest outside a St Kilda Borough Council meeting in Dunedin in March 1933. Relief camps, they argued, meant enforced separation 'with little prospect of being able to earn enough money to keep those homes together'. A compromise was reached whereby men would be medically examined before being sent to camps. The following year, when more than 1,000 married men were offered work in camps, the vast majority presented medical certificates declaring them unfit.[130] Whereas men would once have gone in search of any work to relieve their family of privation, by the 1930s many opted to suffer at home, alongside their wives and children.

After the Labour Party's victory in the 1935 general election, Michael Joseph Savage became prime minister. While promising to deliver a wage sufficient to keep a man, his wife and three children, and to make sure that 'the luxuries of today' became 'the necessities of tomorrow', Savage was himself single, and found a home in the family of his good friends Alf and Elizabeth French.[131] His party was committed to the idea of the male breadwinner supporting his family; women would be the 'professional' managers of households, guarding the health of future citizens and buying New Zealand-made goods to support the economy.[132] The reality of the Depression, however, had undercut the ideal of the male breadwinner, as necessity forced all family members (including wives) to find work wherever they could, with the result that more women entered the workforce.[133]

Photographer Thelma Kent, seated at the head of the table, took this photograph of herself and five women having breakfast during a camping trip in 1939. Kent travelled around New Zealand in the 1930s and '40s and has left an extensive photographic record of these trips. *Alexander Turnbull Library, Wellington, 1/2-010114-F*

By the end of the Depression, Melanie Nolan argues, a 'striking and public consensus had emerged among women's organisations' that single women should be treated no differently from single men.[134] They were now taken seriously as participants in the paid workforce. The right of married women to paid work, however, remained highly contested.

Modern discontents

New Zealand was thrown into disarray by the economic upheaval of the worldwide Depression. The interwar years also saw concern about another kind of upheaval: an apparent decline in the sanctity of marriage. In 1920, Jane Mander's *The Story of a New Zealand River* showed New Zealanders to themselves in a new way. Acclaimed in London where it was published, the novel examined an unhappy marriage; according to one New Zealand reviewer, this placed the book in the category of 'sex problem' fiction.[135]

In October 1924, the Anglican Synod viewed with dismay 'the alarming increase in the number of divorces in the Dominion'. 'All right-thinking persons agreed,' said the Revd G. Gordon Bell, 'that society was going to pieces on this "rock of divorce".' The Revd C. H. Grant Cowan blamed youthful marriages, bad housing and 'lack of parental control' for

The workers at the Bonded Tobacco Company at Wanganui around 1920 were mainly young women. *Alexander Turnbull Library, Wellington, 1/1-017327-G*

the rise in divorce, while others expressed concern about 'objectionable literature' such as 'soul destroying sex novels'.[136] D. H. Lawrence's *Lady Chatterley's Lover*, first published privately in 1928, was regarded as one of those unsuitable for New Zealanders – and was banned.[137] Hollywood movies also picked up on this so-called 'modern divorce age'.[138] Well-known star Norma Shearer took the title role in the 1930 film *The Divorcee*, which brought the New York fast set to New Zealand screens.[139] The 'uproarious' comedy *Peach o' Reno*, based around a 'divorce Mill' in Reno, amused audiences in mid-1932.[140]

But the 'All-Night Vigil' of the New Zealand Cabinet held on 11 December 1936 reminded the country of the seriousness of divorce. At around 4 a.m. ministers gathered around a shortwave radio set to hear of the abdication of King Edward VIII.[141] His determination to marry the twice-divorced American Wallis Simpson led to a constitutional crisis. The King was head of the Church of England, which did not permit the remarriage of divorced people. Had the British Parliament allowed him to marry a woman with two living former husbands, it would have violated the 'widely-accepted moral law' considered fundamental to Christian civilisation.[142] '[A]ll right-thinking people', said the moderator of the Presbyterian Assembly of New Zealand, would acknowledge the King's abdication as 'inevitable', while the chairman of the Auckland Methodist Church saw it as 'a vindication of the nation's moral sense of values'.[143]

In July 1921, the Ngāti Whātua community at Ōrākei welcomed T. W. Ratana during a visit to Auckland; but the city was steadily encroaching on Ngāti Whātua lands and the community was evicted in 1950. *Auckland Weekly News, 14 July 1921, p.35, Auckland Libraries, Sir George Grey Special Collections, AWNS-19210714-35-5*

The abdication of Edward VIII was a highly public affair, and opprobrium was swift. New Zealanders were left in no doubt that divorce was considered a disgrace. However, family tensions continued to force ordinary couples to decide they had no alternative but to separate. The usual resort was to a Magistrate's Court where, from 1910, women could apply for separation and guardianship orders.[144] If granted, women might also receive maintenance from their husbands, but they did not have the right to remarry. The next step, divorce, was expensive, and entailed the risk of women losing their children if they were judged the 'guilty' party. In 1926, women finally achieved equal rights to guardianship under the Guardianship of Infants Act. It was but one sign of a growing desire to transform the balance of power in the marital relationship.

Jean Devanny was one of a small group of women who looked to social revolution to bring about the day when relations between the sexes would be more fully transformed. She believed the possibility of equality for women might exist under socialism. Devanny articulated her analysis of marriage in her 1926 novel *The Butcher Shop*, which the New Zealand Board of Censorship found to be 'sordid, unwholesome and unclean', and was banned in this country and elsewhere.[145] The novel portrays marriage as a terrible trap for women, one in which they are treated as property and unable to assert their sexual and economic freedom; they are kept, like animals in a butcher shop. 'I had taken the stand,' Devanny recorded, 'that the right of a woman to control over her own body was inviolable, irrespective of the marriage bond.'[146] New Zealand was not ready for Devanny's critique of sexual relations within marriage, nor for her view that socialism would release married women from their lowly status as the property of their husbands.[147]

Another novelist and journalist, Robin Hyde, shared Jean Devanny's commitment to discovering a new world in which justice for all might prevail. Her journalism of the 1930s

Te Puea Herangi (wearing a white headscarf) stands in the official party at the opening of Turongo House at Tūrangawaewae Marae, Ngāruawāhia, in 1938. To the left of the photograph is Sir Apirana Ngata. *Alexander Turnbull Library, Wellington, EP-Ethnology-Maori-Marae and meeting houses-01*

reveals the range of women's daily experience. She wrote articles on soup kitchens and vagrant women, as well as commentaries on fashion and society notes. She contributed to the socialist-feminist *Woman Today*, a new periodical that aimed to draw women into public debate on political issues because, as Hyde wrote, 'Woman *is* a backward nation.'[148] Herself an outsider from the ideal of womanhood – independent, the mother of an illegitimate child, living by her writing, and suffering bouts of mental illness – Hyde believed she 'needed madness in order to survive'.[149] Yet her own difficulties never overrode concern for others.

In articles for the *Observer* appearing in 1937, Hyde highlighted the conflicting interests of Māori and Pākehā over land at Bastion Point, Ōrākei, in Auckland. 'In the interests of a garden suburb and a view,' she wrote, 'the white residents of Orakei are perfectly willing to hunt the living natives from lands which have been their ancestral right and property for so many years.' She warned John A. Lee, Labour's Minister of Housing, that 'dispossession' undertaken for a state housing development 'would not be forgiven or forgotten', and that there would 'come hard times and poor times when more is wanted than satisfaction in the houses of the well-paid workers'.[150]

Lee chose to ignore Hyde's warning and the eviction of the Ngāti Whātua community at Bastion Point went ahead. The First Labour Government's vision of happy families in suburban state housing overrode Māori claims to land ownership. Labour's policies were determined by two important and pervasive understandings of the world. The first was that families should be built around mothers who were devoted to domestic pursuits. The implications of this resonated beyond the home to shape views of women's role in the public world. The second understanding was that Pākehā views of home life would eventually triumph over Māori attachment to ancestral lands. Such attachments were regarded as outdated, and simply a matter of cultural difference which might inhibit the economic development of Māori.

Māori, by this thinking, presented problems that Pākehā 'intellectual skills' would solve.[151] Māori, however, had their own solutions, and some lay in the hands of capable women. Heeni Wharemaru, for example, was raised in a prominent Tainui family near Mōkau, north-east of New Plymouth. Usually a woman of such high birth would be expected to make a political marriage, but Heeni's family decided she should dedicate her life to the Methodist Church.[152] Born in 1912, Heeni first attended the Te Kūiti School of Domestic Science and Hygiene, set up in response to concerns about Māori health and as a training ground for young women who would go on to church work. She then went to the Kurahuna Maori Girls' School, where she was senior girl and prepared her application to train as a Methodist deaconess. Initially turned down because she was too young, Heeni spent two years in Auckland and observed the work of Sister Ivy Jones and the charismatic Methodist missioner Colin Scrimgeour, renowned for his radio broadcasts which empathised with the issues facing working people and brought them 'hope and comfort.'[153] Both worked hard for the dispossessed of Auckland: Ivy Jones ran clubs for young Māori in the city and 'Uncle Scrim' gathered the elderly at the Methodist Mission.[154] This proved to be good preparation for Heeni's future role in social work – work that eventually led her to know and admire Te Puea Herangi.

The charismatic Te Puea had a particular vision of Māori regeneration which she persuaded others to share. From 1921, she had been building a community at Tūrangawaewae, near Ngāruawāhia, 'a marae that, one day', she said, 'people will visit from all over the world'.[155] Hard work on the land during the day was complemented by the practising of haka and action songs at night.[156] By 1923, the performance group Te Pou O Mangatawhiri had emerged, ready to tour and raise funds for Tūrangawaewae. By the late 1920s, the settlement was regarded as a model of Māori development: clean orderly houses with gardens, a recreation hall, and a no-alcohol policy. From this base, Te Puea reached out to Apirana Ngata and to the centre of political power in Native Affairs in Wellington. By early 1932, she was the paid supervisor of nearly 5,000 acres under the Māori land development scheme.[157] The scheme provided work and sustenance for hundreds of Waikato families in the depths of the Depression.

Te Puea's example encouraged others, and she continued building cultural capital – developing carved houses, reviving canoe traditions and extending performance repertoires. In March 1938, at Tūrangawaewae, her contribution received national recognition when she was invested with a CBE for her service to Māori.[158] Te Puea found it

A group of women and children enjoy the sunshine at Te Poho-o-Rāwiri marae, Kaitī, Gisborne, in 1939, while listening to a girl reading from a newspaper. *Alexander Turnbull Library, Wellington, PAColl-0785-1-091-001*

difficult to accept an individual honour when she saw her work as a commitment she had made to her people – people who had been wronged and who required recompense. She had planted seeds from which new developments would grow.

Whatever modern discontents and upheavals disrupted the lives of Pākehā and Māori women and men in the interwar years, they were to take a back seat as the clouds of war gathered over Europe. New Zealanders, still British citizens, were called upon to support Britain in battlefields on the other side of the world and closer to home in the Pacific. Once more men embarked to fight for democracy while women were expected, in the words of a famous First World War song, to 'keep the home fires burning'.

When May Smith exhibited this portrait of Marie Conlan at the Auckland Society of Arts annual exhibition in 1941, one reviewer declared that it defied 'all recognised standards of approach'. Others found fault with its expressive rather than naturalistic use of colour, and the cigarette in Conlan's hand. There is more than a hint of challenge in this portrait, and its modernist style was unsettling. Over a decade later city councillors were reluctant to agree to its acquisition for the Auckland City Art Gallery. *Auckland Art Gallery Toi o Tāmaki, purchased 1958, 1958/20*

Chapter Nine

On the Home Front: From Dependence to Independence

In June 1939, Helen Simpson was hard at work on *The Women of New Zealand*, one of the thirteen surveys published to mark New Zealand's centennial in 1940. She wrote:

> I am about to order a case of sherry, 10,000 cigarettes, and 1 cwt of coffee, and to have put up on the front fence a notice in 6ft. letters … I haven't yet decided whether it is to read 'POISON LAID FOR VISITORS', or, more simply, 'KEEP OUT!' I should rather like to have 'DANGER: LIVE WIRE', but my strict regard for the truth prevents that.[1]

The book went on to become a bestseller, but when the all-male National Centennial Historical Committee first considered a volume on women, they put it on the 'maybe' or 'B' list. Members considered the 'sex war' to be 'an anachronism' and such a volume 'illogical', reminiscent of a time when women had to fight for the vote.[2] The centennial was about celebrating the nation's cohesion.

Helen Simpson, one of the first New Zealand women to gain a PhD in English literature, represented a new generation of working women.[3] At the outbreak of the Second World War other young women, drawn in to support the war effort, entered factories and offices where they learned new skills and experienced welcome companionship. Women's work was said to be 'just for the duration', but it became clear that independence in decision-making and financial matters would carry through into the postwar years. Young Māori women were among those embracing opportunities in the urban environment. Women discovered that they had skills in a range of fields both within New Zealand and abroad, and that these needed to be recognised. To women in the public service, for example, it no longer seemed fair that they should be paid less for their work than their male colleagues. Tested for their competence in a variety of workplaces, and found to be as good as men, activists found flaws in a system designed to reward male breadwinners, and began a campaign for equal pay that strengthened in the 1950s.

Uncertainties generated by the demands of wartime spilled over into the peace. How were personal relationships that had been broken or disrupted by the war to be rebuilt? How was postwar reconstruction to proceed, and what were the roles of women and men, and Māori and Pākehā, within it? While the postwar baby boom tied women to the home, the economic boom enticed them out of it once their children had started school. The burgeoning Māori population required initiatives in health, education and welfare. In 1939, the problems facing the Māori community were thought best solved by the efforts of male leaders. By 1951, Māori women were in the vanguard of change. The founding of the Maori Women's Welfare League in that year provided a united voice for different iwi at a time when state pressure was toward assimilation.

Women welcomed the peace and, for many, the chance to embark on family life that had been disrupted by the war. For some that meant moving abroad – especially to the United States to build lives with service men they had met in New Zealand. Some arrived in the country newly wed to returning New Zealand servicemen; even for British women, this meant coming to grips with a different society and culture. Absorption in the demands of home life quickly followed as birth rates boomed. But lessons learned about independence fed into restlessness and a desire to discover new possibilities beyond the domestic realm.

War work

'Nineteen thirty-nine,' recalled Ena Ryan, 'was a great skiing season.' Arriving home in early September to a well-heeled household in Kelburn, Wellington, after a fortnight's holiday at the Chateau Tongariro, she heard British Prime Minister Neville Chamberlain's radio broadcast to announce the outbreak of war. Too tired from her skiing and dancing to care, she grasped the meaning of the war only when her friend Robert enlisted. A young man of twenty-nine without qualifications or a job, he had been in a relief camp. The chance to enlist gave Robert and others like him a new purpose in life – 'somebody wanted them' – as well as a regular job, a pay packet, and a role in defending King, country and family.[4] By April 1940, some 34,900 men had volunteered for the services, and 15,636 of them had gone to a training camp or overseas.[5]

Women also wished to contribute to the war effort, and a group approached the Minister of Defence about forming a Women's Auxiliary Corps even before the out-break of hostilities. They were rebuffed. Undeterred, by mid-1940, volunteer corps of women were training in Auckland, Hamilton, Christchurch and Gisborne.[6] War service helped create a new mould of womanhood: independent, and capable of any task or position of responsibility put before them, from packing parachutes to leading a women's branch of the armed services. Women discovered they were well able to do jobs previously denied them.

Dr Agnes Bennett, now a prominent Wellingtonian, led a deputation to Prime Minister Peter Fraser, seeking official recognition for a Women's War Service Auxiliary to recruit women for national service and assist the war effort in various ways, from the traditional knitting of socks to the new skill of motor mechanics.[7] Fraser supported the service but not the proposed uniform, reportedly commenting: 'We won't have our New Zealand women in trousers.'[8] The Women's War Service Auxiliary was nonetheless formally constituted in July 1940.[9] Janet Fraser, the prime minister's wife, became the first president and Agnes Bennett served as vice-president.[10] The executive council drew in existing women's organisations: the Women's Division of the Farmers' Union, the YWCA, the Women's Institutes, the Women's Branch of the Labour Party, the Federation of Women's Clubs and the Girl Guides.[11] Thirty women were chosen to serve overseas in response to Lieutenant-General Bernard Freyberg's call for some New Zealand women to brighten the drab forces club in Cairo. 'Tuis', as they became known, soon spread their wings to service clubs in Italian towns and, later, in London.[12]

Approximately 140,000 New Zealand men and women eventually enlisted in war service. Almost 60,000 men initially volunteered for the 2nd New Zealand Expeditionary Force, but the need for more men eventually led to the introduction of conscription in 1940. Balloted men left at intervals in the ensuing years to reinforce those already serving. In total, approximately 67 per cent of men aged between eighteen and forty-five served in the armed forces.[13]

As the shortage of men impacted on the armed services in New Zealand, attitudes to women joining up softened, and on 16 January 1941 the War Cabinet approved the formation of a women's auxiliary to the Royal New Zealand Air Force (RNZAF), the first of the services to accept women. They became known as the WAAFs (Women's Auxiliary Air Force).[14] The Cabinet envisaged women being trained in a small number of jobs, the priority being to provide meals for servicemen. Thirty-three-year-old Kitty Kain, a married mother of one and an experienced dietitian, was put in charge of developing the WAAF at Rongotai, in Wellington. By October 1942 the service had proved so valuable that it was incorporated into the RNZAF and the women were given ranks equivalent to those of men. Kitty Kain became Wing Commander Kain. By the war's end, women were employed in thirty-nine RNZAF trades, including as wireless operators, dental mechanics and meteorological assistants.

Before the Women's Royal New Zealand Naval Service (WRENS) was established in 1942, women had already taken over supply and secretariat roles in the Navy in order to release men for service.[15] Old questions were raised as women were sought for new positions. Could women serving in the Navy be asked to work at night?[16] Of course they could, was the answer. Women became visual signallers, coders and telegraphists. They took up accounting and stores work, and took over entirely from men as cooks and stewards in officers' quarters and in some smaller naval establishments.[17] More would have served, but the selection standards set by Chief Officer Ruth Herrick, former chief commissioner for the New Zealand Girl Guides, were high. By January 1943, 350 of the 870 applicants had been declined.[18]

The last of the women's services to be established, in July 1942, the Women's Auxiliary Army Corps (WAAC) soon became the largest. In their magazine *Pro Patria*, the Southern

The Red Cross co-ordinated various patriotic and welfare campaigns during the Second World War. In Wellington, these Red Cross nurses marched in a procession, promoting health and fitness. *Alexander Turnbull Library, Wellington, PAColl-7688-01-24*

Military District WAACs wrote of the 'fun and sportsmanship' being enjoyed in the 'out-of-town camps'. The drama club was busy with preparations for Gilbert and Sullivan's *Trial by Jury*, the basketball team 'was keeping up its good reputation', and the hockey team was 'bloody but unbowed'.[19] Many of the friendships forged in close, all-women communities such as these lasted a lifetime.[20]

Many who enlisted, like the eighteen nursing sisters of the New Zealand Army Nursing Service who departed in January 1940 with the First Echelon, were keen to serve abroad.[21] Given a choice between continuing work in a clothing factory or learning new skills and experiencing the adventure of foreign travel, young women often opted for adventure. Many more sought to serve overseas than were accepted. By 1945, a total of 650 nurses had served outside New Zealand. Some, like Mavis Thyne, serving in Senigallia on the Adriatic coast of Italy, were called upon to administer the miraculous new antibiotic, penicillin, which was to transform healthcare on the battlefield and in the postwar world.[22]

Trained nurses were supplemented by Voluntary Aids (VADs), 300 of whom served in the Middle East, in Italy on hospital ships, and in the Pacific.[23] Nineteen-year-old Theo

These women have made their army hut at Miramar in Wellington comfortable with flowers, a mirror and other personal items. For many young women, communal living in the auxiliary forces brought new and close friendships that they maintained in the postwar world. *Alexander Turnbull Library, Wellington, 1/4-019080-G*

Mountford left her office job in 1941 to work as an aid in a hospital. When the call came for 200 volunteers to serve in the Middle East, she was desperate to be chosen for this 'real work for a real purpose'.[24] Undeterred by the fact that volunteers were to be between twenty-four and thirty-four years of age, Theo doctored her birth certificate and was duly chosen. On 22 December 1941, she left New Zealand aboard the hospital ship *Maunganui*, and proved to be a dedicated nurse, thrown into the 'deep end' at the Helwan Military Hospital outside Cairo. She was also an indefatigable tourist, her VAD uniform serving as protection from unwanted advances when she and her nursing friends used precious leave to visit the ancient sites of the Middle East and Italy.[25]

New experiences were not just the preserve of those abroad. Barbara Foreman grew up in comfortable Fendalton in Christchurch, surrounded by nannies, maids, gardeners and a chauffeur. Pressured into a university education in accountancy and office work, she greeted the opportunity to join the Women's Land Service with glee. Many farmers regarded their work as a male bastion and were reluctant to take on women who might not be able to cope with heavy lifting and dirty conditions, but the government worked with

Left An advertisement of 1942 or '43 called on women to support the war effort by working in agriculture. The Women's Land Service was originally called the Women's Land Army but was renamed in 1942. *Right* Miss M. McLean and Mrs W. Houston of the New Zealand Women's Land Service confer in October 1941. The elegantly dressed Miss McLean, of Christchurch, was organiser of the service, while trouser-clad Mrs Houston was in charge of a working party at Waimate. *Alexander Turnbull Library, Wellington, Eph-C-WOMEN-1942-01; PAColl-0785-1-106-05*

the Farmers' Union and its Women's Division to overcome the prejudices of both farmers and young women, who expressed a preference for urban employment.[26] Barbara was one who readily exchanged city life for the country. She learned to make her bed and do her own laundry, and regarded her two years as a 'land girl' at Rydal Downs, north-west of Rangiora, as 'total magic'. She became a tractor driver and expert at ploughing. Full of mischief, and inspired by fellow land girl and artist Juliet Peter, she sowed mustard into a rape crop in a 100-acre paddock so that from the air it read: 'LONELY LAND GIRLS HERE'. As a result 'we were literally dive-bombed with anything and everything, all kinds of messages, phone numbers'.[27]

Not all land girls had such fun. Sadie Stuart, for example, worked on a high-country farm near Ōmārama, where she lived in 'an appalling hut' without electricity or heat, and had access to the homestead bath only once a week. The stock work was hard, and all done by Sadie and the farmer. But what she really minded was the extreme isolation; she felt 'very lonely'.[28] The initial poor wages of land girls – 35s per week, plus keep, for the

A woman, possibly a member of the Women's Auxiliary Air Force, drives a tractor hauling another machine in front of an Avro Anson training plane during the Second World War. *Alexander Turnbull Library, Wellington, PAColl-6075-17*

first six months – were raised in September 1942 when the service was reorganised to make it more attractive. Women were paid 41s per week, plus keep, on dairy farms and 42s 6d on other farms. The 2,711 women in the Land Service helped maintain essential primary production throughout the war years.

Essential services in country areas, such as rural deliveries and school bus services, were also kept going by women. Mabel Waititi lived in Mōtatau, north of Whāngārei. When her husband George and brother Kahukiwi Henare joined the 28th (Maori) Battalion, Mabel took over the family's business, collecting the cream cans from forty-two suppliers and delivering goods in return, accompanied by her infant son. Once, unloading a four-gallon drum of petrol, she felt a crack in her chest. The local hospital taped her chest with plaster so she could continue her cream run the next morning. On leaving the hospital she remembered she was still breastfeeding her son, so the staff obliged by cutting holes in the plaster for her nipples. Mabel recalled that her son 'was quite happy with that!'[29]

A novel urban employment opportunity arose in 1941 when it was decided that women could enter the police force. That year, thirty-four-year-old kindergarten teacher Edna Pearce became one of the first batch of women police recruits, who received the same training as male officers. Posted to Auckland's Central Police Station, without uniform, the 5 foot 4 inch (163 centimetre) officer was allotted the most menial tasks, searching female offenders and transporting them from police cells to the courts and prisons. The wartime dilemma of what to do with a number of Japanese women evacuated from Tonga to New Zealand led to Officer Pearce's appointment, in December 1941, as supervisor of the internment camp set up for them in an insanitary and damp building at Pōkeno, south of Auckland. She lived in a Public Works Department hut alongside a translator, censoring the letters of the seven Japanese women (one of whom succumbed to mental illness), teaching Correspondence School lessons to their nine school-age children, and ensuring sufficient rice was available to feed them. After being moved to better premises in February 1943, the group was to be repatriated to Japan in exchange for prisoners of war in August. But shortly after lifting off from Whenuapai airport, their transport plane crashed. Two of the women and four of the children who had been under Officer Pearce's care were among those killed; others were injured. Three months later, Officer Pearce accompanied the remaining internees on a ship to Sydney, and they were repatriated to Japan. The Commissioner of Police, D. J. Cummings, commended her work for the detainees.[30]

Law enforcement was one new area of opportunity for women; jury service was another. Military service overseas meant a shortage of suitable male jurors, so in October 1942, legislation sponsored by Labour member Mary Dreaver of Waitematā enabled women aged between twenty-five and sixty to apply for jury service.[31] But women's right to serve on juries as citizens, first raised in the National Council of Women in 1896, remained hedged around with limitations.[32] The age of service was higher than that of twenty-one for men, and, unlike men, women had to apply to go on the jury roll. Enrolments were slow, and it was not until 20 October 1943 that Elaine Rebecca Kingsford of Takapuna became the first woman sworn in – to hear a case of house-breaking.[33]

The other side of the law fell heavily on those who opposed the war. Censorship and Publicity Regulations designed to quell such opposition were introduced in September 1939 and extended by the Public Safety Emergency Regulations in 1940.[34] Twenty-two-year-old Connie Jones, who had boarded in the household of the charismatic Methodist and pacifist Ormond Burton, was a member of the No More War movement and the Christian Pacifist Society. She first attended the Friday night public meetings at which pacifists argued their case in 1941. She stepped onto the podium, stating, 'The Lord Jesus Christ tells us to love one another,' and was promptly arrested by Wellington's chief inspector of police. Charged with obstruction under the Emergency Regulations, she was sentenced to three months' hard labour with harsh conditions at the Point Halswell Reformatory – an experience that did nothing to dampen her commitment to pacifism.[35]

Opposing the war was to go against the tide. One pacifist woman recalled how her 'convictions were sorely tried', even by close relatives; she was 'sickened' by the 'fervent flag-waving and militarism of some – especially women'. On account of the two poems she had written for the *Christian Pacifist Society Bulletin*, she was interviewed by the police. Undeterred, she and her husband took their ex-minister and his wife into their home following his forced resignation from the church because of his pacifist stance. Later the couple were forced to give up their sharemilking business after their employer 'was pressured into telling us to go'.[36]

When Rita Watts married Alan Graham in January 1939, his declared pacifism meant little to her. In the nursing home with her second child in July 1942, she learned that to oppose the war had serious consequences for her small family. Alan was called up for military service and declared his conscientious objection to war while Rita was caring for the new baby in the home. He was taken into detention for an indeterminate period when the child was only about six weeks old. Aware of the condemnation directed at the families of 'conchies', Rita would initially 'dodge the issue' whenever anyone inquired into her husband's whereabouts. And when the news was out, more than one white feather – signifying cowardice – appeared in her mail. However, Rita found that after she had publicly and proudly acknowledged her husband's stance, life became easier. She was also spared the fear and uncertainty of the women whose husbands were on active service overseas. Rita could be sure that her husband would eventually come home.[37]

Pacifists were not the only group under surveillance by the state. Those who had radical political allegiances were also under suspicion. In November 1939, the Wellington branch of the New Zealand Communist Party elected Elsie Freeman as its provincial secretary. The following year she was forced to go into hiding in Nelson as attitudes hardened against communists. Back in Wellington by May 1940, she was subject to police surveillance and became expert at foiling those detailed to follow her. One detective who failed in his mission to find out where she was living noted: 'Mrs Freeman is a very clever individual.'[38] By October 1940, Elsie was working in the Wellington Woollen Mills factory in Petone and was soon the trade delegate to the Trades Council in Wellington. Hearing of government plans to extend working hours, she distributed a pamphlet to her fellow workers headed: 'Urgent! Your Forty Hour Week Is Going To Be Taken Away From You'. The factory's general manager quickly gave her notice. Elsie apparently approached the Minister of Labour, Paddy Webb, asking him whether he condoned 'the dismissal of a competent worker' when looms were standing idle because of the wartime labour shortage. Webb promised to look into the matter, but added that a communist who caused trouble 'in his opinion justified dismissal'.[39]

Elsie Freeman's commitment to communism lost her several jobs and kept her subject to government surveillance, even after the Soviet Union joined the Allies in 1941. Both the Police Special Branch and the Security Intelligence Bureau watched her activities. One sergeant reported: 'She is fanatically devoted to the cause and even the fact that about two years ago she gave birth to a child did not prevent her from carrying on work for the party during a period normally devoted by mothers to nursing.'[40]

By November 1941, divorced from Fred Freeman and married to Jack Locke, Elsie was living in Christchurch. When Jack went into the Air Force in 1942, Elsie took over his role, acting as district secretary of the Communist Party. She held meetings at her home, gave classes in public speaking, and in 1943 began to tour country districts, speaking at Rangiora, Oxford, Springfield, Darfield, Akaroa, Little River, Methven, Rakaia, Ashburton, Geraldine, Tīmaru and Temuka. Communist Party membership grew during the war, no doubt due to new sympathy for the Soviet allies but perhaps also because of Elsie's efforts.

Women 'manpowered'

The ordering of the private sphere was significantly challenged when industrial conscription regulations were introduced in early 1942, although compulsion never went as far as it did in Britain or the United States. All women under forty – Māori and Pākehā – could be drafted into essential work. Women might hope to avoid serving by failing to register, or they might argue for a different placement once called up, but few refused outright, and those who did so on the grounds of conscience got short shrift.[41] Raids by manpower officials on hotels and cinemas in Auckland and Wellington led to fines for women who had failed to register. Their lack of patriotism was advertised through publication of their names in the newspaper.[42]

Perhaps because it threatened the old social order in which women were treated primarily as dependants, 'manpowering' was implemented cautiously, aimed first at young unmarried women who were either not working or in non-essential jobs, and whose skills could be redirected to war purposes. To some, the new directive regulations were a spur to join a branch of the women's services. Joyce Stables, a typist in Dunedin, had been doing VAD work when she was told she would probably be 'manpowered' to work at Seacliff Psychiatric Hospital: 'the man in charge told us it wasn't the sort of work we'd enjoy, so he had signed us up for the air force'. Soon she was trained as a WAAF medical orderly and stationed at the Woodbourne base, outside Blenheim.[43]

As the need for labour grew, married women who were not responsible for the care of children became subject to direction, since their efforts were now needed to maintain desired levels of production.[44] Indeed, a 1941 National Service Department report described women with husbands in the forces as 'redundant'.[45] If they were not needed to look after their husbands or children, they could be called upon to serve the country. This novel idea upset long-cherished beliefs about women's dedication to families and challenged husbands' authority over their wives. A correspondent to the *Dominion* suggested that 'when a married woman applied for a job, the department should check to see whether she had her husband's permission or whether she had "deserted her home"'.[46]

Much of the work considered essential was already done by women. Clothing factories, woollen mills, hospitals, and boot- and shoe-making factories, largely staffed by women at the outbreak of the war, were designated essential industries. Teaching and food processing were also categorised as essential, followed by food services (including waitressing) and government services in late 1942.[47] In September 1943, the New Zealand Manufacturers' Association requested that recruiting of women for the auxiliary services be stopped, because its members required 4,000 women workers.[48] The demand for nurses, too, was so acute (especially in psychiatric hospitals) that by 1945 all single women aged twenty-one and twenty-two were asked to perform twelve months' hospital service as required, including wards-maiding and laundry and kitchen duties.[49]

Young Māori women without large families to care for moved to urban areas, increasing their participation in all kinds of employment. Some, like Mihi Edwards, took jobs assembling hand grenades and mortar bombs in ammunition works, a constant reminder of the realities of the distant war.[50] The 1936 Census recorded 8 Maori women employed in 'Transport and Communications'; this had increased to 50 by 1945. A number of Māori women were directed to work at the De Havilland aircraft construction plant in Wellington. De Havilland supported its employees' association with the Ngati Poneke Young Maori Club, putting up notices informing the members when and where they should meet.[51] Riria Utiku imagined that marriage protected her from manpowering, but by the end of 1943 married women were being directed into work and she was told to work either in the woollen mills or in the Wills tobacco factory in Lower Hutt. Anxious to avoid a workplace that she thought of as 'rough', she successfully approached the Department of Maori Affairs for work. Her married sister, Hinga Timiha, was also directed into work as a tram conductor – though this meant she was not allowed to use her Māori name but 'had to go back to Walker', her family name.[52] The influx of Māori women into the towns was recorded in the 1945 Census: a threefold increase in the number of Māori women in the Public Administration and Professional category, from 222 in 1936 to 699 in 1945.[53] Whereas in 1936 only 12.2 per cent of Māori women were recorded as paid participants in the labour force, by 1951 this had increased to 20.7 per cent, indicating that wartime demands led to a new urban employment trend.[54]

New opportunities in the workforce did not necessarily mean assumptions about women's lower wages and limited working life had changed. By 1944, over 7,000 women were temporarily employed in a public service that was stretched by the new administrative burdens of war and the departure of men into the forces.[55] In 1939, a mere 5 per cent of the clerical workers in the service had been women; by 1947, the proportion had risen to 25 per cent.[56] But from the early 1920s, women in the public service had been restricted to lower wage ceilings and were unlikely to be considered for promotion because their gender rendered them 'not fully suitable for higher positions demanding the control of male officers'.[57] Drafted into the government's employ on a temporary basis during the war, women still found that their pay could be as little as half that of the men they worked alongside.

Women employees of the Westfield freezing works in Ōtāhuhu, Auckland, gather outside in their uniforms prior to the visit of Eleanor Roosevelt, first lady of the United States, who toured the North Island in 1943. *Photograph by John Dobree Pascoe, Alexander Turnbull Library, Wellington, 1/4-000572-F*

If not locked into low-paying work by industrial conscription, women might seek opportunities for work with better pay. The war years opened up professional occupations such as the law, librarianship, accountancy, medicine and academia. Historian Margaret Corner notes that between 1936 and 1945 the number of women lawyers rose by 12, dentists by 2, doctors by 54, university staff members by 39, welfare workers by 63, librarians by 217, accountants and cost accountants by 186, and women police by 30.[58] Women in professional occupations reaped the benefit of the higher education available to a select (and overwhelmingly Pākehā) few, and they expected equal pay rates.

Pay rates and prestige, however, were not the only reasons for working. Social connections were also important. 'Loved working', one woman recalled of her wartime job in the Ministry of Supply, which allowed her to work school hours and to have the school holidays off.[59] Lorna Smith, who joined the WAAF, and worked coding and decoding messages at Woodbourne base, frequently 'felt guilty' about having such a good time. 'The social life was marvellous', she recalled, and she enjoyed the company and the

Women war workers at the Colonial Ammunition Company in Hamilton undertake essential war service by loading rounds of bullets onto clips. *Photograph by John Dobree Pascoe, Alexander Turnbull Library, Wellington, 1/4-000858-F*

opportunities the work brought. By the end of the war, after stints in Auckland and Fiji, she was working in the Prime Minister's Department in Wellington.[60] For those who experienced challenging work and new prospects, the end of the war brought unexpected flatness as things were expected to return to 'normal'. Gwenda Christopher, who worked in meteorology with the WAAFs, recalled: 'I found it hard to settle down after I left the air force.' Most of her fellow WAAFs married and 'soon settled', but she remained unmarried until 1956.[61]

The Front at home

Women responsible for the care of children were automatically exempt from wartime manpowering, but industry's demand for labour did encourage some women with children into employment. The consequent need for childcare fused with new educational currents coming from abroad that emphasised child development through play.

Government funding for kindergarten trainees increased from £50 in early 1942 to £70 in June 1944 in order to attract young women into teaching. Voluntary Playcentres

Women stenographers work in an office in 1939. They were transcribing shorthand notes into typed form. *Alexander Turnbull Library, Wellington, PAColl-0785-1-091-002*

also began to open.[62] Many followed the model of the first Playcentre/day nursery, which opened in Karori, Wellington, in 1941, where mothers paid a small fee, rotated the supervision of children, and enjoyed the child-free afternoons this system created. As the need for women's labour increased, the nursery extended its hours. Daycare services for two- to five-year-olds and holiday supervision for school children became more common, but lack of adequate transport was a barrier to their use.[63] Women were more likely to make arrangements with relatives and neighbours to enable them to juggle the needs of children and work.

Wives of servicemen had their income from war work supplemented by monthly cheques of £10 from the armed forces, and an additional £2 55d for each child. Some women found they had spare cash at their disposal for the first time. As much as they might enjoy additional spending power, however, rationing and the cessation of home grocery deliveries imposed constraints on household shopping. By March 1942, supply shortages were compelling grocers to restrict the amount of tea customers could buy. The following month, the government, via post offices, issued ration books limiting eligibility for sugar and tea, and later for clothing and footwear. Women's ration books had an extra page of coupons specifically for 'fully fashioned stockings of silk, rayon or lisle (cotton), one pair every three months'.[64]

Lois White's mural *Controversy* was painted for the Auckland Workers' Educational Association in 1945, but was destroyed by fire several years later. Its human figures each represent a different walk of life and the composition depicts the tension between them. White was associated with the Elam School of Art from the 1920s to the 1940s, first as a student and then as a teacher. Her sensitivity to social issues and distinctive decorative style gained her a high reputation as an artist in the 1930s and '40s. *Museum of New Zealand Te Papa Tongarewa, Wellington, CA000205/001/0001/0001*

Women's productive enterprises, usually undertaken in the privacy of the home, were now noted in the daily newspapers as various patriotic committees competed for recognition. That baking and sewing had a public end meant it was appreciated in a quite different way from women's private efforts. That it was undertaken cooperatively meant that women were released from the isolation in which most domestic tasks were performed. Women's Institutes, the Women's Division of the Farmers' Union, Townswomen's Guilds and church groups set to work knitting socks, mittens, gloves, skull caps, jerseys and scarves for the troops. More than one million garments passed through the National Patriotic Organisation. The Red Cross and St John societies packed hospital supplies, while thousands of individuals prepared parcels of foodstuffs, including home-baked goods, and items such as cigarettes, razor blades, playing cards, books and handkerchiefs.[65] In the Tairāwhiti region, the Manutūkē Maori Mothers' Union sewed garments 'for hospital or war needs' and set about translating a prayer for peace into te reo Māori to be placed in every home.[66] Te Puea Herangi organised dances, garden parties and the sale of produce to assist the Red Cross. Under her leadership, a group of women made camouflage nets for home defence, and each Sunday at Tūrangawaewae she provided entertainment for troops from army camps. 'We sent £100 for our Maori prisoners of war in camp in Germany,' she recorded of one week in October 1941, '£100 for a marquee tent for the Maori Battalion overseas … and £200 towards comforts for the battalion, also £100 for the general purpose fund of the Waikato Red Cross.' Over six years of fundraising, Te Puea's efforts contributed between £30,000 and £40,000 to the war effort.[67]

Cooperative efforts turned fundraising into fun. The East Coast Patriotic Council organised a fundraising Queen Carnival that involved local communities organising dances, concerts, euchre parties and bring-and-buys. The opening street parade in Gisborne in September 1940 attracted thousands. Arapera (Bella) Halbert, crowned the Māori Queen, sat in a raupō whare, carried on a large truck, in the final carnival parade. In total, the carnival raised £15,000.[68]

There were, however, limits to the cooperative enterprise. Whina Cooper joined the Hokianga Patriotic Committee only to find that although Māori participation was welcomed, it was on limited terms. The Māori members were not trusted to control any funds. This insult inspired her to form a Māori war effort committee, which eventually became one of more than 400 set up around the country as part of the Maori War Effort Organisation. Led by Ratana MP Paraire Paikea, the organisation worked to enlist men and to direct Māori into essential industries. Women contributed voluntary labour, knitting socks and balaclavas, holding fundraising hangi, and packing comforts for the troops.

In the absence of men, Māori and Pākehā women alike found they had to mow lawns, chop wood, tend the vegetable garden, see to household repairs, and manage finances and sometimes family businesses, on top of the usual cleaning, laundry and cooking.[69] This shifting of boundaries, together with women's war work, enabled questions about domesticity to surface. In 1941, the *Listener* asked three prominent women for their opinions about an 'income for wives', a proposal first voiced (to public bewilderment) by Kate Sheppard in 1899. While the *Listener* respondents varied in their replies, all were convinced of the need for greater recognition of the work undertaken in the private sphere.[70] The widespread dissatisfaction with the burdens women carried in the home led a number of women's organisations, including the Plunket Society and the Christchurch Home Service Organisation, to request the Minister of Health, A. H. Nordmeyer, to call for a conference on women's work in the home.

In the winter of 1943, hatted and gloved representatives of prominent women's organisations gathered in Wellington to meet with the minister, the four women members of Parliament, the wife of the prime minister, Janet Fraser, and Mr Bockett of the

Manpower Department. The representatives from the Women's Division of the Farmers' Union, the Home Service Association, the Women's War Service Auxiliary, Wellington Mothers' Helpers, the Dunedin and Wellington Townswomen's Guilds, and the Canterbury Women's Institutes detailed the urgent need for domestic help for the mothers of the country. 'I hope to arouse public interest in the cause of the average housewife,' Christina Guy wrote. The housewife was 'usually so busy looking after home, husband and family that she takes but little interest in public life herself, and so her voice, unlike the organised voice of industrial workers, is not heeded'.[71] Women caring for families found it difficult to understand, for example, that while hotel domestic work was classed as 'essential' in wartime, there was no provision allowing domestic workers to be sent to assist mothers in hard-pressed households, and little recognition of the extent of women's domestic labour.[72] Vivid vignettes of hardship were given: the case of a family with nine children under fifteen and the mother going to the nursing home to give birth to the tenth child; a farm woman about to have her sixth child at a time when her husband had urgent tasks on the farm; an ill woman about to have her third child while her husband was away serving in the forces.

'The emancipation of women,' Christina Guy wrote after the Wellington conference, 'has been rather unevenly distributed. The one to receive the least benefit has been the seven-day-week worker – the mother.'[73] The invited delegates all wanted the status of the household worker to be raised and a comprehensive scheme of domestic assistance introduced by the government, utilising the many schemes already being run by voluntary women's groups. The assembled women stressed the very real difficulties of running a home with young children, and endorsed the expansion of kindergartens, creches and nursery schools.[74] In the absence of household help, new solutions had to be found to assist with the care of young children.

The government's response was, in part, to ameliorate the conditions of domestic workers by greater regulation. The Annual Holidays Act of 1944 instituted a fortnight's paid holiday, while the Minimum Wage Act of 1945 set a minimum wage for female and male workers over twenty-one years.[75] Women's wages were set at 60 per cent of the male wage (£5 5s for adult male workers and £3 3s for adult female workers). The conditions of paid domestic workers were now regulated in the manner of shop and factory workers (demarcating their work from that of wives). The consequent rise in cost to employers probably accelerated the decline of formal domestic service. At the end of 1945, the government established a Home Aid Service in the hope that a new name might raise the status of 'domestic service'.[76]

The daily battles of women on the home front were heightened by the rising birth rate. From an all-time low of 16 births per 1,000 in 1935, the rate had risen to 22.8 per 1,000 in 1941. Births were welcomed in the *Listener* as a 'fine way of saying "Yah" to Hitler', and "Yah" to Hirohito too'.[77] Yet even as the work of households increased with more babies and absent men, other job opportunities accelerated the flight of women from the poor

The Wellington Free Kindergarten in Taranaki St, pictured about 1944, was open during the war to the children of parents 'engaged in work of national importance.' *Alexander Turnbull Library, Wellington, PAColl-0981-1-06*

conditions of domestic service. The Dean of the Otago University Medical Faculty was only one of a number of prominent citizens who called for the state subsidy of trained domestic workers to raise the status of the worker in the 'most important factory in the land, the home'.[78] Only 9,169 women were classified as domestic workers by 1945, compared to more than 29,000 in 1936. As a result, housewives across the class spectrum were ever more firmly tied to household tasks. Formerly, those with resources hired others to help with childcare and household work; now all women with families, whatever their social class, had to do more. Housework, partly in response to new postwar ideas about the dangers to children of maternal deprivation, came to be reinterpreted as an expression of love for one's family, best undertaken by mothers alone.[79]

Financial recognition of the importance of mothers finally came in the month after the war ended, when the government committed to the introduction of a universal Family Benefit. 'We have to create such enthusiasm for the service the mother renders, that it will be lifted to the highest pinnacles of the service in the nation,' the Minister of Internal

Polish refugees arrive in Wellington in November 1944. Some 800 people, most of them orphaned children, were accepted for permanent settlement in New Zealand because of the situation in Poland as the war drew to a close.
Photograph by John Dobree Pascoe, Alexander Turnbull Library, Wellington, 1/2-003624-F

Affairs argued.[80] Introduced in 1946, the benefit was paid directly to the mother and set at a generous 10s per week per child (nearly $40 in today's terms). It gave Māori and Pākehā women a reliable means to pay for groceries and clothing when the family income might vary greatly from week to week.[81] Some Pākehā officials took it upon themselves (with no authority) to monitor Māori spending of the benefit – a list in Ruatōria, for example, forbade spending on soft drinks and biscuits, amongst a number of other items.[82] But for Māori with large families, the universal Family Benefit was a significant and welcome innovation. Previously unregistered births were quickly registered, since birth certificates were required in order to receive benefits.[83] Marriage was also a prerequisite, and some couples decided to formalise their customary marriages.[84] Heni Brown had married Ned Brown according to Māori custom by being blessed in the Mangatū River. Three or four years and two children later, they married in accordance with European law because 'social security was so important'.[85] The postwar world was one in which women were enjoined by the state to dedicate themselves to home and family.

Wartime relationships

Constant anxiety about brothers, lovers, husbands and fathers overshadowed the self-reliance wrought by the war. No one was sure if families would survive intact. Losses seemed inevitable, and memories of loved ones killed in or damaged by the First World War were still sharp. Prior to the introduction of conscription in June 1940, some mothers refused to let their sons volunteer. 'I said no,' said one woman whose twenty-year-old son wanted to enlist. 'My husband suffered from the effects of warfare. It was the trenches then, and my son is not going.'[86] Dorothy Goddard took her children to live with her mother in Wellington when her husband left with the Second Echelon. She had a feeling that something was wrong on a day in early August 1942, and it was confirmed with the news that a man had called from the Post Office to deliver a telegram but had refused to leave it. She knew immediately that her husband, the father of her two children, had been killed in action.[87]

Other women were conscious of the importance of assisting the men abroad by writing to them. Kate packed parcels for the Patriotic Fund in Christchurch, and at Christmas she put a greeting message in a parcel. The note ended up in the hands of a soldier in Egypt, who asked her to write to him. Already writing 'to six or seven chaps', she added the new contact to her correspondence list and they wrote to each other for two years. One mail delivery brought twenty-one letters from him, leading the postman to remark, 'Somebody loves you.' The couple finally met at the Christchurch railway station when he returned in December 1945, and they married in May 1946.[88] Correspondence had the opposite effect for Olive Brookes, whose mail from her fiancé contained a letter 'to another girl'. Olive recalled, 'The war was an unsettling time for relationships.'[89]

The uncertainty of the future led many couples to invest in the moment. June Fleming refused the two engagement offers she had received 'before the chaps went away'. But she understood that the men wanted some anchor at home before they left and promised to write regularly to both of them.[90] Sheila Greenwood and Ken Smith met at a Red Cross dance in 1943 and became engaged after eight or nine weeks of courting. She recalled purchasing the five-diamond engagement ring the week before her fiancé's departure: '[H]e was on final leave and he was off overseas. He wanted to book me before he went away!'[91]

Edna May Warren married Gordon Law Familton in St Paul's Presbyterian Church at Ōamaru in January 1940. Unlike many wartime weddings, at which women made do with whatever clothes they possessed, the bride wore ivory and was attended by two bridesmaids. Nurses from the public hospital formed a guard of honour as the couple left the church. The reception was held at the Star and Garter tearooms, followed by dancing at the Lyric Hall. Not long after the wedding, the bridegroom sailed from New Zealand with the First Echelon.[92]

Mihi Edwards also married a departing soldier, but in less grand style, at the Anglican church at Arapuni in the Waikato, not far from Putāruru. It was a hasty decision, prompted by her sisters' enthusiasm and a sense that it would be wrong to let down a young man about to depart for war service. She quickly regretted marrying a man she did not love, but she remained married in name until 1950 when she sought a divorce.[93]

Wartime doubts about the future brought challenges to conventional relationships, especially when from 1942 American forces began coming to New Zealand for training before facing battle in the Pacific, or for rest and recreation after a time at the Front. In excess of 80,000 American troops spent time in New Zealand during the war years.[94] The Americans brought a new code of manners to relations between the sexes. '[T]hey gave us,' one woman recalled, 'the gentle, careful attentions that we were starved of, and moreover did it in a way that made us expect more of our boys when they came back.'[95] It was not only the gifts of flowers, chocolates and stockings that were attractive, but the fact that the American men seemed to want to talk and to socialise with women, rather than to spend time with their mates, as so many New Zealand men preferred to do.

Mihi Edwards met 'a very handsome Marine one day in a launderette'. He brought her six red roses on their first date. She fell head over heels in love with him, and they spent as much time as they could together before he shipped out to Tarawa. He sensed, rightly, that he would not come back alive. Half a century later, the memory of that wonderful time still made her weep.[96] Sonja Davies also fell in love, with a 'tall red-headed marine' from Nebraska who 'brought a new dimension' to her life as well as a sense 'of living on borrowed time'. Sonja knew nothing of contraception and would not have used it anyway. After her marine departed for the Pacific, where he too was killed, she learned she was pregnant. Her horrified stepfather refused to have her at home. She was seven months' pregnant when she was finally forced to give up nursing and went to stay with friends in Benneydale, in the King Country. She gave birth to her daughter, Penny, among the Māori mothers in Te Kūiti Hospital.[97]

The wartime sense of living on borrowed time broke down inhibitions, and the risk of unplanned pregnancy was ever-present. Contraception was still not mentioned, or was regarded as cold, calculated planning for an activity that was usually spontaneous. If it was to be used, men were expected to take charge either through the use of condoms (which few women would purchase for fear of being thought a prostitute) or by 'withdrawal' or coitus interruptus. Many shared Dr Hilda Northcroft's view that it was not 'the bad girls who have babies, it [was] the more innocent ones'.[98]

The social stigma of bearing an 'illegitimate' child led women to seek refuge in homes run by the Salvation Army or the non-sectarian Alexandra Home in Wellington.[99] The number of illegitimate births increased from 4.27 per cent of total births in 1938 to 6.01 per cent in 1944. For the mothers of these children, adoption presented one alternative to social shame and financial uncertainty, and the number of adoptions rose.[100] One young woman wrote feelingly to the *Evening Post* in October 1944:

The despair of a soldier's wife who finds herself bereft of a husband but compensated with a pension for life receives sympathetic consideration. The despair of a destitute unmarried mother, handicapped with a new baby, deserted, unwanted, can expect little sympathy or help, I find.[101]

The consequences of sex outside marriage could indeed be disastrous. After concealing the birth of her dead infant, a twenty-two-year-old woman was sentenced to two years' probation – even though her employer wanted her to return to her job because she was a 'very industrious girl, a good worker'.[102] The father of the child was an American soldier serving in the Pacific who had promised to marry the woman 'if anything happened'. Another young woman who became pregnant to a marine with whom her parents had forbidden her to associate went to a backstreet abortionist and died as a result of septicaemia.[103] In March 1943, the chairman of the Auckland Hospital Board reported that the hospital saw between twenty and thirty abortion cases each week.[104] Nationally, thirty-two women died from septic abortion in 1942, although sulphonamide drugs that were administered at the slightest sign of infection helped to keep the death toll down.[105]

The churches responded to the wartime climate of 'living for the moment' with a 'Campaign for Christian Order'. Joan and Bruce Cochran, who were active Methodists, produced a discussion pamphlet for the campaign, entitled *Sex, Love and Marriage*; they claimed that young girls were congregating to 'entertain' servicemen and that prostitution was 'becoming a game for the respectable "amateur" to play at'.[106] The pamphlet grouped masturbation, sadism and homosexuality together, and while the Cochrans noted that these activities varied in significance, they were described as 'but three of the ugly, and largely unrecorded, forms that sexual aberration may take'.[107] The dance hall and, according to the Cochrans, the easy availability of contraceptives in fruit and bicycle shops, encouraged moral decay. The pamphlet maintained that '[t]he only right reason for marriage is love', but emphasised the importance of a spiritual as well as a sexual component in such love.[108]

Moral arguments aside, the attraction between American servicemen and New Zealand women sometimes gave rise to bitterness and antagonism between New Zealand and American men. A young woman going out with an American might even be regarded as unpatriotic.[109] In a few cases, women themselves faced the brunt of men's anger. One husband beat his wife to death with a hammer after she told him she wanted to leave him for an American.[110] Even the barriers put in place by the American authorities – mandatory interviews by chaplains and company officers, final approval by battalion commanders – could not discourage almost 1,500 New Zealand women from marrying American servicemen.[111] In approximately one in seven of these marriages (often hastily contracted), the husbands deserted their brides. In the United States, divorce could be arranged in a few months, but the New Zealand partners had to wait three years. The women, therefore, might find themselves still married under New Zealand law to a man who had remarried in America. The Matrimonial Causes (War Marriages) Act 1947 was introduced to deal with this problem. The Act recognised decrees and orders issued in the United States, and shortened the period of desertion or separation from three years to twelve months.[112]

New Zealand men abroad also fell in love, and brought back wives to settle in a country many of them knew little about. Thalia Christidou was told by a friend prior to leaving Greece that in New Zealand 'the black people ate the white people'.[113] Over 4,700 dependants of servicemen, including over 3,000 wives, 700 fiancées and 1,000 children, arrived between 1942 and 1948.[114] Joyce McMurtry, from the Isle of Wight, found New Zealanders 'ultra conservative and a little difficult' when she arrived. She, at least, had a shared language; this was not the case for most women coming from Italy, Greece and other parts of Europe, or from the Pacific. Homesickness was compounded by strange food and different social customs. Plonerl Priest had met her husband when he worked as a prisoner of war on her family's farm in Austria. In New Zealand he provided her with a cookbook which she used with dictionary in hand. 'I had no idea what shape a rock cake should be. Was it like a pebble in the river or the rock of Gibraltar?'[115] Even more mysterious for many of these women was the way New Zealanders segregated by sex at social gatherings and the way 'rugby, racing and beer seemed the main topics of interest'.[116]

Foreign brides shared the impetus wrought by the dislocation of war to seek stability in family life. Wartime saw a dramatic alteration in marriage patterns as couples married at younger ages. From the 1890s through to the 1940s, 70 per cent of women under twenty-four were single. The 1940s saw a dramatic drop in the age at first marriage for Pākehā women, making it increasing likely they would marry in their early twenties. Marriage itself rose in popularity, reaching an all-time high of 12.4 marriages for every 1,000 New Zealanders in 1946.[117] Marriage remained the ideal to which all women should aspire, and the state envisioned its responsibility to women in terms of wifehood and motherhood. A 'married woman', it seemed, immediately acquired a degree of maturity and the ability to accept responsibility.

But for many women of this generation, like the First World War generation before them, the loss of men in the war meant loss of opportunity to marry. Martha, for instance, recalled, 'I lost my friend in the War and you don't start again.'[118] One single woman who had a fulfilling career as a deaconess spoke of the loss she felt in never having experienced 'an emotionally fulfilled sexual life'. Her energies were devoted to caring for the families of the Anglican parishes in which she worked.[119] Unmarried women felt their exclusion particularly when their friends joined the popular club for mothers, the Plunket Society. New Zealand was a 'couples' society.[120] Those couples were, of course, heterosexual, and in such a society lesbian women might live under cover of a committed friendship rather than openly acknowledging their sexual preference.

The influx of Māori women and men into the towns during the war years led to increased intermarriage. Yet there could be strong opposition from both Pākehā and Māori

Mrs R. S. Kain, mother of Second World War air ace Edgar (Cobber) Kain who was killed in the early years of the war, buys a war bond in 1947. Bonds were used to fund the war effort and support reconstruction. *Alexander Turnbull Library, Wellington, PAColl-0785-1-105-002*

parents. Māori kin might object to offspring marrying out of the iwi as much as to their marrying Pākehā, while European parents might object to religious differences, as well as expressing unease about racial difference.[121] Disputes unresolvable within families could end up in court. In 1944, a nineteen-year-old Pākehā woman pursued her case for marrying her Māori boyfriend and father of her prospective child as far as the Supreme Court. Her father had refused his consent to the marriage 'on account of [her fiancé's] dark blood'. A magistrate had upheld the father's refusal, stating that the objection was reasonable, and adding that 'during his sixteen years' experience on the Bench he had known a number of marriages of white women with Maori men, and he did not know of one that had not ended disastrously in the Maintenance or Divorce Court'.[122] In fact, the young woman's fiancé was the son of a happily married Māori man and English woman. The Supreme Court reversed the magistrate's decision, the judge maintaining that the well-being of the young woman and the interests of the unborn child were the prime consideration.

While marriage had reached new heights of popularity and was undertaken at a younger age, divorce was also on the rise. Increased stress on the social and, particularly, the sexual compatibility of couples led more people to seek marital dissolution when

Those on the home front were urged to grow their own fruit and vegetables to support the war effort. These Wellington women are planting a community garden in October 1940. *Alexander Turnbull Library, Wellington, PAColl-5927-24*

these expectations were unmet. In 1939, there were 1,092 decrees nisi and 1,032 decrees absolute; by 1946, the numbers had risen to 2,137 and 2,133 respectively.[123] One woman described the men's return from war as:

> a mixed-up time, and far more upsetting in personal relationships than can easily be imagined. Both men and women had changed. We women were now not so submissive or willing to take a back seat. We were capable and independent – qualities we needed to help men adjust to civilian life. But the men (and New Zealand as a whole) did not see it that way. We were expected to go back to the kitchen and to maternity. The post-war baby boom began.[124]

The grieving families of the 11,625 New Zealanders killed in action (along with 634 missing, 17,000 wounded, and at one point 8,086 held as prisoners of war) fostered agreement that the needs of those who served should have priority in the postwar world.[125] But meeting men's needs demanded a shift in outlook. The war had allowed many women to assume authority within the family, an authority it was difficult to relinquish when

American servicemen and New Zealand women socialise at the Majestic Cabaret in Wellington, in December 1944. All the American sailors in the photograph were killed on 29 January 1945 when the *USS Serpens* exploded off Lunga Beach, Guadalcanal, Solomon Islands, while servicemen were loading depth charges. *Alexander Turnbull Library, Wellington, PAColl-0089-1-16*

husbands returned. One nurse recalled: 'I was more mature than my years, self reliant, used to making decisions. For nearly two years we had experienced entirely different lifestyles.' She and her husband needed time to readjust to each other.[126] But women were being urged to return to old roles. Even before the war's end, WAACs were being offered courses on 'Planning your Trousseau', 'Adjusting Yourself to Married Life' and 'Furnishing and Managing your Home'.[127] Marriage, home and family were to remain the women's domain. In late 1945, the *Woman's Weekly* ran a number of articles on 'Rehabilitating the Men': women were advised to be self-abnegating and, when they felt overburdened, to 'remember those who never came back'.[128]

Some men 'never really settled down'. As one woman recalled, she 'copped it' because she was the only one her husband would talk to about his experiences – and 'he would talk by the hour'.[129] Many men chose to remain silent, but nightmares, depression and irritability corroded family life.[130] Much had been learned about war neurosis (what is now called post-traumatic stress disorder) from the First World War and there was greater public understanding about the effects of military service. Christchurch psychiatrist Maurice Bevan-Brown stressed that a supportive family atmosphere was crucial to recovery from wartime neurosis.[131]

With many men still overseas, women danced together at socials such as this Women's Institute gathering in Denniston on the West Coast in 1945. *Photograph by John Dobree Pascoe, Alexander Turnbull Library, Wellington, 1/4-001249-F*

The adjustment in relations between the sexes, previously regarded as a personal matter, began to attract more attention from interested groups. Marriage was increasingly seen as an arrangement requiring preparation and understanding. Prior to the war, the Domestic Proceedings Act of 1939 had introduced the first provision for conciliation into New Zealand divorce law (a magistrate could refer a couple to a counsellor to try and effect a reconciliation).[132] After the war, the New Zealand National Council of Churches, inspired by the British example, promoted home and family weeks that involved lectures and literature displays relating to family life, along with various church activities. These weeks gave direct impetus to the creation of Marriage Guidance Councils in three towns and indirect impetus to their development in others.[133] The Dunedin Marriage Guidance Council, for example, first met in November 1948; it was made up of representatives of the church, the medical and legal professions, and the National Council of Women. The council quickly organised a lecture series in 1949 for married couples, addressing 'man and woman', 'successful marriage', 'parents and children', and another series for youth focused on 'thinking of marriage', 'a sound attitude to sex' and 'what marriage is for'.[134]

A woman farewells a soldier in the Maori Battalion reinforcements at Rotorua railway station in January 1944. *Photograph by John Dobree Pascoe, Alexander Turnbull Library, Wellington, 1/4-000828-F*

Owing to the disruptions of war and rising divorce rates, marriage, once seen as natural and thus unquestioned, was now the focus of educational campaigns. One woman recalled:

> Young women in the years at the end of the Second World War were among the last of those raised in a society whose main expectations were that they would make good wives and mothers, and which gave the title of 'respectable' to a woman because she was married.[135]

Maintenance of that status required effort, and new organisations were designed to help women in that endeavour.

Political lives

It fell to an unmarried woman, Mabel Howard, to advocate for women in Parliament. The first woman to preside in the male world of labourers' unions, Mabel Howard moved from the local to the national scene when she was made national secretary of the 11,000-member New Zealand Labourers' Union in 1942.[136] Denied her father's Labour seat for Christchurch South on his death in 1939, Howard won the Christchurch East seat in 1942 for Labour. In

Women belonging to the Women's Army Auxiliary Corps welcome the 28th Maori Battalion at Wellington, on the battalion's return to New Zealand in January 1946. *Photograph by John Dobree Pascoe, Alexander Turnbull Library, Wellington, 1/4-001636-F*

her maiden speech in February 1943, she sounded a warning: 'The men of this country and of every other country have yet to realize that the whole outlook of women has changed, and that they are no longer going to be the servile creatures they have been.'[137]

The women's branches of the Public Service Association (PSA) exemplified this new outlook. From 1942 they had attacked the procedures that kept women relegated to the lowest ranks in terms of pay and promotion opportunities. The level of discontent among women was so high, they suggested, that 'but for Manpower direction, a large percentage of the female office assistants and shorthand writers and typists would seek positions outside the service'.[138] The issue was also raised by the Amalgamated Society of Railway Servants and discussed by Kathleen Ross, a public service worker, in a 1944 article entitled 'Are they 80% Efficient?' The answer was a resounding 'no' – women fulfilled their duties with the same efficiency as men and therefore deserved the same remuneration. Equal pay, the activists argued, was a just cause, and was a vital issue to the 'new world order'

Rationing during the war meant that many goods were highly sought-after. These women are queuing outside Salisbury's egg and poultry store in Dixon Street, in Wellington. *Alexander Turnbull Library, Wellington, 1/4-041095-G*

that would come with the end of the war.[139] In this new order, women were to be regarded as individuals, and not as the dependants of men. The loss of many thousands of men in war underlined the arguments of those who pointed out that not all women could expect to marry but might choose to pursue a career.

Caroline Webb, a teacher and member of the Parents' National Educational Union, charted the change in 1946:

> It was the generation of our grandmothers who won for us legal equality, or at any rate, laid the foundations of equality in the Marriage and Divorce Laws and the Married Women Equality Acts. Then our mother's generation won political equality for us, in winning the right to vote. But it still remains for us to complete their work by winning economic equality.[140]

The war years prompted Pākehā women to organise specifically on this issue. In fact, the Women's Committee of the Wellington section of the PSA won acceptance of the principle of equal pay from a consultative committee formed to examine salary scales. The National Council of Women and the Business and Professional Women's Association

Women relax in their swimsuits on the deck of the launch Royal Saxon, at Matakana in January 1949. *Photograph by W. Walker, Alexander Turnbull Library, Wellington, 1/2-027529-F*

supported their cause, fuelling the drive of other women's groups to fight for equal pay, even in the face of stiff resistance.

When Mabel Howard became the first woman in New Zealand's Cabinet in May 1947, more than 2,000 women in New Zealand and abroad wrote to congratulate her. She believed that gender should be irrelevant in determining the wage for a job, and was determined that her colleagues in the House should take the matter seriously. In 1950, when the National government introduced a Bill to raise the minimum wage, women (not covered by industrial awards) were to receive 25 per cent less than the male rate. Under the award system, men were paid more on the assumption that they were supporting a wife and children. Howard made her objection clear: 'If a man and woman are ... doing the same job, whatever it is, they should get the same wage. There is no reason whatever for any differentiation.'[141]

Meanwhile, as Minister of Health and Minister of Mental Hospitals, Howard was determined to make a difference. Her concern for polio sufferers led her to advocate for a new treatment developed by an Australian nurse, Sister Kenny, that was in use in other countries but opposed by the British (New Zealand Branch) Medical Association.

Howard organised for Sister Kenny to visit New Zealand and persuaded representatives of the association to attend a large public meeting in Wellington. Dr Charles Burns, opening the meeting, thanked the audience for their attendance and then announced, 'Now it's over to the Minister of Health.' Mabel Howard promptly responded, 'Since it's over to me, we'll have it' – and it was agreed that New Zealanders would be trained in the Kenny treatment.[142]

Perhaps Mabel Howard's most subversive action, and the one that garnered the greatest publicity, was her displaying of two pairs of outsized bloomers before the bemused men of the House in 1954. While her innovations in preventative health services such as childhood immunisation for diphtheria and whooping cough, and a free ambulance service, ensured better health outcomes for many people, this highlight of her campaign on behalf of women consumers had the potential to appear frivolous. But Mabel Howard was deeply serious. Customers could not try on underwear in shops, and disparities in sizing meant they were often cheated. The 'pinching of material out of women's clothing', she said, required redress. The establishment of both consistent sizing standards and a Consumer Council in 1959 were significant achievements in Howard's work to protect the interests of all consumers.[143]

Very different issues were at the heart of Iriaka Ratana's political career. Born Iriaka Te Rio in 1905, she was descended from Ngāti Hauā, Ngāti Ruru, Te Āti Haunui-a-Pāpārangi, Ngā Poutama and Ngāti Uenuku. Spending her childhood on the upper Whanganui River, she was educated at Hiruhārama School by the Sisters of Compassion, who encouraged her interest in music and singing. In her mid-teens, Iriaka and her family made a lengthy visit to the settlement of the religious leader Tahupotiki Wiremu Ratana that became known as Rātana Pā, and Iriaka remained behind when her family returned home. She joined the concert party (as the piano player in the girls' band) that toured with Ratana around New Zealand as well as Britain, Europe and Japan.[144] Ratana took with him on tour a copy of the Treaty of Waitangi, hoping to discuss it with the King and the British prime minister. The New Zealand government, however, advised the British government that the group had no official status, so they were denied an audience with the King. A visit to the League of Nations proved similarly abortive because it was not in session.[145]

In the mid-1920s, with the encouragement of his first wife, Iriaka became a second wife to Ratana, following Māori customary law.[146] She bore two children, one of whom died aged six. After Ratana's death in 1939, Iriaka married his younger son from his first wife, Matiu Tahupotiki Ratana, and together they farmed and raised their growing family at Whangaehu, on a Māori development scheme fostered by Apirana Ngata. Matiu Ratana, who became MP for Western Maori in 1945, was injured in a motor accident and died in October 1949. Iriaka decided to run for his seat in the forthcoming general election, although there were many in the Labour Party who held that 'the mother of a large family has heavy enough domestic duties without taking on the responsibility of watching the affairs of a large and scattered constituency'.[147] Opposition to her and another independent woman candidate, Katarina Nutana, was voiced by Māori men unwilling to contemplate women in politics. Having herself declined to stand, Tainui leader Te Puea Herangi also objected, on the grounds that a woman should not captain 'the Tainui canoe'.[148] The National Party candidate, Hoeroa Marumaru, expressed the views of other tribal leaders with the saying, 'If the hen crows, screw its neck. It is a bad omen.'[149] The voters thought otherwise, and Iriaka Ratana, who was pregnant at the time, won the seat by a very large majority. She was the first Māori woman member of Parliament, and served for twenty years.

Iriaka Ratana represented a new generation of Māori – those, she said, who had lost their 'tribal affiliations'. Rātana Pā was her home, and it became so for others who no longer identified with a tribal place. She had travelled the world, and been exposed not only to other cultures but also to Ratana's deep commitment to social equality for landless Māori. In her maiden speech to Parliament, she reminded the House of the great increase in the Māori population and the consequent desperate need for housing. In years to come she promoted welfare issues, including flats for the aged, and hostels and trade training for Māori youth moving to the towns. She described the Treaty of Waitangi 'as a "beacon light" for race relations'.[150]

Te ao hou: the new world

Iriaka Ratana emphasised that the foundations 'of Maori wellbeing are laid in the home, the starting-point of social progress and structure'.[151] When a conference of young Māori was held at the University of Auckland in the 1930s, it was assumed young Māori men were the key leaders. Iriaka Ratana's rise signalled an important shift, and in 1951 a meeting of Māori women was called to address matters of concern to Māori. The founding of the Maori Women's Welfare League ushered in a new era in which the national voice of Māori was heard most strongly from its women. A number of factors influenced this transition.

The Second World War had made Labour Prime Minister Michael Savage's 1936 promise of 'economic equality with racial individuality' seem hollow.[152] In the 1940s, the Labour government could not ignore the fact that two very different standards of living operated within New Zealand. An observer wrote about Ōhinemutu, a Māori village on the shores of Lake Rotorua: 'The contrast is indeed painful between the home life and surroundings of the Maori children in the area and that of their pakeha school-fellows.' The houses of the former, he suggested, should be 'condemned by the health department'.[153] A conference of the four Northern District Hospital Boards in November 1943 viewed 'with alarm the present housing, food, and general living conditions of the Natives in the North'.[154] And in the Manawatū, where Māori were drawn to Ōpiki to work in market gardens, they lived in such appalling conditions that the local medical officer of health commented that, though the Department of Health had few statutory responsibilities, it

Soldiers returning from the war were warmly greeted by their communities. Delight is evident in the faces of the young women – Gina Wineera, Olive Elkington, Erina (Edna) Daymond and Maria Wineera – at this welcome for the 28th Maori Battalion. The hākari or feast plays an important part in such gatherings. *Photograph by John Dobree Pascoe, Alexander Turnbull Library, Wellington, 1/4-001663-F*

'had many moral ones'.[155] Job opportunities also drew Māori families to Hamilton where, in one instance, more than forty people 'exist[ed] in some 3 to 4 dilapidated sheds with earthern [*sic*] floors' and without suitable sanitary facilities.[156] In July 1944, the Auckland Maori Tribal Executive Committee wrote to Peter Fraser, the minister in charge of the Maori War Effort Organisation, asking for urgent consideration of 'the dire need for housing to accommodate the Maoris of Panmure, Auckland and Pukekohe'. Families there were living in tents or one-room hovels.[157] In February 1945, a camp at Pukekohe was home to 110 young women from the Gisborne district who had been brought in to work on market gardens and at the quick-freeze plant that had opened there.[158]

In the mid-1930s, about 1,800 Māori lived in the Auckland metropolitan area. By 1943, the number of Māori in Auckland had grown to 10,000, more than a tenth of the whole

Women members of the Gisborne Kiwi Club, wearing warm coats over their traditional dress, practise a traditional action song before the hui at Ruatōria to celebrate the posthumous award of the Victoria Cross to Ngāti Porou soldier Te Moananui-a-Kiwa Ngarimu. He was awarded the VC for outstanding bravery in battle at Tebaga Gap in Tunisia. The hui on 6 October 1943 was attended by 7,000 Māori. The women are (from right) Paranihi Kahaki, Kura Johnson, Mate Kaua, Cissy Ryland and Miria Kaua. On the far left is Peggy Pitt Kaua. *Photograph by John Dobree Pascoe, Alexander Turnbull Library, Wellington, 1/4-000679*

Māori population of 97,000. Elders were concerned about young women going to the cities and joining the auxiliary services, but they also acknowledged: '[W]hat girl does not want to appear in uniform and strut down the street in uniform? That has its attraction for the Maori girl, just as for the Pakeha.'[159] The war expanded the type of work available to young Māori women, and many were employed in the essential boot and shirt factories, and in domestic work in hotels and restaurants. Many of these new urban dwellers found themselves subject to discrimination and housed in substandard accommodation. A few hostels for Māori girls were created (although never enough to meet the demand) and the Methodist Church organised a club for young Māori.[160] But the poor living conditions experienced by large numbers of Māori women working in Auckland hotels and restaurants led the Maori War Effort Organisation to recommend that the government appoint Māori women welfare officers to the Native Department.[161] These officers became crucial in the efforts to address Māori living conditions in the postwar world.

Care of the young was vital in Māori communities where the birth rates were high. Māori, noted a Methodist minister in 1943, were increasing in number three times as fast as Pākehā.[162] In 1939, the non-Māori birth rate stood at 18.73 per 1,000, while the Māori rate was 46.20 per 1,000. From approximately one-fourteenth of the North Island population in 1935, Māori were around one-twelfth in 1943. In 1940, it was calculated that 53 per cent of the Māori population was under 21, compared to 35 per cent of Pākehā; 44 per cent of Māori males were 'children or scholars', compared to 27 per cent of Pākehā boys; for girls, the figures were 46 per cent for Māori and 25 per cent for Pākehā.[163]

The youthful Māori population led to new concerns about education. 'The Maori child attending the Pakeha School,' noted the Wanganui Education Board, 'is in a cleft stick … while at school he must be a Pakeha, at home he must be a Maori or lose the respect of his own community.' The problems raised by the young Māori population were 'of tremendous importance to the whole of our New Zealand community', the board said, and its *Report on Character Training and Citizenship* urged that the matter be given urgent attention.[164] That attention came from the New Zealand Council for Educational Research which commissioned a study of Māori needs at the behest of the New Zealand Vocational Guidance Association. The author, H. C. McQueen, assumed that the life course of Māori women would be the same as that of Pākehā women: '[M]ost women will make their careers in their homes and children, and … therefore we must think in terms of a relatively short period of gainful employment for them, followed by domestic life for the remainder of their days.' He continued: 'So to think does not rule out the possibility of women giving their whole lives to careers, or of their returning to careers after a period of childbearing and rearing.'[165] McQueen noted that the twenty girls in one Māori college who wrote an essay on 'My Future Career' had similar career aspirations to their Pākehā counterparts. Nine intended to become teachers, eight wanted to be nurses and three planned to be shorthand typists.[166] However, these were girls who had remained in school; the career options for those who left school early were much more restricted.

Keeping Māori girls at school was seen as essential. According to McQueen: 'Girls who had earned independent incomes, who had lived and worked on equal terms with Europeans, who had, in other words, enjoyed pakeha standards of life, would not be content to marry and live in squalid conditions with few of the material comforts of the New Zealand home.'[167] Providing girls with educational opportunities would, in his view, ensure better futures. He recommended that accessible high schools should be built for Māori communities to prepare young people for work of all kinds.[168]

While the churches had done well in providing residential schools for girls, such as Queen Victoria (Auckland), Hukarere and St Joseph's (Hawke's Bay), and Turakina (Whanganui), more high schools were needed because the number of Māori children attending native and public primary schools had doubled over twenty-five years. In 1941, three native district high schools were established on the East Coast. Apart from fundamental subjects, they concentrated 'on home-making': boys received carpentry and building lessons, while girls learned 'practical home management, home crafts and infant welfare'. A fourth native district high school was opened at Te Kao, in the far north, in 1945. When the school leaving age was raised to fifteen on 1 February 1944, this had significant implications for girls. In effect, secondary schooling ceased being an optional extra for Māori girls; it was now the standard.[169]

From the late 1930s, Māori girls with two to four years' post-primary training, who were employed as pupil teachers or junior assistants, were encouraged by the Education Department to study via the Correspondence School or to qualify for teachers' training college.[170] As the young population increased, the need for teachers was clear. Mira Petricevich, of Te Aupōuri and Te Rarawa descent on her mother's side, entered teachers' training college 'as one of a group of Maori on a quota'.[171] As a child, Mira had loved reading and the worlds it opened up. She left the comfort of her community at Te Hāpua in the far north for secondary schooling at Queen Victoria in Auckland, and teaching seemed an obvious career. Mira also began an Education degree in Auckland but was told she had to do country service, a requirement of all newly qualified teachers at that time. Mira wrote to Prime Minister Peter Fraser, requesting an education bursary to finish her university study. Her request was accepted, and in 1945 she became the first Māori woman on record to complete a degree.[172]

Between 1940 and 1945, sixty-five Māori students, including Mira Petricevich (later Szászy), went to training college, many of them the recipients of continuation scholarships that had made it possible for them to complete secondary school. In 1947, university scholarships specifically for Māori enabled one woman to study home science at Otago University.[173] Thirty-five Māori women were listed as being assisted with re-establishment in occupations after the war, thirty-four after leaving the home services and one from the overseas services.[174]

In the face of the expanding youthful population, Peter Fraser used his powers both as prime minister from 1940 and as native minister from 1946–49 to push through policies that would facilitate educational and employment opportunities for Māori, and enhance the contribution of Māori women. He encouraged the promotion of Māori into positions of authority as well. Tipi Ropiha, of Ngāti Kahungunu, was one of these. It was he, together with Chief Welfare Officer Rangi Royal, who saw the potential of the women's committees promoted by Māori women welfare officers after the Second World War to help raise the standard of living in Māori communities. From these committees Ropiha and Royal sponsored the development of the Maori Women's Welfare League.[175]

At the time of the league's founding in 1951, Ernest Corbett, Minister of Maori Affairs in the National government, made clear his resolute stance against anything that savoured of segregation or separate development. In housing, for example, the policy was 'to disperse Maori households among European and not to segregate Maoris in separate

Four nurses leave the nurses' home to go on duty at Kaitaia Memorial Hospital, in August 1949. *Photograph by Edward Percival Christensen, Alexander Turnbull Library, Wellington, 1/2-040735-F*

communities'.[176] Ironically, he had no trouble welcoming the formation of a separate women's organisation which, in his eyes, would serve to promote integration. Members of the league were also opposed to segregation. As Mira Petricevich stated:

> Our organization does not exist because of segregation, but because of the very fundamental needs of our women, the most important of which is the need to identify themselves as self-determining individuals, with the right to choose what was best for themselves in this ever-changing world.[177]

Reporting on the progress of the Maori Women's Welfare League in 1954, poet and writer J. C. Sturm was asked why it was that Māori women were providing leadership on welfare issues in the 1950s.[178] She replied that:

> nearly all the disadvantages of the Maoris' position are felt most acutely in the home, so that it is the women, not the men, who have to cope with them daily, understand them more fully, and are most strongly moved to do something about them.[179]

The New Dance Group was founded in Wellington in 1945 by Rona Bailey, Olive and Philip Smithells and Edith Sipos. Its women members performed expressive modern dance works that often had political themes. The group was photographed performing in 1947, the year before it disbanded. *Photograph by Neville Lewers, Alexander Turnbull Library, Wellington, PAColl-6180-10-25*

In urban areas, Māori women provided the buffer between traditional expectations and the aspirations of the young people who sought, in many ways, to live like Pākehā.

The independence in decision-making and financial matters that women experienced during the war years carried through into the postwar years. Young Māori women embraced opportunities in the urban environment. Women had discovered they were competent in a range of fields both within New Zealand and abroad. To those in the public service, for example, it no longer seemed fair that they should be paid less for their work than their male colleagues. Tested for their capabilities in a variety of workplaces, and shown to be as good as men, activists found flaws in a system designed to reward male breadwinners and began a campaign that strengthened in the 1950s.

Arapera Kaa (Ngāti Porou, Ngāti Kahungunu) married Swiss photographer Pius Blank at St John's Church, Rangitukia, in 1958. Arapera was one of New Zealand's first bilingual poets, whose work offers insights into Māori culture, feminism, and the dual Māori–Pākehā world she lived in. *From* For Someone I Love – A Collection of Writing by Arapera Blank, *Anton Blank Ltd (June 2015); courtesy of Anton and Marino Blank*

Chapter Ten
Suburbia: Expansiveness and Confinement

Twenty years old and pregnant, Catherine Maclean married aspiring politician Bob Tizard in 1951 and, for a time, put an end to her studies.[1] 'The first years of our marriage,' she recalled, 'were all politics and babies; I had four children within five years and eight months.'[2] Cath Tizard's married life began near the start of an exceptional period during which the pattern of New Zealand women's family life, based around early marriage and childbearing, differed from what had come before.[3] Age at marriage for both women and men dropped significantly by international standards, and marriage became almost a universal experience for young women.[4] Hence, the 1950s saw a unique social climate of young couples raising larger families, and the needs of the children who would become known as the postwar baby-boom generation were paramount.

The 1950s began with industrial strife, but optimism gradually prevailed as full employment enabled high rates of home ownership; children safely walked to school and explored neighbourhoods, and the balance of women's domestic load changed as access to household appliances increased. Generous benefits made it possible to support large families: typically, married women had four children, the third highest fertility rate among developed countries in the western world. Busy mothers found themselves called upon for a wide range of voluntary endeavours, which also provided them with training in public life.

Māori death rates declined and the Māori population nearly doubled between 1951 and 1966. Many found new homes in the growing city of Auckland, though the standard of accommodation was variable.[5] New schools had to be quickly built for Pākehā and Māori children alike, and innovative organisations arose to assist with parenting, including its psychological aspects.[6] The latter appeared urgent as the baby-boom children absorbed exciting new trends in music and fashion from abroad, and threatened to become troublesome teenagers. Continually rising illegitimacy rates signalled new norms of sexual behaviour that were reinforced by the introduction of the contraceptive pill in 1961. Change was in the air.

In her 1963 book *The Feminine Mystique*, American author Betty Friedan powerfully dissected middle-class women's dissatisfaction with their lives, apparent in the New

Louise Henderson painted this cubist-influenced portrait of Betty Curnow in 1954. Dressed in red, gazing directly at the viewer and holding a cigarette and a white rose, Curnow is presented as the epitome of the independent modern woman.
Collection of Christchurch Art Gallery Te Puna o Waiwhetu, purchased 1972

Zealand campaign for equal pay. Friedan's work gave voice to the discontents of well-educated women who felt trapped in the home and unable to use their talents to the full.

Home lives

In February 1951, the postwar commitment to nation-building was marred by political strife at a time when those with communist affiliations were regarded as suspect. Confrontation between the National government and the leftist Waterside Workers' Union began over wages, and escalated when the watersiders refused to work overtime and the shipping companies responded by locking them out. The government brought in troops to run the waterfront, and enforced draconian emergency regulations. The conflict lasted 151 days and involved 22,000 waterside workers and unionists who supported them, including coal miners and freezing workers (in total about 8 per cent of the country's unionised workers).[7] Mabel Howard decried the government's harsh response to the unions as a 'war on women', because the emergency regulations apparently did not allow any assistance to the wives and families of the locked-out workers.[8] The National government used the confrontation to call a snap election, winning a victory that consolidated its position and effectively undid the united power of the Waterfront Workers' Union. The chilly climate of the Cold War dampened dissent, often discredited as 'communist-inspired'.

The waterfront confrontation highlighted, among other things, the centrality of women's unpaid labour in most households. The dispute was over male wages, but the length of the lockout called into question the notion of the male breadwinner. In Port Chalmers, as elsewhere, wives of locked-out men went to work to keep their families out of debt. Their husbands accepted responsibility for cooking and childcare, usually as a temporary necessity.[9] A longer-term reversal of roles was hardly appealing. Gwen Percy, working overtime in Dunedin, arrived home late one evening:

> [I]t was snowing. It was cold and I was miserable. I thought, well, I'll get home and I'll have something nice and hot to eat waiting for me … He'd cooked me some chips and eggs. Well, have you ever had chips cooked in cold fat … there he was, he had a pot of chips and some dripping on the fire … there he was stirring away with a wooden spoon and it was all mushed up and fatty. I thought that is it, I can't stand it any more …[10]

If the wives of the locked-out workers were distressed by having to leave their children, and by the decline in domestic standards, the end result was nevertheless a new-found independence and an increased voice in family budgeting. At a time when a judge in the Auckland Supreme Court had ruled that a wife's savings from housekeeping money must be returned to her husband, any sense of financial independence was very welcome.[11]

The Dunedin Tudor Clothing Company was among a number of employers to benefit from women's work during the waterfront dispute and offer women permanent jobs. But poor wages in general were a disincentive to remaining in employment once the men were

In this 1946 photograph, Dunedin mothers and children wait to see a Plunket nurse in a mobile clinic that visited the suburbs. Mothers valued the advice Plunket nurses provided and were keen to chart their children's development.
Otago Daily Times, *Evening Star Collection*

back at the docks. Nationally, women were paid on average about 60 per cent of the male wage, because it was assumed they were not supporting families. In addition, the social pressure on women with small children to return home was too great to resist when the men went back to work.

The national disunity caused by the waterfront strike was nowhere to be seen when the name Elizabeth flashed in neon light to welcome to the country the twenty-seven-year-old mother of two, Queen Elizabeth II, in the royal summer which began in late December 1953. Crowds assembled everywhere, from Waitangi to Bluff, to wave flags and greet the new young Queen.[12] She appeared to embody fairytale romance. Having been smitten with her distant cousin, Philip, at the age of thirteen, Elizabeth married him at twenty-one. Two children quickly followed, Charles born in November 1948 and Anne born in August 1950. Queen Elizabeth embodied grace, charm, young motherhood and evening-gown glamour. She was, as her visit to New Zealand illustrated, in fact a working woman who put duty to her role as head of the Commonwealth ahead of spending Christmas with her young children.

Readers of the *Woman's Weekly*, which reported on the royal tour with great enthusiasm, were expected to know the bargain that marriage entailed for most families: men worked to become homeowners and married women maintained the domestic side of

Women found many opportunities to knit and sew, as this photograph shows. Dorothy Pascoe talks to a woman who continues her work, on a mail launch in the Marlborough Sounds in January 1945. *Photograph by John Dobree Pascoe, Alexander Turnbull Library, Wellington, 1/4-045757-F*

life, even if they returned to part-time work once their children were in school. To assist young women in imagining their futures, the magazine ran a series about a young engaged couple, Judy and John, which exemplified the division of labour and ownership thought appropriate in 1954. The couple were planning to build a house: John would be the homeowner while Judy, preoccupied with 'the kitchen, the laundry, the decorating and the cleaning', was to provide the 'extras'.[13] The series exhorted young working women to save for the future and to be '*a great help to your future husband when you start planning your dream home*': Judy, the model fiancée, intended to work for two years after marriage so that she and her husband could 'buy extras like a refrigerator, washing machine, floor polisher, good radiogram and vacuum cleaner, in that order'.[14]

'Homes Weeks' and 'Parades of Homes' held in the major centres nationwide provided encouragement for young couples like Judy and John to build a house.[15] More houses were desperately needed, and suburbs like Hillcrest in burgeoning Hamilton, Ōtara in Auckland, Porirua East in Wellington and Aranui in Christchurch developed quickly, not always with adequate infrastructure.[16] Companies advertised economical house plans, and *Pictorial Parade*, the National Film Unit 'shorts' shown before a feature film, screened the 'Parades of Homes' in picture theatres.[17] *The Newsview Book of House Plans*, one of two booklets produced in a series by Wellington publisher A. H. & A. W. Reed, was aimed at the young family, 'and especially the most important member of the young family – the mother'.[18] The Architectural Centre of Wellington had a rather different focus in mind in its booklet *Demonstration House*. Here 'the hypothetical owner was to be a family man interested in his home, his garden, his books and his music'.[19]

Local authorities were encouraged to assist home ownership through a manual entitled *Housing the Citizen*, which began by advising that '[c]ontented citizens are a country's best assets, and adequate housing is essential to the welfare and happiness of the family group.'[20] The benefits of home ownership were regarded as so important by the government that they were to be conveyed to school children in a booklet entitled *Houses to Live In*. This told the story of the Walton family (father, mother, Peter, Annie and baby), whose lives were cramped by unsatisfactory housing design. Father and mother each made a list of their requirements for a new house. Mr Walton's list was primarily concerned with leisure, and house and garden maintenance, while Mrs Walton's much longer list revealed priorities to do with convenience for housework and childcare.[21] The home was clearly Mrs Walton's workplace and she wanted it to be well organised. Men were much more likely to associate their work around the home with leisure, which they saw as a 'welcome change from work'. Women, on the other hand, saw leisure as something done for pleasure: gardening, knitting, sewing and reading were listed as favourite activities.[22] These contained the satisfaction of creativity and completion – unlike other household tasks, such as washing and cleaning, which had to be repeated weekly, if not daily, and were remarked upon only if left undone.

Mrs C, the thirty-four-year-old wife of a clerk in the public service and mother of five children, dealt with the reality of household life rather than any ideal. Her work began at 6.15 a.m. Her young baby was asthmatic; her seven-year-old had contracted cerebro-spinal meningitis at eight months and was assisted by the family's association with the Crippled Children's Society. Mrs C herself had bad varicose veins and bronchial asthma. Busy as her days were, she found time in the evenings to belong to the Kindergarten Mothers' Club, a church club, the Mothers' League and the Plunket Mothers' Club. Mrs C was also on the committee of the local intermediate school and involved in Girl Guides and Brownies.[23] A great many other women shared Mrs C's commitment to service, enriching their communities through their energy and skills – all voluntarily provided.

Women were linked in the rhythm of their household days by radio programming, and the ability to receive radio broadcasts became an important consideration in home design.[24] A 1954 social survey of Hāwera noted the home-centred leisure activities of Māori and Pākehā.[25] In all households, the sound of the radio provided the main leisure activity, as well as a window into the world beyond the home. Adored radio personality Maud Ruby Basham, better known as 'Aunt Daisy', began endorsing products over the national ZB network at 9 a.m. In the Roxburgh hydro town, 'shops did little business until the 4ZB Feature Hour finished at 11 am'.[26] Rotorua's 1YZ began the housewife's Monday (after the children had gone to school) with *Washtub Tunes* at 9.15. At 9 a.m. Wanganui's 2XA aired *Homemakers' News and Views*. An hour later, Christchurch's 3YA devoted a half-hour to 'Mainly for Women', which included *Town Topics* and *Artists New to Listeners*. A devotional service followed at 10.30; 'Mainly for Women' resumed at 2.30. All the ZB stations in the main centres had a *Woman's Hour* at 2.30, which might include news from women's organisations, a travel item, entertaining tips ('Let's Give a Party') and book reviews.[27] Dunedin's 4YA *Topics for Women* included segments on 'Life among the Maoris' and 'This is the Law: Property'. A number of stations ran 'Home Science Talks' and had a 'shopping reporter'.

'The housewife's social conscience,' a radio reviewer commented in 1951, 'so often diluted by dishwater and beginning and ending at home [was] offered a chance to develop a little': 2YA's well-presented Tuesday morning series *Other People's Problems* addressed topics such as 'Speech Therapy', 'Child Welfare', 'The Play Centre Movement' and 'The After Care Association'. If the housewife preferred romance to reality, she could always avoid such worthy programming and listen in to *My Husband's Love*, *The Woman in Black*, *The Second Mrs Manning* or *The Crossroads of Life*.[28] The power of *Dr Paul: Radio's Great Story of Adult Love* and *Portia Faces Life*, a story 'taken from the heart of every woman who has dared to love completely', was such that some listeners had them taped when they were unable to listen to them.[29]

From 1961, television promised a widening of horizons, but transmission and coverage were initially limited and the entertainment not to everyone's taste. 'Has it ever occurred to those who select our TV programmes,' one irate viewer wrote to the *Listener* in August 1963, 'that half of New Zealand's population are women and that they too would like to enjoy television? Like most other things in this country, our programmes are chosen by men, for men.' Men seemed to prefer westerns with guns and 'bashings', in contrast to the human interest in the medical drama *Dr Kildare*.[30]

The telephone was available only to a select few early in the century, but had become much more ubiquitous by the 1950s, the numbers growing tenfold from 1910 to 1950.[31] For a time, demand outstripped supply: in 1960, for example, 28,711 applicants were waiting to have a telephone installed.[32] 'Great store is placed on the telephone in the country,' one study noted, where 'long daily conversations replace to a certain extent the afternoon tea parties one meets within towns.'[33] For Māori who had moved to the city, the telephone provided a personal, if expensive, way of keeping in touch with whānau who had access to a phone line. By 1961, New Zealand ranked fifth in the world in telephone ownership, with 42.63 telephones per 100 of the population. Other amenities were also increasingly sought after. By the mid-1950s, more than 50 per cent of Pākehā households had a washing machine and a refrigerator.[34] Indeed, piped water, hot water on tap, a bath and shower, a flush toilet, a refrigerator and a washing machine were becoming the norm for Pākehā; rural-dwelling Māori families were far less likely to have such amenities.[35]

The proportion of those buying houses increased steadily over the 1950s, while renting declined.[36] By the end of the 1950s, 69 per cent of houses were in the keep of owners (with or without a mortgage) – an increase of 8 per cent since the start of the decade.[37] Home ownership was much more difficult for Māori, whose incomes were well below those of Pākehā.[38] In 1951, 32 per cent of all Māori houses were classed as shacks or overcrowded houses, and more than 500 households lived in tents.[39] State housing provided better amenities but might be occupied by more people than planned for. In Wellsford in 1954, for example, four married couples, three babies and eight older children shared a five-bedroom state house. There, close quarters and lack of a town water supply assisted the spread of impetigo and summer gastroenteritis among the Māori community.[40]

Government policy supported the desire of many Māori to move to the cities for employment. Waerete Norman's mother was the 'driving force' behind the family's leaving the 'corrugated tin shack' community of Ngātaki, on Northland's Aupōuri Peninsula, for Auckland. The family of five first moved in with other whānau members to a boarding house on Grafton Road, sharing cooking and bathroom facilities with other Māori, Rarotongan and Samoan families. Eventually they moved into a Maori Affairs Department-built 'little matchbox three-bedroom home' in Mt Roskill. Waerete recalled that the house was built with cheap apprentice labour, and the toilet (on the back porch) had a door that could neither open nor shut until the side of the toilet seat was sawn off. The Norman house nonetheless provided a starting point for the extended family keen to live and work in the city.[41]

Māori migration to the cities gave rise to new problems of housing and welfare. During the war, women welfare officers had been appointed on the recommendation of the Maori War Effort Organisation to help the young Māori women moving into the cities to find work and accommodation. This initiative was coopted by the government in late 1944, when the Department of Maori Affairs created a new welfare branch and appointed welfare officers. By 1947, thirteen of these officers were women, and they provided invaluable assistance to families bewildered at how to apply for various benefits or for housing.

By 1950, over 12,000 Māori were living in Auckland, many of them in substandard housing.[42] Whina Cooper, newly elected president of the Maori Women's Welfare League, instituted a housing survey that exposed gross overcrowding and a lack of basic amenities.[43] As a result, the league forwarded 519 applications from Māori and 32 from Pacific Islanders for state rentals, and both the Auckland City Council and the Departments of Maori Affairs and Housing began to demolish slums and increase the number of state houses being built for Māori.[44] *Te Ao Hou*, a bilingual quarterly magazine published by the Department of Maori Affairs from 1952 as a vehicle for discussion of Māori interests, canvassed a range of matters relating to home ownership. In 1959, for example, the magazine reported on the forty-one entries for the Mangōnui County best-kept Māori home competition, sponsored by local businesses. The competition, seeking the best of 'Maori arts combined with western comforts', was judged to be an outstanding success.[45]

State housing was concentrated in urban areas where employment was available, but not all Māori were attracted by city living. Many were 'reluctant to move' from their home areas because they had 'deep-rooted affiliations' with their districts. Officials suggested that the government should 'help the people reorient their thinking'.[46] Eruera Tirikatene, Ratana MP for Southern Maori from 1932 (knighted in 1960), believed that racism, rather than Māori intransigence, was the problem to be addressed; he condemned the 'rampant' discrimination against Māori seeking accommodation. In a 1964 parliamentary debate, he suggested that such discrimination should be made a punishable offence.[47] The following year, the Minister of Maori Affairs, Ralph Hanan, claimed that about 32,000 Māori had been rehoused, and that this would provide a 'firm platform' to enable 'Maori children to attain better health, better education and better opportunities of employment'.[48] The Maori Women's Welfare League was in the vanguard of action, so that by 1960 it was said to be 'generally more alive than the tribal organisations'. By that year, 'that grand band of voluntary workers' had spawned 358 branches, with more than 3,200 members committed to health and welfare issues.[49]

Iriaka Ratana regarded the Labour government's 1958 Family Benefit (Home Ownership) Act, which enabled parents to capitalise the family benefit to buy a new home, as a great boon to her people. The provision of housing, she believed, encouraged 'better citizenship'.[50] When the average price of a new house without a section was around £3,050 (approximately $134,000 in 2015), capitalisation allowed families a maximum of £1,000 as a deposit.[51] In 1960, senior civil servant J. K. Hunn was asked to prepare a report on Māori assets. Published the following year, his report was much more far-reaching and included discussion of the disparity between Pākehā and Māori standards of living, including housing.[52] It recommended that Māori homes be 'pepper-potted' through Pākehā areas in an effort to improve the conditions of Māori and advance the assimilation of the races. In effect, the policy expected Māori to conform to Pākehā ways; Pākehā houses, with women at their centre, would provide the frame in which the transformation of values would be enacted.

The Maori Women's Welfare League's dedication to improving houses up to the standard of those inhabited by Pākehā sprang from a desire to promote health. The Minister of Maori Affairs also emphasised the necessity of presenting 'a good image to the Pakeha'.[53] The latter imperative was one of the reasons for the anger felt by league members when *Washday at the Pa* was published by the Department of Education in 1964. Produced for use in primary schools, the booklet was intended as one of a series designed to illustrate family life in different parts of New Zealand.[54]

Twenty-one-year-old Ans Westra, the freelance documentary photographer commissioned for the project, had come to New Zealand in 1957 from Holland, one of the 1950s influx of Dutch immigrants. She brought a fresh eye to her adopted country and soon received commissions from the Education Department's School Publications Branch and

Traditional crafts survived through women passing on their skills. In this photograph women from Ōtaki are making tukutuku panels at a Māori crafts workshop held at the Dominion Museum in Wellington in February 1936. *Alexander Turnbull Library, Wellington, PAColl-5927-60*

Te Ao Hou. As an outsider and new immigrant, Westra 'wanted to document particularly Maori things – in the rural rather than the urban area', for she was aware that she was witnessing a period of rapid change.[55] Westra's photographs in *Washday at the Pa* show a Māori family carrying out daily tasks in a house lacking electricity and hot water. The images are of a happy, if materially deprived, family, whose apparent richness of life is contrasted with the somewhat bleak image of the new state house they are soon to occupy. Members of the Maori Women's Welfare League objected to the booklet on a number of levels, arguing that Māori women themselves should determine the ways in which their lives were represented. The league unanimously called for the Minister of Education to withdraw the publication, lest it have 'a detrimental effect on the efforts of our people to establish themselves in better living conditions'.[56] In August 1964, the minister ordered the destruction and withdrawal of all 38,000 copies of the booklet. While many liberal Pākehā were annoyed at apparent government censorship and saw the league's stance as conservative, they failed to appreciate the extent of the prejudice against Māori.

Mira Petricevich, later Dame Mira Szászy, speaks at the inaugural conference of the Maori Women's Welfare League in 1951. She was the league's first secretary and its president in the 1970s. The league brought together Māori women from around the country to work for improvements in health, education and employment; by 1956, some 300 branches had been established nationwide. *Archives New Zealand The Department of Internal Affairs Te Tari Taiwhenua, National Publicity Studios, AAQT 6401 W3537 A24594*

Discrimination in hotels and rental accommodation was common. At a time when Māori women were made to feel unwelcome even in local restrooms, the booklet's depiction of their way of life could easily foster misunderstanding.[57]

The picture of Māori life that appeared in *Washday at the Pa* differed little from that in earlier *School Journal* stories.[58] By the 1960s, however, the equation of domestic modernity with social worth was such that the league could only be outraged at a depiction of Māori as pre-modern. Pride in the home was central to women's self-esteem in the 1950s and 1960s, and *Washday* was 'hardly encouraging', one league supporter stated, to the 'very real efforts of the Maori to improve the welfare of his race'.[59] In fact, it was the women's efforts that were being overlooked. The home was both central and marginal: central as a mark of status and the site of familial relations which held society together, and marginal in that the work within it was unpaid and unnoticed, except during times of public concern about the state of the family.

Food was cooked in pots over an open fire for the feast after the wedding of Arapera and Pius Blank in 1958. *From* For Someone I Love – A Collection of Writing by Arapera Blank, *Anton Blank Ltd (June 2015); courtesy of Anton and Marino Blank*

Working women

The controversy over *Washday at the Pa* occasioned cries of nostalgia from some who wished for women's interests to be safely located within the bounds of home and family – for a world where happiness was seen to lie in mothers' absorption in domesticity rather than engagement in the workforce. In fact, a subterranean shift in women's lives was going on – the proportion of married women employed in work outside the home increased from 12.9 per cent in 1956 to 20 per cent by 1966.[60]

The 1950s saw growth in the New Zealand economy, as wool suppliers profited from the Korean War of 1950–53 and employment expanded in both construction and manufacturing. The state invested not only in house building but also in other major

Winnie Te Tai, Mrs Russell and Mrs Parker prepare peaches for preserving in the kitchen at Te Ūnga Waka Marae, Auckland. Te Ūnga Waka, established by the Catholic church in 1966, was one of a number of urban marae that provided a community base for Māori coming to the city. *Auckland Diocesan Catholic Archives, File 668C(I)*

public works: hydroelectricity, highways and airports.[61] Import controls protected local manufacturers, who were desperate for more employees to meet production. Social security, the government reminded the public, could 'only be paid for by a high level of production' from everyone. Workers must put in effort not merely for themselves but 'to keep New Zealand prosperous'.[62] Women's 'nimble fingers and racing machines' were needed to supply garments for New Zealanders. Women were also sought for the production of new light electrical goods such as kettles and radios, and for the growing clerical and service sectors.[63] Businesses offered complimentary holidays, discounts on company goods and free cigarettes 'to entice women workers'.[64]

Women's increasing involvement in the labour force highlighted the gap between women's and men's wages. Women were clustered in female-dominated occupations where wage rates were traditionally low: they were nurses and midwives; primary teachers; stenographers, typists and clerical workers; tailors, cutters, furriers; salespeople, shop assistants; and housekeepers, cooks, maids.[65] The annual wage bracket for most nurses was between £100 and £299 a year, whereas the comparative wage bracket for policemen and firefighters was between £700 and £899. Under the category 'typists, stenographers

Women greet the manuhuri (visitors) at a tangi at Tūrangawaewae Marae, Ngāruawāhia, in 1963. *Photograph by Ans Westra*

and other related workers', men predominated in the £700 to £899 annual wage bracket, while women were more likely to earn £300 to £499 a year.[66] Lida Weterman-Opdam, the head waitress at the New Zealand Tourist Bureau hotel at Milford Sound in 1957, earned £6 a week, while her chef husband earned £10 a week. They could save for their future because the hotel provided free board and lodging (in a basic cabin).[67]

The postwar baby boom heightened demand for teachers and health workers. Throughout the 1950s, employers desperate for staff called on the idea of women's commitment to service in an effort to fill jobs. 'Be a nurse,' a much-repeated advertisement in the pages of *Te Ao Hou* urged, and by the age of twenty, 'be assured of a position in an honoured profession either in New Zealand or overseas'.[68] '[N]o woman gains greater pleasure,' another advertisement suggested, 'than the nurse, through her sense of service to mankind.'[69] In the light of these exhortations, it is perhaps not surprising that women were concentrated in such service occupations: in 1951, more than half the workers in community, social and personal services were women. Their numbers had grown markedly too. Between 1956 and 1961, women wage and salary earners increased by more than 19 per cent, due to the rising number of married women entering the workforce. In 1956, married women made up 33 per cent of the female labour force; by 1961, this had increased to 38 per cent.[70] Ten years later, married women made up the majority of the female workforce, at 55.8 per cent.[71]

Māori women's participation in the service sector grew as opportunities in the primary sector, such as agriculture and fishing, declined.[72] By 1956, records suggest that 38 per cent

A kuia performs while another plays a mouth organ during celebrations at a hui at Tūrangawaewae Marae, Ngāruawāhia, in 1963. *Photograph by Ans Westra*

of Māori women aged between twenty and twenty-five lived in urban areas, compared to 31 per cent of Māori men.[73] Eighty-nine young Māori women took up apprenticeships in Christchurch between 1958 and 1962.[74] But Auckland was a particular focus for those seeking work in the early 1960s.[75] The Auckland Hospital Board advertised for cooks, housemaids, laundry assistants, waitresses and kitchen assistants in the pages of *Te Ao Hou*, hoping to attract young single Māori women by the offer of full board and accommodation and good pay.[76] By the late 1950s, Waerete Norman's mother was working shifts at the Auckland Hospital laundry in Newmarket, alongside Pacific Island women.[77]

Māori women were also recruited for careers in general and psychiatric nursing, and as nurse aids. In 1958 alone, 100 Māori women were assisted to take up nursing training by the Department of Maori Affairs.[78] Dental nursing and teaching provided other avenues of employment for those with secondary education. Vivian Hauraki (later Kahi) was lucky enough to find work at home in the Hokianga. Her commercial practice teacher recommended her for a clerical position at the Rāwene hospital in March 1957. Vivian's father had recently died; her mother was caring for her new baby sister (the latest addition to the family of ten sisters and two brothers), and Vivian had no desire to milk cows on the farm. A novice typist at the beginning, Vivian learned fast, using the hospital's only typewriter, working for everyone who needed it and fielding the telephone calls. As her skills grew, Vivian played a central role in the hospital's administration. A chance opportunity to try out for a post turned into more than fifty-two years of dedicated service.

She took particular pleasure in seeing some of the local young women who began as nurse aids train as registered nurses.[79]

About a quarter of the total female labour force worked in the secondary sector of industrial production in 1951, concentrated mainly in manufacturing.[80] The latter provided an important avenue of employment for Māori women as well as the increasing number of Pacific Island women coming to New Zealand. Caroline Munokoa Tuteru, for example, arrived in New Zealand in 1942, one of a group of young women recruited from Rarotonga as domestic servants. After working as a housemaid and cook for a doctor's family for six years, she moved into factory work, 'making expensive dresses', for which she was paid much more than she was as a housemaid.[81] The shortage of labour in manufacturing was such that one Wellington soft goods company approached the Department of Labour to find workers for its factory. In collaboration with the Department of Maori Affairs, it recruited twelve young women from Wairoa. The company paid for the women's transport to Wellington, helped them to find accommodation and paid their first week's board.[82] In Auckland, a food manufacturing plant employed a number of Te Rarawa women who had moved to the city from Panguru in the Hokianga.[83] The New Zealand Post Office urged young women to join the telephone service with the words: 'Mahia nga mahi kei tamariki ana/Make the most of your time while you are young'.[84]

A buoyant economy and demand for women's labour were only two of the factors challenging the concept of the male breadwinner in the postwar years. Universal Family Benefits also undercut the idea that a man needed a better wage to support his family.[85] After the Arbitration Court dropped the concept of the breadwinner wage in 1954, the Labour Party, then in Opposition, became more active in the equal pay campaign. Labour's 1954 manifesto promised it would encourage 'a progressive reduction in the margins of pay between men and women until the ideal of equal pay for equal work for the job is attained'.[86]

Quiet encouragement from supporters of equal pay turned to uproar in August 1956 over the case of Jean Parker. A senior public servant, Parker appealed against the appointment of three junior cadets who, by virtue of being male, automatically received seniority over her because of their potential for higher maximum salaries. The Public Service Commission responded that equal pay for women 'would be an injustice for the majority of men as family living standards would suffer'.[87] The Public Service Association (PSA) replied that many male wage earners did not have dependants, while a number of women did. Jean Parker was, in fact, supporting her medical student husband. On 29 August, the Public Service Commission announced its decision in the case. Parker's salary was to be reduced from £695 to a cadet's salary of £460 per annum, and she was to be transferred from her position of responsibility as a section leader to take on the junior duties of a cadet. The PSA immediately protested, joined by the National Council of Women, which was able to mobilise support instantly because its national conference was just then taking place. The forty-two branches of the council sent telegrams of protest to Prime Minister Sidney Holland, Opposition leader Walter Nash and other members of Parliament. The government denied responsibility for the fixing of public service salaries and defended the Public Service Commission. However, to stave off criticism of its stance, the prime minister announced a meeting with representatives of national women's organisations to discuss their interests.

After meeting with representatives of the National Council of Women, the Business and Professional Women's Club, the Post Primary Teachers' Association, the Federation of University Women, the Maori Women's Welfare League, the PSA, the New Zealand Educational Institute and the Country Women's Institute, among others, the prime minister was forced to modify his view. 'Times have changed,' he announced. 'Men used to be the breadwinners, but now I know that thousands of women have dependants and these women should be getting as much pay as men.'[88]

The Parker case highlighted the shift in public opinion towards the justice of equal pay for women. Jean Wishart, the dynamic editor of the *New Zealand Woman's Weekly*, saw equal pay as 'inevitable and logical', and believed that the only question was when it would be enacted.[89] From 1957, the Council for Equal Pay and Opportunity, a national body made up of organisations supporting equal pay, took the initiative on the issue, with the result that both National and Labour made equal pay part of their election platform in November 1957. Labour's victory at that election led to the passing of the Government Service Equal Pay Act 1960. By the time it was fully implemented in 1963, approximately one-fifth of all women in paid employment were working in the public service.[90]

Women outside government employment, often in service occupations, remained poorly paid. At the opening of the Maori Women's Welfare League conference in 1963, the Minister of Maori Affairs, Ralph Hanan, reminded his audience of 'the sacrifices Maori women are making to give their families a home life'. He noted that 'between 60% and 80% of the small army of state building cleaners in Wellington, who get out of bed to go to work at 2 o'clock, 3 o'clock or 4 o'clock in the morning are Maori women'. The minister asked what induced these women to do it, and the general answer was 'that they wanted to provide their children with a better education than they themselves had, and to enable their families to have better homes'.[91]

Recognising that marriage and paid work might now be combined, and in an attempt to lure women back into the workforce, in 1962 the government changed the tax status of married women: they would now be taxed as individuals, creating a consequent shift in the balance of power within marriage.[92] Women were marrying earlier, at around twenty-two years, bearing children, and then, at about thirty, were more able to re-enter the workforce, if only on a part-time basis. Work, as historian Megan Cook has noted, 'became an on-going and important part of female life and identity, and the conditions under which it was done were no longer a short term problem'.[93]

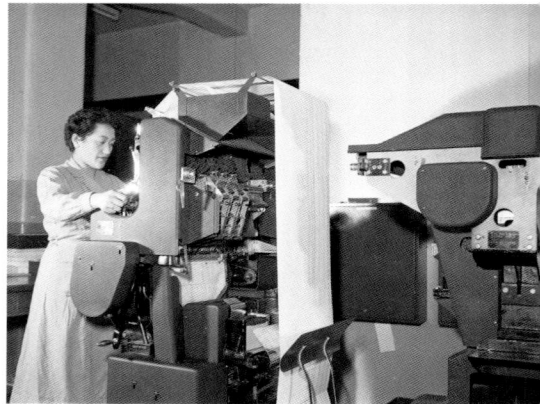
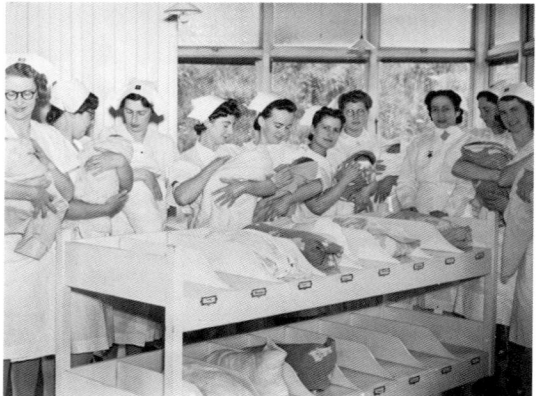

In mid-twentieth-century New Zealand, opportunities for women in paid employment (or their own businesses) expanded.

TOP: *Left* New domestic appliances proliferated over these years. In 1950, young women pack electric jugs at H. C. Urlwin Ltd, a Christchurch electrical goods manufacturer. *Right* Tangiora Ruawai from Wairoa operates a tabulating machine at the Post and Telegraph accounts branch at Herd Street in Wellington in the 1950s. After the Second World War, many young Māori from rural areas moved to the cities, taking up opportunities for employment, training and education.
Alexander Turnbull Library, Wellington, 1/2-033698-F; 1/2-040760-F

Appreciation of this issue led the New Zealand Federation of University Women and the New Zealand Federation of Business and Professional Women's Clubs to organise a conference on 'Women's Contribution to a Changing Society' in 1964. As a senior member of the Department of Industry and Commerce pointed out at the conference:

> If married women stopped work overnight, 100,000 children would have to be sent home from school because over 2,500 married women are active teachers, 10 per cent of the people in hospital would lack adequate nursing care because almost 1,400 nurses would have to be withdrawn, the equivalent of 20 per cent of shops of all kinds would have to close down, something like 2,000 businesses of various types would lose their managers, almost a quarter of the country's stenography and typing services would stop, and industry of all kinds would be hit to a greater or less degree. Many firms would be forced to close and for many others production would fall heavily.
> And this would be merely the first wave effect.[94]

The second wave would be the disappearance of around £750,000 in purchasing power and a significant drop in tax revenues, not to mention the decline in living standards in homes reliant on women's wages.[95]

The Labour Department, swayed by the growing numbers of married women in employment, responded to demands from women's groups to examine the issues raised by women's labour force participation more closely. In 1966, it set up the National Advisory Council on the Employment of Women 'to create the conditions for women to make their full contribution to the national economy consistent with their individual freedom and their responsibilities as wives and mothers'.[96] This brief enabled the committee to consider the educational levels of men and women, childcare issues, community attitudes to Pākehā working women, questions around part-timers, and the difficulties facing Māori and Pacific Island workers.[97] The role of women was opened up to analysis and debate. Most apparent was the gap between women's 'potential and their achievement'.[98]

In and out of school

One day in 1955, fourteen-year-old Beatrice Hill knocked on the door of the science teacher's laboratory. That teacher, Joyce Jarrold, had been dissuaded from studying mathematics at university in 1940: 'Girls don't become mathematicians. You had better do home science,' her headmistress had declared. Back teaching at her old school, New

OPPOSITE: *Middle left* Women of the Red Cross Voluntary Aid Detachment did a variety of nursing work; these VAD nurses are holding babies at the Alexandra Maternity Home in Wellington in January 1944. *Right* Rona Armstrong (right) works with an assistant in the family's store in Fitzroy, New Plymouth, around 1957. *Alexander Turnbull Library, Wellington, PAColl-6203-01; Private collection*

OPPOSITE: *Bottom left* Mrs Joan Hamilton ran a tourist bus service in the Lake Wakatipu area in the 1960s. Some women began driving long-distance coaches in the 1930s, but met with resistance from male bus drivers. *Right* Dental nurses work under supervision at the Mt Eden Dental Centre in the 1950s. The School Dental Service, set up in 1921, provided a popular career opportunity for young women. *Alexander Turnbull Library, Wellington, PAColl-0785-1-067; Auckland War Memorial Museum Tāmaki Paenga Hira PH-NEG-H1651*

Left A young woman bank teller is shown at work behind the counter in the 1950s. *Right* A 1950 pamphlet advertises jobs for Hutt Valley women at the tobacco factory of W. D. and H. O. Wills. The factory offered part-time and full-time work, provided free uniforms and a chartered bus to take women to and from work, and had a cafeteria for its employees. *BNZ Heritage Collection; Alexander Turnbull Library, Wellington, Eph-A-EMPLOYMENT-1950-01*

Plymouth Girls' High, Joyce Jarrold introduced physics as an option, and opened a door for a girl who, as Beatrice Tinsley, would become an internationally renowned astronomer whose research on galaxies had implications for understandings of the universe. There were not many women role models for physicists in the 1950s, but Beatrice decided that this was a subject asking fundamental questions she wanted to answer. Her school (with help from New Plymouth Boys' High) eventually accommodated her desire to study mathematics, chemistry and physics.[99]

Home science was no longer compulsory for girls, as it was between 1917 and 1942, but few girls were encouraged to venture into other, less domestically focused fields of science.[100] The teaching of physics remained poor in most girls' schools, making it difficult for pupils to qualify for entry to well-paid and prestigious professions like medicine, engineering and pharmacy. Instead, the academic streams in most secondary schools still encouraged young women to imagine professional futures in areas such as teaching and nursing. Commercial streams remained popular with parents, who saw them as offering their daughters an immediate passport to office life. Typewriters clattered as young

Tokelauans leave for New Zealand in 1966 as part of the Tokelau Islands Resettlement Scheme. The Tokelau Islands have been administered by New Zealand since 1925, and from 1948 Tokelauans have had New Zealand citizenship. In the 1960s, the New Zealand government became concerned that the Tokelauan population was becoming too large for the small islands, so assisted families to emigrate to New Zealand. *Archives New Zealand The Department of Internal Affairs Te Tari Taiwhenua, AAQT 6539/69 A81,257*

women learned to touch type at speeds that made them excellent secretaries. Oven doors clanged as girls in home science classes checked their freshly baked goods, perfecting skills invaluable in the home and potentially useful in the working world.

Beatrice Hill was one of the baby-boom generation who poured into secondary school in the 1950s. High school attendance was the norm after the school leaving age was raised to fifteen in 1944. Parents could no longer argue that secondary education for their daughters was a waste of time: on the contrary, it opened up opportunities, despite the limitations of the professional streams in most girls' schools. The number of pupils attending all types of secondary school increased from 38,800 in 1943 to 67,478 a decade later.[101] New suburbs in the urban areas, particularly Auckland, also meant that more schools were needed. A total of 92 per cent of primary school pupils went on to secondary school (compared to 10 per cent in 1900), and in 1952 alone 589 new classrooms were required.[102]

As girls remained longer in education, they were likely to begin menstruating at school, and a subject once hidden, and almost absent in the historical record, came in for public

Athlete Yvette Williams trains at St Clair Beach, Dunedin, in the late 1940s or early 1950s. She is leaping from a sand dune and using a technique called the hitch kick to gain extra length. Williams won the gold medal for long jump at the Helsinki Olympics in 1952. Otago Daily Times

discussion. But what girls learned in the classroom about human biology and menstruation in particular often conflicted with teaching at home. In one 1948 study at Otago Girls' High, 44 per cent of the girls said they were forbidden to bathe during their periods, 'following their mothers' teaching'. At school, in contrast, the biology mistress taught them that bathing daily during menstruation was essential for good hygiene. Arguments in the home ensued.[103] Mothers who adhered to the traditional view that menstruation demanded rest did not support their daughters' participation in school sports. Judith, who had her first period in 1957, was warned by her mother not to wash her hair, swim or do physical education at school while menstruating. Cheryl began menstruating in 1960. She was chosen to be the angel in the school play in the fifth form. She recalled, 'I had the embarrassment of fronting up to our very with it English teacher and telling her my mother said I couldn't go barefoot because I had my period.' Coming from 'a clean middle-upper-class family', Cheryl said she always felt dirty 'at the wrong time of the month'

Left This puberty and menstruation education booklet was written by Mary Pauline Callender in 1928 and went through various editions during the next ten years. Such pamphlets were designed to assist mothers in explaining the onset of menstruation to their daughters and to market sanitary products. *Right* Two of the contestants in a Mount Maunganui Bathing Beauties contest, Rewa Dow and Phyl Belcher, play leapfrog on the beach. When this photograph was taken, in the late 1940s or 1950s, a swimsuit parade was part of summer activities at many coastal resorts. *Private collection; photograph by W. Walker, Alexander Turnbull Library, Wellington, 1/2-027522-F*

because her mother insisted on no baths or hair washing, reflecting earlier views of the dangers of getting cold at this time of the month.[104]

Now more and more girls were taking to school the paraphernalia of belts, pads, safety pins and wrapping paper: the hidden baggage of their most intimate lives. Homemade sanitary towels, which required soaking and washing, remained common into the 1960s. Tampons, marketed increasingly after the Second World War, were thought unsuitable for virgins in the 1960s. One young woman recalled not understanding why her mother had the convenience of using Meds tampons while she herself was made to use uncomfortable thick pads and nylon pants with plastic lining. Only when she went away to university did she realise she could use and buy tampons herself.[105]

Secondary school was a place where young women made lifelong friends and took up new opportunities. Caroline, who was seventeen when she left boarding school in 1960, loved it 'because of the company'. She continued: 'I was never homesick, loved it. I played sport – hockey for the school, and I did quite well at gym and athletics. I belonged to the choir and I was on the library committee.'[106] Sporting inspiration for schoolgirls was provided by Yvette Williams, who had become the first New Zealand woman to win an Olympic medal – a gold for the long jump in Helsinki on 23 July 1952. New Zealanders also gloried in her achievement when she broke the world record in Gisborne in 1954 by jumping 6.29 metres. Her three gold medals, for discus, long-jump (new world records for both) and shot put, at the 1954 Empire and Commonwealth Games in Vancouver made up nearly half of New Zealand's total of seven gold medals.

Some were concerned that women's participation in sport might come at a cost. In 1960, the *Listener*'s editor, Monte Holcroft, agreed that women could enter whatever fields they wished 'provided only that in doing so they do not lose what men treasure most in them – not beauty, though that is precious too, but womanly grace and charm'.[107] Schools had their own notions of female decorum. Sandra Pearse (later Coney), who went on to become a prominent feminist activist, was one of a group of high-achieving pupils at Auckland Girls' Grammar in the late 1950s and early 1960s that included Rosslyn Noonan (future Chief Human Rights Commissioner), Anne Else (writer and social commentator) and Susan St John (economist). School rules – such as not appearing in the street without hat and gloves – were a constant irritation to Sandra. Her bleached hair, later dyed brunette, caused offence, as did her self-assertion. Her jewellery was confiscated and she was banned from the hockey team because of her appearance. Not wanting to give up the game she loved, Sandra chose to join a team not associated with the school, the one that would 'displease' the school the most, and kept playing for three more seasons.[108]

In rural areas, the demands of work on the land might override schooling at certain times. Merata Mita, born in 1942, grew up in a Māori-speaking community in Maketū, in the Bay of Plenty. Secure in her Ngāti Pikiao identity, and the eldest daughter and third child in a family of nine children, Merata understood her responsibility to the whānau. When labour was needed for planting, weeding or harvesting potatoes, she stayed home from school. Whenever her mother was ill, or was called away, Merata remained at home to do the domestic chores. None of these demands proved a barrier to her academic success at Te Puke High School, where she became head girl. Identified as a potential teacher, Merata was sent to Auckland to train. Later, while teaching at Kawerau College, she found that her difficult Māori and Polynesian pupils responded better to the visual than the textual. The purchase of a second-hand Super 8 camera began what was to be a lifelong engagement with film-making. From that classroom experience, born of desperation to engage her pupils, Merata Mita found the medium in which she became New Zealand's foremost documentary maker.[109]

New postwar co-educational schools like Kawerau College attracted young women teachers away from traditional girls' schools, but men continued to dominate administrative positions.[110] No Christchurch women teachers were invited to a heads of schools meeting in the 1950s: women principals organised their own meetings and invited the senior mistresses from the co-ed schools.[111] The number of women teachers in state secondary schools rose from 795 in 1946 to 2,503 in 1966, mirroring the expansion of the education sector. But the proportion of female to male teachers in secondary and district high schools rose only slowly, from 34 per cent in 1957 to 37.6 per cent in 1967.[112]

Young women and the new youth culture

'[T]op conflict with Mum,' reported the 1957 *Woman's Weekly*'s new 'Teenage Pages', 'is helping out at home.' This section (and others like it in women's magazines) marked a new cultural category, which addressed adolescent girls as citizens and consumers. And there were magazines published specifically for this market, such as *Seventeen*, founded in America in 1944.[113] It had once been expected that daughters would help out with housework as a form of training for their future, but educated adolescent girls had now begun to imagine different lives.[114] The burgeoning secondary schools became crucibles for an emerging youth culture defined by distinctive music, dancing and fashion. Rowena Hill's prize trophy from a school exchange visit to Canada in 1954 was a pair of pedal-pushers – tight, calf-length pants that were the vanguard of American fashion. So novel was this new teenage look that the pedal-pushers were 'remembered in New Plymouth for decades'.[115] Hollywood movies, too, popularised new fashions: in 1954 Grace Kelly lounged in denim jeans in Hitchcock's *Rear Window*, while denim and leather jackets translated to rebellion on the bodies of movie stars James Dean and Marlon Brando.[116]

Fashions like these made it easier to 'Rock around the Clock' to the new music popularised by the film of that title that was a New Zealand box-office hit and ran for five weeks in 1956.[117] Significantly, historian Redmer Yska notes, the film censor removed 'the advice one jiving teenage girl gave to another in the film: "Have fun, you'd be amazed at the number of men around the country who don't want to get married."'[118] The New Zealand *Hit Parade*, half an hour of popular music sponsored first by Lifebuoy soap and then by the Lever Brothers Company, became 'like church' for New Zealand teenagers.[119] If half an hour of hits was too little, teenagers could head to the local milk bars to listen to their favourite music on jukeboxes.

Parents' worries about their daughters' taste in music and fashions erupted into a national concern in June 1954 when school friends Pauline Parker and Juliet Hulme brutally murdered Pauline's mother, Honora Parker, in Victoria Park in Christchurch by bashing her head with a brick. The intense friendship between middle-class Hulme and working-class Parker at Christchurch Girls' High had given rise to their creation of a fantasy world which, they believed, would lead them to Hollywood. When it became clear that their relationship would be broken by Juliet's departure overseas, the girls hatched a plan to kill Pauline's mother, who had expressed concern about their 'retreat from reality'.[120] Details of the girls' relationship, their 'abnormally homosexual' behaviour and the calculated murder were widely reported in the press.[121] As details of the trial emerged, a father of five girls expressed his horror at his daughters' scuffles to get hold of the evening paper.[122]

The Parker-Hulme case heightened fears that young people, influenced by new music and movies, were out of control.[123] That the opinion of adults might no longer matter to the young seemed even more apparent when girls aged between thirteen and fifteen attending the Hutt Valley Memorial Technical College were found to be engaging in sex with older boys – motorcycle riders whom they met at Elbe's Milkbar in Lower Hutt. One fifteen-year-old girl told a police officer, 'I have had it. Sex, sex, sex.'[124]

Coming as this scandal did on the heels of the Parker–Hulme trial, the government appointed a Special Committee on Moral Delinquency in Children and Young People, under the chairmanship of Baptist Oswald Mazengarb, QC. The committee's brief was to inquire into the influences undermining the 'sexual morality of children and adolescents' and to make recommendations to remedy the situation. Roman Catholic Lucy O'Brien, vice-president of the Women's Auxiliary of the Inter-church Council on Public Affairs, and Rhoda Bloodworth, a Justice of the Peace associated with the Auckland Children's Court, were the two women on the committee of seven middle-class and middle-aged professionals. Submissions were taken from a variety of groups ranging from milk-bar proprietors to educational and church organisations.[125] Discussion about the 'precocity of girls' who took little notice of their parents' opinion took up much of the committee's time.[126] One such young woman was the daughter of Petone Senior Sergeant Frank Le Fort. Disturbed by her modelling of the new black velvet pedal-pushers she had made for herself, and her announcement that she was going to the local milk bar, her father demanded that she cut her new pants to shreds – an order with which she complied, in much distress.[127]

Puzzled by the fact that some 'delinquent teenagers' came from materially well-off homes, the committee looked to psychology for answers. It concluded that new child-raising patterns emphasising the 'free expression' and development of the child's personality had the potential to 'lead to licence'.[128] Absent working mothers were neglecting their duties, and emotional insecurity could be attributed to a flawed bond between the mother and child from (or even before) birth.[129] Young people, moreover, had too much money, and too much access to salacious comics, literature, films and radio serials – and even to condoms. Blocking such access through legislative controls appeared to be the way forward: a way to prevent 'moral drift'. Bills were introduced in Parliament to amend legislation around indecent publications, child welfare and police offences. The definition of 'obscenity' was widened to control literature; 'delinquent' children guilty of indecent behaviour could now be dealt with under the law; and it became an offence to sell contraceptives to those under sixteen.[130]

Psychological subjects

For the Mazengarb committee, psychological theories were seen as both a source of danger (too much emphasis on free expression in children) and a source of security (proper emotional development lay in fostering the bond between mother and child).

From 1951, the *New Zealand Woman's Weekly* had featured an advice column entitled 'The Psychologist's Consulting Room', which encapsulated the shifting ethos of the time. Secure incomes had made couples more confident that they could provide well for their children, and family size increased; the emphasis now shifted to questions about how children might best be raised and how marital relationships might best be managed. On 2YA's *Let's Talk it Over*, for example, listeners could hear the animated opinions of panel members Allona Priestley, housewife and mother; an unnamed doctor; and Quentin Brew, psychologist, on common family problems. Members of the public wrote in for advice on topics such as jealousy of a new baby, bullying, petty pilfering and 'difficulties with resident in-laws'. Listeners were also encouraged to write in with solutions to problems.[131]

There was a consistent theme to the responses of these and other opinion-makers. Responsibility for child welfare clearly lay with mothers. New psychological theories, derived from studies of children evacuated in Britain during the Second World War, put great emphasis on the importance of the maternal bond. 'It is a commonplace in psychology nowadays,' a psychiatrist stated in a 1957 YC network lecture on the family, 'that adult personality and beliefs, customs and manners which characterise the social order are largely the outcome of childhood experience.'[132] Maurice Bevan-Brown, a London-trained psychiatrist, pioneered analytical psychotherapy on his return to New Zealand in 1940. His book *The Sources of Love and Fear* was the New Zealand manifestation of an international trend that saw a child's early relations with its mother as setting 'the pattern for all subsequent relationships'.[133] Out of this view grew a critique of the rigidity of Plunket child-rearing prescriptions and of maternity services pre-occupied with hygiene and pain relief rather than emotional fulfilment.[134] The most important factor in birth, Bevan-Brown believed, was for a mother to fall in love with her baby at first sight.[135]

What had once been regarded as natural was now the subject of debate, and issues around parenting came to the fore. Immigrants from Britain and Holland, where mid-wives attended home births with husbands present, were critical of the strict rules surrounding birth in New Zealand hospitals. As researchers Jane and James Ritchie later put it, the 'early mother–child system' was 'very abnormal indeed. Hospital nursery, the crib, cot and "pram"' indicated 'the distance put between mother and child'.[136] To visitors from overseas, corporal punishment also signified the authoritarian nature of New Zealand parenting.[137]

The increasing attention paid to theories of child psychology, as well as the sheer number of young children, led to a new generation of parents interested in preschool education of different kinds, both to give relief to overburdened mothers and to benefit their children.[138] Kindergartens flourished, and mothers found support in the kinder-garten mothers' clubs in which they shared ideas about child-raising. New ideas about childbirth were also subject to discussion. Helen Brew, one of New Zealand's first trained speech therapists (and whose husband Quentin dispensed psychological advice on the radio), pushed for reform through an organisation that developed into the Wellington Parents' Centre.[139] She described her first experience of childbirth as 'horrendous': she was anaesthetised, 'and I didn't even know if I'd had a baby or not ... I actually didn't get to see the baby for another six to eight hours'. The second birth was equally disastrous: her feet 'were put in stirrups' and she felt humiliated. These experiences were a spur to action.[140]

The founding of the Parents' Centre movement in 1954 was based on the premise that parents needed an educational programme to equip them 'for their demanding but rewarding role'.[141] Advice for families proliferated in both specialist magazines such as the *New Zealand Parent and Child* and in women's magazines. The Justice Department, too, aimed to heighten community concern about the welfare of home and family as a means of curbing future delinquency of the kind revealed by the Mazengarb Inquiry.[142] Auckland psychologist A. E. Manning's book *The Bodgie,* an analysis of the disturbing black-clad teenage male who was likely to be wearing fluorescent green or orange socks and was often accompanied by a female 'Widgie', was subtitled *A Study in Psychological Abnormality.* Parents, and especially mothers, were held responsible for the behaviour of children and adolescents. There were dangers if mothers were 'away from home too much, working or enjoying themselves'.[143] The 1962 Report of the Commission on Education in New Zealand (the Currie Report) reinforced this message, locating the seeds of delinquency 'in emotional and psychological factors from childhood'.[144]

The government considered the best childcare to be that provided in the home. The officially sanctioned and supported childcare providers (kindergartens and Playcentres) offered only part-time care, and the latter involved input from mothers. Women who required longer daycare for their children were forced to make informal arrangements or use charitable services. Nuns of the Order of the Good Shepherd who ran a crèche in Auckland had to turn away hundreds of children annually.[145] The once-popular Wellington Railway Station crèche, commandeered for military purposes in 1941, was not reopened in the 1950s, despite vigorous lobbying.[146] In 1952, the Canterbury Housewives' Union decided to initiate a local day nursery themselves, having found that 'scores of toddlers' were cared for in backyard nurseries.[147]

Standards of care varied enormously. The worst were revealed in 1958 when children had to be removed from an Auckland centre where Mabel Howard, Minister of Child Welfare, declared conditions were '[t]oo shocking to give full details'.[148] Most of the children had skin diseases or scabies; one child had an unattended fractured leg; and the carer did not know the surnames or the home addresses of most of the children. The incident led to regulations issued in 1960 that set standards for children's physical safety in all childcare centres, from kindergarten and Playcentres to private fee-paying kindergartens and parents' cooperative centres.[149] The number of childcare centres steadily grew, though

Teacher Rose Parekowhai works in her classroom at Parikino Maori School on the Whanganui River in 1963, as two curious boys look on. *Photograph by Ans Westra*

they remained firmly categorised as social welfare rather than educational services. In the early 1960s, Sonja Davies, frustrated at the lack of government support for early childhood services, set up the New Zealand Association for Child Care Centres.[150]

Preschool groups developed among Māori communities in the Whanganui district, Northland and the East Coast. The Maori Women's Welfare League lent its support to the development of preschool centres by its branch committees, by school committees and by parent teachers' associations.[151] While Pākehā women might have the resources to stay at home while their children were young, the incomes of many Māori women were vital to their families' survival in the cities. Childcare was a whānau obligation: older relatives might care for mokopuna (grandchildren) and other young ones, and those young people were aware they would do the same later in life.[152] In the early 1960s, Māori became involved in Playcentre. Historian Aroha Harris records Letty Brown's initiative in creating a Māori session at the Te Atatū Playcentre to make Māori mothers more comfortable in the environment.[153] The Maori Education Foundation, and in particular Alex (Lex) Grey, the foundation's officer for preschool education, 'adapted the Playcentre model to suit Maori culture and perspectives and achieved enormous, almost immediate success; even in areas where the original Pakeha-inspired groups had failed'.[154] Large families, and the care of grandchildren, meant that Māori mothers might spend more time associated with a preschool 'than they themselves had spent at school'.[155] In 1965 a twenty-minute National Film Unit educational film, *As the Twig is Bent*, featured mainly Māori families in showing the importance of play and of parental (and especially mothers') engagement with children.[156]

Working against the primacy of the mother–child bond was the movement towards closed stranger adoption, in which the birth parent had no knowledge or contact with the adoptive parents. By the 1950s, adoption was often seen by social workers as the perfect solution to the problem of unmarried motherhood.[157] The child's needs for 'happiness in a family', according to a Child Welfare official, overrode the birth mother's attachment to her child.[158] Through adoption, the child was placed in a stable family and removed from the influence of a 'sexually wanton "girl"' who was nevertheless given a fresh start.[159] The 1950 Infant Amendment Act changed the property rights of adopted persons, making severance from the natural parents almost complete. This was followed, in 1955, by the Adoption Act which ensured confidentiality of the court's records and so denied children a right of access to information about their birth parents. The government's response to the rising illegitimacy rate was to encourage adoption by making it as close to 'natural' parenthood as possible.[160] The unquestioned model was the Pākehā family. The Act 'openly reject[ed] Maori beliefs and practices' by specifically stating that 'adoption in accordance with Maori custom' would not henceforth be recognised as lawful.[161] The legislation thus overrode the tradition of openness, in which Māori children might be brought up within the extended family by people who were not their biological parents. Tamariki whāngai might 'know many homes, but still, one whanau'.[162] For Māori, illegitimacy was of little note: children were embedded in the whānau.

Sexual subjects

Adoption appeared necessary as the wartime reluctance to wait for marriage before having sex continued well into the postwar years. The rate of ex-nuptial births per 1,000 unmarried Pākehā women rose continually from 11.67 in 1945, to 14.85 in 1951 and 17.79 in 1956, reaching 24.14 in 1961. At 5.77 per cent of live births, the New Zealand illegitimacy rate was higher than the rates of Australia, Canada, the United Kingdom and the United States, but lower (the government statisticians consoled themselves) than that of Sweden.[163]

While young women's overt sexuality was the cause of anxiety, and opprobrium if she became pregnant, judging women's looks and femininity had long been a national pastime. Bathing suit contests became particularly popular in the 1950s and 1960s, ranging from 'Miss Tiny Tot' to the ubiquitous 'Miss Locality' and 'Mother and Daughter' competitions.[164] In 1956, Jeannette de Montalk became New Zealand's first representative at the Miss World competition.[165] 'Miss University' contests were held at Victoria University between 1962 and 1968, and at Otago University from 1965 to 1971.[166] In 1962, cinema-goers were treated to a short feature entitled *North Island: Five Pretty Girls*, about the finalists from the Miss New Zealand show visiting the tourist spots. The following year, Maureen Te Rangi Rere I Waho Kingi interrupted her training as a radiographer in Auckland to enter the Miss New Zealand contest, which she went on to win. A former top Māori student at Rotorua High, Maureen was judged to be an expert at 'action songs and double and triple poi' by *Te Ao Hou*, which remarked that she had 'considerable talent as well as beauty'.[167]

A new kind of beauty came to the fore in the 1960s, epitomised by British teenage model Lesley Hornby, better known as 'Twiggy', whose thin, waif-like appearance took the fashion world by storm. She was named British woman of the year in 1966. Another top British model, twenty-three-year-old Jean Shrimpton, wore a white shift dress that ended 10 centimetres above the knee when she attended the Victoria Derby at Flemington Racecourse in Melbourne in 1965. Hatless, gloveless and bare-legged, and wearing a man's watch, the 'Shrimp' caused a sensation amongst the formally dressed women. The shift minidress was an assertion of the importance of youth above any trappings of social status.[168] The miniskirt quickly became the emblem of modern womanhood. Hemlines rose, and a generation of New Zealand schoolgirls became subject to measurement inspections to ensure their gym frocks were no more than 3 inches (7.5 centimetres) above the knee.

Young women of the 1960s, Māori and Pākehā, took up where their 1950s counterparts had left off, setting new fashion trends and embracing new idols. Glenda Reti recalled going to a rock 'n' roll jamboree at the Wellington Town Hall in 1961. She spent all day getting ready with her girlfriends; they had their hair set, checked their homemade frocks (Ming blue, shocking pink and burnt orange) and practised their dance steps in front of the mirror. That was the start of many dances at the Wellington Trades Hall, the Downtown Club and the Ngati Poneke Young Maori Club.[169] Named by Apirana Ngata in 1937 ('Poneke' being a transliteration of Port Nicholson), Ngati Poneke provided a home for Māori migrants to Wellington. Young people could find traditional performance culture there, as well as the latest music and dancing.

In Auckland, four young women aimed to take centre stage: Linda Williams, Val Tapene, Faye Reid and Norma Stacey formed New Zealand's first all-female pop group, the Fair Sect. But limits remained on female ambitions. Arriving for a gig at the Peter Pan Cabaret, they were advised by a representative of the Auckland Musicians' Union that they would not be able to perform because they were not members of the union. They offered to join the union on the spot, but were told they were ineligible because they were women.

Scores of couples took part in a rock 'n roll jamboree at the Wellington Town Hall on 11 March 1957. Rock 'n roll dancing arrived in New Zealand in the mid-1950s and was embraced with enthusiasm by young people, but viewed with suspicion by many of the older generation. Swing skirts were a 'must'. *Alexander Turnbull Library, Wellington, EP/1957/0643-F*

According to music historian Roger Watkins: 'Sanity prevailed and a compromise was reached whereby they paid their dues, did their spot, resigned and got their money back.'[170]

New music flooded in through any channels available. The June 1964 visit of the Beatles showed a new side to young women: screaming fans prepared to go to any lengths to make contact with their pop idols. 'She's a Mod', a 1964 hit song by New Zealand group Ray Columbus and the Invaders, described a girl who 'was a rocker for the week' and then became a 'Mod', her new look causing her lover to go broke.[171] Ray Columbus might well have been singing about Dinah Lee, the New Zealand singing sensation whose blunt haircut and short skirts were coveted by the young. '[I] didn't sing cute and pretty,' Lee recalled, 'I belted out songs.'[172] Her 1966 rendition of 'Night Time is the Right Time' reinforced many mothers' fears that sexual assignations were foremost on their daughters' minds.

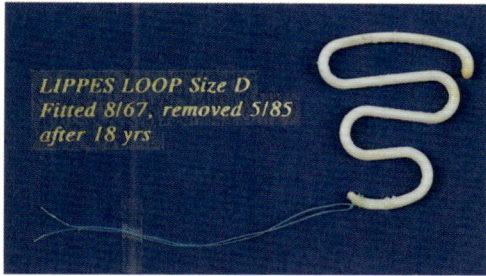

Top left This Lippes Loop intrauterine device (IUD) was one of the contraceptive devices that provided a reliable alternative to the contraceptive pill from the mid-1960s. *Bottom left* The rubber diaphragm, pictured here in its tin case, was the barrier contraceptive chosen by many women from the 1940s. It was fitted over the cervix and used with pessaries made of cocoa butter and quinine. *Right* Loette was a brand of the Pill, the revolutionary form of contraception for women that was introduced in New Zealand in 1961. This advertisement from 2000 suggests that young women could rely on the Pill more than they could on any young man. *From top left: Museum of New Zealand Te Papa Tongarewa, Wellington, GH022288; Museum of New Zealand Te Papa Tongarewa, Wellington, GH022217; reproduced with the permission of Pfizer Australia*

Sexuality, according to the American expert Alfred Kinsey, was not shaped by God but instead by social factors and cultural expectations. In two best-selling reports, *Sexual Behavior in the Human Male* (1948) followed by *Sexual Behavior in the Human Female* (1953), Kinsey had lifted the lid on discussion of sexuality. People were not either heterosexual or homosexual: most had a spectrum of sexual desire that changed over the life course.[173] What was important, Kinsey said, was individual sexual fulfilment. The *Woman's Weekly* psychologist advised: 'In a woman's case especially, marriage is a career and although sex is not all there is to marriage, it plays an important part.'[174] British author Barbara Cartland warned women in the same publication that 'sexual love must colour every action every day, recognizing that the physical act is just an ingredient of life. Ignore sex – and a bitter, unforgivable hatred is born.'[175]

The tremor in the conventional social fabric caused by the Kinsey reports became an earthquake when the news spread via American magazines such as *Time, Life* and *Readers' Digest* that a new oral contraceptive giving women complete protection from unwanted pregnancy would soon be available. Earlier methods of birth control, such as the diaphragm, condom or withdrawal, relied on some type of intervention during the act of intercourse. The Pill, as it became known, promised to be revolutionary in that it could be taken daily at any time and entirely forgotten during the sexual act itself.

Many doctors welcomed the advent of a contraceptive that was simple and quick to prescribe, unlike diaphragms and spermicidal jellies that required embarrassing and time-consuming lessons in fitting technique.[176] Wellington GP Roger Ridley-Smith was one of those who 'just thought it was marvellous, there was no question about it, the pill virtually took over, it was just fabulously convenient'.[177] The Branch Ethical Committee of the New Zealand Medical Association, however, remained exceedingly cautious about contraception, declaring in 1961 that 'only danger to the health and life of a patient should be adequate prerequisites when providing contraception'; and that 'on no account were "reasons of convenience or indulgence" admissible'.[178] This did not seem to deter the majority of doctors who, by the 1950s, appear to have accepted that married couples were entitled to use contraceptives.[179] Some doctors wished to go further and prevent rising illegitimacy rates by prescribing the Pill to single women, but in 1966 the Branch Ethical Committee made its opposition clear: 'the supply of prescriptions by medical practitioners of contraceptives to unmarried persons, thereby facilitating extra-marital relationships, is not in keeping with the highest principles of the medical profession'.[180] By that year, New Zealand already had one of the highest rates of Pill usage in the western world.[181]

For married women who had been using condoms and diaphragms and had experienced contraceptive failure, the Pill offered a new peace of mind. There were other advantages as well. 'He thinks it's marvellous' was the 'almost uniform' reply of married women surveyed about their husbands' attitudes to the contraceptive.[182] Mrs D reported how the use of condoms had 'caused ill-feeling' between her and her husband over the years, but they had persisted in the interests of family planning. Her husband's delight with the Pill had improved their sexual relationship and this, she believed, was 'a prerequisite for a happy marriage'.[183] Other women reported that one reason for their preferring the Pill over other methods was 'that their husband's enjoyment and aesthetic appreciation is much increased'.[184] For themselves, the fact that the Pill involved 'no mechanics' or 'mucking about' was also a great attraction.

The Pill held out life-changing promises for women: not only could they enjoy sex without worrying about pregnancy, but they could also plan their lives to include both a career and children. Married women were the first to benefit, and many, like Cath Tizard who had given birth to four children in her twenties, chose to end childbearing and to explore horizons beyond the home. By the 1960s, a new generation of young women could invest in education and career training secure in the knowledge they could prevent pregnancy without having to practise abstinence. They looked to the future with new expectations, and imagined lives different from those of their mothers. Their confidence could be unsettling.

In 1963, Geoffrey Palmer, editor of Victoria University's student magazine *Salient*, described the newly independent young women he was encountering in the university's halls:

> For thousands of years men have expected women to be feminine, warm, even demure. The 'New Woman' is a hard and brash super-sophisticate, with dyed hair and drip dry morals. She can take her drink like a man and chooses who she will go to bed with. The one thing this woman does not have is the respect of men … By all means women should be intelligent and realistic. So should they be attractive and vivacious.
>
> The most important thing a woman can do is to maintain her femininity. She must maintain her taste in clothes and makeup, while avoiding becoming loud.[185]

In the future prime minister's view, 'what was right for a man may not be forgiven in a woman', yet the same young women he wished to instruct were no longer willing to listen.[186]

'The problem that has no name'

Mothers worried, but they perhaps also admired their baby-boom daughters' aspirations. As American Betty Friedan described it, women were aware of 'a strange stirring, a sense of dissatisfaction, a yearning' for something more than lives devoted to home and family.[187] Lindsey Dawson, a noted New Zealand author and journalist, recalled sitting up in bed in the 1960s 'feverishly' reading *The Feminine Mystique*, 'riveted' by Friedan's arguments about the constraints on women's lives in the 1950s. For Dawson, the book's message that women were conned into believing they could truly fulfil themselves only through homemaking explained her mother's frustrations with life.[188] In 1964, the same year Friedan's book was published in paperback, Wellington women listened attentively to economist and public servant William Sutch's discussion of 'Women's Contribution to a Changing Society' at a study conference organised by the Department of Adult Education at Victoria University.[189] The conference, though barely advertised, was vastly oversubscribed; many women were turned away.[190] Clearly Friedan's book spoke to bubbling discontent about the way in which women's talents were underutilised.[191]

That is not to say that New Zealand women were idle. Their talents might be poured into coping with young families and new housing, but they also found time for – and enjoyed – voluntary endeavours. In the towns and countryside, women banded together to lobby for childbirth education, natural childbirth and increased childcare options. Women involved in churches and community groups welcomed a wave of new immigrants to the country. The YWCA social groups, in particular, provided a welcome for refugees from war-ravaged Europe, including women from Poland, Hungary, Greece, Eastern Germany, Czechoslovakia and the Baltic States.[192]

Playcentres, school committees, Girl Guides, marching groups and craft groups were but some of the other activities that brought women together to plan and discuss the future, as well as to enjoy each other's company in a socially approved forum. New Zealand's largest women's organisation in 1965 was the Federation of Country Women's Institutes: it had more than 1,000 local branches in New Zealand and 200 members in the Cook Islands. Members who moved to towns urged the creation of branches there, and the rural–urban divide, always blurred in the lives of individuals, became blurred in the organisation but did not damage its appeal.[193] Part of the popularity of the Country Women's Institute for its 35,000 members lay in its encouragement 'to take an active part in rural life and its development in the widest sense'.[194] The 27,000 members of the Women's Division of Federated Farmers, originally a more exclusive rural group, aimed to better the conditions for women and children living in the country, in cooperation with farming organisations.[195] In the towns, Business and Professional Women's Clubs and Townswomen's Guilds promoted interest in civic and international affairs.

But for many of the rising generation of baby-boom women, neither these organisations nor the traditional church women's fellowships, such as the Mothers' Union or the League of Mothers, appeared to fit their needs. Women's groups that upheld commitment to the family or stressed civic duty seemed unlikely to provide answers for the daily discontent that many young mothers shared as they attended Playcentre or dropped off their children at kindergarten. Duty seemed obvious and, at times, overwhelming; denying it seemed wrong. Yet some women were beginning to question the extent to which their identity was bound by motherhood. In Margot Roth's words, they were asking whether they were 'Housewives or Human Beings?'[196]

Life in the suburbs, so sought after in the postwar world for the new housing and amenities it offered, began by the 1960s to reveal its bleak side, often referred to as 'suburban neurosis'. '[I]ncreasing numbers of young mothers are experiencing emotional disturbance,' the *Listener* reported, 'because they are staying at home in the new urban area often cut off from other adults.'[197] Isolated in their houses, 'listening to childish prattle' all day, tested a woman's 'nervous system'.[198] Some took to drink: the first women-only Alcoholics Anonymous formed in Wellington in the 1960s. Others took to drugs. Forty million doses of the minor tranquilliser, Valium, were prescribed by New Zealand doctors in 1969, the great proportion to women to take the edge off their unexplained misery.[199]

In 1966, inspired by a *Voice of America* programme played by the New Zealand Broadcasting Service on 'Women's contribution to a changing society', members of the Linden Playcentre in the Wellington suburb of Tawa organised a lecture series to explore this question in the New Zealand context. The six lectures analysing 'The changing role of women' drew large and enthusiastic audiences. 'It is time,' sociologist Miriam Gilson urged them, 'we stopped thinking that work is either male or female.'[200] New Zealand, once proud of its record of women's rights, now appeared to be lagging behind the times, she said; fewer women worked outside the home than in the USA, England, France or Japan, and few women held positions of responsibility. Economist William Sutch argued that

Rita Angus painted her Wellington studio around 1962. By this time Angus was a mature artist who had attained a degree of recognition as a pioneer of modern art in New Zealand. Her style remained distinctive and highly personal, and she was sustained by a strong belief in her vocation: 'As a woman painter, I work to represent love of humanity and faith in mankind in a world, which is to me, richly variable and infinitely beautiful'. *Courtesy of the Rita Angus Estate*

a workforce predicated on ideas about appropriate male and female roles limited girls' educational aspirations and hobbled the contribution women could make to society.[201] The newspapers' employment columns segregated into 'male' and 'female' jobs were the manifestation of societal blinkers. If employment opportunities could be seen as open to all, the speakers suggested, suburban neurosis would be a thing of the past and women's talents would contribute to all spheres of society.

The message of the lectures in Tawa soon reverberated in meeting halls throughout the country. The position of women had become a legitimate subject for examination. Galvanised by currents outside New Zealand, the volunteer impulse so evident in the range of women's traditional activities outside the home encouraged a group of women to establish a new and very different type of organisation: the Society for Research on Women. Its founders believed that 'the popular practice of declaiming on what women should or should not be doing with their lives was irresponsible in view of the paucity of factual information available on the subject'.[202] They set out to remedy this deficiency by planning and undertaking an agenda of research about their own position, not as distanced objects of someone else's study.

The question 'Why make studies of women?' was the one that Mrs L. W. Tiller posed for herself. As president of the National Council of Women and a member of the Society for Research on Women, she was ready with the answer:

> The accepted role of women has changed for a number of reasons. Women are better educated than they used to be. The intellectual pursuits that used to give satisfaction no longer seem enough for many women. Family planning has made it possible for people to limit their families. Labour-saving devices have cut down the time needed to do domestic jobs. People want more in a material sense, and so women who are in a two-pay-packet situation find it difficult to adjust to the one-pay packet situation.[203]

The Society for Research on Women drew support from university-educated women who were frustrated by a narrow focus on domestic pursuits but felt it important to put the care of their families ahead of any career aspirations. That women were seeking higher education in increasing numbers was attracting attention. At Victoria University, for example, the number of women had risen from 25 per cent of the student body in the 1950s to 31 per cent by 1970. 'Should Mother be a Career Girl?' the *Listener* asked in April 1967, before pointing out that although the female workforce was growing at twice the rate of the male workforce, women held 'only a minute percentage of administrative and managerial jobs':

> Except in rare instances, such as four women Members of Parliament, New Zealand's public life is left to the men. The traditional feeling that a married woman's place is in the home still prevails – though it has become accepted that a young married woman will work

for a few years before having a family. The primary function of the New Zealand woman of the formation and care of a family has not changed.[204]

What had changed, Miriam Gilson pointed out, was that Pākehā women were marrying younger and having smaller families. As a consequence, women had more than forty years of life ahead of them after their last child went to school. Those who remained at home were likely to become depressed, while those who sought work lacked confidence and, in many cases, adequate education.[205]

The introduction of the Pill had placed a brake on Pākehā birth rates, and by 1966 Māori birth rates were also on the decline. The traditional trajectory of women's lives – marriage, home and family – was unravelling in the face of women's potential for greater social and economic independence which created alternatives to marriage and homemaking. The outline of a new ideal of self-fulfilment for women appeared on the horizon, though no one could be sure what its lineaments would be.

Photographer Marti Friedlander, whose work captured social change in New Zealand from the 1970s, took this self-portrait in Paris in 1972. *Reproduced by permission of Marti Friedlander*

Chapter Eleven
Decade of Discovery

'Nineteen-seventy was extraordinary,' recalled Therese O'Connell:

> It was the year that I left my home, my family, and New Plymouth and came to Wellington,
> I was just eighteen and I was going to university and I joined a women's liberation group.
> Everything happened for me that year – it was an incredibly exciting time. I was involved
> in the setting up of the Women's Liberation Front, the Vietnam war was on, there was the
> rugby tour to South Africa ... I was confident that all these were the things that needed to be
> changed and I was going out to bloody well do it.[1]

At university, Therese learned that young men could earn more over one summer break
than she had earned in four years of various part-time jobs. Now, equal pay became a
cause worth fighting for, soon followed by a raft of other issues taken up by the newly
formed Women's Liberation Front Club. They included opposition to the Miss Victoria
beauty contest, liberating 'men-only' bars, promoting a free twenty-four-hour crèche
on campus, and contraception on demand. Not content with minor aims, the women's
liberationists argued for the removal of all discriminatory social practices that confined
women, and stressed their commitment to 'fighting exploitation of any group whether
national or international'.[2]

From 1967 to 1977, arguments about the role of women were everywhere in New Zealand society. When prominent psychiatrist Dr Fraser McDonald announced in 1968 that
women were 'the Negroes of New Zealand society', many women, like the 30,000 members
of the Country Women's Institutes which upheld the role of women as homemakers and
mothers of the 'citizens of the future', were baffled.[3] Very different perspectives were
generated by studies undertaken by the Society for Research on Women, by ideas put
forward in a new publication, *Broadsheet*, and in overseas feminist literature.

The slogan 'the personal is political' meant that the arrangement of everyday life was
opened out to analysis in homes throughout the country. Some women who wished to
attend the United Women's Convention in 1972 felt comfortable about leaving home only
if they cooked all their husband's meals in advance. After attending the convention, they

Left Historian Judith Binney and Sebastian Black were photographed at their Auckland home in the 1970s. At this time Binney had embarked on her landmark research into the history of Ngāi Tūhoe, paying particular attention to Māori belief systems and understandings of the past. *Right* Gil and Pat Hanly were photographed by Marti Friedlander in Auckland in 1969. Pat was an artist who then taught drawing at Auckland University School of Architecture; Gil was to establish herself as a documentary photographer from the late 1970s. *Private collection; photograph by Marti Friedlander, Museum of New Zealand Te Papa Tongarewa, Wellington, O.031284*

might ask why on earth they had done so. Novel forms of organising and protest emerged to highlight the position of women, both Pākehā and Māori, in New Zealand society.

The government could not ignore the pressure for change coming from currents inside and outside the country. The 1967 United Nations Declaration on the Elimination of Discrimination Against Women was just one of the many spurs to the 1972 Labour government's appointment of a Select Committee on Women's Rights, which had a wide brief to investigate the extent of discrimination against women in New Zealand. While many could agree that women were entitled to equal pay and opportunities, controversy raged over whether or not women had a right to abortion. The vision of sisterhood that sparked so many initiatives in the early 1970s began to wane with the passing of a tightened abortion law and the Human Rights Commission Act in 1977.

Electrifying ideas

'Students,' commented English activist Polly Toynbee in 1968, 'form one of the few pressure groups that *can* exist. They have time to think, and the leisure to be idealistic without having to face the immediate responsibilities borne by their seniors.'[4] That year, as student

Overseas travel was increasingly part of New Zealand women's experience. Gretchen Albrecht (left) and a friend were photographed in Greece in 1979. During the 1970s Albrecht rose to prominence as an abstract artist and her works were exhibited both in New Zealand and overseas. *Courtesy of Gretchen Albrecht*

protests proliferated around the western world, a great many young New Zealanders eagerly took up the call for social, political and economic change. Student unions, emulating their counterparts elsewhere, moved away from representative to participatory democracy, potentially opening up their executives to women and minorities.[5]

Baby boomers coming of age were well educated, and determined they should make a difference. Television and music contributed to the creation of an international youth culture that sought new ways to live, free of the constraints of the suburbs and nuclear families, deliberately eschewing the safety and security valued by an earlier generation. Bob Dylan's 1964 song 'The Times They Are A-Changin'' warned parents they could no longer 'command' their sons and daughters.[6] Young people raised in the shadow of the nuclear bomb were, according to Elsie Locke, tired of the hypocrisy, complacency and self-seeking they saw in their elders.[7] Energised by the achievements of the American civil rights movement, by the student demonstrations that in 1968 nearly brought France to its knees, by international and local youth protests against the war in Vietnam, and by local organising against apartheid in South Africa, young New Zealanders began to imagine they could create change in many spheres. HART (Halt All Racist Tours) was formed in 1970 to protest against the proposed All Black tour of South Africa. The radical young Māori group Nga Tamatoa (Young Warriors) formed that same year to fight racism within New Zealand. Young women like Therese O'Connell threw themselves into organising for a new society.

Left Two schoolgirls head off to play basketball in Auckland, 1969. Although their skirts are short to allow freedom of movement and they wear gym shoes, their uniform includes a shirt and tie, a heavy tunic cinched in with a belt, and thick tights. *Right* Young soprano Kiri Te Kanawa was photographed wearing a formal concert gown in February 1966, the year she left New Zealand for further study and a glittering international opera career overseas. By this time Te Kanawa had been placed in a number of prestigious competitions, including the Mobil Song Quest and the Melbourne Sun Aria. *Photograph by Marti Friedlander; Alexander Turnbull Library, Dominion Post Collection, EP/1966/0479-F*

By the late 1960s, the 'generation gap' featured increasingly in the popular media, usually in respect of young men. But as American historian Ruth Rosen has written, while young men might reject parental expectations in terms of seeking security and stability in conventional careers, they did not reject their future as fathers. Young women, however, saw that their mothers' lives had been, and were, consumed by domesticity. 'The ghost haunting these young women,' Rosen wrote of the American context, 'wore an apron and lived vicariously through the lives of husband and children.'[8] Young New Zealand women were also questioning this legacy. More young women than men spread their wings by embarking on ships in the 1960s, and planes in the 1970s, for the great 'OE' ('Overseas Experience') to the United Kingdom. Some ventured onto the 'Hippie Trail' from London to Nepal, seeking in the East a culture completely different from that at home. Indeed, going abroad was regarded as more acceptable for young women than moving out of home to go flatting.[9] The divide between older and younger women was widening – manifest in young women's greater mobility, as well as their tastes in fashion, music and leisure activities, higher levels of education and greater sexual freedom.

Pantihose, as advertised in *thursday: The Magazine for Younger Women* in early 1972, were an innovation that did away with the need to wear a cumbersome suspender belt with stockings. Here the advertiser plays with ideas about women's liberation while at the same time displaying a long leg shot. *thursday* itself was an innovation, one of a group of women's magazines aimed at readers interested in social issues. thursday: The Magazine for Younger Women, *advertisement, 20 Jan 1972, Alexander Turnbull Library, Wellington*

New ideas were everywhere. In 1969, American Kate Millett's *Sexual Politics* explored sexism in the writing of prominent male authors and the way in which sex roles ensured women were subservient to the so-called patriarchy. *Sisterhood is Powerful* was the American feminist Robin Morgan's 1970 message. She had become increasingly critical of the sexism that pervaded the American civil rights and left-wing political movements in which she had been active in the 1960s, and became a founder of New York's Radical Feminist Group. Her edited collection of radical writings from the women's movement became an international bestseller. Twenty-three-year-old Wellingtonian Sue Kedgley read it in 1971:

> Every page of the book seemed to speak directly to me and I was filled with indignation at the way society was organised to suit men's needs at the expense of women. I became an instant convert and an ardent advocate of the cause of women's liberation.[10]

In that same year, Australian author and activist Germaine Greer visited New Zealand; she was smart, learned, independent, funny and sexy. For the first time it appeared possible to be all these things, and a feminist as well. Greer's iconoclastic bestseller, *The Female Eunuch*, rapidly disappeared from bookshop shelves and into the homes of New Zealand women. Unlike the 'genteel middle-class ladies who clamoured for reform' during the first wave of feminism at the end of the nineteenth century, Greer called for revolution. In her view, the first wave had failed to unseat God, marriage, the family, private property and the state – all things women's liberation should do.[11] The publicity surrounding Greer's visit turned to a media frenzy when she announced that she had received a summons on two charges for using the word 'bullshit' and one for saying 'fuck' (indecent and obscene language, respectively). Soon students were taking to the streets and shouting the words in acts of solidarity. So great was the reaction to Greer's outspokenness that the New Zealand Broadcasting Association placed a temporary ban 'on the subject of politics and Dr Germaine Greer' on its open-line-telephone programmes.[12] But Greer's visit helped push feminism from the margins to the centre of debate and, according to the *Sunday Herald*, 'put an end to the laughter surrounding women's liberation'.[13]

In response to Greer's claims, Miriam Dell, president of the National Council of Women (which represented combined women's groups), commented that while a lot was being said about women's liberation, women had in fact already been 'liberated from household chores'. By 1972, she argued, families averaged only 2.4 children, so women could choose how to spend their time and should be free to do so. 'I sympathise,' she said, 'with the women who don't want to be liberated because they are very happy.'[14] Long-time trade union organiser and social activist Connie Purdue, president of the National Organisation for Women, was particularly outraged by Greer's disdain for the union movement, claiming she did a 'disservice in pouring scorn on the effort of a few'.[15] Feelings 'ran high' in the pages of that barometer of New Zealand women's interests, the *Woman's Weekly*.[16] 'From

'Momma don't allow me to whistle
Poppa don't allow me to sing
They didn't raise me to be a dyke
but I am one just the same'

Six young lesbian women pose with motorbikes in this 1977 photograph by Mary Bailey. The verse at the bottom by Alix Dobkin encapsulates the 1970s lesbian critique of authoritarian heterosexual beliefs. *Alexander Turnbull Library, Wellington, Eph-C-LESBIAN-1977-02*

Toss and Edith Woollaston were photographed by Marti Friedlander in 1969. They had met at art school in Dunedin and married in 1936. While Woollaston established himself as one of New Zealand's leading painters, Edith raised four children, often in difficult living circumstances. *Reproduced by permission of Marti Friedlander*

what is it that women's liberation plans to liberate women?' wrote one reader. In her view, all Greer offered was 'liberation from the shackles of decency and self-respect'.[17]

Journalist Rosemary McLeod has suggested that it was the 'nice girls' who had been well educated but had no other expectation than marriage who were galvanised by *The Female Eunuch*. These women had married the right boys, had one or two children, and then discovered they were bored with suburban life. From Greer they learned that they could experiment sexually and 'had a brain that they were entitled to use'.[18]

The term liberation signalled that 1970s feminists considered themselves oppressed and that men were the oppressors. Unlike the feminists of the 1890s, who fought for women's rights under the banner 'For God, Home and Humanity', the new-wave agitation generally regarded Christianity as patriarchal, the home as a prison, and the term 'humanity' too often used as a code word for men, thus negating women's interests. Women's neglected interests were legion. 'The personal is political' turned the question of who cooked the meals or took out the rubbish bins into a political one. Husbands, whose

Jacqueline Fahey's paintings, such as *Christine in the Pantry* (1973), often depicted women in domestic settings from a feminist perspective. Christine Massey was about eighteen years old at the time of this painting, and her parents disapproved of her decision to dress like a 'hippy'. Fahey captures Christine's sense of alienation and withdrawal, as she stands partly obscured by a wall. Influenced by Fahey, Christine decided to go to art school and later worked as a sculptor.
Aigantighe Art Gallery, Timaru, 1978.005

The growth of cities in the post-war years led to the creation of new suburbs. Marti Friedlander photographed a raw suburban development in Henderson, Auckland, in 1966. *Museum of New Zealand Te Papa Tongarewa, Wellington, O.031288*

main domestic exemplars were mothers at home, were asked to cook, clean the toilets and do their share of childcare. Private life was opened out to scrutiny as never before, and a number of marriages failed.

Lesbianism, the visibility of which was promoted by groups such as Sisters for Homophile Equality (begun in Christchurch in 1973), offered a critique of the supposedly natural state of heterosexual relations. Activists who had witnessed their mothers servicing the needs of husbands and families argued that women should no longer plan their lives around men – a stance summarised in the popular feminist slogan 'A woman without a man is like a fish without a bicycle'. Women like Robyn Du Chateau became enraged by 'the fact that men had these things called wives that did just everything for them and for nothing'.[19]

The advent of women's liberation spawned powerful forces. Feminist activists, inspired by electrifying ideas, began questioning the central organising concepts of

'Eglinton Valley, 1970' by Marti Friedlander evokes an older rural way of life in contrast to the rapidly changing urban scene shown opposite. *Auckland Art Gallery Toi o Tāmaki, 2000/28/43*

society. Why were women housewives and men were not? Why was women's labour worth less than that of men? Why were men doctors and women nurses? Why were men the bosses and women their secretaries? Why were women's sexual histories on trial when men were charged with rape?[20] A new word entered the vocabulary of New Zealanders. 'Sexism', first used in the United States in 1968, named the act of 'judging people by their sex where sex doesn't matter'.[21] Suddenly its implications could be seen everywhere: in newspaper advertisements, where the 'Wanted' columns separated jobs into 'male' and 'female' categories; in sport, where male sports took the spotlight and the lion's share of public funding; and in the household, where gender seemed to determine who cooked the meals or mowed the lawn. Housework, once a series of mundane but necessary tasks, now had a 'politics'.[22]

The more women inquired, the more men appeared to be privileged in New Zealand society. Married women, financially dependent on their husbands, had much lower rates of participation in the paid workforce than women elsewhere. In 1971, just 26.1 per cent of married women in New Zealand were working – still well below the 1951 figure for England and Wales of 40 per cent.[23] New Zealand's reputation as a great place to bring up children relied on an environment in which the priority for mothers was to be at home when their children were young. But the buoyant economic climate of the 1950s and 1960s allowed families to educate their daughters to new levels. This education inspired them to question the limited employment choices of their mothers and the very domestic environment in which they had been raised. To a generation of younger women pondering their futures, discrimination, once identified, appeared rampant. Women made up 29.6 per cent of students graduating from university in 1969, and many of them chafed at lower pay packets and other barriers to their ambitions.[24] A February 1969 cover of *thursday* – the New Zealand magazine founded in October 1968 to appeal to just this generation – pictured four young women students above the caption: 'I have been to university, worked hard, passed exams, got my B.A., grown up and now nobody wants me'.[25]

Women's liberation groups set out to analyse and dismantle male privilege, and in sharing their experiences women found themselves moved in profoundly personal ways. The Manifesto of Auckland Women's Liberation declared:

> Women's Liberation is a movement for human equality, a movement aimed to liberate women from the deeply embedded image of their own inferiority. It is a movement aimed to liberate women from narrow, limiting social roles, so that women in New Zealand can grow up facing an open future with many and varied opportunities for development and fulfilment. It is a movement aimed to liberate persons, both men and women from stultifying social roles and stereotypes, in order that men and women may be fairly assessed as PERSONS.[26]

The 'fusion of personal life and political action' released great energy and creativity, leading to demonstrations, alternative institutions, street theatre, art installations, challenges to the churches, and political organising.[27] Feminists were empowered by the idea of sisterhood: that women shared a system of oppression which they could work together to undo. If the 50 per cent of the population regarded as second-class citizens organised to challenge their status, the results would be revolutionary – or so many women hoped.

Socialist feminists – those who argued that women could be truly liberated only by both cultural and economic reform – argued that 'deep ongoing social changes' were required to 'remove from individual women the responsibility for child-rearing and domestic work, placing this on society as a whole'.[28] American feminist Dorothy Dinnerstein's *The Mermaid and the Minotaur: Sexual Arrangements and the Human Malaise* (1976) argued that women's sole responsibility for childcare reproduced 'asymmetry in sexual roles'.[29] The family, she said, needed to be taken apart and childcare seen as a social responsibility, with men as equal participants. Christine Wren of the Wellington Organisation for Women pointed out that the 'physical structure' of women 'no more suits them to washing floors, cooking, cleaning or for that matter looking [after] children than the equivalent parts of the male'.[30] As a gesture in support of this argument, men ran the crèche at the Women's Liberation Conference held at Victoria University in Wellington in 1972. The call for twenty-four-hour childcare centres to provide coverage for families who needed care to be available at different times to suit their circumstances was a central demand of the first women's liberation groups.[31]

Predictably, the intensity of the feminist movement inspired a counter-movement led by women and men who wished to shore up what they regarded as 'traditional values' of women as homemakers and men as breadwinners. A fissure grew between those women who wished to be free agents and those who, like many of the women who had so disapproved of Germaine Greer, were committed to an ideal of family life in which mothers provided a domestic anchor for their spouse and children. The battle was not just about individual lifestyles; it was over the future shape of New Zealand society.

Translating new ideas into action

While the Society for Research on Women had members (including some men) in the main centres collecting data on New Zealand women as a means of promoting changes in the existing social structure, 'liberationist' groups wanted to overturn that structure altogether. In the Dunedin Collective for Women, the 'prime movers' were married women with children, some of whom had returned from the USA where feminist groups were agitating for change.[32] Angered by the wrongs of male hierarchies, the collective sought equality through a women-only organisation that had no leaders and, as its name suggested, shared responsibilities. Through consciousness-raising – the sharing of personal feelings of oppression – women found 'themselves empowered to challenge and change situations as small as a word or as large as the structure of their lives'.[33]

Liberationists saw the traditional committee structures of organisations such as the Society for Research on Women and the National Council of Women as oppressive. They looked beyond women's rights to the whole issue of sex-role stereotyping: the way in which the future of children was determined from birth by different expectations of girls and boys.[34] To 'free children from rigid characterisation by sex', two members of the collective, Andrée Lévesque and Jocelyn Harris, wrote a seventeen-page booklet entitled *First Sex, Second Sex*. The title illustrated the way in which primary school readers published by the Education Department portrayed boys as the central actors in stories and girls as secondary and passive.[35]

Members of the collective were also writing a newsletter, *Woman*, from 1972; they gave talks on women's liberation to the YWCA, the Plunket Society, the Young Wives Coffee Club, local high schools, Lions Clubs and Round Table groups, and participated in talkback radio. Members might be found picketing Miss New Zealand contests, surveying Dunedin residents on attitudes to abortion, providing a 'Knowhow' service on sexual matters, setting up a cooperative preschool, or performing satire on sex roles in the 'Cure-All Ills All Star Women's Travelling Medicine Show'.[36]

Shock tactics to get media attention appealed to liberationists. An Auckland group, which included Ngahuia Te Awekotuku and Donna Awatere (who composed a special song for the event, 'How much longer must we wait?'), succeeded in getting front-page coverage in the *New Zealand Herald* and TV airtime.[37] They dressed in black and staged a mock

Two girls' netball teams compete in a Saturday morning game at Papakura, Auckland, in 1983. Netball has been a leading women's sport in New Zealand since the beginning of the twentieth century. *Manukau Libraries/Footprints 00503. Courtesy of Fairfax Media*

funeral in Albert Park to mourn the progress women had made since enfranchisement in 1893.[38] Christchurch liberationists also took advantage of the immediacy of television news in July 1972, dressing in nineteenth-century garb and chaining themselves to the railings of Christchurch Cathedral to protest at this lack of progress. Their banner, 'Yesterday's suffragettes; today's marionettes', guaranteed media attention.[39]

Health stamps were introduced in New Zealand in 1929 and the proceeds from sales supported health camps for children. This stamp of 1969 showed girls playing cricket. *Courtesy of New Zealand Post*

The commitment to 'political action and public education' was exemplified by *Broadsheet*, a product of the publications subcommittee of Auckland Women's Liberation.[40] It first appeared in July 1972 and went on to become one of the longest-running feminist magazines in the world. The founders, tertiary-educated women and students, aimed to use their skills to overcome the belittling of feminism that occurred in the mainstream media.[41] Under the editorship of Sandra Coney, *Broadsheet* presented the face of a younger generation of feminists than those represented in the pages of the National Council of Women's *Viewpoint*. *Broadsheet* determinedly eschewed the coverage of fashion and celebrities that was becoming increasingly common in the much more widely read *New Zealand Woman's Weekly*. But even that popular magazine was charting important changes. For example, the *Woman's Weekly* celebrated the 1974 graduation of Innes Asher, who topped the class of Auckland Medical School's first intake of students, and who was confident that women GPs, once a rarity, would become mainstream.

For developing new ideas, new types of organisation were necessary, and groups such as Broadsheet were based on feminist principles. At a broader level, new structures were needed as social mores changed rapidly. With sexuality no longer confined within marriage, provision for the support of children had to be reviewed. The Status of Children

Left Established in 1932, *The New Zealand Woman's Weekly* was still going strong in 2015. Its stories, which focused on the royal family, celebrities and domesticity, appealed to a wide readership. *Right* Female and male roles in marriage were amongst the contemporary – and sometimes contentious – issues discussed in *thursday*. Woman's Weekly, *cover, 16 March 1970.* thursday: The Magazine for Younger Women, *cover, 20 March 1969. Both Alexander Turnbull Library, Wellington*

Act 1969 had abolished the concept of illegitimacy and made all children of equal status, whatever the circumstances of their birth.[42] The same year, the National government established a Royal Commission of Inquiry into Social Security, which provided a forum for disenfranchised groups to demand inclusion in New Zealand's welfare system.[43]

Single women supporting children were prominent among those vocal in requesting state support. In 1970, Joss Shawyer founded the Single Parents' Association (later called the Council for the Single Mother and her Child) to fight for the rights of single women with children. The parent of twins born in 1969, Shawyer had refused to give the children up for adoption, and was appalled at attitudes towards single mothers and the lack of information about their benefit entitlements. She went on to co-author a short book on *Everything a Single Parent Needs to Know* (1975); the demand for this led to many reprints.[44]

In response to the pressure for reform, and in recognition of the growing number of children born out of wedlock, the increasing difficulty of finding adoptive homes, and the financial needs of single mothers who kept their children, the Labour government introduced the Domestic Purposes Benefit (DPB) in 1973.[45] Solo parents and women wanting to leave abusive relationships, in particular, benefited from the DPB, although

Left A poster produced by the Committee on Women for International Women's Year, 1975, encouraged women to leave aside domestic chores in favour of political activity. *Right* The second United Women's Convention held in Auckland in September 1973 coincided with the eightieth anniversary of women's suffrage in New Zealand. *Alexander Turnbull Library, Wellington, Eph-D-WOMEN-1975-02; Eph-C-WOMEN- 1973-01*

it was hedged around with restrictions, and eligibility was constantly tightened. Many New Zealanders, including some politicians, continued to argue that women whom they believed had taken sexual risks should not be supported by the state.[46]

The DPB made it possible for some women to leave violent marriages. Domestic abuse was not a new issue, but feminist action ensured that it gained a high profile in the 1970s. Between 1956 and 1969, some 30 per cent of all common assaults involved domestic violence, according to Justice Department statistics.[47] It was clear that the home, customarily identified as a site of partnership and love, might also contain 'violence and domination'.[48] Like the DPB, the refuge movement was a practical response to the situation some women found themselves in. The aim was to provide safe houses for women trapped in violent relationships who did not have the resources to extricate themselves or their children. Christchurch feminist groups – Radical Feminists, University Feminists, and Sisters for Homophile Equality – established the first refuge in 1973 with financial support from women living in two local communes. By 1977, five women's refuges were operating in New Zealand, run by volunteers committed to providing a supportive environment for women and their children wanting to escape violent relationships.

Such developments were not always warmly received. In 1976, the *Otago Daily Times* described the planned Dunedin refuge as 'a house for women who are running away from men'.[49] Such hostility meant that some of the organisers feared for their personal safety. Sue Culling, who chaired the first planning meeting about the Dunedin refuge, found it necessary to take her husband with her for support.[50] A group of Auckland women who proposed to set up a refuge were even told that family violence 'could not happen in New Zealand'.[51]

'House for Battered Wives and Rape Victims', read the public notice announcing the Dunedin refuge. It was one of a number of signals that the issue of physical and sexual violence against women was to be brought into the stark light of day. American feminist Susan Brownmiller's 1975 book *Against Our Will: Men, Women and Rape* provided a powerful analysis of rape as a weapon that shored up male power by keeping women in fear. In 1976, *New Zealand Herald* reporter Ann Lloyd published *Rape: An Examination of the Crime in New Zealand: Its Social and Emotional Consequences.* The cover quotations summed up the range of attitudes, from 'There's no such thing as rape' to 'Every hetero-sexual act is rape'. The book's chilling interviews with rapists demonstrated the close link between rape and violence – a connection made by the feminists also interviewed for the book.[52] Nonetheless, the everyday trivialisation of rape was all too apparent in 1977 when a menswear shop in Auckland's Queen Street dressed its windows to represent prison cells, and announced that a 'macho man in one window was in for "Rape, and more rape"'.[53] In the same year, the first permanent rape crisis hotline was established, in Auckland.

Challenging longstanding inequalities

At the same time as new issues were coming to the fore almost daily, old matters remained unresolved. In the late 1960s, Elsie Awatere, of Ngāti Whakaue descent, mother of five and wife of a war hero, worked quickly and efficiently as an egg packer at Egg Distributors in Wellesley Street, Central Auckland. She was her family's main breadwinner. The man next to her worked much more slowly, broke eggs because of his clumsiness, and was paid substantially more than Elsie. Her daughter Donna, who would become well known as a Māori and feminist activist, worked in the factory in the school holidays and noted that her mother's weekly pay of about $37 was $20 less than that of the male worker who stood beside her. Elsie was indignant about the situation, but she had had little education and 'wasn't particularly articulate in English'. Donna wrote that:

> her generation had a fear of Pakeha and a fear of authority that I hadn't learned. Most of the people in the factory were Maori and Pacific Islands and all the managers were Pakeha men. My mother saw the injustice of it, but she loved her work, she loved the environment, and she didn't want to change her job.[54]

When Donna complained to the management, she was told that the men were paid more for heavy work such as lifting boxes. In fact, she had observed that the women were just as likely to be involved in heavy work as the men were. Donna was eventually sacked for not fitting in. When, some years later, she read the Government Service Equal Pay Act

1969, she understood that it would never deliver equal pay to women like her mother. Her response was to organise action on the issue by visiting factories to educate the workers – an effort that was not well received. Women workers at the Egg Distributors factory ejected the young students onto the street and pelted them with eggs.[55] The Māori and Pacific Island workers had too much to lose in confrontations with management.

The labour market was segmented into jobs for men and jobs for women, the latter paid at lower rates. Married women, in particular, were regarded as a reserve army of labour, to be dispensed with when times were tough. Facing a downturn in the economy, the Bank of New Zealand announced in 1967 that it would dismiss all female employees 'when they marry'.[56] In 1970, out of a total of 778 awards (pay rates set by the Arbitration Court), only 50 had full equal pay.[57] In 1971, young Canterbury women training to be hairdressers (the only full apprenticeship option for women) received $10.58 a week; this was nearly $3 below the unemployment benefit, while their male equivalents received more than $6 above the benefit.[58] In banking and the insurance industry, where women and men did substantially the same job, women's top annual income was more than $1,000 less than that of men.[59] No matter how competent women were, their earnings in the insurance industry could never match those of men: the women's salary scale had eleven steps, the men's eighteen.[60]

The first National Women's Liberation Conference was held in Auckland in 1972, the same year as the passage of the Equal Pay Act which extended equal pay to the private sector. Historian Megan Cook has charted how the Act resulted from the quiet work of an older generation of activists – members of traditional women's rights groups such as the New Zealand Federation of Business and Professional Women's Clubs and the Federation of University Women. In January 1971, the National government, under electoral pressure, set up a Royal Commission of Inquiry into Equal Pay. Miriam Dell was the only woman appointed to the five-person inquiry. (She was described as a 'Married Woman', while the marital status of the four men remained unnoted.) Reporting in September 1971, the commission was unequivocal: that there should be no distinction in remuneration on the basis of sex.[61] The 1972 Labour government responded to the challenge, and set out a five-year implementation plan.[62]

In June of that year, Mabel Howard, who had been an MP for twenty-six years (the only woman in Parliament for two of those years) and New Zealand's first woman Cabinet minister, died in Sunnyside Hospital; in her last few years she had been ill, isolated and uninvolved in the issues that had once consumed her time.[63] It would have disappointed Howard to know that, at the 1972 Federation of Labour conference, only twelve of the 263 delegates were women, that the women workers whom she had long championed were represented by men, and that no woman had ever been elected to the Federation's national executive.[64] Trained in the union movement, Howard was staunch in advocating for equal pay, arguing in the 1950s that remuneration should be based on the requirements of the job, not the sex of the worker.[65] She cared deeply about health and social welfare, and

Whetu Tirikatene-Sullivan was the first Māori woman to become a cabinet minister. She was Minister of Tourism and Minister for the Environment in the Labour government of 1972–75. *Archives New Zealand The Department of Internal Affairs Te Tari Taiwhenua, KIRK W1394/2*

about the welfare of animals, and was forthright in expressing her views.[66] Few of the younger generation of feminists recognised Howard's political achievements.

Young women with seemingly urgent and modern preoccupations looked to the future, and regarded with disdain the apparently limited gains and conventional tactics of the women who immediately preceded them in fighting for women's rights. Historian Charlotte Macdonald has noted that the first significant effort to close the gap between the older generation of women's organisations and the new liberationists took place in Auckland in 1973, when the Labour government established the Select Committee on Women's Rights in September.[67]

The seven-member committee included two new women MPs with a strong commitment to women's rights: Mary Batchelor and Dorothy Jelicich, both of whom were experienced in the union movement. Batchelor's experience with the Clerical Workers' Union had taught her that no matter how well or hard women worked, there were two rates for the job and the male rate was higher.[68] Jelicich tried to increase the effectiveness of the shop assistants' union by joining its executive and working as a union organiser. Both Batchelor and Jelicich wanted women to be free to choose their futures, and saw the provision of equal opportunities and equal pay as key elements in that choice.[69] They brought their experience to a committee that had a wide brief to report on evidence of discrimination against women in New Zealand and to suggest remedies. Evidence was

In May 1975 Wellington's *Evening Post* published this photograph of MPs Dorothy Jelicich and Mary Batchelor playing pool in Bellamy's at Parliament. At the time there were only four women MPs and Bellamy's was a male preserve – one that the women were determined to challenge. *Alexander Turnbull Library, Wellington, EP/1975/2033/24A-F*

Women workers package cartons of ice cream at the Tip Top Ice Cream Factory, Johnsonville, Wellington, in 1972.
Alexander Turnbull Library, Wellington, 1/4-021010-F

collected from around the country, and the committee accepted 'without reservation the need for an accelerated effort to remove all impediments to the equal participation of women in society'. Such discrimination was based not only on sex, 'but also on marital and parental grounds'. To remedy the situation, its 1975 report suggested initiatives in five areas: education and training; earnings and employment support; legal and commercial transactions; family and social welfare; and all aspects of public life.[70]

According to the Select Committee on Women's Rights, the term 'breadwinner' was still 'universally identified with males'.[71] Along with this identification went male authority and consequent female dependency. A woman alone, therefore, had difficulty in raising mortgage finance or securing credit.[72] Evidence of this was reported elsewhere. One unmarried career woman with a good job asked for credit at a large Wellington department store, only to be asked for the name of a referee. She asked if this was a 'request for a male guarantor' and was told 'no' – but when she then supplied the name of a woman, 'she was immediately told that the name of a man was required'.[73] In 1974, a married woman deposited $625 of her own savings for the purchase of a car, the remainder to be paid by a finance company, but the salesman insisted that her husband's name go on the ownership papers, despite the couple's objections. The woman paid the car off early and was entitled to a rebate, but the finance company sent the cheque to her now-departed husband. Although he could not be found, the company 'refused to re-write the cheque to her'.[74]

In 1966 National Airways Corporation (NAC) air hostesses began wearing colourful, specially designed uniforms in place of black suits. Miniskirts were a daring feature of the uniform introduced in 1970. *Archives New Zealand The Department of Internal Affairs Te Tari Taiwheuna, AEPK 20231 W2774/12*

In the absence of financial autonomy, it was difficult for women to leave unsatisfactory marriages, even with the assistance of the Domestic Purposes Benefit. Nonetheless, divorce became increasingly common during the 1970s, rising from 13.7 decrees absolute (decrees which officially ended a marriage) per 100 marriages in 1973 to a rate of 23.8 per 100 in 1977.[75] Divorce was made more practicable for women with the passing of the Matrimonial Property Act 1976, which attempted to remedy the deficiencies of the 1963 Act. The latter had allowed a great deal of judicial discretion, under which women were consistently awarded one- third or less of the family home.[76] The 1976 reform meant that, should a marriage break down, matrimonial property was to be shared equally between the husband and the wife.[77] Māori land was exempted from the provisions of the Act.[78]

Behind the 1976 Act was 'a new philosophical underpinning: the partnership concept', which took heed of the contribution to the household of women's work that had not been rewarded by direct payment.[79] Marriage was now legally a partnership of equals.[80] The problem lay in working out what equality meant in day-to-day life. Partnership involved sharing not only income but also childcare. And, for women to have a genuine choice about combining career and family commitments, attention had to be paid to the question of maternity leave.

The Islanders, first published as a series of articles about Pacific Island peoples in the *Auckland Star* newspaper, was produced as a booklet in 1976. The cover shows a view of Karangahape Road, Auckland. *Fairfax Media, The* Auckland Star *Collection*

Although some limited progress had been made toward recognition of unpaid maternity leave in public-sector employment, social disapproval of pregnant women working continued.[81] A musician noted in the mid-1970s that her employers were 'surprised and disapproving when she performed publicly late in pregnancy'.[82] In July 1976, very few industrial awards contained maternity leave provisions and 'none included an obligation on the employer to re-hire the woman taking leave'.[83]

The Pacific Islanders Congregational Church Bible class on the steps of the church in Newton, Auckland, in the 1960s. Through the church, these formally dressed young people kept alive values brought from their home communities. *M. Anae, Fofoa-i-vao-'ese: the identity journeys of New Zealand-born Samoans, PhD thesis (Anthropology), University of Auckland, 1998, p.150*

The majority of women in the early 1970s were reluctant to take on paid work outside the home while their children were young, but those who wished to do so faced a strong social stigma. The 1972 Royal Commission on Social Security, for example, found it reasonable to assume that mothers of children under three, including single mothers, should not be in paid employment outside the home.[84] But women were also faced with an unsatisfactory array of childcare options. A 1971 study of childcare provision in Auckland found that of the forty-seven existing day nurseries, only eleven had at least one staff member trained in early childcare. Thirty-one of the nurseries took children from two to five years of age, while only sixteen took children under two. Standards of care were low, and the study team was convinced that the government had a responsibility to require better-trained staff, and to subsidise accommodation and equipment.[85] Moreover, the fees for registered daycare centres, ranging from $5.50 to $10 a week in 1972, were beyond the means of many women.[86] Approximately 31 per cent of three- and four-year-olds were in fact in part-time care in 1969, but the restricted hours of kindergartens and the parental involvement expected at Playcentres meant that the services of these organisations were not designed to release mothers for employment.[87]

Those wanting an end to discrimination against women in New Zealand found their arguments bolstered by the United Nations' declaration of 1975 as the International Year for Women, followed by the Decade for Women, 1976–85, when international pressure would be brought to bear on governments to improve the status of women. New Zealand branches of the Women's Electoral Lobby (WEL) were established in 1975 when two Wellington feminists, Judy Zavos and Marijke Robinson, decided that New Zealand needed an equivalent of the Australian organisation that promoted women in politics. Prior to the 1975 election, only eleven women had ever been elected to Parliament, and very few women stood for local bodies. The organisation grew like wildfire, gaining 2,000 members and eighteen branches in eight months.[88] The immediate focus became the forthcoming election, and WEL undertook a survey of all parliamentary candidates on a range of issues to do with women's rights. National's leader, Robert Muldoon, was dismissive of the group, but the survey results became a media event.[89] WEL was concerned with discrimination against women in employment, with the provision of good childcare, with equal opportunity in education and with women's health.[90] Its call for greater representation of women on statutory bodies led Muldoon to comment that 'the government wanted intelligent, balanced women to appoint to statutory bodies, not beady-eyed ladies who scream slogans'.[91]

WEL was only one of a number of groups engaged in analysing the barriers to women's independence. Also in 1975, women within the Labour Party organised a Labour Women's Council, partly out of frustration with the way in which women's issues were sidelined within the party. Members Dorothy Jelicich and Mary Batchelor were both members of the Select Committee on Women's Rights; another member, Pauline Penny, organised a workshop on 'Women and Politics' for the second United Women's Convention in 1975; and Margaret Shields and Sonja Davies were part of the delegation, headed by Whetu Tirikatene-Sullivan, that attended the conference for International Women's Year in Mexico.[92]

The 1975 election brought twenty-three-year-old Marilyn Waring into Parliament as the National member for Raglan. In her first speech, she signalled that she would represent not only her electorate but also 'the youth and the women of this country who are grossly under-represented in this House. From time to time, when I feel a pressing need to advance the interests of those two groups, I will do so.'[93] Colleen Dewe, representing the Lyttelton electorate, was the only other woman elected for National, joining Mary Batchelor (Labour, Avon) and Whetu Tirikatene-Sullivan (Southern Maori) in the House. Waring's stated support for women's rights at the outset, and her decision to take a Caucus seat directly opposite Prime Minister Muldoon, made it clear that she would be fearless in asserting her views rather than always toeing the party line.

The first conference of Pacific women took place as part of the United Nations International Year of Women. Some of those who attended decided to form an organisation to empower women from the Cook Islands, Samoa, Fiji, Tonga, Niue and Tokelau. Samoan-born Paddy Walker, encouraged by Mira Szászy, worked with Fanaura Kimiora Kingstone, Johnnie Frisbe, Louisa Crawley and Eti Laufisa Moira Walker to set up an inaugural conference in 1976; this was attended by 400 women, who became members of the organisation known as PACIFICA. Fanaura Kingstone described it as 'a tremendously exciting and inspiring time'.[94] The organisation worked to assist Pacific Island women in adjusting to New Zealand while at the same time valuing their cultural heritage.[95] For many of these women, the churches, such as the Pacific Islanders' Congregational Church and the Pacific Islanders' Presbyterian Church, provided pan-Pacific meeting places and continuity with Pacific cultures. The churches' values echoed those of the first wave of feminism – a strong faith, 'love, family and God' – values often rejected by women's liberationists.[96]

'Houses have been developed,' Germaine Greer had told her captivated New Zealand audience in 1972, 'to keep women off the streets, when really we ought to be out there in the streets.'[97] Two months after Greer's electrifying visit, large numbers of Christian New Zealanders – including some from the Pacific Islands churches – took to the streets to express their concern about the moral state of New Zealanders in a 'March for Righteousness'. Greer's message of female sexual assertiveness was exactly the kind of individual permissiveness that the 'Jesus marchers' opposed.[98] The Marchers for Righteousness believed the family itself to be under attack from women who wished to put their own desires ahead of commitment to husbands and children. Upholding family values became central for those women who found meaning within the home and had no desire to enter the competitive marketplace. Furthermore, the 'Jesus marchers', along with groups such as Women for Life, held to the view that communist countries were promoting their atheistic lifestyles through international organisations such as the United Nations. Countries that rejected God, they believed, also rejected the nuclear family. From this perspective, the United Nations' commitment to human rights – and its influence on New Zealand – was a Trojan horse used to destabilise the traditional family.

Māori resurgence

In 1967, Whetu Tirikatene-Sullivan won the by-election for Southern Maori with a large majority. For the next two years, there were two Māori women members in the House – Tirikatene-Sullivan and Iriaka Ratana, who retired in 1969. When, in November 1970, Tirikatene-Sullivan became the first member of the House to have a baby during a parliamentary session, she took care to ensure that she missed only six working days, despite having had a Caesarian section.[99] To have done otherwise would have reinforced views that women's childbearing capacity was a barrier to their full political participation – the kind of attitude that commonly disadvantaged women in the workplace.

Whetu Tirikatene's preparation for political leadership had been thorough. Her family life was infused with politics: in the year she was born, 1932, her father, Eruera Tirikatene, became the first Rātana Independent MP. After her secondary schooling at

People gather at Rātana Pā in the 1960s at the annual celebration of the prophet T. W. Ratana's birthday on 25 January.
Photograph by Ans Westra

Rangiora High School and Wellington East Girls' College, Whetu worked in the Public Service Commission and was selected to assist with the royal tour of Queen Elizabeth II in 1953. Employed as a welfare officer in Wellington in the 1950s, Whetu and others devised a programme to encourage Māori children into tertiary education. Like her siblings, she also gave her time freely to promote Māori interests through acting as secretary to the Maori Policy Council and assisting her father in his political work. Once she became a student in 1958, studying social science at Victoria University, it was natural to participate in student politics, and Whetu became the first Māori elected to the University Students' Association – holding, as vice president, the highest position open to women. As president of the fledgling Maori Students' Federation, she played an important role in lobbying for Māori language and Māori Studies to be introduced at Victoria University.[100]

In her maiden speech to Parliament, Whetu Tirikatene-Sullivan reminded the House of the 'predatory land confiscations' and other injustices that had crippled Māori, including

Marti Friedlander took this photograph of kuia at Tūrangawaewae Marae, Ngāruawāhia, in 1971. *Reproduced by permission of Marti Friedlander*

the deficiencies of a Pākehā-oriented education system. Pākehā required knowledge of Māori language and culture, she said, in order to engender mutual respect. She delivered a prescient warning:

> There is a glaring disparity between the apparently harmonious situation in New Zealand's race relations and the real socio-economic levels, a disparity which must be eliminated if we are to take our rightful stand in the international forums of the world.[101]

At the first Women's Liberation Conference in 1972, the position of Māori women was not addressed. University-educated Donna Awatere and Ngahuia Te Awekotuku were among the few who attended. Māori women's perspectives were, however, sought at the 1973 United Women's Convention, where Mira Szászy, former president of the Maori Women's Welfare League, spoke about the position of Māori women:

> I said we were like the crippled member of the children's group who followed the Pied Piper of Hamlin. We were being left behind. Pakeha women were being led to the mountaintop while we were still picking ourselves up to start walking. As I saw it, we were still trying to survive.[102]

Szászy's analysis identified oppression on two fronts: race and sex. Māori men were drinking and being violent in the home; Māori women were 'so trapped in their lifestyles they didn't see the oppression'.[103] Her fear was that middle-class Pākehā women committed to feminism might not see the 'poverty, cultural deprivation and poor education' that impacted on the lives of many Māori women. With the support of the Department of Maori Affairs, the Maori Women's Welfare League had focused on health, education and welfare, striving to raise Māori living standards to those of Europeans. At the same time, it campaigned for the teaching of Māori language in schools, requested a Chair in Māori at the University of Auckland, fostered cultural traditions, and criticised the misrepresentation of Māori in tourist items, films and school publications.[104] A new generation of activists, however, was impatient with the league's accommodation with the state.

Māori activism had gathered pace during the 1960s as increasing numbers of Māori moved into urban areas, and disparities in health, education and housing became obvious. Levels of teenage pregnancy among Māori were more than twice the Pākehā rate in 1971, and Māori women had larger families, averaging five births per woman.[105] By 1976, those under the age of fifteen made up 45.3 per cent of New Zealand's Māori population, compared to 29.7 per cent of the total population; such a young population had many urgent needs in terms of health and educational opportunities. At the other end of the life cycle, high Māori mortality rates were reflected in the fact that, while 13 per cent of the total population was aged sixty and over, only 3.6 per cent of the Māori population fell into this category.[106]

Those who saw their people more poorly housed, poorly paid and with lower life expectancy could only raise questions about New Zealand's own racial politics at a time when the international spotlight was falling on the injustices of apartheid in South Africa. Young radicals were not interested in the conciliatory approach taken by their predecessors such as the Maori Women's Welfare League. When Hana Jackson, active in Nga Tamatoa, began a petition for the teaching of Māori language in schools, the league did not support it. 'Mind you,' Jackson recalled, 'they had been passing remits every year since 1952 for the teaching of Maori Language in schools and they felt that was enough.'[107] She felt caught between the radicalism of Donna Awatere, who challenged her on feminism, and the conservatism of the league. When Jackson wrote a paper on Māori women in 1975, Donna Awatere 'thought it was pathetic', while the league 'thought it was so radical they wanted to take me to court over it'.[108]

In 1975, it was an elderly woman who brought together elements of these two strands of Māori activism and came to the forefront of national attention. Eighty-year-old Whina Cooper led a new Māori organisation, Te Roopu o te Matakite (Those with Foresight), in a land march from Te Hāpua in the far north to Wellington to deliver a petition demanding an end to the alienation of Māori land. The organising committee included members of the older organisations and the young radicals. Whina Cooper's motivations were clear:

I wanted to draw attention to the plight of Maoris who were landless. I wanted to point out that people who were landless would eventually be without culture. I wanted to stop any further land passing out of Maori ownership, and I wanted the Crown to give back to Maoris land that it owned that was of traditional significance to Maoris. The march itself was to dramatise these things, to mobilise Maori opinion, to awaken the Pakeha conscience.[109]

Whina Cooper's slight, bent body, supported by a will of iron, became a symbol for a new phase of Māori activism. The march began symbolically on 14 September 1975, the first day of that year's Māori Language Week. The spectacle of the marchers crossing the Auckland Harbour Bridge attracted extensive media coverage, which continued as the marchers made their way down the North Island, and came to a peak as the 5,000-strong group led by Whina Cooper arrived at Parliament. Labour Prime Minister Bill Rowling greeted Cooper and promised the marchers that their concerns would be heeded. Cooper felt much had been accomplished, but others, including Nga Tamatoa's Titewhai Harawira, were dissatisfied. The unity the march had engendered dissolved as those who wanted immediate results began an occupation of Parliament grounds in a tent embassy; they were evicted (with Whina Cooper's approval) three months later by the new National government under Robert Muldoon.[110]

The politics of abortion

The generation of women coming of age in the 1970s saw fertility control as a choice. But that sense of control could easily be undermined by an accidental pregnancy. Legal abortion was a rare option, unless a woman had the contacts and the funds to get to Australia. Access to abortion was governed by the Crimes Act 1961, under which therapeutic abortion was lawful only 'for the preservation of the life of the mother' – a judgement made by doctors.

By the mid-1960s, activist women in England, where access to legal abortion was similarly restricted, were speaking of abortion as an urgent social issue for all 'who take seriously the notion of the emancipation and full equality of women'.[111] The English abortion law was reformed in 1967, providing access to therapeutic abortion on more liberal grounds, including mental health and familial considerations. Change came much later in New Zealand. Norman Kirk, leader of the 1972–1975 Labour government that had appointed the Select Committee on Women's Rights, was firmly opposed to abortion. The 1967 British Act, he suggested, was the first step on a slippery slope that would lead to the elimination of those who were 'incurably ill or cripples'.[112] To prevent liberalisation of the New Zealand abortion laws, those opposed to abortion founded the Society for the Protection of the Unborn Child (SPUC) in 1970. Norman Kirk's wife, Ruth, became a patron of the organisation in 1974, and that year SPUC could claim 32 out of 87 parliamentarians as members.[113] Conflict with radical feminists arose from the start: the Wellington Women's Liberation Front leafleted an early SPUC meeting with pamphlets entitled 'Abortion – or compulsory pregnancy'.[114]

Pro-abortion demonstrators were photographed outside Parliament in 1974. They were protesting against the closure of the Auckland Medical Aid Centre (which provided a therapeutic abortion service for women) and the introduction of a Hospital Amendment Bill to restrict abortions to public hospitals. Cath Tizard, then a member of the Auckland City Council (later Auckland mayor, and then Governor-General), is speaking to the demonstrators. *Alexander Turnbull Library, Wellington, 1/4-021836-F*

One woman was at the vanguard of opposition to both permissiveness in sexual relations and greater access to contraception and abortion. Patricia Bartlett, a former Catholic nun, represented those who believed the sea change in sexual behaviour would be the undoing of all that was good about New Zealand. A tireless campaigner, and often a figure of derision among liberals, Bartlett founded the Society for the Promotion of Community Standards in 1970 and pressed for censorship of 'scenes of nudity or sexual intercourse in public entertainment'.[115] Nearly 50,000 people were willing to support her petition on this issue.[116]

Abortion was, however, a matter of ongoing concern for both Māori and Pākehā women. A well-trained Māori midwife used her skills to assist women who might otherwise have resorted to dangerous backstreet abortions. She recalled:

> I had worked in theatres and had seen abortions being carried out, including some for fetal abnormality or intellectual impairment, these done at the wish of the parents. I had seen badly deformed children being born and not resuscitated for humane reasons.[117]

A man debates with two pro-choice demonstrators during the International Women's Day march in Wellington in 1978.

Photograph by Lee Switzer, Alexander Turnbull Library, Wellington, 35mm-00525-d-F

She regarded her own actions, in providing distressed women with safe abortions, as equally humane. But the hospitalisation of one panicked young girl she had helped led to charges against her. During the trial, she felt tremendously supported by her parents and their Māori community. 'Where I come from,' she noted, 'children are often accepted into the extended family, but Maori women not in a position to look after a child will often resort to abortion.' As Prisoner 60/71 she served seven-and-a-half months of her twelve-month sentence in Mount Eden prison.[118]

The abortion debate heated up during the 1970s, as did SPUC's level of organisation. As historian Grace Millar has noted, the English law was reformed before the height of second-wave feminism, but in New Zealand feminists' agitation on the issue led to strengthened opposition. In 1974, the Auckland Medical Aid Centre was set up as a charitable trust to provide a therapeutic abortion service for women. SPUC was quick to respond, first by taking steps to close down the centre through the charge that it was breaking the law, and second by using sympathetic MPs to introduce a Hospital Amendment Bill to restrict abortions to public hospitals. A police raid on the centre in September 1974 and confiscation of records outraged the feminist community, as did the 1975 trial of one of the clinic doctors, Jim Woolnough. After twice being tried in the Auckland Supreme Court for performing an abortion at the woman's request, rather than for reasons of mental health, Woolnough was eventually acquitted on the charge of procuring unlawful abortions.

But the passing of the Hospital Amendment Act in May 1975 (between Woolnough's two trials) by a House that included only four women out of eighty-seven MPs caused a storm of controversy. The original Bill had been designed to close down the Auckland Medical Aid Centre by requiring all abortions to be done in public hospitals, but an amendment extended the provisions to licensed private hospitals, which the centre quickly became.[119] The Labour government responded to the public outcry by setting up a Royal Commission of Inquiry into Contraception, Sterilisation and Abortion, which began its work in June 1975.

The Royal Commission posed a dilemma for radical feminist groups: did they participate in the process (which, by its very membership, seemed likely to resist any possibility of liberalisation), or did they continue their disdain for male politics by refusing to take part? One of those groups was the Women's National Abortion Action Campaign (WONAAC), which had an intermittently high profile but never gained a significant mass membership. Its more radical members argued that the state had no role in determining women's reproductive decisions:

> It is control of our bodies, control of our lives that we want, the abortion laws are the most blatant denial of that control. These laws should be repealed, abolished, so that women can make a free choice. No doctor, no priest, no government, no man, no-one at all should be able to override her right to decide.[120]

WONAAC, the Dunedin Collective for Women, the Broadsheet Collective and the Women's Health Workshop of the Values Party (an alternative 'green' party founded in 1972) all made submissions to the Royal Commission, but the efforts of feminists were overshadowed by the large number of group submissions from anti-abortion groups.[121]

To conservatives in Parliament, the issue was about moral values. As Bill Birch, the National member for Franklin, put it: 'One must recognise that there is a tide of change anxious to displace the moral values of society. For those of us who want to stem the tide, this is a crucial debate and critical legislation.'[122]

Those like Birch who equated permissive abortion legislation with the downfall of society won the day. The Royal Commission's recommendation for a more restrictive law was enacted, despite Heylen polls indicating that 61 per cent of the public supported the contention that 'abortion to terminate any unwanted pregnancy should be made legal'.[123] The Contraception, Sterilisation and Abortion Act 1977 gave precedence to the rights of the unborn child rather than the rights of women. Access to abortion was to be closely monitored under a complex system involving an Abortion Supervisory Committee and certifying consultants. A woman seeking an abortion had to convince two certifying consultants (one of whom had to be a practising obstetrician and gynaecologist) that continuing the pregnancy would constitute 'a serious danger' to her 'life or physical or mental health'.[124] All four women members of the 1977 Parliament, from opposing sides of the House, voted against the Bill. Once more, male politicians appeared oblivious to the voice of women. Colleen Dewe supported an amendment to drop the legislation; it would, she argued, 'bring the House into disrepute'.[125] And, to feminists, it did.

The Act threw New Zealand's abortion services 'into chaos'.[126] The best facility, the Auckland Medical Aid Centre, closed down. Doctors were uncertain how to interpret the law and afraid of prosecution. Women in need of terminations once more took flight to Australia, and feminists formed Sisters Overseas Service (SOS) to assist them. It is estimated that around 4,000 to 4,500 women went to Australia over two years.[127] Marilyn Waring was behind efforts to support a repeal petition, which gathered more than 319,000 signatures but was rejected by the House.[128] The heat died from the issue only after sufficient time had passed for operating doctors to feel secure in their understanding that they could interpret the law liberally without fear of prosecution.

Critiquing heterosexuality

Just as SPUC framed debates about abortion in terms of a decline in moral values, so too did the Society for the Promotion of Community Standards in its defence of traditional family values. Patricia Bartlett and her supporters believed that heterosexual sex within marriage should be the socially upheld norm. These beliefs came under increasing attack as activists began organising to legalise male homosexuality and reform the law to prevent state interference in the private sexual acts of all adults. A feminist critique of

The flamboyant Carmen, born Trevor Rupe, became a drag-performer in the 1950s. In the 1960s Carmen opened a coffee lounge in Wellington whose staff provided refreshments, entertainment and sexual services. In 1977 she ran for mayor in Wellington, then left for Australia, and spent her last years in Sydney. Carmen is pictured at the 'Miss Drag NZ' ball in Auckland in 1975. *Photograph by Fiona Clark*

heterosexuality emerged, too, fuelled by issues of domestic violence and rape. This was given a sharper edge by new forms of lesbian organising. Female homosexuality, though not illegal, was so stigmatised that lesbian groups were denied both advertising in newspapers and telephone listings into the late 1970s.[129]

In the late 1960s, Sharon Alston lived with her female lover quietly in Christchurch. In 1974, she attended a lesbian conference. She recalled:

> To experience the high I got from attending the conference in Wellington is to understand far more of what it means when women say 'Sisterhood is Powerful'. The conference provided an opportunity for approximately 125 gay woman [*sic*] from many cities in New Zealand to find a consensus based on a common bond of oppression and the increasing sense of self-identity and pride which is enabled to grow within our groups. We now have groups for gay women established in Christchurch, Wellington and Auckland. The dichotomy between 'women's liberation' and 'gay women's liberation' is weakened by our working together.[130]

Sharon Alston became a regular cartoonist and designer for *Broadsheet*, as well as a noted lesbian feminist artist. In Auckland, Ngahuia Te Awekotuku was a founding member of Gay Liberation in 1972. In May of that year, she and other student protesters disrupted a meeting of the Society for Promotion of Community Standards held in the Auckland Sunday School Union's Hall. Activist Tim Shadbolt took over the microphone, shouting 'The worst obscenity is war!' while other protesters, bearing fake blood and wooden guns, further disrupted the meeting. They unfurled a 4-metre banner that read 'Lesbian and gay liberation'.[131]

Sisters for Homophile Equality formed in Christchurch in 1973, and lesbian rights were among the many issues discussed at the Auckland United Women's Convention that year. The voices of those supporting lesbian interests became louder in later conventions. Lesbian women could claim a high moral ground by accusing heterosexual women of sleeping with the enemy. '[T]o be a consistent feminist,' some lesbians argued at a Radical Feminist Weekend in Hamilton, 'one must also be a lesbian.'[132] The visibility of homosexuality increased remarkably as gay men and women began to assert their sexual preferences openly. They pointed out that, while the church and wider society had long emphasised that the primary purpose of sex was procreation, non-procreative sex had become the norm for heterosexuals: what then could the rationale be for objecting to homosexual sex?

Arguments about what was 'natural' were difficult to sustain at a time when ideas about women's 'natural' place in the home were being dismissed. In Parliament, National MP Venn Young took up the campaign for homosexual law reform in 1974, introducing a Private Member's Bill to decriminalise homosexual acts between consenting males aged twenty and over. The Bill was narrowly defeated, but gay liberation groups had not supported it wholeheartedly, arguing that the age of consent should be sixteen, the same as for heterosexuals.[133]

Although the climate was changing, accusations of homosexuality remained damaging for public figures. Not long after Marilyn Waring entered Parliament in 1975, the *Truth* newspaper alleged that she was living with a woman who had left her family to pursue the relationship. The newspaper's revelations were undoubtedly intended to shock, but both Prime Minister Muldoon and Waring's electorate chairman were unwavering in support of her. The latter said firmly: 'Marilyn Waring's private life is no one else's bloody business.'[134] Muldoon's support may have been based primarily on party loyalty, but the public backing Waring received from these unlikely allies reflected a more general change in social attitudes.

Human rights

If an increasing number of New Zealanders were of the view that the behaviour of consenting adults was not the business of the state, feminists insisted that when consent was lacking or enforced, the state needed to do more. In fact, feminists increasingly looked to the state to right the wrongs of family life. The Select Committee on Women's Rights noted with concern in its 1975 report that there were no women judges or magistrates in New Zealand, and women could opt out of jury service merely on the grounds of their sex.[135] Few women served in the police. If women were to get justice in cases of domestic violence or rape, the state needed to step in to promote change.

The Select Committee on Women's Rights suggested that New Zealand needed to come into line with the United Nations Declaration on the Elimination of Discrimination Against Women (1967). Either the government should create a statutory body to fight discrimination against women and promote equal opportunities, the committee argued, or it should establish a broader human rights commission that would have women's rights part of its brief.[136] In the event, the National government opted for the latter.

Whetu Tirikatene-Sullivan, who served as a member of the select committee that took submissions on the Human Rights Commission Bill in 1977, kept the focus on the position of women. She noted the number of submissions from women's groups, and saw their interest as articulating the urgent concerns of 'a group that has felt its human rights were inadequately recognised'.[137] According to David Lange, the Labour MP for Māngere, the Bill was 'a cautious first step', since it allowed employers, most of whom had made no provision for separate toilets for women and men, to continue to discriminate on the grounds of sex until 1982. Lange wryly commented that five years seemed an unduly generous amount of time to provide another lavatory.[138]

During the final reading of the Bill, Tirikatene-Sullivan reminded members of the House of a certain irony. 'While groups are enthusiastically lobbying for the rights of the unborn child, the cause of the born but neglected children excites less interest and emotion.'[139] She expressed her disappointment that the rights of children were not clearly articulated in the Bill. Tirikatene-Sullivan's stance was not uncommon: it recognised the need both for abortion to protect women's rights and for advocacy on behalf of children already born. But for opponents of abortion, the rights of the unborn child trumped the rights of women. The ongoing abortion debate revealed the fraught nature of New Zealand's sexual politics.

In introducing the Human Rights Commission Bill in 1977, Minister of Justice David Thomson declared the necessity of passing legislation 'to prohibit discrimination on the grounds of sex or marital status in the crucial field of employment and in other key areas'. Such legislation, he claimed, was 'fundamental to the aims and objects of the women's movement', and followed directly the recommendations of the Select Committee on Women's Rights.[140] Adopting the language first used by feminists, Barry Brill, National member for Kapiti, argued: '[W]e must do away with the traditional stereotyping that a man is a person of particular ambitions or abilities and a woman is a person of different abilities and ambitions.' It was this stereotyping, he said, that had 'rebounded in the past against the interests of women'.[141]

The Human Rights Commission Act 1977 aimed to abolish discrimination on the grounds of sex, marital status, race, colour, ethnic or national origins, and religious or ethical belief. The Act also created an Equal Opportunities Tribunal to hear cases referred to it by the commission. 'Sexual harassment', a term coined by feminists in the 1970s, turned what had been seen as a man's right to flirt, use sexual innuendoes, and even suggestively touch women workers, into unacceptable behaviour.

Yet one sector of New Zealand society continued to uphold a commitment to the distinct roles of women and men. The Pentecostal New Life Churches launched a 'Save our Homes' campaign with a convention in Christchurch in 1977. The crusade advocated 'family values' and was underpinned by the long-held belief that 'home' was the repository of certain moral values, particularly that of service above self, which women performed in the family. Feminism was threatening to 'belittle the dedicated wife and mother – [to] howl down women who cling to real values'.[142] The 'home' acted as a metaphor for the role of a domestic mother.

The great majority of women, however, were neither fervent Pentecostal believers devoted to home and family nor radical feminist activists questioning heterosexism, and they had to negotiate their lives through a period of upheaval and challenging change. In Porirua, Novena Petelo, an immigrant from the Tokelau Islands, kept on juggling the needs of her family with the demands of her cleaning job. For four years from 1973 she worked at night because she had to look after the children during the day. For her, 'the main thing was to do the right thing for my family'.[143] Other women shared that commitment, continuing their lives along pathways very similar to those of their mothers, though perhaps expecting different opportunities for their daughters.

This famous photograph shows Whina Cooper, leader of the 1975 Māori Land March, setting off on the hīkoi from the far north with her three-year-old mokopuna, Irene Cooper. *Photograph by Michael Tubberty,* New Zealand Herald, *NZH-1045886*

Those daughters might be involved in feminist organisations based on 'principles of collectivity, consensus and co-operation'.[144] They jettisoned the old-fashioned parliamentary procedures of groups such as the National Council of Women as hierarchical and unnecessarily bureaucratic. But the new structures often held within them the seeds of destruction. The politics of identity – whether one was heterosexual, lesbian, Pākehā, Māori, middle or working class – could become a substitute for political analysis, and alienated those who were committed to feminism but whose 'identities' apparently aligned them with culpable privilege.[145] Collective structures often lacked the resilience of the old-style organisations in which adherence to procedural rules provided a mechanism for accommodating differences of opinion.

The decade from 1967 to 1977 saw women's rights asserted in new and urgent ways. Individual acts and group initiatives led to the reverberation of feminism throughout New Zealand society. 'Ms' became the preferred form of address for women who did not wish to be defined by their marital status. Young women no longer automatically wanted to be 'given away' by their fathers in marriage, or to promise 'to obey' their husbands – if indeed they wanted to be married at all. Marriage did not now mean a woman automatically abandoned her surname.

Demonstrations, street theatre and pub invasions signalled women were serious about social change. Lively debate filled the pages of *Broadsheet*; the *Woman's Weekly* charted women's advances; and television brought feminist issues into the heart of the family home. It was hard to ignore the Auckland buses graffitied with 'Smash Sexism' and 'Disarm the Rapist' on International Women's Day in April 1977. The following month, a Third United Women's Convention gathered in Christchurch. But, as Sandra Coney wrote, some women were 'heaven-bent on taking the "united" out of the United Women's Convention'.[146] Those divisions, so apparent in the Contraception, Sterilisation and Abortion Act and in debate around the Human Rights Commission Act, were about to widen. The aspirations of socialist feminists, who looked to the state to create social justice, were undercut by the political aims of those, like future Minister of Finance Ruth Richardson, who believed that only the dismantling of the state would lead to a buoyant economic future for New Zealand.

Golden Sky Stream (1973) is by Auckland artist Gretchen Albrecht. Early in her career Albrecht painted figurative works, but from the 1970s began increasingly to favour an abstract style. *Reproduced by permission of Gretchen Albrecht*

Chapter Twelve
Into the Corridors of Power

In 1978 an ambitious woman lawyer won the National Party nomination for the Tasman seat. Ruth Richardson was defeated in the election by the incumbent, Labour's Bill Rowling, but Richardson was determined to try again. The 1970s had seen her, along with other women, devote considerable energy to the work of the Women's Electoral Lobby and to reform of family law, including the Matrimonial Property Act.[1] Soon her keen attention would be directed to economic matters. New Zealand, which had once had one of the highest living standards in the world, had entered the doldrums. Fresh approaches were needed to stimulate the economy and solve rising unemployment. Socialist feminists had looked to the state to create better conditions for women through the promotion of equal opportunities; to Ruth Richardson, the answer lay in individual initiative, promoted through the progressive dismantling of an over-regulated economy and an over-stretched welfare system.

The United Nations had declared 1976 to 1985 a 'Decade for Women', to promote equal rights and opportunities. Those years, however, saw rising levels of unemployment throughout New Zealand and heightened debate about women's work, especially around the issue of access to parental leave. Women took on new roles and sought to have their career aspirations taken seriously in all types of endeavours, from firefighting to early childhood education, and in the sciences and arts. The Māori protest movement of the mid-1970s also continued into the 1980s, with land issues again to the fore. Māori women joined forces with Pākehā protesters, too, in the campaigns against the 1981 Springbok tour. But while that national protest movement held groups together, Māori women increasingly sought their own solutions to the problems facing their communities, particularly those to do with health.

Longstanding divisions among women were brought to a head with the creation of the Ministry of Women's Affairs as a separate department in March 1985. Conservative women's organisations were among those to disrupt the ministry's attempts to consult the community through forums held throughout the country to prioritise issues. Their concerns about the erosion of family life were heightened further by the removal of spousal immunity from rape law in 1985 and the passing of the Homosexual Law Reform Act in 1986. The feminist onslaught, which threatened to undermine traditional marriage, appeared to conservatives to have won the day.

Girls take their ponies for a swim during a pony club event at Tauherenīkau in the 1980s. Pony clubs were established in New Zealand in 1944 and taught children horse-riding skills through competitive games and activities such as camps and treks. *Alexander Turnbull Library, Wellington, EP/1980/0070*

Girls can do anything

In the 1970s and 1980s, increasing numbers of girls remained longer at college, reversing older patterns that saw girls leaving school earlier than boys and with fewer qualifications. But traditional patterns of subject choice were slow to change: girls still opted for arts, languages, and typewriting and shorthand courses, while boys were more likely to choose science and technical subjects.[2] The proportion of girls taking physics, for example, rose only from 13 per cent in 1967 to 16 per cent in 1988. A doubled participation in mathematics over the same period, from 36 per cent to 69 per cent, was more encouaraging.[3] Nonetheless, the gradual improvements in girls' science education resulted in new career opportunities. In 1976 the New Zealand Census recorded 23 women veterinarians; by 1981 the number had risen to 60. The number of women surgeons had risen from 4 to 27; the number of dentists from 14 to 54. Increasingly, women clients were asking for women professionals, and previously all-male practices in medicine and law responded by employing new graduates.

Women take part in a surf lifesaving carnival at Paekākāriki in 1979. Women's lifesaving teams were established before the Second World War, and from 1944 women competed for national titles. However, mixed teams of men and women were not accepted until the 1970s. *Alexander Turnbull Library, Wellington, EP/1979/0256/25-F*

Left From the 1980s, the Department of Labour encouraged girls to train for trades traditionally dominated by males. This poster of 1985 features a female butcher. *Right* In 1977 National Minister of Social Welfare Bert Walker implied that women were abusing the Domestic Purposes Benefit (DPB), sparking protests such as this one. Women with dependent children could receive the benefit from 1973, but the level of financial support was low and there was a cap on the amount of additional money recipients could earn through part-time work. *Alexander Turnbull Library, Wellington, Eph-B-WOMEN-1985-02-front; 1/4-028309-F*

Attention-grabbing stories of women's 'firsts' dominated the media in the late 1970s and early 1980s. Barbara Johns, who became a traffic officer, was described as 'like one of the boys' in the *Press* in October 1978.[4] The following year, Julie Gibbs, aged seventeen, became the first female coach-building apprentice, and sixteen-year-old Justine Hampson became the first female apprentice fitter at Addington Railways Workshops.[5] All but combat roles were opened to women in the Royal New Zealand Airforce under the Human Rights Commission Act of 1977, and in 1979 the country's first female airforce engineers graduated.[6]

In 1981, Anne Barry of Auckland won her two-year battle to join the New Zealand Fire Service after the Human Rights Commission overturned the service's decision to decline her application because she was a woman.[7] Barry faced all sorts of discrimination – she was too short (though senior officers were shorter than her), her vision was not up to par (thought multiple tests showed it was) – as well as union opposition. The 600-strong

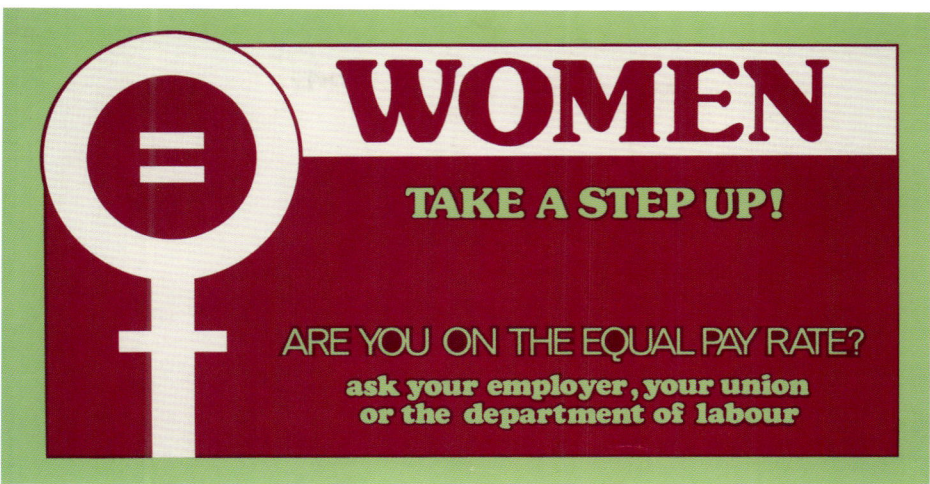

Legislation requiring employers to pay equal pay for equal work was passed in 1960 for the public sector, and in 1972 for the private sector. This Department of Labour poster of 1976 urged women to check that they were being paid the same rate as men. *Alexander Turnbull Library, Wellington, Eph-D-ROTH-Women-1976-01*

South Island branch of the Firemen's Union voted against admitting women firefighters. They followed the lead of their president, who said:

> Women in the working environment can be very restricting to some men's ability to express themselves. There is no doubt that a certain amount of sexual activity will take place, however much supervision is imposed ... as those who have dealt with women will realise, they will be harder to discipline and cannot be handled in the normal way ... We are going to have to cope with pregnancy, menstrual cycles and associated unpredictable behaviour, menopause and associated depression and ill-health.[8]

After the Human Rights Commission backed her, Anne Barry met the male culture of fire brigade life full-on, proving she could do the job as well as her male colleagues.

While attractive avenues opened up for the well educated, the majority of women were not in well-paid occupations, and those seeking work were doing so in a period of economic recession. The 1981 Census showed that the main full-time occupations for women were clerical and sales related, followed by work in teaching or in the healthcare sector. Part-time work reflected a similar distribution but also indicated a growing trend: more than 10,000 women were employed as 'caretakers, charworkers or cleaners', while another 5,000 were part-time 'housestaff and related housekeeping service workers'.[9] Many of the cleaners were Māori and Pacific Island women. The part-time labour force (generally without any security or benefits) increased by 261 per cent between 1966 and 1981, as more women sought work that would help balance the family budget while also fitting in with the needs of preschool or school-aged children.

A woman works in the factory of Allied Industries, Māngere, Auckland, in 1981. The photographer, Glenn Jowitt, commented on the irony 'that people who were experts at weaving were now weaving wiring looms for cars'.
Photograph by Glenn Jowitt, Museum of New Zealand Te Papa Tongarewa, Wellington, O.003178

Women committed to improving working conditions worked doggedly within the trade union movement, despite the scepticism of those in the unions, like the firemen, who had long enjoyed a male-only membership. Sonja Davies, a veteran of community union activism, campaigned vigorously for trade union support of the Working Women's Charter, 'essentially a Bill of Rights for all women'.[10] Endorsed by the Working Women's Councils formed in the mid-1970s to promote the rights of women and their families, the charter supported the elimination of discrimination against women, improved working conditions for women, the provision of quality childcare and the '[i]ntroduction of adequate paid parental leave without loss of job security, superannuation or promotion prospects'.[11] Davies saw the charter as having a 'significant impact on the labour movement' because it prompted major labour organisations to take women's issues seriously.[12] In 1980, the Federation of Labour set up a Women's Advisory Council. The union movement, traditionally a male stronghold, was responding to the demands of New Zealand's women workers at a time when it needed all the combined strength it could muster.

Whereas women had formerly been expected to abandon paid employment on the birth of a child, parental leave was based on the expectation that motherhood should not be a barrier to employment. New Zealand lagged well behind some European countries in

Actor and producer Joanna Paul of Ngāi Te Rangi became the first Māori woman to front television news when in 1989 she presented the inaugural breakfast bulletin for TV3, and then from 1990 its late night news show *Nightline*. She went on to front *One Network News*, and from 2002 to 2004 was general manager of programmes and production at Māori Television. *Photograph by Jenny Scown*

this regard. Sweden, for example, had introduced parental leave in 1974 in the expectation that it would both increase employment opportunities for women and enable men to be more involved with their children.[13] New Zealand's much more limited Maternity Leave and Employment Protection Act 1980 safeguarded the employment of women who had been working for eighteen months or more for the same employer by stipulating that they could not be dismissed for reasons of pregnancy or childbirth, and were entitled to twenty-six weeks' unpaid maternity leave. But the Act made no provision for paid leave for either mothers or fathers.[14] Ann Hercus, the Labour MP for Lyttelton, was critical of the legislation, suggesting the National government saw parenting as a role 'for mothers, not fathers', whereas Labour held 'most strongly that parenting and childrearing are the responsibility of men and women, and of society at large'.[15]

A new assertiveness among women in traditional female occupations led to a number of campaigns for better working conditions and wages. The registration of the Early Child-hood Workers' Union in March 1982, for example, acknowledged that childcare work could no longer be seen as an extension of women's mothering role but was an occupation delivering a professional service. By 1986, the union had achieved a national award covering all workers.[16] In the mid-1980s, nurses ran a 'Nurses are worth more' campaign and gave unprecedented notice of strike action. The creation of a National Council of Maori Nurses in 1983 drew attention to longstanding cultural insensitivity in the healthcare system.[17]

Women in work sought better conditions and the flexibility to integrate work and motherhood. But what if no work could be found? Women had higher unemployment rates than men, and the rate was particularly high in the part-time workforce where women predominated.[18] A 1982 Palmerston North study revealed the dilemmas that faced women seeking work. A thirty-two-year-old divorced woman, Louise, had trained as an obstetric nurse before marriage. By the time her children were aged nine and six, her qualification was obsolete, but retraining as a general nurse required three-and-a-half years of full-time study – an impossible time and financial commitment for her. Louise was offered a full-time job, working weekdays from 8.30 a.m. to 5.30 p.m. as a receptionist. The researcher reported that:

> [Louise] calculated that if she took this job, she would have to pay for after-school child-care for her two children, and pay someone to mow the lawns and do 3 hours' housework per week (so that she would be free to spend her evenings and weekends with the children). All this would cost at least $60 per week. This would be a sizeable proportion of her salary, so she decided that, on balance, it was not worth accepting the job.[19]

Women raising children alone found the juggle of childcare and work particularly difficult, but those in stable relationships were just as likely to seek work limited to school hours.[20]

Those in receipt of the Domestic Purposes Benefit were grateful for the state support that allowed them to leave abusive relationships, but found the policing of their private lives and the social stigma hard to bear. Many sought part-time work to show that they were not 'bludgers' on the state and to earn enough to subsist above the breadline. They were hampered by the fact that additional annual income (above $1,300 in 1981) would lead to an abatement of their benefit. In addition, associated childcare costs could well undermine any financial gains from employment. Given this, and the costs of travel to paid employment, women sometimes used their homes as places of work – taking in boarders, minding children, doing laundry, ironing, knitting and dressmaking, as well as typing, and giving music lessons.[21]

Domestic demands continued to constrain women's working lives in a multitude of ways, from the care of children and other family members to the expectation that cleaning and cooking in the home were women's work. More likely than men to move out of employment when they became parents, and concentrated in a narrow range of occupations, women found the return to the workforce difficult when the skills required were changing rapidly. They continued to be paid substantially less than men. Māori women were at a particular disadvantage: the 1981 Census revealed that they had an unemployment rate of 17.5 per cent, compared with 4.3 per cent for non-Māori women.

Independence and creativity

'Every fortnight when I draw National Super,' wrote J. C. in her prize-winning letter to the *Woman's Weekly* in October 1983, 'I give silent thanks for something I have lacked all my married life – a personal allowance. It may not amount to much after a housekeeping contribution, but it's *mine*.' A beneficiary of the Muldoon government's universal national superannuation scheme to which women had the same entitlement as men at the age of sixty, J. C. revelled in the fact that she no longer had to ask her husband for money. Although she had accepted financial dependence within her marriage, she had been determined 'to instill into my own children as young adults the concept of marriage as a sharing partnership in which no wife worth her salt deserves to be treated as an unpaid servant or secondary citizen'.[22]

A new generation of young women seemed to be responding to her call. They opened bank accounts and expected that they could determine their financial futures. Women with education and opportunity began to delay family commitments, seeking work and adventure. In 1966, just 28 per cent of women gave birth to their first child after the age of twenty-five; 50 per cent did so by 1981. The years of independent living were lengthening.

Jane Campion was one of those young women bent on new futures. She completed her BA in Anthropology at Victoria University of Wellington in 1975 and then headed over-seas, studying in London and travelling in Europe before settling in Sydney in 1979. She made her first short film, *Tissues*, in 1981. Campion's career as an internationally renowned film-maker has been remarkable, but her initial trajectory – university, then overseas travel – was one shared by an increasing number of tertiary-educated women in the late 1970s and 1980s. For these women, the period of working and travelling in the UK, Europe and beyond extended the commitment-free period of their lives and delayed family formation. Many high achievers chose to continue their academic careers abroad.

The *New Zealand Woman's Weekly* charted the successes of women in different occupations but avoided political controversy, appealing instead to the desire for advice on fashion, cooking and family life – as did a range of imported women's magazines. In 1981, the *Weekly*'s wide readership, far in excess of anything *Broadsheet* could hope for, was provided with a steady diet of detail about the forthcoming marriage of Prince Charles to Lady Diana Spencer. Dreams of romance and glamour, fed through the fashion industry, the movies and the royal family, were an escape from otherwise mundane routines of life. No matter how much second-wave feminism critiqued the beauty industry, a visit to the hairdresser, or the purchase of a new dress or a lipstick, still had a powerful allure for most women. Indeed, the righteousness of some feminists about appropriate clothing, appearance and behaviour seemed like a new form of puritanism to a younger generation. Magazines aimed at the young, such as *Cosmopolitan*, also appealed to women as sexual subjects determining their lives in new ways. A 1978 *Cosmopolitan* quiz headed 'How Liberated Are You?' asked readers: 'Is it right that more men than women

WORKBOOKS/ DIARIES

Anne Morris/ Ans Westra & Sylvia Bowen/ Carole Shepheard/ Di Ffrench/ Heather McPherson/ Janet de Wagt/ Jo Cornwall/ Joanna Paul/ Juliet Batten/ Keri Hulme/ Lani Morris/ Lynnsay Francis/ Robin White/ Sarah Parkinson/ Shirley Cameron/ Sky Isaacs

I November — I7 December

**The Women's Gallery 323 Willis Street Wellington
phone 850179
12-4pm Tuesday-Saturday   -5pm Fridays**

with thanks to Media Collective and to Rawa House

The Women's Gallery, a product of the feminist art movement, was established by Anna Keir, Bridie Lonie and Marian Evans in Wellington in 1980. This poster, designed by Sarah Parkinson, advertises an exhibition in 1983, reproducing a print by Robin White entitled 'The name of this girl is Florence.' *Alexander Turnbull Library, Wellington, Eph-C-WOMENS-Gallery-1983-01*

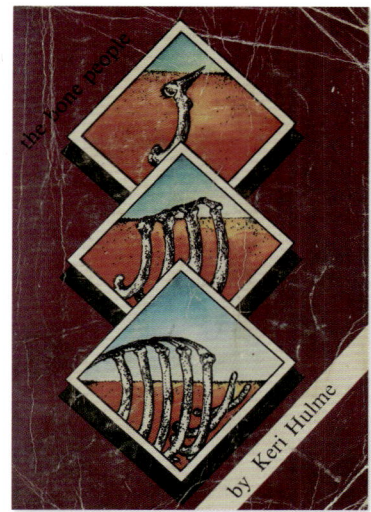
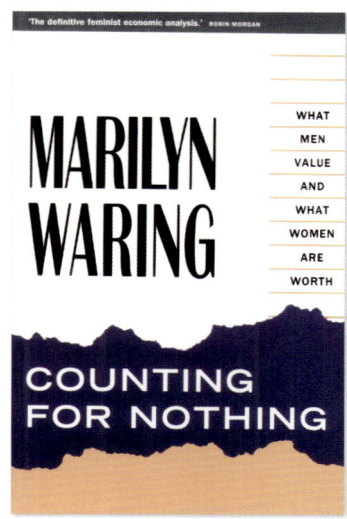

Influential books that appeared from the 1980s included Lauris Edmond's *Autobiography* (published 2001, appearing earlier in three volumes); the winner of the Booker Prize, *the bone people* (1983) by Keri Hulme (shown here in a much-read first edition, with artwork by Keri Hulme); and Marilyn Waring's *Counting for Nothing* (1988), an analysis of the economic value of women's work. *Covers reproduced with permission from Bridget Williams Books (left, right) and Spiral Collective (centre)*

go to university?' and 'Do you agree that women are expected to juggle too many roles?'[23] The message of *Cosmopolitan*'s editor, Helen Gurley Brown, was that 'a woman should have men complement her life, not take it over', and she unashamedly promoted women's sexual pleasure.[24]

Sex, drugs and rock 'n' roll were all part of youthful experimentation. When 65,000 young women and men attended the 1979 Nambassa Festival in Waihī to rock to the Little River Band and Split Enz, young women were more likely to be in the audience than on stage. But music, whether local or from offshore, shaped their generation, and for women it was 'empowering and freeing': no longer did they have to follow a dance script where men led and women followed; they could dance alone or with a group, with women or with men.[25] By the late 1970s, women were beginning to make it in local bands. Jenny Morris became the lead vocalist for an all-girl group, Wide Mouth Frogs, going on to perform with the Crocodiles.[26] Jane Dodd played bass for the Chills before going overseas in 1981, while Look Blue Go Purple, an all-women band formed in 1983, became part of the Dunedin sound scene.

The visual arts provided another outlet for creativity, although women found it difficult to be taken seriously as full-time practitioners – as they had done for centuries. Robin White built her career in the 1970s 'conscious of the extra effort that's involved in being female and trying to do something like paint'. Women, she believed, faced certain 'inbuilt prejudices and preconceived ideas' about their role.[27] Painter and printmaker Claudia Pond Eyley recalls the day she told Colin McCahon, one of her teachers at Elam School of Fine Arts in Auckland, that she was going to have a baby:

McCahon threw his hands up in the air and said, 'Oh, what a waste, all that effort and energy, here goes another one, you'll never do any painting again.' I remember saying, 'Yes I will, if it's in me to paint, I'll paint no matter what.'

She did indeed continue to paint 'even with little babies around.'[28]

By the late 1970s, Pond Eyley was energised by the growing feminist art movement, which encouraged not only independence but also new forms of collective creativity. In 1980, Anna Keir, Bridie Lonie and Marian Evans opened the Women's Gallery in Wellington, and eight years later they, together with Tilly Lloyd, produced the groundbreaking *A Women's Picture Book*, celebrating twenty-five women artists of Aotearoa.[29] The Women's Gallery was theme-based, and ran exhibitions associated with multidisciplinary seminars and forums on such issues as 'Women and Violence', 'Women and Sexuality', 'Women and the Environment' and 'Women and Spirituality'. 'Mothers', which had an associated publication and toured to several galleries in New Zealand as well as to Sydney, was an interrogation of the role of the mother in art and in life, and included *Hinetitama*, a striking work by Robyn Kahukiwa. A separate Māori women's art collective, Haeata, was formed in 1983 and held a major group exhibition with Waiata Koa, the Auckland collective of Māori women writers and artists.[30]

Women's words were at the centre of the June 1979 issue of New Zealand's premier literary magazine, *Landfall*, which devoted its 130th issue to women writers under an editorial entitled 'Liberation and Literature'. Edith Campion and Annabel Fagan were among the eight short-story writers, while the twenty poets included Lauris Edmond, Anne French and Riemke Ensing. In the same year, the writers' workshop run by the playwright, poet and novelist Renée at the United Women's Convention led to the writing group Womenspirit, which produced a collection entitled *Roses and Razorblades* in 1981.[31] More often, though, women poets, novelists and playwrights were working on their own, as they had always done, and increasingly looking to local publishers to take their work to an audience eager for New Zealanders' lives to be reflected in what they read.

One writer who found her voice after several decades of commitment to home and family was Lauris Edmond, mother of six, who was fifty-one when she published her first volume of poetry, *In Middle Air*, in 1975. She went on to become internationally recognised for her work, and was awarded the Commonwealth Poetry Prize for her *Selected Poems* in 1984.[32] The following year, Keri Hulme's *the bone people*, published in New Zealand by the small publishing collective Spiral, won the prestigious Booker Prize, bringing global recognition to a little-known New Zealand Māori woman writer.[33] For many women with the leisure and inclination to read, such home-grown novels changed their view of the world; these included Fiona Kidman's *A Breed of Women* (1979) or Marilyn Duckworth's *Disorderly Conduct* (1984), alongside internationally acclaimed works such as Doris Lessing's *The Golden Notebook* (1962) or Marilyn French's *The Women's Room* (1977).

Non-fiction and academic writing offered new opportunities for women as well. The history of the suffrage campaign was the subject of Patricia Grimshaw's Auckland MA thesis in 1963, later published as *Women's Suffrage in New Zealand* (1972). The past of Māori women was investigated that same year by Berys Heuer in a volume published by the Polynesian Society entitled *Maori Women*. Alongside those examinations of the past, Sue Kedgley and Sharyn Cederman's edited volume *Sexist Society* (1972) was an indictment of the present.

These books were supplemented through the 1970s and 1980s by a raft of studies of women's past, present and possible futures. In 1974, the study of women entered the academy: the University of Waikato established courses on women in Psychology (third year), in Sociology (graduate level) and in University Extension Women's Studies courses. Rosemary Seymour, the driving force behind Women's Studies at Waikato, noted how attitudes shifted from the challenges of 1973 ('What can there be to teach about women?') to the 1979 endorsement that 'there is no student and no subject that would not benefit from women's studies'.[34] In her view, the development of Women's Studies within the universities had 'powerful political implications'; it would be 'an activator for deep and wide change that is radical'.[35] Her prediction that university and public libraries would build up resources that would contribute to a changing social climate was accurate. One of these resources was Rosemary Barrington and Alison Gray's *The Smith Women: 100 New Zealand Women Talk About Their Lives* (1981), which gave voice to the everyday life experiences of New Zealand women.

The excitement generated by women's writing and Women's Studies extension courses was contagious, and led to vibrant national conferences at which a range of topics, from employment, mental health and the effects of pornography to science education for girls and women's humour, was explored. In 1980 (to give but two examples) Margaret Wilson, future Attorney-General, gave a paper entitled 'The Relationship Between the Law and Equal Opportunity for Women', while Prue Hyman, who became Associate Professor of Economics and Gender and Women's Studies at Victoria University, spoke on 'Women's Labour Force Participation and Unemployment of Women in New Zealand Cities'.[36] Both women would become leaders in the campaign for equal pay for work of equal value.

The enthusiasm for a burgeoning new field led to the founding of the New Zealand *Women's Studies Journal* in 1984, the same year the first postgraduate course on women's history was taught at the University of Otago. Feminist bookstores such as Dunedin's Daybreak, which opened in 1976, and the Broadsheet bookshop in Auckland, were founded to meet the need of a generation of women seeking new ways to plan their lives.

As the study of women consolidated in universities, the subject itself fragmented: 'woman' became myriad women from different class, ethnic, educational and regional backgrounds. Similarly, the hope that Women's Studies would have a transformative effect on other academic disciplines began to be realised as more Humanities departments

Activists Donna Awatere and Ripeka Evans, pictured in the 1980s, were pioneering members of Māori protest group Nga Tamatoa and part of the Patu Squad, a Māori group that worked to undermine the Springbok rugby tour of 1981. *Photograph by Gil Hanly*

began to employ a generation of women whose feminist analyses informed their research. An analytical move away from the study of sex roles to an understanding of the ways in which gender is socially constructed suggested that masculinity required study as much as the development of femininity.

Just as Women's Studies initiated different kinds of inquiry in the universities, so too did Māori Studies, where the teaching of language and tikanga empowered students to critique the current state of New Zealand society.

Women at the forefront of Māori activism

Among Māori, women were often at the forefront of campaigns in the mid- to late 1970s and early 1980s that sought some redress for land loss. Tauiwa (Eva) Rickard, for example, picked up the baton passed to her by her dying mother when she led the campaign for the return of lands of the Tainui Awhiro people at Te Kōpua, near Raglan.

The community had been forced to leave their homes, cultivations and urupā (burial grounds) during the Second World War after the land was taken for an emergency airstrip on the promise that it would be given back at the end of the war. That promise was broken when the Raglan Golf Club was given the lease of the land in 1967. Eva Rickard began petitioning for return of the land from 1972, joined the 1975 march from Te Hāpua in

MAORI SOVEREIGNTY

DONNA AWATERE

Donna Awatere's powerful indictment of the ravages of colonialism was first published in instalments in *Broadsheet* magazine, and the book asserted the importance of cultural renewal and political action. Maori Sovereignty, *Broadsheet Collective, Auckland, 1984, with permission of the publishers*

Northland to Parliament in Wellington to highlight the injustice, and was a leading figure in the civil disobedience that led to a large protest occupation of the Raglan land in 1978. The arrest of Rickard and seventeen others, as well as police brutality and the continued occupation, generated considerable media attention. It was 1983 before the land at Te Kōpua was returned to its traditional Tainui owners.[37] Eva Rickard also advocated for Māori sovereignty and the right of women to speak on marae. The slow pace of change on the latter issue became clear when fellow activist Annette Sykes faced a challenge as she rose to speak at Rickard's tangi in 1997.[38]

The right to speak on marae was a matter of concern for some Māori feminists, but not central for Donna Awatere, who saw honouring the Treaty of Waitangi as the key issue. For a brief time she formulated her critique of society in terms of 'racism, sexism and capitalism', finding common ground with socialist feminists. With the first Nga

Tamatoa activists exhausted by the 1975 land march, Awatere with Hilda Halkyard and Ripeka Evans sought to revitalise Nga Tamatoa and bring a feminist perspective to the group. They confronted Māori men who had relationships with Pākehā women, claiming, in Awatere's words, 'that if they couldn't see the beauty in Maori women, and see us as partners, we were lost'.[39] They also confronted the way in which male activists relied on the organisational work of Māori women without giving them any credit. Donna Awatere attended the United Women's Conventions which she found 'spiritually refreshing', but she became increasingly frustrated with middle-class Pākehā feminists' lack of interest in Māori issues.

The future for Māori was at the heart of the September 1977 Young Maori Leaders Conference, where Mira Szászy was invited to speak, drawing on her experience as president of the Maori Women's Welfare League to inspire younger women to take leadership roles. At the end of the day, a number of those present called for a 'women-only' session to occur. According to Ngahuia Te Awekotuku, who was one of the vocal young women at the conference, 'the patriarchs felt threatened' by this demand, but a number of the women made it clear they wanted to discuss current issues such as abortion and contraception, and the perennial issue of the 'hardship of being a Maori woman', on their own terms. The women-only session brought heated discussion and a resolution in te reo Māori that called for another meeting of Māori women 'to discuss their present and future roles'.[40]

That meeting occurred at the Freeman's Bay Daycare Centre in early November 1977; it was, according to Te Awekotuku, a stimulating and empowering experience. In that venue and with that group, it was possible to have open discussion of challenging issues, such as the prohibitions around menstruation associated with the concept of tapu, which some understood to mean it was seen as unclean. One woman commented, '[D]oesn't it make you feel powerful to know you can scare away the fish, rot the flax, and turn the kumara crop off?' Such questions, and others relating to violence in the home, could be safely debated in a women-only environment.[41] Those who attended discovered new allies in making connections between the personal and the political.

A different kind of connection – between being passionate about film and being Māori – was deeply felt by Merata Mita when, in 1977, she became disenchanted with her role of assisting a Pākehā documentary-maker in gaining access to Māori interviewees. In 1978, she answered a call to film the events at Bastion Point, where the government had sent in 600 police to evict the occupiers of traditional Ngāti Whātua land, led by Joe Hawke and the Orakei Maori Committee Action Group.[42] Witnessing those months of dispossession and resistance had a huge impact upon Mita.[43] The resulting documentary, *Bastion Point: Day 507*, co-directed with Gerd Pohlmann and Leon Narbey, meant that future generations could witness that protest. Merata Mita also documented the greatest confrontation over race New Zealand had seen: the protests that took place during the 1981 Springbok tour. Her riveting 1983 film *Patu!* followed the clashes between anti-tour protesters and the police, and showed New Zealanders themselves in a disturbing light. It was also the first feature-length documentary ever made by a New Zealand woman.[44]

Women had long been sideline supporters of the game played by their husbands and sons. They had willingly washed rugby jerseys and brought oranges for half-time. Now, in 1981, the playing of New Zealand's national game asked all of its supporters to examine their consciences: were they for or against apartheid in South Africa? Did they expect their government to abide by the 1977 Gleneagles Agreement, which bound all Commonwealth states to take 'every practical step to discourage contact or competition by their nationals with sporting organisations, teams or sportsmen from South Africa'?[45] Women took different sides, but for Māori women such as Merata Mita, Ripeka Evans and Donna Awatere, the tour brought together the issues of domestic and South African racism. Awatere later summed up its importance:

> Before the tour, about half of all non-Maori New Zealanders considered racism to be abhorrent. After the tour those same people realised that what was happening in New Zealand was different in degree but not in kind from what was happening in South Africa.[46]

For radical feminists, the New Zealand Rugby Football Union (NZRFU) and the government that supported the tour were representative of the way men wielded power in New Zealand society.[47] Some saw rugby as a form of institutionalised violence at the heart of a national culture that sanctioned male aggression in the domestic sphere. The belligerence of the police force (only about 6 per cent of which was female) during the tour reinforced this view. Robert Muldoon's National government, in failing to press the NZRFU to cancel the tour, appeared dismissive of the concerns of tens of thousands of New Zealanders, and of the rights of minorities. The formation of 'Dykes Against the Tour' signalled lesbian insistence on connecting racism in South Africa with repression of homosexuals in New Zealand.[48] Women active in a range of church denominations, Roman Catholic, Methodist, Presbyterian, Baptist, Anglican and the Society of Friends, also showed their support for social justice by joining the anti-apartheid movement.[49]

In Christchurch, a 'well-organised and vocal women's group', Women Against the Tour, tried to promote non-sexist ways of organising. But the most radical women's group arose in Auckland, where lesbian and Māori women combined to create the core of the Patu squad, in which thirty-three out of the thirty-seven protest marshals were women. For some within the Patu squad, the confrontations with police were as much about domestic racism as about apartheid. Ripeka Evans explained the arrest of a large number of Māori women as 'a combination of sexism, racism and a recognition by the police of the militant role played by Maori women'.[50] For some Pākehā women, too, participation in the protests was a way of affirming their commitment to political action. One remarked:

> At the start of the tour I did not make connections between racism and sexism. As the tour went on I became more aware of women's views and I now have a more Feminist outlook to

Top Women watch participants in the Tūhoe Festival at Rūātoki. Since the 1970s, Tūhoe have held a sports and cultural festival at one of their communities every two years. Photographer Terry O'Connor attended these gatherings through the 1970s and 1980s, documenting the rural lives of the people he came to know.

Bottom In the home of Harry and Nawarihi Melbourne at Rūātoki, the piano is adorned with portraits of relatives Harry and Taiha, with the prophet Rua Kenana in the centre.

Both photographs courtesy Terry O'Connor Estate & McNamara Gallery

things in general. In mixing with others I became more aware of the rights of others. I saw sexism in the police and the rugby supporters. It made me more politically aware ...[51]

In the aftermath of the tour, Pākehā feminists examined their white privilege in anti-racism teach-ins. There they might be subjected to having their names mispronounced and their language misunderstood to remind them of Māori experience. *Broadsheet* underwrote the anti-racism agenda by its publication of a series of articles by Donna Awatere, later published as a book entitled *Maori Sovereignty*.

The original series of articles had a profound effect on one group of feminist activists, Women for Aotearoa, who met to analyse the challenge Awatere presented. Her 'totally Maori-identified politics' meant 'for once we were forced to find our theory in New Zealand', as Gay Simpkin put it. With intense intellectual excitement, the women debated the Pākehā legacy of colonialism and the contrast between Pākehā individualism and Māori communal values. Inspired by Marxism, the women analysed the individualism at the heart of the phrase 'the personal is political'. They became active in anti-racism groups such as People Opposed to Waitangi to express their commitment to anti-racism within New Zealand.[52]

Maori Sovereignty built on the Māori radicalism of the 1970s and presented a strident call for a battle plan against Pākehā who were 'captives of their own culture'.[53] Māori were enjoined to seek self-determination in their own country; Pākehā New Zealanders were confronted with their shallow roots in the land and their lack of a culture beyond adherence to Britain. Awatere challenged New Zealanders to mainstream Māori culture. At the same time she saw, as had the Maori Women's Welfare League in the 1950s, that the 'basic unit for change is the mother and her child'. The youthfulness of the Māori population, 80 per cent of whom were under twenty-five, held revolutionary potential; Awatere envisaged Te Kohanga Reo turning 'from a palliative into a tidal wave of self-determination' through the efforts 'and struggle of thousands of young Maori mothers'.[54]

Kōhanga reo – literally, language nests, preschools aimed at immersing children in Māori language and culture – emerged as a positive way to retain language and values. Women were instrumental in the initiative. Iritana Tawhiwhirangi, of Ngāti Porou, Ngāti Kahungunu, Ngāpuhi, Canadian and English descent, was one of those who took a leadership role. She had begun teaching on the East Coast in 1948 before becoming the first Māori woman district officer in the Department of Maori Affairs.[55] She took her experience from the Playcentre movement into Māori community development after a hui in 1981 charged her and others with the development of kōhanga reo.[56] Frances Williams and Iritana Tawhiwhirangi toured marae throughout the country to inspire groups to launch their own initiatives, bringing together elders fluent in the language with preschoolers and their parents. The first kōhanga reo opened at Pukeatua, Wainuiomata, in April 1982. By 1986 there were 466 kōhanga reo in operation, mostly staffed by women volunteers.[57]

Gaylene Preston, photographed here in the early 1990s, has made an important contribution to women's history as a film maker. From the late 1970s, Preston made feature films and documentaries about New Zealand, including *Bread and Roses* (1993), a television mini-series about the life of trade union activist Sonia Davies, and *War Stories Our Mothers Never Told Us* (1995), a documentary in which women (including her mother, Tui) recalled their experiences during the Second World War. *Photograph by Jenny Scown*

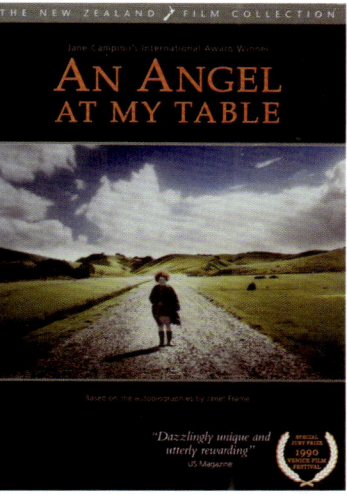

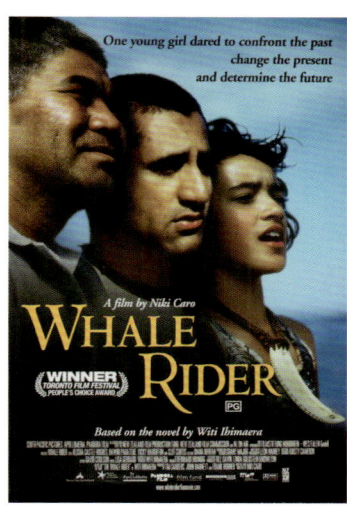

Left Film-maker Jane Campion adapted Janet Frame's immensely popular three-volume autobiography published in the 1990 as *An Angel at my Table*; like the book, the film was acclaimed. *Middle* The 1981 Springbok rugby tour divided New Zealand. In 1983 film maker Merata Mita produced *Patu!*, a graphic feature-length documentary (the first in New Zealand to be made by a woman), showing the widespread civil disobedience that occurred during the tour. The film was highly controversial; major cinemas refused to screen it, and Mita was forced to hide footage used in the film when police tried to obtain it to assist with prosecution of anti-tour protesters. Eventually *Patu!* was shown at film festivals around the world. *Right* Witi Ihimaera's novel was the basis for the internationally successful film *Whale Rider* (2002). Written and directed by Niki Caro, the main protagonist is a young Māori girl, Pai, played by Keisha Castle-Hughes. *From left: Courtesy of Hibiscus Films; New Zealand Film Archive Ngā Kaitiaki O Ngā Taonga Whitiāhua, Patu, Awatea Film Productions, Poster Collection, (1) P02077; © South Pacific Pictures Limited/ApolloMedia GmBH & Co 5 Filmproduktion KG 2002; Photographer Kirsty Griffin*

Women and health

Women volunteers were integral to the success of a 1977 Maori Women's Welfare League initiative to research the health status of Māori women. Dr Eru Pomare's study of Māori health from 1955 to 1975, which suggested very high rates of coronary heart disease among Māori women, came together with Minister of Lands and of Maori Affairs Matiu Rata's challenge to the league in 1975 to ensure that their programmes met the current needs of Māori.[58] When Elizabeth Murchie became the league's president in 1977, she decided to focus on research. The result was a survey of the health of 1,177 women carried out by 200 volunteers who went into communities from South Auckland, down through the Waikato and out into the East Cape. Murchie believed that the work of the volunteers was crucial in achieving a high participation rate: only twelve women refused to be interviewed.[59]

The resulting report, *Rapuora: Health and Maori Women*, suggested that Māori women were 'at crisis point'. Their rates of lung cancer and coronary heart disease were among the highest in the world. Rheumatoid arthritis, circulatory and respiratory diseases, and diabetes were common. But for Elizabeth Murchie, the most revealing finding lay in the difference between the older and the younger generation. While young women were subject to stress and depression and lacked knowledge of their culture, older women were 'robustly secure' in their cultural background. Health, then, was inseparable from culture, and the young required greater access to tribal support systems.[60]

Māori women were likely to give birth at a much earlier age than Pākehā women, and took longer to complete their larger families. In 1981, the Māori fertility rate was 2.6 children per woman, compared with the Pākehā rate of 1.9. For the Maori Women's Welfare League, the health of mothers was of particular concern because of their importance to Māori youth whose lack of achievement 'set the alarm bells ringing'.[61]

Linda Erihe belonged to both the Maori Women's Welfare League and the Māori women's movement. The youngest of five children, she had a rural upbringing, went to boarding school on a scholarship, and trained as a nurse. The mother of a young daughter, she worked at the Manukau Health Centre as a public health nurse from 1978. There she saw Māori 'destroying' themselves: 'We smoke too much. We drink too much. We are deaf and we are filling up the prisons.'[62] She was one of a number of younger Māori women speaking out about problems within their communities. Teachers' college lecturer Te Aroha McDowell was another who argued that Māori needed to be deciding policies for themselves. Erihana Ryan and Paparangi Reed, both medical graduates, and Irihapeti Ramsden, a trained nurse, worked within the medical system to promote sensitivity to Māori spiritual and cultural needs.[63] Outside the health system, new community-based organisations such as the Otara Maori Women's Movement ran health seminars to assist women in the community. Many were aware, however, that poor health was but one symptom of a deeper social malaise. As the Minister of Maori Affairs noted, Māori health could not 'be seen in isolation from the social, economic, and cultural influences which affect the well-being of people'.[64]

Women from other cultures, too, were seeking a variety of alternatives to a health system that appeared insensitive to their needs. Both the Auckland Women's Health Centre and The Health Alternatives for Women (THAW) in Christchurch developed out of the Sisters Overseas Service, whose members had found that women needed information about not only abortion but also a raft of health issues. The Auckland Women's Health Centre, organised by a collective, included the services of regular medical practitioners as well as alternative services such as those of an iridologist. THAW became both a centre for advice on women's health issues and a consumer pressure group for improved services. THAW trained workers to offer smear-taking, pregnancy testing, breast self-examination and vaginal examination until pressure from local gynaecologists led to the cessation of these services in 1985. THAW continued, however, to offer an advice service for low-income women and to fight for consumers' rights in the health system.[65]

Many women were inspired to take charge of their health by *Our Bodies, Ourselves*, an international bestseller published by the Boston Women's Health Collective in 1973. The book offered 'comprehensive woman-positive information about health care by women, in a cheap and accessible format' and, literary scholar Susan Wells argues, introduced a new rhetorical space that brought previously private issues into the open.[66] Norma Swenson, one of the original members of the Boston collective, addressed the first National Women's Health Conference, held in Auckland in September 1982. She reminded her audience of the ways in which race and class impacted on health.[67] The Māori women at the conference were only too well aware of how ill-health affected their communities. They accused 'Pakeha health workers of racism in concentrating on uterine issues to the exclusion of more pressing issues for Maori, such as ownership of the land, and a nuclear-free, independent Pacific'.[68]

The definition of health issues was infinitely broad, but for many women pregnancy and childbirth brought their first major interaction with the healthcare system, and it galvanised some of them into action. The New Zealand Home Birth Association formed in 1978 out of a determination to maintain the independence of domiciliary midwives. The closure of maternity hospitals in smaller centres in the interests of centralising services at larger general hospitals in the 1970s and 1980s led to a loss of the intimacy that smaller units promoted. This change, along with the medicalisation of childbirth, reduced opportunities for women to feel in control of the birthing process.[69] Home birth, attended by a midwife, provided a fresh alternative. Support after birth might come from home and clinic visits with Plunket nurses, from more informal mothers' support groups, or from the La Leche League which promoted breastfeeding. Whether women were active in alternative women's health centres, or more comfortable embracing motherhood supported by the La Leche League, all were empowered to see medicine as a 'consumer product' and that women had rights as consumers to insist that their particular needs – be it contraception, abortion, home birth, or rooming-in with baby in hospital – be met.[70]

One woman whose needs as a new mother were not met was Ruth Richardson, who became National MP for Selwyn from 1981 to 1994. Careful planning and preparation had led to her success in politics, but despite scheduling the arrival of her first child for the April 1982 parliamentary recess, the pregnant MP's waters broke at the Hororata National Party AGM on 14 February, and her daughter was born early. The chief Opposition whip, Jonathan Hunt, had promised Richardson a pair (that is, to pair her with an absent Opposition MP on parliamentary votes) should she not be able to attend the House after the birth of her child. However, Ann Hercus, supported by the other Labour women, led the move to refuse Richardson the right to a pair that would enable her to attend to the needs of her premature baby. Richardson believed, 'I had failed the political correctness test in their eyes; failed to conform to some code of sisterhood of which I knew not.' She recalled:

> Lucy was six weeks old, and there were no facilities for breastfeeding parliamentarians, let alone tiny infants who need quiet sleeping conditions. To add insult to injury, Standing Orders forbade me to take Lucy into the voting lobbies if the vote clashed with breastfeeding time. She would have been categorised as a 'stranger in the House' and presumably evicted by the Sergeant at Arms had I pushed my luck.[71]

This poster, designed by Denese Black for the New Zealand University Students' Association's Women's Rights Action Committee, urges people to support the Working Women's Charter. Developed by labour activists in the late 1970s, the Charter has been described as a 'bill of rights' for working women, with provisions including the right to work, elimination of workplace discrimination, equal pay and equal opportunity, childcare and paid parental leave, and access to sex education, contraception and abortion. Conservative groups including Feminists for Life, Save Our Homes and the Catholic Women's League vigorously opposed the Charter. *Alexander Turnbull Library, Wellington, Eph-C-WOMEN-1980-02, with permission of the New Zealand Union of Students' Associations*

A supportive husband enabled Richardson to cope with the ensuing 'logistical nightmare'. The Labour women regarded Ruth Richardson's concern to provide for her child as selfish, because she had not responded to their earlier calls for a childcare service for all women in Parliament.[72] Here the National creed of individual responsibility came directly up against the Labour women's vision of collective provision for children. Feminists' optimistic creed – that women working together would bring about change – confronted the realities of party politics.

Great expectations? Women and politics

After Colleen Dewe, National MP for Lyttelton, lost her seat in 1978 to Ann Hercus, she was asked to chair the government's Advisory Committee on Women's Affairs. As a result, she led the New Zealand delegation to the 1980 Vienna Conference on the Status of Women, followed by the United Nations Conference on Women at Copenhagen, where she signed the Convention on the Elimination of Discrimination Against Women (CEDAW) on behalf of New Zealand.

The culmination of a long history of concern about the status of women, CEDAW was the United Nations' 'Bill of Rights' for women, aiming to eliminate any discrimination on the basis of sex in 'the political, economic, social, cultural, civil or any other field'. In a wide-ranging approach, it targeted 'cultural patterns which define the public realm as a man's world and the domestic sphere as women's domain', affirming 'the equal responsibilities of both sexes in family life and their equal rights with regard to education and employ-ment'.[73] CEDAW's articles laid out a number of principles, including equal pay for work of equal value, and the promotion of family planning and childcare, to guide governments on the elimination of discrimination. Some groups, inside and outside New Zealand, feared that CEDAW was one more nail in the coffin of the family as they knew it, and that male prerogatives were being undermined by legislation. When, in May 1984, Prime Minister Muldoon said his government had no intention of ratifying the convention, Connie Purdue, now a stalwart of the conservative anti-abortion group Women for Life, replied that this was 'the best Mother's Day present the mothers of New Zealand could get'.[74]

Within the Labour Party, women had been energised by the creation of a Labour Women's Council in the mid-1970s. The council pursued a two-pronged strategy by, first, encouraging women to stand for positions of responsibility within the party hierarchy and for Parliament and, second, developing a women's policy that would become part of the Party Manifesto. Separate women's policy conferences allowed women to develop a strategic agenda that they hoped would inform policy should Labour come to power. Labour's success came in the snap election of 1984, prompted by Marilyn Waring's decision to withdraw from the National Caucus after she refused to support the government's opposition to a nuclear-free New Zealand. She retired from Parliament aged thirty-one. Labour was now in power and, for the first time, attracted more women

National MP Ruth Richardson is pictured with her daughter Lucy in 1983. Lucy's birth sparked a controversy over how new mothers should cope with traditional parliamentary practises which took no account of infants. *Photograph by Gail Selkirk, Alexander Turnbull Library, Wellington, EP/1983/1483/3-F*

voters than National. Ten Labour women had become MPs and two of those were elected to Cabinet: Margaret Shields and Ann Hercus.[75]

Both had honed their political skills in organisations supporting the interests of women, Shields as a founder of the Society for Research on Women, and Hercus in the Playcentre movement and in consumer rights. Shields was given two portfolios: Consumer Affairs and Customs, while Hercus was given three: Police, Social Welfare, and the new portfolio of Women's Affairs. In Women's Affairs, Hercus had the task of overseeing the creation of the 'first independent ministry for women in the world' – one opposed by Ruth Richardson, who argued that women's issues knew 'no bounds' and 'must be dealt with in an integrated manner'.[76]

The brief of the Ministry of Women's Affairs was:

1. To advise the Minister of Women's Affairs on the implications of the government's policies and public sector plans and expenditure programmes in terms of their differential impact on women;
2. To monitor and initiate legislation and regulations in order to promote equality of opportunity for women;

Cheryl Glensor took her nine-month-old son Kim with her to the well-attended women's forum at Petone in November 1984. *Photograph by John Nicolson, Alexander Turnbull Library, Wellington, EP/1984/5460*

3. To advise the Minister of Women's Affairs of suitable nominees for the appointment of women to statutory bodies and other quasi-governmental bodies;

4. To advise the Minister of Women's Affairs on any matter relevant to the implementation of the government's manifesto where this has implications or explicitly refers to women.[77]

Mary O'Regan was appointed Secretary of Women's Affairs, the first woman to head a New Zealand government department. She saw her challenging task as two-fold: first, to create an organisation that made policies and legislation work in the interests of women; and, second, to provide a new way of working 'to which women could relate'. The latter, in O'Regan's view, 'made the Ministry unique'.[78] The ministry's 'disarming' pink offices, together with the children's playpen in the reception area, signalled a determination that things would be done differently.[79] Recognising the existence of two very different constituencies, the ministry also created a Māori secretariat, launched in May 1986.[80] The ministry's small staff of twenty meant it would be difficult to achieve all that was expected, but it had taken more than 100 years for women to win influence in the centre of government, and O'Regan was prepared to be patient. She believed firmly that, in developing policy, 'the way you get there greatly affects the quality of the outcome'.[81] Summing up feminism in one word, O'Regan said it was about 'choice'.[82]

Ann Hercus decided that the women of New Zealand should be consulted about determining priorities for the new ministry from the 30-point Labour women's policy list. In October and November 1984, a series of women's forums was held throughout the country. Much to the surprise of the organisers, a large number of women who attended the forums came 'not to prioritise the policies but to oppose them and to oppose the very idea of a Ministry of Women's Affairs'.[83] Opponents came together in regarding feminists – and by extension the new ministry – as denigrating women's role as mothers.

Nola McGowan, the youngest woman to open her own legal practice in New Zealand, touched a chord in her audience when she addressed a charity luncheon in Whanga-paraoa. 'Man-hating', she proclaimed, had 'gone on too long'. She deplored 'the pressures for men and women to be considered equal' and claimed that the Minister of Women's Affairs was concentrating too much on equality: 'We have roles equal to men but they are different. The "uniqueness" of women is being downgraded.' McGowan, a high achiever, did not want to be labelled as a feminist: 'I don't want to be identified with people who seem intent not on building a better future together but on building – more hate – more resentment – more separatism.' In her view, feminist actions had made 'too many men into angry, hurt people, grown sour with resentment'. She noted that Germaine Greer, 'once a shining tower of independence and spunkiness for the followers of Feminism', had published a new book which urged women 'to consider the delights of babies, home, human values and chastity'.[84]

Marilyn Pryor, a devout Catholic who opposed abortion, wrote of the women's forums:

> For more than a decade, mothers and homemakers had taken a back seat while feminists set the agenda on women's issues. This agenda not only ignored concerns of mothers and homemakers – it also embraced items capable of undermining the family. Until the 1984 Forums, there had been no arena where mothers and homemakers could effectively challenge the feminist agenda. And so, when Mrs Hercus provided that arena, mothers doffed their pinnies, told Dad he could look after the children, and they went in their thousands to defend the family.[85]

The forum organisers repeatedly made it clear that the task of participants was to prioritise, not debate, the items on the policy list. This unwillingness to debate, however, was used by opponents to suggest that feminists were ramming their anti-family agenda down the throats of New Zealanders. Historian Raewyn Dalziel has charted the disruptions at forums throughout the country. In Auckland, a group of protesting women rose to sing the national anthem, interrupting the pōwhiri and ignoring instructions to sit down. They attempted to force a motion against the ratification of CEDAW. In Nelson, police had to be called; in New Plymouth, a majority of the attendees voted against the formation of a

Ministry of Women's Affairs; in Christchurch, four men were mistakenly admitted to the women-only gathering and refused to leave when asked. Any good the forums achieved, Dalziel argues, 'was totally overshadowed by the spectacle and reports of major dissension amongst women'.[86]

Feminists were taken by surprise. Despite divisions amongst themselves, support for the ministry had largely been taken for granted. The forums were intended to set the agenda on women's issues for the next three years, but they were subverted by an organised campaign against the ratification of CEDAW, one of the aims on the Labour women's policy list.

Opposition to CEDAW had been building in Australia through the evangelical crusade known as the Festival of Light, and through the actions of a group called Women Who Want to be Women. Carolyn Moynihan noted in the pages of the Catholic periodical *Zealandia* that the 'recurring theme' in such critiques of CEDAW was that it was 'a communist conspiracy against the family'. Yet she pointed out that New Zealand's delegates to the World Union of Catholic Women's Organisations in June 1983 had voted 'in favour of pressing their governments towards ratification'. In Moynihan's view, participation in the convention was essential 'to ensure that such instruments are really effective in promoting justice for all human beings'.[87] Labour ratified CEDAW in January 1985, with three reservations: one related to the participation of women in underground mining; the second was about the right of women to engage in armed combat; and the third was about the right to paid maternity leave.[88]

Whereas first-wave feminists in the 1880s and 1890s had emphasised women's rights, feminists of the 1970s and 1980s focused on choice, particularly reproductive choice, since there was no 'right' to be pregnant or not pregnant. The problem was that choice could quickly be detached from its feminist moorings and become associated with 'individualistic, market-like behaviour' – the kind of economic behaviour championed by National's Ruth Richardson and keenly promoted by the same Labour government that established the Ministry of Women's Affairs.[89]

Women were now expected to be in the marketplace, and many were in low-paid, unrewarding jobs in retail and service industries. But high-achieving women found their political voices and campaigned for change within Parliament. For Ann Hercus, 'all issues' were 'women's issues'. Women's voices had to be heard, she said: '[T]he women's perspective can be different from men's – equally valuable, equally deserving of being heard, but different. The best decisions, the best policies and the best leadership have to reflect that reality.'[90]

The United Nations' Decade for Women from 1976 to 1985 had seen a series of re-markable changes in New Zealand, including the increasing educational aspirations of young women and legislation creating a Ministry of Women's Affairs. Nine women were returned with the new Labour government in 1984; two were on the Opposition benches.

Helen Mason (left) and the Pramazons were photographed by Gil Hanly in Tokomaru Bay in November 1983. The Pramazons, a women's theatre group, travelled around the country with an anti-nuclear production called 'Pacific Paradise', performing in schools and local halls. Mason was a well-known potter, who lived in Tokomaru Bay. *Photograph by Gil Hanly*

As Raewyn Dalziel has written, 'Women had come into the political arena in 1893; 1984 claimed to bring them into the corridors of power.'[91] But in those corridors, some chose to walk to the left, others to the right. Despite hopes of sisterhood, they did not always see eye to eye. As the Decade for Women drew to a close, some believed feminism to be outmoded, while others saw it as ever more urgent. Whatever one's view, no one was untouched by the profound changes wrought in the lives of New Zealand women. By 1986, there was no one 'place' for a woman to be.

The politics of sex

In the early 1970s, Germaine Greer and magazines like *Cosmopolitan* were encouraging women to become active sexually. Speaking about sex, and its pleasures and dangers, was now permissible in ways unimaginable when the subject had been seen as private or, if it reached the public arena, possibly obscene. International events fed into local debates. In England, the 1957 Wolfenden Report had advocated for decriminalising consensual sex between adult men, a recommendation implemented in 1967. The 1969 Stonewall riots in New York highlighted discrimination against gay men in America.[92]

 Greater openness about sexual matters encouraged the development of a feminist critique of sexual violence. Historian Jacqueline O'Neill has traced the way in which the meaning of rape shifted between the mid-1970s and the mid-1980s as feminists contested

Women of the Pacific Peace Band sing before a lecture by Helen Caldicott at the YMCA stadium, Auckland, in April 1983. An outspoken advocate of citizen action to remedy global nuclear and environmental crises, Dr Caldicott was visiting from the United States. *Photograph by Gil Hanly*

the way in which women's sexual history was put on trial in rape cases. Women in the early 1970s, O'Neill argues, were positioned 'as provocateurs' in a way that 'served to uphold male sexual privilege and made women responsible for the standards of sexual propriety'.[93] Women, according to this view, had to mind how they dressed and be careful where they went if they were to avoid unwanted advances from men. Increasingly, however, feminism empowered women to speak out. In the 1980s, Rape Crisis Centres were set up throughout the country to provide immediate support for victims, 'individual and group counselling; advocacy work within the Court system and in dealings with the police, doctors, Accident Compensation Corporation and the Department of Social Welfare'.[94] Feminists also worked to change the dominant meanings of rape, challenging the view of women as provocateurs and identifying rape instead as a crime of violence against women.[95] Displacing the responsibility for violence on to men fuelled the work of the refuge movement, which gave women a place to go to escape abuse.

Domestic and sexual violence often went together, and married women had no legal redress against sexual coercion. In 1978, Labour's Mary Batchelor introduced a Private Member's Bill to protect women in violent marriages and to give police training in dealing with domestic violence.[96] Her Bill failed to pass, but it did garner enough support to encourage the government to introduce a Domestic Violence Bill in 1981, supported by all eight women in Parliament. The resulting Domestic Protection Act 1982 gave de facto spouses the same protections against violence as the married. Jacqueline O'Neill suggests that this Act marked an important shift: it brought domestic violence out of the privacy of the home and into the public arena.[97] The next step would be a reform of the rape law to remove spousal immunity.

Women took to the streets in 'Reclaim the Night' marches to highlight the way in which fear of sexual violence controlled them. Women and their daughters nationwide enrolled in self-defence courses to enhance their assertiveness, and the Women's Self Defence Network – Wahine Toa emerged in the 1980s.[98] History was called into service to highlight the way in which sex and violence were closely interlinked. On Anzac Day 1978, a women's group in Auckland controversially laid a wreath to commemorate the women raped in wartime.[99] The most dramatic action, however, took place on 1 February 1984, when six women ambushed Auckland playwright and university lecturer Mervyn Thompson, tied him to a tree and spray-painted the word 'rapist' on his car. The women believed Thompson had abused his position as a lecturer to sexually harass women, and that 'white middle class professional men' were rarely prosecuted for their sexual crimes.[100]

Debate over the case raged in the media. The offices of *Metro* magazine were first graffitied and then invaded after the magazine published an article headed 'From Feminism to Fascism, Is This What Wimmin Want?' by Carroll Wall, who was accused by her interviewees of writing a 'slanderous piece of gutter journalism' which portrayed lesbian feminists as 'avowed man-haters'. The heat of the debate was such that the Auckland University bookshop banned *Metro* and the *Metro* office received used sanitary pads in the mail.[101] Mervyn Thompson's play *Songs for Uncle Scrim* was pulled from the programme at Wellington's Depot Theatre after submissions from the Wellington Unemployed Workers' Union and women's groups such as Women Against Pornography.[102]

'Don't Get Mad, Get Even' was the motto that inspired the women responsible for the Thompson attack. The redefinition of rape by radical feminists into the slogan 'All Men are Rapists' had tapped into a deep vein of fear in the community. Carroll Wall claimed that radical lesbian feminists had staged the assault on Thompson and that this extreme wing of feminism was in danger of alienating others. Sandra Coney agreed, suggesting that the climate of feminism was failing 'to talk to women about their day to day problems, about their work, jobs and child care'.[103] In a letter to the editor printed in the *Woman's Weekly*, 'Sane Feminist' saw no place for vigilante attacks by women. 'The judge,' she wrote, 'must sentence them as he would any group of loutish males who abducted a female in like circumstances.'[104] The assailants, however, were never identified, and there were a number of women who applauded their actions: 'Women have played the victim game long enough. We must fight back and turn fear into outrage.'[105]

The fact that women themselves were prepared to engage in violence to highlight the issue of sexual harassment troubled many who had hoped that women might seek non-violent solutions. Groups such as the Women's League for Peace and Freedom, which

Badges from the 1980s show some of the feminist concerns of that time, including the abortion, anti-nuclear, anti-Springbok tour and peace campaigns. *From top, left to right: Museum of New Zealand Te Papa Tongarewa, Wellington, GH014497; GH012534; GH014893; GH011846; GH014500; GH011836; GH011840; FE012454*

dated from 1916 in New Zealand, and Women for Peace, founded by Dorothy Ballantyne in Dunedin in the early 1960s, believed that women 'through their natural concern for the family' were more likely to oppose all forms of aggression.[106] Yet now women's anger about sexual predation had made women themselves predators. Rape became a powerful metaphor for all kinds of exploitation – the oppression of women generally and, for Māori activists, the dispossession of Māori land.

The ongoing failure to recognise rape within marriage came to stand for a wider societal expectation that men were free to demand sexual access to women. In response to rising public concern about the incidence of rape and its effect on victims, in 1983 the Minister of Justice, Jim McLay, requested that the Institute of Criminology and the Department of Justice undertake a study of rape law and procedure. A number of victims of rape were interviewed for the study, and many of them reported that pursuing the matter through the courts amounted, in effect, to a further violation.[107] After publication of the *Rape Study*, the Minister called for submissions in response to it. The 'great majority' who responded favoured abolition of spousal immunity, but one of the nine submissions that supported retention came from the organisation Feminists for Life.[108] Connie Purdue, editor of the *Feminists for Life* magazine, had long been active in what she described as the 'third stage' of feminism which was 'truly "for women" only if it is also pro-family and pro-life'. Purdue believed that 'destructive hatred' divided the feminist movement and that women were misguided in seeking 'sameness' with men. Although opposed to having the law intervene in sexual relations within marriage, Purdue was concerned that girls and women were 'pressurised into too-early sex' and was clear that 'women and girls suffer from sexual exploitation'. But for her the answer lay in revaluing the family.[109] By 1984, however, even the mainstream *Woman's Weekly* was raising the issue of whether a wife should be able to charge her husband with rape.

The government set up a select committee to investigate changes in rape law. It recommended higher sentences for rapists, overturning the concept of spousal immunity, and replacing the term 'rape' with 'sexual violation'. In the event, three separate pieces of legislation in 1985 signalled new standards with regard to rape prosecutions. The Crimes Amendment Act (No 4), the Evidence Amendment Act (No 2) and the Summary Proceedings Amendment Act (No 4) saw the end of spousal immunity, created a new offence of 'obtaining sexual consent by coercion', and recognised that women 'could be perpetrators and victims'.[110]

Reformulating the place of sex within relationships by emphasising consent opened up the further possibility of reforming the law, decriminalising male homosexuality, and making discrimination on the grounds of sexual orientation illegal. In January 1981, lesbians and gay men had picketed the offices of the Human Rights Commission to protest the commission's 1980 decision that discrimination against lesbians and gay men was justified.[111] By late 1984, the Labour MP for Wellington Central, Fran Wilde, was meeting with lesbians and gay men to discuss sponsoring a Bill to recognise homosexual rights. In March 1985, Wilde introduced the Homosexual Law Reform Bill, which aimed 'to legalise homosexual activity and anal intercourse between consenting adults, to protect boys as well as girls by making 16 the age of consent, and to outlaw discrimination on the grounds of sexual orientation'.[112]

Fran Wilde's Bill was the culmination of organisation at the grassroots level by members of the gay liberation movement. Historian Laurie Guy titled his book on the reform movement *Worlds in Collision* to highlight the way in which the proponents of sexual freedom came up against those who organised against the Bill in the Coalition of Concerned Citizens (many of whom were conservative Christians).[113] For gay rights activists, the advent of AIDS in 1981 made it imperative to create 'a climate of openness' surrounding sexual behaviour in order to prevent new infections.[114] But it was this very openness that offended groups such as the Society for the Promotion of Community Standards who worked alongside the Coalition of Concerned Citizens. Normalising homosexuality, in their eyes, put young men at risk of seduction and corruption. 'Family men with homosexual tendencies,' they argued, 'would face stronger temptation to seek homosexual outlets and so cause breakdown of their families.'[115] Patricia Bartlett was vigilant in campaigning against what she regarded as obscenity and pornography. The Society for the Promotion of Community Standards, along with the Coalition of Concerned Citizens, opposed the view that 'all sexual activity is morally equal', believing that only heterosexuality was ordained by God, and that sodomy was unnatural and sinful.[116]

Those opposed to the Homosexual Law Reform Bill argued that they were working 'for the common good' that was being undermined by anti-family values. Laurie Guy argues that the mass mobilisation by the Coalition of Concerned Citizens, who presented to Parliament a petition signed by 800,000 people opposed to Wilde's Bill, in fact 'provoked a counter-mobilisation of pro-reform people'. By April 1986, a Heylen Poll indicated that 64 per cent of respondents were in favour of decriminalisation.[117] On 9 July 1986, the first part of the Bill, decriminalising homosexuality, passed by 49 votes to 44. Ten women voted for homosexual law reform while Ruth Richardson and Whetu Tirikatene-Sullivan voted against it. Though the second part of the Bill (outlawing discrimination on the basis of sexual orientation) was lost, Fran Wilde had won an important victory in a hard-fought campaign.

But there were other battles to be fought, and feminists were working on them outside the corridors of power, gathering information, poring over medical papers, and asking women about their experience of the health system. Whereas the issue of consent to sex had come to the forefront of public discussion of rape, women's consent appeared to matter little at the National Women's teaching hospital in Auckland. There, trainees might practise vaginal examinations or the insertion of intrauterine devices on unknowing women anaesthetised for other purposes. The era of women not being asked, because the doctor knew best, was about to come to an end.

Broadsheet was a long-running monthly feminist magazine produced in Auckland from 1972 to 1997 and sold throughout New Zealand. It contained articles on wide range of topics including politics, social issues, health, sexuality and culture, and provided an important forum for discussing women's concerns. *Cover designed by Sharon Alston. Auckland Libraries, Broadsheet, cover, September 1986*

Chapter Thirteen

Reckoning with Women

Sandra Coney embarked on a risky career as a freelance journalist in 1984. As a key member of the Broadsheet Collective for fourteen years and a counsellor at the Auckland Medical Aid Centre, Coney's feminist advocacy skills had been honed through editing New Zealand's premier feminist magazine and working with women seeking safe abortions. Abortion counselling, she said, was 'a job I loved and in which I learned a good deal about the health system'.[1] Not all she learned was positive, and Coney, together with Women's Studies academic Phillida Bunkle, founded Fertility Action to advocate for reproductive rights. One of their first campaigns was to draw attention to the dangers of the Dalkon Shield, an intrauterine device (IUD) that was implicated in causing pelvic inflammatory disease in women fitted with it. Apart from lobbying for government action to check the safety of all IUDs, Fertility Action assisted 258 New Zealand women to make legal claims against the United States manufacturer of the Dalkon Shield.[2] The expertise that Coney and Bunkle had developed soon led to another challenging investigation, this time into Dr Herbert Green's study of carcinoma in situ at National Women's Hospital.

Women worked for social transformation in a variety of arenas. Many hoped that the Ministry of Women's Affairs would be a catalyst for change, lobbying for employment equity, working for a more responsive healthcare system, and ensuring women were not disadvantaged in the workplace by parental responsibilities. Great irony lay in the fact that the creation of the ministry occurred at the same time as the Labour government sought to dismantle the state's role in the egalitarian redistribution of resources. The ministry's highpoint came with the celebration of a century of women's suffrage in 1993, followed by continual downgrading. At the same time, women's ever-increasing commitment to the workforce was remaking New Zealand – from a society in which men worked in paid employment outside the home and women did unpaid work raising children in the home, to one in which families were smaller, both partners worked, and children might be cared for outside the home. Women's lives were being rethought on a number of fronts.

Experiments at National Women's

Women's health was central to the business of Auckland's National Women's Hospital, whose flagship new building for modern treatment opened in 1964.[3] In 1983, twenty-seven-year-old Felicity Bell and her husband Stephen were desperate to try anything to conceive a second longed-for child. They were offered the opportunity to participate in an experimental programme of in vitro fertilisation (IVF) at National Women's by Felicity's obstetrician, Celia Liggins.[4] At that time, New Zealand women diagnosed as infertile could seek this new treatment only at great expense in Australia.[5] Felicity was warned to keep her treatment secret: it was very 'hush hush'.[6] To her delight, she became pregnant on the second attempt, and gave birth to a healthy daughter on 24 June 1984. Between July 1983 and July 1985, twenty-two pregnancies eventuated for the 100 couples accepted into the programme.[7] The relatively low success rate appeared to be no deterrent to those longing to conceive. The experimental programme in IVF at National Women's went on to become a stunning success.

Another experimental programme at the hospital, however, became a national disaster and signalled a significant turning point in New Zealand's health system. That system was already under pressure from a younger generation concerned about the outmoded attitudes of a number of senior doctors. Some of these doctors had trained in the 1950s or earlier, when professors at the Otago Medical School were apt to remind women of their place. In 1958, the twelve women students in a class of 120 were told that they were 'taking a man's place' and that premenstrual tension 'was more common in women who had not adapted fully the woman's role in society'. One professor took it upon himself to declare that 'girls were useful only for routine duties, like dishes and anaesthetics'.[8] By the 1980s, the number of women medical students was on the rise – in part because of better science teaching in girls' schools – and such views were seen as beyond the pale. In October 1985, the Auckland and Otago Medical Schools, with the blessing of the Director General of Health, organised a national 'Role of the Doctor' conference. Among 230 public submissions received were many that criticised doctors for, among other things, their 'cultural insensitivity and sexist attitudes'.[9]

Doctors were the gatekeepers of both abortion services and modern methods of fertility control: the Pill and the IUD. Both were at first welcomed unconditionally for their ease of use and effectiveness, but the risks of high-dosage Pills and the potential for infection associated with IUDs became increasingly apparent. Women became dissatisfied with doctors who continued to assume they always knew what was best for patients and felt it unnecessary to discuss side-effects. Activist women, such as those in Hecate, the Wellington women's health collective, compiled 'hot and cold' doctor files to record women's positive and negative experiences of doctors and to make these available as a resource for others.[10] Hospitalised childbirth and dehumanising procedures, such as pubic shaving, enemas and the separation of infants from their mothers, fuelled the demand for alternative birthing services and increased status for midwifery.

A New Zealand Women's Health Network had been established in 1977, and women's health centres like Hecate and The Health Alternatives for Women in Christchurch served a demand for information about women's health issues. The Homebirth Association

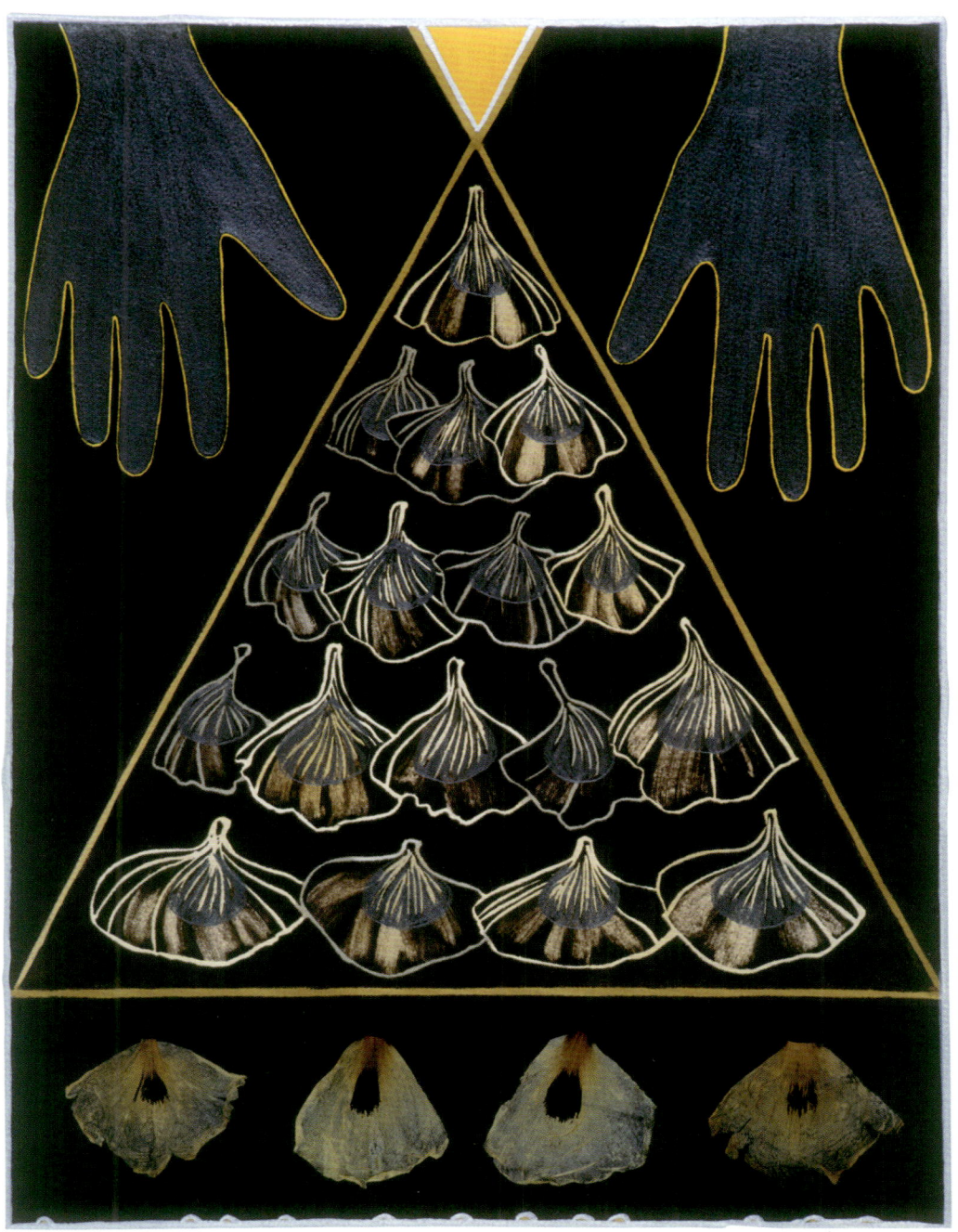

Marilynn Webb, one of New Zealand's finest printmakers, made this etching, 'Protection work – pale poppy 2' in 1987. Like much of her work, it focuses on connections between the natural environment and people, and the place of women in art. *Reproduced by permission of Marilynn Webb*

became a national grouping in 1979, as women active in the traditional female occupations of nursing and midwifery sought to improve their status and challenge practices they saw as demeaning to women. In September 1982, an inaugural National Women's Health Conference was held in Auckland, an event at which Māori women once again highlighted the poor health status of women in their communities. Two years later, Hecate 'had run out of funds and energy'.[11]

Then, in June 1987, just when the lay women's health movement seemed to be losing steam, Sandra Coney and Phillida Bunkle published an article in *Metro* magazine entitled '"An Unfortunate Experiment" at National Women's'. Its publication brought new and urgent attention to the issue of women's health.[12]

Coney and Bunkle revealed that a number of women, referred to the National Women's Hospital for treatment after positive cervical smear tests had shown carcinoma in situ (a precursor to cervical cancer), had been unknowingly subjected to a study by Associate Professor Herbert Green in which he merely observed, rather than treated, their cervical lesions. One woman under Green's care recalled:

> Having to visit the hospital so frequently became a strain. I was very uptight and I felt diseased. My husband got rather sick of it too. We lived a long way from the Hospital and he was always left with the children to look after and at the time we had two businesses to run … Eventually I used to visit the Hospital in a taxi because my husband didn't want to take me. I eventually got sick of going to the Hospital. I was worried that I had cancer but they didn't seem to be doing anything about it …
>
> Every time I went there, there were several doctors who talked about me in my presence as if I was a piece of furniture. They talked amongst themselves about me instead of to me and I would be lying on a bed with my legs in stirrups and a sheet in front of me …[13]

Her testimony, along with that of other women who had been subject to similar neglect, became central to the work of the government-initiated Inquiry into Allegations Concerning the Treatment of Cervical Cancer at National Women's Hospital and into Other Related Matters, prompted by the *Metro* article. District Court Judge Silvia Cartwright was appointed to lead the inquiry, and she interviewed eighty-one patients or relatives of patients to assess their treatment at National Women's. Many of the patients were from Māori and Pacific Island communities; all were encouraged to speak and were listened to with respect.

In the course of the inquiry, other aspects of Green's practice were also revealed. In one research project, swabs had been taken from the vaginas of newborn girls to examine their cervical cells; Green had lost interest in this study, but failed to stop it until swabs had been taken from 2,244 babies.[14] Permission had not been sought from the parents. Wider practices at the hospital came to light, too, such as students practising the insertion of IUDs in anaesthetised women without their knowledge or consent.

In its final submission to the Cartwright Inquiry, the Ministry of Women's Affairs noted its symbolic significance: 'Ultimately the issues are about who controls medicine and how; about who benefits from it and who are its victims. Thus, as so many witnesses have so clearly stated, the central issue, above all others, is power.'[15] Traditionally regarded as a caring profession, medicine was now charged with having 'victims' – and they were women.

The women who had been seen by Green implicitly trusted that a professor at a respected teaching hospital in reproductive health would be doing his best for them. Green believed this himself, but his unwillingness to take criticism and to re-evaluate his beliefs about the non-invasive nature of carcinoma in situ meant that he was unable to see how he was endangering his patients. Because their lesions remained untreated, women had a higher risk of developing invasive cancer, and several died as a result. One of the medical advisers to Judge Cartwright, epidemiologist Charlotte Paul, observed that the women showed 'extraordinary patience' with multiple visits to the hospital 'for an endless series of examinations and biopsies' – a patience born, she suggested, from an innate trust that they were being well cared for.[16] To Coney and Bunkle, Green's actions were representative of the unwarranted power of the medical profession – a power that required dismantling.

Certainly some doctors at National Women's had sought to expose the inadequacies of Herbert Green's approach to carcinoma in situ, but they had made no headway in changing practices in a hospital where powerful personalities held sway. A carefully researched magazine article by two lay people brought immediate action. That these women were also feminists meant there were those who saw the subsequent inquiry (and the fact that it was chaired by a woman) as a 'witch hunt', but the vast majority of New Zealanders were appalled that the elite of New Zealand's obstetrics and gynaecology community had been found so wanting.

Cartwright's report was damning. There had indeed been 'a failure to adequately treat cervical carcinoma in situ' at National Women's, and a research programme about which the women involved had not been informed had been carried out. Judge Cartwright made strong recommendations, and major changes and new initiatives were instituted nationally. Ethics committees became mandatory to review research projects; informed consent was placed high on the agenda; and health professionals were reminded of their duty to pay attention to the rights of patients. Patient advocates were employed to assist patients in hospitals, and the Health and Disability Commissioner Act of 1994 established the role of a commissioner dedicated to protecting the rights of those in receipt of health and disability services.[17] A Code of Health and Disability Services Consumers' Rights Regulation was established in 1996.[18]

The pendulum had swung away from full autonomy for the medical profession towards lay input into medical services and external regulation. But perhaps more important for the changing climate of opinion was the rapid growth in the number of women in medicine. Once a rarity, the increased numbers of women entering medical school from

This group held a twenty-four-hour vigil outside Parliament in July 1984 to draw attention to the plight of women victims of violence. *Photograph by Phil Reid, Alexander Turnbull Library, Wellington, EP/1984/3321/9-F*

the 1970s meant that the profession could no longer be seen as a male stronghold impervious to the needs of women.

Policing boundaries

If the medical profession was changing, there were few signs that the upholders of community law and order – the police – were doing the same. When the first woman police prosecutor requested permission to plead in court in 1972, the magistrate involved reportedly replied, 'Why not? Anything's good for a laugh.'[19] Yet the police were the first line of call when women experienced domestic or sexual assault. That officers might not take the matter seriously was explicit in the 1950s *Police Practice for Constables*, which advised: 'These assaults are usually minor.'[20] Such attitudes lingered. Research by historian Jacqueline O'Neill indicated that violence in the home was regarded as a private rather than a police matter. The police saw themselves as preserving the family unit rather than protecting at-risk individuals within the home.[21] And as long as corporal punishment was practised in schools, violence as a means of chastising family members could be seen as unremarkable. Attitudes began to change after the passing in 1982 of the Domestic Protection Act, which separated domestic violence out from matrimonial law and also gave legal protection to de facto spouses.[22] It put the police on notice that women deserved protection within the home.

Rape, already a statutory offence, appeared to be a more complicated matter. Marilyn Waring reported in the early 1980s, before the Rape Reform Act 1985 that overturned spousal immunity, on the 'omnipresent boys' brand of humour' at Bellamy's, the members-only dining room at Parliament. She gave an example:

MP no. 1: How can you legislate against rape in marriage? It couldn't be implemented.
MP no. 2: That's not the point – why should you be able to rape your wife in the bedroom but not beat her up in the kitchen?
MP no. 3: Then beat her in the bedroom and rape her in the kitchen?
Honourable Members: Ha Ha ...[23]

Many police officers, too, were out of step with the changing social climate. Those whose training had been influenced by advice in the 1964 manual for police detectives that rape complaints were likely to be false found it difficult to believe that women had a right to say no. There were few women in their workplace to tell them otherwise. In 1990, women comprised only 6.9 per cent of the police force, and they were most likely to be deployed in the control room.[24] One of the reasons the numbers remained low may have been that until the mid-1990s the dominant police culture 'enabled a few male officers to sexually harass women officers and staff'.[25] The police lacked any code of conduct around sexual behaviour in respect of either fellow staff or the public.

In Wellington, the Ministry of Women's Affairs worked hard after the Rape Reform

Act to ensure sexual violence was taken seriously, but in small communities such as Murupara, in an isolated area in the Bay of Plenty, a local police officer saw nothing wrong in assuming that a thirteen-year-old girl, Louise Nicholas, had consented to his sexual abuse in the early 1980s. In a pattern of male behaviour in which women were treated as objects of sexual desire – through sexual banter, and acts such a bottom-pinching and wolf-whistling – rather than as individuals with complex needs of their own, a distressing series of police incidents occurred. In 1989, a twenty-year-old woman was lured into a lifeguard hut at Mount Maunganui by a businessman, a fireman and two police officers. There she was bound, raped, forced to perform oral sex, and violated with a police baton up to twenty times. Encouraged by Louise Nicholas speaking out in the media about her own experiences, she brought a case against the perpetrators, and in 2005 all four of the accused were found guilty; the two police officers, Brad Shipton and Bob Schollum, received eight-year sentences.[26] These two men, along with Assistant Police Commissioner Clint Rickards, were alleged to have been involved also in the repeated abuse of Louise Nicholas but had not been convicted, in part because the police had failed to investigate the complaints properly. In 2007, the detective in charge of handling Nicholas's initial complaint was convicted of obstructing the course of justice and sentenced to a prison term of four-and-a-half years.[27] Nicholas showed great personal courage in pursuing her case in the face of the closed ranks of the police, and has remained a tireless advocate for rape victims.

A police culture that both belittled and excluded women was one barrier to change. A second lay in the lack of transfer and promotion opportunities. Catherine Handley-Packham spent seven years on general duties as a policewoman. She applied for a transfer to New Brighton, in Christchurch, 'but the sergeant there said he didn't want any policewomen. He already had one and didn't want any more!' Later, married with children, she asked to job-share with the other woman at New Brighton: 'The department wouldn't hear of it.' In 1994 she left the police, but she was persuaded to go back on a casual basis, serving as a police matron at Christchurch District Court – a job that grew into a permanent position.[28]

Recognition of the vital role women could play in the force, and across all ranks, improved considerably during the 1990s and beyond. The 1988 State Sector Act's emphasis on equal opportunities added fuel to the calls for change, and led to the widening participation of women in the police force. In 1993, a Women's Consultative Committee was set up as an equal opportunities initiative. At first treated as a suspicious sisterhood, the committee showed itself willing to deal with difficult issues and highlight persistent inequities.[29] From a proportion of only 6.9 per cent of sworn officers in 1990, women's participation had risen to 15.3 per cent by 2000. Nonetheless, only one of 33 superintendents was a woman, all the top officers were men, and the greatest representation of women (17.8 per cent) was at the lowest rank of constable. In contrast, women made up nearly 70 per cent of non-sworn staff, only 26 per cent of whom were in the top salary bands.[30] After the consultative committee expressed concern, the police commissioned Associate Professor Prue Hyman of Victoria University to prepare a report on women in the Criminal Investigation Branch. Issued in the year 2000, the report suggested that a 'climate of mild gender harassment and workplace bullying' still required remedy and the police needed to develop a more 'family friendly' culture.[31]

In contrast to the slow pace of change in the police, the number of women studying law grew quickly, from 10 per cent of students in 1970 to 46 per cent by 1986, so that by the 1990s more women than men were graduating from the country's law schools.[32] Women were also entering the top echelons of the profession. In 1988, Sian Elias and Lowell Goddard were the first women to be appointed Queen's Counsel. Lowell Goddard, of Ngāti Kahungunu descent, went on to become Deputy Solicitor General for New Zealand in 1992 and a judge of the High Court in 1995. From 2007 to 2012, Justice Goddard served as chair of the Independent Police Conduct Authority, a body created in 1998 to provide independent investigation and resolution of complaints against the police.[33] Sian Elias became a judge of the High Court in 1995, and head of the New Zealand judiciary with her appointment as Chief Justice in 1999.

Advocating for women at a time of deregulation

The Ministry of Women's Affairs had begun with a burst of optimism and enthusiasm. Mary O'Regan was committed to doing the business of government differently, with less hierarchy and more consensus decision-making, and a commitment to biculturalism that made the ministry a model of practice for other departments.[34] Consultation was a high priority. Between May 1986 and March 1987, for example, staff from the Maori Women's Secretariat, Te Ohu Whakatupu, attended 215 hui.[35] Expectations from the community were high, and the ministry had to pay attention to these as well as to government priorities. But difficulties quickly arose as the Fourth Labour Government sought to solve the country's economic woes by loosening up restrictions on previously protected markets, reducing the state's role in New Zealand's economy and welfare system, and cutting public spending. Public spending on health, education and social services, which had consumed 13 per cent of GDP in the 1950s, had reached 23 per cent of GDP in the late 1970s. High inflation and a budget deficit of over $3 billion called for drastic measures.[36] Under the 1988 State Sector Act, the ministry was restructured to meet goals of cost-effectiveness, and by the late 1980s a new language of accountability had entered the public service. The ministry was now required to measure outputs.[37]

Those who worked there were acutely aware of the irony that the ministry had been set up at the very time the policies of economic rationalism espoused by the reforming Labour government were impacting on the lowest paid – many of whom were women. The introduction of the goods and services tax (GST) in 1986, for example, added 10 per cent to families' supermarket bills.[38] The impact on unskilled workers, in particular, led

Artist Claudia Pond Eyley designed this poster to promote the work of the Ministry of Women's Affairs around 1990. It incorporates the ministry's logo in the bottom right corner and an image of a woman's moko in the bottom left corner.
Alexander Turnbull Library, Wellington, Eph-E-WOMEN-1990-01

to ministry initiatives to improve educational outcomes for women. But this was just one of the myriad causes to capture the ministry's attention, from the general concern with equal employment opportunities to the specific issues around the high incidence of cervical cancer among Māori and the implications of new birth technologies.[39] The ministry became a catalyst for action by creating a Women's Appointment File to increase the representation of women on statutory boards and committees, and by working with other departments to ensure that, under the State Sector Act, they were 'good employers' and committed to equal opportunities programmes.[40]

'Good employers' were obliged to work towards equity for Māori, ethnic or minority groups, women, and people with disabilities. Change in this area was slow. In 1997, for example, although women made up 54 per cent of public servants, they were only 29 per cent of the well-paid senior managers.[41] As a sign of the downsizing of welfare, government policy suggested that women be treated primarily as workers. Hence, two of the 'measurable outcomes' the ministry sought were, first, an increase in the number of women in the paid labour market and, second, a reduction in the number of women on state benefits.[42] The decline of the male breadwinner wage meant it was increasingly difficult for families to survive on one income.[43]

Charged with the identification of policy issues, the ministry initiated a number of studies to assess the situation of women. In 1988, this led to the publication of two reports: *Women in the Economy* and, more specifically, *Maori Women in the Economy*. The former found that women worked long hours but that much of their work was unpaid. Age, marital status and employment status (rather than income level) governed the way women were treated by the tax and social welfare systems. Low pay and a high level of involvement in voluntary work meant that women were unable to accumulate savings; were less likely to have money to spend on education, training or childcare; and were 'at risk of experiencing poverty'.[44] The companion report revealed that Māori women were likely to be even more impoverished, and that in 1986 nearly 65 per cent of Māori women left school without any formal qualifications. Most problematically, education services, and New Zealand culture more widely, failed to value Māori culture and language.[45]

Effective lobbying by the Ministry of Women's Affairs and the Equal Employment Opportunities Unit within the State Services Department led to the creation of a Working Group on Equal Pay and Equal Opportunity in 1988. Margaret Wilson, president of the Labour Party from 1984 to 1987, chaired the group, which produced a report entitled *Towards Employment Equity* that same year. The report argued that women's segregation into certain occupations kept their earnings low. The 1986 Census revealed that 51 per cent of women in paid work were concentrated in six occupational groups: clerical, sales, teaching, medical, typing and book-keeping. Women were over-represented in the wholesale and retail trades, restaurants and hotels; in finance and insurance; and in community, social and personal service sectors.

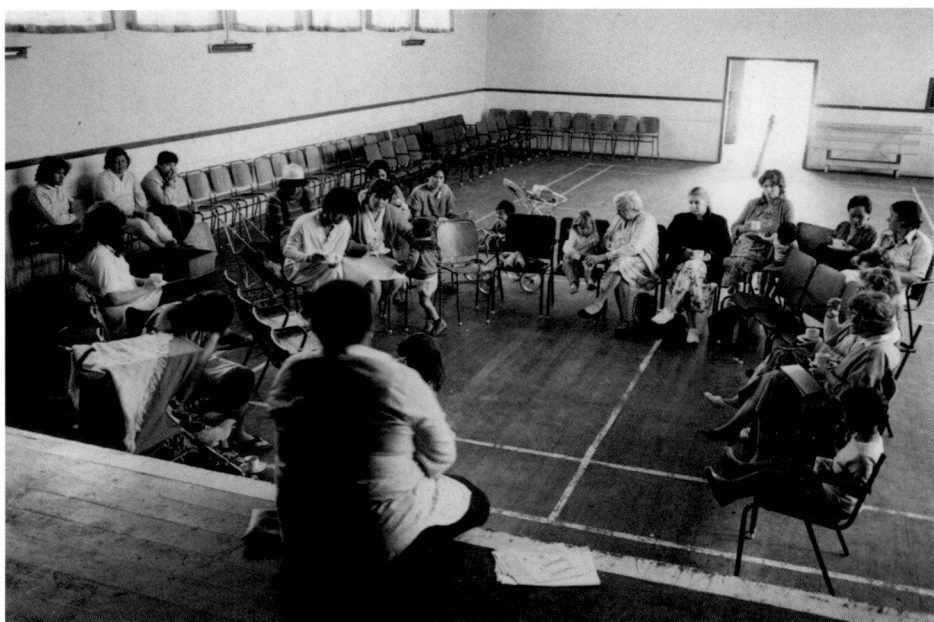

Top In 1979 State Coal Mines announced a plan to demolish the township of Rotowaro south-west of Huntly to build a huge opencast coal mine; residents were to be relocated. State Coal Mines Liaison Project Officer, Nancy Buckley, is pictured at a meeting held to discuss the concerns of the women of Rotowaro. *Photograph by David Cook/Waikato Museum*

Bottom Clare Tomelty, State Coal Mines pay clerk, was photographed in the about-to-be-closed Rotowaro office in 1984. *Photograph by David Cook/Waikato Museum*

Why, women workers asked, was their labour worth less than men's? Clerical workers at Todd Motors in Porirua (and soon at General Motors and Ford Motors in the Hutt Valley) went on strike in February 1986 in an attempt to achieve pay parity with factory staff. The workers maintained round-the-clock picket lines every day for a month. Voicing the feelings of many, union delegate Robin Dick said: 'It hurt us a lot going without the money for so long. People seem to think that we work to supplement our husband's incomes but we work because it's our bread and butter.'[46] In the end, the companies agreed to arbitration. In this case, workers were subject to the kind of structural and institutional discriminatory practices that the *Towards Employment Equity* report argued required a legislative remedy. It proposed an Employment Equity Act.[47]

Although employers and politicians paid lip service to the ideal of equity, many could not imagine how whole occupations could be revalued. How was one to judge that the work of a nurse was worth the same as that of a firefighter? According to the historian of the campaign, Megan Cook, employers saw equity as being achieved by women moving 'outside their traditional occupations' and committing themselves to the same working patterns as men.[48] Bureaucrats within government who were focused on labour-market deregulation and greater efficiency wanted the market, not government, to determine wage rates.[49] Helen Clark, the rising star of the Labour Party, took on the labour portfolio in order to see through pay equity legislation – although perhaps not quickly enough for the campaigners.[50] Those in the Labour government who were committed to winding back the role of the state saw such legislation as yet another barrier to free enterprise. Most National MPs certainly saw it this way, and repeal of any legislation became part of their election policy. Nevertheless, the Employment Equity Bill was first read in the House in December 1989, passed into statute in July 1990, and came into effect in October 1990.

The landslide victory of the National Party, led by Jim Bolger, in the late-October 1990 elections meant that repeal was almost certain. The new Minister of Labour, Bill Birch, introduced the Labour Relations Amendment Bill, clause 4 of which repealed the Employment Equity Act. Helen Clark, acting leader of the Opposition, described the repeal as 'a black day for women', but the newly appointed Minister of Women's Affairs, Jenny Shipley, argued that it was a stand 'in favour of women who wish to participate in the future'. That future, she said, was one in which individuals should make their own way in the workforce, free from obligations to other workers through unions, and hence capable of 'flexibility'.[51] As Shipley's ministry held its Christmas party on 19 December 1990, the repeal of the Employment Equity Act was passed.[52]

The National government was committed to workers' rights being covered by individual contracts rather than collective bargaining – a position that took legislative form in the 1991 Employment Contracts Act. Politicians like Jenny Shipley argued that male unions had historically used 'their strength to blackmail the economy'. Women's progress, she said, had been inhibited by the way male unions 'dominated the industrial

Manuhiri arrive at the Roma Marae at Ahipara in Northland, following the release of the Waitangi Tribunal's report on the Wai 262 claim in 2011. The claim was originally lodged with the Tribunal in 1991 and concerned Māori control of their culture, identity and traditional knowledge. The visitors are carrying photographs to honour the memory of those who passed away while the claim was being heard. *Photograph by Peter de Graaf,* Northern Advocate

relations system', winning 'wage settlements not related to productivity' that thus distorted the labour market.[53] Freeing up the workforce under the new Act would allow women to realise new opportunities. But this liberalisation, in effect, allowed employers to offer contracts that ignored hard-won protections such as the eight-hour day.

Ruth Richardson, now Minister of Finance, presented what she called the 'mother of all budgets' in 1991 – a budget designed to severely constrain government spending. A believer in 'individual liberty and small government', Richardson wanted to 'redesign the welfare state' by removing the notion of universal entitlement and, instead, providing targeted assistance to those most in need.[54] Asset testing for superannuation entitlement, fees for tertiary students, and charges for public hospital care as well as for prescriptions and doctors' visits were designed to remove entitlements from the well-paid and to target assistance at those who were eligible for a 'community services' card, issued by Department of Social Welfare. Not all these changes were achieved, but Richardson believed she had done much to stop 'middle-class welfare' and had 'lifted the burden of the state from people'.[55]

The costs of restructuring the economy, the labour market and welfare entitlements fell heavily on Māori. Between March 1986 and March 1990, Māori unemployment rates increased from 8.5 per cent to 20.6 per cent (the non-Māori rate rose from 3 per cent to 6.5 per cent). Unemployment exacerbated health problems, alcohol abuse and violence.

Miriata Te Hiko and other representatives of Ngāti Raukawa sign the Central North Island Deed at the Beehive on 25 June 2008. Nicknamed 'Treelords' (after the Sealords fisheries settlement), the agreement returned $196 million worth of forest lands to seven central North Island tribes. *Photograph by Mark Mitchell*, New Zealand Herald, *NZH-1036765*

Māori women, the Ministry of Women's Affairs pointed out, bore 'the brunt of this physically, emotionally, spiritually, as well as financially'.[56] However, optimism about the possibilities for redress of longstanding grievances that were raised by the Waitangi Tribunal Act 1985 (which enabled the hearing of historic claims dating back to 1840), spurred some Māori women into action. They joined with their men in preparing claims to the Tribunal, and sometimes prepared submissions of their own. In 1993, the Maori Women's Welfare League made an urgent Tribunal claim which alleged:

> The Crown's actions and policies have been inconsistent with its obligations under the Treaty of Waitangi to protect and ensure the rangatiratanga of Maori women as individuals and members and leaders of tribes and families. These actions and policies have resulted in an undermining of Maori women so that their status as rangatira has been expropriated due to the Crown's failure to accord Maori women status and power within the political, social and economic structures it has created.[57]

Early childhood teachers march in 1994. As more women with pre-school children moved into the workforce, early childhood learning centres were in demand. Teachers sought recognition of their educational work previously regarded merely as child 'care'. *NZEI Te Tiu Roa collection*

To strengthen the claims of Māori women, and to reinforce claims like those of the Maori Women's Welfare League, in 1997 the Ministry of Women's Affairs produced *Te Mana Wahine: Hei Ara Whakatupu: Recognition of Women's Mana is the Pathway to Equality*.[58]

Concerned to facilitate all women's employment in a range of sectors, the Ministry of Women's Affairs also paid attention to issues around childcare and parental-leave policies. The provisions of the Maternity Leave and Employment Protection Act 1980, which allowed women to take unpaid maternity leave for up to twenty-six weeks and prohibited dismissal on the grounds of pregnancy and maternity leave, were extended in 1987. The new Act also made it possible for fathers to take unpaid leave after the birth of a child. It did not, however, include provisions for payments – a situation the Secretary of Women's Affairs described as 'indefensible'.

Despite pressure from a 1994 coalition of groups from the community and from legal, women's and union representatives, the government remained obdurate that paid parental leave would be too expensive for the country. Kathleen O'Regan, National MP for Waipā and Deputy Minister of Women's Affairs, was one who broke ranks. She pointed out:

Margaret Wilson, president of the Labour Party from 1984 to 1987, speaks at the party's conference in 1986. Wilson, a lawyer and academic, went on to become a Labour MP, Attorney-General and later Speaker of the House of Representatives. *Photograph by Ross Giblin, Alexander Turnbull Library, Wellington, EP/1986/4169/16-F*

Somehow the state and employers manage to fund a system of Accident Compensation that provides for the sorts of things that happen to men. Let's not call them accidents, but a temporary inability to be in paid work. Equally pregnancy provides a 'temporary absence from work'. Why should one be more worthy of compensation then the other?[59]

While campaigners argued that paid parental leave would remove discrimination against women, allow them to participate more effectively in the workforce, and assist employers to retain skilled staff, the government consensus remained that the economics of family formation remained a matter for couples alone.

Laila Harré, former trade unionist and future Minister of Women's Affairs, brought energy to the campaign when, under the new mixed member proportional (MMP) voting system, she was elected on the Alliance Party list in 1996. After the Labour–Alliance coalition came to power in November 1999, she was instrumental in the introduction of a Bill that committed the government to funding paid parental leave through general taxation. The Parental Leave and Employment Protection Amendment Acts of 2002 entitled those who had worked for the same employer for an average of ten hours per week for twelve months before the baby's expected due date to twelve weeks' paid leave.[60]

The advent of paid parental leave, however meagre, recognised that women's earnings were often central to the family economy but that gendered life cycles shape women's careers very differently from men's. Māori women's participation in the workforce fell while they were in their twenties, as did Pākehā women's participation in their thirties, while male rates remained steady during these years.[61]

After parental leave, working parents looked to childcare options. The term 'child-care' gave way to 'early childhood education', signifying the role and qualifications of the experienced workers in the field. Successive governments put more resources into early childhood education during the late 1980s and 1990s (while at the same time introducing a fee system for tertiary education from the late 1980s). The expansion of childcare meant that by the end of the twentieth century, increasing numbers of children were likely to spend time with paid carers, most of whom were women. In 1995, there were 8,804 women employed in the early childhood sector and only 106 men. The numbers of men involved in primary and secondary teaching declined during the 1990s, from 36 per cent of full-time teacher equivalents in 1992 to 31 per cent in 1997. Within the teaching profession, however, men remained greatly over-represented in positions of authority.[62]

A career or a family had once been the stark alternatives facing women. By the 1980s, women at home found they increasingly had to explain themselves: it was hard not be ashamed of being 'just a housewife'. As one woman said defensively: 'I have to lay out all my reasons for staying home and being with the children. Sometimes I get very miserable about it ... Everyone I meet says "where are you working now?" Because they know I've finished studying.'[63] By 1996, 30 per cent of women with an infant under one, and 50 per cent of women with children aged one to four, were in paid work. Seventy-five per cent of mothers with teenagers were in paid work.[64] Mothers were clearly bearing children and continuing their employment in any way they could, not least because they needed the money. In the mid-1990s, the Ministry of Women's Affairs promoted a proposal for the funding of before- and after-school programmes for the children of working parents. The resulting OSCAR (Out of School Care and Recreation) funding was to be targeted at high-needs communities.[65]

However well children were cared for during work hours, the household tasks of food preparation, cleaning up afterwards, house cleaning and laundry remained. A 1991 pilot 'time-use' study revealed that 31 per cent of women's time was spent in unpaid work, compared with 12 per cent of men's time.[66] A 1998–99 survey suggested that little had changed: women did most of the housework, spending an hour per day more than men on these tasks. Caring for others, whether children or the elderly, ill or disabled, also took twice as much of women's time as men's.[67] There continued a double standard of expectation that working women would 'not compromise their family obligations – a standard by which fathers were rarely judged'.[68] Data from the 1996 Census also suggested

Jane Kelsey was captured in an informal kitchen moment by photographer Jenny Scown in the early 1990s. A prominent critic of globalisation and neoliberalism, she has taught at the University of Auckland since 1979. *Photograph by Jenny Scown*

that women working full time in senior-level positions were unlikely to have children. Clearly, it remained difficult to combine family responsibilities and demanding work.[69]

Pushing boundaries and celebrating success

Riwia Brown, daughter of a Pākehā father and a mother of Ngāti Porou and Te Whānau-a-Apanui descent, took to playwriting after she had seen a performance of her brother Apirana Taylor's play *Kohanga*. *Roimata* (1988) was her first play, and in 1989 she overcame her reluctance to adapt and direct it for television, recognising the importance of raising the profile of Māori women directors, represented at that time by Merata Mita alone. Brown continued to write for theatre as well as to act until she eventually decided to quit her day job to pursue full-time writing. A chance meeting with director Lee Tamahori in Wellington in 1992 led to the opportunity to work Alan Duff's novel *Once Were Warriors* into a compelling film script. Brown reshaped the novel so that it centred on the story of Beth Heke, a woman caught in a violent relationship on a South Auckland housing estate. Unemployment, drinking and gangs marked the lifestyle of the urban Māori portrayed in both the book and the film; they were 'disconnected from their tribal roots' and hovered over by the Pākehā state.[70] *Once Were Warriors* was a confronting, 'very real and raw expose of life'.[71] New Zealanders were challenged, as Paul Stanley Ward suggests, 'with life beyond the clichés of sheep and pretty scenery'.[72]

Riwia Brown's favourite moment in the film is when the abused woman, Beth Heke (played by Rena Owen), takes a stand against Jake the Muss (Temuera Morrison):

> Our people once were warriors. But unlike you, Jake, they were people with mana, pride; people with spirit. If my spirit can survive living with you for eighteen years, then I can survive anything.[73]

In the spirit of earlier women leaders such as Te Puea Herangi and Whina Cooper, Beth Heke fictionally represents the role of strong women who act as leaders and nurturers of cultural tradition.

Once Were Warriors portrayed a fictional South Auckland. In the real South Auckland, June Jackson of Ngāti Maniapoto in 1986 became chief executive of the Manukau Urban Maori Authority (MUMA), 'the largest urban organisation in the country'.[74] The authority developed a number of small businesses that gave employees training that would lead to full-time employment. Nga Whare Waatea Marae, an urban marae in Māngere, became the hub of MUMA's operations; here the authority built a kōhanga reo, and a complex of buildings that included meeting halls, workshops, dining room and kitchen, and some flats for elderly residents. MUMA went on to develop night markets. At the same time, Jackson worked in the jails and, as a member of the National Parole Board, served on various government committees. She embraced the concept of self-determination; the 1990s, she believed, was 'a decade for the courageous and the strong, not for the weak' as Māori strove to build a future that retained their culture 'while competing for the elusive dollar'.[75]

Sandra Lee, another activist in local government after her 1983 election to the Waiheke County Council, had taken steps to create change for Māori through the founding, with others, of the Mana Motuhake Party in 1979. In 1991, she became president of the party and agreed to go into coalition with other minor parties in the Alliance. Lee successfully stood for the Auckland Central electorate in 1993 and became the first Māori woman to gain a general seat in the New Zealand Parliament.[76] After losing her seat in 1996, she returned to Parliament in 1999 as a minister in the Labour–Alliance government. As

Minister of Local Government, Minister of Conservation and Associate Minister of Maori Affairs, Lee saw her role as ensuring that the government developed 'a full and sincere relationship with te iwi Maori' to ensure future success for marginalised people.[77]

One way to build success in the future was to develop healthy lifestyles through a commitment to sport. In 1987, the new president of the Maori Women's Welfare League, June Hinekahukura Mariu, decided to act on the league's report on women's health, *Rapuora*, by making netball a vehicle for change. She herself had excelled at sport, captaining the New Zealand basketball team in 1960, and playing for the national indoor basketball and softball teams. Through promoting netball field days, the league encouraged young and older players to enhance their levels of physical activity.[78] Many young players benefited, and netball gained even greater national prominence when New Zealand won the World Championships in 1987.

New Zealand women had long had good role models in sporting high achievers. Runner Alison Roe took the spotlight when she won the 1981 Boston and New York marathons in record times. In 1984, the first year women could compete in the marathon at the Olympics, Lorraine Moller came fifth wearing the New Zealand colours. At the Edinburgh Commonwealth Games in 1988, Moller ran her best time of 2:28:17, winning silver. An Olympic medal came in 1992, when she won the bronze at Barcelona. Such examples encouraged others, and young women took to a variety of sporting endeavours that their mothers would never have considered.

Eight hundred thousand New Zealanders crowded around their television sets in 1990 to watch Susan Devoy battle for the title of World Open Squash Champion, a title she had won in 1985 and 1987; in 1989 she was runner-up. She won again in 1990 and in 1992. Devoy represented a new type of late-twentieth-century woman: one who was keen to take on remarkable physical challenges. The youngest of seven siblings and the only girl in a squash-mad family, Devoy 'spent much of the early years of her life in a carrycot being carried from squash court to squash court'.[79] As soon as she was able to grip a racket she was given one of her own, followed soon by a specially cut-down version more appropriate to her size. Devoy was a natural left-hander, but one of her brothers insisted she play with her right hand, unwittingly improving her on-court advantage. By age sixteen she was able to demolish much older competitors, and became New Zealand Under-22 Champion. At seventeen, she boarded a plane for London, determined to try her luck on the English professional squash circuit, and in 1984 she won the British Open Squash Champion-ships, a competition she went on to win eight times.

By the 1990s, myths about what women might achieve in sport well and truly fell away as women athletes excelled in a range of fields, from Barbara Kendall's Olympic gold for boardsailing in 1992 to skier Annalise Coberger's triumph on the slopes at Albertville, France, that same year. Coberger was the first person from the southern hemisphere to win a medal (silver for the slalom) at a Winter Olympics.

New Zealand's Valerie Adams is shown in action during the Olympic Games women's shot put qualifying round at the Olympic Stadium in London, on 6 August 2012. As Valerie Vili, Adams had won gold at the 2008 Beijing Olympics, and she repeated the feat at London in 2012. *Photograph by Mark Mitchell*, New Zealand Herald, *NZH-1065229*

Louisa Wall, seen here playing rugby, represented New Zealand in both netball and women's rugby before entering Parliament as a Labour list MP in 2008. In 2012 she introduced a bill to legalise same-sex marriage, which was passed into law in July 2013. Of Tūwharetoa and Waikato descent, Wall identifies as a lesbian. *Photograph by David Rogers, Getty Images Sport*

Celebration of all kinds increasingly became the focus of the Ministry of Women's Affairs as the Centennial of Women's Suffrage drew closer in 1993. Dame Miriam Dell, a leader in the National Council of Women, and the first New Zealander elected president of the International Council of Women (1970–74), was appointed to chair the Suffrage Trust set up in July 1991 to disburse $5 million to projects that reflected every aspect of women's lives. The theme for Suffrage Year was to be 'Celebrating the Past: Challenging the Future'. The year began on 14 and 15 February with 'Summits for Suffrage', when all-women teams climbed the nation's peaks from Mount Ruapehu in the north to Aoraki/Mount Cook in the south. The less experienced climbed local hills, and 4,000 women saw the world from a new perspective. That weekend also saw the start of the 'Kiwi Women in Action' programme aimed at encouraging all girls and women to take part in physical activity.[80]

As part of their commitment to the centennial of suffrage, all government departments agreed to mark the year with a project. Some produced histories focused on women, among them Ann Beaglehole's *Benefiting Women: Income Support for Women 1893–1993* and Fiona McKergow's *The 'Taxwoman': 101 Years of Women Working in the Inland Revenue Department*. Other initiatives included booklets on women's participation in various sectors, and forums on women's perspectives and decision-making in conservation. Crown Law undertook a study on women lawyers' representation in small towns and women's progress into law firm partnerships. The Customs Department worked to enhance policing of child pornography through improved liaison with international agencies. Women with disabilities and women who had arrived as refugees between 1982 and 1992 were also the subjects of special projects, as were the workings of the Parental Leave and Employment Protection Act.[81]

The biggest history projects published during the suffrage centennial were *The Vote, the Pill and the Demon Drink: A History of Feminist Writing in New Zealand, 1869–1993*, a collection edited and introduced by Charlotte Macdonald; *Women Together: A History of Women's Organisations in New Zealand*, edited by Anne Else; and Sandra Coney's lavishly illustrated *Standing in the Sunshine: A History of New Zealand Women since the Vote*, and the accompanying television series. A much more modest volume, Tania Rei's *Maori Women and the Vote*, threw light on a little-explored topic. Once invisible in histories, women now appeared to be everywhere.

The milestone of 100 years of women's enfranchisement also led to conferences and discussions about the meaning of women's citizenship. The *New Zealand Official Yearbook* profiled more than ninety women, many of them trailblazers in politics and the professions, and activists on behalf of women, but also mountaineers, sports people, farmers, scientists, television presenters, actors, comedians, musicians, educationalists, dancers, artists, models, photographers, inventors, businesswomen, motor mechanics, stockbrokers and writers. The Rt Revd Dr Penny Jamieson was featured as the world's first woman Anglican bishop to lead a diocese. That women should be free to do anything and work in whatever field they chose had been recognised by the Health and Safety in Employment Act 1992 which removed all restrictions on where women could work, apart from those governing women in combat. The latter restriction remained until the year 2000.

A women jockeys' race in Te Awamutu, a Suffragists Terrific Education Retreat on Stewart Island, a Grannies Galore weekend in Buller, and a formation fly-past by New Plymouth women pilots were some of the other innovative ways in which women celebrated the suffrage centenary. In the Te Aroha district, ninety women were served dinner that had been prepared by their male farming colleagues.[82] While few New Zealanders had been aware of the significance of Kate Sheppard prior to 1993, after that year most could identify the woman pictured on the new ten-dollar bank note.[83] National and local events instilled in New Zealanders a sense of pride at being the first independent nation to enfranchise women. Most felt that the suffrage celebrations had communicated that fact well, though they were less sure that the events had led to any greater understanding of the current position of women.[84]

In government offices, women like Ripeka Evans, who had a long tradition of activism, were working within the system to foster Māori development. By 1985 she was a member of the Maori Economic Development Commission, working hard to find solutions to Māori poverty. 'I saw that,' she has remarked, 'as following on from storming the barricades at Hamilton[,] storming the barricades in the cabinet room. And it was brilliant.'[85] In 1993, Evans became the inaugural chief executive of Te Māngai Pāho, a Crown entity charged with promoting Māori language and culture through allocating funds to broadcasting. Working within the system she once opposed, Evans contributed to a number of significant Māori initiatives, such as the Waitangi Tribunal and Māori Television.

In 1996, National's Jenny Shipley was still the Minister of Women's Affairs. A close colleague of Ruth Richardson, she had trained as a teacher and, while her children were young, honed her skills in educational and childcare organisations. Aged thirty-five when she entered Parliament in 1987, Shipley had risen quickly through the National Party ranks, becoming Minister of Social Welfare and of Women's Affairs in 1990. The ministry marked its tenth anniversary by commissioning *The Full Picture: Te Tirohanga Whanui: Guidelines for Gender Analysis* to assist with mainstreaming a gender perspective in policy and programmes.[86] New ways of doing the work of government, with an emphasis on efficiency, led to templates that could be applied across the public service. That year, 1995, new ways of communication were introduced, including email and a ministry homepage.[87] But further change was in the wind.

Mainstreamed or swimming against the tide?

Second-wave feminism stressed the limitation of sex roles that confined women to the home and men to the workplace, and imagined that the elimination of gender roles would create equality. The Labour government elected in 1984 had outlined a series of commitments to 'economic equality', 'social and cultural equality' and 'legal and political equality' for women. The Ministry of Women's Affairs had been, in its turn, committed to overseeing the implementation of measures that would enhance women's opportunities to participate in all areas of society. But the same Labour government had been concerned to roll back the reach of the state in order to reduce public spending. The succeeding National government worked only to accelerate the achievement of that aim.

The new economic climate led the government to emphasise individual responsibility for health and welfare. The language of individual responsibility was one that feminism had fostered, claiming women's independence from the family and individual right to self-fulfilment. Held within the wider critique of society made by the women's liberation movement, feminism focused on social change. Detached from a wider political critique, however, liberation could quickly slide into a matter of 'individual women's achievement and choice'.[88] In a significant transition, the overall purpose of the Ministry of Women's Affairs was 'downsized' in the early 1990s from a role assisting government 'in enabling women to gain autonomy in all aspects of their lives, and within the social and cultural context of their own family, Iwi or other groups', to assisting government 'in developing

This necklace is by Auckland artist and jeweller Niki Hastings-McFall. Her Samoan heritage has influenced her style and imagery. *Museum of New Zealand Te Papa Tongarewa, Wellington, FE010610*

opportunity and choice for women in all aspects of their lives'.[89] In 1997, the status of the ministry was downgraded further, and the Minister of Women's Affairs exiled from Cabinet, the key decision-making body of government.

Choices were nevertheless the prerogative of those who had education and employment. From the 1980s, a new and sharp polarisation had emerged between the well-educated women who expected to have careers and so might delay childbearing, and women with little education who were more likely to become pregnant at a young age and find themselves immersed in a cycle of poverty. Government policy attempted to address gaps such as this by targeted assistance rather than universal entitlements. By 1996, unemployment was highest for Māori women (19 per cent), Pacific Island women (17.5 per cent) and Asian women (14.3 per cent). Pākehā women were much more likely to be in work, with an unemployment rate of 5.8 per cent.[90] While Māori women were likely to give birth between the ages of twenty and twenty-four, Pākehā women were more often

Dancers from Atiu in the Cook Islands prepare to perform at an Auckland event in 1992. *Photograph by Glenn Jowitt, Museum of New Zealand Te Papa Tongarewa, Wellington, O.027955*

between twenty-five and twenty-nine when their children were born. Overall, Māori and Pacific Island women had more children (2.1 per woman) compared to Pākehā women (1.9), and were also much more likely to be sole parents and nearly twice as likely to live in rental accommodation.[91]

The housing needs of Māori women became a particular concern of Helen Clark, who in 1987 became the first woman appointed Minister of Housing. A veteran of anti-Vietnam and anti-tour campaigns, she had entered Parliament in 1981 as Labour member for Mt Albert. On being chosen over six male contenders as the candidate for the safe Labour seat, Clark remarked: 'A decade of feminism is starting to have its effect.'[92] Making her mark from the time she entered the House, she successfully championed anti-nuclear policies in the heightened debate caused by the bombing of the anti-nuclear protest ship, the *Rainbow Warrior*, by French agents in 1985.

Helen Clark was promoted to Cabinet in 1987 as Minister of Conservation and of Housing. In the latter role she encouraged the papakāinga housing policy, allowing houses to be built on communally owned Māori land. In 1989, she became Minister of Health and occupied the government front bench, becoming the first woman to do so.[93] In August of that year, when Geoffrey Palmer succeeded David Lange as prime minister, she became

Women celebrate the launch of Vaine Mo'oni , the new Tongan Methodist Church complex, in New Lynn, Auckland, in 1994. The name of the church translates as 'the new vine', and its opening was a highly significant event for Auckland's large Tongan community, providing them with a spiritual and social centre. *Photograph by Glenn Jowitt, Museum of New Zealand Te Papa Tongarewa, Wellington, O.027953*

deputy prime minister. The aspirations of the feminists of the 1890s appeared to be fulfilled when, in December 1993, almost precisely a century after women's suffrage, Helen Clark became the first woman to lead a major political party when she was elected leader of the Opposition Labour Party.[94]

Those men, and some were politicians, who had thought women were to be judged for their looks or were merely 'good for a laugh', faced a new climate by the late 1980s and 1990s as women took on more and more positions of responsibility. The boys' club atmosphere in Parliament noted by Marilyn Waring seemed, however, to have changed little from the 1890s: as MP Anne Fraser walked past the bench in 1984 to be sworn in, front bencher Michael Cox still felt free to say: 'You're a real cutie, Anne.' In the late nineteenth century, members had worried that if women were allowed to stand for Parliament, their presence in the house 'might excite a great deal of sentiment' and detract from the work of politics.[95] Annette King, who entered the house as Labour MP for Horowhenua 100 years later, in 1984, found Parliament '*incredibly*' sexist'.[96] All this had to change when New Zealand had two women prime ministers in a row.

In December 1997, Jenny Shipley became leader of the National-led coalition government and the first woman prime minister of New Zealand. The previous year had seen an important change to the electoral system, the introduction of MMP, a development supported by groups such as the Women's Electoral Lobby who argued that it would lead to greater representation of women in the House. That faith was borne out by the fact that women members comprised 30 per cent of the new Parliament.[97]

Jenny Shipley faced Helen Clark in the November 1999 general election. By that time, Labour had reached its goal of having women as 50 per cent of its candidates. The results of that election saw Helen Clark become prime minister; the election of New Zealand's first Pacific Island woman MP, Winnie Laban; and the election of the first transsexual MP, Georgina Beyer.[98] The new millennium looked to be promising for diversity.

Singer Lorde performs at the Fonda Theatre on 24 September 2013 in Los Angeles, California. Born Ella Marija Lani Yelich-O'Connor in Auckland in 1996, Lorde rose to international fame as a singer-songwriter with her hit single, 'Royals' in 2013. She won numerous awards, including two Grammy awards, and was named one of the world's most influential teenagers by *Time* magazine. *Photograph by Chelsea Lauren, Getty Images, 181783642*

Chapter Fourteen
Shaping the New Millennium

Ella Yelich-O'Connor was just three years old when New Zealand entered the twenty-first century. By 2016 everyone knows her as Lorde, and her music can be heard throughout the world. A confident young woman with a number one on the *Billboard* Hot 100, she has been fêted at international award ceremonies and honoured at home. Assured in her songwriting and singing, Lorde is also unafraid to express her opinions. Of American singer Selena Gomez's song 'Come and Get It', she said, 'I'm sick of women being portrayed in this way.' Lorde is a declared feminist, and has spoken out against artists who say they are not feminists because they 'love guys'. 'A lot of girls think it's not shaving under their arms and burning bras and hating boys,' she has said, 'which just seems stone age to me.'[1]

Louise Upston (b.1971), aged twenty-nine at the turn of the new century, never called herself a feminist, saying proudly: 'I'm not interested in being a flag waver.' From a generation that benefited from the efforts of second-wave feminism to ensure that 'girls can do anything', Upston grew up in a world where it was not unusual for women to be members of Parliament – and from a young age she was determined to be one of them.[2] She became a management consultant and mother of three children, then, at the age of thirty-seven, received the National Party nomination for the Taupō electorate, winning the seat in the election of 2008. Louise Upston believes 'political correctness has invaded our homes, lives and minds'.[3] When appointed Minister of Women's Affairs in 2014, she was quick to reassure the public that she was not a feminist and that she thought beauty contests were good for women's confidence.[4]

Merimeri Penfold (1920–2014), aged eighty at the advent of the new millennium, regarded herself as a 'quiet feminist'. 'It's in the nature of women,' she commented in 2005, 'that they're close to the real issues and very often they're more committed.'[5] A trained teacher, she promoted total-immersion Māori language education, worked alongside others in the Maori Women's Welfare League, and became the first woman to teach Māori language at a New Zealand university. She became an authority on classical Māori spoken on the marae but, as a woman, could not speak there herself. Comfortable with the pace of change, Penfold recognised that 'it takes time for Maori to make adjustments to centuries-old protocol and tikanga. It will take time to convince Maori men that women should have a marae voice.'[6]

JE ARE KARIOI

Tivaevae are treasured quilts made by Cook Islands women, appliqued and embroidered with geometric, plant and animal designs in bright colours. This tivaevae was made in 1996–97 by Mi'i Quarter. Commissioned by TV2, it features the TV2 logo and was used in an advertising campaign, suggesting the important place of Pacific Island culture in New Zealand. *Museum of New Zealand Te Papa Tongarewa, Wellington, FE011186*

Skilled cooks have always been celebrated. Chelsea Winter and Nadia Lim join a long line of writers such as Alison Holst, Lois Daish and Annabel Langbein who have published cookbooks for the general market. *Chelsea Winter*, Homemade Happiness, *Random House NZ, Auckland, 2015. Nadia Lim*, Easy Week Night Meals, *Allen & Unwin, Auckland, 2015*

The vocabulary of feminism may be found across the generations, and whether that language is accepted or rejected, it is likely that most women welcome the changes in education, law and social expectations that have reshaped women's lives in the nineteenth and twentieth centuries. The new millennium saw a raft of new challenges: from individual dilemmas around career and family to demographic shifts that include Pākehā women outnumbering men in older age groups and the Māori birth rate declining. Although the country is seen by many from outside New Zealand as a 'Woman's Land' where, in 2000, all the highest positions of state were held by women, longstanding issues about the work of caring, the feminisation of poverty with the decline of the breadwinner wage, and the real meaning of equality remain unresolved.

Recreating the family

Tahlia first saw Phillippa at Auckland's Hero Party. Soon the pair became friends and lovers, and in January 2010 they became engaged. For them marriage through a civil union meant they could 'formalise their relationship and share their love for each other with family and friends'. Fifty family members and close friends, most of whom had never attended a civil union before, joined them for the ceremony at the Stonewillow Café in Pukekohe in March 2011. One guest was moved to ask Tahlia's mother: 'Is the ceremony so lovely because they are gay?'[7] Tahlia and Phillippa were amongst 133 female couples who married in 2011 under the Civil Union Act 2004. That Act, and the accompanying

Relationships (Statutory References) Act, enabled all couples, whether married, in a civil union or in a de facto relationship, to have the same general rights and obligations.[8]

Earlier, in 1996, three lesbian couples in long-term relationships had sought marriage licences and been denied them. They took their case to the High Court to determine whether the Human Rights Act 1993, which protected all New Zealanders from discrimination on the grounds of sexual orientation, and the New Zealand Bill of Rights, overrode the Marriage Act 1955 that did not allow marriage of persons of the same sex. At the time of the 1955 Act, the purpose of marriage was still held to be procreation. The advent of effective contraception, however, and the fact that the law did not prohibit marriage for the elderly or those otherwise unable to have children would seem to have undermined this purpose. In holding that the denial of marriage to gay couples was not discriminatory, Justice Tipping concluded: '[The question] as to whether modern society wished to maintain the traditional concept of marriage was one for the legislature and not the courts to decide'.[9] In 2005, the legislature decided that a majority of New Zealanders supported civil unions for gay couples: marriage remained a step too far.

Couples united through civil union were denied a right that heterosexual partners could exercise: that of adopting children. 'Currently a gay individual can adopt a child, but a gay couple can't,' noted Labour MP Jacinda Ardern, sponsor of the Care of Children Law Reform Bill in August 2012, which she introduced the day after a Bill to recognise gay marriage passed its first reading in Parliament. Ardern sought to iron out inconsistencies in the law under which a de facto heterosexual couple could adopt a child but a civil union couple could not.[10]

By 2012, the majority of New Zealanders appeared ready to accept gay marriage, recognising that the sex of the partners made no difference to marriage as a personal commitment. The Marriage (Definition of Marriage) Amendment Bill was introduced that year by Labour MP Louisa Wall, a former Silver (netball) and Black (rugby) Fern of Ngāti Tūwharetoa and Waikato ancestry. Wall, who had worked for the Children's Commission and the Ministry of Women's Affairs, was in a civil union partnership with Prue Kapua, a lawyer, whom she had met through the Maori Women's Welfare League.[11] Nikki Kaye, National MP for Auckland Central, commended the Bill's introduction, saying that it enshrined 'a principle that society supports loving and committed relationships between two individuals'.[12] Labour's Su'a William Sio, however, made it clear he would be voting against the Bill, which he said offended the Pacific Islanders in his Māngere electorate.[13] Sio wrote in the *Samoan Observer*:

> I have received strong views from our Pacific community, the Asian community as well as Muslims regarding this topic. I believe the majority [of them] hold to the belief that a marriage is a divine covenant made between a man and a woman and that covenant remains from beginning until the end of time.[14]

In its October/November 2015 issue, *Mana* magazine ran a feature on marriage, family and diversity in sexual relationships. Featured on the cover were (from left) Rev. Hirini Kaa, Louisa Wall, Ramon Te Wake, Miki-Tae Tapara and Ray Pye. Ramon Te Wake was one of the three presenters of Takatāpui, which was Māori Television's first ever lesbian, gay, bisexual, and transgender (LGBT) show. A transwoman of Te Rarawa, Ngāpuhi and Ngāti Whātua descent, she has made her mark as a television presenter, director and a singer-songwriter. Mana Magazine, *No.125, cover, photograph by Qiane Matata-Sipu*

Le'au Asenati Lole-Taylor, of New Zealand First, shared this stance, calling the debate a 'waste of time' when there were more urgent issues facing the country.[15] But most MPs disagreed, and the Act was passed on 17 April 2013, in front of a full public gallery. The vote was eighty votes to forty, with one abstention.

Marriage, once the ceremony in which women promised to 'love, honour and obey', was being reshaped in the twenty-first century as a ceremony of commitment between two people who may be of the same sex. Yet marriage itself had been on the decline from 1971. Women with educational opportunities became more likely to plan their lives around careers than marriage, with relationships alongside work and childbearing, they hope, strategically timed. In 2011, the median age at marriage was 32.1 years for men and 30 for women; it was 23.5 and 21.2, respectively, in 1971. The proportion of Pākehā and Asian women born in the 1950s who do not have children has risen to around 11.5 per cent, whereas the rise in childlessness for Māori and Pacific Island women has been much smaller; around 9 per cent of Māori and 8 per cent of Pacific Island women born in the 1950s remained childless.[16] Young women who bear children early and hence interrupt their education are often left to raise the child alone, facing financial and emotional stress. Gender makes childbearing an issue for all women, but social class and ethnic identity determine the outcomes in very different ways.

Susan Baragwanath made it her business to assist young single mothers. The associate principal of Porirua College, in a low-income area of Wellington, she despaired that pregnancy meant the end of education for some of her pupils.[17] In the early 1990s, she began campaigning for a daycare centre at the school so that young women would not automatically drop out of school after the birth of their children. In November 1994, He Huarahi Tamariki School for teenage mothers – and later fathers – opened. There, students who had had their education interrupted received lessons while their children were looked after. Among the many success stories, Susan Baragwanath pointed to Carrie Trevathan as the 'face of the future' in 2001. From a family of eleven children, Carrie had Māori, Samoan, German, Jewish and Pākehā ancestors. Carrie's son was born when she was sixteen. At twenty she was sitting Bursary examinations and planning to study arts and languages at Victoria University in 2002.[18] The school continues to thrive and there is now a network of teen parent schools throughout the country, from Northland to Southland, which have allowed young women to set new goals for themselves. When Helen Woolner, sixteen years old and pregnant, enrolled at He Huarahi Tamariki in 2005, 'primarily because they were offering a free lunch', she never imagined that by 2010 she would be enrolled for PhD study in Chemistry at Victoria University.[19]

By 2002, the number of children born within marriage in New Zealand had plummeted to 56 per cent, from 91 per cent in 1962.[20] But as the importance of legal marriage declined, the government moved to ensure that those who entered de facto unions had their contribution to the partnership – monetary or otherwise – recognised in the case of relationship breakdown. In 2002, in recognition that marriage was no longer the essential precursor to long-term relationships, the existing marital property legislation was renamed the Property (Relationships) Act, and was extended to cover same-sex and de facto relationships.[21]

While choices for entering coupledom have increased, the number of sole parents has risen. In 1998, for example, 28.3 per cent of all families with children were headed by only one parent – usually a woman.[22] Apart from choosing to bear and raise children alone, women might be widowed, separated or divorced. Compared to men, women generally have lower incomes and lower standards of living after divorce, largely because they remain primarily responsible for the children and therefore limit their commitment to employment.[23] The divorce rate, at 12 per 1,000 existing marriages, remained fairly stable during the 1980s and 1990s, but as cohabitation became much more common, divorce became a less reliable indicator of relationship breakdown.

Another new trend lay in the willingness of fathers to care for their children. In 2001, a total of 6,400 children under five lived with a solo father – an increase of almost 300 per cent from 1981. Forty per cent of these children were Māori.[24] The rising number of men caring for children may have had less to do with a desire to expand traditional sex roles than with the fact that it has become easier for women to get paid work and young women have aspirations beyond full-time motherhood.

In 2004, the co-leader of the Māori Party, Tariana Turia, addressed the first National Māori Sexual and Reproductive Health Conference and reminded the delegates of 'respect for whare tangata', the women through whom the children of the ancestors enter the world. She could see little good in a declining Māori birth rate.[25]

By 2005, the Māori fertility rate stood at 2.6 births per woman, and the rate for Pacific Island women was slightly higher. Asian and Pākehā women have the lowest rates, and women in the major urban centres have lower fertility rates than women in rural areas.[26] Couples are delaying and limiting births, and the connection between childbirth and marriage has become increasingly tenuous.

A revolution in conceiving children took place in the last decades of the twentieth century. Children may now be born to numerous parents: a biological mother who donated an embryo, a birth mother, a donor father who gifted sperm, and a social father. The earlier bedrock of family formation – a father and a mother – has been expanded by parenting by homosexual couples. And the control of fertility that the Pill promised is now sought in the reverse situation – the control of infertility. Women seek fertility treatment for a variety of reasons: some delay childbearing until beyond their most fertile years, others may find their fertility compromised by their own or their partner's health status, or some may choose to bear children with another woman, or alone.[27] The demand for infertility services grew quickly over the 1980s and beyond so that the government had to increase funding for hospital boards in order to assist people seeking treatment.[28]

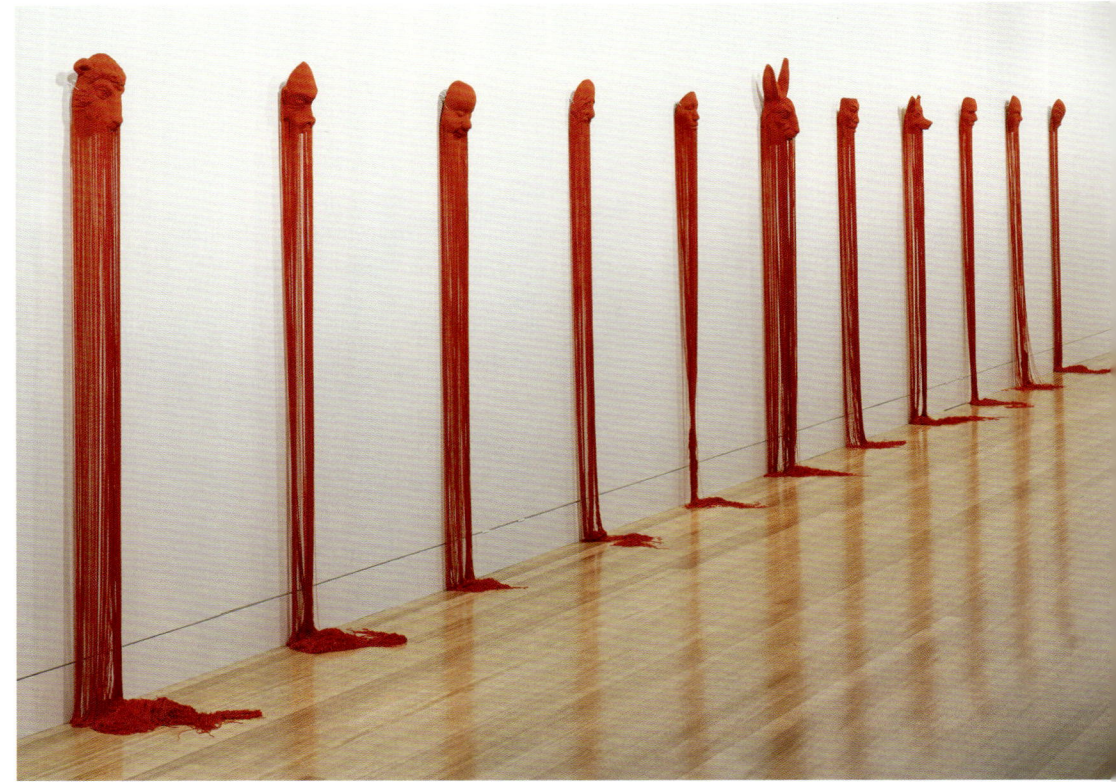

Chinese New Zealander Yuk King Tan made this work, a series of red masks, in 1998. The eleven masks represent symbolic animals from the Chinese calendar, an 'alien' mask, and a wax mask of the artist's face. Masks both hide and reveal facial features, and Tan uses them to draw attention to stereotypes of 'alien' cultures within society. *Museum of New Zealand Te Papa Tongarewa, Wellington, 1999-0012-1/A-K to K-K*

The potential for multiple parents through IVF is also present through family dissolution and reformation. One in five children today grows up, mostly for a short time, in a blended family that includes children from former partnerships.[29] Step-parents, once the dreaded figures of fairy tales, and common through the death of one or other parent, are now common through serial relationships. And their position is seldom easy. One stepmother commented:

> Once he and I set up house together, his sons didn't want to stay with their mother after all, but they came to live mostly with us. If they got fed up with their father or me, they [went] back to her.[30]

Step-parents do extraordinarily well in the difficult task of parenting, but at times it all proves too much. Children are much more at risk of violence from step-parents than from biological parents.[31] And child abuse statistics reveal that children who live in households with unrelated adults are almost fifty times as likely to die from an inflicted injury as children raised in households with two biological parents.[32] New Zealand's high levels of child abuse have spurred public outrage.[33] In 2007, Māori Party co-leader Pita Sharples expressed the view that 'problems of child abuse stemmed from a dysfunctional culture which happened among poverty-stricken and underachieving communities, a group in which Maori were too highly represented'. These, he believed, were 'people who had stopped dreaming and were just coping'.[34] Lacking hope for their own lives, they were unable to imagine positive futures for children in their care.

In 2005 one young woman's view of the future included:

> A career to get passionate about, a healthy balanced lifestyle, some travel and an active social life ... I think that every working class girl's dream now is to be able to choose to improve herself and her options without getting into extreme debilitating debt.[35]

Until the 1960s, a woman's future depended upon marrying a good provider – a form of dependency rejected by to feminists. Women's move into the workforce, and better employment opportunities, put the emphasis on their independence. Political changes have supported the idea of individual responsibility, and this has manifested itself in ways unimaginable even fifty years ago. Students now pay for their tertiary education (women, who in general still earn less than men, find it more difficult to do so); 30 per cent of New Zealanders now have private health insurance; and women and men need to save for retirement.[36] The latter is of crucial importance to the generation of baby-boom women who are now making up the swelling ranks of senior citizens.

Whose traditions?

New Zealand/Aotearoa has become home to an immense diversity of immigrants who bring different customs with respect to gender roles. In the nineteenth century, migrants from various regions of Great Britain and Europe brought their own traditions, which contrasted with those of Māori and, in the case of property, disadvantaged Māori women. Settlers from different places had different expectations of their wives and daughters. Some came from communities where, for example, it was expected that men would hand over their wages publicly to their wives as a matter of masculine honour, whereas in other migrant groups women might see little of their husband's earnings.[37] As the generations of New Zealand-born increased, the various aspirations of the original migrants flattened out and new settlers brought different traditions. For all migrant people, it takes time to change deep-seated beliefs and practices.

Samoa was the main source of Pacific migration to New Zealand in 2005, followed by Fiji, Tonga and the Cook Islands. A growing proportion of immigrant women now come from various parts of Asia, such as South Korea, China, India and Sri Lanka, and from Africa – South Africa, Zimbabwe and Somalia.[38]

Luisa Avaiki, long-serving captain of the New Zealand women's rugby league team, believes her Samoan family instilled the values of commitment, hard work and faith in God that allowed her to succeed. She advises younger women to believe in who they are as Polynesian women, to know that their cultures, personalities and differences are 'valuable and unique'. Such differences are made manifest in the arts and in other areas of life, as well as in sport, but Avaiki sees the 'physicality and athleticism' that Māori and Pacific Island women bring to her chosen game as leading to the high regard in which the women's rugby team is held.[39]

Golf is the game at which Lydia Ko excels, and one that many Koreans enjoy. Born in Seoul on 24 April 1997, Ko was five when she moved to New Zealand with her family as part of a wave of migrants from South Korea in the 2000s. Like many Koreans, Ko's family settled in Auckland. Lydia attended Pinehurst School in Albany, but by the age of fourteen was winning professional golf tournaments (and continuing her education by correspondence). She took a number of 'youngest ever' titles, and on 2 February 2015 became the world's number one ranked woman professional golfer.[40]

According to the 2013 Census, 12 per cent of New Zealanders identified with at least one Asian ethnicity.[41] 'Banana' is a slang self-identification of Asians who have grown up in the west: 'yellow on the outside, white on the inside'. *Banana in a Nutshell* was the title chosen by Chinese New Zealander Roseanne Liang for her award-winning 2005 autobiographical documentary.[42] Like many new immigrants, Roseanne's Hong Kong-born parents expected their New Zealand-born children to work hard. Roseanne became dux of her high school and achieved entry to medical school. In the event, she deferred her place in order to follow her passion for film-making and telling stories.[43] Her debut feature film, *My Wedding and Other Secrets* (2011), built on the original documentary and her own experience of falling in love with a Pākehā man. *New Zealand Herald* reviewer Peter Calder described it as 'a cracker of a film' about the stress of being stranded between two cultures.[44]

Around 46,000 New Zealanders are Muslim.[45] In 2004, two Afghani Muslim women refused to remove their burqas (all-encompassing cloaks that have only a slit for the eyes) when appearing as witnesses in court. The requirement that women be covered is often perceived by those in the west as the key 'highly visible symbol of the subordination of women in Islam'.[46] The Islamic Women's Council apparently supported the women's wish to remain veiled, but the judge ruled that the women should unveil, wear headscarves and give testimony from behind a screen, so that they would be seen only by the judge, lawyers and female court staff.[47] The two women were asserting their right to dress as they wished – a right most women in the west take for granted.

The challenge to ideas about gender equality has come not just from outside the country, however. When Māori-language proponent Cathy Dewes was elected to the Te Arawa Trust Board in 1994, it took a High Court decision to enable her to take her seat

Farah and Aalia Mohammed of Auckland play netball in 2010. The sisters stopped playing for their local netball league because they were expected to wear short skirts, which was not acceptable in their Muslim faith. Their mother, Tasneem, later set up the Muslimah Sports Association with funding from Manukau City Council. *Photograph by Michelle Hyslop*, The Aucklander, *AUC-1006300*

A tino rangitiratanga flag flies among other banners of Māori independence as thousands of marchers gather outside Parliament on 5 May 2004 to protest against legislation that asserted Crown ownership of the foreshore and seabed. Marchers regarded this as a further act of confiscation. *Photo by Kenny Rodger,* New Zealand Herald, *NZH-1002071*

against the wishes of the male incumbents.[48] In other arenas, a new respect for indigenous traditions could conflict with ideas about women's rights. In 1999, a Northland iwi expressed concern that the Department of Conservation had hired a woman of childbearing age as a weeds officer, because her job would take her into sacred sites in the Waipoua Forest. Te Roroa spokesman Garry Hooker said 'it was culturally inappropriate for women of childbearing age to go into wahi tapu (reserved ground) areas due to menstruation'. The department undertook to work alongside Te Roroa to ensure that their concerns were respected while at the same time not discriminating against the best-qualified employee for the job.[49]

The Treaty of Waitangi and the Census speak in terms of Māori and Pākehā, but nearly 70,000 New Zealanders live in relationships that combine Māori and non-Māori. Anthropologist John Harré studied marriage between Māori and Pākehā in New Zealand in the 1960s. One of his respondents, a Pākehā woman, described the impact of her marriage and the fluidity of identity:

Belli Faha, Suzanne Antony and Nairata Hari (with others) perform traditional dances at the 2015 Diwali festival at Tīmaru. Diwali, the Hindu Festival of Lights, is now celebrated around the country, with events that are attended by many New Zealanders. *Photograph by John Bisset, Fairfax Media,* Timaru Herald

I said to Charlie: 'Now either we're going to be Maoris or Pakehas but we can't mix the two – apart from anything else it wouldn't be fair on the kids.' We were pretty sure that everyone would look on them as Maoris, and I was very happy to live as a Maori, so that's what we decided … One thing it meant for me [was] becoming a Ratana, but the main thing was I started to think of myself as a Maori.[50]

Not clearly identifying with one group or the other, however, brought its own problems. Deirdre Walker, a Pākehā married to distinguished Māori author and academic Ranginui Walker, observed that: '[S]ociety treated kids from cross-cultural marriages unfairly. Society labelled them "Maori" and then blamed them for not knowing what that meant, and in the same breadth challenged them, "What's Maori about you?"'[51] For her, ideas about equality between the sexes created more issues than race. 'Rangi was talking about dividing his mother's property for the boys, not including our daughter. I had to talk to him about that!'[52]

Official ethnicity statistics in New Zealand are based on an individual's self-definition. Māori, according to current analysis, are the 'most likely to identify with more than one ethnic group'.[53] In 2006, nearly 20 per cent of children aged under fifteen were reported as belonging to two or more ethnic groups. In 2013, around one in ten people identified with more than one ethnic group: 'Europeans' made up 67.6 per cent of the population and Māori 14.6 per cent. The fastest-growing population groups were people of Asian and Pacific Island descent.[54]

Marriage, home and family have brought together people from many backgrounds, so that marriage (whether formal or informal) is the place where New Zealand is truly multicultural. The complexity of this has to be resolved on a daily basis, and mothers are often at the centre of family conflicts caused by children 'caught between cultures' and who require a lot of support.[55] Higher birth rates among Māori and Pacific Island people may lead to the 'browning' of New Zealand; one prediction is that by 2031, close to one-third of all New Zealand school-age children will be Māori.[56] Yet family forms themselves are now multiple, and the expectations of roles within them have been recast. Māori families increasingly contain members 'with no whakapapa links to other whānau members', whereas Pacific Island women, followed by Asian women, are those most likely to live in an extended family.[57]

Senior women

Still working at age ninety-two, Dulcie Richards regarded the toilets and changing shed at Tongapōrutu Recreation Reserve in Taranaki as her 'gold mine'. Aboard her mobility scooter, and accompanied by her broom and Dettol, Dulcie travelled to the reserve from her riverside bach nearby. What had once been a labour of love had turned into a paid job, perhaps the final one for a woman who had worked since the age of fourteen. The oldest worker employed by the New Plymouth District Council, Dulcie earned around $995 in 2005. Dulcie said her needs were small: 'I am one of those people that's content with a jam tin and a beer crate to sit on. As long as I have a roof that doesn't leak I am happy.' But one thing she was determined to preserve was her right to live in her bach, and she led a campaign to seek preservation of the baches on the Tongapōrutu River as 'Kiwiana icons'.[58]

While Dulcie's independence and longevity are exceptional, they are part of a pattern in which, between 1950 and 2000, women's life expectancy increased dramatically – by nearly ten years. The life expectancy of Pākehā women at birth was by then 81.9 years, while for Māori women it was 73.2 years. Māori women were more likely than other women to keep working over age sixty-five, perhaps because of greater financial need.[59]

The experience of a long working life, of raising a family and participating in a multitude of other pursuits means that a great many women in their sixties, seventies and older have benefited from the gains advanced by the second wave of feminism that began in the 1960s and 1970s. But old pressures and assumptions persist. Airbrushed advertisements exhort older women to buy an ever-proliferating range of 'anti-ageing' products. Expensive creams promise to erase wrinkles; 'control' or 'shapewear' undergarments are marketed to remove 'unsightly bulges'; and time can apparently be 'reversed' through the use of hair dye.[60] There are few role models for an attractive old age, though British actors Judi Dench and Helen Mirren are frequently held up as successful models of 'youthful ageing'.[61]

In the early 1990s, Anne Noble took a series of photographs of Gladys Thetford and her daughter Audrey, entitled *Hidden Lives: The Work of Care*. Audrey was disabled, and lived at home with her mother. But as these photographs show, the care was mutual. In the top photograph, 'The Thetfords cooking together', Gladys supports Audrey as she works in the kitchen; in the bottom photograph, Audrey assists her mother as she washes her hair. *Photographs by Anne Noble, Museum of New Zealand Te Papa Tongarewa, Wellington, O.027961/3; O.027961/2*

In 2015 Trina Nesbitt spent five months living in a caravan with her two children because she could not find affordable rental accommodation in Christchurch. After the earthquake of February 2011, the house she was living in was renovated and the landlord tripled the rent. She was forced to move from one short-term home to another, and her situation became desperate when she lost her job. She finally secured a state house in North Canterbury. *Photograph by John Kirk-Anderson, Fairfax Media,* The Press

In New Zealand, Geraldine Brophy, Lynda Milligan and Jude Gibson, who make up the theatre group Grumpy Old Women, take a satirical approach to the subject of ageing gracefully. In their show entitled *Fifty Shades of Beige*, described as an 'orgy of middle-aged mayhem', they teach the art of 'grumpy grooming', 'the joy of large pants, a free nagging master class (how to get your own way without him even noticing)', and 'beards for women, which style will suit you'.[62] For Grumpy Old Women, humour is an essential antidote to the earnest, dreary manner in which old age is usually depicted.

Women are likely to outlive men by five years, meaning that an increasing proportion of women live in homes alone. In 2001, women made up 62 per cent of those over seventy-five, and most of these women (over 95 per cent) were Pākehā.[63] At sixty-five, women are entitled to universal superannuation, so that there is less difference between the incomes of retired women and men than there is in countries with contributory pensions.[64]

Of those aged eighty-five-and over, 19 per cent of men and 31 per cent of women are in residential care.[65] *Caring Counts* is the title of a 2012 Human Rights Commission report into the aged-care workforce. As many as 48,000 workers, the great majority of whom are women, perform the work of care in residential homes for the elderly.[66] Nearly a quarter of

Maria Patau (right) packs Mallowpuff biscuits alongside other workers at the Griffins factory, Lower Hutt, in February 1995. All the packers are women, while the white coat of inspection is worn by a man. *Photograph by Melanie Burford, Alexander Turnbull Library, Wellington, EP/1995/C0513/24-F*

those carers are migrants from the Philippines, China, the Pacific Islands and elsewhere.[67] Because the work is done by women and is caring in nature, it is underpaid: one worker said that an eighteen-year-old working at the fast-food restaurant Burger King was paid more than she was.[68] Maintenance men and gardeners at residential facilities are routinely paid more than the women who do arduous daily tasks assisting residents with showering, dressing, eating and general mobility, as well as providing essential social contact.[69] The Human Rights Commission concluded:

> Low wages and pay inequality and inequity are three issues which dominated the Inquiry. The fact that thousands of (mainly women) are caring for vulnerable older people for barely the minimum wage is an injustice grounded in historical undervaluation of the role. It is an indignity New Zealand can no longer afford. Pay inequality between home and residential based caring and those doing much the same work in public hospitals cannot continue to be condoned when it is publicly funded. Quite simply it is a fundamental breach of human rights.[70]

Given the growing numbers of elderly (who are mainly women), the issue of proper payment is a challenge for the state, which has to meet the financial burden of

People queue for food outside the Auckland City Mission, 20 December 2012. *Photograph by Brett Phibbs,* New Zealand Herald, *NZH-1067110*

underwriting residential care. Valuing caring in a number of domains, not least in the family, remains an unsolved problem.

Working for families

Once the expectation was that men worked for families and provided for them through the breadwinner wage; the state stepped in to assist families when that wage was insufficient, through universal family benefits and unemployment assistance. The decline of the breadwinner wage reflects a new reality, one in which it cannot be assumed that people live in heterosexual nuclear families that can be supported by a single male wage.[71] Yet women continue to do the bulk of caregiving work and domestic labour. And young women who bear children without partners are likely to be in poverty.

At 30 pregnancies per 1,000 women aged between ten and nineteen, New Zealand has the second highest teenage pregnancy rate in the developed world, second only to the United States.[72] Those who choose to keep their babies often do so in a hostile climate. Once New Zealand was regarded as a great place to bring up children because most women were homemakers, but rates of child poverty doubled between 1982 and 2012. Now 25 per cent of children live in households below the poverty line (in 2013, calculated at about

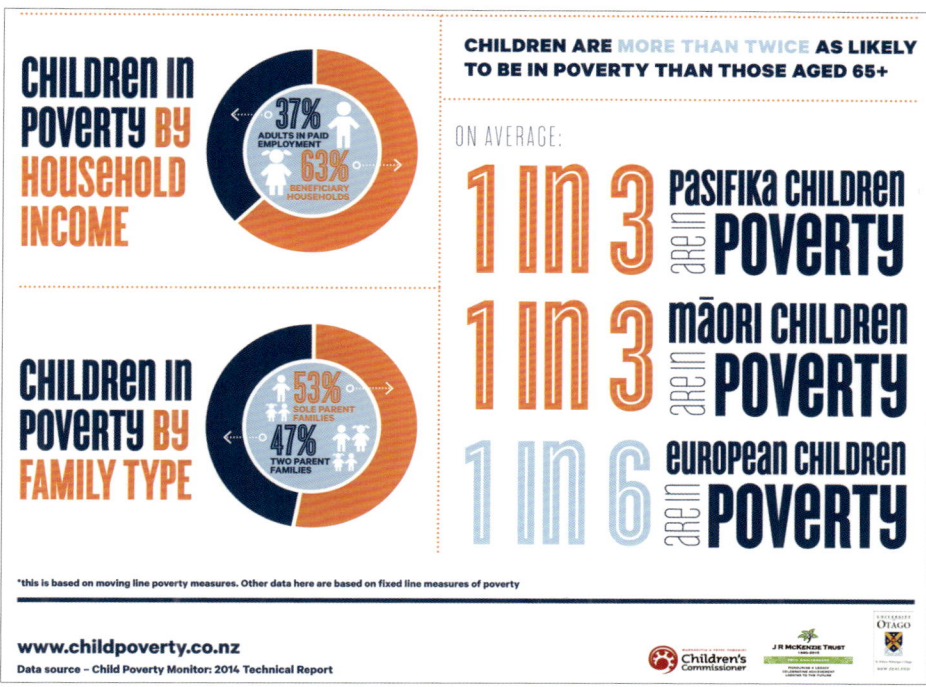

Child poverty has become a major social concern in New Zealand in the 2000s. This infographic on a poster highlighting the issue summarises the statistics in 2014. *Child Poverty Monitor*

$19,500 per annum for a sole parent with one child), and many of these are Māori and Pacific Island children.[73] In those households it is mothers who, most frequently, do the work of caring. And young mothers raising children alone are more at risk of poor physical and mental health.

With the decline in formal marriage and a move towards cohabitation, the state has been increasingly called upon to provide support once supplied by male partners. At the start of the new millennium, women made up 90 per cent of those in receipt of the Domestic Purposes Benefit.[74] The number of recipients doubled between 1981 (39,000) and 1991 (97,000), and reached 100,087 in 2001; Māori women represented over one-third of beneficiaries. From 1981 to 2001, there was a dramatic 22 per cent increase in parents with children who had not had a long-term relationship, signalling the rapid decline of the link between marriage and reproduction.[75]

Growing concern about welfare dependency in Māori communities, and the view that it leads to a cycle of generational poverty, prompted some activists to look for radical solutions. One of them was Donna Awatere Huata, MP for the ACT Party from 1996 to 2003, and briefly an Independent before leaving Parliament in 2004. Awatere Huata was a radical promoter of free-market reform. 'I live in Bridge Pa, Hastings,' she said in

2001, 'where about 80 per cent are on some sort of benefit. I see young Maori sole mothers raising kids from serial fathers.'[76] In her view, teenagers should not be eligible for the DPB. The benefit, she believed, had become an easy option for young women, and it had done nothing to change men's behaviour: 'They can carry on being abusers rather than providers because our welfare system takes over their responsibilities.'[77] She also had advice for young people, and made it her business to visit high schools to tell them: 'Don't you dare bring another human being into this world until you can give them the security they deserve. Two committed parents, financial security, time, wisdom, and the gifts of your own sense of achievement and happiness.'[78]

But it wasn't just young Māori in the reformers' sights. From March 2003, all those in receipt of the DPB came under increased pressure to get jobs, and were required to work with case managers in developing 'Personal Development and Employment Plans'. By then, the numbers on the DPB were declining, and the new policy accelerated the change. In 1998, a total of 10.5 per cent of women aged between eighteen and forty-nine were receiving the DPB; by 2001, the proportion stood at 7 per cent.[79]

Despite the changing social climate, and the increasing pressure even for young women beneficiaries to join the paid workforce, mothers remain the primary caregivers for children. In 2001, Statistics New Zealand recorded that 68 per cent of mothers with dependent children worked in paid employment, compared with 91 per cent of men. Mothers with children under one were the least likely to participate in the labour force (39 per cent), but 83 per cent of women were in work by the time their youngest child was at secondary school.[80]

To facilitate combining work and family, in 2002 the Labour–Alliance government passed the Parental Leave and Employment Protection (Paid Parental Leave) Act. In July 2006, its twelve weeks' paid parental leave provisions were extended to fourteen weeks.[81] In Sweden, a couple can take up to thirteen months between them, with government recompense for lost wages up to 80 per cent, and men are encouraged to take parental leave; in comparison New Zealand's recognition of the work of childcare appears minimal. Various proposals to improve the situation have been mooted, but to date little has changed. Policy analysts Paul Callister and Judith Galtry suggest that longer leave and creating eligibility for fathers would contribute to child health and gender equity.[82]

Nonetheless, a raft of policies entitled 'Working for Families' (introduced in 2002) improved the childcare subsidies for both preschool and after-school care available to low-income families. The new tax credits associated with the programme also benefited middle-income families with dependent children. One aim was to make the income derived from working more attractive than being on a benefit. The policies, introduced at a time of economic buoyancy, appeared to have been effective.[83] But difficulties arose with the international economic downturn of 2008. Getting people into jobs was possible when work was available but much less feasible when the unemployment rate rose to between 6 and 7 per cent (with some of those in employment working fewer hours). By March 2014, women's labour-force participation rate was 63.7 per cent, compared to 75 per cent for men. Women were more likely to be unemployed than men (6.4 per cent compared to 5.6 per cent), and unemployment rates were highest for Māori and Pacific Island women.[84]

Despite the considerable social advances since women began entering the workforce in numbers after the Second World War, most jobs remain organised on the traditional model of the male worker without family commitments. It is not surprising that some women prefer to cut down on paid work rather than sacrifice family time. In the first New Zealand survey of work–life balance taken in 2006, 40 per cent of New Zealanders reported having 'some or a lot of difficulty' in getting the balance they wanted, and 46 per cent said they experienced 'some degree of work–life conflict'. Employees particularly wanted flexible start and finish times. Thirty-one per cent wanted to be able to take school holidays off.[85]

In response, in 2007 the government introduced the Flexible Working Hours Arrangement Act which enables employees to request flexibility, and encourages employers to treat such requests with due consideration. The intention was to assist parents to cope with the needs of their children, and children to assist with the needs of elderly parents. A great many working women of the baby-boom generation find themselves having to juggle the needs of both children and elderly parents. In other families, one or other parent will choose to work at night so that someone is there for the children during the day. As the survey of work–life balance revealed, this kind of arrangement has 'significant costs', including fatigue and a divided family life.[86]

Earning and spending

The spending power of the increased number of women workers has fuelled consumer industries in fashion, restaurants and household goods. Women can now shop, or serve in shops, during the weekend or (in the case of supermarkets) late into the night. From 1990, shops could be open for twenty-four hours a day. In the 1970s, in comparison, most businesses shut down for the weekend and workers were recompensed for working outside 'normal hours'.[87] While the flexibility of supermarket hours suits working women well, couples may now be working at different times. 'Family time' that was a given when most workplaces shut down in the weekend and shop trading hours were more limited might now require planning and coordination.

In 2005, the most common paid occupation for a woman was as a service worker or sales assistant.[88] Despite hopes that the 'girls can do anything' campaign would broaden women's options, old patterns of expectation regarding feminine service mean these remain the staple and low-paid occupations of unskilled women. Pacific Island women, especially, are more likely to work as cleaners than as anything else.[89] Lily described the precarious nature of such work:

I work 15 hours a day. We have low-skilled jobs which give low pay. We keep getting more work but fewer hours. A company may come along and drive down the hours. What you used to do in 40 hours a week, it's now 30 hours or 25. You do the same amount of work, or more, and get less pay.[90]

Deregulation of working hours, while benefiting consumers in terms of convenience, can take a heavy toll on these workers who are expected to be available at all hours yet may not be able to predict those hours from week to week.

But perhaps the most dramatic change for workers has been the disappearance of the forty-hour week. According to Annie Newman, assistant secretary of the Northern Region of the Service and Food Workers' Union:

It is quite common in the cleaning industry for women to be working three jobs in order to get enough hours to make ends meet. And you could say 'Well, we should go back to the eight-hour day' but a lot of our members wouldn't give a thank you for the eight-hour day, because they actually need a lot more to bring up their families. There are a lot of problems in trying to deliver a reasonable standard of living to workers, which go way beyond the rate of pay that they are getting.[91]

Women's labour-force participation has grown at double the rate of men's in recent decades. Whether to work or not is no longer a choice. But the assumption that women are mainly responsible for the unpaid work at home, for taking care of children, and for supporting the elderly means that the cost of being a mother remains higher than the cost of being a father.

Glowing stories about women who have made it to the top feature frequently in the media but can mask the fact that the majority of women earn less than men, remain responsible for housework, and occupy a limited range of occupations that involve 'caring for others, serving others and/or assuming a position of comparatively lower status'.[92] Whereas once a service economy operated within marriage, with unpaid women working for the families of breadwinning men, it now operates in the market, with women as the main providers in service and caring occupations. As Ellen from Northland commented in a Federation of Graduate Women survey: 'Women have always worked. The thing is, occasionally they now get paid.'[93]

OPPOSITE: *Top left* In 1981 Peri Drysdale established Snowy Peak Ltd as a small business in Christchurch, with ten outworkers knitting garments from natural fibres. Later the company brought production in-house, and in 1996 launched Merinomink, a luxury yarn incorporating possum fur. In 1998 the Untouched World brand of clothing was established. Snowy Peak is now an international business regarded as an innovative leader in sustainable development. *Snowy Peak*

OPPOSITE: *Top right* Victoria Ransom, raised on a farm near Bulls, was a technology entrepreneur by her twenties, moving to the United States and establishing several successful companies. In 2012 she sold Wildfire, the social media company she had founded in 2008, to Google for around US$350 million. *Fairfax Media NZ,* Dominion Post

OPPOSITE: *Bottom* Mai Chen, who arrived in New Zealand from Taiwan with her family at the age of six, graduated as a lawyer in New Zealand, then gained a master of laws at Harvard University. In 1994 she became a foundation partner of Chen Palmer, New Zealand's only specialist public law firm. Author of legal and constitutional publications, she has held a number of government posts, and chaired the Advisory Board of New Zealand Global Women. *Fairfax Media NZ,* Dominion Post

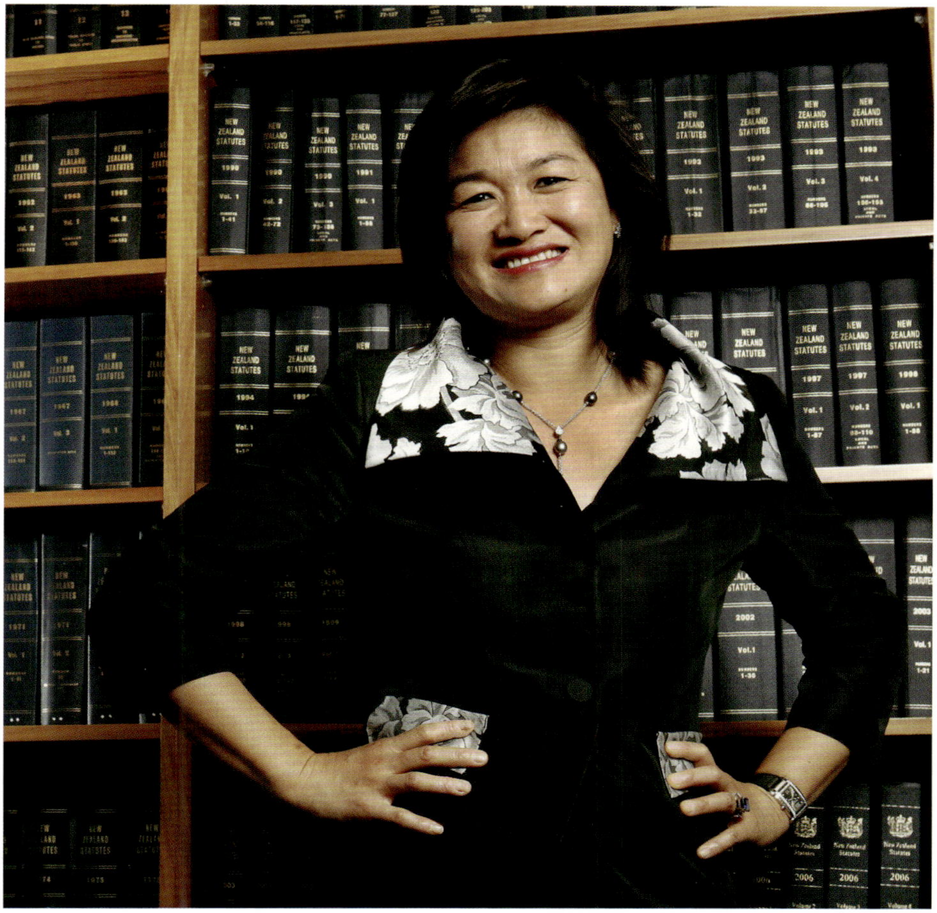

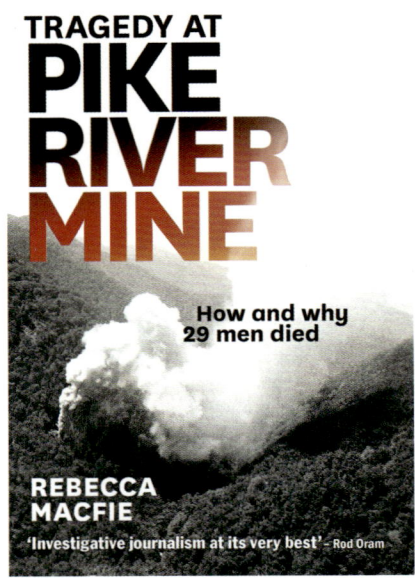

Award-winning journalist Rebecca Macfie investigated the Pike River coal mine disaster of 2010, in which twenty-nine men lost their lives. The book presented damning evidence about the causes of the mine's collapse, and identified significant management failures; Macfie also underlined the devastating impact on the miners' families and the West Coast mining community. Tragedy at Pike River Mine, *Awa Press, Wellington, 2013*

For those in the professions, and in administration and management, women's improved educational achievements have continued to open up better-paid work opportunities. By 2001, over 11 per cent of women had a degree or higher qualification, compared to only 1 per cent in 1971.[94] But the wages available to many women and the need for flexible time has encouraged some to set up businesses of their own. Peri Drysdale joined the Company of Women's New Zealand Hall of Fame for Women Entrepreneurs in 2012 for having created a 'multimillion-dollar export company'.[95] She had been brought up on a high-country sheep station and initially trained as a nurse, that quintessential service role for middle-class women. In 1981, at home with two children under three, Drysdale wanted to 'exercise the grey matter a little' and contribute to the family finances. At that time she knew little about business – not even the difference 'between an invoice and a statement, a debtor or a creditor' – but she knew that she could add value 'to some of New Zealand's primary produce' and merino wool in particular.

Drysdale created innovative knitwear designs using high-quality fibre (including possum fur combined with merino), and took women's traditional knitting skills in a new direction. She began with ten outworkers, and as demand grew, imported new generation computerised knitting machines.[96] Drysdale's vision kept production in New Zealand at a time when women were being laid off in droves from New Zealand's clothing manufacturing plant as the market was opened to China (where low-paid workers make

Flowers lie at the entrance to the Pike River coal mine as Mines Rescue staff prepare to enter on 28 June 2011 to search for the men trapped there after the methane gas explosions in November 2010. This and other recovery and inspection efforts were unsuccessful. Families continue to hope for the return of the bodies of their loved ones. *Photograph by Iain McGregor-Pool, Getty Images, 117547115*

garments for the world). A commitment to environmental sustainability underlies her business platform – and women have benefited from her entrepreneurship, both as employees and as consumers.

Drysdale's company, Snowy Peak, which encompasses the brands Untouched World and Merinomink, has achieved international acclaim: two United States Presidents, Bill Clinton and Barack Obama, have been photographed wearing Untouched World sweaters.[97] The company also became a training ground for a number of other women. The first sales manager, Ann Lockhart, went on to become CEO of the Chamber of Commerce in Queenstown. Drysdale's's first PA, Tui Crerar (later McBeath), became the head of Work and Income and then Workbridge.[98] The company has also nurtured women like the 2012 production manager who began in a very junior role, has had four children in the course of her employment, and will 'go on much further', according to Drysdale.[99] Whatever support women find within the company, Drysdale believes that the business world demands that women 'have to work harder, and you have to be better to be equal'. But she also insists they have a real advantage in that 'women are inherently able to multi-task'.[100]

The working conditions of one particular group of women – those in the sex industry – took centre stage in 2003, when the decriminalisation of sex work became the subject of parliamentary and public debate. Lobbying by the Prostitutes' Collective – who also saw discrimination against sex workers as a human rights issue – led to a coalition of some unlikely partners: the Venereological Society, the Maori Women's Welfare League, the Young Women's Christian Association, the Public Health Association, the Massage Institute, the Council of Trade Unions, and some nuns and churches who supported decriminalisation of sex work.[101] For these groups, New South Wales, where most forms of sex work had been decriminalised, provided a model.

The Prostitution Reform Act passed on 25 June 2003 by a margin of one vote. Support from Prime Minister Helen Clark and the 'near universal support of a strong group of women MPs' was crucial.[102] Clark said that she personally found prostitution abhorrent, but that unless the law was reformed sex workers had 'no proper protection of the law' and it was impossible to institute health and safety measures or to deal with employment matters.[103] Evidence suggested that most women went into sex work primarily for economic reasons: they could earn more money than in the other types of work available to them, and the flexible hours suited women with children.[104]

Rather than supporting the decriminalisation of sex workers, the National Council of Women initially supported criminalising clients as well as sex workers, following the Swedish model – a view that veteran feminist Sandra Coney also supported.[105] In 1998, Sweden had made the selling of sex illegal as a way of 'signalling to the world that sex work is not acceptable in a gender-equal society'.[106] In 2010, Iceland (named as the best country for women in 2011) went further, outlawing strip clubs.[107] 'I guess the men of Iceland,' said singer Gudrun Jonsdottir, 'will have to get used to the idea that women are not for sale.'[108] But New Zealanders took a different view. In so doing, the Prostitution Reform Act, perhaps more than any other legislation, signifies the distance between the aims of first- and second-wave feminists. Whereas the first were concerned to eliminate prostitution through raising men to a higher moral standard, the second wave rejected moralistic judgements on sexual behaviour. Hence, the right to work safely in the sex industry appeared a logical development to many.

One hundred and fourteen years after women's suffrage was won, the final barrier to women's full citizenship, the right to bear arms in defence of the country, was eliminated in May 2007. Supported by all parties, the Human Rights (Women in Armed Forces) Amendment Act removed the right of the armed forces to restrict the employment of women in combat roles. The services had been aiming for the full integration of women by 2005, so the law change, in effect, recognised what had happened in practice, and removed the only reservation to the United Nations Convention on the Elimination of All Forms of Discrimination against Women (CEDAW).[109] By 2011, women made up 16 per cent of the armed forces. Those forces serve abroad, in the Pacific and the Middle East, for example,

Dame Sian Elias (centre) was appointed Chief Justice in 1999, the first woman to hold that position in New Zealand. In 2015 she was also presiding judge of the Supreme Court. Dame Sian is shown here with other Royal Commissioners Hon. Ellen Dolour France (right) and Hon. Helen Diana Winkelmann in the Debating Chamber of Parliament during the swearing in ceremony after the 2014 election. *Setford News Photo Agency, SNPA201014001*

but they also serve at home. After the 2011 Canterbury earthquake, the army catering crew – including women and men – produced 1,646 breakfasts, 1,893 lunches, 2,009 dinners and 600 midnight meals.[110]

A woman's land?

In April 2001, the British magazine the *New Statesman* called New Zealand a 'Woman's Land' where 'virtually every top job is held by a woman'. The list of prominent women would be reeled off many times as proof of the country's egalitarian character: Helen Clark, Prime Minister; Dame Silvia Cartwright, Governor-General; Margaret Wilson, Attorney-General; Dame Sian Elias, Chief Justice; and Theresa Gattung, chief executive of Telecom New Zealand.

Telecom was the country's largest private company; the services it provided had once been state owned. The roll-back of the state had provided new opportunities for women like Theresa Gattung. But other women, such as Helen Kelly, first woman president of the New Zealand Council of Trade Unions (from 2007 to 2015), fought to preserve New Zealand's egalitarian tradition. Unionists watched with dismay as the protectionist welfare state that inhibited extremes of wealth and poverty gave way to greater gaps between the

TOP: *Left* Dame Silvia Cartwright, Governor-General of New Zealand, inspects an Army, Airforce and Navy guard at her state farewell on 2 August 2006. Previously a lawyer and High Court judge, she presided over the 1988 Cartwright Inquiry into treatment of women with cervical cancer at National Women's Hospital. After her term as Governor-General, she was appointed an international judge on the Cambodian War Crimes Tribunal. *Photograph by Marty Melville, Getty Images, 71564852*

TOP: *Right* Prime Minister Helen Clark is pictured with the US Deputy Secretary of Defense, Paul Wolfowitz, in 2002. Clark entered Parliament as a Labour MP in 1981 and became leader of the party in 1993. After victory in the 1999 election she was prime minister for three consecutive terms, during which she implemented a number of economic and social reforms. After Labour was defeated at the polls in 2008, she became Administrator of the United Nations Development Programme. *Photograph by R. D. Ward, Department of Defence*

richest and poorest. Reducing inequalities has proved elusive for the governing parties in power during the last thirty years, and some of the biggest gaps may not be between men and women, or Māori and non-Māori, but between those doing well and those doing badly within those groups.

Helen Clark proved to be a consummate politician, leading the Labour Party to power, albeit in strategic alliance with other parties, for three successive terms from 1999. During her time as prime minister, she joined the Council of Women World Leaders (allied with the United Nations Foundation), which works for collective action on women's issues.[111] The council advises the World Economic Forum through its Women Leaders Advisory Board and supports a greater voice for women in democracies everywhere.[112] In April 2009, after Labour lost the 2008 election, Clark took up a New York appointment as the first woman to lead the United Nations Development Programme.[113]

The following year, the co-leader of the Green Party, Jeanette Fitzsimons, retired from Parliament after serving for thirteen years. Formed in May 1990, the Green Party, built on the earlier commitment of the Values Party to environmental issues and gender equity. Fitzsimons was proud to be a member of the first Parliament elected under MMP, which gave greater representation to minority groups. Along with fellow Green members, she raised awareness of climate change, promoted home-insulation and solar-heating initiatives, and doggedly fought for the environment and a sustainable future. Co-leader Rod Donald called her the 'Steel Magnolia': 'gracious, generous, fair-minded, and under all that, toughly persistent'.[114] Metiria Turei, of Ngāti Kahungunu descent, replaced Fitzsimons as co-leader when the latter stepped down in 2009. By then, the Greens had become the third largest party in Parliament.

In 2004, Tariana Turia (of Ngāti Apa, Ngā Rauru and Ngāti Tūwharetoa descent) had acted decisively with Pita Sharples to form the Māori Party when Labour passed the controversial foreshore and seabed legislation – which the new co-leaders saw as extinguishing Māori rights in an action akin to the nineteenth century land confiscations. Both were former Labour MPs, but the Māori Party agreed to support John Key's

OPPOSITE: *Middle left* Tariana Turia (right), formally hands over her co-leadership of the Māori Party to Marama Fox at Whangaehu Marae on 1 November 2014. Turia entered Parliament as a Labour MP in 1996 but broke with the party over its stance on foreshore and seabed legislation in 2004. She won the Te Tai Hauāruru by-election that year as co-leader with Pita Sharples of the new Māori Party. *Photograph by Lewis Gardner,* Wanganui Chronicle*, WIC-1000043*

OPPOSITE: *Middle right* Jacinda Ardern (left) and Annette King are both high-ranking Labour MPs. King held major portfolios in Labour governments of 1987-1990 and 1999-2008, and was in 2015 Deputy Leader of the Opposition. Jacinda Ardern was first elected in 2008 and by 2015 was on Labour's front bench. *Photograph by Kevin Stent, Fairfax Media,* Dominion Post

OPPOSITE: *Bottom left* Green Party co-leader Metiria Turei, seen here arriving at the Party's election night celebrations in 2014, entered Parliament in 2002 and was elected co-leader in 2009. A corporate lawyer before she entered politics, she has backed protection of the marine environment and campaigned to end child poverty. *Setford News Photo Agency, SNPA200914401*

OPPOSITE: *Bottom right* Paula Bennett, National MP and in 2011 the Minister of Social Development and Employment, launched a Green Paper on Children that year. Focusing on issues surrounding child abuse and the protection of children, the paper provoked fierce debate. *Photograph by Brett Phibbs,* New Zealand Herald*, NZH-1058513*

minority National government after the election of 2008. In 2009, Turia, as Minister of the Community and Voluntary Sector, commissioned a task force on whānau-centred initiatives. Twenty-two hui were held throughout the country to discuss reforms to benefit whānau. The resulting report observed that the devolution of state enterprises since 1984 had delivered some benefits for Māori, in new systems of healthcare, education and social work that facilitated the development of some Māori provider organisations.[115] The potential transformation of services by flaxroot initiatives, however, was being hampered by the fragmentation of social services, the separation of social and economic development, and an emphasis on crisis intervention rather than positive development.[116] The Whānau Ora initiative promoted the well-being and self-determination of the group by focusing on whānau rather than the individual, embracing the knowledge of elders and placing an emphasis on cultural values. The policy aimed to provide coordinated and positive support for Māori families.[117]

Parmjeet Parmar, elected as a National list MP in the 2014 election, represents the changing face of New Zealand. One of four sisters raised by a father in the Indian Airforce and a mother who cared for the family during the multiple moves associated with her husband's job, Parmar was encouraged to work hard and get a good education. Her traditional arranged marriage brought her to New Zealand in 1995, and she went on to complete a doctorate in biological sciences at the University of Auckland. She has worked as operations director of the family business, Kiwi Empire Confectionery; is the proud mother of two; and has served as chair of the New Zealand Sikh Women's Association. In addition, she has worked weekends as a broadcaster on Indian radio and in the community organising against domestic violence. Thirty-nine per cent of Parmar's Mt Roskill electorate is of Asian ethnicity; 50 per cent of the electorate were, like her, born overseas. In her maiden parliamentary speech, she spoke of her commitment both to gender equality and to family values. Eliminating domestic violence is one of her priorities along with promoting science, innovation and small business. She is proud to be a member of a party that does not support a quota system for women, as Labour did in 2013, and grateful she was chosen 'purely on merit'.[118]

The diversity of women's voices now represented in Parliament was illustrated by the results of the 2014 election. Thirty-eight of the 121 members were women: sixteen National, twelve Labour, seven Green, two New Zealand First, and one Māori Party. Māori women can be found in all the main parties, among them Hekia Parata for National, Meka Whaitiri for Labour, Metiria Turei for the Greens, and Marama Fox as co-leader of the Māori Party. Pacific Island women are more likely to be found in the Labour Party; they include Jenny Salesa, committed to representing the people of Manukau East, and Carmel Sepuloni, New Zealand's first MP of Tongan descent. Melissa Lee, a list MP for National, was born in South Korea and grew up in Malaysia before moving to New Zealand via Australia in 1988. She is the first Korean woman to be elected in a non-Korean legislature.

New feminisms

Innovative forms of communication such as Facebook (2004), YouTube (2005) and Twitter (2006) made for new types of expression and relationships, and have helped shape the conversation among women in the twenty-first century, as among countless other groups. The conversations can be local or international, and sometimes lead to worldwide protests – as was the case with the #Bringbackourgirls campaign to highlight the plight of more than 200 Nigerian schoolgirls abducted in 2014 by Islamic Jihadist organisation Boko Haram, which opposes the education of girls.[119] Wellington Girls' College Year 13 student Dawape Giwa-Isekeije organised for 270 girls (the number abducted) to march on Parliament to urge the government to do more to bring pressure on the Nigerian government to find the girls and return them to their families.[120]

Local internet conversations include those from the Wellington Young Feminists Collective, who display their support for Māori sovereignty; from Kiwi Mummy Blogs, the first blog aggregation site in New Zealand, which asks others, among other things, to join in making dresses for street girls in Cambodia; and from Jan Pentecost, secretary of Grey Power and chair of its advocacy standing committee, who reports on lobbying for the rights of senior citizens.[121] The banner heading on the feminist blog site The Hand Mirror proclaims: 'Feminism is the radical notion that women are people'. Begun in 2008, the site has been home to more than 2,500 posts and has consistently been in the top twenty New Zealand political blogs as ranked by the Tumeke blogosphere.[122] Bloggers include 'Elsewoman' (Anne Else), 'Undomestic Goddess' and 'Luddite Journo'. On the Feminist Mothers Aotearoa site, mothers find support for raising children in non-sexist ways.

YouTube provides instant access to the music of young New Zealand women. Caitlin Moran, British columnist and author of the award-winning *How to be a Woman* (2011), has said that pop music is 'the cultural bellwether of social change', and New Zealand is part of an international trend away from the male rock stars of the 1970s towards domination by female artists.[123] In New Zealand, these would include Bic Runga, Anika Moa, Gin Wigmore, Kimbra and Lorde, whose 2013 smash hit 'Royals' encapsulated a disdain New Zealanders have traditionally had for the high life, preferring 'a different kind of buzz'.[124]

While Lorde dominated the domestic and international sound waves in 2013, Eleanor Catton's novel *The Luminaries* flew off the bookshelves after she won the prestigious Man Booker Prize, the youngest author (at twenty-eight) ever to do so. Glowing accolades from the Man Booker judges contrasted with 'a "bullying reception" from certain New Zealand reviewers of an older generation' (to use Catton's words). Under the dismissive title 'All that glistens', C.K. Stead found some things to admire about *The Luminaries,* but was lukewarm in his praise in London's *Financial Times*.[125] Another Auckland writer, Michael Morrissey, dismissed Catton's talent in these terms:

Eleanor Catton won the Man Booker Prize in 2013 for her second novel *The Luminaries*. At the age of twenty-eight, she was the youngest-ever winner. Catton has been outspoken about how older male critics in New Zealand have dismissed her work, and has defended her right to state her political opinions publicly. *Photograph by Matt Bialostocki*

> Her first novel, *The Rehearsal*, written when the author was virtually a child of 21 (or so) set a new hallmark in schoolgirlish bitchiness, as well as including flashes of purple writing – understandable in one so young. Femmes were impressed; chaps less so.[126]

To this chap, what other chaps thought mattered. What seemed to interest him about Catton was that she was 'pensive-featured [and] marginally beautiful': not attributes that book reviewers usually take into consideration.[127]

Catton has been outspoken about the difficulty women writers have in being taken seriously, noting that 'male writers get asked what they think, women what they feel'. She has been frank about the way in which women's success is attributed to luck rather than talent, and how women writers are unlikely to be seen as serious thinkers, as philosophers or as people 'with preoccupations that are going to sustain them for a lifetime'.[128] And there are those in New Zealand who object to Catton's right to speak out on politics. In 2015, radio host Sean Plunket called Catton an 'ungrateful hua' for criticising New Zealand's National government. Many heard the word 'hua' (not one in common parlance) as 'whore', though Plunket denied having used that term.[129]

Parris Goebel, hip hop dancer and choreographer, was photographed in her Auckland dance studio in 2012. The creator of a dance style called Polyswagg, Goebel dances with an all-women crew ReQuest which has won major competitions in the United States. She has also received awards as a choreographer. By 2015 she was travelling regularly overseas to work with stars such as Janet Jackson and Jennifer Lopez. *Photograph by Steven McNicholl*, New Zealand Herald, *NZH1064825*

Plunket's comment was heard – and debated – by radio listeners. Young people are more likely to get their news via Facebook. At a Canadian university safety forum on 24 January 2011, a policeman who spoke on crime prevention said: 'Women should avoid dressing like sluts in order not to be victimised.'[130] A great many young women were angered by this statement, which appeared to blame the victim rather than the rapist. They also wanted to rehabilitate the word 'slut'. Women, they said, were tired of being oppressed by 'slut-shaming' – by being judged by their sexuality and feeling unsafe as a result. News quickly spread through Facebook and Twitter, and New Zealand women added their voices to the call for change. On 25 June 2011, hundreds of women and men marched in Auckland and Wellington in a contemporary version of 1970s and 1980s 'reclaim the night' marches. Twenty-one-year-old Natalie Thorburn said she joined the walk because rape 'was never the victim's fault and she wanted to change the culture of blame'.[131] Addressing 'slut shaming' remains a key issue for many young feminists.

The same year, a group of young men in Auckland calling themselves the Roast Busters boasted about intoxicating and raping underage girls; they discussed their activities and named their victims on their Facebook page. Despite a thirteen-year-old girl laying a complaint with the police, no action was taken against the young men. Public anger grew,

Two works by contemporary jewellers show strong New Zealand influences. Lisa Walker, who trained and worked in Germany for many years, used pounamu (New Zealand jade) for her powerful geometric pendant. Dunedin artist Lynn Kelly created her 'lacebark necklace' from maps on silver leaves that resemble the New Zealand tree, lacebark or houhere. *Photograph by Michael Couper, courtesy of Lisa Walker; necklace photograph courtesy of Lynn Kelly*

culminating in thousands of people throughout the country protesting against a 'rape culture' that sanctioned unwanted sexual advances to women, blamed the victim, and denied the seriousness of sexual abuse. Tania Domett, an Auckland mother, marched with her twelve-year-old daughter:

> I think it's really time to get out there from all walks of life in New Zealand and show that this is not acceptable and we need to effect a culture change in how we deal with the issues of sex and our young people.
>
> I think the sexualisation of children is really a big issue. I think there's not enough discussion about consent, I think consent is the main critical factor here and I think boys and girls need to know what that is.
>
> I think it's a difficult conversation that parents need to have with their children.[132]

C. K. Stead was moved to write to the *New Zealand Herald* decrying the 'Roast Busters' controversy, claiming that the nation had 'become gripped by a collective hysteria'. He suggested 'it was now universally accepted that anything immoral or illegal between sexually active minors was the fault of the male and the female was the victim'. It was time to change the subject, he suggested.[133] An outraged Eleanor Catton tweeted in response: 'Rape culture is: people who want to shut down conversations about rape. From a NZ writer, this is disgusting.'[134] Stead backed down, saying Catton might be right and he had no wish to quash the conversation.

The report of the Independent Police Conduct Authority found the police had failed in their duty to the victims of the Roast Busters. The police, in their focus on the behaviour of young women, 'overlooked the importance of holding the young men accountable for their

New Zealand fashion label NOM*D was established in Dunedin in 1986 by Margarita Robertson (sister of Zambesi designer Elisabeth Findlay). NOM*D flourished, and in 1999 its collections were shown with those of other New Zealand designers at London Fashion Week. This brought the label international recognition and a reputation for being 'edgy, dark and intellectual'. *Photograph by Karen Inderbitzen-Waller, courtesy of NOM*d*

behaviour and preventing its recurrence'.[135] There was clearly still much to be done by the media, the police and other agencies to create a culture in which women feel safe reporting sexual violence.

Continuing conversations

In the second decade of the twenty-first century, there are many voices in the conversation about women, and many languages and venues in which that conversation might take place, from traditional media outlets, Facebook and Twitter, to the family, Parliament and the marae. Old forums of advocacy for women, such as a Ministry of Women's Affairs, seemed to some to be outdated; in December 2014, the Ministry was renamed the Ministry for Women, with the mission of advising the government 'on achieving better outcomes for women'.[136] Just what those 'better outcomes' might be is subject to debate.

Promoting 'family values' might be central to the aspirations of new migrants such as Parmjeet Parmar, while those who participate in the Breaking Boundaries internet forum are committed to 'a safe place to chat for all Lesbian, Gay, Bisexual, Transgender, Intersex and Queer identifying individuals of all ages'.[137] New media serve to amplify gendered stereotypes but also provide a means of resistance. The old question 'What do women want?' will generate new answers in the decades to come, but the question itself is unlikely to go away.

Auckland string quartet *Geist*, consisting of school students Lauren Bennett (first violin), Britta Balzat (second violin), Sophia Lee (viola) and Sally Kim (cello), won the New Zealand Chamber Music Contest two years in a row, in 2011 and 2012. As a result of their second win, they were invited to play at the New Zealand Music Festival in Shanghai in 2012. *Simon Darby Photography, courtesy of Chamber Music New Zealand*

Educated women will be key contributors to the debate on a national and at a personal level – and many of the debates, particularly to do with child abuse, child poverty and the shape of working lives, are urgent. In terms of education, New Zealand girls do better than boys in national school qualifications, and more women than men in the 20–24 age group complete degrees.[138] The rise in women's educational achievements has been named a 'gender educational transition'.[139] Whereas once men might have married women who had less education than they did, today's couples are more likely to have comparable levels of education. In fact, old patterns may be reversed, with women having higher educational qualifications than their male partners.[140]

One might think that the educational transition would lead smoothly to equal pay for women, but this goal remains elusive. In 2015, the Public Service Association's national secretary, Erin Polaczuk, pointed out that the wage gap of 5.3 per cent had worsened since 2008, and that 'the issue of wage inequity was pervasive across the public sector'.[141] Overall, women still earn less than men, in part because of occupations segregated by gender, 'unconscious bias', and lack of flexible working hours.[142] Caring still remains mostly women's responsibility and little will change, according to theorist Nancy Fraser, until men are induced to do primary care work. If jobs were built around a universal, rather

Patricia Grace, of Ngāti Toa, Te Āti Awa and Ngāti Raukawa, has been publishing fiction since the 1970s, exploring Māori experience through themes such as loss, isolation and family. Her collection of short stories, *Waiariki* (1975), was the first by a Māori woman writer, and her work has been translated into several languages. Her many honours and awards include the Deutz Medal for Fiction, the Neustadt International Prize for Literature, and the Prime Minister's Lifetime Achievement Award for Fiction; in 2007 Grace was made a Distinguished Companion of the New Zealand Order of Merit for her services to literature. *Photograph by Grant Maiden*

than a gendered, concept of caring, she suggests, there would be a shorter working week and policies that facilitated the integration of work and family life – whatever shape those families take.[143]

In her ground-breaking book *Counting for Nothing*, Marilyn Waring advocated the recognition of the economic contribution of women's unpaid caring work, pointing out that such work, although unmarked in national accounting, underpins national life.[144] While Waring's work has had an international impact, market forces continue to dominate the New Zealand economy, and there has been little accommodation with New Zealand women's lives. Many women work part time, and this has an impact on their working conditions and their pay packets.[145] To ensure that women's work is valued, some workers see the way forward in court action, as in recent challenges to the low wages of carers, such as those who work in the aged-care industry.[146]

Women who have opted for traditionally male professions are currently transforming them. The numbers suggest that if entries and exits from the legal profession remain the same, by 2018 women lawyers will outnumber their male colleagues. The number

Teitei is one of the principal tīpuna wahine (women ancestors) in the Tahu Pōtiki meeting house, Te Rau Aroha Marae, Awarua, Bluff. The meeting house celebrates the contribution of women as anchors for their communities; the carvings were a cooperative community project led by Cliff Whiting. *With permission of Hana Morgan, Graham Metzger and Tā Tipene O'Regan at Te Rūnaka o Awarua, and Cliff Whiting and He Kupenga Hao i te Reo*

of Māori lawyers is increasingly slowly, with advocacy from groups such as Te Hunga Rōia Māori o Aotearoa – The Māori Law Society. Women made up 43.2 per cent of doctors in 2015, and outnumber men in training for general practice, and obstetrics and gynaecology (their numbers are low in surgery). Only a very small proportion of medical graduates or students, however, are of Māori or Pacific Island descent.[147] Engineering, once a male bastion, has been slowly infiltrated by women, who now make up 13 per cent of professional engineers.[148] Change is a little more rapid in architecture, where women comprise 29 per cent of the New Zealand Institute of Architects. And while there has been change in dentistry, where 34.2 per cent of dentists are now women, the gender hierarchy looks traditional when the whole pattern of the profession is observed: 96.6 per cent of dental therapists and 95.7 of dental hygienists are women. In the traditionally male trades of plumbing, building and electrical work, women remain marginally represented (1 per cent).[149]

Gender segregation remains apparent in nursing, for example, where over 90 per cent of the nursing workforce is female, though the profile is changing as more men enter the profession. And within nursing major disparities exist. At the 2015 Indigenous Nurses Conference organised by Te Kaunihera o Ngā Neehi Māori (National Council of Māori Nurses), delegates discussed how those working for Whānau Ora agencies may earn up to 25 per cent less than their District Health Board colleagues.[150]

In classrooms throughout the country, women are largely those educating the coming generation. Over three-quarters of the teaching staff at state and integrated schools are women – but fewer than half of the principals are.[151] A census of teachers taken in 2004 indicated that 79 per cent identified as Pākehā, 10 per cent as Māori and 2 per cent as Asian. While the census did not break down the gender statistics by ethnicity, women made up 82 per cent of primary teachers, 83 per cent of special-school teachers, and 58 per cent of high school teachers.[152]

Women have ventured into new fields in work, in sport and leisure, and in their personal lives. Few people now imagine that their daughters will be dependent on a man for their financial well-being. Women's voices are raised in the academy and in Parliament, debating the direction of New Zealand for the future. They can no longer be dismissed as the 'shrieking sisterhood', as the women's rights advocates of the nineteenth century often were. But finding a basis for sisterhood at the same time as celebrating cultural diversity frequently proves difficult.

Younger women, benefiting from the success of past campaigns, might feel that women no longer have to argue for rights and that feminism is outmoded. They may find it hard to imagine the world, charted in this history, when women's position was, for a good many, subservient to the needs of others. We now rely on them to imagine a future where the challenges of both respect for diversity and a commitment to equality can be met.

Acknowledgements

In addition to those named in the introduction, Stephen Robertson, Sandy Bardsley, Bridget Waldron, Victoria Timpany, Pat Sargison, Cameron Duder, Judy Gould, Louise Shaw, Claire Gooder, Megan Cook, Nancy de Castro, Diana Brown, Frances Steel, Angela Findlay and Jane Adams provided valuable assistance at various stages of the project. I have learned a great deal from Honours and postgraduate students I have supervised, and I thank all of them for their work and discussions that have ranged over a wide range of topics from women's health, to paid work (as, for example, politicians, hairdressers, clerical workers, pharmacists, missionaries, nurses, dental nurses and doctors), to voluntary and cultural endeavours (such as in the suffrage campaign and the Plunket Society). Examining work by excellent postgraduate students from other universities in New Zealand has similarly been a great learning curve. Teaching and researching alongside my former teachers, Dorothy Page and Erik Olssen, taught me much.

I am grateful to Marilyn Waring, Margaret Wilson and Raewyn Dalziel for presenting thoughtful Women's Suffrage Commemorative lectures at Otago that influenced my understanding of the years post-1980. Input from readers has been crucial at various times. I thank Margaret Tennant, Charlotte Macdonald, Atholl Anderson, Alison Carew, Margaret Wilson, Patricia Grimshaw, Aroha Harris, Melissa Matutina Williams, Michael Reilly and Bronwyn Dalley for the care they took considering my text. They offered different points of view and will, I am sure, continue to do so in the future. Grappling with their challenges assisted me to sharpen my thinking. The wider community of History and Gender Studies scholars in New Zealand and abroad has provided a vital testing ground for ideas. Reviewers for articles I have published in the *New Zealand Journal of History* and *Gender and History* have been generous in making suggestions.

I am indebted to administrative assistance from Sue Lang, the superb linchpin of our department. Librarians and archivists at the University of Otago library, the National Library of New Zealand, Archives New Zealand and the Hocken Collections have been unfailingly helpful, and the latter library provided a refuge when I needed to escape from the office.

Bridget Williams has been at the forefront of publishing essential texts on the history of women in New Zealand, as many of the endnotes in this volume attest. Her confidence in this project sustained mine. It has been a delight and a revelation to work with editor Jane Parkin. My thanks to Jo Scully, Hannah August, Jill Livestre, Moira Long, Melanie Lovell-Smith, Nancy Swarbrick and the rest of the team at Bridget Williams Books for their professionalism and care.

I am indebted to the University of Otago, and the Division of Humanities in particular, in two crucial respects. First, for nurturing the enterprise of women's history over the years I have been teaching in the History and Art History Department. Second, for vital financial and academic support, which enabled this project to come to completion. I am indeed fortunate to have such an intellectual home.

Barbara Brookes

Editorial Note

Māori language and names

In general, the form and spelling of Māori words and names follows *Guidelines for Māori Language Orthography* (Te Taura Whiri i te Reo Maori/Māori Language Commission, 2009), available at www.tetaurawhiri.govt.nz. This includes the placement of hyphens, and the use of macrons to mark long vowels. However, macrons are not used on personal names, and titles (such as groups, organisations, government departments) take the form of their time. Likewise, quotations retain the original spelling and punctuation. Māori words are glossed in the text on their first usage, or where this is helpful. See also www.maoridictionary.co.nz, available in print as *Te Aka Māori–English, English–Māori Dictionary* by John Moorfield (3rd edn, Pearson, 2011), or *A Dictionary of the Māori Language* by Herbert Williams (7th edn, Government Print, 1971).

Illustrations

The artworks, photographs, texts and other items appearing in the images through this book are intended to be read not simply as illustrations for the immediate text but as a narrative in themselves. The selection of images was made within the framework set out in the introduction – that is, presenting a woman's perspective. Thus, alongside the photographic record, the work of women artists, craftswomen and photographers has been included. But the significance of this creativity in women's history can only be briefly signalled in a general history, and we would like to make a general acknowledgement to the strength of the many artistic traditions that women have contributed to.

For permission to reproduce their work in this book, the publishers would particularly like to thank photographers Marti Friedlander, Gil Hanly, Anne Noble, Jenny Scown and Ans Westra, and artists Gretchen Albrecht, Jacqueline Fahey, Star Gossage, Robyn Kahukiwa, Yuk King Tan, Kura Te Waru Rewiri, and Marilynn Webb. We would like to acknowledge also works such as Anne Kirker's *New Zealand Women Artists* (Reed Methuen, 1986), Ann Calhoun's *The Arts and Crafts Movement in New Zealand 1870–1940* (Auckland University Press, 2000) and Awhina Tamarapa's edited work *Whatu Kākahu: Māori Cloaks* (Te Papa Press, 2011) that have, amongst other publications, documented women's artwork over time.

Captions for the images are based primarily on information provided by the organisation supplying the image (museum, library, newspaper); they draw also on *Te Ara: The Encyclopedia of New Zealand* (www.teara.govt.nz), the sources in the endnotes for the relevant chapter, and the books listed in the introduction and above. All efforts have been made to provide correct information relating to these images, and any further information is gratefully received.

Many institutions, iwi and individuals have granted permission for images to be included in this book, and we thank here: Aigantighe Art Gallery; Alexander Turnbull Library; Auckland Art Gallery; Auckland Diocesan Catholic Archives; Auckland Libraries, Sir George Grey Special Collections; Auckland War Memorial Museum Tāmaki Paenga Hira; Archives New Zealand; British Library Board; British Museum; Christchurch Art Gallery; Christchurch City Libraries; Dunedin Public Art Gallery; Fairfax Media; Hocken Collections at the University of Otago Library; Macmillan Brown Library, University of Canterbury; Masterton District Library and Archive; Museum of New Zealand Te Papa Tongarewa (and particularly Claire Regnault, Stephanie Gibson, Kirstie Ross and Lynette Townsend); Nelson Provincial Museum; Otago Museum; Owaka Museum; Palmerston North City Library; Puke Ariki; Sarjeant Gallery; Tairawhiti Museum; Te Manawa Museums; Te Runaka o Awarua and Cliff Whiting; Toitū Otago Settlers Museum; Waikato Museum; Waikato University Library; Whanganui Regional Museum.

Endnotes

List of Abbreviations

Note: All newspapers were accessed in Papers Past, National Library of New Zealand.

A&U   Allen and Unwin
AJHR   *Appendices to the Journals of the House of Representatives*
ANZ   Archives New Zealand
ATL   Alexander Turnbull Library
AUP   Auckland University Press
BWB   Bridget Williams Books
CUP   Canterbury University Press
DIA   Department of Internal Affairs
DNZB   *Dictionary of New Zealand Biography*
NZPD   *New Zealand Parliamentary Debates*
OUP   Oxford University Press
VUP   Victoria University Press

Introduction

1   Steven Oliver, 'Tautari, Hemi and Tautari, Mary', *DNZB*, www.teara.govt.nz/en/biographies/2t12/tautari-hemi; 'Waitangi Treaty copy', www.nzhistory.net.nz/media/interactive/waitangi-treaty-copy (accessed 14 October 2015).

2   'Honey bees brought to NZ', www.nzhistory.net.nz/mary-bumby-brings-the-first-honey-bees-in-new-zealand (accessed 14 October 2015).

3   Angela Wanhalla, *Matters of the Heart: A History of Interracial Marriage in New Zealand*, AUP, 2013, pp.62–67.

4   Rosemary Killop, *To Find a Fortune: Women of the Thames Goldfield, 1857–1893*, Women's Studies, Victoria University of Wellington, Wellington, 1995, pp.31, 53.

5   Megan Cook, 'Women's movement – The 19th-century women's movement', *Te Ara: The Encyclopedia of New Zealand*, www.teara.govt.nz/en/document/27884/polly-plum-speaks-out (accessed 14 October 2015).

6   Letter to the Editor, 'What Women Want,' *New Zealand Herald*, 31 July 1871, p.3.

7   'Ko kā wāhine ēnei, ko rātou puka i mau ai': "These women they anchor us; the women who anchored the men'. Bill Dacker, *The Neck or Te Wehika a Te Wera; History notes for Rakiura Māori Land Trust*, September 2009, cited in Suzanne Spencer, 'Cross Cultural Encounters on the Shores of Foveaux Strait,' Dissertation for Masters of Indigenous Studies, University of Otago, 2011, p.18.

8   *DNZB*, Vols 1–5; Charlotte Macdonald, Merimeri Penfold and Bridget Williams (eds), *The Book of New Zealand Women, Ko Kui Ma te Kaupapa*, BWB, Wellington, 1991.

9   Frances Porter and Charlotte Macdonald (eds), *'My Hand Will Write what my Heart Dictates': The Unsettled Lives of Women in Nineteenth-century New Zealand as Revealed to Sisters, Family and Friends*, AUP/BWB, Auckland, 1996; Angela Ballara, *Iwi: The Dynamics of Māori Tribal Organisation from c. 1769 to c. 1945*, VUP, Wellington, 1998.

10   Patricia Grimshaw, *Women's Suffrage in New Zealand*, AUP/OUP, Auckland, 1972; 2nd edn, AUP, 1987; Tania Rei, *Maori Women and the Vote*, Huia, Wellington, 1993; Margaret Lovell-Smith, *The Woman Question: Writings by the Women who Won the Vote*, New Women's Press, Auckland, 1992: Dorothy Page, *The Suffragists: Women Who Worked for the Vote*, BWB/*DNZB*, Wellington, 1993.

11   Judith Binney and Gillian Chaplin, *Ngā Mōrehu: The Survivors*, OUP, Auckland, 1986.

12   Nancy Taylor, *The Home Front: New Zealand in the Second World War*, Vols 1 and 2, Historical Branch, DIA, Government Printer, Wellington, 1986; Deborah Montgomerie, *The Women's War: New Zealand Women 1939–45*, AUP, Auckland, 2001; Eve Ebbett, *When the Boys were Away: New Zealand Women in World War II*, A. H. & A. W. Reed, Wellington, 1984.

13   Margaret Corner, *No Easy Victory: Towards Equal Pay for Women in the Government Service, 1890 to 1960*, New Zealand Public Service Association, Dan Long Trust, Wellington, 1988.

14   Christine Dann, *Up From Under: Women and Liberation in New Zealand, 1970–1985*, A&U/Port Nicholson Press, Wellington, 1985.

15   Janet McCallum, *Women in the House: Members of Parliament in New Zealand*, Cape Catley, Wellington, 1993.

16   Anne Else (ed.), *Women Together: A History of Women's Organisations in New Zealand*, Historical Branch, DIA/Daphne Brasell Associates, Wellington, 1993; Sandra Coney,

Standing in the Sunshine: A History of New Zealand Women Since They Won the Vote, Penguin, Auckland, 1993.

Chapter 1

1   Elsdon Best, *The Maori*, Memoirs of the Polynesian Society, Vol. 5, Board of Maori Ethnological Research, Wellington, 1924, p.41. The limitations of the work of Best, Percy Smith and others are discussed in Angela Ballara, *Iwi: The Dynamics of Māori Tribal Organisation from c.1769–c.1945*, VUP, Wellington, 1998, chapter 8.

2   Judith Binney, 'Some Observations on the Status of Maori Women', in Barbara Brookes, Charlotte Macdonald and Margaret Tennant (eds), *Women in History 2*, BWB, Wellington, 1992, pp.19–20.

3   S. P. Smith, *The Lore of the Whare-Wānanga. Part 1. Te Kauwae-runga or 'Things Celestial'*, Memoirs of the Polynesian Society, Vol. 3, Thomas Avery, New Plymouth, 1913, pp.117–19.

4   Ibid., p.121.

5   Best, *The Maori*, p.113.

6   Elsdon Best, *Maori Religion and Mythology*, New Zealand Dominion Museum, Bulletin No. 10, W. A. G. Skinner, Wellington, 1924, p.74.

7   For another version of the creation story and the creation of woman, see Anaru Reedy (ed. and trans.), *Ngā Kōrero a Mohi Ruatapu*, CUP, Christchurch, 1993, pp.117–18.

8   Best, *The Maori*, p.118.

9   Smith, *The Lore of the Whare-Wānanga*, p.178.

10 Judith Binney and Gillian Chaplin, *Ngā Mōrehu: The Survivors*, OUP, Auckland, 1986, p.26.

11 Ibid., and Anne Salmond, 'TIPUNA: Ancestors in Maori', unpublished paper.

12 Donna Durie-Hall and Joan Metge, 'Kua Tutū Te Puehu, Kia Mau: Māori Aspirations and Family Law', in M. Henaghan and B. Aitken, *Family Law Policy in New Zealand*, OUP, Auckland, 1992, p.81, n.26.

13 I am indebted to Atholl Anderson for this discussion.

14 Binney and Chaplin, *Ngā Mōrehu*, pp.24–26. See also F. Allan Hanson, 'Female Pollution in Polynesia?' *Journal of the Polynesian Society*, 91, 3 (1982), pp.343–59.

15 Manuka Henare, cited in Leonie Pihama, 'Tīhei Mauri Ora: Honouring Our Voices: Mana Wahine as Kaupapa Māori Theoretical Framework', PhD thesis, University of Auckland, 2001, p.187.

16 Hanson, 'Female Pollution in Polynesia?', p.358.

17 Caroline Ralston, introduction to 'Sanctity and Power: Gender in Polynesian History', Special Issue, *Journal of Pacific History*, 22 (1987), p.116.

18 Best, *Maori Religion and Mythology*, p.74.

19 Rangimarie Rose Pere, cited in Pihama, 'Tīhei Mauri Ora', p.187.

20 Best, *Maori Religion and Mythology*, pp.74–75.

21 Annie Mikaere, 'Maori Women: Caught in the Contradictions of a Colonized Reality', *Waikato Law Review*, 2 (1994), www.waikato. ac.nz/law/research/waikato_law_review/ volume_2_1994/7 (accessed 15 October 2015).

22 Maharaia Winiata, 'Leadership in Pre-European Society', *Journal of the Polynesian Society*, 65, 3 (1956), p.219; Pihama, 'Tīhei Mauri Ora', p.184.

23 Winiata, 'Leadership in Pre-European Society', p.221.

24 George Grey, *Polynesian Mythology & Ancient Traditional History*, John Murray, London, 1855, pp.260–72.

25 Ibid., pp.296–300.

26 Ariana Simpson, 'Puhi: Memories and Experiences in their Ceremonial Role in Traditional and Contemporary Māori Worlds', MAI Review: Intern Research Report 9, www. review.mai.ac.nz/index.php/MR/article/ viewFile/18/18 (accessed 13 March 2015).

27 Joan Metge, *The Maoris of New Zealand*, Routledge & Kegan Paul, London, 1967, pp.25–26.

28 Ibid., p.26.

29 Berys Heuer, *Maori Women*, A.H. & A.W. Reed, Wellington, 1972, p.19.

30 Ibid., p.54.

31 Raymond Firth, *Economics of the New Zealand Maori*, Government Print, Wellington, 1959, p.124.

32 Ibid., p.209.

33 Ibid., pp.357–58.

34 Awhina Tamarapa (ed.), *Whatu Kākahu: Māori Cloaks*, Te Papa Press, Wellington, 2011, p.21.

35 'Kahu kuri style of cloak', http://collections. tepapa.govt.nz/topic/3631 (accessed 13 March 2015).

36 Tamarapa (ed.), *Whatu Kākahu*, p.25.

37 Ibid., p.26.

38 Angela Ballara, 'Wāhine Rangatira: Māori Women of Rank and their Role in the Women's Kotahitanga Movement of the 1890s', *New Zealand Journal of History*, 27, 2 (1993), pp.133–34.

39 Ibid., p.134.

40 Bruce Biggs, *Maori Marriage: An Essay in Reconstruction*, A.H. & A.W. Reed for the Polynesian Society, Wellington, 1960, pp.24–25.

41 'Riri – traditional Māori warfare', *Te Ara: The Encyclopedia of New Zealand*, www.teara.govt. nz/en/riri-traditional-maori-warfare/page-2 (accessed 6 May 2013).

42 Rangimarie Rose Pere, *Ako: Concepts and Learning in Maori Tradition*, Working Paper No. 17, Department of Sociology, University of Waikato, 1982, p.22.

43 Tuta Nihoniho, *Narrative of the Fighting on the East Coast, 1865–71*, with a Monograph of Bush Fighting, Dominion Museum, Wellington, 1913, p.51, cited in A. P. Vayda, 'Maori Women and Maori Cannibalism', *Man: A Monthly Record of Anthropological Science*, 60 (1960), pp.70–71.

44 Elsdon Best, 'Notes on the Art of War', *Journal of the Polynesian Society*, 11 (1902), pp.20–27.

45 Firth, *Economics of the New Zealand Maori*, p.215.

46 Angela Ballara, 'Hinematioro', *DNZB*, www.teara.govt.nz/en/biographies/1h23/ hinematioro (accessed 12 October 2012).

47 Best, *The Maori*, p.353.

48 The Holy Bible, Revised Standard Version, Genesis 2:18.

49 Genesis 3:16.

50 Genesis 3:19.

51 Jane Rendall, *The Origins of Modern Feminism: Women in Britain, France and the United States 1780–1860*, Macmillan, London, 1985, p.76.

52 Genesis 24:16–65; 1 Samuel 1:20–2:19; Ruth 4:13.

53 Roy Porter, *The Creation of the Modern World: The Untold Story of the British Enlightenment*, W. W. Norton & Co, London, 2000, p.99.

54 Lenore Davidoff and Catherine Hall, *Family Fortunes: Men and Women of the English Middle Class 1780–1850* (1st edn 1987), Routledge, London, 2002, p.74.

55 Ibid., p.178.

56 Erica Harth, 'The Virtue of Love: Lord Hardwicke's Marriage Act', *Cultural Critique*, 9 (1988), p.154.

57 Roy Porter, *English Society in the Eighteenth Century*, Allen Lane/Penguin Books, London, 1982, p.39.

58 Ibid., p.38.

59 William Alexander, *The History of Women, from the Earliest Antiquity to the Present Time*, Vol. 2, 1779, p.336, quoted in Linda Colley, *Britons: Forging the Nation 1707–1837*, Yale University Press, New Haven, 1992, p.238.

60 Colley, *Britons*, p.248.

61 Lyndall Gordon, *Vindication: A Life of Mary Wollstonecraft*, HarperCollins, New York, 2005, p.152.

62 Ibid.

63 Cited in Karen O'Brien, *Women and Enlightenment in Eighteenth Century Britain*, Cambridge University Press, Cambridge, 2009, p.185.

64 Mary Wollstonecraft, 'A Vindication of the Rights of Woman', in Janet M. Todd (ed.), *A Wollstonecraft Anthology*, Indiana University Press, Bloomington, 1977, p.112.

65 Cited in Gordon, *Vindication*, p.152.

66 Cited in Todd, *A Wollstonecraft Anthology*, p.84.

67 Ibid.

68 Mary Wollstonecraft, *Maria: or, The Wrongs of Women* (1st edn 1798), with an introduction by Anne K. Mellor, W. W. Norton & Co, New York, 1994, p.11.

69 Susie Steinbach, *Women in England, 1760–1914: A Social History*, Palgrave MacMillan, New York, 2004, p.226.

70 Anna Clark, review of Amanda Vickery, *The Gentleman's Daughter: Women's Lives in Georgian England*, www.history. ac.uk/reviews/paper/anna.html (accessed 11 September 2015).

71 Bridget Hill, *Women, Work and Sexual Politics in Eighteenth Century England*, UCL Press, London, 1994, p.260.

72 Ibid.

73 Porter, *English Society in the Eighteenth Century*, p.39.

74 Gordon, *Vindication*, p.4.

75 Porter, *English Society in the Eighteenth Century*, pp.225–30.

76 Anna Clark, *The Struggle for the Breeches: Gender and the Making of the British Working*

Class, University of California Press, Berkeley, 1995, p.19.

77 Ibid., p.22.

78 Steinbach, *Women in England*, p.49.

79 Ibid.

80 Estimate from 1759. See Maxine Berg, 'Women's Work and the Industrial Revolution', *ReFresh: Recent Findings of Research in Economic & Social History*, 12 (Spring 1991), www.ehs.org.uk/ehs/refresh/assets/Berg12a.pdf (accessed 14 June 2013).

81 Steinbach, *Women in England*, p.10.

82 Mary Louise Ormsby, 'Charlotte Badger', *DNZB*, Vol. 1, A&U/DIA, Wellington, 1990, p.11.

83 Ibid.

84 *Sydney Morning Herald*, 26 October 1937, p.21.

85 Trevor Bentley, *Captured by Maori: White Female Captives, Sex and Racism on the Nineteenth-century New Zealand Frontier*, Penguin, Auckland, 2004, p.27.

86 Anne Salmond, *Between Worlds: Early Exchanges Between Maori and Europeans, 1773–1815*, Viking/University of Hawaii Press, Honolulu, 1997, p.360.

87 Trevor Bentley, *Pakeha Maori: The Extraordinary Story of the Europeans Who Lived as Maori in Early New Zealand*, Penguin, Auckland, 1999, p.37.

88 J. A. James, *Female Piety or the Young Woman's Friend and Guide Through Life to Immortality* (5th edn), 1856, p.63, quoted in Davidoff and Hall, *Family Fortunes*, p.115.

89 A. W. Beasley, *Fellowship of Three*, Kangaroo Press, Kenthurst, NSW, 1993, p.73. See also https://anmm.wordpress.com/tag/elizabeth-cook (accessed 9 July 2015). The Australian National Maritime Museum holds the embroidery attributed to Elizabeth Cook.

90 Beasley, *Fellowship of Three*, p.50.

91 Anne Salmond, *Two Worlds: First Meetings Between Maori and Europeans, 1642–1772*, Viking/University of Hawaii Press, Honolulu, 1991, p.87.

92 'Every Maori, especially if he came of a good family, knew his or her genealogy and exact relationship to every relative.' Makereti, *The Old-Time Maori* (1st edn 1938), New Women's Press, Auckland, 1986, p.37.

93 Lisbet Koerner, 'Carl Linnaeus in his Time and Place', in N. Jardine, J. A. Secord and E. C. Spary, *Cultures of Natural History*, Cambridge University Press, London, 1996, p.151.

94 Ibid., pp.146–47.

95 Margaret T. Hodgen, *Early Anthropology in the Sixteenth and Seventeenth Centuries*, University of Pennsylvania Press, Philadelphia, 1964, pp.425–26, cited in Salmond, *Two Worlds*, p.116.

96 Clare Midgley, *Feminism and Empire: Women Activists in Imperial Britain, 1790–1865*, Routledge, London, 2007, p.14.

97 Nancy Cott, *Public Vows: A History of Marriage and the Nation*, Harvard University Press, London, 2002, p.22.

98 Ibid., p.3.

99 Salmond, *Two Worlds*, p.95.

100 Ibid., p.361.

101 Porter, *The Creation of the Modern World*, p.361.

102 Joseph Banks in J. C. Beaglehole (ed.), *The Endeavour Journal of Joseph Banks 1768–1771*, Vol. 2, 1962, p.33, cited in Salmond, *Two Worlds*, p.289.

103 Ibid., pp.275–76.

104 James Cook in J. C. Beaglehole (ed.), *The Journals of Captain James Cook on His Voyages of Discovery. Vol. 1. The Voyage of the Endeavour 1768–1771*, Cambridge University Press, for the Hakluyt Society, 1968, pp.538–39, cited in Salmond, *Two Worlds*, pp.178–79.

105 William Monkhouse in Beaglehole (ed.), *The Journals of Captain James Cook, Vol. 1*, p.575, cited in Salmond, *Two Worlds*, p.144.

106 Sydney Parkinson, *A Journal of a Voyage to the South Seas in His Majesty's Ship, The Endeavour*, facsimile edn, Libraries Board of Australia, Adelaide, 1972, p.210, cited in Salmond, *Two Worlds*, p.228.

107 Banks in Beaglehole (ed.), *The Endeavour Journal of Joseph Banks*, Vol. 2, p.16, cited in Salmond, *Two Worlds*, pp.275.

108 J. C. Beaglehole (ed.), *The Endeavour Journal of Joseph Banks*, Vol. 1, Trustees of the Public Library of New South Wales in association with Angus & Robertson, Sydney, 1962, p.457, cited in J. M. Davidson, 'The Polynesian Foundations', in W. H. Oliver and B. R. Williams (eds), *The Oxford History of New Zealand*, OUP, Wellington, 1981, p.24.

109 Salmond, *Two Worlds*, pp.270–71.

110 Kathryn Rountree, 'Maori Bodies in European Eyes: Representations of the Maori Body on Cook's Voyages', *Journal of the Polynesian Society*, 107, 1 (1998), pp.43–44.

111 Ibid., pp.35–59.

112 Beaglehole (ed.), *The Journals of Captain James Cook, Vol. 2*, 1961, pp.174–75, cited in ibid., pp.38–39.

113 Michael E. Hoare (ed.), *The Resolution Journal of Johann Reinhold Forster, 1772–1775*, Vol. 2, the Hakluyt Society, London, 1982, p.254.

114 Rountree, 'Maori Bodies in European Eyes', pp.54–55.

115 J. R. Forster, *Observations Made During a Voyage Round the World on Physical Geography, National History and Ethical Philosophy*, G. Robinson, London, 1778, p.237, cited in ibid., p.40.

116 Rountree, 'Maori Bodies in European Eyes', pp.53–55.

117 Antoinette Burton, *Burdens of History: British Feminists, Indian Women, and Imperial Culture, 1865–1915*, University of North Carolina Press, Chapel Hill, 1994, p.75.

118 Jane Rendall, *The Origins of Modern Feminism: Women in Britain, France and the United States 1780–1860*, Macmillan, London, 1985, p.76, quoting F. A. Cox, *Female Scripture Biography: Including an Essay on What Christianity has Done for Women*, Vol. 2, London, 1817, p.xcvi.

119 Du Clesmuer Journal, in I. Ollivier and J. Spencer, *Extracts from Journals relating to the Visit to New Zealand in May–July 1772 of the French Ships Mascarin and Marquis de Castries under the command of M. J. Marion de Fresne*, ATL Endowment Trust with Indosuez, N.Z. Ltd, Wellington, 1985, p.23, cited in Salmond, *Two Worlds*, p.372.

120 Edwin Palmer related meeting a Māori 'regarded as the son of one of Captain Cook's crew, from a liaison in Queen Charlotte Sound'. Atholl Anderson, 'Race Against Time', Hocken Lecture, University of Otago, 1991, p.2. For an 1801 comment on 'that destructive disease the venereal is among them', see Paul Monin, *Hauraki Contested 1769–1875*, BWB, Wellington, 2001, p.32.

121 Kate Riddell, 'A "Marriage of the Races": Aspects of Intermarriage, Ideology and Reproduction on the New Zealand Frontier', MA thesis, Victoria University of Wellington, 1996, p.3.

122 Ibid., p.32.

123 J. M. R. Owens, 'New Zealand before Annexation', in Oliver and Williams (eds), *The Oxford History of New Zealand*, p.48.

124 Stephen Donaldson, 'Hineawhitia Williams

(circa 1810–circa 1853)', in Jane Thomson (ed.), *Southern People,* Longacre Press, Dunedin, 1998, p.547.

125 Monin, *Hauraki Contested*, p.40.

126 Angela Wanhalla, '"One White Man I Like Very Much": Interracial Marriage and the Cultural Encounter in Southern New Zealand, 1829–1850', *Journal of Women's History*, 20, 2 (2008), pp.34–51.

127 Ibid., p.51.

128 Angela Wanhalla, *In/visible Sight: The Mixed Descent Families of Southern New Zealand*, BWB, Wellington, 2009, pp.37–68.

129 Edward Jerningham Wakefield, *Adventure in New Zealand, from 1839 to 1844*, Vol. 1, John Murray, London, 1845, p.324.

130 J. W. Barnicoat, a surveyor's assistant on the *Deborah*, recorded this exchange in his journal, 8 May 1844, p.56, cited in Sheila Natusch and Bridget Williams, 'Makariri', in Charlotte Macdonald, Merimeri Penfold and Bridget Williams (eds), *The Book of New Zealand Women: Ko Kui Me Te Kaupapa*, BWB, Wellington, 1991, pp.407–8.

131 Ernest Dieffenbach, *Travels in New Zealand*, John Murray, London, 1843, p.38.

132 Wakefield, *Adventure in New Zealand*, p.324.

133 'Further Papers Relative to Native Affairs. Report from Mr Fenton, R. M. as to Native Affairs in the Waikato District', *AJHR*, 1860, E-1C, p.17.

Chapter 2

1 Eliza White, Journals, 1829–1926, cited in Sandra Coney, 'Eliza White, 1809–1883,' in Charlotte Macdonald, Merimeri Penfold and Bridget Williams (eds), *The Book of New Zealand Women: Ko Kui Ma Te Kaupapa*, BWB, Wellington, 1991, p.723.

2 Coney, 'Eliza White', p.723.

3 Megan Hutching, *Over the Wide and Trackless Sea: The Pioneer Women and Girls of New Zealand*, HarperCollins, Auckland, 2008, pp.22–23.

4 Coney, 'Eliza White', p.724.

5 Ibid.

6 See Basil Keane, 'Traditional Māori religion: Ngā karakia a te Māori', in *Te Ara: The Encyclopedia of New Zealand*, www.teara. govt.nz/en/traditional-maori-religion-nga-karakia-a-te-maori (accessed 20 March 2015).

7 'John King and Hannah Hansen family', https://sites.google.com/site/

pre1839settlersinnz/home/more-details-3/
john-king-and-hannah-hansen-family
(accessed 26 June 2013).

8   J. C. Stanley, 'Giving Honour Unto the Wife',
    *Journal of the New Zealand Federation of
    Historical Societies*, 1, 11 (1981), p.10.

9   Quoted in S. J. Goldsbury, 'Behind the Picket
    Fence: The Lives of Missionary Wives in Pre-
    Colonial New Zealand', MA thesis, University
    of Auckland, 1986, p.107.

10 Cited in Angela Middleton, *Te Puna: A New
    Zealand Mission Station*, Springer, Dortrecht,
    2009, pp.57–58.

11 Ibid., pp.114–15.

12 John King, Letter to the Church Missionary
    Society, cited in Middleton, *Te Puna*, p.114.

13 'British Land Pattern Musket (Brown Bess)
    Muzzle-Loading Service Musket (1722)',
    www.militaryfactory.com/smallarms/detail.
    asp?smallarms_id=361 (accessed 17 March
    2015); Matthew Wright, *Guns and Utu: A
    Short History of the Musket Wars*, Penguin,
    Auckland, 2011, pp.126–27.

14 'Musket Wars', www.nzhistory.net.nz/war/
    musket-wars/overview (accessed 17 March
    2015).

15 Angela Ballara, *Iwi: The Dynamics of Māori
    Tribal Organisation from c.1769 to c.1945*,
    VUP, Wellington, 1998, p.236.

16 Ibid., p.245.

17 Raina Meha, 'Rangi Topeora', in Macdonald,
    Penfold and Williams (eds) *The Book of New
    Zealand Women*, pp.685–87.

18 J. B. Pratt, 'Instructions to the Rev. Henry
    Williams', 6 August 1822, cited in Goldsbury,
    'Behind the Picket Fence', p.73.

19 S. J. Brittan, George, Charles and Arthur
    Grace (eds), *A Pioneer Missionary Among
    the Maoris, 1850–1879*, G. H. Bennett & Co.,
    Palmerston North, 1928, p.14.

20 Mami Harada, 'Women's Suffrage in New
    Zealand: What Made it Possible?' unpublished
    paper in author's possession.

21 Eugene Stock, *History of the Church
    Missionary Society*, Vol. 1, Church Missionary
    Society, London, 1899, p.215, cited in Frances
    Porter (ed.), *The Turanga Journals 1840–1850:
    Letters and Journals of William and Jane
    Williams, Missionaries to Poverty Bay*, Price
    Milburn for VUP, Wellington, 1974, p.26.

22 J. M. R. Owens, *Prophets in the Wilderness: The
    Wesleyan Mission to New Zealand, 1819–27*,
    AUP, Auckland, 1974, p.143.

23 Leonore Davidoff, Megan Doolittle, Janet
    Fink and Katherine Holden, *The Family Story:
    Blood, Contract and Intimacy, 1830–1960*,
    Longman, London, 1999, p.8.

24 Sarah M. Williams, 'Marianne Williams',
    DNZB, Vol. 1, A&U/DIA, Wellington, 1990,
    p.595.

25 John Houghton (trans.), *J. F. H. Wohlers
    Missionary at Ruapuke, New Zealand: An
    Autobiography*, Otago Daily Times and
    Witness Newspapers Company, Dunedin,
    1895, p.169.

26 Cited in D. M. Stafford, *Te Arawa: A History of
    the Arawa People*, Reed, Auckland, 1967, p.346.

27 Claudia Orange, 'The Maori and the Crown',
    in K. Sinclair (ed.), *The Oxford Illustrated
    History of New Zealand*, OUP, Auckland, 1990,
    p.36.

28 David Martin, 'The Maori *Whare* After
    Contact', MA thesis, University of Otago, 1996,
    p.115.

29 Owens, *Prophets in the Wilderness*, p.120.

30 Nancy M. Taylor (ed.), *Early Travellers in New
    Zealand*, Clarendon Press, Oxford, 1959, p.71.

31 June Starke, 'Sarah Selwyn', in Macdonald,
    Penfold and Williams (eds), *The Book of New
    Zealand Women*, p.595.

32 Angela Ballara, 'Wāhine Rangatira', *New
    Zealand Journal of History*, 27, 2 (1993), p.134.

33 Hazel Petrie, *Chiefs of Industry: Māori Tribal
    Enterprise in Early Colonial New Zealand*,
    AUP, Auckland, 2006, p.39.

34 Ibid., p.48.

35 Mary Ann Martin, *Our Maoris*, Society for
    Promoting Christian Knowledge, London,
    1884, p.12.

36 Ibid., p.67. Emphasis in the original.

37 Hugh Carleton, *The Life of Henry Williams
    Archdeacon of Waimate*, A. H. & A. W. Reed,
    Wellington, 1948, p.55.

38 Cited in Kathryn Rountree, 'Re-making the
    Maori Female Body: Marianne Williams'
    Mission in the Bay of Islands', *Journal of
    Pacific History*, 35, 1 (2000), p.57.

39 Cited in ibid., p.59.

40 Ruth Fry, *Out of the Silence: Methodist Women
    of Aotearoa, 1822–1985*, Methodist Publishing,
    Christchurch, 1985, p.37.

41 M. P. K. Sorrenson, 'Maori and Pakeha',
    in W. H. Oliver and B. R. Williams (eds),
    The Oxford History of New Zealand, OUP,
    Wellington, 1981, p.171.

42 Cited in Owens, *Prophets in the Wilderness*, pp.142, 135.

43 Bruce Biggs, *Maori Marriage*, A. H. & A. W. Reed, Wellington, 1960, p.74.

44 Goldsbury, 'Behind the Picket Fence', p.14.

45 J. L. Nicholas, *Narrative of Voyage to New Zealand*, Black & Son, London, 1817, pp.170–71, cited in Goldsbury, 'Behind the Picket Fence', p.64.

46 Salmond, 'TIPUNA: Ancestors in Maori', unpublished paper, p.2.

47 A. E. Brougham and A. W. Reed, *Maori Proverbs*, Reed Methuen, Auckland, 1987, p.21.

48 Rangimarie Rose Pere, 'Te Wheke: Whaia te Maramatanga me te Aroha', in Sue Middleton (ed.), *Women and Education in Aotearoa*, A&U/Port Nicholson Press, Wellington, 1988, p.8.

49 A. J. Ballantyne, 'Reforming the Heathen Body: C.M.S. Missionaries, Sexuality, and the Maori, 1814–1850', BA Hons History dissertation, University of Otago, 1993, p.41.

50 John Hobbs, cited in Owens, *Prophets in the Wilderness*, p.50.

51 Biggs, *Maori Marriage*, p.12.

52 Bernard Smith, *European Vision and the South Pacific*, Yale University Press, New Haven, 1985, p.322; Judith Binney, *The Legacy of Guilt: A Life of Thomas Kendall* (2nd edn), BWB, Wellington, 2005, p.134.

53 Cited in Rountree, 'Re-making the Maori Female Body', p.62.

54 Fry, *Out of the Silence*, p.26.

55 J. M. R. Owens, 'Christianity and the Maoris to 1840', *New Zealand Journal of History*, 2, 1 (1968), p.36.

56 Owens, *Prophets in the Wilderness*, p.50.

57 Ibid., p.74. Emphasis in original.

58 Ibid., p.126.

59 Judith Binney, 'Kendall, Thomas', *DNZB*, www.teara.govt.nz/en/biographies/1k9/kendall-thomas (accessed 15 March 2015).

60 Richard Cruise, *Journal of a Ten Months Residence in New Zealand [1820]*, London, 1823, cited in Monin, *Hauraki Contested*, p.55.

61 J. M. R. Owens, 'New Zealand before Annexation', in Oliver and Williams (eds), *The Oxford History of New Zealand*, p.105.

62 Cited in Joan Druett, *Petticoat Whalers: Whaling Wives at Sea 1820–1920*, Collins, Auckland, 1991, p.106.

63 Edward Markham (ed. E. H. McCormick), *New Zealand or Recollections of It*, Government Printer, Wellington, 1963, p.65.

64 Philip Andrews, *Ko Mata: The Life in New Zealand of Anne Chapman, Missionary at the Bay of Islands, Rotorua and Maketu, 1830–1855*, Rotorua and District Historical Society, Rotorua, 1991, p.9.

65 F. Allan Hanson argues that the concept of sexuality as sinful is 'utterly alien to Maori culture': 'Female Pollution in Polynesia?', *Journal of the Polynesian Society*, 91, 3 (1982), p.354. For similar ideas considered in another cultural context, see Jo-anne Fiske, 'Colonisation and the Decline of Women's Status: The Tsimshian Case', *Feminist Studies*, 17, 3 (1991), p.524.

66 Cited in J. R. Elder, *Marsden's Lieutenants*, A. H. Reed, Dunedin, 1934, p.82.

67 Elsdon Best noted the absence of a prostitute class in Māori society: Best, 'Maori Marriage Customs', *Transactions and Proceedings of the Royal Society of New Zealand*, Vol. 36, 1903, p.33.

68 Best was basing his observations on the Tūhoe people, ibid., pp.15, 29, 34–35.

69 Cited by Biggs, *Maori Marriage*, p.57.

70 Porter (ed.), *The Turanga Journals*, p.493.

71 Cited in K. R. Howe, 'The Maori Response to Christianity in the Thames-Waikato Region', *New Zealand Journal of History*, 7, 1 (1973), p.35.

72 Owens, *Prophets in the Wilderness*, p.37.

73 Ibid., p.142.

74 Biggs, *Maori Marriage*, pp.44–45.

75 Florence Keene, *By this We Conquer*, F. Keene, Whāngārei, 1974, p.55.

76 Fry, *Out of the Silence*, p.37.

77 Ibid., p.38.

78 James Belich, *The New Zealand Wars and the Victorian Interpretation of Racial Conflict*, AUP, Auckland, 1986, p.66.

79 W. T. Parham, 'Tapsell, Phillip, 177?–1873', *DNZB*, Vol. 1, pp.425–26.

80 Russell Caldwell, *Tapihana: Brothers in Arms*, Iwi-link Management, Christchurch, 2004, p.7.

81 Sheila Natusch, 'Johann Friedrich Heinrich Wohlers', *DNZB*, Vol. 1, p.606.

82 Atholl Anderson, *Race Against Time*, Hocken Library, University of Otago, 1991, pp.28–29.

83 Owens, 'New Zealand before Annexation', p.48.

84 Ibid., p.46.

85 Ibid., p.41.

86 Ibid., p.42.

87 Ged Martin, 'Wakefield's Past and Futures', in The Friends of the Turnbull Library, *Edward Gibbon Wakefield and the Colonial Dream: A Reconsideration*, GP Publications, Wellington, 1997, pp.20–46.

88 Raewyn Dalziel, 'Men, Women and Wakefield', in The Friends of the Turnbull Library, *Edward Gibbon Wakefield and the Colonial Dream*, p.29.

89 Cited in ibid., p.80.

90 Edward Gibbon Wakefield, *A Letter from Sydney*, in M. F. Lloyd Prichard, *The Collected Works of Edward Gibbon Wakefield*, Collins, Glasgow, 1968, p.111.

91 Cited in Ngatata Love, 'Edward Gibbon Wakefield: A Maori Perspective', in The Friends of the Turnbull Library, *Edward Gibbon Wakefield and the Colonial Dream*, p.4.

92 Cited in Dalziel, 'Men, Women and Wakefield', pp.81–82.

93 Ibid., pp.83–84.

94 Edward Gibbon Wakefield, *A Letter from Sydney*, p.163.

95 James Belich, *Making Peoples: A History of the New Zealanders: From Polynesian Settlement to the End of the Nineteenth Century*, Allen Lane, Auckland, 1996, p.187.

96 Claudia Orange, *The Treaty of Waitangi*, A&U/Port Nicholson Press, Wellington, 1987, pp.11–12.

97 'Report from the Select Committee of the House of Lords, Appointed to Inquire into the Present State of the Islands of New Zealand, and the Expediency of Regulating the Settlement of British Subjects Therein, 1837–38' (680) XXI, 69, in Tony Ballantyne, 'Humanitarian Narratives: Knowledge and the Politics of Mission and Empire', *Social Sciences and Missions*, 24 (2011), p.257.

98 Ballantyne, 'Humanitarian Narratives', pp.259–60.

99 Comment by the Chief Surveyor, Felton Mathew, cited in Elsie Locke and Janet Paul, *Mrs Hobson's Album*, AUP/ATL, Auckland, 1989, p.11.

100 K. A. Simpson, 'Hobson, William', *DNZB*, www.teara.govt.nz/en/biographies/1h29/hobson-william (accessed 20 March 2015).

101 The Treaty of Waitangi (English text) in Orange, *The Treaty of Waitangi*, p.258.

102 Orange, *The Treaty of Waitangi*, p.90.

103 Locke and Paul, *Mrs Hobson's Album*, p.22.

104 Ibid., p.11.

105 *Auckland Times* cited in Locke and Paul, *Mrs Hobson's Album*, p.11.

106 G. W. A. Bush, *Decently and in Order: The Government of the City of Auckland 1840–1971*, Collins, Auckland, 1971, p.22.

107 John Wilson, 'The voyage out – Personal accounts: 1840–1899', *Te Ara: The Encyclopedia of New Zealand*, www.teara.govt.nz/en/community-contribution/4309/determination-rewarded (accessed 19 March 2015).

108 Jim McAloon, *Nelson: A Regional History*, Cape Catley, Whatamangō Bay, 1997, p.15.

109 Ibid., p.16.

110 Patricia A. Sargison, 'Rymill, Mary Anne', *DNZB*, www.teara.govt.nz/en/biographies/1r23/rymill-mary-anne (accessed 10 February 2015).

111 Ibid.

112 W. J. Gardner, 'A Colonial Economy', in Oliver and Williams (eds), *The Oxford History of New Zealand*, pp.60–62. On protests by immigrants, see Tony Simpson, *The Immigrants: The Great Migration from Britain to New Zealand, 1830–1890*, Godwit, 1997, pp.94–97.

113 Erik Olssen, *A History of Otago*, John McIndoe, Dunedin, 1984, p.34.

114 Ibid.

115 Ralph Johnson, *The Trust Administration of Maori Reserves*, Rangahaua Whanau National Theme L, August 1997, www.waitangi-tribunal.govt.nz/doclibrary/public/researchwhanui/theme/ThemeL-JohnsonTrustadminofMaorireserves.pdf (accessed 5 July 2013).

116 Cited in ibid., p.16.

117 The Māori communities in Massacre Bay, Nelson, for example: see McAloon, *Nelson*, p.50.

118 Kathleen A. Coleridge, 'Revans, Samuel', *DNZB*, www.teara.govt.nz/en/biographies/1r5/revans-samuel (accessed 15 January 2015)

119 Rachel Barrowman, 'Davis, Rowland Robert Teape', *DNZB*, www.teara.govt.nz/en/biographies/1d4/davis-rowland-robert-teape (accessed 15 January 2015).

120 *New Zealand Colonist and Port Nicholson Advertiser*, 23 September 1842, p.3.

121 W. Sidney Smith, *Women's Franchise Movement in New Zealand*, Whitcombe & Tombs, Christchurch, 1905, p.vi.

122 A. H. McLintock, *Crown Colony Government in New Zealand*, Government Printer, Wellington, 1958, p.419.

123 W. David McIntyre, *The Journal of Henry Sewell, 1853–7*, Vol. 1, Whitcoulls, Christchurch, 1980, p.229.

124 Ibid., p.258.

125 F. D. Fenton, 'Memorandum as to Domiciliary Conditions of the Natives', 'Papers relative to the Right of Aboriginal Natives to the Elective Franchise', *AJHR*, 1860, E-7, pp.3–4.

126 Richard Bethel and Henry S. Keating, 'The Law Officer of the Crown to the Duke of Newcastle', 'Elective Franchise', *AJHR*, 1860, E-7, 3, p.8.

127 Hugh Carleton, 'Memorandum', 'Elective Franchise', *AJHR*, 1860, E-7, p.5. Emphasis in original.

128 *Daily Southern Cross*, 5 April 1859. Emphasis in original, p.3.

129 John Gorst, *The Maori King: Or The Story of Our Quarrel With the Natives of New Zealand* (1st edn 1864), Paul's Book Arcade, Auckland, 1959, http://nzetc.victoria.ac.nz// tm/scholarly/tei-GorMaor-t1-body-d2.html pp. 16-17 (accessed 6 July 2013).

Chapter 3

1 Charlotte Godley, *Letters from Early New Zealand*, Bowering Press, Plymouth, 1936, p.19.

2 Ibid., p.25.

3 Ibid.

4 'Immigrant Ships Transcribers Guild Barque Lady Nugent',www.immigrantships. net/v3/1800v3/ladynugent18410317.html (accessed 5 June 2015).

5 Godley, *Letters from Early New Zealand*, pp.8–9.

6 Passenger list of the *Oriental*, http://freepages. genealogy.rootsweb.ancestry.com/~donegal/ family/oriental.htm, (accessed 5 June 2015).

7 'Mrs Sole's Memories, 1841–1926', in Airini E. Woodhouse (ed.), *Tales of Pioneer Women*, Whitcombe & Tombs, Christchurch, 1940, p.81.

8 Woodhouse (ed.), *Tales of Pioneer Women*, p.82; David Hastings, *Over the Mountains of the Sea: Life on the Migrant Ships 1870–1885*, AUP, Auckland, 2006, p.84.

9 See Hastings, *Over the Mountains of the Sea*, pp.73–96.

10 Ibid., p.85.

11 Ibid., pp.84–85.

12 Queen's Order-in-Council, 7 January 1864; Instructions to Captains, Surgeons and Matrons of Emigrant Ships, 1873–4; regulations on emigrant ships, cited in Hastings, *Over the Mountains of the Sea*, p.175.

13 Hastings, *Over the Mountains of the Sea*, p.175.

14 Jane Findlayson, Journal, 4 October 1876, TS, MS-Papers-1678, Manuscripts Collection, ATL. Cited in Lilja Mareika Sautter, 'Femininity and Community at Home and Away: Shipboard Diaries by Single Women Emigrants to New Zealand', *Victorian Literature and Culture*, 43 (2015), pp.311–12.

15 Hastings, *Over the Mountains of the Sea*, p.94.

16 Godley, *Letters from Early New Zealand*, pp.13–15. Emphasis in the original.

17 Woodhouse (ed.), *Tales of Pioneer Women*, p.82.

18 Frances Porter, *Born to New Zealand: A Biography of Jane Maria Atkinson*, A&U/Port Nicholson Press, Wellington, 1989, p.59.

19 Woodhouse (ed.), *Tales of Pioneer Women*, p.154.

20 Charlotte Macdonald, *A Woman of Good Character: Single Women as Immigrant Settlers in Nineteenth-century New Zealand*, A&U/Historical Branch, Wellington, 1990, p.193.

21 Woodhouse (ed.), *Tales of Pioneer Women*, pp.152–53.

22 Charlotte Warburton, MS War, ATL, p.70.

23 Cited in Roberta McIntyre, *The Canoes of Kupe: A History of Martinborough District*, VUP, Wellington, 2002, pp.68–69.

24 'M 8.2 - 8.3, Wairarapa, 23 January 1855', http://info.geonet.org.nz/display/quake/ M+8.2+-+8.3,+Wairarapa,+23+January+1855 (accessed 27 July 2015).

25 G. Downes and R. Grapes, 'The 1855 Wairarapa, New Zealand, Earthquake – Historical Data', in *Institute of Geological and Nuclear Sciences Science Report 99/16* (1999), pp.14–15, cited in McIntyre, *The Canoes of Kupe*, p.69.

26 *Nelson Examiner and New Zealand Chronicle*, 21 February 1855, p.2.

27 *Wellington Independent*, 11 January 1861, p.2.

28 *Taranaki Herald*, 19 January 1861, p.4.

29 Ibid.

30 *Hawke's Bay Herald*, 2 February 1861, p.1.

31 C. Warburton, MS War, ATL, p.68.

32 Godley, *Letters from Early New Zealand*, pp.33–35.

33 Edward Brown Fitton, *New Zealand: Its Present Condition, Prospects and Resources*, Edward Stanford, London, 1856, cited in John Macgibbon, *Piano in the Parlour: When the Piano was New Zealand's Home Entertainment Centre*, Ngaio Press, Wellington, 2007, p.12.

34 Mary Ann Martin, *Our Maoris*, Society for Promoting Christian Knowledge, London, 1884, pp.12–13.

35 Warburton, MS War, ATL, p.74.

36 Cited in Katherine Raine, 'Domesticating the Land: Colonial Women's Gardening', in Bronwyn Dalley and Bronwyn Labrum (eds), *Fragments: New Zealand Social and Cultural History*, AUP, Auckland, 2000, p.82.

37 Cited in Raine, 'Domesticating the Land', p.80.

38 Jane Ann Moorhouse, Journal and Household Account Book, 1867–1869, May 6, 1868, MS Moo, ATL.

39 Nancy Swarbrick. 'Flax and flax working – Māori use of flax', *Te Ara: The Encyclopedia of New Zealand*, www.teara.govt.nz/en/flax-and-flax-working/page-2 (accessed 14 October 2015).

40 *New Zealand Gazette and Wellington Spectator*, 23 November 1842, p.2.

41 *New Zealand Gazette and Wellington Spectator*, 20 May 1843, p.3.

42 *Nelson Examiner and New Zealand Chronicle*, 10 July 1847, p.71.

43 *Taranaki Herald*, 29 September 1852, p.2.

44 Catherine E. Bishop, 'Commerce Was a Woman: Women in Business in Colonial Sydney and Wellington', PhD thesis, Australian National University, 2012, p.83.

45 Louise George Rose to her sister Constance, Journal, 8 November to 20 December 1853, S Papers 2314, ATL, cited in Jane Malthus, 'Dressmakers in 19th Century New Zealand', in B. Brookes, C. Macdonald and M. Tennant (eds), *Women in History 2*, BWB, Wellington, 1992, p.86.

46 Bishop, 'Commerce Was a Woman', p.66.

47 Ibid., p.81.

48 Mary Taylor to Ellen Nussey, 9 February 1849, WS no. 422 MS Berg Collection, New York Public Library, in Joan Stevens (ed.), *Mary Taylor: Friend of Charlotte Brontë*, John McIndoe, Dunedin, 1972, p.80.

49 Pat Sargison, 'Mary Taylor, 1817–1893', in Charlotte Macdonald, Merimeri Penfold and Bridget Williams (eds), *The Book of New Zealand Women: Ko Kui Ma Te Kaupapa*, BWB, Wellington, 1991, pp.657–59.

50 Mary Taylor to Ellen Nussey, 4 to 8 January 1857, WS no. 977 MS Berg Collection, New York Public Library, in Stevens (ed.), *Mary Taylor*, p.130.

51 Ibid., pp.130–31.

52 Raewyn Dalziel, 'Grace Hirst, 1805–1901', *DNZB*, Vol. 1, A&U/DIA, Wellington, 1990, p.193.

53 Sarah Amelia Courage, *Lights and Shadows of Colonial Life*, Whitcoulls, Christchurch, 1976, pp.92–95.

54 *Press*, 28 August 1866, p.3.

55 *New Zealand Herald*, 8 May 1877, p.6.

56 See Bishop, 'Commerce Was a Woman'.

57 *Evening Post*, 21 January 1887, p.4.

58 Jacob F. Field, 'Domestic Service, Gender, and Wages in Rural England c.1760–1860', *Economic History Review*, 66, 1 (2013), pp.249–72.

59 *Timaru Herald*, 18 June 1864, p.4.

60 *New Zealand Spectator and Cook's Strait Guardian*, 4 March 1854, p.3.

61 Ibid.; see also Angela Ballara, 'Te Puni-kokopu, Honiana', *DNZB*, www.teara.govt.nz/en/biographies/1t58/te-puni-kokopu-honiana (accessed 13 February 2015).

62 *New Zealand Spectator and Cook's Strait Guardian*, 4 March 1854, p.3.

63 Godley, *Letters from Early New Zealand*, p.38. Emphasis in the original.

64 Raewyn Dalziel, 'Marital and Reproductive Behaviour among European Women in Colonial New Zealand', unpublished paper.

65 See Macdonald, *A Woman of Good Character*.

66 Charlotte Macdonald, '"Too Many Men and Too Few Women": Gender's "Fatal Impact" in Nineteenth-Century Colonies', in Caroline Daley and Deborah Montgomerie (eds), *The Gendered Kiwi*, AUP, Auckland, 1999, p.26.

67 Ian Pool, Arunachalam Dharmalingam and Janet Sceats, *The New Zealand Family from 1840: A Demographic History*, AUP, Auckland, 2007, p.74.

68 Porter, *Born to New Zealand*, p.50.

69 Ibid., p.76.

70 S. M. Goldsbury, 'Behind the Picket Fence: The Lives of Missionary Wives in Pre-colonial New Zealand', MA thesis, Auckland University, 1986, p.109.

71 *Daily Southern Cross*, 1 May 1869, p.3.

72 Macdonald, *A Woman of Good Character*, p.70.

73 *Invercargill Times*, 14 October 1863, p.2.

74 Jock Phillips, *A Man's Country: The Image of the Pakeha Male*, Penguin, Auckland, 1987, p.36.

75 Macdonald, *A Woman of Good Character*, p.140.

76 Sarah Courage, *Lights and Shadows of Colonial Life*, p.42, cited in Raine, 'Domesticating the Land', p.84.

77 30 May 1857, in Robin Homes and Allan J. Farley (eds), *Dear Sister: Letters Between a Pioneer Wairarapa Family and Relatives in Rural England, 1856–1883*, Wairarapa Archive, Masterton, 2006, pp.45–46.

78 Jean Garner, 'Rural Society Expands and Adapts', in Garth Cant and Russell Kirkpatrick (eds), *Rural Canterbury: Celebrating its History*, Daphne Brasell Associates and Lincoln University Press, Wellington, 2001, p.105.

79 O. A. Gillespie, *Oxford: The First Hundred Years* (1st edn 1953), Cadsonbury Publications, Oxford, 2001, p.26.

80 Ibid., p.97.

81 Ibid., p.101.

82 Margaret Tennant, 'Matrons with a Mission: Women's Organisations in New Zealand 1893–1915', MA thesis, Massey University, Palmerston North, 1976, p.9.

83 Rosemary Killip, *To Find a Fortune: Women of the Thames Goldfield, 1867–1893*, Women's Studies, Victoria University of Wellington, 1995, p.20.

84 A. J. T. Fraser, 'The Social Work of the Presbyterian Church in New Zealand up till 1930', MA thesis, University of Otago, 1933, p.81.

85 Raewyn Dalziel, 'Marriage and Reproduction in a Colonial Community', unpublished paper presented to the Otago Historical Association Society, Dunedin, April 1992, n.p.

86 Ibid.

87 G. H. Sutherland, 'Sarah Ann Cripps, 1821/22?–1892', *DNZB*, Vol. 1, pp.94–95.

88 David Thomson, 'Marriage and the Family on the Colonial Frontier', in Tony Ballantyne and Brian Moloughney (eds), *Disputed Histories: Imagining New Zealand's Pasts*, University of Otago Press, Dunedin, 2006, p.131.

89 'Sarah Ann Taylor, 1856–1924', in Tauranga Women's Centre (eds), *New Zealand Herstory*, John McIndoe, Dunedin, 1982, p.27.

90 Alison Clarke, *Born to a Changing World: Childbirth in Nineteenth-Century New Zealand*, BWB, Wellington, 2012, p.174.

91 J. Graham, 'The Pioneers: 1840–1870', in Keith Sinclair (ed.), *The Oxford Illustrated History of New Zealand*, OUP, Auckland, 1990, p.72.

92 Raewyn Dalziel, '"Making Us One": Courtship and Marriage in Colonial New Zealand', *Turnbull Library Record*, 19, 1 (May 1986), p.24.

93 Homes and Farley (eds), *Dear Sister*, p.126.

94 MS Moo, ATL, 1869.

95 Macdonald, *A Woman of Good Character*, p.168.

96 Ibid., pp.168–69.

97 Warburton, MS War, ATL, p.71.

98 Porter, *Born to New Zealand*, p.156.

99 *Wanganui Herald*, 2 March 1872, p.2.

100 *New Zealand Herald*, 29 April 1873, p.2.

101 *Evening Post*, 13 May 1885, p.2.

102 Jean Garner and Kate Foster, *Letters to Grace: Writing Home from Colonial New Zealand*, CUP, Christchurch, 2011, pp.122–23.

103 MS Moo, ATL, 15 September 1869.

104 Wilding Family, Julia Wilding, 'Life Events', Box 14, Item 2, Folder 65, Canterbury Museum Archives.

105 Shelley Richardson, '"Striving After Better Things": Julia Wilding and the Making of a "New Woman" and a "Noble Gentleman"', MA thesis, University of Canterbury, 1997, p.187.

106 Frances Porter (ed.), *The Turanga Journals, 1840–1850*, Price Milburn for VUP, Wellington, 1974, p.373.

107 Frances Porter, 'Jane Maria Atkinson', in Macdonald, Penfold and Williams (eds), *The Book of New Zealand Women*, p.27.

108 Raeburn Lange, *May the People Live: A History of Maori Health Development 1900–1920*, AUP, Auckland, 1999, p.85.

109 *Wellington Independent*, 26 March 1851, p.2; *Nelson Examiner and New Zealand Chronicle*, 3 February 1844, p.397.

110 *Taranaki Herald*, 29 September 1852, p.2.

111 Cited in Lange, *May the People Live*, p.18.

Lange's book has an excellent discussion of concerns about Māori population decline.

112 *New Zealand Herald*, 11 June 1866, p.4.

113 *New Zealander*, 28 September 1850, p.2.

114 *Nelson Examiner and New Zealand Chronicle*, 10 January 1867, p.7.

115 Lange, *May the People Live*, p.85.

116 Edward Markham wrote in the 1830s of the decline of aboriginal peoples: 'my belief is that the Almighty intended it to be so'. Edward Markham (ed. E. H. McCormick), *New Zealand or Recollections of It*, Government Printer, Wellington, 1963, p.83. See James Belich, 'European ideas about Māori – The dying Māori and Social Darwinism', *Te Ara: The Encyclopedia of New Zealand*, www.teara.govt.nz/en/european-ideas-about-maori/page-4 (accessed 14 March 2015).

117 *Daily Southern Cross*, 31 August 1849, p.2; *New Zealander*, 25 August 1849, p.2.

118 *New Zealander*, 25 August 1849, p.2.

119 'New Zealand's Lost Cases', www.victoria.ac.nz/law/nzlostcases/CaseDetails.aspx?casenumber=00562 (accessed 9 August 2013). Bettina Bradbury, 'From Civil Death to Separate Property: Changes in the Legal Rights of Married Women in Nineteenth Century New Zealand', *New Zealand Journal of History*, 29, 2 (1995), pp.45–46.

120 *NZPD*, 1854, pp.220–23, quoted in Bradbury, 'From Civil Death to Separate Property', p.45.

121 Nancy F. Cott, *Public Vows: A History of Marriage and the Nation*, Harvard University Press, Cambridge, Mass., 2002, p.11.

122 Bradbury, 'From Civil Death to Separate Property', p.42.

123 Courage, p.93, cited in ibid., p.44.

124 Angela Ballara, 'Wāhine Rangatira: Māori Women of Rank and their Role in the Women's Kotahitanga Movement of the 1890s', *New Zealand Journal of History*, 27, 2 (1993), p.130. Emphasis in original.

125 Ibid., p.131.

126 Frances Porter and Charlotte Macdonald (eds), *'My Hand Will Write What My Heart Dictates': The Unsettled Lives of Women in Nineteenth-Century New Zealand as Revealed to Sisters, Family and Friends*, AUP, Auckland, 1996, p.107.

127 Ballara, 'Wāhine Rangatira', p.134.

128 Bradbury, 'From Civil Death to Separate Property', p.47.

129 Hon. George Marsden Waterhouse, MLC, Wellington, recounting the history, in *NZPD*, 21 June 1881, Vol. 38, p.133.

130 Bradbury, 'From Civil Death to Separate Property', p.51.

131 *NZPD*, 13 August 1860, Vol. 28, p.284.

132 Ibid.

133 W. B. Sutch, *Women with a Cause* (2nd edn), New Zealand University Press, Wellington, 1974, p.87.

134 Quoted in Macdonald, *A Woman of Good Character*, p.155.

135 Paul Husbands, 'The People of Freeman's Bay, 1880–1914', MA thesis, University of Auckland, 1992, pp.83, 87.

136 Margaret Tennant, *Paupers and Providers: Charitable Aid in New Zealand*, A&U/Historical Branch, DIA, Wellington, 1989, p.106.

137 Ibid., p.18.

138 Ibid., p.17.

139 Margaret Tennant, *The Fabric of Welfare: Voluntary Organisations, Government and Welfare in New Zealand, 1840–2005*, BWB, Wellington, 2007, p.30.

140 *Daily Southern Cross*, 4 December 1875, p.1.

141 *Daily Southern Cross*, 20 March 1872, p.7.

142 Bradbury, 'From Civil Death to Separate Property', p.42.

143 *Wellington Independent*, 21 September 1869, p.2.

Chapter 4

1 Janet C. Angus, 'Catherine Carran, 1842–1935', *DNZB*, Vol. 2, BWB/DIA, Wellington, 1993, p.78.

2 'Curiosus' in the *New Zealander*, 3 July 1858, cited in M. P. K. Sorrenson, 'Maori and Pakeha', in W. H. Oliver and B. R. Williams (eds), *The Oxford History of New Zealand*, OUP, Wellington, 1981, p.180.

3 Philippa Mein Smith, *A Concise History of New Zealand*, Cambridge University Press, Cambridge, 2005, p.69.

4 Peter Adds, 'Te Āti Awa of Taranaki – Origins and lands', *Te Ara: The Encyclopedia of New Zealand*, www.teara.govt.nz/en/map/786/te-ati-awa-lands (accessed 24 July 2013).

5 Cited in James Belich, *The New Zealand Wars and the Victorian Interpretation of Racial Conflict*, AUP, Auckland, 1986, p.79.

6 Ibid., p.126.

7   Waitangi Tribunal, *The Taranaki Report: Kaupapa Tuatahi*, chapter 4, section 4.5, www.justice.govt.nz/tribunals/waitangi-tribunal/Reports/wai0143/chapt04 (accessed 24 July 2015).

8   Valerie Burr and Lydia McLennan-Boman, 'Lydia Burr, 1838–1930', in Charlotte Macdonald, Merimeri Penfold and Bridget Williams (eds), *The Book of New Zealand Women: Ko Kui Ma Te Kaupapa*, BWB, Wellington, 1991, p.110.

9   Frances Porter and Charlotte Macdonald (eds), *'My Hand Will Write What My Heart Dictates': The Unsettled Lives of Women in Nineteenth-Century New Zealand as Revealed to Sisters, Family and Friends*, AUP, Auckland, 1996, p.116.

10 S. McLean, 'Nga Tamariki O Te Rohe O Waikato: Maori Children's Lives in the Waikato Region 1850–1900, A Case Study', MA thesis, University of Waikato, 1990, p.24.

11 K. Riddell, 'A "Marriage of the Races": Aspects of Intermarriage, Ideology and Reproduction on the New Zealand Frontier', MA thesis, Victoria University of Wellington, 1996, p.75.

12 McLean, 'Nga Tamariki O Te Rohe O Waikato', p.23.

13 Riddell, citing the May Summary, *Daily Southern Cross*, 9 May 1863, p.3, in 'A "Marriage of the Races"', p.80.

14 Porter and Macdonald (eds), *'My Hand Will Write What My Heart Dictates'*, p.125.

15 Belich, *The New Zealand Wars*, p.86.

16 Maria Atkinson to Emily Richmond, 3 June 1860, in Porter and Macdonald (eds), *'My Hand Will Write What My Heart Dictates'*, p.119.

17 Maria Atkinson to Emily Richmond, May 1860, in ibid., p.121.

18 Grace Hirst to her sisters, 27 February 1860, in ibid., p.115.

19 Mary Martin to Mary Anne Palmer, 21 May 1860, in ibid., p.118.

20 Margot Fry, *Tom's Letters: The Private World of Thomas King, Victorian Gentleman*, VUP, Wellington, 2001, p.209.

21 Fry, *Tom's Letters*, p.223.

22 Ibid., p.222.

23 Porter and Macdonald (eds), *'My Hand Will Write What My Heart Dictates'*, p.104.

24 Ann Parsonson, 'The Pursuit of Mana', in Oliver and Williams (eds), *The Oxford History of New Zealand*, p.159.

25 Ibid.

26 J. B. Condliffe and W. T. Airey, *A Short History of New Zealand*, Whitcombe & Tombs, Christchurch, 1957, p.103.

27 Vincent O'Malley and David Armstrong, *The Beating Heart: A Political and Socio-economic History of Te Arawa*, Huia, Wellington, 2008, p.72.

28 Mark Iles, 'A Maori History of Tokomaru Bay East Coast, North Island', MA thesis, University of Auckland, 1981, p.253.

29 Timothy Walker, *Robley: Te Ropere, 1840–1938*, University of Auckland, 1985, p.66, http://nzetc.victoria.ac.nz/tm/scholarly/tei-WalRobl-t1-body-d1-d4.html (accessed 27 July 2015).

30 Cited in Iles, 'A Maori History of Tokomaru Bay', p.247.

31 *Lyttelton Times*, 8 September 1864, p.2.

32 4 July 1863, cited in Belich, *The New Zealand Wars*, p.80.

33 Richard Boast, 'Te tango whenua – Māori land alienation – Crown pre-emption', *Te Ara: The Encyclopedia of New Zealand*, www.teara.govt.nz/en/te-tango-whenua-maori-land-alienation/page-3 (accessed 30 July 2013).

34 Ranginui Walker, *Ka Whawhai Tonu Matou: Struggle Without End*, Penguin, Auckland, 1990, p.135.

35 Keith Sinclair, *Kinds of Peace: Maori People After the Wars, 1870–1885*, AUP, Auckland, 1991, p.11.

36 Te Ahukaramū Charles Royal, *Te Ara: The Encyclopedia of New Zealand,* 'Story: Waikato tribes', www.teara.govt.nz/en/waikato-tribes/page-6 (accessed 20 March 2015).

37 Translation by Margaret Orbell, in Porter and Macdonald (eds), *'My Hand Will Write What My Heart Dictates'*, pp.47–48.

38 Claudia Orange, 'Introduction', *The Turbulent Years, 1870–1900: The Maori Biographies from the Dictionary of New Zealand Biography, Volume Two*, BWB/DIA, Wellington, 1994, p.17.

39 *AJHR*, 1887, G-1, pp.7–8, cited in Angela Ballara, *Iwi: The Dynamics of Māori Tribal Organisation from c.1769–c.1945*, VUP, Wellington, 1998, p.254.

40 Ballara, *Iwi*, p.255.

41 Waitangi Tribunal, *The Hauraki Report*, Vol. 1, www.waitangi-tribunal.govt.nz, pp.336, 358 (accessed 18 June 2015).

42 Ibid., ES 5.2, p.xxix.

43 Ballara, *Iwi*, p.256 and footnote 111, p.355.

44 Steven Oliver, 'Hemi Tautari', 'Mary Tautari', in *The Turbulent Years*, p.141.

45 Quoted in J. Simon and L. Tuhiwai Smith (eds), *A Civilising Mission? Perceptions and Representations of the New Zealand Native Schools System*, AUP, Auckland, 2001, p.72.

46 R. De Z. Hall and Steven Oliver. 'Kahutia, Riperata', *DNZB*, www.teara.govt.nz/en/biographies/2k2/kahutia-riperata (accessed 20 March 2015).

47 Ibid.

48 Porter and Macdonald (eds), *'My Hand Will Write What My Heart Dictates'*, p.133.

49 Ruta Te Manuahura to W. W. Lewis, Under-Secretary Native Office, Wellington, 9 July 1881, in ibid., p.137.

50 Charlotte Macdonald, 'Too Many Men and Too Few Women: Gender's "Fatal Impact" in Nineteenth Century Colonies', in Caroline Daley and Deborah Montgomerie (eds), *The Gendered Kiwi*, AUP, Auckland, 1999, p.24.

51 Philip May, *The West Coast Gold Rushes*, Pegasus Press, Christchurch, 1962, p.283.

52 Macdonald, 'Too Many Men and Too Few Women', p.26; Olive Trotter, *The Maid Servants Scandal: A Page from Otago's Early History*, University of Otago Printing Department, Dunedin, 1993.

53 Charlotte Macdonald, *A Woman of Good Character: Single Women as Immigrant Settlers in Nineteenth-century New Zealand*, A&U/Historical Branch, DIA, Wellington, 1990, pp.41–71.

54 Ibid., p.41.

55 Ibid., p.56.

56 Ibid., p.50.

57 Ibid., p.153.

58 May, *The West Coast Gold Rushes*, p.294.

59 *Lyttelton Times*, 21 August 1852, p.10.

60 May, *The West Coast Gold Rushes*, p.294.

61 Ibid.

62 Rosemary Killip, *To Find a Fortune: Women of the Thames Goldfield, 1867–1893*, Women's Studies, Victoria University of Wellington, 1995, p.13.

63 Ibid., p.31.

64 Steven Eldred-Grigg, *Diggers, Hatters and Whores: The Story of the New Zealand Gold Rushes*, Random House, Auckland, 2008, p.53.

65 Cited in Gordon Ell, *Gold Rush Tales and Traditions of New Zealand Goldfields*, The Bush Press, Auckland, 1995, p.31.

66 'The Takaka Diggings', *Nelson Examiner and New Zealand Chronicle*, 24 October 1857, p.2.

67 Eldred-Grigg, *Diggers, Hatters and Whores*, p.175.

68 *The Cyclopedia of New Zealand*, Vol. 4, The Cyclopedia Company, Christchurch, 1905, pp.699–70.

69 Sandra Quick, '"The Colonial Helpmeet Takes a Dram": Women Participants in the Central Otago Goldfields Liquor Industry, 1861–1901', MA thesis, University of Otago, 1998, p.30.

70 Ibid., p.31.

71 Rosemarie Smith, 'Susan Wood, 1836–1880,' in Macdonald, Penfold and Williams (eds), *The Book of New Zealand Women*, pp.742–44.

72 May, *The West Coast Gold Rushes*, p.323.

73 Ibid., p.310.

74 Ibid., p.303.

75 Ibid., p.292.

76 Ibid., p.303.

77 Ibid., p.311.

78 Killip, *To Find a Fortune*, p.37

79 Ibid., p.39.

80 Ibid., p.15.

81 Eldred-Grigg, *Diggers, Hatters and Whores*, p.409.

82 May, *The West Coast Gold Rushes*, p.292.

83 Lyndon Fraser, '"No one but black strangers to spake to God help me": Irish Women's Migration to the West Coast, 1864–1915', in L. Fraser and K. Pickles, *Shifting Centres: Women and Migration in New Zealand History*, University of Otago Press, Dunedin, 2002, p.45.

84 Ian Pool, *Te Iwi Maori: A New Zealand Population Past, Present and Projected*, AUP, Auckland, 1991, p.75.

85 H. T. Clarke, 'Reports on the Social and Political State of the Natives in Various Districts at the Time of the Arrival of Sir G. F. Bowen', *AJHR* I, 1868, A-04, p.11.

86 G. T. Wilkinson, 'Reports from Officers in Native Districts', *AJHR* II, 1884, G-01, p.6.

87 Translation by Barry Mitcalfe, 1974, in Porter and Macdonald (eds), *'My Hand will Write What My Heart Dictates'*, pp.38–39.

88 Raeburn Lange, 'The Revival of a Dying Race: A Study of Maori Health Reform, 1900–1918, and its Nineteenth-Century Background', MA thesis, University of Auckland, 1972, p.32.

89 Ibid., p.39.

90 George S. Whitmore, *The Last Maori War in*

New Zealand Under the Self Reliant Policy, Sampson Low Marston & Co., London, 1902, pp.165–66. See also Judith Binney, *Encircled Lands: Te Urewera, 1820–1921*, BWB, Wellington, 2009, pp.148–55.

91   *Colonist*, 11 July 1865, p.8.

92   Angela Ballara, 'The Pursuit of Mana? A Re-evaluation of the Process of Land Alienations by Maoris, 1840–1890', *Journal of the Polynesian Society*, 91, 4 (1982), pp.519–42.

93   Transcription and translation by Angela Ballara in Porter and Macdonald (eds), *'My Hand Will Write What My Heart Dictates'*, pp.51–52.

94   Ibid., pp.49–50.

95   Hazel Riseborough, *Days of Darkness: The Government and Parihaka, Taranaki 1878–1884* (revised edn), Penguin, Auckland, 2002, p.51.

96   'Story: Treaty of Waitangi', *Te Ara: The Encyclopedia of New Zealand,* www.teara.govt.nz/en/graph/36364/maori-and-european-population-numbers-1840-1881 (accessed 31 August 2013).

97   See Judith Binney, *Redemption Songs: A Life of Te Kooti Arikirangi Te Turuki*, AUP/BWB, Auckland, 1995; and Binney, *Encircled Lands*.

98   Waitangi Tribunal, *The Taranaki Report: Kaupapa Tuatahi*, chapter 8, Parihaka, www.justice.govt.nz/tribunals/waitangi-tribunal/Reports/wai0143/chapt08 (accessed 24 July 2015).

99   Dick Scott, *Ask That Mountain: The Story of Parihaka*, Raupo/Penguin, Auckland, 2008, p.48.

100   Riseborough, *Days of Darkness*, p.167.

101   Ibid., p.172.

102   Scott, *Ask That Mountain*, p.117.

103   Waitangi Tribunal, *The Taranaki Report: Kaupapa Tuatahi*, chapter 8, Parihaka.

104   Scott, *Ask That Mountain*, p.127.

105   Bronwyn Elsmore, *Mana from Heaven: A Century of Maori Prophets in New Zealand*, Moana Press, Tauranga, 1989, p.276.

106   Judith Binney, 'Ani Kaaro, Maria Pangari, Remana Hane', in Macdonald, Penfold and Williams (eds) *The Book of New Zealand Women*, pp.334–37.

107   *NZPD*, 5 August 1885, Vol. 52, p.515, quoted in M. P. K. Sorrenson, 'Land Purchase Methods and their Effect on Maori Population, 1865–1901', *Journal of the Polynesian Society*, 65, 3 (1956), p.191.

108   *New Zealand Herald*, 18 March 1882, quoted in Sorrenson, 'Land Purchase Methods', p.192.

109   Ibid.

110   *New Zealand Herald*, 9 May 1878, cited in Sorrenson, 'Land Purchase Methods', p.195.

111   Angela Ballara, 'Wāhine Rangatira: Māori Women of Rank and their Role in the Women's Kotahitanga Movement of the 1890s', *New Zealand Journal of History*, 27, 1 (1993), pp.134–35.

112   Ibid., p.135.

113   An Act to Provide for the Better Representation of the Native Aboriginal Inhabitants of the Colony of New Zealand, 10 October 1867, *New Zealand Statutes*, 1867, p.491.

114   Raewyn Dalziel, 'Mary Ann Müller 1819/20?–1901', *DNZB*, Vol. 1, A&U/DIA, Wellington, 1990, p.303.

115   Aorewa McLeod, 'Mary Ann Müller, 1820–1901', in Macdonald, Penfold and Williams (eds) *The Book of New Zealand Women*, p.462.

116   *New Zealand Herald*, 2 August 1871, p.3.

117   Judith Elphick Malone, 'What's Wrong with Emma? The Feminist Debate in Colonial Auckland', in Barbara Brookes, Charlotte Macdonald and Margaret Tennant (eds), *Women in History: Essays on European Women in New Zealand*, A&U, Wellington, 1986, pp.69, 83–84.

118   Frances Porter, *Born to New Zealand: A Biography of Jane Maria Atkinson*, A&U/Port Nicholson Press, Wellington, 1989, p.134.

119   Bradbury, 'From Civil Death to Separate Property', p.54.

120   *NZPD*, 23 June 1870, Vol. 7, p.74.

121   Bradbury, 'From Civil Death to Separate Property', p.52.

122   Ballara, 'Wāhine Rangatira', p.135.

123   Ibid.

124   *NZPD*, 21 June 1881, Vol. 38, p.134.

125   Ibid., p.133.

126   Ibid., p.135.

127   Ibid., p.136.

128   *NZPD*, 6 June 1882, Vol. 41, pp.294–95.

129   Waterhouse, in *NZPD*, 1881, Vol. 38, p.137.

130   Bradbury, 'From Civil Death to Separate Property', p.64.

131   Macdonald, *A Woman of Good Character*, p.135.

132   Simon and Tuhiwai Smith, *A Civilising Mission?*, p.9.

133 *Wairarapa Daily Times*, 20 March 1889, p.2.

134 'The Native Schools Code', 1880, in Simon and Tuhiwai Smith, *A Civilising Mission?*, p.327.

135 Simon and Tuhiwai Smith, *A Civilising Mission?*, p.35.

136 'Directions for Teachers of Native Schools', Circular Memorandum for Teachers of Native Schools, in ibid., p.336.

137 Ibid.

138 'The Native Schools Code', 1880, in Simon and Tuhiwai Smith, *A Civilising Mission?*, p.328.

139 Ibid., p.327.

140 Simon and Tuhiwai Smith, *A Civilising Mission?*, p.45.

141 Ripeka Love, 'Reminiscences', in Porter and Macdonald (eds), *'My Hand Will Write What My Heart Dictates'*, p.54.

142 See Angela Wanhalla, *Matters of the Heart: A History of Interracial Marriage in New Zealand*, AUP, Auckland, 2013.

143 Beryl Hughes, 'Kate Edger', in Macdonald, Penfold and Williams (eds), *The Book of New Zealand Women*, p.202.

Chapter 5

1 *New Zealand Herald and Daily Southern Cross*, 28 January 1885, p.4.

2 *Star*, 12 May 1885, p.3.

3 'Lecture on Woman', *Press*, 23 May 1885, p.2.

4 'WCTU Time Line, Red Letter Days, & a Brief Summary of National Presidents' Terms', www.wctu.org/services.html (accessed 15 July 2015).

5 Judith Binney, 'Ani Kaaro, Maria Pangari, Remana Hane', in Charlotte Macdonald, Merimeri Penfold and Bridget Williams (eds), *The Book of New Zealand Women: Ko Kui Ma Te Kaupapa*, BWB, Wellington, 1991, pp.334–37.

6 Tania Rei, *Maori Women and the Vote*, Huia, Wellington, 1993, p.27.

7 David Green, 'Citizenship – 1840–1948: British subjects', *Te Ara: The Encyclopedia of New Zealand*, www.teara.govt.nz/en/citizenship/page-1 (accessed 12 July 2015).

8 Rahui Papa and Paul Meredith, 'Kīngitanga – the Māori King movement – Tāwhiao, 1860–1894', *Te Ara: The Encyclopedia of New Zealand*, www.teara.govt.nz/en/kingitanga-the-maori-king-movement/page-3 (accessed 12 July 2015).

9 *New Zealand Gazette and Wellington Spectator*, 27 August 1842, p.2.

10 Tony Ballantyne, 'The State, Politics and Power, 1769–1893', in Giselle Byrnes, *The New Oxford History of New Zealand*, OUP, Melbourne, 2009, p.110.

11 John Aramete Wairehu Stedman, 'Rahera Te Kahuhiapo', *DNZB*, Vol. 2, BWB/DIA, Wellington, 1993, pp.516–17.

12 A point made with reference to Aboriginal society by Marilyn Lake in 'A Response to Henry Reynolds', *Australian Humanities Review*, www.australianhumanitiesreview.org/emuse/Mabo/Lake.html (accessed 14 October 2015).

13 'Letters from Native Chiefs to Mr Fitzgerald, M. H. R.', 20 November 1864, *AJHR*, 1864, E-15, p.3.

14 'Waitangi Tribunal', www.waitangi-tribunal.govt.nz/reports/viewchapter.asp?reportID=C04FF009-8245-455E-9BF2-A8998413132F&chapter=8 (accessed 15 January 2015).

15 Claudia Orange, 'Introduction', *The Turbulent Years, 1870–1900: The Maori Biographies from the Dictionary of New Zealand Biography, Volume Two*, BWB/DIA, Wellington, 1994, p.x.

16 Alan Ward, 'Carroll, James', *DNZB*, Vol. 2, p.79.

17 Orange, 'Introduction', *The Turbulent Years*, p.vii.

18 *Tuapeka Times*, 14 November 1868, p.6.

19 *Otago Witness*, 2 January 1869, p.8; *West Coast Times*, 11 August 1869, p.3.

20 *Daily Southern Cross*, 11 December 1869, p.6; *West Coast Times*, 21 December 1869, p.3.

21 *West Coast Times*, 3 June 1871, p.3. Victoria Woodhull was nominated for the presidency of the United States by the Equal Rights Party in May 1872.

22 *Nelson Examiner and New Zealand Chronicle*, 1 April 1871, p.3.

23 On the influence of Mill, see Jean Garner, 'Sir John Hall: Pioneer, Pastoralist and Politician', PhD thesis, University of Canterbury, 1993, pp.233–35.

24 *North Otago Times*, 9 August 1872, p.4.

25 *Tuapeka Times*, 1 August 1874, p.3; *North Otago Times*, 21 August 1874.

26 *NZPD*, 8 August 1878, Vol. 28, p.158 (Robert Stout).

27 *NZPD*, 20 August 1878, Vol. 28, p.347, cited in Patricia Grimshaw, *Women's Suffrage in New Zealand*, AUP, Auckland, 1987, p.16.

28 *Wanganui Herald*, 23 August 1878, p.2.

29   *NZPD*, 25 October 1878, Vol. 30, pp.1105–18.

30   Grimshaw, *Women's Suffrage in New Zealand*, p.16.

31   *NZPD*, 13 August 1878, Vol. 28, p.200, cited in Grimshaw, *Women's Suffrage in New Zealand*, p.16.

32   Grimshaw, *Women's Suffrage in New Zealand*, p.13.

33   Beryl Hughes, 'Mary Richmond', in Macdonald, Penfold and Williams (eds), *The Book of New Zealand Women*, p.565.

34   L. W. Dalrymple, *A Few Words on the Higher Education of Women*, Fergusson & Mitchell, Dunedin, 1872, p.5. Emphasis in the original.

35   Beryl Hughes, 'Kate Edger', in Macdonald, Penfold and Williams (eds), *The Book of New Zealand Women*, p.202.

36   *Press*, 10 December 1886, p.2; Beryl Hughes, 'Kate Milligan Edger, 1857–1935', in *The Suffragists: Women Who Worked for the Vote: Essays from the Dictionary of New Zealand Biography*, BWB/DIA, Wellington, 1993, pp.61–66.

37   *Ten Reasons Why the Women of New Zealand Should Vote*, WCTU leaflet, May 1888, in Margaret Lovell-Smith (ed.), *The Woman Question: Writings by the Women who Won the Vote*, New Women's Press, Auckland, 1992, p.66.

38   Lovell-Smith (ed.), *The Woman Question*, p.74.

39   Kate Sheppard, *The Prohibitionist*, WCTU page, 17 June 1893, p.3, in Lovell-Smith (ed.), *The Woman Question*, p.84.

40   See Suzanne M. Marilley, 'Frances Willard and the Feminism of Fear', *Feminist Studies*, 19, 1 (Spring 1993), pp.123–46.

41   Jeanne Wood, *A Challenge Not a Truce: A History of the New Zealand Women's Christian Temperance Union 1885–1985*, The Union, Nelson, 1986, p.6.

42   Marten Hutt, *Te Iwi Maori me te Inu Waipiro: He Tuhituhinga Hitori. Maori and Alcohol: A History*, Health Services Research Centre, ALAC, Wellington, 1999, p.12.

43   Helen Nichol, letter to editor, *Evening Star*, 13 May 1890, p.2, cited in Grimshaw, *Women's Suffrage in New Zealand*, p.25.

44   Ian Tyrrell, *Woman's World, Woman's Empire: The Woman's Christian Temperance Union in International Perspective, 1880–1930*, University of North Carolina Press, Chapel Hill, 1991, pp.17–18.

45   Alan Ward, *A Show of Justice: Racial 'Amalgamation' in Nineteenth Century New Zealand*, AUP/OUP, Auckland, 1983, p.249; Hutt, *Te Iwi Maori me te Inu Waipiro*, p.23.

46   Hutt, *Te Iwi Maori me te Inu Waipiro*, p.19.

47   Ibid., p.20.

48   Miles Fairburn and Stephen Haslett, 'Violent Crime in Old and New Societies: A Case Study Based on New Zealand 1853–1940', *Journal of Social History*, 20, 1 (Autumn 1986), pp.89–126.

49   Unsourced newspaper cutting, 1896, Seddon Papers 3/11, 45, cited in A. R. Grigg, 'Prohibition and Women: The Preservation of an Ideal and a Myth', *New Zealand Journal of History*, 17 (1983), p.146.

50   Cyril Bradwell, *Fight the Good Fight: The Story of the Salvation Army in New Zealand, 1883–1983*, A. H. & A. W. Reed, Wellington, 1982, p.15.

51   Judith Binney, *Stories Without End: Essays 1975–2010*, BWB, Wellington, 2010, p.321; Harold Hill (ed.), *Te Ope Whakaora: The Army that Brings Life*, Flag Publications, Wellington, 2007, pp.57–59, 88–90. A letter of greeting to the 'two hundred' Māori women who had joined the WCTU under the superintendence of Mrs James Hewett Duff was printed in the *White Ribbon*, December 1896, p.9.

52   'Commission into case of Joshua Jones of Mokau', *AJHR*, 1888, G-4c, p.20.

53   *Southland Times*, 7 August 1884, p.2.

54   Ibid. See also Rosemarie Smith, *The Ladies Are At It Again: Gore Debates the Women's Franchise*, Women's Studies Department, Victoria University of Wellington, p.47.

55   Phillida Bunkle, 'The Origins of the Women's Movement in New Zealand: The Women's Christian Temperance Movement 1885–1895', in Phillida Bunkle and Beryl Hughes (eds), *Women in New Zealand Society*, A&U, Auckland, 1980, p.57.

56   Sandra Coney, *Standing in the Sunshine: A History of New Zealand Women Since They Won the Vote*, Penguin, Auckland, 1993, p.24.

57   Bronwyn Labrum, '"For the Better Discharge of our Duties": Women's Rights in Wanganui, 1893–1903', *Women's Studies Journal*, 6, 1 and 2 (November 1990), pp.136–52.

58   Kate Sheppard, 'The Responsibilities of Women as Citizens', *White Ribbon*, April 1899, pp.8–9, reprinted in Lovell-Smith (ed.), *The Woman Question*, pp.129–32.

59 Judith Devaliant, *Kate Sheppard: A Biography*, Penguin, Auckland, 1992, p.19.

60 On the uses of petitions, see the Special Supplement to the *International Review of Social History*, 46 (2001).

61 Coney, *Standing in the Sunshine*, p.24.

62 9 August 1889, Diary 1899-90 1894-5-6, Godfrey H. Hall Collection, cited in Jean Garner, 'Sir John Hall: Pioneer, Pastoralist and Politician', PhD thesis, University of Canterbury, 1993, p.243.

63 Grimshaw, *Women's Suffrage in New Zealand*, p.37.

64 *Thames Star*, 16 May 1887, p.3.

65 Garner, 'Sir John Hall', p.239.

66 Ibid., p.243.

67 *Evening Star*, 25 June 1891, cited in J. L. Patterson, 'Woman Suffrage in Dunedin, 1890–1893', BA Hons thesis, University of Otago, 1974, p.14.

68 *Evening Star*, 13 April 1892, p.4.

69 *The Globe*, 27 July 1891, cited in Patterson, 'Woman Suffrage in Dunedin', p.21.

70 *Evening Star*, 13 April 1892, p.4.

71 W. Sidney Smith, *Outlines of the Women's Franchise Movement in New Zealand*, p.61, cited in Kirsten Thomlinson, '"We the Undersigned": An Analysis of Signatories to the 1893 Women's Suffrage Petition from Southern Dunedin', MA thesis, University of Otago, 2001, p.18.

72 Garner, 'Sir John Hall', p.246.

73 *Lyttelton Times*, 15 August 1891, cited in Garner, 'Sir John Hall', p.247.

74 *NZPD*, 9 September 1891, Vol. 74, p.410 (Hon. Charles Christopher Bowen, Canterbury). The fate of the suffrage Bills is discussed in Grimshaw, *Women's Suffrage in New Zealand*.

75 *NZPD*, 10 September 1891, Vol. 74, p.468.

76 *North Otago Times*, 27 May 1892, p.3.

77 Letter to the Editor, *North Otago Times*, 1 June 1892, p.3.

78 Letter to the Editor, *North Otago Times*, 2 June 1892, p.3.

79 Bradwell, *Fight the Good Fight*, p.123.

80 Grimshaw, *Women's Suffrage in New Zealand*, p.47.

81 Thomlinson, '"We the Undersigned"', p.26.

82 Annabel Cooper, Erik Olssen, Kirsten Thomlinson and Robin Law, 'The Landscape of Gender Politics: Place, People and Two Mobilisations', in Barbara Brookes, Annabel Cooper and Robin Law (eds), *Sites of Gender: Women, Men and Modernity in Southern Dunedin, 1890–1939*, AUP, Auckland, 2003, p.46.

83 K. R. Dreaver, 'Women's Suffrage in Auckland: 1885–1893', MA thesis, University of Auckland, pp.52–3, cited in Thomlinson, '"We the Undersigned"', p.26.

84 Grimshaw, *Women's Suffrage in New Zealand*, p.51.

85 *Southern Standard*, 23 December 1892, cited in Smith, *The Ladies Are At It Again*, p.43.

86 This paragraph relies on Grimshaw, *Women's Suffrage in New Zealand*, p.92.

87 Cited in ibid., p.93.

88 *New Zealand Herald*, 15 September 1893, p.5.

89 Grimshaw, *Women's Suffrage in New Zealand*, p.94.

90 Dorothy Page, 'Introduction', in *The Suffragists*, p.1.

91 *Otago Daily Times*, 21 September 1893, p.3.

92 Grimshaw, *Women's Suffrage in New Zealand*, pp.92–96.

93 *Grey River Argus*, 29 November 1893, p.2.

94 *Taranaki Herald*, 29 November 1893, p.2; *Wanganui Herald*, 29 November 1893, p.2.

95 *Colonist*, 29 November 1893, p.4.

96 *North Otago Times*, 29 November 1893, p.3.

97 *Otago Daily Times*, 29 November 1893, p.3.

98 Ibid.

99 Ibid.

100 Neill Atkinson, 'Voting rights – Votes for women', *Te Ara: The Encyclopedia of New Zealand*, www.teara.govt.nz/en/voting-rights/page-4 (accessed 20 January 2015).

101 *Otago Witness*, 30 November 1893, p.21.

102 'Beginnings', www.nzhistory.net.nz/politics/temperance-movement/beginnings (accessed 12 July 2015).

103 David Hamer, *The New Zealand Liberals: The Years of Power, 1891–1912*, AUP, Auckland, 1988, pp.115–19, 358.

104 *Evening Post*, 29 November 1893, p.2.

105 Judith Devaliant, *Elizabeth Yates: The First Lady Mayor in the British Empire*, Exisle Publishing, Auckland, 1996, p.46.

106 *Press*, 7 February 1896, p.6.

107 Ihaka Te Tai Hakuene, ?–1887, in *The Turbulent Years*, p.179.

108 *Otago Daily Times*, 8 August 1885, p.3.

109 *AJHR*, 1886, Vol. 3, G-1, p.1.

110 *Star*, 20 June 1888, p.4.

111 In 1879, Māori votes on European rolls were substantially reduced when their household franchise was abolished. The Māori seats were retained out of fear that, if abolished, Māori votes would flood North Island seats. *Towards a Better Democracy: Report of the Royal Commission on the Electoral System*, Appendix B; M. P. K. Sorrenson, *A History of Maori Representation in Parliament*, p.B-24, V. R. Ward, Government Printer, Wellington, 1986.

112 *AJHR*, 1886, Vol. 3, G-2, pp.15–16.

113 Angela Ballara, 'Mangakahia, Meri Te Tai', *DNZB*, www.teara.govt.nz/en/biographies/2m30/mangakahia-meri-te-tai (accessed 10 June 2015).

114 Charlotte Macdonald, with Charles Royal, 'Meri Mangakahia', in Macdonald, Penfold and Williams (eds) *The Book of New Zealand Women*, pp.413–15.

115 Carol Rankin, *Women and Parliament 1893–1993: 100 Years of Institutional Change*, Office of the Clerk of the House of Representatives, Wellington, 1993, p.11.

116 *Auckland Star*, 6 October 1893, p.4.

117 *Otago Witness*, 25 October 1893, p.15.

118 Although the papers report the chief's name as Hone Nea Nea, this was likely to be Hori Niania, a leading chief of Ngāti Kahungunu. My thanks to Lachy Paterson for his assistance here.

119 *Taranaki Herald*, 15 January 1895, p.2.

120 *Otago Daily Times*, 15 January, 1895, p.2.

121 Angela Ballara, 'Wāhine Rangatira: Māori Women of Rank and their Role in the Women's Kotahitanga Movement of the 1890s', *New Zealand Journal of History*, 27 (1993), pp.127–39.

122 Ranginui Walker, *Ka Whawhai Tonu Matou: Struggle Without End*, Penguin, Auckland, 1990, p.139.

123 'Maori Women', in Regional Women's Decade Committee, *Canterbury Women Since 1893*, Pegasus, Christchurch, 1979, p.38.

124 In this case, examining title to Tuahiwi lands, *AJHR*, 1911, G-5, p.13.

125 On gum-digging, see P. W. Hohepa, *A Maori Community in Northland*, A. H. & A. W. Reed, Wellington, 1964, pp.42–45. On making kits for sale, see Bill Dacker, *Te Mamae me te Aroha: The Pain and the Love: A History of the Kai Tahu Whanui in Otago, 1844–1994*, University of Otago Press, Dunedin, 1994,

p.76. On guiding, see Jenifer Curnow, 'Sophia Hinerangi, 1830–4?–1911', *DNZB*, Vol. 2, p.216. On tourism, see Paul Diamond, 'Te tāpoi Māori – Māori tourism – 19th-century Māori tourism', *Te Ara: The Encyclopedia of New Zealand*, www.teara.govt.nz/en/te-tapoi-maori-maori-tourism/page-1 (accessed 10 October 2014).

126 Paul Diamond, *Makereti: Taking Māori to the World*, Random House, Auckland, 2007.

127 Alexander MacKay, cited in Dacker, *Te Mamae me te Aroha*, p.76.

128 *AJHR*, 1886, Vol. 3, G-1, p.2.

129 Ibid., p.15.

130 *AJHR*, 1886, Vol. 3, G-12, p.3.

131 Ibid., p.11.

132 Ibid., p.12.

133 *Otago Daily Times*, 14 August 1885, p.2.

134 F. S. McLean, *Challenge for Health: A History*, R. E. Owen, Wellington, 1964, p.190.

135 R. T. Lange, 'The Revival of a Dying Race: A Study of Maori Health Reform 1900–1918, and its Nineteenth Century Background', MA thesis, University of Auckland, 1972, pp.32–39.

136 Ibid., p.41.

137 Ibid., p.40.

138 See, for example, report of George Preece, Napier, 20 May 1891, 'Census of the Maori Population, 1891', *AJHR*, 1891, G-2, p.4.

139 'Census of the Maori Population', *AJHR*, 1896, H-13b, p.12.

140 B. Elsmore, *Mana from Heaven: A Century of Maori Prophets in New Zealand*, Reed, Auckland, 1999, p.141.

141 Ian Pool and Rosemary Du Plessis, 'Families: a history – Late 19th and early 20th century families', *Te Ara: The Encyclopedia of New Zealand*, www.teara.govt.nz/en/families-a-history/page-3 (accessed 12 June 2015).

142 Alison Clarke, *Born into a Changing World: Childbirth in Nineteenth-Century New Zealand*, BWB, Wellington, 2012, pp.25–26.

143 Ian Pool, *Te Iwi Maori: A New Zealand Population: Past, Present and Projected*, AUP, Auckland, 1991, p.101.

144 E. and P. Beaglehole, *Some Modern Maoris*, New Zealand Council for Educational Research, Wellington, 1946, p.80; D. I. Pool, *The Maori Population of New Zealand 1769–1971*, AUP, Auckland, 1977, pp.87–88.

145 Judith Binney and Gillian Chaplin, *Ngā Mōrehu: The Survivors*, OUP, Auckland, 1986, pp.58–60.

146 *New Zealand Herald*, 5 June 1901, p.3.

147 Orange, 'Introduction', *The Turbulent Years*, p.xvi.

148 *White Ribbon*, 6, May 1901, p.5.

149 *Auckland Star*, 4 January 1945, p.3; *New Zealand Herald*, 4 January 1945, p.2.

150 BAAA1001/275a, ANZ, cited in Judith Simon and Linda Tuhiwai Smith, *A Civilising Mission? Perceptions and Representations of the New Zealand Native Schools System*, AUP, Auckland, 2001, pp.217–18.

151 *Mataura Ensign*, 17 March 1911, p.7.

152 *Auckland Star*, 15 April 1909, p.2.

153 Graham Butterworth, 'Pomare, Maui Wiremu Piti Naera', *DNZB*, www.teara.govt.nz/en/biographies/3p30/pomare-maui-wiremu-piti-naera (accessed 15 June 2015).

154 *AJHR*, 1904, H-31, pp.58–9, cited in R. Fry, *It's Different for Daughters*, New Zealand Council for Educational Research, Wellington, 1985, pp.158–59.

155 Miria Louise Woodbine Pomare, 'Pomare, Mildred Amelia Woodbine', *DNZB*, www.teara.govt.nz/en/biographies/4p16/pomare-mildred-amelia-woodbine (accessed 12 June 2015).

156 Sheila Robinson, 'Carroll, Heni Materoa', *DNZB*, www.teara.govt.nz/en/biographies/3c5/carroll-heni-materoa (accessed 14 June 2015).

157 Elsmore, *Mana From Heaven*, pp.310–11.

158 David Young, 'Mere Rikiriki', in Macdonald, Penfold and Williams (eds), *The Book of New Zealand Women*, pp.568–69.

159 'Our Maori Sisters', *White Ribbon*, September 1908, p.7.

160 Joy Hippolite, 'Wetekia Ruruku Elkington', in Macdonald, Penfold and Williams (eds), *The Book of New Zealand Women*, pp.205–7.

Chapter 6

1 Anna P. Stout, 'The New Woman', in the *Citizen*, 1 (December 1895), pp.153–59, reprinted in *Women and the Vote*, Victorian New Zealand – A Reprint Series, No. 7, Hocken Library, 1986, p.16.

2 Ibid., p.17.

3 Ibid., p.20.

4 *Free Lance*, 20 October 1900, p.8.

5 Ibid.

6 Indigenous women could not vote in Federal elections until 1962. South Australia was the first state to grant women both the right to vote and the right to seek election in 1895. www.australia.gov.au/about-australia/australian-story/austn-women-in-politics (accessed 27 July 2015).

7 For a similar view on the Australian situation, see Judith Allen, *Sex and Secrets: Crimes Involving Australian Women Since 1880*, OUP, Melbourne, 1990, p.45.

8 See Lucy Bland, *Banishing the Beast: Feminism, Sex and Morality*, Tauris Parke Paperbacks, London, 2001, pp.95–101; Lesley A. Hall, *Sex, Gender and Social Change in Britain since 1880*, Macmillan, London, 2000, pp.30–46.

9 'Whose Daughter', *White Ribbon*, July 1896, p.1

10 Margaret Sievwright, 'The New Woman', *Lyttelton Times*, 30 April 1896, p.2, reprinted in Margaret Lovell-Smith (ed.), *The Woman Question: Writings by the Women who Won the Vote*, New Women's Press, Auckland, 1992, p.119.

11 *Daybreak*, 8 June 1895, p.5.

12 The Offences Against the Person Act 1889, sections 1&2.

13 *The Prohibitionist*, 11 August 1894, p.3.

14 *White Ribbon*, February 1897, p.4.

15 WCTU page, 26 January 1895, 3, cited in Lovell-Smith, *The Woman Question*, p.177.

16 *NZPD*, 1894, Vol. 86, pp.780, 918.

17 *NZPD*, 1895, Vol. 88, p.215.

18 *White Ribbon*, August 1895, p.5.

19 Raewyn Dalziel, *Focus on the Family: The Auckland Home and Family Society, 1893–1993*, Home and Family Society, Auckland, 1993, p.9.

20 Ibid.

21 *NZPD*, 1895, Vol. 88, p.273.

22 *NZPD*, 1894, Vol. 83, p.407.

23 *NZPD*, 1895, Vol. 87, p.635; *NZPD*, 1894, Vol. 83, p.568.

24 *NZPD*, 1895, Vol. 88, pp.273–74. On Rigg, see 'The Late Mr John Rigg', *Evening Post*, 24 February 1944, p.3.

25 *NZPD*, 1895, Vol. 88, pp.273–74.

26 *White Ribbon*, October 1895, p.2.

27 *Press*, 11 October 1895, p.7.

28 *White Ribbon*, October 1895, p.2.

29 Ibid.

30 Ibid.

31 *Star*, 2 July 1896, p.3.

32 *NZPD*, 1896, Vol. 94, p.527.

33 Ibid., p.532.

34 *Daybreak*, 8 June 1895, p.5.

35 On the WCTU Convention, see *Press*, 17 February 1910, p.8; Findlay quoted in the *Dominion*, 5 September 1910, cited in Philip J. Fleming, '"Shadow over New Zealand": The Response to Venereal Disease in New Zealand, 1910–1945', PhD thesis, Massey University, 1989, pp.21–22.

36 *NZPD*, 1910, Vol. 149, p.314.

37 For a discussion of these issues in the British context, see Lucy Bland, 'The Married Woman, the "New Woman" and the Feminist: Sexual Politics of the 1890s', in Jane Rendall (ed.), *Equal or Different: Women's Politics 1800–1914*, Basil Blackwell, Oxford, 1987, pp.141–64.

38 *White Ribbon*, November 1900, pp.9–10, cited in Lovell-Smith, *The Woman Question*, p.183.

39 Bronwyn Dalley, citing *NZPD*, 1910, Vol. 153, pp.405–15 in 'Lolly Shops "of the red-light kind" and "soldiers of the King": Suppressing One-Woman Brothels in New Zealand, 1908–1916', *New Zealand Journal of History*, 30, 1 (1996), p.12.

40 'Report of the Committee of the Board of Health Appointed by the Minister of Health on Venereal Diseases in New Zealand', 1922.

41 Ada Wells, 'A Short Review of the Political, Social and Economic Position of Women', *The Prohibitionist*, 26 January 1895, pp.3–4, reprinted in Lovell-Smith, *The Woman Question*, pp.111–12.

42 *NZPD*, 1900, Vol. 113, p.472.

43 *NZPD*, 1896, Vol. 94, p.469.

44 Ibid.

45 *NZPD*, 1900, Vol. 111, p.532.

46 Ibid., p.477.

47 *R. v Hon Maaka Mokomoko* [1904] 23 NZLR 829. *R. v Stanley* [1904] 23 NZLR 378. In the latter case, the fact that the daughter was adopted was raised in defence but rejected by the Court of Appeal. See also Scott Gallacher, '"Publishing Our Own Dinosaur": The Criminalisation of Incest in New Zealand and the Judicial Response', BA Hons dissertation, University of Otago, 1993.

48 *Truth*, 17 August 1907, p.5.

49 J. S. Mill, *On the Subjection of Women*, 1869, www.marxists.org/reference/archive/mill-john-stuart/1869/subjection-women/ch04.htm (accessed 19 July 2015).

50 Bland, *Banishing the Beast*, p.124; see, for one example, *Observer*, 17 November 1888, p.4.

51 *Wanganui Chronicle*, 21 November 1888, p.2.

52 Roderick Phillips, *Divorce in New Zealand: A Social History*, OUP, Auckland, 1981, p.146.

53 *New Zealand Tablet*, 3 August 1894, p.16.

54 *NZPD*, 1894, Vol. 83, p.572.

55 Public Petitions, *AJHR*, 1895, I-1; I-2.

56 Public Petition No. 227, *AJHR*, 1895, I-2.

57 *NZPD*, 1895, Vol. 89, p.319; *NZPD*, 1895, Vol. 88, p.185.

58 *NZPD*, 1896, Vol. 93, p.433.

59 Ibid., p.432.

60 *White Ribbon*, October 1896, p.7.

61 Phillips, *Divorce in New Zealand*, p.65.

62 *Lees v Lees*, *Gazette Law Reports*, 8 (10 August 1906), pp.709–11.

63 *Pybus v Pybus*, *Gazette Law Reports*, 9 (8 March 1907), p.286.

64 All quotations above from *Rex v Leonard*, *New Zealand Law Reports*, 41 (1922), pp.721–47.

65 Heather Ward, 'Making the World More Like Home: The Women's Christian Temperance Union in World War One', BA Hons Long Essay, University of Otago, 1991, p.62.

66 *The Maoriland Worker*, 4 August 1915, p.4.

67 'Report of the Chief Justice', *AJHR*, 1916, I-2a, p.3.

68 Claudia Geiringer, 'The Alice Parkinson Release Campaign, 1915–20: A Study of Contemporary Attitudes to the "Fallen Woman"', History 452 essay, University of Otago, 1989.

69 'Poor Alice Parkinson', *Truth*, 26 June 1915, p.5.

70 'A Woman Wronged', *Truth*, 3 July 1915, p.7.

71 Miss H., 'Report of the Royal Commission appointed to inquire into certain relations between the employers of certain kinds of labour and the persons employed therein [Sweating commission]', *AJHR*, 1890, I H-5, p.14.

72 John Bartlett, 'Woven Together: The Industrial Workplace in the Otago Woollen Mills 1871–1930', MA thesis, University of Otago, 1987, p.16.

73 Louise Shaw, 'Hallenstein Brothers and Company 1876–1906: Early Years of Mass Retailing in New Zealand', BA Hons dissertation, University of Otago, 1994.

74 *NZPD*, 1896, Vol. 92, p.294.

75 *NZPD*, 1896, Vol. 94, p.299.

76 Ibid., p.300.

77 Rod Fabish, 'Fabish, Agnes', *DNZB*, www.teara. govt.nz/en/biographies/3f1/fabish-agnes (accessed 12 June 2015).

78 Diana Unwin, 'Women in New Zealand Industry', MA thesis, University of Otago, 1944, pp.6–7.

79 Ibid., p.18.

80 Ibid., p.26.

81 Erik Olssen, 'Working Gender, Gendering Work: Occupational Change and Continuity in Southern Dunedin', in B. Brookes, A. Cooper and R. Law (eds), *Sites of Gender: Women, Men and Modernity in Southern Dunedin, 1890–1939*, AUP, Auckland, 2003, p.55.

82 'Report on the Government Printing Department', *AJHR*, 1881, H-10, p.2.

83 John Stenhouse, 'The Passionate Pastor: The Cultural Performances of the Reverend Rutherford Waddell', *Journal of New Zealand Studies*, 15 (2013), pp.22–35.

84 Ian Hunter, 'Factory industries', www. teara.govt.nz/en/factory-industries/page-2 (accessed 8 April 2015).

85 *Star*, 4 August 1893, p.2.

86 See advertisement for Remington Typewriters, *Otago Daily Times*, 15 January 1892, p.3.

87 Tolerton, *Ettie*, pp.25–26.

88 Olssen, 'Working Gender, Gendering Work', in Brookes, Cooper and Law (eds), *Sites of Gender*, pp.54–55.

89 Bronwyn Karran, 'She Stoops to Conquer: The Feminization of the Clerical Workforce in New Zealand, 1890–1935', BA Hons dissertation, University of Otago, 1991, p.33.

90 Dorothy Page, Howard Lee and Tom Brooking, 'Schooling for a Gendered Future: Gender, Education and Opportunity', in Brookes, Cooper and Law (eds), *Sites of Gender*, p.116.

91 Angela Findlay, 'Widening Women's Sphere? Women, Work and Ideology in the New Zealand Post Office, 1900–1920', BA Hons dissertation, University of Otago, 2000, p.23.

92 Karran, 'She Stoops to Conquer', p.55.

93 *Press*, 9 April 1904, p.4.

94 'Women Clerks and the Birthrate', *Press*, 7 June 1904, p.9.

95 'Women Clerks and their Salaries', *Press*, 6 June 1904, p.9.

96 *White Ribbon*, June 1904, p.6.

97 *White Ribbon*, August 1914, p.15.

98 'Report of a Commission appointed to Inquire and Report upon the Unclassified Departments of the Public Service of New Zealand', *AJHR*, 1912, H-34, p.29.

99 *White Ribbon*, August 1914, p.16.

100 Kuni Jenkins and Kay Morris Matthews, *Hukarere and the Politics of Maori Girls' Schooling 1875–1995*, Dunmore Press, Palmerston North, 1995, p.31.

101 *Hawera & Normanby Star*, 30 January 1912, p.8.

102 Jenkins and Morris Matthews, *Hukarere*, p.16.

103 Michael King, 'Cooper, Whina', *DNZB*, www. teara.govt.nz/en/biographies/5c32/cooper-whina (accessed 14 June 2015).

104 John Barrington, *Separate But Equal? Maori Schools and the Crown 1867–1969*, VUP, Wellington, 2008, p.142.

105 *Evening Post*, 4 December 1897, p.5.

106 'Report of Dr. Pomare, Health Officer to the Maoris,' *AJHR*, 1904, H-31, p.58.

107 Hamiora Hei, 'Maori Girls and Nursing', Papers and Addresses read before the Second Conference of the Te Aute College Students Association, Napier, 1898, p.30, cited in A. H. McKegg, '"Ministering Angels": The Government Backblock Nursing Service and the Maori Health Nurses, 1909–1939', MA thesis, University of Auckland, 1991, p.62.

108 *Press*, 12 April 1904, p.4.

109 Alexandra McKegg, 'The Maori Health Nursing Scheme: An Experiment in Autonomous Health Care', *New Zealand Journal of History*, 26, 3 (October 1992), p.174, n.10.

110 Cited in ibid., pp.150–51.

111 *Otago Daily Times*, 4 July 1896, p.2.

112 *Otago Daily Times*, 28 July 1905, p.3.

113 Margaret Tennant, '"Missionaries of Health": The School Medical Service in the Inter-War Period', in Linda Bryder (ed.), *A Healthy Country: Essays on the Social History of Medicine in New Zealand*, BWB, Wellington, 1991, pp.128–48.

114 See Barbara Brookes, 'A Corresponding Community: Dr Agnes Bennett and her Friends from the Edinburgh Medical College for Women of the 1890s', *Medical History*, 52, (2008), pp.237–56.

115 *Population Census 1926*, Vol. 9, p.6.

116 Angela Ballara, 'Love, Ripeka Wharawhara',

DNZB, www.teara.govt.nz/en/
biographies/3l14/love-ripeka-wharawhara
(accessed 20 June 2014).

117 Ballara, 'Love, Ripeka Wharawhara'.

118 Hiria Moffat, 'Hiria Kokoro Barrett, 1890–
1943', *DNZB*, Vol. 3, AUP/BWB/DIA, 1996,
pp.268–70.

119 Charlotte Macdonald, 'Strangers at the
Hearth: The Eclipse of Domestic Service
in New Zealand Homes c. 1830s–1940s', in
B. Brookes (ed.), *At Home in New Zealand:
History, Houses, People*, BWB, Wellington,
2000, pp.50–52. See also the *1926 Population
Census*, Vol. 14, 'Maori and Half Caste', in
which 90% of Māori are recorded as living in
country districts.

120 *Auckland Star*, 6 October 1904, p.4.

121 *Otago Witness*, 16 August 1905, p.44.

122 *Auckland Star*, 2 February 1906, p.2.

123 *Auckland Star*, 26 March, 1914, p.5.

124 Judith Binney and Gillian Chaplin, *Ngā
Mōrehu: The Survivors*, OUP, Auckland, 1986,
p.57.

125 Ibid., p.63.

126 John E. Martin, *The Forgotten Worker: The
Rural Wage Earner in Nineteenth-Century
New Zealand*, A&U/Trade Union History
Project, Wellington, 1990, p.41.

127 King, 'Cooper, Whina'.

128 Ann Parsonson, 'Herangi, Te Kirihaehae
Te Puea', *DNZB*, www.teara.govt.nz/en/
biographies/3h17/herangi-te-kirihaehae-te-
puea (accessed 14 April 2014); Michael King,
Te Puea (3rd edn), Sceptre, Auckland, 1987,
pp.52–53.

129 King, *Te Puea*, pp.55–63.

130 Ibid., p.78.

131 Ibid., p.77.

132 Ann Parsonson et al., 'Te Kirihaehae Te Puea
Herangi', *DNZB*, Vol. 3, pp.208–9.

133 King, *Te Puea*, 1988, p.86.

134 Jane Tolerton, 'Women and the First World
War', in Ian McGibbon (ed.), *The Oxford
Companion to New Zealand Military History*,
OUP, Auckland, 2000, p.613.

135 Eru Woodbine Pomare, 'Maria Woodbine
Pomare', in Charlotte Macdonald, Merimeri
Penfold and Bridget Williams (eds), *The
Book of New Zealand Women: Ko Kui Ma Te
Kaupapa*, BWB, Wellington, 1991, pp.527–30.

136 Sheila Robinson, 'Carroll, Heni Materoa'.

137 *Tapanui Courier*, 26 October 1914, p.8.

138 Quoted in Nicholas Boyack, *Behind the Lines:
The Lives of New Zealand Soldiers in the First
World War*, A&U/Port Nicholson Press,
Wellington, 1989, p.117.

139 Edna Valentine Trapnell, in the *Maoriland
Worker*, 20 January 1915, p.1.

140 Margaret McClure, *A Civilised Community:
A History of Social Security in New Zealand
1898–1998*, AUP/Historical Branch, DIA,
Auckland, 1998, pp.35 n.94, 267.

141 'Fortune Tellers Sent to Gaol', *Wanganui
Chronicle*, 19 October 1917, p.2.

142 'Report of the Department of Labour', *AJHR*,
1918, H-11, p.1, cited in Jan McLeod, 'Activities
of New Zealand Women During World War
1', BA Hons dissertation, University of Otago,
1993, p.83.

143 Natalie Wright, 'Clutha at War! The Impact
of the First World War on the Residents of
Clutha', BA Hons dissertation, University of
Otago, 1993, p.46.

144 McLeod, 'Activities of New Zealand Women',
pp.85–86.

145 *Ashburton Guardian*, 16 November 1915, p.7;
McLeod, 'Activities of New Zealand Women',
p.89.

146 McLeod, 'Activities of New Zealand Women',
p.88.

147 Ibid., pp.89–90.

148 'Annual Report of the Post and Telegraph
Department', *AJHR*, 1917, F-01, 'Post and
Telegraph Department', p.4.

149 McLeod, 'Activities of New Zealand Women',
p.39.

150 Tolerton, 'Women and the First World War',
p.613.

151 Kerry Stratton, '"Doing their Bit": The Impact
of the First World War on the Inhabitants
of Tuapeka County', BA Hons dissertation,
University of Otago, 1992, p.25.

152 Dorothy Page, *The National Council of Women:
A Centennial History*, AUP/BWB, Auckland,
1996, p.52.

153 *Maoriland Worker*, 8 November 1916, p.7,
cited in McLeod, 'Activities of New Zealand
Women', p.26.

154 Megan Hutching, '"Mothers of the World",
Women, Peace and Arbitration in Early
Twentieth Century New Zealand', *New
Zealand Journal of History*, 27, 2 (October
1993), pp.173–85.

155 'Anti-Compulsion', *Otautau Standard and*

Wallace County Chronicle, 20 June 1916, p.2. See also Charlotte Macdonald, *The Vote, the Pill and the Demon Drink: A History of Feminist Writing in New Zealand, 1869–1993*, BWB, Wellington, 1993, pp.76–78.

156 'Anti-Compulsion', *Otautau Standard and Wallace County Chronicle*, 20 June 1916, p.2.

157 McLeod, 'Activities of New Zealand Women', pp.69–70.

158 *Otago Daily Times*, 4 April 1916, p.4.

159 Beryl Hughes, 'Bennett, Agnes Elizabeth Lloyd', *DNZB*, www.teara.govt.nz/en/biographies/3b28/bennett-agnes-elizabeth-lloyd (accessed 12 August 2015).

160 Dunedin City Council, TC 33 Finance, A7, 1918, cited in Karran, 'She Stoops to Conquer', p.59.

161 McLeod, 'Activities of New Zealand Women', pp.92–93.

162 'A Great Need in the City', *Dominion*, 30 August 1918, p.3.

163 Bronwyn Dalley, '"Fresh Attractions": White Slavery and Feminism in New Zealand, 1885–1918', *Women's History Review*, 9, 3 (2000), pp.585–606.

164 'A Great Need in the City', *Dominion*, 30 August 1918, p.3.

165 'Gabrielle', *Otago Witness*, 21 August 1918, p.55.

166 *Auckland Star*, 25 October 1917, p.9.

167 Tolerton, *Ettie*, chapters 8, 9, 10.

168 *Colonist*, 21 March 1915, p.6.

169 'Social Hygiene: Bringing the new Act into operation', *Press*, 10 November 1917, p.13.

170 *Press*, 12 October 1918, p.2.

171 *Colonist*, 16 July 1919, p.3.

172 Page, *The National Council of Women*, pp.65–66.

173 McLeod, 'Activities of Women', p.100.

174 *Maoriland Worker*, 15 November 1916, p.7.

175 Page, *The National Council of Women*, p.54.

176 *Evening Post*, 2 April 1918, p.9.

Chapter 7

1 Michael King, *Whina: A Biography of Whina Cooper*, Hodder & Stoughton, Auckland, 1983, p.82.

2 Ibid., p.83.

3 Maureen Hickey, 'Negotiating Infant Welfare: The Plunket Society in the Interwar Period', MA thesis, University of Otago, 1999.

4 Charles W. Budden, MD, *The Way of Health:*

Plain Counsels in Personal Hygiene, Pilgrim Press, London, 1920, p.24.

5 Ibid. p.100.

6 M. A. Blackmore, *Housewifery for Use in School and Home*, Whitcombe & Tombs, Auckland, n.d.

7 Geoffrey Rice, *Black November: The 1918 Influenza Epidemic in New Zealand*, A&U, Wellington, 1988, p.159.

8 Ibid., p.160.

9 Ibid., p.63.

10 Ibid., p.105.

11 Michael King, *Te Puea* (3rd edn), Sceptre, Auckland, 1987, p.112.

12 Ranginui Walker, *Ka Whawhai Tonu Matou: Struggle Without End*, Penguin, Auckland, 1990, p.187.

13 Rice, *Black November*, p.173.

14 Melanie Nolan, *Breadwinning: New Zealand Women and the State*, CUP, Christchurch, 2000, p.85.

15 Margaret Tennant, '"Missionaries of Health": The School Medical Service During the Inter-war Period', in Linda Bryder (ed.), *A Healthy Country: Essays on the Social History of Medicine in New Zealand*, BWB, Wellington, 1991, p.128.

16 Dr G. F. McLeary addressing the Eugenics Society in London, reported in the *Evening Post*, 24 February 1938, p.5.

17 *Evening Post*, 18 January 1932, p.8.

18 Mark Krivan, 'The Department of Maori Affairs Housing Programme, 1935 to 1967', MA thesis, Massey University, 1990, p.26.

19 Philippa Mein Smith, *Maternity in Dispute: New Zealand 1920–1939*, Historical Branch, DIA, Wellington, 1986, p.4.

20 F. S. McLean, *Challenge for Health: A History of Public Health in New Zealand*, R. E. Owen, Government Printer, Wellington, 1964, p.216.

21 J. C. Smith, 'The Obstetrical Society and the Effects on Maternal Care of the Changes in Medical Education in New Zealand 1920–1940', BA Hons dissertation, University of Otago, 1985, p.63.

22 See Mein Smith, *Maternity in Dispute*, for a detailed analysis of maternal welfare policies in the interwar years.

23 *Otago Daily Times*, 7 March 1935, p.10; 8 March 1935, p.7. Maureen Hickey, unpublished 'Johnson's Paper', Passions of the Past Symposium, University of Otago, 1996.

24 Letter 10 February 1936, AG7 2-300, Plunket Society Records, Hocken Library, cited by Maureen Hickey in 'Johnson's Paper'.

25 Linda Bryder, *A Voice for Mothers: The Plunket Society and Infant Welfare 1907–2000*, AUP, Auckland, 2003.

26 Ibid., p.68, and see chapter 4.

27 H. B. Turbott, 'Health and Welfare', in I. L. G. Sutherland (ed.), *The Maori People Today: A General Survey*, New Zealand Institute of Economic Affairs, New Zealand Council for Educational Research, Institute of Pacific Affairs, Wellington, 1940, p.253.

28 'Report of the Committee of Inquiry into Maternity Services', *AJHR*, 1938, H-31A, p.56.

29 Judith Binney and Gillian Chaplin, *Ngā Mōrehu: The Survivors*, OUP, Auckland, 1986, p.66.

30 J. P. Broad and J. Steven, 'A General Survey of Ratana', fifth year Medical Preventive Medicine thesis, University of Otago, 1940, p.94.

31 Ibid., p.79.

32 Derek Dow, *Maori Health and Government Policy 1840–1940*, VUP, Wellington, 1999, pp.161–73.

33 'Report of the Committee of Inquiry into Maternity Services', *AJHR*, 1938, H-31-A, p.25.

34 Ibid., p.6.

35 Barbara Brookes, 'Aspects of Women's Health, 1885–1945', in Bryder (ed.), *A Healthy Country*, pp.157–58.

36 The Māori figure is based on live births registered from January to March 1937. *Special Report Series 8: Maori Patients in Mental Hospitals*, Department of Health, Wellington, 1962, p.12. On non-Māori figures, see Philippa Mein Smith, 'Mortality in Childbirth in the 1920s and 1930s', in B. Brookes, C. Macdonald and M. Tennant (eds), *Women in History: Essays on European Women in New Zealand*, A&U/Port Nicholson Press, Wellington, 1986, p.139.

37 D. Gordon, 'Comparative Obstetrics: A Paper Read before the Taranaki Division of the British Medical Association, November 1925', *New Zealand Medical Journal*, 25, 126 (1926), p.69, cited in Charlotte Parkes, 'The Medicalisation of New Zealand's Maternity Services, 1904–1937', in Bryder (ed.), *A Healthy Country*, p.170.

38 Mrs Ryburn, South Auckland Provincial Committee, Women's Division New Zealand Farmers' Union, to Committee of Inquiry into Maternity Services, Hamilton, 9.9.37, Ms.78, Vol. 2, cited in Parkes, 'The Medicalisation of New Zealand's Maternity Services', p.170.

39 *Auckland Star*, 4 September 1937, p.17.

40 Naomi Brell, 'Nurse Cameron', in Charlotte Macdonald, Merimeri Penfold and Bridget Williams (eds), *The Book of New Zealand Women: Ko Kui Ma Te Kaupapa*, BWB, Wellington, 1991, pp.121–23.

41 *Evening Post*, 1 November 1920, p.6. For just one of the politicians' speeches extolling the 'mothers of the race', see the report of Mr J. Anstey, Liberal candidate for Waitaki, *Mt Ida Chronicle*, 21 November 1919, p.3.

42 *Evening Post*, 9 May 1919, p.2; *New Zealand Herald*, 29 July 1918, p.6; 31 July 1918, p.9; *Auckland Star*, 29 May 1919, p.12.

43 *Grey River Argus*, 11 April 1919, p.1.

44 'Where Are My Children?', http://en.wikipedia.org/wiki/Where_Are_My_Children%3F (accessed 28 July 2015).

45 *Evening Post*, 9 May 1917, p.3.

46 *Auckland Star*, 24 January 1924, p.12. For conversion into 2015 currency, see www.rbnz.govt.nz/monetary_policy/inflation_calculator/

47 The average annual income of a male industrial worker in 1922 was £208 4s (about $18,800), according to the *New Zealand Official Yearbook*, 1924, p.453.

48 MSS. 58575, Stopes Collection, British Library. See Barbara Brookes, 'Reproductive Rights: The Debate over Abortion and Birth Control in the 1930s', in Brookes, Macdonald and Tennant (eds), *Women in History*, p.121.

49 Marie Carmichael Stopes, *Married Love: A New Contribution to the Solution of Sex Difficulties* (7th edn), G. P. Putnam's Sons, London, 1919, p.94.

50 Stopes, *Married Love*, p.102.

51 *Otago Witness*, 11 January 1927, p.75, cited in Sarah Fyfe, 'The Topsy-Turvy Twenties: Urban Society 1921–1928', BA Hons dissertation, University of Otago, 1984, p.40.

52 Ettie Rout, *Safe Marriage: A Return to Sanity*, William Heinemann, London, 1922, chapter 2.

53 See Jane Tolerton, *Ettie: A Life of Ettie Rout*, Penguin, Auckland, 1992. The publishers classified the book as a 'medical text': see Jo Richdale, 'Ladies' and Gentlemen's Toilet and Rubber Requisites: The Development

of New Zealand's Commercial Trade in Contraceptives and Birth Control Literature 1900s–1940', *Health and History*, 15, 2 (2013), p.80.

54   *New Zealand Dairy Exporter*, 1 January 1936, pp.71–79. For more on the availability of contraceptive advice, see Richdale, 'Ladies' and Gentlemen's Toilet and Rubber Requisites', pp.72–92.

55   *New Zealand Truth*, 12 July 1924, p.6.

56   *New Zealand Truth*, 29 August 1929, p.8.

57   *Auckland Star*, 17 May 1933, p.19.

58   Ruth Hall (ed.), *Dear Dr. Stopes: Sex in the 1920's*, Deutsch, London, 1978, p.121.

59   Kate Fisher, *Birth Control, Sex and Marriage in Britain, 1918–1960*, OUP, Oxford, 2006, p.153.

60   'Richards case, Maiden name Miss Hinemoa Hopkins L.L.B', *New Zealand Truth*, 19 March 1931, p.5.

61   Doris Gordon, *Backblocks Baby-Doctor: An Autobiography*, Faber & Faber, London, 1955, p.94.

62   Kate Fisher and Simon Szreter, '"They prefer withdrawal": The Choice of Birth Control in Britain, 1918–1960', *Journal of Interdisciplinary History*, 24, 2 (2003), pp.263–91.

63   For more on the availability of contraceptive advice, see Richdale, 'Ladies' and Gentlemen's Toilet and Rubber Requisites', p.85.

64   Brookes, 'Reproductive Rights', in Brookes, Macdonald and Tennant (eds), *Women in History*, pp. 123–24.

65   Letter to Editor, *Eugenics Review*, 13 (1920–21), p.375.

66   *Birth Control News*, 20 (October 1931), p.85.

67   H. K. Lovell-Smith Papers, ATL.

68   Labour Party National Executive Report, 1935–36, p.21. Labour Party Papers, MSS.270, F23, ATL.

69   Margaret Sanger, 'Woman of the Future,' p.29. SH&BRS Papers, MS 1388, F6, ATL.

70   Elsie Freeman, 'Towards Happier Parenthood', *Woman Today*, April 1937, p.10.

71   *Woman Today*, April 1937, p.10.

72   Barbara Brookes, 'Aves, Isabel Annie', *DNZB*, www.teara.govt.nz/en/biographies/4a25/aves-isabel-annie (accessed 28 July 2015).

73   *Dominion*, 12 April 1937, p.8.

74   Barry Martin, 'The Family Allowance Act 1926', BA Hons research essay, Massey University, 1990.

75   Ibid., p.22. The Labour Party's interest in 'motherhood endowment' was registered in the three unsuccessful Bills that Michael Joseph Savage lodged with the General Assembly in 1922, 1924 and 1925.

76   See discussion in Nolan, *Breadwinning*, pp.137–41.

77   Elizabeth Hanson, *The Politics of Social Security*, AUP/OUP, Auckland, 1980, p.24.

78   Margaret McClure, *A Civilised Community: A History of Social Security in New Zealand 1898–1998*, AUP/Historical Branch, DIA, Auckland, 1998, pp.28–29.

79   W. B. Sutch, *The Quest for Security in New Zealand: 1840–1966*, OUP, Wellington, 1966, p.152.

80   Martin, 'The Family Allowance Act 1926', p.34.

81   Michael Belgrave, 'Needs and the State: Evolving Social Policy in New Zealand History', in B. Dalley and M. Tennant (eds), *Past Judgement: Social Policy in New Zealand History*, University of Otago Press, Dunedin, 2004, p.28.

82   Nolan, *Breadwinning*, p.137.

83   Ibid.

84   Ibid., pp.137–38.

85   McClure, *A Civilised Community*, p.54.

86   'Report of the Committee of Inquiry into Mental Defectives and Sexual Offenders', *AJHR*, 1925, H-31A, p.28.

87   James Bennett, 'Maori as Honorary Members of the White Tribe', *Journal of Imperial and Commonwealth History*, 29, 3 (September 2001), pp.33–54.

88   'Report of the Committee of Inquiry into Mental Defectives and Sexual Offenders', *AJHR*, 1925, H-31A, p.22.

89   'Report of the Inquiry into Venereal Diseases in New Zealand', *AJHR*, 1922, H-31A, p.12.

90   Cited in Angela Wanhalla, 'To "Better the Breed of Men": Women and Eugenics in New Zealand, 1900–1935', *Women's History Review*, 16, 2 (April 2007), p.164. On Howlett, see *Auckland Star*, 19 February 1913, p.6.

91   Wanhalla, 'To "Better the Breed of Men"', p.165.

92   See 'Mental Defectives', *Evening Post*, 26 August 1926, p.10.

93   'Obituary: Lady Luke', *Evening Post*, 15 March 1937, p.16.

94   'Report of the Committee on Venereal Diseases in New Zealand', *AJHR*, 1922, H-31A, p.11.

95   Ibid., p.12.

96   Ibid., p.11.

97   *New Zealand Truth*, 29 April 1922, p.5.

98   'Report of the Committee on Venereal Diseases in New Zealand', p.22.

99   Margaret Tennant, 'Paterson, Ada Gertrude', *DNZB*, www.teara.govt.nz/en/biographies/3p13/paterson-ada-gertrude (accessed 20 June 2015).

100 'Report of the Committee of Inquiry into Mental Defectives and Sexual Offenders', *AJHR*, 1925, H-31A, p 5.

101 Bronwyn Dalley, 'From Demi-mondes to Slaveys: Aspects of the Management of the Te Oranga Reformatory for Delinquent Young Women, 1900–1918', in B. Brookes, C. Macdonald and M. Tennant (eds) *Women in History 2*, BWB, Wellington, 1992, pp.148–67.

102 'Report of the Committee of Inquiry into Mental Defectives and Sexual Offenders', pp.23–24.

103 Stephen Robertson, '"Production not Reproduction": The Problem of Mental Defect in New Zealand, 1900–1939', BA Hons dissertation, University of Otago, 1989, p.131.

104 Tennant, 'Paterson, Ada Gertrude'.

105 Sandra Coney, 'Jean Begg, 1887–1971', in Macdonald, Penfold and Williams (eds), *The Book of New Zealand Women*, pp.70–74.

106 Hilary Stace, 'Fraser, Janet', *DNZB*, www.teara.govt.nz/en/biographies/4f21/fraser-janet (accessed 21 June 2015).

107 Robertson, '"Production not Reproduction"', pp.133–34.

108 1931 Dominion Conference of the Women's Division of the Farmers' Union, cited in Robertson, '"Production not Reproduction"', p.151.

109 Associate Members Association, Minutes, 26 April 1926–12 April 1937, MS 879, Auckland Museum Library.

110 Associate Members Association, Minutes, 14 July; 8 September 1927; 12 September; 10 October 1929, MS 879, Auckland Museum Library.

111 The 1936 Census recorded 2,432 Chinese males and 511 females. Manying Ip, *Home Away from Home: Life Stories of Chinese Women in New Zealand*, New Women's Press, Auckland, 1990, p.20.

112 'Maori Hygiene', H1, 11685, ANZ.

113 Bennett, 'Maori as Honorary Members of the White Tribe', pp.49–50.

114 Te Rangi Hiroa, 'The Passing of the Maori', *Transactions and Proceedings of the New Zealand Institute*, 55 (1924), pp.370–74, cited in Toelesulusulu D. Salesa, 'Half-castes Between the Wars', *New Zealand Journal of History*, 34 (2000), p.107.

115 Bennett, 'Maori as Honorary Members of the White Tribe', p.48.

116 Evidence of Dr Mildred Staley, H1, 11685, ANZ, p.58.

117 Evidence of Mr Goffe, H1, 11685, ANZ, p.46.

118 H1, 11685, ANZ, p.57.

119 Ibid., p.109.

120 Mr Slaughter, Evidence to the Committee of Inquiry into the Employment of Maoris on Market Gardens, H1, 11685, ANZ.

121 H1, 11685, ANZ, p.28.

122 *Auckland Star*, 6 September 1929, p.12.

123 *New Zealand Herald*, 10 September 1929, p.12. Robert J. C. Young, *Colonial Desire: Hybridity in Theory, Culture and Race*, Routledge, London, 1995, examines the ways in which sex was integral to cultural contact and ideas about race. On commerce, see p.182.

124 Press clipping, 11 November 1929, unsourced, H1, 194, 11685, ANZ.

125 Unattributed clipping, 10 November 1929, L1, 10/3/268, ANZ.

126 Labour Inspector to the Department of Labour, 22 July 1929, L1, 10/3/268, ANZ; unattributed clipping, July 1929, L1, 10/3/268, ANZ.

127 Apart from this letter, and an article in the *Auckland Star*, 11 June 1931, which indicated that the league was assisting unemployed women, nothing is known of this organisation except that it preceded the national Maori Women's Welfare League, founded in 1951. See Barbara Brookes, 'Nostalgia for "innocent homely pleasures": The 1964 New Zealand Controversy over *Washday at the Pa*', *Gender & History*, 9 (1997), pp.242–61.

128 Mere Newton to Apirana Ngata, 8 August 1930, L1, 10/3/268, ANZ.

129 *NZPD*, 26 September 1919, Vol. 184, p.967, cited in Sandra Wallace, 'Powder-Power Politicians: New Zealand Women

Parliamentary Candidates', PhD thesis, University of Otago, 1992, p.397.

130 *NZPD*, October 1919, Vol. 185, p.6.

131 Sandra Coney, 'Ellen Melville, 1882–1946', in Macdonald, Penfold and Williams (eds), *The Book of New Zealand Women*, p.437.

132 Sandra Coney, 'Melville, Eliza Ellen', *DNZB*, www.teara.govt.nz/en/biographies/3m51/melville-eliza-ellen (accessed 21 June 2015).

133 Geoffrey Rice (ed.), *The Oxford History of New Zealand* (2nd edn), OUP, Auckland, 1992, chapters 8 and 14.

134 Carole Pateman discusses C. B. Macpherson's argument about the taming of the democratic franchise through the party system and extends it to the case of women's suffrage in 'Three Questions about Womanhood Suffrage', in C. Daley and M. Nolan (eds), *Suffrage and Beyond: International Feminist Perspectives*, AUP, Auckland, 1994, pp.343–44.

135 Ibid., pp.343–44.

136 Cited in Coney, 'Ellen Melville, 1882–1946', p.440.

137 Ibid., p.438.

138 Margaret Thorn in Elsie Locke and Jacquie Matthews (eds), *Stick Out, Keep Left: An Autobiography by Margaret Thorn*, AUP/BWB, Auckland, 1997, p.55.

139 Wallace, 'Powder-Power Politicians', p.392.

140 Janet McCallum, *Women in the House: Members of Parliament in New Zealand*, Cape Catley, Wellington, 1993, p.7.

141 *Evening Post*, 14 September 1933, p.12.

142 *Evening Post*, 7 September 1933, p.12.

143 *Evening Star* (Dunedin), 19 September 1914, cited in Charlotte Macdonald, 'Kate Sheppard, 1848–1934', in Macdonald, Penfold and Williams (eds), *The Book of New Zealand Women*, p.606.

144 Cited in McCallum, *Women in the House*, p.7.

145 Liz Gordon, 'Women's Place in the Sun: A History of Women in the Labour Party', unpublished MS, p.99, cited in McCallum, *Women in the House*, p.8.

146 *Auckland Star*, 25 September 1934, p.10.

147 *Auckland Star*, 22 September 1934, p.10.

148 'Parliament's people Page 2 – Women MPs', www.nzhistory.net.nz/politics/parliaments-people/women-mps (accessed 2 December 2008).

149 *Akaroa Mail and Banks Peninsula Advertiser*, 11 June 1935, p.2.

150 Robert Robertson, 'The Tyranny of Circumstances: Responses to Unemployment in New Zealand, 1929–1935, with particular reference to Dunedin', PhD thesis, University of Otago, 1978, pp.122–58.

151 Thorn, in Locke and Matthews (eds), *Stick Out, Keep Left*, p.71.

152 *New Zealand Herald*, 21 November 1935, p.13. See also Wallace, 'Powder-Power Politicians', p.397.

153 *Auckland Star*, 13 November 1935, p.16.

154 *New Zealand Herald*, 21 November 1935, p.13.

155 *Auckland Star*, 27 November 1935, p.10.

156 Labour Party Papers, MS 270, F23, ATL.

157 E. Olssen and A. Levesque, 'Towards and History of the European Family in New Zealand', in P. G. Koopman-Boyden (ed.), *Families in New Zealand Society*, Methuen, Wellington, 1978, pp.1–20.

158 Annabel Cooper and Maureen Molloy, 'Poverty, Dependence and "Women": Reading Autobiography and Social Policy from 1930s New Zealand', *Gender & History*, 9, 1 (April 1997), p.46.

159 McClure, *A Civilised Community*, p.66.

160 *Evening Post*, 23 February 1938, p.16; see also Wallace, 'Powder-Power Politicians', pp.412–13.

161 *Evening Post*, 20 September 1938, p.19.

162 Janet Frame, *To the Is-land*, Vintage, Auckland, 1991, p.119.

163 *New Zealand Herald*, 12 September 1938, p.13.

164 McClure, *A Civilised Community*, p.85.

165 Ibid., p.89.

166 M. Soljak, 'Social Security: Women and Children Last!', *Woman Today*, 3, 5 (1939), pp.10–11, cited in McClure, *A Civilised Community*, p.88.

167 *Otago Daily Times*, 10 June 1929, p.10, cited in Asmir Bashir, 'Skirting the Issues: Women Teachers in New Zealand During the Inter-war Period', MA thesis, University of Otago, 2001, p.100.

168 Eileen Soper, born 1901, oral interview with Sarah Fyfe, 11/6/1984, quoted in Fyfe, 'The Topsy-Turvey Twenties', p.61.

Chapter 8

1 *New Zealand Free Lance*, 5 December 1925, pp.1, 2. For a description of the women's exhibit, see *New Zealand Free Lance*, 25 November 1925, p.48.

2   In conversation with Marie Bonaparte in 1925, quoted in Ernest Jones, *Sigmund Freud: Life and Work*, Vol. 2, Hogarth Press, London, 1955, p.468, www.freud.org.uk/about/faq (accessed 29 July 2015).

3   John Brown, *NZPD*, 1918, Vol. 183, p.753.

4   Erik Olssen, 'Working Gender, Gendering Work: Occupational Change and Continuity in Southern Dunedin', in B. Brookes, A. Cooper and R. Law (eds), *Sites of Gender: Women, Men and Modernity in Southern Dunedin*, AUP, Auckland, 2003, p.75; Melanie Nolan, *Breadwinning: New Zealand Women and the State*, CUP, Christchurch, 2000, p.189.

5   Nolan, *Breadwinning*, p.166.

6   For a full history of the service, see Susan Moffatt, 'From Innovative to Outdated: New Zealand's School Dental Service 1921–1989', PhD thesis, University of Otago, 2015.

7   *Evening Post*, 19 November 1920, p.6.

8   *Grey River Argus*, 3 December 1920, p.4.

9   Marie Burgess, 'Hester Maclean', in Charlotte Macdonald, Merimeri Penfold and Bridget Williams (eds), *The Book of New Zealand Women: Ko Kui Ma Te Kaupapa*, BWB, Wellington, 1991, pp.389–91.

10 *Kai Tiaki*, October 1925, p.176.

11 Patricia Sargison, '"Essentially a Woman's Work": A History of General Nursing in New Zealand, 1830–1930', PhD thesis, University of Otago, 2001, p.93.

12 Deborah Dunsford, 'The Privilege to Serve Others: The Working Conditions of General Nurses in Auckland's Public Hospitals, 1908–1950', MA thesis, Auckland University, 1994, pp.149–50; Patricia Sargison, 'The Wages of Sin: Aspects of Nurse Training at Dunedin Hospital in the 1920s and 1930s', *Women Studies Journal*, 11 (August 1995), pp.172–73.

13 Sargison, 'The Wages of Sin', p.173.

14 Hare Hemi Wehipeihana, Betty Goldsmith and Cushla Parekowhai, 'Mirika Powhirihau Wehipeihana', in Macdonald, Penfold and Williams (eds) *The Book of New Zealand Women*, pp.715–18.

15 Judith Binney, 'Irene Paulger, 1899–1966', in Macdonald, Penfold and Williams (eds), *The Book of New Zealand Women*, pp.502–4.

16 Asmir Bashir, 'Skirting the Issues: Women Teachers in New Zealand During the Inter-war Period', MA thesis, University of Otago, 2001, pp.19–22.

17 Phoebe Meikle, *Accidental Life*, AUP, Auckland, 1994, p.59.

18 Ibid., p.68.

19 Mere Hall, 'The Secondary Education of Maori Girls', in Patrick M. Jackson (ed.), *Maori and Education: Or the Education of Natives in New Zealand and its Dependencies*, Ferguson & Osborn, Wellington, 1931, p.278.

20 Dorothy Page, Howard Lee and Tom Brooking, 'Schooling for a Gendered Future', in Brookes, Cooper and Law (eds), *Sites of Gender*, pp.113–20.

21 Sandra Coney, *Standing in the Sunshine: A History of New Zealand Women Since They Won the Vote*, Penguin, Auckland, 1993, p.163.

22 *New Zealand Dairy Exporter*, 1 February 1936, p.28.

23 Ibid.

24 *New Zealand Dairy Exporter*, 1 May 1936, p.41.

25 Arbitration Court of New Zealand, *Awards*, Department of Labour and Employment, Wellington, 1919, p.162.

26 Ibid., p.603.

27 Janice Delaney, Mary Jane Lupton and Emily Toth, *The Curse: A Cultural History of Menstruation*, University of Illinois Press, Urbana, 1988, pp.14–15.

28 *Awards*, 1921, Part 1, p.695.

29 Ibid., 1930, pp.512–13.

30 Ibid., 1921, Part 2, p.1113.

31 Ibid., 1921, Part 1, pp.758–59.

32 Ibid., 1921, Part 2, p.1270; 1922, p.624.

33 Ibid., 1936, Part 2, p.1334.

34 Ibid., 1928, pp.380–81.

35 Ibid., 1938, Part 2, p.2505.

36 Evidence of Mr Grieve, H1, 11685, ANZ, p.26.

37 Evidence of Sister Ivy, H1, 11685, ANZ, p.43. On the role of Methodist deaconesses, see Margaret Tennant, 'Pakeha Deaconesses and the New Zealand Methodist Mission to Maori, 1893–1940', *Journal of Religious History*, 23 (1999), pp.309–26.

38 'Report of the Department of Labour', *AJHR*, 3, 1925, H-11, p.4.

39 Diana Unwin, 'Women in New Zealand Industry', MA Hons dissertation, University of Otago, 1944, p.91.

40 *Northern Advocate*, 17 November 1923, p.2. See B. Brookes and C. Smith, 'Technology and Gender: Barbers and Hairdressers in New Zealand, 1900–1970', *History and Technology*, 25, 4 (December 2009), pp.365–86.

41   *Auckland Star*, 11 February 1930, p.6.

42   Charlotte Macdonald, *Strong, Beautiful and Modern: National Fitness in Britain, New Zealand and Canada*, BWB, Wellington, 2011, p.18.

43   *NZPD*, 1925, Vol. 208, p.710.

44   Society for Research on Women, *In Those Days: A Study of Older Women in Wellington*, Wellington Branch, Society for Research on Women, Wellington, 1982, p.37.

45   '1928 – key events', www.nzhistory.net.nz/culture/the-1920s/1928 (accessed 19 June 2014).

46   Patricia Grace, Irihapeti Ramsden and Jonathan Dennis, *The Silent Migration: Ngati Poneke Young Maori Club 1937–1948*, Huia, Wellington, 2001, pp.24–25.

47   *Evening Post*, 14 August 1929, p.2.

48   Society for Research on Women, *In Those Days*, p.43.

49   Ernest and Pearl Beaglehole, *Some Modern Maoris*, Whitcombe & Tombs and OUP, Christchurch and London, 1946, pp.105–6.

50   Charlotte Macdonald, 'Organisations in Sport, Recreation and Leisure', in Anne Else (ed.), *Women Together: A History of Women's Organisations in New Zealand: Nga Ropu Wahine o te Motu*, Historical Branch, DIA/Daphne Brasell Associates, Wellington, 1993, pp.405–16. See the 'YWCA Girl Citizen's creed' in Helen Dollery, 'Youth organisations – Christian youth organisations', *Te Ara: The Encyclopedia of New Zealand*, www.teara.govt.nz/en/youth-organisations/page-1 (accessed 14 October 2015).

51   Hilda Maher (b.1912), interviewed 1996, Caversham Oral History Project, Transcript Series One, Vol. 4, pp.46–48. See Brookes, Cooper and Law (eds), *Sites of Gender*, pp.168–69.

52   Elizabeth Wilson, *Adorned in Dreams: Fashion and Modernity*, University of California Press, Berkeley, 1987.

53   Jodine Lyons, 'The "Grands Magasins" of the South: The World of Dunedin Department Stores 1890–1960', BA Hons dissertation, University of Otago, 1999, pp.56–75.

54   Fiona McKergow, 'Shopping for Clothes in Palmerston North', in Bronwyn Labrum, Fiona McKergow and Stephanie Gibson (eds), *Looking Flash: Clothing in Aotearoa New Zealand*, AUP, Auckland, 2007, p.148.

55   Ibid., p.147.

56   *New Zealand Free Lance*, 4 February 1925, p.10.

57   *Ladies' Mirror*, 2 July 1923, p.30, cited in Catherine Smith, 'The Business of Beauty: A History of Hairdressers 1920s–1960s', PhD thesis, University of Otago, 1998, p.39. On Club women, see Susan Upton, 'Women in the Club', *Women's Studies Journal*, 12, 1 (1996), pp.43–60; Nancy Swarbrick, 'Women's networks and clubs – Women's self-improvement groups', *Te Ara: The Encyclopedia of New Zealand*, www.teara.govt.nz/en/womens-networks-and-clubs/page-3 (accessed 12 July 2015).

58   *New Zealand Truth*, 15 August 1925, p.1. See also 'Flapper (the cause of all the trouble)', *New Zealand Herald*, 1 June 1929, p.12; 21 March 1931, p.2. *Auckland Star*, 1 November 1927, p.16.

59   Smith, 'The Business of Beauty', p.43.

60   Ibid.

61   *Auckland Star*, 7 December 1929, p.27.

62   Grace, Ramsden and Dennis, *The Silent Migration*, pp.27; 36.

63   Judith Binney and Gillian Chaplin, *Ngā Mōrehu: The Survivors*, OUP, Auckland, 1986, p.164.

64   Anna Rogers and Miria Simpson (eds), *Te Timatanga Tatau Tatau: Early Stories from Founding Members of the Maori Women's Welfare League*, BWB, Wellington, 1993, p.142.

65   A. Ngata and I. L. G. Sutherland, 'Religious Influences', in I. L. G. Sutherland (ed.), *The Maori People Today: A General Survey*, New Zealand Council for Educational Research and New Zealand Institute of International Affairs, Wellington, 1940, p.360.

66   *Woman's Weekly*, 12 January 1933, p.21.

67   Quoting Charlotte, in Society for Research on Women, *In Those Days*, p.43.

68   *Maoriland Worker*, 20 December 1922, p.12.

69   Gwendolen Somerset, *Sunshine and Shadow*, New Zealand Playcentre Federation, Wellington, 1988, p.89.

70   Ibid., p.169.

71   Ian Pool, Arunachalam Dharmalingam and Janet Sceats, *The New Zealand Family from 1840: A Demographic History*, AUP, Auckland, 2007, p.61.

72   See 'Love's Young Dream', *Auckland Star*, 8 March 1928, p.8.

73   Jill Trevelyan, *Rita Angus: An Artist's Life*, Te Papa Press, Wellington, 2008, p.39.

74 *New Zealand Dairy Exporter*, 2 March 1936, p.72.

75 *Hutt News*, 8 July 1936, p.5.

76 *New Zealand Dairy Exporter*, 1 April 1936, p.61.

77 *New Zealand Dairy Exporter*, 1 May 1936, p.88.

78 *New Zealand Dairy Exporter*, 1 August 1936, p.71.

79 H. W. Scott, 'The "Electric Home"', *The Young New Zealander incorporating New Zealand Woman and Home*, 2 (February–15 March 1926).

80 Jane Neville, 'The "Electric Servant" in Rural New Zealand: A Study of the Impact of Electrification on Rural Domestic Life', BA Hons long essay, University of Otago, 1985, p.89.

81 Jean-Marie O'Donnell, '"Electric Servants" and the Science of Housework: Changing Patterns of Domestic Work, 1935–1956', in B. Brookes, C. Macdonald and M. Tennant (eds), *Women in History 2*, BWB, Wellington, 1992, p.171.

82 G. R. Hawke, 'Economic Decisions and Political Ossification: The New Zealand Retail Electricity Tariff', in Peter Munz (ed.), *The Feel of Truth: Essays in New Zealand and Pacific History*, A. H. & A. W. Reed, Wellington, 1967, p.232.

83 Charlotte Macdonald, 'Strangers at the Hearth: The Eclipse of Domestic Service in New Zealand Homes c.1830s–1940s', in B. Brookes (ed.), *At Home in New Zealand: History, Houses, People*, BWB, Wellington, 2000, p.53.

84 Cited in Sandra Coney, *Everygirl*, Young Women's Christian Association, Auckland, 1986, p.100.

85 Katie Pickles, 'Empire Settlement and Single British Women as New Zealand Domestic Servants during the 1920s', *New Zealand Journal of History*, 35, 1 (2001), pp.22–44.

86 J. P. Broad and J. Steven, 'A General Survey of Ratana', fifth year Preventive and Social Medicine thesis, University of Otago Medical School, 1940, p.73.

87 Grace, Ramsden and Dennis, *The Silent Migration*, p.10.

88 *NZPD*, 1933, Vol. 236, p.719.

89 Ruth Fry, *Out of the Silence: Methodist Women of Aotearoa, 1822–1985*, Methodist Publishing, Christchurch, 1987, pp.60–61.

90 Macdonald, 'Strangers at the Hearth', p.53.

91 Sarah Boyd, 'Images of Femininity', BA Hons long essay, University of Otago, 1985, p.87.

92 15 August 1935, p.31, cited in Boyd, 'Images of Femininity', p.88.

93 'Lucy Jacob, 1896–1976', in Macdonald, Penfold and Williams (eds), *The Book of New Zealand Women*, p.325.

94 Ruth Dallas, *Curved Horizon: An Autobiography*, University of Otago Press, Dunedin, 1991, pp.36–39.

95 *Kai Tiaki*, 12 (January 1929), p.44.

96 Yvonne Robertson, *A Victorian Lady in an Age of Change: Mary Downie Stewart, 1876–1957*, BA Dip Arts dissertation, University of Otago, 1990.

97 Helen Frizzell, recorder, 'Bessie Turnbull', in Macdonald, Penfold and Williams (eds), *The Book of New Zealand Women*, p.700.

98 Dorothy Butler, 'Born to Read', in Michael Gifkins (ed.), *Through the Looking Glass: Recollections of Childhood from 20 Prominent New Zealanders*, Century Hutchinson, Auckland, 1980, pp.2–3.

99 Ibid., p.6.

100 Ibid.

101 *Marlborough Express*, 9 May 1919, p.6.

102 Barbara Brookes, '"Cherishing Hopes of the Impossible": Mothers, Fathers and Disability at Birth in Mid-Twentieth Century New Zealand', in T. P. Light, B. Brookes and W. Mitchinson, *Bodily Subjects: Essays on Gender and Health, 1800–2000*, McGill-Queens University Press, Montreal, 2014, pp.178–99.

103 Margaret Tennant, 'Missionaries of Health', in L. Bryder (ed.), *A Healthy Country: Essays on the Social History of Medicine in New Zealand*, BWB, Wellington, 1991, pp.144–45.

104 Nolan, *Breadwinning*, p.171.

105 *NZPD*, 1931, Vol. 228, p.405.

106 Coney, *Every Girl*, p.201; Margaret Tennant with Kate Flintoff, 'Women's Unemployment Committees 1931–1939', in Else (ed.), *Women Together*, p.139; Nolan, *Breadwinning*, p.170.

107 Nolan, *Breadwinning*, p.175.

108 Megan Cook, 'Women's Labour Organisations: Women and unemployment', *Te Ara: The Encyclopedia of New Zealand*, www.teara.govt.nz/en/womens-labour-organisations/page-3 (accessed 30 June 2015).

109 Nolan, *Breadwinning*, p.174.

110 *Press*, 2 June 1931, p.12.

111 *White Ribbon*, 18 August 1932, p.1.

112 *White Ribbon*, 18 May 1931, p.1.

113 Bashir, 'Skirting the Issues', p.80.

114 Ibid., p.38.

115 One of the leaders of the NZWTA was Jean Park, who had been dismissed from teaching in 1921 for selling books thought to be seditious. Eventually reinstated by the Supreme Court, Jean Park became active in the association and the New Zealand Education Institute. Ibid., p.79.

116 Ibid., p.107.

117 *Press*, 25 August 1931, p.15, cited in Jo Aitken, 'Wives and Mothers First: The New Zealand Teachers' Marriage Bar and the Ideology of Domesticity, 1920–1940', *Women's Studies Journal*, 12, 1 (Autumn 1996), p.85.

118 Bashir, 'Skirting the Issues', p.39.

119 28 January 1937, cited in ibid., p.106.

120 Ibid., p.111.

121 Aitken, 'Wives and Mothers First', p.92.

122 Ibid., p.93.

123 *NZPD*, 1932, Vol. 231, p.50.

124 *New Zealand Woman's Weekly*, 5 November 1936, p.28.

125 Ibid.

126 H1, 11685, ANZ.

127 *NZPD*, 1933, Vol. 236, p.734.

128 Robert Robertson, 'The Tyranny of Circumstances: Responses to Unemployment in New Zealand, 1929–1935, with Particular Reference to Dunedin', PhD thesis, University of Otago, 1978, pp.311–22.

129 *New Zealand Herald*, 22 January 1936, p.16.

130 This paragraph draws on the work of Annabel Cooper and Marian Horan, 'Down and Out on the Flat: The Gendering of Poverty', in Brookes, Cooper and Law (eds), *Sites of Gender*, p.225, and Penny Isaac, '"No Room for Luxuries": Aspects of Life in a Working Class Community in the 1930s', MA thesis, University of Otago, 1999, pp.32–36.

131 Barry Gustafson, *From the Cradle to the Grave: A Biography of Michael Joseph Savage*, Reed Methuen, Auckland, 1986, p.229.

132 Tim Frank, 'Bread Queues and Breadwinners: Gender in the 1930s', in Caroline Daley and Deborah Montgomerie (eds), *The Gendered Kiwi*, AUP, Auckland, 1999, p.119.

133 Ibid., p.130.

134 Nolan, *Breadwinning*, p.186.

135 *Dominion*, 28 August 1920, p.11.

136 *New Zealand Herald*, 22 October 1924, p.13.

137 See Ian Gordon, 'Book Censorship in New Zealand', *Salient*, 26, 6 (4 June 1963), http://nzetc.victoria.ac.nz/tm/scholarly/tei-Salient26061963-t1-body-d19.html (accessed 29 July 2015). See also David McGill, *The Guardians at the Gate: The History of the New Zealand Customs Department*, Silver Owl Press, Wellington, 1991, pp.122–43.

138 'Easy to Love', *Auckland Star*, 18 August 1934, p.20; *New Zealand Herald*, 28 May 1931, p.15; 'Peach o' Reno', *New Zealand Herald*, 21 May 1932, p.11.

139 *Press*, 11 October 1834, p.24.

140 *Press*, 31 May 1932, p.3.

141 *Auckland Star*, 11 December 1936, p.11.

142 Ibid.

143 Ibid.

144 Megan Cook, 'Divorce and separation – Growth in divorce: 1898–1979', *Te Ara: The Encyclopedia of New Zealand*, www.teara.govt.nz/en/divorce-and-separation/page-2 (accessed 20 June 2015).

145 Bill Pearson, 'The Banning of the Butchershop', in Jean Devanny, *The Butcher Shop*, introduction by Heather Roberts, AUP/OUP, Auckland, 1981.

146 Carole Ferrier (ed.), *Point of Departure: The Autobiography of Jean Devanny*, St Lucia, Queensland, 1986, p.94. See also Pearson, 'The Banning of the Butchershop', p.11.

147 Heather Roberts, 'Devanny, Jean', *DNZB*, www.teara.govt.nz/en/biographies/4d13/devanny-jean (accessed 20 June 2015).

148 'Woman Today', *Tomorrow*, 14 April 1937, p.196, cited in Gillian Boddy and Jacqueline Matthews (eds), *Disputed Ground: Robin Hyde, Journalist*, VUP, Wellington, 1991, p.196.

149 R. Hyde, *A Home in this World*, p.92, cited in J. Matthews, 'Robin Hyde', in Macdonald, Penfold and Williams (eds), *The Book of New Zealand Women*, p.320.

150 Macdonald, Penfold and Williams (eds), *The Book of New Zealand Women*, p.321; Robin Hyde to J. A. Lee, 18 August 1937, cited in Boddy and Matthews (eds), *Disputed Ground*, p.124.

151 H. G. R. Mason, *Education Today and Tomorrow* (2nd edn), Government Printer, Wellington, 1945, p.57.

152 Heeni Wharemaru, with Mary Katharine Duffié, *Heeni: A Tainui Elder Remembers*, Harper Collins, Auckland, 1997, p.19.

153 Allan K. Davidson, 'Scrimgeour, Colin Graham', *DNZB*, www.teara.govt.nz/en/biographies/4s16/scrimgeour-colin-graham (accessed 5 July 2015). Quote from Allison Oosterman, 'Everybody's Uncle', *Pacific Journalism Review*, 18, 1 (2012), p.255.

154 Wharemaru and Duffié, *Heeni*, p.99.

155 Michael King, *Te Puea* (3rd edn), Sceptre, Auckland, 1987, p.108.

156 Ibid., p.116.

157 Ibid., p.153.

158 Ibid., p.194.

Chapter 9

1 Rachel Barrowman, 'History and Romance: The Making of the Centennial Historical Surveys', in William Renwick (ed.), *Creating a National Spirit: Celebrating New Zealand's Centennial*, VUP, Wellington, 2004, p.172.

2 Ibid., p.167.

3 Bronwyn Labrum, 'Simpson, Helen Macdonald', *DNZB*, www.teara.govt.nz/en/biographies/5s19/simpson-helen-macdonald (accessed 14 March 2014).

4 Cited in Ena Ryan, 'On the Home Front', in Anna Rogers (ed.), *The War Years: New Zealanders Remember 1939–1945*, Platform Publishing, Wellington, 1989, pp.44–46.

5 Nancy M. Taylor, *The Home Front*, Vol. 1, Historical Branch Department of Internal Affairs, Government Printer, Wellington, 1986, p.90.

6 Deborah Montgomerie, *The Women's War: New Zealand Women 1939–45*, AUP, Auckland, 2001, pp.44–45.

7 Joanne Thrush, 'World War Two and its Post-war Repercussions on New Zealand Women', BA Hons dissertation, University of Otago, 1986, p.9.

8 Montgomerie, *The Women's War*, p.45.

9 Ibid.

10 Ibid., pp.45–46.

11 Ibid., p.46.

12 Ibid., p.54.

13 'Second World War – overview', www.nzhistory.net.nz/war/second-world-war/counting-the-cost (accessed 29 September 2014).

14 'NZWAAF', www.diggerhistory.info/pages-nz/nz-waaf.htm (accessed 17 March 2014).

15 D. O. W. Hall, 'Women at War', War History Branch, DIA, Wellington, 1948, electronic text at www.nzetc.org/tm/scholarly/tei-WH2-1Epi-c2-WH2-1Epi-c.html, p.4.

16 Ibid.

17 Ibid., p.5.

18 Ibid.

19 *Pro Patria*, 1, 2 (July 1943), Southern Military District Magazine, Hocken collections.

20 Jim Sullivan (ed.), *Doing Our Bit: New Zealand Women Tell Their Stories of World War Two*, Harper Collins, Auckland, 2002, p.88.

21 Anna Rogers, *While You're Away: New Zealand Nurses at War 1899–1948*, AUP, Auckland, 2003, p.197.

22 Mavis Bracegirdle, in Sullivan (ed.), *Doing Our Bit*, p.47.

23 Thrush, 'World War Two and its Post-war Repercussions', p.11.

24 Alan Paisey, *Bedpans and Ruins: A Young Woman Soldier's Experience of War 1940–1945*, Campaid Graphics, Preston UK, 2008, p.10.

25 Ibid.

26 Nancy M. Taylor, *The Home Front*, Vol. 2, Historical Branch, DIA, Wellington, 1986, p.1105.

27 Dianne Bardsley, *The Land Girls: In a Man's World, 1939–1946*, University of Otago Press, Dunedin, 2000, p.89.

28 Ibid., p.39.

29 Gaylene Preston and Judith Fyfe, *War Stories Our Mothers Never Told Us*, Penguin, Auckland, 1995, pp.129–42, quotation, p.135.

30 Jamie Mackay, 'Edna Bertha Pearce', *DNZB*, Vol. 5, AUP/DIA, Auckland, 2000, pp.404–5.

31 Taylor, *The Home Front*, Vol. 2, pp.1100–1.

32 Dorothy Page, *The National Council of Women: A Centennial History*, AUP/BWB, Auckland, 1996, p.25.

33 Taylor, *The Home Front*, Vol. 2, p.1101.

34 Taylor, *The Home Front*, Vol. 1, pp.190–91.

35 Murray Horton, Obituary – Connie Summers, *Peace Researcher*, 38 (July 2009), www.converge.org.nz/abc/pr38-176b.htm (accessed 12 November 2014).

36 Anonymous, in Lauris Edmond (ed.), *Women in Wartime: New Zealand Women Tell Their Story*, Government Printing Office, Wellington, 1986, pp.28–29.

37 Preston and Fyfe, *War Stories Our Mothers Never Told Us*, pp.143–61.

38 Maureen Birchfield, *Looking for Answers: A*

Life of Elsie Locke, CUP, Christchurch, 2009, p.213.

39 Ibid., pp.215–16.

40 Cited in ibid., p.220.

41 Montgomerie, *The Women's War*, pp.104–5.

42 Ibid., p.107.

43 'Joyce Carr', in Sullivan (ed.), *Doing Our Bit*, p.60.

44 Pamela Alison Mason, 'The Redistribution of Womanpower: Women in the Workforce, 1940–1945', BA Hons dissertation, University of Otago, 1983, p.17.

45 Deborah Montgomerie, 'Man-powering Women: Industrial Conscription during the Second World War', in B. Brookes, C. Macdonald and M. Tennant (eds), *Women in History 2*, BWB, Wellington, 1992, p.186.

46 J. F. Bates, *Dominion*, 8 October 1943, p.4, cited in Montgomerie, 'Man-powering Women', p.190.

47 Montgomerie, 'Man-powering Women', pp.187–88.

48 Hall, *Women At War*, p.30.

49 Thrush, 'World War Two and its Post-war Repercussions', p.12.

50 Mihi Edwards, *Mihipeka: Early Years*, Penguin, Auckland, 1990, p.163.

51 Ruria Utiku, in Alison Parr, *Home: Civilian New Zealanders Remember the Second World War*, Penguin, Auckland, 2010, p.112.

52 Ibid.

53 *Population Census*, 1945, Vol. 3, I, 'Maori Census', p.iii.

54 G. V. Butterworth, *The Maori People in the New Zealand Economy*, Department of Social Anthropology and Māori Studies, Massey University, Palmerston North, 1974, p.29.

55 J. V. T. Baker, *The New Zealand People at War: War Economy*, Historical Branch, DIA, Wellington, 1965, p.437.

56 Ibid.

57 Bert Roth, *Remedy for Present Evils: A History of the New Zealand Public Service Association from 1890*, New Zealand Public Service Association, Wellington, 1987, p.66.

58 Margaret Corner, *No Easy Victory: Towards Equal Pay for Women in the Government Service 1890–1960*, New Zealand Public Service Association, Dan Long Trust, Wellington, 1988, p.30.

59 Society for Research on Women, *In Those Days: A Study of Older Women in Wellington*, Wellington Branch, Society for Research on Women, Wellington, 1982, p.54.

60 'Lorna Gayton', in Sullivan (ed.), *Doing Our Bit*, pp.98–101.

61 'Gwenda Birnie', in ibid., p.40.

62 Taylor, *The Home Front*, Vol. 2, pp.1125–27.

63 Thrush, 'World War Two and its Post-war Repercussions', pp.25–26.

64 Taylor, *The Home Front*, Vol. 2, pp.789–90.

65 Ibid., p.1054.

66 Monty Soutar, *Nga Tamatoa: The Price of Citizenship: C Company 28 (Maori) Battalion 1939–1945*, David Bateman, Auckland, 2008, p.110.

67 Michael King, *Te Puea: A Biography*, Hodder & Stoughton, Auckland, 1977, pp.209–10.

68 Soutar, *Nga Tamatoa*, p.112.

69 Eve Ebbett, *When the Boys Were Away: New Zealand Women in World War II*, A. H. & A. W. Reed, Wellington, 1984, pp.38–40.

70 *New Zealand Listener*, 27 June 1941, p.42.

71 Christina Guy, *Women on the Home Front: An S.O.S. from Mothers*, Progressive Publishing Society, Wellington, 1943, p.5.

72 Ibid., p.27.

73 Ibid., p.16.

74 Ibid., pp.62–64.

75 Minimum Wage Act, 1945, No. 44. See also Melanie Nolan, '"Politics Swept Under a Domestic Carpet"? Fracturing Domesticity and the Male Breadwinner Wage: Women's Economic Citizenship, 1920s–1940s', *New Zealand Journal of History*, 27 (October 1993), p.216.

76 John E. Martin, *Holding the Balance: A History of New Zealand's Department of Labour, 1891–1995*, CUP, Christchurch, 1996, pp.229–30.

77 Montgomerie, *The Women's War*, p.129.

78 C. E. Hercus, 'Women and National Survival', Wilding Memorial Lecture, Christchurch, 1940, p.19.

79 John Bowlby, *Maternal Care and Mental Health*, World Health Organization, Geneva, 1951.

80 'Children and adolescents, 1930-1960', www.nzhistory.net.nz/culture/children-and-adolescents-1930-1960 (Ministry for Culture and Heritage) (accessed 30 July 2015)

81 *New Zealand Official Yearbook*, 1946, p.439.

82 Margaret McClure, *A Civilised Community: A History of Social Security in New Zealand*,

1898–1998, AUP/Historical Branch, DIA, Auckland, p.122.

83 I. Pool, A. Dharmalingam and J. Sceats, *The New Zealand Family from 1840: A Demographic History*, AUP, Auckland, 2007, p.176.

84 A. Ngata and I. L. G. Sutherland, 'Religious Influences', in I. L. G. Sutherland, *The Maori People Today: A General Survey*, New Zealand Institute of International Affairs, New Zealand Council for Educational Research, Institute of Pacific Affairs, Wellington, 1940, p.360.

85 Judith Binney and Gillian Chaplin, *Ngā Mōrehu: The Survivors*, OUP, Auckland, 1986, p.45.

86 Society for Research on Women, *In Those Days*, p.89.

87 Ebbett, *When the Boys Were Away*, pp.51, 146.

88 Society for Research on Women, *In Those Days*, p.39.

89 'Olive Bennett', in Sullivan (ed.), *Doing Our Bit*, p.35.

90 Parr, *Home*, p.163.

91 Ibid., p.166.

92 *Otago Daily Times*, 9 January 1940, p.13.

93 Mihi Edwards, *Mihipeka: Time of Turmoil: Ngā Wā Raruraru*, Penguin, Auckland, 1992, pp.90–100, 160.

94 Bronwyn Dalley and Gavin McLean (eds), *Frontier of Dreams: The Story of New Zealand*, Hodder Moa Beckett, Auckland, 2005, p.298.

95 Edmond (ed.), *Women in Wartime*, p.140.

96 Edwards, *Time of Turmoil*, pp.139–41.

97 Sonja Davies, *Bread and Roses: Her Story*, Fraser Books, Masterton, 1984, pp.55–58.

98 Cited in Taylor, *The Home Front*, Vol. 2, pp.1039–40.

99 Ibid., p.1041.

100 Ibid.

101 *Evening Post*, 14 October 1944, p.6.

102 *Truth*, 7 March 1945, p.5.

103 Davies, *Bread and Roses*, p.43.

104 *Truth*, 31 March 1943, p.5, cited in Taylor, *The Home Front*, Vol. 2, p.1040.

105 Taylor, *The Home Front*, Vol. 2, p.1040.

106 Joan and Bruce Cochran, *Sex, Love and Marriage*, Presbyterian Bookroom for the National Council of Churches, Christchurch, 1942, p.8.

107 Ibid., p.10.

108 Ibid., p.13.

109 Preston and Fyfe, *War Stories*, p.102.

110 Jock Phillips, *Brief Encounter: American Forces and the New Zealand People 1942–1945: An Illustrated History*, Historical Branch, DIA, Wellington, 1992, p.40.

111 Ibid.

112 Thrush, 'World War Two and its Post-war Repercussions', p.67.

113 Val Wood, *War Brides: They Followed Their Hearts to New Zealand*, Random Century, Auckland, 1991, p.99.

114 Gabrielle Fortune, '"Mr Jones' Wives": War Brides, Marriage, Immigration and Identity Formation', *Women History Review*, 15, 4 (September 2006), p.588. See also G. Fortune, '"Mr Jones' Wives": World War II War Brides of New Zealand Servicemen', PhD thesis, University of Auckland, 2005.

115 Wood, *War Brides*, p.153.

116 Ibid., pp.143, 149.

117 Statistics New Zealand, 1855–2003. Long term data series table A2-1, 2004–2008: Demographic table 3.01, *Te Ara: The Encyclopedia of New Zealand*, www.teara.govt.nz/files/30774-data.txt (accessed 30 July 2015).

118 Society for Research on Women, *In Those Days*, p.41.

119 Glenys Lewis, in Glenn Busch, *You Are My Darling Zita*, Temple University Press, Philadelphia, 1991, p.67.

120 Edmond (ed.), *Women in Wartime*, p.237.

121 John Harré, *Maori and Pakeha: A Study of Mixed Marriages in New Zealand*, Frederick A. Praeger, New York, 1966, pp.80–84.

122 In 're A B (An Infant)', *New Zealand Law Reports* (1944), pp.675–76.

123 *New Zealand Official Yearbook*, 1947–49, p.61.

124 Edmond (ed.), *Women in Wartime*, p.250.

125 Ebbett, *When the Boys Were Away*, p.147.

126 Edmond (ed.), *Women in Wartime*, p.242.

127 Thrush, 'World War Two and its Post-war Repercussions', pp.35–36.

128 *New Zealand Woman's Weekly*, 20 September 1945, cited in Helen May, *Minding Children, Managing Men: Conflict and Compromise in the Lives of Postwar Pakeha Women*, BWB, Wellington, 1992, p.51.

129 May, *Minding Children, Managing Men*, p.49.

130 Alison Parr, *Silent Casualties: New Zealand's Unspoken Legacy of the Second World War*,

Tandem Press, Birkenhead, 1995, p.165.

131 M. Bevan-Brown, *War Neurosis: Designed for the Guidance of Relatives and Friends of Ex-service Men and Women*, J. W. Baty, Christchurch, 1945, p.2.

132 Domestic Proceedings Act 1939, www.enzs. auckland.ac.nz/docs/1939/1939A013.pdf (accessed 30 July 2015); Brenda L. Stedman, 'The Origins and Development of the Dunedin Marriage Guidance Council, 1948–1970', BA Hons long essay, University of Otago, 1988, p.7.

133 Stedman, 'The Origins and Development of the Dunedin Marriage Guidance Council', p.19.

134 Ibid., p.21.

135 Edmond (ed.), *Women in Wartime*, p.234.

136 Janet McCallum, *Women in the House: Members of Parliament in New Zealand*, Cape Catley, Wellington, 1993, p.37. In 1934, Mabel Howard had been appointed secretary of the Canterbury General Labourers' Union, the first woman to hold such a position.

137 *NZPD*, 1943, Vol. 262, p.43, cited in McCallum, *Women in the House*, p.38.

138 'The Case for Equal Pay for Equal Work Presented on Behalf of the Women of the New Zealand Public Service to the Consultative Committee', 4 April 1944, reprinted in Charlotte Macdonald, *The Vote, the Pill, and the Demon Drink: A History of Feminist Writing in New Zealand, 1869–1993*, BWB, Wellington, 1993, p.125.

139 Kathleen Ross, 'Are they 80% Efficient?', *Public Service Journal* (December 1944), reprinted in Macdonald, *The Vote, the Pill and the Demon Drink*, pp.130–33.

140 Caroline Webb, 'Social Aspects of Equal Pay', *Public Service Journal* (January 1946), reprinted in Macdonald, *The Vote, the Pill and the Demon Drink*, pp.133–35.

141 McCallum, *Women in the House*, p.42.

142 Ibid., p.39.

143 Ibid., p.44.

144 Angela Ballara, 'Ratana, Iriaka Matiu, 1905–1981', *DNZB*, Vol. 5, pp.432–33.

145 McCallum, *Women in the House*, p.58.

146 Ballara, 'Ratana, Iriaka Matiu, 1905–1981', p.433.

147 McCallum, *Women in the House*, p.59.

148 Angela Ballara, 'Ratana, Iriaka Matiu', *DNZB*, www.teara.govt.nz/en/biographies/5r7/ ratana-iriaka-matiu (accessed 20 July 2015).

149 McCallum, *Women in the House*, p.60.

150 Ballara, 'Ratana, Iriaka Matiu, 1905–1981', p.433.

151 *NZPD*, 12 July 1950, Vol. 289, p.336.

152 Prime Minister M. J. Savage, *New Zealand Herald*, 26 October 1936, cited in Claudia Orange, 'A Kind of Equality: Labour and the Maori People', MA thesis, University of Auckland, 1977, p.53.

153 Letter to *Rotorua Morning Post*, 10 January 1941. HD Acc WI353 3/211 P1, ANZ.

154 HD Acc WI353 3/211 P1, ANZ.

155 *Manawatu Evening Standard*, 19 December 1944. HD Acc wI353 3/211 P1, ANZ.

156 HD Acc WI353 3/211 Pt 1, ANZ.

157 HD Acc W1353 3/211, ANZ.

158 Taylor, *The Home Front*, Vol. 2, p.1242.

159 *NZPD*, 1943, Vol. 263, pp.149–50; Taylor, *The Home Front*, Vol. 2, p.1241.

160 Taylor, *The Home Front*, Vol. 2, pp.806–7, 1240.

161 Claudia Orange, 'Maori War Effort Organisation', in Ian McGibbon (ed.), *The Oxford Companion to New Zealand Military History*, OUP, Auckland, 2000, p.307.

162 *Evening Post*, 10 May 1943, p.4, cited in Taylor, *The Home Front*, Vol. 2, p.1037, n.132.

163 Henry C. McQueen, *Vocations for Maori Youth*, New Zealand Council for Educational Research, Whitcombe & Tombs, Christchurch, 1945, p.2.

164 Wanganui Education Board, *Report on Character Training and Citizenship*, pamphlet, 1944, p.52.

165 McQueen, *Vocations for Maori Youth*, p.133.

166 Ibid., pp.133–34.

167 Ibid., p.134.

168 Ibid., pp.133–35.

169 H. G. R. Mason, *Education Today and Tomorrow* (2nd edn), Government Printer, Wellington, 1945, p.39.

170 *AJHR*, 1937, I, E-03, p.3.

171 'Mira Szaszy', in Virginia Myers, *Head and Shoulders: Successful New Zealand Women Talk to Virginia Myers*, Penguin, Auckland, 1986, p.237.

172 Ibid., p.235.

173 *AJHR*, 1948, E-3, p.6.

174 *AJHR*, 1945, Vol. 2, G-11, p.1; H-18, p.19.

175 G. V. Butterworth and H. R. Young, *Maori Affairs*, Iwi Transition Agency/GP Books, Wellington, 1990, pp.89–99.

176 HD Acc W 1353 3/211 Pt 1, ANZ.

177 Maori Women's Welfare League, Fourth Annual Conference, 1955, MS Papers-1396-002, ATL.

178 Sturm was married to James K. Baxter at the time but chose to write under her own name. For biographical information, see Paul Millar, 'Jacquie Baxter/J. C. Sturm', www.nzepc. auckland.ac.nz/kmko/09/ka_mate09_millar. asp (accessed 31 July 2015).

179 *Te Ao Hou*, 9 (1954), p.58.

Chapter 10

1 Cath Tizard, *Cat Among the Pigeons: A Memoir*, Random House, Auckland, 2010, p.36.

2 Cath Tizard, 'A Happy Series of Accidents', in Margaret Clark (ed.), *Beyond Expectations: Fourteen New Zealand Women Write About Their Lives*, A&U/Port Nicholson Press, Wellington, 1986, p.86.

3 Steven Mintz and Susan Kellogg, *Domestic Revolutions: A Social History of American Family Life*, Collier Macmillan, New York, 1988, p.178.

4 I. Pool, A. Dharmalingam and J. Sceats, *The New Zealand Family from 1840*, AUP, Auckland, 2007, p.179; Ian Pool and Rosemary Du Plessis, 'Families: A history – Baby boom continues: 1960s – early 1970s', *Te Ara: The Encyclopedia of New Zealand*, www. teara.govt.nz/en/graph/30214/age-at-first-marriage-1935-2005 (accessed 12 June 2015).

5 On the vitality of Māori communities during this period, see Aroha Harris, 'Dancing with the State: Maori Creative Energy and the Policies of Integration, 1945–1967', PhD thesis, University of Auckland, 2007.

6 Doubling of the Māori population is noted in B. Dalley and G. McLean (eds), *Frontier of Dreams: The Story of New Zealand*, Hodder Moa Beckett, Auckland, 2005, p.326.

7 'The 1951 waterfront dispute', www.nzhistory. net.nz/politics/the-1951-waterfront-dispute (accessed 4 August 2015).

8 Quoted in Bert Roth and Janny Hammond, *Toil and Trouble: The Struggle for a Better Life in New Zealand*, Methuen New Zealand, Auckland, 1981, p.158.

9 For an in-depth discussion of the dispute and its impact on families, see Grace Millar, 'Families and the 1951 Waterfront Lockout', PhD thesis, Victoria University of Wellington, 2013.

10 Andrea Hotere, 'The 1951 Waterfront Lockout in Port Chalmers', BA Hons dissertation, University of Otago, 1989, p.93.

11 *Truth*, 19 April 1950, p.26.

12 Jock Phillips, *Royal Summer: The Visit of Queen Elizabeth II and Prince Philip to New Zealand 1953–54*, DIA/Daphne Brasell Associates, Wellington, 1993; John Hardingham, *The Queen in New Zealand*, A. H. & A. W. Reed, Wellington, 1954; 'The Royal Tour of New Zealand, 1953–54', www.nzonscreen.com/title/royal-tour-1953-54-1954 (accessed 4 August 2015).

13 *New Zealand Woman's Weekly*, 16 December 1954, p.14.

14 *New Zealand Woman's Weekly*, 4 March 1957, p.89. Emphasis in the original.

15 *New Zealand Official Yearbook*, 1959, p.639.

16 Erica Marian O'Flaherty, 'Keeping up with the Joneses? Representation and Reality in the Postwar Private Suburb of Hillcrest, 1949–1962', MA thesis, Waikato University, 2004.

17 National Film Unit, 'Parades of Homes', *Pictorial Parade*, 62, 1957; 'New Developments', *Pictorial Parade*, 79, 1958.

18 Advertisement in J. G. Sowerby, *Economical House Planning in New Zealand*, A. H. & A. W. Reed, Wellington, 1954, cited in W. Unkovich, 'Shelter and Haven: State Tenants and Home-ownership in New Zealand 1945–1955', BA Hons long essay, University of Otago, 1984, p.58.

19 Architectural Centre Inc. Wellington, *Demonstration Home*, p.1, cited in Unkovich, 'Shelter and Haven', p.55.

20 Ministry of Housing, *Housing the Citizen: A Manual for Local Authorities*, Government Printer, Wellington, 1954, p.5.

21 School Publications Branch, *Houses to Live In: A School Bulletin*, Education Department, Wellington, 1949, pp.9–10.

22 A. Congalton, *Hawera: A Social Survey: A Report of a Community Venture*, Hawera District and Progressive Association, Hawera Star Publishing, Hawera, 1954, pp.117–38.

23 T. Gebbie, 'The Health and Conditions of Some Working Class Housewives', fifth year Preventive Medicine thesis, University of Otago, 1953, pp.11–12.

24 See, for example, C. Firth, *State Housing in New Zealand*, Ministry of Works, 1949, p.32.

25 See Congalton, *Hawera*.

26 W. J. Campbell, *Hydrotown: The Social History*

of an Industrial Boom Settlement, University of Otago, Dunedin, 1957, p.50.

27 *New Zealand Listener*, 6 January 1950.

28 Ibid., p.30; 1 September 1950, p.29.

29 Campbell, *Hydrotown*, p.50.

30 *New Zealand Listener*, 9 August 1963, pp.8–9.

31 A. C. Wilson, 'Telecommunications – Post and Telegraph, 1914–1945', *Te Ara: The Encyclopedia of New Zealand*, www.teara.govt.nz/en/telecommunications/page-4 (accessed 25 June 2015).

32 *New Zealand Official Yearbook*, 1969, p.365.

33 M. Jerram and J. Hamlin, 'Public Health Conditions in Country Districts', fifth year Preventive Medicine thesis, University of Otago, 1941.

34 J.-M. O'Donnell, '"Electric Servants" and the Science of Housework: Changing Patterns of Domestic Work, 1935–1956', in B. Brookes, C. Macdonald and M. Tennant (eds), *Women in History 2*, BWB, Wellington, 1992, p.178.

35 *New Zealand Population Census*, 1956: Bath or shower 58% Māori 93% Pākehā; Piped water 51% M 86% P; Hotwater service 48% M 88% P; Flush toilet 31% M 80% P; Refrigerator 20% M 55% M; Washing machine 19% M 58% P. 'Report on Department of Maori Affairs: Hunn Report' (1960), *AJHR*, Vol. 2, 1961, G-10.

36 *New Zealand Population Census*, 1951, Vol. 12, *Dwellings and Households*, p.11; 1956, Vol. 9, *Dwellings and Households*, p.29; 1961, Vol. 9, *Dwellings and Households*, p.9.

37 Dunstall, 'The Social Pattern', in W. H. Oliver and B. R. Williams (eds), *The Oxford History of New Zealand*, OUP, Auckland, 1981, p.458; C. Orange, 'A Kind of Equality: Labour and the Maori People', MA thesis, University of Auckland, 1977, p.208.

38 *New Zealand Population Census*, 1951: 87.70% of Māori incomes were below £500 per annum, compared with 63.13% for Pākehā.

39 Michael King, *After the War: New Zealand Since 1945*, Hodder & Stoughton with Wilson & Horton, Auckland, 1988, p.288.

40 L. K. Harries, 'Family Life in Wellsford', fifth year Preventive Medicine thesis, University of Otago, 1956, p.5.

41 Waerete Norman, 'Taura', in Witi Ihimaera (ed.), *Growing Up Maori*, Tandem Press, Auckland, 1998, pp.110–32.

42 The 1951 Census suggests 7,621 Māori lived in the urban Auckland area. Citing internal correspondence within DIA, Claudia Orange puts the figure at over 12,000 in 1945. *New Zealand Population Census*, 1951, Vol. 6, *Maori Census*, R. E. Owen, Government Printer, Wellington, 1954, p.14; Orange, 'A Kind of Equality', p.169.

43 *Te Ao Hou*, 2 (Spring 1952), pp.53–54.

44 Michael King, *Whina: A Biography of Whina Cooper*, Penguin, Auckland, 1991, p.176–77.

45 *Te Ao Hou*, 7, 3 (1959), p.79.

46 *AJHR*, 1959, G-9, p.28.

47 *NZPD*, 10 June–17 July 1964, Vol. 338, p.231.

48 *AJHR*, Vol. 2, 1965, C-H16.

49 *NZPD*, Vol. 301, 1953, p.2215; 'Report on the Department of Maori Affairs: Hunn Report' (1960), *AJHR*, Vol. 2, 1961, G-10, p.80.

50 *NZPD*, 26 July–7 September 1962, Vol. 331, p.812.

51 P. Koopman Boyden and C. Scott, *The Family and Government Policy in New Zealand*, A&U, Sydney, 1984, p.127. In 1969, the Family Benefit (Home Ownership) Act was amended to allow the purchase of an existing home (p.127).

52 Dan Morrow, 'Tradition and Modernity in Discourses of Māori Urbanisation', *Journal of New Zealand Studies*, 18 (2014), pp.8–9.

53 D. S. Walsh, 'Inter-Ethnic Relations in New Zealand: A Recent Controversy', *Journal of the Polynesian Society*, 73, 3 (1964), p.340.

54 For an in-depth discussion of this episode, see Barbara Brookes, 'Nostalgia for "innocent homely pleasures": The 1964 New Zealand Controversy over *Washday at the Pa*', in Barbara Brookes (ed.), *At Home in New Zealand: Houses, History, People*, BWB, Wellington, 2000, pp.210–55.

55 Ans Westra, quoted in Janet Bayley, 'Finding a "Place" in New Zealand', in Janet Bayley and Athol McCreadie (eds), *Witness to Change: Life in New Zealand*, Photoforum, Wellington, 1985, p.68. See also *Handboek: Ans Westra Photographs*, BWX, Wellington, 2004.

56 Publisher's note inserted in Ans Westra, *Washday at the Pa*, Christchurch, 1964, p.2.

57 Congalton, *Hawera: A Social Survey*, p.175.

58 Noel Harrison, 'Maori Attitudes and School Publications', in *National Education*, 1 February 1965.

59 The Dean of Dunedin, the Very Revd P. E. Sutton, quoted in *National Education*, 1 September 1964, p.347.

60 *New Zealand Official Yearbook*, 1968, p.898.

61 Geoff Bertram, 'The New Zealand Economy, 1900–2000', in Giselle Byrnes (ed.), *The New Oxford History of New Zealand*, OUP, Melbourne, 2009, p.543.

62 *New Zealand National Review*, 15 November 1946.

63 *New Zealand Official Yearbook*, 1958; see illustrations of women making radios, shirts, pottery.

64 Joanne Thrush, 'World War Two and its Post-war Repercussions on New Zealand Women', BA Hons dissertation, University of Otago, 1986, p.88.

65 Gordon A. Carmichael, 'Post-war Trends in Female Labour Force Participation in New Zealand', *Pacific Viewpoint*, 1975, p.95.

66 *New Zealand Population Census*, 1956, Vol. 10, *Incomes*, pp.34–37.

67 Lida Weterman-Opdam, 'Life Has Been Good', in Judi Doornbos (ed.), *Swapping Country and Culture*, Inlet View Press, Wellington, 2005, pp.152–54.

68 *Te Ao Hou*, 33, December 1960, p.36.

69 *New Zealand Woman's Weekly*, 4 March 1954, p.56.

70 'The New Zealand Official Year-Book, 1966', www3.stats.govt.nz/New_Zealand_Official_Yearbooks/1966/NZOYB_1966.html#idchapter_1_359212 (accessed 14 June 2015).

71 Gordon A. Carmichael, 'The Labour Force', in R. J. W. Neville and C. J. O'Neill (eds) *The Population of New Zealand: Interdisciplinary Perspectives*, Longman Paul, Auckland, 1979, p.214.

72 Lisa Davies, with Natalie Jackson, *Women's Labour Force Participation in New Zealand: The Past 100 Years*, Social Policy Agency, Wellington, 1993, pp.95, 108.

73 G. V. Butterworth, *Maori in the New Zealand Economy*, Department of Industries and Commerce, Wellington, 1967, p.42.

74 Megan C. Woods, 'Integrating the Nation: Gendering Maori Urbanisation and Integration, 1942–1969', PhD thesis, University of Canterbury, 2002, p.189.

75 Ibid.

76 Ibid., p.199.

77 Waerete Norman, 'Taura', in Ihimaera (ed.), *Growing Up Maori*, p.131.

78 Woods, 'Integrating the Nation', p.203.

79 Christine Williams, *Hokianga Health: The First Hundred Years: Te Rautau Tuatahi*, Hokianga Health Enterprise Trust, Whāngārei, 2010, pp.109–12.

80 Davies with Jackson, *Women's Labour Force Participation*, p.93.

81 'Profile of a House-Girl: Caroline Munokoa Tuteru Masters', in Sean Mallon, Kolokesa Māhina-Tuai and Damon Salesa, *Tangata O Le Moana: New Zealand and the People of the Pacific*, Te Papa Press, Wellington, 2012, p.171.

82 Woods, 'Integrating the Nation', p.203.

83 Melissa Williams, *Panguru and the City: Kāinga Tahi, Kāinga Rua: An Urban Migration History*, BWB, Wellington, 2015, pp.180–99.

84 Woods, 'Integrating the Nation', p.206.

85 M. Nolan, 'Employment Organisations', in Anne Else (ed.), *Women Together: A History of Women's Organisations in New Zealand*, Historical Branch, DIA/Daphne Brasell Associates, Wellington, 1993, p.201.

86 M. Corner, *No Easy Victory: Towards Equal Pay for Women in the Government Service, 1890–1960*, New Zealand Public Service Association/Dan Long Trust, Wellington, 1988, p.36.

87 Ibid., p.53.

88 Ibid., p.70.

89 'Equal Pay – Another Setback for Public Service Women', Editorial, *New Zealand Woman's Weekly*, 4 March 1957, p.1.

90 Nolan, 'Employment Organisations', in Else (ed.), *Women Together*, p.202.

91 *NZPD*, 20 June 20–2 August 1963, Vol. 335, p.914.

92 P. G. Koopman-Boyden and C. D. Scott, *The Family and Government Policy in New Zealand*, A&U, Sydney, 1984, p.126.

93 M. Cook, 'A History of the Campaign for the 1972 Equal Pay Act', BA Hons long essay, University of Otago, 1994, p.17.

94 J. C. Holden, 'The Changing Economic Contribution of Women in New Zealand and Overseas', JCWE/1 ATL, cited in Cook, 'A History of the Campaign for the 1972 Equal Pay Act', pp.16–17.

95 Ibid.

96 Cook, 'A History of the Campaign for the 1972 Equal Pay Act', pp.33–36.

97 Ibid., p.36.

98 Beverley Morris, 'Women's Role in Perspective' (1966), in Charlotte Macdonald

(ed.), *The Vote, the Pill and the Demon Drink: A History of Feminist Writing in New Zealand, 1869–1993*, BWB, Wellington, 1993, p.148.

99 Christine Cole Catley, *Bright Star: Beatrice Hill Tinsley, Astronomer*, Cape Catley, Auckland, 2006, pp.69–76.

100 Nancy Swarbrick, 'Primary and secondary education – Curriculum changes', *Te Ara: The Encyclopedia of New Zealand*, www.teara.govt. nz/en/photograph/36652/a-home-science-class-1939 (accessed 17 June 2015).

101 Nancy Swarbrick, 'Primary and secondary education – Education from the 1920s to 2000s', *Te Ara: The Encyclopedia of New Zealand*, www.teara.govt.nz/en/primary-and-secondary-education/page-3 (accessed 17 June 2015).

102 Noeline Alcorn, *To the Fullest Extent of his Powers: C. E. Beeby's Life in Education*, VUP, Wellington, 1999, p.184.

103 Margaret Wray, 'Some Aspects of Menstruation in Fifth Form Girls at Otago Girls' High School', Department of Preventive and Social Medicine, fifth year thesis, University of Otago, 1948. The following two paragraphs are derived from joint research carried out by the author and Margaret Tennant. I am grateful for Margaret's permission to reproduce the material here.

104 B. Brookes and M. Tennant, 'Making Girls Modern: Pakeha Women and Menstruation in New Zealand, 1930–1970', *Women's History Review*, 7, 4 (1998), p.572.

105 Ibid., pp.575–76.

106 Rosemary Barrington and Alison Gray, *The Smith Women: 100 New Zealand Women Talk about their Lives*, A. H. & A. W. Reed, Wellington, 1981, p.21.

107 *New Zealand Listener*, 22 April 1960, p.10.

108 Sandra Coney, *Out of the Frying Pan: Inflammatory Writing, 1972–89*, Penguin, Auckland, 1990, pp.35–37.

109 'Merata Mita: film-maker', in Virginia Myers, *Head and Shoulders: Successful New Zealand Women Talk to Virginia Myers*, Penguin, Auckland, 1986, pp.38–71.

110 Ruth Fry, *It's Different for Daughters: A History of the Curriculum for Girls in New Zealand Schools, 1900–1975*, New Zealand Council for Educational Research, Wellington, 1985, p.102.

111 Ibid., p.103.

112 *New Zealand Official Yearbook*, 1959, 1969,
www3.stats.govt.nz/New_Zealand_Official_Yearbooks (accessed 20 June 2015).

113 Kelley Massoni, *Fashioning Teenagers: A Cultural History of* Seventeen *Magazine*, Walnut Creek, CA, 2010.

114 Report from an American survey, in *New Zealand Woman's Weekly*, 9 December 1957, p.19.

115 Cole Catley, *Bright Star*, p.65.

116 'Who's Wearing the Pants Now? A Look Back at Women's Right to Wear Jeans', www.cottoninc.com/corporate/Pressroom/PressReleases/2012/item10419.cfm 9 (accessed 5 December 2014).

117 Redmer Yska, *All Shook Up: The Flash Bodgie and the Rise of the New Zealand Teenager in the Fifties*, Penguin, Auckland, 1993, pp.108–9.

118 Lists of New Zealand Censorship Deletions 1950–1957, IA 2/7/2, ANZ, in ibid., pp.109–10.

119 Chris Bourke, *Blue Smoke: The Lost Dawn of New Zealand Popular Music, 1918–1964*, AUP, Auckland, 2012, pp.182–86.

120 Yska, *All Shook Up*, p.61.

121 'Report of the Special Committee on Moral Delinquency in Children', *AJHR*, 1954, H-47, p.8; Julie Glamuzina and Alison J. Laurie, *Parker and Hulme: A Lesbian View*, New Women's Press, Auckland, 1991.

122 Yska, *All Shook Up*, p.61.

123 Ibid., p.63.

124 Ibid., p.65.

125 Ibid., pp.69–70.

126 'Report of the Special Committee on Moral Delinquency in Children', p.18.

127 Yska, *All Shook Up*, p.73

128 'Report of the Special Committee on Moral Delinquency in Children', p.31.

129 Ibid., pp.37–39. For discussion of the report's gendered assumptions, see Maureen Molloy, 'Science, Myth and the Adolescent Female: The Mazengarb Report, the Parker-Hulme Trial, and the Adoption Act of 1955', *Women's Studies Journal*, 9, 1 (1993), pp.1–25.

130 Yska, *All Shook Up*, p.79.

131 *New Zealand Listener*, 3 April 1959, p.19.

132 *New Zealand Listener*, 4 October 1957, p.4.

133 M. Bevan-Brown, *The Sources of Love and Fear* (3rd edn), Raven Press, Christchurch, 1960, p.10.

134 Heather Knox, 'Feminism, Femininity and Motherhood in Post-World War II New Zealand', MA thesis, Massey University, 1995.

135 Mary Dobbie, *The Trouble with Women: The Story of Parents' Centre New Zealand*, Cape Catley, Whatamangō Bay, 1990, p.3.

136 Jane and James Ritchie, *Child Rearing Patterns in New Zealand*, A. H. & A. W. Reed, Wellington, 1970, p.148.

137 David P. Ausubel, *The Fern and the Tiki: An American View of New Zealand National Character, Social Attitudes, and Race Relations*, Holt, Reinhart & Winston, New York, 1965, pp.88–91.

138 Marie Bell, 'The Pioneers of Parents' Centre: Movers and Shakers for Change in the Philosophies and Practices of Childbirth and Parent Education in New Zealand', PhD thesis, Victoria University of Wellington, 2004, p.73

139 'History', www.parentscentre.org.nz/about/ history.asp (accessed 4 August 2015).

140 Bell, 'The Pioneers of Parents' Centre', p.117.

141 *Parents Centre Bulletin*, 13 (June 1959), p.2, cited in S. Bishop, '"Married with Children": Perceptions of New Zealand Women's Lives in the 1950s: A Social and Literary Study', BA Hons dissertation, University of Otago, 1991, p.94.

142 Brenda Stedman, 'The Origins and Development of the Dunedin Marriage Guidance Council, 1948–1970', Hons long essay, University of Otago, 1988, p.45.

143 A. E. Manning, *The Bodgie: A Study in Abnormal Psychology*, Reed, Wellington, 1958, p.68.

144 Claire Gooder, 'A History of Sex Education in New Zealand, 1939–1985', PhD thesis, University of Auckland, 2010, p.127.

145 Helen May, *Mind that Child: Childcare as a Social and Political Issue in New Zealand*, Blackberry Press, Upper Hutt, 1985, pp.25–26, citing *New Zealand Herald*, 30 September 1950.

146 Ibid., p.19.

147 Ibid., p.26.

148 *NZPD*, Vol. 316, 18 July 1958, cited in May, *Mind that Child*, p.26.

149 Anne Meade and Valerie Podmore, *UNESCO: Early Childhood and Family Policy Series n.1* (March 2002), p.8, http://unesdoc.unesco.org/ images/0011/001102/110281e.pdf (accessed 27 June 2015).

150 Ibid.

151 Geraldine McDonald, *Maori Mothers and Pre-school Education*, New Zealand Council

for Educational Research, Wellington, 1973, pp.1–2.

152 Ibid., p.37.

153 Harris, 'Dancing with the State', pp.168–71.

154 Knox, 'Feminism, Femininity and Motherhood', p.83.

155 McDonald, *Maori Mothers and Pre-school Education*, p.49.

156 *As the Twig is Bent*, National Film Unit, 1965.

157 Bronwyn Dalley, *Family Matters: Child Welfare in Twentieth Century New Zealand*, AUP /Historical Branch, DIA, Auckland, 1998, pp.224–35; Anne Else, *A Question of Adoption*, BWB, Wellington, 1991, chapter 3.

158 Else, *A Question of Adoption*, p.25.

159 Molloy, 'Science, Myth and the Adolescent Female', p.16.

160 Koopman-Boyden and Scott, *The Family and Government Policy*, pp.130–31.

161 D. Durie-Hall and J. Metge, 'Kua Tutu te Puehu, Kia Mau: Maori Aspirations and Family Law', in M. Henaghan and W. R. Aitken (eds), *Family Law Policy in New Zealand*, OUP, Auckland, 1992, p.59.

162 Ministerial Advisory Committee on a Maori Perspective for the Department of Social Welfare, *Puao-te-ata-tu (Daybreak)*, Appendix, Wellington, 1988, pp.32–33, cited in Else, *A Question of Adoption*, p.175.

163 *New Zealand Official Yearbook*, Government Printer, Wellington, 1968, pp.94–95.

164 '1960s bathing suit contest', www.nzhistory. net.nz/media/photo/1960s-bathing-suit-contest (accessed 28 June 2015).

165 'Miss New Zealand at Miss World 1956–2009', http://missnzl.blog.com/2010/01/02/66 (accessed 28 June 2015).

166 B. Hughes and S. Ahern, *Redbrick and Bluestockings: Women at Victoria, 1899–1993*, VUP, Wellington, 1993, p.145; Sam Elworthy, *Ritual Song of Defiance: A Social History of Students at the University of Otago*, Otago University Students' Association, Dunedin, 1990, pp.103, 124.

167 *Te Ao Hou*, 40 (September 1962), p.2.

168 Sylvia Harrison, 'Jean Shrimpton, the "Four-inch Furore" and Perceptions of Melbourne Identity in the Sixties', in Seamus O'Hanlon and Tanja Luckins, *Go! Melbourne in the Sixties*, Melbourne Publishing Group, Melbourne, pp.72–86.

169 Georgina White, *Light Fantastic: Dance Floor*

Courtship in New Zealand, HarperCollins, Auckland, 2007, p.174.

170 Roger Watkins, *Hostage to the Beat: The Auckland Scene 1955–1970*, Tandem Press, Auckland, 1995, pp.54–55.

171 "She's a mod' by Ray Columbus and the Invaders', www.nzhistory.net.nz/media/video/shes-a-mod (accessed 14 November 2014).

172 Claire Hedger, 'Saluting Our Seminal Woman Rockers', www.australianmusician.com.au/saluting-our-seminal-woman-rockers (accessed 23 April 2015).

173 In this paragraph I am indebted to the discussion of the American context in Jessica Weiss, *To Have and to Hold: Marriage, the Baby Boom and Social Change*, University of Chicago Press, Chicago, 2000, pp.141–75.

174 *New Zealand Woman's Weekly*, 6 July 1956.

175 *New Zealand Woman's Weekly*, 27 January 1955.

176 D. C. Moreau, 'Living with the Pill: Oral Contraceptive Use in New Zealand, 1960–1975', MA thesis, University of Auckland, 1997, p.43.

177 Nancy de Castro, interview with Dr Roger Ridley-Smith, 26 October 2004, tape in author's possession. See also Barbara Brookes, Claire Gooder and Nancy de Castro, '"Feminine as her Handbag, Modern as her Hairstyle": The Uptake of the Contraceptive Pill in New Zealand', *New Zealand Journal of History*, 47, 2 (2013), pp.208–31.

178 Moreau, 'Living with the Pill', p.42.

179 Fay Hercock, 'Professional Politics and Family Planning', in Linda Bryder (ed.), *A Healthy Country: Essays on the Social History of Medicine in New Zealand*, BWB, Wellington, 1991, p.193.

180 *New Zealand Medical Journal*, 65, 409 (September 1966), p.619.

181 Alan F. Guttmacher, 'The Pill Around the World', *IPPF Medical Bulletin*, 1, 1 (October 1966), pp.1–2.

182 F. T. Bostock, 'The Pill', Preventive and Social Medicine dissertation, University of Otago, 1963, unpaginated.

183 R. J. Somerville, 'Attitudes Towards and Use of the Pill and Other Methods of Contraception in the 30 to 50 Age Group of Women, and Related Use of the Family Planning Association', fifth year Preventive Medicine dissertation, University of Otago, 1971, p.25.

184 Bostock, 'The Pill'.

185 Editorial, *Salient*, 25 February 1963, cited in Hughes and Ahern, *Redbrick and Bluestockings*, p.147.

186 Ibid.

187 Betty Friedan, *The Feminine Mystique*, W. W. Norton & Co, New York, 1963.

188 'Book Lover: Lindsey Dawson', *New Zealand Herald*, 16 May 2011, www.nzherald.co.nz/lifestyle/news/article.cfm?c_id=6&objectid=10725990 (accessed 18 June 2015).

189 William Sutch, *Women's Contribution to a Changing Society*, Department of Industries and Commerce, Wellington, 1964.

190 Elizabeth Orr, 'The Continuing Education of Women – Some Suggestions', *Comment*, 6, 2 (January–February 1965), p.17.

191 Stephanie Coontz, *A Strange Stirring: The Feminine Mystique and American Women at the Dawn of the 1960s*, Basic Books, New York, 2011, p.145.

192 Jacqueline Leckie, 'Immigration, Ethnicity and Women's Organisations', in Else (ed.), *Women Together*, p.500.

193 Rosemarie Smith, 'New Zealand Federation of Country Women's Institutes, 1921', in Else (ed.), *Women Together*, p.391.

194 'Dominion Federation of New Zealand Country Women's Institutes (Inc.)', *Te Ara: The Encyclopedia of New Zealand*, www.teara.govt.nz/en/1966/womens-organisations/2 (accessed 22 June 2015).

195 'Women's Division Federated Farmers of New Zealand (Inc.)', *Te Ara: The Encyclopedia of New Zealand*, www.teara.govt.nz/en/1966/womens-organisations/13 (accessed 23 June 2015).

196 *New Zealand Listener*, 20 November 1959, pp.6–7, reprinted in Macdonald (ed.), *The Vote, the Pill and the Demon Drink*, pp.138–41.

197 *New Zealand Listener*, 14 April 1967, p.66.

198 Beverley Morris, 'Women's Role in Perspective', in Macdonald (ed.), *The Vote, the Pill and the Demon Drink*, p.146.

199 Caroline Daley, 'Men and women in the city', *Te Ara: The Encyclopedia of New Zealand*, www.teara.govt.nz/en/men-and-women-in-the-city/3 (accessed 23 June 2015). See also 'Mum the Drug Addict', *thursday*, 10 May 1973, pp.48–51.

200 Linden Playcentre, *The Changing Role of Women: Record of a Series of Public Lectures,*

Wellington Play Centres' Association, Wellington, 1966, p.52.

201 Ibid., pp.54–64.

202 Margaret Shields, *The Society for Research on Women: A Case Study of a Recent Voluntary Organisation*, Society for Research on Women, Wellington, 1971, p.1.

203 Society for Research on Women, *An Introduction to Social Research*, Wellington, 1969, p.13.

204 *New Zealand Listener*, 14 April 1967, p.66.

205 Ibid., pp.66–67.

Chapter 11

1   Therese O'Connell, 'Singing to Survive', in Maud Cahill and Christine Dann, *Changing our Lives: Women Working in the Women's Liberation Movement, 1970–1990*, BWB, Wellington, 1991, pp.71–73.

2   Beryl Hughes and Sheila Ahern, *Redbrick and Bluestockings: Women at Victoria, 1899–1993*, VUP, Wellington, 1993, pp.166–68.

3   Marcia Russell, 'Memo from the Editor', *thursday*, 3 October 1968, p.3, reprinted in Charlotte Macdonald (ed.), *The Vote, the Pill and the Demon Drink: A History of Feminist Writing in New Zealand, 1869–1993*, BWB, Wellington, 1993, p.154; Rosemarie Smith, 'Rural Organisations', in Anne Else (ed.), *Women Together: A History of Women's Organisations in New Zealand*, Historical Branch, DIA/Daphne Brasell Associates, Wellington, 1993, pp. 377–78.

4   *thursday*, 6 February 1969, p.30.

5   Stephen Hamilton, *A History of the Victoria University of Wellington Students' Association 1899–1999*, Victoria University of Wellington Students' Association, Wellington, 2002, p.127.

6   'The Times They Are A-Changin' Lyrics', www.lyricsfreak.com/b/bob+dylan/the+ti mes+they+are+a+changin_20021240.html (accessed 10 June 2015).

7   Elsie Locke, *Peace People: A History of Peace Activities in New Zealand*, Hazard Press, Christchurch, 1992, p.259.

8   Ruth Rosen, *The World Split Open: How the Modern Women's Movement Changed America*, Viking, New York, 2000, p.39.

9   Jude Wilson, *Flying Kiwis: A History of the OE*, University of Otago Press, Dunedin, 2014, pp.38–39, 56–57.

10   Sue Kedgley, *The Sexual Wilderness: Men and Women in New Zealand*, Reed Methuen, Auckland, 1985, p.1.

11   Germaine Greer, *The Female Eunuch*, Paladin, London, 1971, p.11.

12   *New Zealand Herald*, 18 March 1972, p.3. For a full discussion of this event, see Barbara Brookes, 'A Germaine Moment: Style, Language and Audience', in T. Ballantyne and B. Moloughney (eds), *Disputed Histories: Imagining New Zealand's Pasts*, University of Otago Press, Dunedin, 2006, pp.191–203.

13   *Sunday Herald*, 12 March 1972, p.7.

14   *New Zealand Herald*, 8 March 1972, p.2.

15   *Sunday Herald*, 12 March 1972, p.23.

16   Megan Cook, 'Gender and Paid Work in New Zealand, 1950–1972', MA thesis, University of Otago, 2000, p.45.

17   *New Zealand Woman's Weekly*, 1 May 1972, p.88.

18   Rosemary McLeod, 'Things Changed Abruptly', in Jane Tolerton (ed.), *60s Chicks Hit the Nineties*, Penguin, Auckland, 1997, p.133.

19   Robyn Du Chateau, 'Fluffy Bantam to Masseuse', in Tolerton (ed.), *60s Chicks Hit the Nineties*, pp.61–62.

20   Susan Kedgley, cited by Grace Millar, 'Because We Are All Women: The Relationship between the Ideas of Women's Liberation and the Development of the New Zealand Feminist Movement', MA thesis, Victoria University of Wellington, 2003, p.29.

21   *Oxford English Dictionary*.

22   Millar, 'Because We Are All Women', p.30.

23   English figures cited in Jane Lewis, *Women in England, 1870–1950: Sexual Divisions and Social Change*, Wheatsheaf, Brighton, 1984, p.152. New Zealand figure from *New Zealand Official Yearbook*, 1976, p.855. The Female Labour Force Participation Rate – the percentage of women between 15 and 64 who are working – was 38.9 in New Zealand in 1971. Comparative rates for 1970 from the *International Labour Office Year Book* were: Britain 50.1; France 43.5; USA (estimated) 42.4; Australia 40.1. National Council of Women, *What Price Equality? Women and Work in New Zealand*, National Council of Women, Dunedin, 1974, p.14.

24   Department of Statistics, *Profile of Women: A Statistical Comparison of Females and Males in New Zealand 1945–1984*, Department of Statistics, Wellington, 1985, p.24.

25 *thursday*, 6 February 1969.

26 'Women's Liberation: An Introduction to the Aims and Ideas of the Women's Liberation Movement in Auckland', date unknown, c.1971, reprinted in Macdonald (ed.), *The Vote, the Pill and the Demon Drink*, pp.164–65.

27 Sara E. Evans, *Tidal Wave: How Women Changed America at Century's End*, Free Press, New York, 2003, p.59.

28 'The New Rise of Feminism: A Socialist Programme for Women's Liberation', *Socialist Action*, 13 April 1973, p.1.

29 Ann Snitow, 'Thinking about *The Mermaid and the Minotaur*', *Feminist Studies*, 4, 2 (June 1978), pp.190–98.

30 Christine Wren, *The Synthetic Woman – In a Plastic World*, pamphlet book 2, Organisation for Women, Wellington, 1972, p.1.

31 'Women's Liberation: An Introduction to the Aims and Ideas of the Women's Liberation Movement in Auckland', pamphlet, Kathleen Johnson, MS papers 4580, f.8, ATL.

32 Elizabeth Harrison, 'Women's Liberation in the Far South: The Dunedin Collective for Women', BA Hons dissertation, University of Otago, 1988, p.19.

33 Evans, *Tidal Wave*, p.62.

34 Harrison, 'Women's Liberation in the Far South', pp.21–22.

35 Ibid., pp.68–69.

36 Harrison canvasses the range of activities in ibid.

37 Donna Awatere, 'Walking on Eggs', in Sue Kedgley and Mary Varnham (eds), *Heading Nowhere in a Navy Blue Suit and other Tales from the Feminist Revolution*, Daphne Brasell Associates, Wellington, 1993, p.122.

38 Kedgley, *The Sexual Wilderness*, p.1.

39 Christine Dann, *Up from Under: Women and Liberation in New Zealand, 1970–1985*, A&U/ Port Nicholson Press, Wellington, 1985, p.1.

40 Margaret Tennant, 'Welfare Organisations', in Else (ed.), *Women Together*, p.117.

41 Carmel Daly, '*Broadsheet* Collective 1972', in ibid., p.100.

42 For debates over the status of the 'illegitimate child', see Mark Henaghan and Pauline Tapp, 'Legally Defining the Family', in M. Henaghan and Bill Aitken, *Family Law Policy in New Zealand*, OUP, Auckland, 1992, pp.15–16.

43 Margaret McClure, *A Civilised Community: A History of Social Security in New Zealand 1898–1998*, AUP/Historical Branch, DIA, Auckland, 1998, pp.164–75.

44 Sandra Coney, *Standing in the Sunshine: A History of New Zealand Women Since They Won the Vote*, Viking, Auckland, 1993, pp.78–79; Joss Shawyer, Julie Maddison and Robert Ludbrook, *Everything A Single Parent Needs to Know* (revised 4th edn), Council for the Single Mother and her Child, Auckland, 1981.

45 Sam Elworthy, 'Social Change and the State: The Emergence of a Benefit for Unmarried Mothers in New Zealand', BA Hons long essay, University of Otago, 1988.

46 Members of the organisation Birthright argued that the state should not support single women and that they should give up their children for adoption, but a 1974 Heylen poll suggested only 4% of New Zealanders shared this view. Anne Else, *A Question of Adoption: Closed Stranger Adoption in New Zealand 1944–1974*, BWB, Wellington, 1998, p.165.

47 Raewyn Dalziel, *Focus on the Family: The Auckland Home and Family Society, 1893–1993*, Home and Family Society, Auckland, 1993, p.58.

48 Fran Crammock, 'A History of the Establishment of Dunedin Women's Refuge, 1967–1977', BA Hons dissertation, University of Otago, 1994, p.1.

49 *Otago Daily Times*, 27 February 1976, p.11, cited in Crammock, 'A History of the Establishment of Dunedin Women's Refuge', p.12.

50 Crammock, 'A History of the Establishment of Dunedin Women's Refuge', p.11.

51 Toni McCallum, 'National Collective of Independent Women's Refuges 1981', in Else (ed.), *Women Together*, p.144.

52 Ann Lloyd, *Rape: An Examination of the Crime in New Zealand: Its Social and Emotional Consequences*, Wilson & Horton, Auckland, 1976.

53 *Broadsheet*, December 1988, p.34, cited in Jacqueline O'Neill, '"She Asked for It": A Textual Analysis of the Re-negotiation of the Meaning of Rape in the 1970s–1980s', MA thesis, Massey University, 2006, p.64.

54 Donna Awatere, 'Walking on Eggs', in Kedgley and Varnham (eds), *Heading Nowhere in a Navy Blue Suit*, pp.120–21.

55 Donna Awatere Huata, *My Journey*, Seaview Press, Auckland, 1996, p.35.

56 *Otago Daily Times*, 30 August 1967, p.1.

57 William Sutch, *Equal Pay for New Zealand*, Commission of Inquiry into Equal Pay, Wellington, 1961, p.161, cited in Megan Cook, 'A History of the Campaign for the 1972 Equal Pay Act', BA Hons dissertation, University of Otago, 1994, p.18.

58 *Evening Post*, 7 March 1972, cited in Cook, 'A History of the Campaign for the 1972 Equal Pay Act', p.20.

59 New Zealand Insurance Guild Industrial Union of Workers, *Annual Report*, October 1971, cited in Robin Ingram, 'The Politics of Patriarchy: The Response of Capital and Organised Labour to the Movement of Women into the Paid Workforce in New Zealand', MA thesis, University of Auckland, 1988, p.149, cited in Cook, 'A History of the Campaign for the 1972 Equal Pay Act', p.20.

60 Ingram, 'The Politics of Patriarchy', p.149, cited in Cook, 'A History of the Campaign for the 1972 Equal Pay Act', p.21.

61 Report of the Commission of Inquiry, *Equal Pay in New Zealand*, A. R. Shearer, Government Printer, Wellington, 1971.

62 Dorothy Page, *The National Council of Women: A Centennial History*, AUP/BWB, Auckland, 1996, pp.132–33.

63 Margaret Wilson, 'Mabel Howard', in Charlotte Macdonald, Meremere Penfold and Bridget Williams (eds), *The Book of New Zealand Women: Ko Kui Ma Te Kaupapa*, BWB, Wellington, 1991, p.311.

64 Herbert Roth, *Trade Unions in New Zealand: Past and Present*, Reed Education, Wellington, 1973, p.130.

65 *NZPD*, 18 August 1950, Vol. 290, p.1664.

66 Wilson, 'Mabel Howard', in Macdonald, Penfold and Williams (eds), *The Book of New Zealand Women*, p.310.

67 Macdonald (ed.), *The Vote, the Pill and the Demon Drink*, p.162.

68 Janet McCallum, *Women in the House: Members of Parliament in New Zealand*, Cape Catley, Wellington, 1993, p.106.

69 *NZPD*, 20 and 23 February 1973, Vol. 382, pp.67, 239.

70 'Select Committee on Women's Rights', June 1975, *AJHR*, 1975, I-13, Vol. IV.

71 Ibid., p.17.

72 Ibid., p.71.

73 Society for Research on Women, *Women and Money: A Study of Financial Management in New Zealand Households*, Society for Research on Women, Wellington, 1981, p.15.

74 *Consumer Review*, May 1976, cited in Society for Research on Women, *Women and Money*, p.15.

75 *New Zealand Official Yearbook*, 1978, p.113.

76 Mark Henaghan and Bill Atkin (eds), *Family Law Policy in New Zealand*, OUP, Auckland, 1972, p.234.

77 Sara Rowan, 'Matrimonial Property and the Status of Women', BA Hons dissertation, University of Otago, 1996, p.2.

78 Joan Metge and Donna Durie-Hall, 'Kua Tutū te Puehu, Kia Mau: Maori Aspirations and Family Law', in Henaghan and Atkin (eds), *Family Law Policy*, p.67.

79 Caroline Bridge, 'Reallocation of Property after Marriage Breakdown: The Matrimonial Property Act 1976', in Henaghan and Atkin (eds), *Family Law Policy*, p.234.

80 Bridge, 'Reallocation of Property', in Henaghan and Atkin, *Family Law Policy*, p.234.

81 As early as the late 1940s, the demand for women's labour had brought some concessions towards recognising that some women might combine work and motherhood. In March 1948, the Public Service Commission introduced six months' maternity leave without pay to encourage women to remain in work. From 1951, women teachers received 'salary recognition for full-time maternity care'. See Melanie Nolan, *Breadwinning: New Zealand Women and the State*, CUP, Christchurch, 2000, p.221; David Grant, *Those Who Can Teach: A History of Secondary Education in New Zealand*, Steele Roberts, Wellington, 2003, p.91.

82 Society for Research on Women, *Career, Marriage, Family*, report of a survey conducted by the Wellington Branch, Johnsonville, 1976, p.22.

83 'Industrial Health and Welfare', paper in Kathleen Johnson, MS papers 4580 f7, ATL.

84 Else, *A Question of Adoption*, p.164.

85 Society for Research on Women, Auckland Branch, 'Childcare in Auckland', typescript, 1971.

86 Costs cited in Society for Research on Women, *Urban Women*, Society for Research on Women, Dunedin, 1972, p.29.

87 Ibid., p.8.

88 Rae Julian, 'Women's Electoral Lobby of New Zealand, 1975', in Else (ed.), *Women Together*, p.104.

89 Elspeth Preddey, *The WEL Herstory: The Women's Electoral Lobby in New Zealand 1975–2002*, WEL NZ, Wellington, 2003, p.11.

90 Ibid., pp.176–78.

91 Ibid., p.13.

92 Rae Julian, 'Labour Women's Council', in Else (ed.), *Women Together*, pp.102–3; Margaret Wilson, 'Women and the Labour Party', in Margaret Clark (ed.), *The Labour Party after 75 Years*, Occasional Publication No. 4, Department of Politics, Victoria University of Wellington, 1992, p.45.

93 'Marilyn Waring', in McCallum, *Women in the House*, pp.125–27.

94 Sandra Kailahi (ed.), *Pasifika Women: Our Stories in New Zealand*, Reed, Auckland, 2007, p.124.

95 Cluny MacPherson, 'Empowering Pacific Peoples', in Sean Mallon, Kolokesa Māhina-Tuia and Damon Salesa, *Tangata O Le Moana: New Zealand and the People of the Pacific*, Te Papa Press, Wellington, 2012, pp.192–96.

96 Francis Campbell, in Kailahi (ed.), *Pasifika Women*, p.92.

97 *New Zealand Woman's Weekly*, 3 April 1972, p.6.

98 Tobias Innis Powell, 'New Zealand in God: Conservative Christianity in New Zealand, 1970–2006', MA thesis, University of Auckland, 2006, pp.38–133.

99 McCallum, *Women in the House*, p.97.

100 'Whetu Tirikatene-Sullivan', in McCallum, *Women in the House*, pp.93–95.

101 Ibid., p.96.

102 Dame Mira Szaszy, 'Opening My Mouth', in Kedgley and Varnham (eds), *Heading Nowhere in a Navy Blue Suit*, p.75.

103 Ibid., p.76.

104 Barbara Brookes, '"Assimilation" and "Integration" in the Maori Women's Welfare League in the 1950s', in *The Turnbull Library Record*, 36 (2003), pp.5–18.

105 Ian Pool, *Te Iwi Maori: A New Zealand Population*, AUP, Auckland, 1991, p.172.

106 *New Zealand Official Yearbook*, 1978, p.70.

107 Hana Jackson, *Broadsheet*, July/August 1982, reprinted in Pat Rosier (ed.), *Been Around for Quite a While: Broadsheet*, New Women's Press, Auckland 1992, p.69.

108 Ibid., p.70.

109 Michael King, *Whina*, Hodder & Stoughton, Auckland, 1983, p.209.

110 Ibid., p.224.

111 Dora Zimmerman, Letter to the Editor, *New Society*, 31 December 1964, cited in B. Brookes, *Abortion in England: 1900–1967*, Croom Helm, Beckenham, 1988, p.153.

112 Alison McCulloch, *Fighting to Choose: The Abortion Rights Struggle in New Zealand*, VUP, Wellington, 2013, pp.25–26.

113 Ibid., p.29.

114 Fiona Clayton, 'A Womb of One's Own: Feminist Political Activity in Relation to the Abortion Debate in New Zealand, 1970–1979', BA Hons research dissertation, University of Otago, 1996, p.5.

115 L. D. Guy, 'The Cinematograph Film Censorship Debate in New Zealand, 1965–1976', MA dissertation, University of Auckland, pp.1–3, cited in Innis Powell, 'New Zealand for God', p.47.

116 Innis Powell, 'New Zealand for God', p.47.

117 Margaret Sparrow, *Abortion Then and Now: New Zealand Abortion Stories from 1940 to 1980*, VUP, Wellington, 2010, p.158.

118 Ibid., pp.157–61.

119 McCulloch, *Fighting to Choose*, p.113.

120 WONAAC poster, 'Repeal All Abortion Laws', cited in Clayton, 'A Womb of One's Own', p.21.

121 Royal Commission on Contraception, Sterilisation and Abortion, *Contraception, Sterilisation and Abortion in New Zealand*, E. C. Keating, Government Printer, Wellington, 1977, pp.399–409.

122 Mr Birch (Franklin, National), Contraception, Sterilisation and Abortion Bill, *NZPD*, 11 October 1977, Vol. 414, p.3539.

123 Jocelyn Brooks, *Ill Conceived: Law and Abortion Practice in New Zealand*, Caveman Press, Dunedin, 1981, p.68.

124 Ibid., p.97.

125 McCallum, *Women in the House*, p.122.

126 Brooks, *Ill Conceived*, p.107.

127 McCulloch, *Fighting to Choose*, p.189.

128 Clayton, 'A Womb of One's Own', p.41.

129 Ngahuia Te Awekotuku, Shirley Tamihana, Julie Glamuzina and Alison Laurie, 'Lesbian Organising', in Else (ed.), *Women Together*, p.547.

130 Sharon Alston, *Broadsheet*, March 1974.

131 Carolyn Moynihan, *A Stand for Decency: Patricia Bartlett and the Society for the Promotion of Community Standards*, Society for the Promotion of Community Standards, Wellington, 1995, p.126.

132 P. Simmonds, 'The Feminist Camp ... or Taking the Top Off Feminism', *Circle*, April 1975, cited in Julie Glamuzina, *Out Front: Lesbian Political Activity in Aotearoa 1962–1985*, Lesbian Press, Hamilton, 1993, p.25.

133 The vote was 34 against to 29 in favour: Moynihan, *A Stand for Decency*, p.128. See also www.nzhistory.net.nz/culture/homosexual-law-reform/birth-of-the-gay-movement (accessed 14 October 2015).

134 Barry Gustafson, *His Way: A Biography of Robert Muldoon*, AUP, Auckland, 2000, pp.196–97. Muldoon was, however, to use an accusation of homosexuality against Opposition Labour politician Colin Moyle in 1976.

135 'Women's Rights Committee', *AJHR*, 1975, I-13, Vol. IV, pp.39–41.

136 Ibid., pp.96–102.

137 *NZPD*, 7 July 1977, Vol. 411, p.1251.

138 Ibid., p.1254.

139 *NZPD*, 2 November 1977, Vol. 415, p.4134.

140 *NZPD*, 20 July 1977, Vol. 411, p.1474.

141 *NZPD*, 17 August 1977, Vol. 412, p.2291.

142 Sandra Coney, Editorial, *Broadsheet*, May 1977, p.27.

143 Novena Petelo, in Adrienne Jansen (ed.), *I Have In My Arms Both Ways: Stories by Ten Immigrant Women*, BWB, Wellington, 1995, p.50.

144 Margaret Tennant, 'Welfare Organisations', in Else (ed.), *Women Together*, p.118.

145 For this critique, see Alison Jones and Camille Guy, 'Radical Feminism in New Zealand: From Piha to Newtown', in Rosemary Du Plessis (ed.), *Feminist Voices: Women's Studies Texts for Aotearoa/New Zealand*, OUP, Auckland, 1992, pp.300–16.

146 Editorial, in Rosier (ed.), *Been Around for Quite a While*, p.27.

Chapter 12

1 Ruth Richardson, *Making a Difference*, Shoal Bay Press, Christchurch, 1995, p.21.

2 Department of Statistics and Ministry of Women's Affairs, *Women in New Zealand*, Wellington, 1990, p.49.

3 Ibid., p.50.

4 *Press*, 6 October 1978, p.13.

5 *Press*, 25 January 1979, p.6.

6 *Press*, 15 June 1979, p.2.

7 *Press*, 10 September 1981, p.7.

8 Anne Barry, *Playing with Fire*, Hazard Press, Christchurch, 2007, pp.62–63.

9 Anne Horsfield, *Women in the Economy*, Ministry of Women's Affairs, Wellington, 1988, pp.279–80.

10 Sonja Davies and Mary Sinclair, 'New Zealand Working Women's Council 1975–1980', in Anne Else (ed.), *Women Together: A History of Women's Organisations in New Zealand*, Historical Branch, DIA/Daphne Brasell Associates, Wellington, 1993, p.232.

11 See the text of the charter in Charlotte Macdonald (ed.), *The Vote, the Pill and the Demon Drink: A History of Feminist Writing in New Zealand, 1869–1993*, BWB, Wellington, 1993, p.213.

12 Davies and Sinclair, 'New Zealand Working Women's Council', in Else (ed.), *Women Together*, p.234.

13 Anita Nyberg, 'Parental Leave, Public Childcare and the Dual Earner/Dual Carer-Model in Sweden', Discussion Paper, Swedish National Institute for Working Life, www.mutualearningemployment.net/uploads/.../disspapSWE04.pd (accessed 30 June 2015).

14 Sarah Crichton, *Work Patterns after Paid Parental Leave*, Department of Labour and Statistics, Wellington, December 2008, p.5.

15 *NZPD*, 25 June 1980, Vol. 430, p.993, cited in Janet McCallum, *Women in the House: Members of Parliament in New Zealand*, Cape Catley, Wellington, 1993, p.140.

16 Helen May, 'Combined Early Childhood Union of Aotearoa: Te Rau o te Aroha o te Kohanga ki Aotearoa, 1982', in Else (ed.), *Women Together*, pp.235–37.

17 Patricia Sargison, 'New Zealand Nurses' Association', in Else (ed.), *Women Together*, pp.218–19.

18 Susan Shipley, *Women's Employment and Unemployment: A Research Report*, Department of Sociology, Massey University, 1982, p.xi.

19 Ibid., p.176.

20 Ibid., pp.170, 176.

21 Ibid., p.178.

22 J.C., 'National Super her first personal allowance', *New Zealand Woman's Weekly*, 31 October 1983, p.155.

23   Kathryn Hunter, review of 'Between the Covers: Women's Magazines and Their Readers' exhibition, Women's Library, London, www.guardian.co.uk/books/2008/dec/20/women-pressandpublishing (accessed 14 April 2012).

24   'Cosmopolitan (magazine)', https://en.wikipedia.org/wiki/Cosmopolitan_%28magazine%29 (accessed 14 April 2012).

25   Barbara Ehrenreich, *Dancing in the Streets: A History of Collective Joy*, Metropolitan Books, New York, 2006, pp.214–15.

26   'Jenny Morris Profile', www.audioculture.co.nz/people/jenny-morris (accessed 25 April 2015).

27   Alister Taylor and Deborah Coddington, *Robin White: New Zealand Painter*, Alister Taylor, Martinborough, 1981, p.19.

28   Marian Evans, Bridie Lonie and Tilly Lloyd, *A Woman's Picture Book: 25 Women Artists of Aotearoa (New Zealand)*, Government Print, Wellington, 1988, p.102.

29   Ibid.

30   'Allie Eagle and Me', www.allieeagleandme.com/eduResource/NZwomensMove.html (accessed 15 April 2012). Thanks also to Bridie Lonie for information on the Women's Gallery.

31   Jane Nicole Le Marquand, '"I'm not a woman writer, but …": Gender Matters in New Zealand Women's Short Fiction 1975–1995', PhD thesis, Massey University, 2006, pp.2–3, 10.

32   'Edmond, Lauris', www.bookcouncil.org.nz/writers/edmondl.html (accessed 30 April 2012).

33   'Hulme, Keri', www.bookcouncil.org.nz/writers/hulmek.html (accessed 30 June 2015).

34   Rosemary Seymour, 'Women's Studies: What For? What Now? What Next?', in Rosemary Seymour (ed.), *Research Papers '79: Women's Studies*, Papers of Women's Studies Association Conference, University of Waikato, 29 August–1 September 1979, pp.158–59.

35   Ibid., p.159.

36   *Women's Studies Association Conference Papers '80*, Women's Studies Association, Auckland, pp.137–44, 6–16.

37   Aroha Harris, *Hīkoi: Forty Years of Māori Protest*, Huia, Wellington, 2004, p.60.

38   Penelope Carrol, 'Will the keepers of marae culture remain silent? Biculturalism and Gender in Aotearoa', *New Zealand Herald,* 11 February 1997.

39   Donna Awatere, 'Walking on Eggs', in Sue Kedgley and Mary Varnham (eds), *Heading Nowhere in a Navy Blue Suit and other Tales from the Feminist Revolution*, Daphne Brasell Associates, Wellington, 1993, p.123.

40   Ngahuia Te Awetokutu, *Mana Wahine Maori: Selected Writings on Maori Women's Art, Culture and Politics*, New Women's Press, Auckland, 1991, pp.52–59.

41   Ibid.

42   Harris, *Hīkoi*, pp.78–87.

43   'Kete Aronui – Merata Mita', www.nzonscreen.com/title/kete-aronui-merata-mita-2007 (accessed 10 April 2012).

44   'Merata Mita Director, Writer, Producer [Ngāti Pikiao, Ngāi Te Rangi]', www.nzonscreen.com/person/merata-mita/biography (accessed 10 April 2012).

45   Trevor Richards, *Dancing On Our Bones: New Zealand, South Africa, Rugby and Racism*, BWB, Wellington, 1999, p.183.

46   Donna Awatere Huata, *My Journey*, Seaview Press, Auckland, 1996, p.64.

47   Jillian Dempster, 'The Women's Stand: A Study of the Participation of Women in the 1981 Springbok Tour Protest Movement', BA Hons dissertation, University of Otago, 1992, p.13.

48   Ibid., pp.16, 60.

49   Richards, *Dancing on our Bones*, p.208.

50   Sandra Coney, 'Women Against the Tour', *Broadsheet*, September 1981, p.9.

51   Marvin Allan, 'Women and the Tour', unpublished essay, pp.24–25, cited in Dempster, 'The Women's Stand', p.75.

52   Gay Simpkin, 'Women for Aotearoa: Feminism and Maori Sovereignty', *Hecate*, 20, 2 (October 1994), p.226, http://go.galegroup.com/ps/i.do?id=GALE%7CA16490499&v=2.1&u=otago&it=r&p=AONE&sw=w&asid=80c01773057142de056ed763a7a466ed (accessed 21 June 2014).

53   Donna Awatere, *Maori Sovereignty*, Broadsheet, Auckland, 1984, p.9.

54   Ibid., p.92.

55   'Iritana Tawhiwhirangi', http://gg.govt.nz/node/2738 (accessed 10 April 2012).

56   Richard S. Hill, *Maori and the State: Crown–*

Maori Relations in New Zealand/Aotearoa, VUP, Wellington, 2009, p.196.

57 Tania Rei and Carra Hamon, 'Te Kohanga Reo 1982', in Else (ed.), *Women Together*, pp.40–42.

58 Elizabeth Murchie, *Rapuora: Health and Maori Women*, Maori Women's Welfare League, Wellington, 1984, p.11.

59 *New Zealand Woman's Weekly*, 16 May 1983, p.6.

60 *New Zealand Woman's Weekly*, 11 March 1985, pp.18–19.

61 Murchie, *Rapuora*, p.12.

62 *New Zealand Woman's Weekly*, 26 December 1983, p.6.

63 *New Zealand Women's Weekly*, 10 February 1986, pp.56–57.

64 Koro Wetere, 'Foreword', in Murchie, *Rapuora*, p.5.

65 The THAW Collective, 'The Health Alternatives for Women, 1980', in Else (ed.), *Women Together*, pp.281–83.

66 Susan Wells, *Our Bodies Ourselves and the Work of Writing*, Stanford University Press, CA, 2010, pp.2–3.

67 Christine Dann, *Up From Under: Women and Liberation in New Zealand, 1970–1985*, BWB, Wellington, 1985, p.87.

68 Sandra Coney, 'Health Organisations', in Else (ed.), *Women Together*, p.251.

69 Joan Donley and Brenda Hinton, 'New Zealand Home Birth Association 1978', in Else (ed.), *Women Together*, pp.278–81.

70 On the La Leche League, see Louise Shaw, *Latching On: 50 Years of Breastfeeding Support: La Leche League in New Zealand 1964–2014*, La Leche League of New Zealand, Porirua, 2014.

71 Richardson, *Making a Difference*, p.28.

72 McCallum, *Women in the House*, 1993, p.162.

73 'Convention on the Elimination of All Forms of Discrimination against Women', www.un.org/womenwatch/daw/cedaw/text/econvention.htm (accessed 13 April 2012).

74 *New Zealand Herald*, 3 and 4 May, 1984, cited in Raewyn Dalziel, 'A Century of Suffrage Ends: 1984 and 1993', Women's Suffrage Commemorative Lecture, University of Otago, 19 September 2010. I am grateful to Emeritas Professor Dalziel for permission to draw extensively on her lecture for this discussion.

75 Margaret Wilson, 'Women and the Labour Party', in Margaret Clark (ed.), *The Labour Party After 75 Years*, Occasional Paper No. 4, Department of Politics, Victoria University of Wellington, 1992, pp.46–47.

76 McCallum, *Women in the House*, p.163.

77 Mary O'Regan in interview with Mary Varnham, 'Daring or Deluded? A Case Study in Feminist Management', in Rosemary Du Plessis, *Feminist Voices: Women's Studies Texts for Aotearoa/New Zealand*, OUP, Auckland, 1992, pp.197–98.

78 Ibid., p.198.

79 Jane Westaway, 'The Ministry of Women's Affairs: Do We Really Need It?', *New Zealand Woman's Weekly*, 24 March 1986, pp.6–7.

80 McCallum, *Women in the House*, p.143.

81 O'Regan, 'Daring or Deluded?', in Du Plessis, *Feminist Voices*, p.203.

82 Westaway, 'The Ministry of Women's Affairs: Do We Really Need It?', p.6.

83 Dalziel, 'A Century of Suffrage Ends', p.3.

84 *Zealandia*, 9 December 1984, p.9.

85 Marilyn Pryor, 'A Funny Thing Happened … An Alternative Report on the 1984 Women's Forums', typescript, Hocken Library, p.1.

86 Dalziel, 'A Century of Suffrage Ends', p.13.

87 Carolyn Moynihan, 'Move Over, Comrade Biryukova', *Zealandia*, 4 December 1983, p.2.

88 'New Zealand First Report to the United Nations General Secretary under Article 18 of the Convention on the Elimination of All Forms of Discrimination Against Women', www.women.govt.nz/sites/public_files/nz-cedaw-1986.pdf (accessed 2 October 2015).

89 Rickie Solinger, *Beggars and Choosers: How the Politics of Choice Shapes Adoption, Abortion and Welfare in the United States*, Hill & Wang, New York, 2001, p.220.

90 McCallum, *Women in the House*, pp.143–45.

91 Dalziel, 'A Century of Suffrage Ends', p.3.

92 Chris Brickell, *Mates and Lovers: A History of Gay New Zealand*, Random House, Auckland, 2008, pp.267, 290.

93 Jacqueline O'Neill, '"She Asked For It": A Textual Analysis of the Negotiation of the Meaning of Rape in the 1970s–1980s', MA thesis, Massey University, 2005, p.27.

94 Alexis Harvey and Mary Moon, 'National Collective of Rape Crisis and Related Groups of Aotearoa 1986', in Else (ed.), *Women Together*, p.147.

95 Jacqueline O'Neill, '"She Asked For It"', pp.156–57.

96 McCallum, *Women in the House*, p.108.

97 Jacqueline O'Neill, 'Men's Violence Against Wives and Partners: The State and Women's Experience, 1960–1984', PhD thesis, Massey University, 2012, p.340–41.

98 'Women's Self Defence Network – Wāhine Toa', www.wsdn.org.nz (accessed 16 June 2015).

99 O'Neill, '"She Asked for It"', p.90.

100 *Broadsheet*, May 1984, p.11.

101 *Metro*, September 1984, p.187.

102 A. K. Grant, 'The Silencing of "Uncle Scrim"', *New Zealand Listener*, 28 April 1984, p.29.

103 Carroll Wall, 'The New Feminism?', *Metro*, July 1984, p.109.

104 *New Zealand Woman's Weekly*, 19 March 1984, p.4.

105 Ibid., pp.4–6.

106 Elsie Locke, *Peace People: A History of Peace Activities in New Zealand*, Hazard Press, Christchurch, 1992, pp.176–77.

107 Jan Jordan, 'Women, Rape and the Police Reporting Process', *British Journal of Criminology*, 41 (2001), p.681; W. Young, *Rape Study, Vol. 1: A Discussion of Law and Practice*, Department of Justice and Institute of Criminology, Wellington, 1983.

108 J. Petterson, *Submissions to the Minister of Justice on the Rape Study*, Department of Justice, Wellington, 1983, p.2.

109 Connie Purdue, in Robyn Rowland (ed.), *Women Who Do and Women Who Don't Join the Women's Movement*, Routledge & Kegan Paul, London, 1984, pp.185–91.

110 O'Neill, '"She Asked for It"', pp.130–37.

111 Julie Glamuzina, *Out Front: Lesbian Political Activity in Aotearoa 1962 to 1985*, Lesbian Press, Hamilton, 1993, p.44.

112 McCallum, *Women in the House*, p.181.

113 Laurie Guy, *Worlds in Collision: The Gay Debate in New Zealand, 1960–1986*, VUP, Wellington, 2002.

114 Brickell, *Mates and Lovers*, p.349.

115 Carolyn Moynihan, *A Stand for Decency: Patricia Bartlett & The Society for the Promotion of Community Standards, 1970–1995*, The Society for the Promotion of Community Standards, Wellington, 1995, p.128.

116 Ibid., pp.128, 130; Guy, *Worlds in Collision*, p.124.

117 Guy, *Worlds in Collision*, p.208.

Chapter 13

1 Sandra Coney, *The Unfortunate Experiment: The Full Story Behind the Inquiry into Cervical Cancer Treatment*, Penguin, Auckland, 1988, p.17.

2 'Our History', www.womens-health.org.nz/about-us/our-history (accessed 6 August 2015).

3 Linda Bryder, *The Rise and Fall of National Women's Hospital*, AUP, Auckland, 2014, p.1.

4 Donna Chisholm, 'Exclusive interview NZ's First Test Tube Baby Turns 25', www.fertilityassociates.co.nz/Downloads/North-and-South_IVF-children-research_RF-and-FG_11.aspx (accessed 26 June 2015).

5 Bryder, *The Rise and Fall of National Women's Hospital*, p.113.

6 Donna Chisholm, 'Exclusive Interview NZ's First Test Tube Baby Turns 25'.

7 Bryder, *The Rise and Fall of National Women's Hospital*, p.114. See also the forthcoming analysis of the history of infertility and its treatment in New Zealand since 1945 by Jane Adams, PhD student in History, University of Otago.

8 Robyn Hewland, 'From Hats, Gloves and Brandy Snaps to Sexual Abuse', in Jill McIlraith (ed.), *The Goods' Train Doctors: Stories of Women Doctors in New Zealand, 1920–1993*, New Zealand Medical Women's Association, Dunedin, 1999, p.46.

9 Dorothy Page, *Anatomy of a Medical School: A History of Medicine at the University of Otago 1875–2000*, University of Otago Press, Dunedin, 2008, p.256.

10 'Story: Primary health care', www.teara.govt.nz/en/photograph/31527/hot-and-cold-doctor-file (accessed 28 July 2015).

11 Christine Dann, *Up From Under: Women and Liberation in New Zealand 1970–1985*, A&U/Port Nicholson Press, Wellington, 1985, p.87. See chapter 5 for a discussion of feminist health initiatives.

12 S. Coney and P. Bunkle, 'An "Unfortunate Experiment" at National Women's', *Metro*, June 1987, pp.47–65.

13 S. R. Cartwright, *The Report of the Committee of Inquiry into Allegations Concerning the Treatment of Cervical Cancer at National Women's Hospital and into Other Related Matters*, Government Printing Office, Auckland, 1988, p.117.

14   Ibid., pp.140–41.

15   Quoted in Coney, *The Unfortunate Experiment*, p.6.

16   Charlotte Paul, 'The New Zealand Cervical Cancer Study: Could It Happen Again?', *British Medical Journal*, 297 (20–27 August 1988), p.537.

17   'History', www.hdc.org.nz/about-us/history (accessed 15 October 2015).

18   Joanna Manning and Ron Paterson, 'New Zealand's Code of Patients' Rights', in Joanna Manning (ed.), *The Cartwright Papers: Essays on the Cervical Cancer Inquiry 1987–88*, BWB, Wellington, 2009, pp.150–69.

19   Valerie Redshaw, *Tact and Tenacity: New Zealand Women in Policing*, Grantham House in association with the New Zealand Police, Wellington, 2006, p.120.

20   Susan Butterworth, *More Than Law and Order: Policing a Changing Society 1945–1992*, University of Otago Press, Dunedin, 2005, p.163.

21   Jacqueline Marie O'Neill, 'Men's Violence against Wives and Partners: The State and Women's Experience, 1960–1984', PhD thesis, Massey University, 2011.

22   Ibid., pp.337–41.

23   Marilyn Waring, *Women, Politics and Power*, A&U/Port Nicholson Press, Wellington, 1985, p.56.

24   Butterworth, *More Than Law and Order*, p.293.

25   Margaret Bazley, *Report of the Commission of Inquiry into Police Conduct*, p.11, www.parliament.nz/resource/0000055162 (accessed 5 August 2015).

26   'Men jailed for Mt Maunganui pack rape', www.nzherald.co.nz/nz/news/article.cfm?c_id=1&objectid=10339317 (accessed 5 August 2015).

27   Louise Nicholas with Philip Kitchin, *My Story*, Random House, Auckland, 2014.

28   Redshaw, *Tact and Tenacity*, p.201.

29   Gail Gibson, 'The New Zealand National Women's Consultative Committee', paper presented at the Australian Criminology Conference, First Australasian Women Police Conference, Sydney, 29–31 July 1996, www.aic.gov.au/media_library/conferences/policewomen/gibson.pdf (accessed 14 October 2015).

30   Prue Hyman, *Women in the CIB*, New Zealand Police, Wellington, 2000, p.16, http://nzpca.co.nz/wp-content/uploads/2014/04/women-in-cib.pdf (accessed 15 October 2015).

31   Ibid., pp.1–3.

32   John Pask, 'Submission on the Report of the Working Group on Equal Employment Opportunities and Equal Pay', Wellington, October 1988, p.27, www.lawsociety.org.nz/about-nzls/women-in-the-legal-profession/by-the-numbers (accessed 22 July 2015).

33   'The Judges of the High Court', www.courtsofnz.govt.nz/about/high/judges/#the-honourable-justice-goddard1995 (accessed 17 July 2015).

34   Jennifer Curtin and Marian Sawer, 'Gender Equity in the Shrinking State: Women and the Great Experiment', in F. Castles, R. Gerritsen and J. Vowles (eds), *The Great Experiment: Labour Parties and the Public Policy Transformation in Australia and New Zealand*, AUP, Auckland, 1996, p.157.

35   'Report of the Ministry of Women's Affairs', *AJHR*, 1986–87, Vol. 8, G-39, p.5.

36   Margaret McClure, *A Civilised Community: A History of Social Security in New Zealand 1898–1998*, AUP/DIA, Auckland, 1998, p.211.

37   'Report of the Ministry of Women's Affairs', *AJHR*, 1990–91, Vol. 3, G-39.

38   'How GST affected retail sales in the 1980s', www.stats.govt.nz/browse_for_stats/industry_sectors/RetailTrade/historical-impact-gst-introduction-and-increase-on-retail-sales.aspx (accessed 21 July 2015).

39   'Report of the Ministry of Women's Affairs', *AJHR*, 1986–87, Vol. 8, G-39, pp.5–8.

40   Ibid., p.7.

41   State Services Commission/Te Komihana O Nga Tari Kawanatanga, *Equal Employment Opportunities: Progress in the Public Service* (August 1988), www.ssc.govt.nz/display/document.asp?NavID=127 (accessed 7 August 2015).

42   'Report of the Ministry of Women's Affairs', *AJHR*, 1991–93, Vol. 11, G-39, p.19.

43   For discussion of the implications of the loss of the breadwinner wage, see Nancy Fraser, *Fortunes of Feminism: From State-Managed Capitalism to Neoliberal Crisis*, Verso, London, 2013, pp.111–35.

44   Anne Horsfield, *Women in the Economy: A Research Report on the Economic Position of Women in New Zealand*, Ministry of Women's Affairs, Wellington, 1988, p.234.

45   Anne Horsfield and Miriama Evans, *Maori Women in the Economy*, Ministry of Women's

46 Coalition for Equal Value Equal Pay, *Just Wages: History of the Campaign for Pay Equity 1984–1993*, Coalition for Equal Value Equal Pay, Wellington, 1994, p.8.

47 Report of the Working Group on Equal Employment Opportunities and Equal Pay, *Towards Employment Equity*, The Working Group, Wellington, 1988.

48 Coalition for Equal Value Equal Pay, *Just Wages*, p.53.

49 Ibid., p.62.

50 Ibid., p.64; Denis Welch, *Helen Clark: A Political Life*, Penguin, Auckland, 2009, p.229.

51 *NZPD*, 6 December 1990, Vol. 511, pp.108–11.

52 Coalition for Equal Value Equal Pay, *Just Wages*, p.35.

53 *NZPD*, 6 December 1990, Vol. 511, p.112.

54 Colin James, 'National Party – Shifting rightwards', www.teara.govt.nz/en/photograph/33885/the-mother-of-all-budgets (accessed 10 August 2015); Janet McCallum, *Women in the House: Members of Parliament in New Zealand*, Cape Catley, Wellington, 1993, p.165.

55 McCallum, *Women in the House*, pp.165–66.

56 Department of Statistics and Ministry of Women's Affairs, *Women in New Zealand*, Department of Statistics and Ministry of Women's Affairs, Wellington, 1990, p.18.

57 'Particulars of Urgent Claim', cited in Annie Mikaere, 'Maori Women: Caught in the Contradictions of a Colonized Reality', *Waikato Law Review*, 2 (1994), n.87. See also Ministry of Women's Affairs, *Status of Women in New Zealand, CEDAW Report 1998*, Ministry of Women's Affairs, Wellington, 1998, p.24.

58 'Report of the Ministry of Women's Affairs', 30 June 1997, *AJHR*, 1997, G-39, p.21.

59 K. O'Regan, National MP for Waipa, quoted in Anna Smith, 'Families to the Fore', *Management*, June 1994, p.20, cited in *Mazengarb's Employment Law*, p.3300.3.

60 Sarah Crichton, *Work Patterns after Paid Parental Leave*, Department of Labour and Department of Statistics, Wellington, 2008, p.6, www.stats.govt.nz/browse_for_stats/income-and-work/employment_and_unemployment/LEED-reports/work-patterns-after-paid-parental-leave.aspx (accessed 17 November 2015).

61 Janet Sceats in Dale Williams (ed.), *Looking Back: Moving Forward: The Janus Women's Convention, 2005*, Janus Trust, Masterton, 2006, p.52.

62 Ministry of Women's Affairs, *Status of Women in New Zealand*, p.34.

63 Rosemary Barrington and Alison Gray, *The Smith Women: 100 New Zealand Women Talk About Their Lives*, A. H. & A. W. Reed, Wellington, 1981, p.145.

64 Arthur Watson Savage, 'Paid Parental Leave', www.findlaw.com/12international/countries/nz/articles/2044.html (accessed 10 August 2015).

65 'Report of the Ministry of Women's Affairs', *AJHR*, 1996, G-39, p.18.

66 Joyce Herd, *Cracks in a Glass Ceiling: New Zealand Women, 1975–2004*, New Zealand Federation of Graduate Women (Otago Branch), Dunedin, 2005, p.vii.

67 Matt Morris, 'Unpaid domestic work: Housework and caregiving', *Te Ara: The Encyclopedia of New Zealand*, www.teara.govt.nz/en/unpaid-domestic-work/page-2 (accessed 3 August 2015).

68 Tahu Kukutai, 'Qualitative Interviews on Work-Family Balance', in Williams (ed.), *Looking Back: Moving Forward*, p.60.

69 Sceats in Williams (ed.), *Looking Back: Moving Forward*, p.53.

70 Maraea Rakuraku, 'A Maori Perspective', www.nzonscreen.com/title/once-were-warriors-1994/background#critique_1 (accessed 5 August 2015).

71 Ibid.

72 Paul Stanley Ward, 'A Perspective', www.nzonscreen.com/title/once-were-warriors-1994/background (accessed 14 October 2015).

73 Riwia Brown, 'Writer's Perspective', www.nzonscreen.com/title/once-were-warriors-1994/background#critique_1 (accessed 5 August 2015).

74 'He Pae Arahi, June Jackson', in Amy Brown (ed.), *Mana Wahine: Women Who Show the Way*, Reed Books, Auckland, 1994, p.196.

75 Ibid., pp.196–97.

76 'He Pu Korero, Sandra Lee', in Brown (ed.), *Mana Wahine*, pp.32–39.

77 Ibid., p.36.

78 'Historical Summary', www.sportsground.co.nz/ikaroa/62467 (accessed 22 July 2015).

79 Allan R. Kirk, *Susan Devoy: Squash Champion*, Capital Letters Publishing, Masterton, 2006, p.7.

80 *Suffrage News* (1993); 3 (Dec 1992).

81 Ibid., p.44.

82 *Suffrage News* (1993); 4 (June 1993).

83 In 1992, only 4% of the population sampled knew of Kate Sheppard; by September 1993, the figure had risen to 83%. Andrew Fletcher Consulting, 'Report on Suffrage Centennial Monitor', p.4.

84 Ibid., p.6.

85 'Ripeka Evans', www.stuff.co.nz/sunday-star-times/features/profiles/38628/Ripeka-Evans (accessed 10 August 2015).

86 'Report of the Ministry of Women's Affairs', *AJHR*, 1996, G-39, p.5.

87 Ibid., p.39.

88 Rajeswari Sunder Rajan, *Real and Imagined Women: Gender, Culture and Postcolonialism*, Routledge, London, 1993, p.131.

89 'Report of the Ministry of Women's Affairs', 10 June 1991, *AJHR*, 1991–93, G-39, p.19; 'Report of the Ministry of Women's Affairs', 30 June 1992, *AJHR*, 1991–93, G-39, p.4.

90 Department of Statistics and Ministry of Women's Affairs, *Women*, Wellington, 1999, p.98.

91 Ibid., pp.42, 45, 53.

92 *Auckland Star*, 15 April 1980, cited in Welch, *Helen Clark*, p.46.

93 Mabel Howard and Ruth Richardson had sat on the front bench in Opposition. Elspeth Preddy, *The WEL Herstory: The Women's Electoral Lobby in New Zealand, 1975–2002*, WEL New Zealand, Wellington, 2002, p.18.

94 Welch, *Helen Clark*, p.135.

95 *NZPD*, 1894, Vol. 83, pp.407, 568, 570.

96 Welch, *Helen Clark*, p.98. Emphasis in original.

97 Preddy, *The WEL Herstory*, p.158.

98 Ibid., p.159.

Chapter 14

1 Noah Michelson, 'Lorde, 16-Year-Old New Zealand Musician, Talks "Royals" Video, Feminism And More', www.huffingtonpost.com/2013/07/24/lorde interview_n_3644831.html (accessed 5 June 2015).

2 Martha McKenzie-Minifie, 'National's big push paints Rotorua blue', www.nzherald.co.nz/nz/news/article.cfm?c_id=1&objectid=10537297 (10 January 2015).

3 'Support the police, says Taupo's new MP', www.stuff.co.nz/national/politics/766011 (accessed 10 January 2015).

4 Kate Dickie-Davis, 'Louise Upston: Minister of Girl Power, Post Feminism Backlash and Being a Babe', http://thedailyblog.co.nz/2014/12/01/louise-upston-minister-of-girl-power-post-feminism-backlash-and-being-a-babe (accessed 14 January 2015).

5 Judy McGregor (ed.), *Lifeswork: Celebrating Older Workers in New Zealand*, Dunmore Publishing, Wellington, 2005, p.111.

6 Ibid., p.112.

7 Jacqui Stanford, 'Tahlia and Phillippa's Civil Union', www.gaynz.com/articles/publish/41/article_10258.php (accessed 22 October 2012).

8 'Civil union in New Zealand', http://en.wikipedia.org/wiki/Civil_union_in_New_Zealand (accessed 22 October 2012).

9 'Quilter v. Attorney-General [1998] 1 NZLR 523', www.equalrightstrust.org/ertdocumentbank/Quilter%20v.pdf (accessed 3 March 2015).

10 Sunnivie Brydum, "New Zealand Parliament Considers Adoption by Gays", www.advocate.com/politics/marriage-equality/2012/08/30/new-zealand-parliament-considers-adoption-gays (accessed 3 March 2015).

11 Michele Hewitson, 'Michele Hewitson interview: Louisa Wall', www.nzherald.co.nz/nz/news/article.cfm?c_id=1&objectid=10718092 (accessed 3 March 2015).

12 'Nikki Kaye's marriage equality bill speech', http://yournz.org/2012/08/30/nikki-kayes-marriage-equality-bill-speech (accessed 4 March 2015).

13 Dayna Levy, 'Labour MP: Dump same-sex marriage bill', www.stuff.co.nz/dominion-post/news/politics/7436056/Labour-MP-Dump-same-sex-marriage-bill (accessed 23 October 2012).

14 AccidentalAnarchist, 'Gay marriage, the Samoan community and its hypocrisy', https://polyanarchist.wordpress.com/2012/06/19/gay-marriage-the-samoan-community-and-its-hypocrisy-14 (accessed 23 October 2012).

15 Ibid.

16 Statistics New Zealand, *Fertility of New Zealand Women by Ethnicity Based on the 1996 Census of Population and Dwellings*, Statistics New Zealand, Wellington, 2004, p.10.

17 Report of the United Nations Commission on the Status of Women 2011, https://docs.google.com/viewer?a=v&q=cache:IUDRXcajK9kJ:presbyterian.org.nz/sites/default/files/apw/Report_on_UN_Commission_on_the_Status_of_Women_for_2011 (accessed 24 October 2012).

18 *North and South*, May 2001, p.42.

19 'Helen Woolner', http://teenparentsschools.org.nz/success-story/helen-woolner (accessed 8 August 2015).

20 Ian Pool, Arunachalam Dharmalingam and Janet Sceats, *The New Zealand Family from 1840*, AUP, Auckland, 2007, p.225.

21 Butterworths, *Family Law in New Zealand* (11th edn), Vol. 2, LexisNexis, Wellington, 2003, pp.1281–82.

22 Ministry of Women's Affairs, *Status of Women in New Zealand, CEDAW Report 1998*, Ministry of Women's Affairs, Wellington, 1998, p.73.

23 Ibid., p.71.

24 Judith A. Davey, *Two Decades of Change in New Zealand: From Birth to Death V*, Institute of Policy Studies, VUP, 2003, pp.11–12.

25 Marewa Glover, *Māori Attitudes to Assisted Human Reproduction: An Exploratory Study*, Department of Social and Community Health, University of Auckland, 2008, p.3.

26 Janet Sceats, in Dale Williams (ed.), *Looking Back: Moving Forward. The Janus Women's Convention, 2005*, Janus Trust, Masterton, 2006, p.50.

27 Glover, *Māori Attitudes to Assisted Human Reproduction*, p.4.

28 Joyce Herd, *Cracks in a Glass Ceiling: New Zealand Women, 1975–2004*, New Zealand Federation of Graduate Women (Otago Branch), Dunedin, 2005, p.55.

29 Pool, Dharmalingam and Sceats, *The New Zealand Family from 1840*, p.368.

30 Herd, *Cracks in a Glass Ceiling*, p.12.

31 Colin Trudge, 'Relative Danger: Research Reveals Stepparents Are More Likely to Fatally Abuse Their Children than Biological Parents', report on the research of Marin Daly and Margo Wilson, McMaster University, 1997, *Natural History Magazine*, http://findarticles.com/p/articles/mi_m1134/is_n8_v1066/ai_20147994 (accessed 3 March 2015).

32 'Family structure, context and processes', www.corrections.govt.nz/research/over-representation-of-maori-in-the-criminal-justice-system/3.0-early-life-environmental-influences/3.2-family-structure,-context-and-processes/3.2-3.html (accessed 4 March 2015).

33 Raema Merchant, in 'Who Are Abusing Our Children? An Exploratory Study on Reflections on Child Abuse by Media Commentators', MA thesis, Massey University, 2010, argues that the media encourage the public to believe child deaths are mainly a Māori problem. The thesis has been criticised for using raw numbers and not using rates to estimate the actual numbers of abuse cases by ethnic group.

34 'Sharples horrified at child's alleged abuse', www.stuff.co.nz/national/13239/Sharples-horrified-at-childs-alleged-abuse (accessed 6 March 2015).

35 Erin Polaczuk, 'A Young Women's Experience', in Williams (ed.), *Looking Back: Moving Forward*, p.100.

36 'Fact File – Health Insurance in New Zealand', www.healthfunds.org.nz/pdf/HFANZ_Fact_File_April_2013.pdf (accessed 11 March 2015).

37 Melanie Tebbutt, *Making Ends Meet: Pawnbroking and Working-class Credit*, Methuen, London, 1984; Viviana Zelizer, *The Social Meaning of Money: Pin Money, Paychecks, Poor Relief and Other Currencies*, Princeton University Press, Princeton, 1997.

38 Statistics New Zealand, *Focusing on Women*, Wellington, 2005, p.24.

39 Luisa Avaiki, 'Passion', in Sandra Kailahi, *Pasifika Women: Our Stories in New Zealand*, Reed, Auckland, 2007, pp.68–69.

40 'My Profile', www.lydiako.co.nz/profile (accessed 18 March 2015).

41 '2013 Census – Major ethnic groups in New Zealand', www.stats.govt.nz/Census/2013-census/profile-and-summary-reports/infographic-culture-identity.aspx (accessed 19 March 2015).

42 'Banana in a Nutshell', http://banana-film.com (accessed 27 April 2015).

43 Renee Liang, 'My sister, the film maker', www.nzherald.co.nz/entertainment/news/article.cfm?c_id=1501119&objectid=10714482 (accessed 27 April 2015).

44 Peter Calder, 'Movie Review: *My Wedding and Other Secrets*', www.nzherald.co.nz/entertainment/news/article.cfm?c_id=1501119&objectid=10711715 (accessed 27 April 2015).

45 '2013 Census QuickStats about culture and identity', www.stats.govt.nz/Census/2013-census/profile-and-summary-reports/quickstats-culture-identity/religion.aspx (accessed 15 October 2015).

46 Erich Kolig, 'Muslim Traditions and Islamic Law in New Zealand', in Henry Johnson and Brian Moloughney (eds) *Asia in the Making of New Zealand*, AUP, Auckland, 2006, p.222.

47 Ibid., p.204.

48 'Waikato University honour for Maori language proponent', www.waikato.ac.nz/news-events/media/2011/waikato-university-honour-for-maori-language-proponent2 (accessed 8 October 2015).

49 *Otago Daily Times*, 19 June 1999. For an in-depth discussion of conflicting women's and indigenous rights, see Claire Charters, 'Universalism and Cultural Relativism in the Context of Indigenous Women's Rights', www.victoria.ac.nz/law/centres/nzcpl/publications/human-rights-research-journal/publications/vol-1/Charters.pdf (accessed 20 June 2015); Kerensa Johnston, 'Maori Women Confront Discrimination: Using International Human Rights Law to Challenge Discriminatory Practices', *Indigenous Law Journal*, 4 (2005), pp.31–36, www.hdl.handle.net/1807/17122 (accessed 20 June 2015).

50 John Harre, *Maori and Pakeha: A Study of Mixed Marriages in New Zealand*, Praeger, New York, 1966, p.96. For a recent overview study of intermarriage in New Zealand, see Angela Wanhalla, *Matters of the Heart: A History of Interracial Marriage in New Zealand*, AUP, Auckland, 2013.

51 Carol Archie, *Skin to Skin: Intimate Stories of Maori–Pakeha Relationships*, Penguin, Auckland, 2005, p.20.

52 Ibid., p.22.

53 Statistics New Zealand, *2013 Census: Quick Stats About Culture and Identity*, Statistics New Zealand, Wellington, 2013, p.7.

54 'QuickStats About Culture and Identity', www.stats.govt.nz/Census/2006CensusHomePage/QuickStats/quickstats-about-a-subject/culture-and-identity/ethnic-groups-in-new-zealand.aspx; '2013 Census – Major ethnic groups in New Zealand', www.stats.govt.nz/Census/2013-census/profile-and-summary-reports/infographic-culture-identity.aspx (accessed 16 June 2015).

55 Valeti Finau, in Adrienne Jansen, *I Have in My Arms Both Ways: Migrant Women Talk about their Lives* (new edn), BWB, Wellington, 2015, p.98.

56 Ministry of Social Development, *Whānau Ora: Report of the Taskforce on Whānau-Centred Initiatives*, 2.2.3, p.13, www.msd.govt.nz/documents/about-msd-and-our-work/publications-resources/planning-strategy/whanau-ora/whanau-ora-taskforce-report.pdf (accessed 20 June 2015).

57 *Whānau Ora: Report*, 2.2.6, p.14; Statistics New Zealand, *Focusing on Women*, p.37.

58 'Dulcie Richards', in McGregor (ed.), *Lifework*, pp.115–24.

59 Statistics New Zealand, *Focusing on Women*, p.63.

60 Nina Judar and Melanie Rud, '2013 Anti-Aging Awards: Skin Products', www.goodhousekeeping.com/product-reviews/beauty-products/anti-aging-skin-awards#slide-1; Deborah Boland, 'Look Slim With Shapewear this Summer', www.fabulousafter40.com/look-slim-with-shapewear-this-summer (accessed 22 July 2015); Alina Dizik, '10 Ways You Make Yourself Look Older Without Realizing It', www.womansday.com/style-beauty/beauty-tips-products/hair-color-for-older-women#slide-2 (accessed 4 August 2015).

61 *Otago Daily Times*, 12 February 2015, see www.odt.co.nz/opinion/opinion/332818/how-do-women-age-gracefully (accessed 4 August 2015).

62 'Grumpy Old Women – 50 Shades of Beige', www.eventfinder.co.nz/2014/grumpy-old-women-50-shades-of-beige/hamilton (accessed 5 August 2015).

63 Statistics New Zealand, *Focusing on Women*, p.109.

64 Ibid., p.94.

65 Davey, *Two Decades of Change in New Zealand*, p.161.

66 'Caring Counts', www.hrc.co.nz/eeo/caring-counts-report-of-the-inquiry-into-the-aged-care-workforce (accessed 6 August 2015).

67 Ibid., p.10.

68 Ibid., p.53.

69 Ibid., p.52.

70 Ibid., p.60.

71 Nancy Fraser, 'After the Family Wage: A Postindustrial Thought Experiment', in N. Fraser, *Fortunes of Feminism: From State-*

Managed Capitalism to Neoliberal Crisis, Verso, London, 2013, p.111.

72 Louisa Allen, 'Sexualities: Young people', *Te Ara: The Encyclopedia of New Zealand*, www.teara.govt.nz/en/graph/30862/teenage-pregnancy-international-comparisons (accessed 7 August 2015).

73 Poverty line calculation 'an income level set at 60% of median household disposable income after housing costs is a reasonable level of income to protect people from the worst effects of poverty', from https://nzccss.org.nz/work/poverty/facts-about-poverty (accessed 8 August 2015).

74 Ministry of Social Development, *The 2002 Domestic Purposes and Widow's Benefit Reform: Evaluation Report*, Ministry of Social Development, 2007, p.7, www.msd.govt.nz/about-msd-and-our-work/publications-resources/research/dpb-widows-reform (accessed 10 July 2015).

75 Davey, *Two Decades of Change in New Zealand*, p.82.

76 *North and South*, May 2001, pp.43–44.

77 Ibid., p.44.

78 Ibid.

79 Statistics New Zealand, *Focusing on Women*, p.93.

80 Ibid., p.64.

81 Paul Callister and Judith Galtry, 'Paid Parental Leave in New Zealand: A Short History and Future Options', *Policy Quarterly*, 2, 1 (2006), pp.41–42, http://igps.victoria.ac.nz/publications/files/843decb51aa.pdf (accessed 18 June 2015).

82 Ibid.

83 Jacinta Dalgety, 'Changing Families' Financial Support and Incentives for Working', www.msd.govt.nz/documents/about-msd-and-our-work/publications-resources/evaluation/receipt-working-for-families/wff-full-report.pdf (accessed 16 June 2015).

84 'New Zealand Women', http://mwa.govt.nz/new-zealand-women (accessed 16 June 2015).

85 Lindy Fursman, *Work-Life Balance in New Zealand: A Snapshot of Employee and Employer Attitudes and Experiences*, Department of Labour, Wellington, 2006, www.dol.govt.nz/er/bestpractice/worklife/research/flexibility2006/worklife-full-2006.pdf (accessed 17 June 2015).

86 Ibid., p.17.

87 Herd, *Cracks in a Glass Ceiling*, p.47; Carl Walrond, 'Food shops: Shopping hours', *Te Ara: The Encyclopedia of New Zealand*, www.teara.govt.nz/en/food-shops/page-7 (accessed 18 June 2015).

88 Williams (ed.), *Looking Back: Moving Forward*, p.93.

89 Ibid.

90 Herd, *Cracks in a Glass Ceiling*, p.37.

91 Ibid., pp.44–45.

92 Rebecca Stringer, 'Is New Zealand a Post-Feminist Paradise?', in Claire Freeman and Michelle Thompson-Fawcett (eds), *Living Together: Towards Sustainable Settlements in New Zealand*, University of Otago Press, Dunedin, 2006, p.84.

93 Herd, *Cracks in a Glass Ceiling*, p.31.

94 Statistics New Zealand, *Focusing on Women*, p.53.

95 Vincent Heeringa, 'How Peri Drysdale risked it all to build Untouched World', http://idealog.co.nz/venture/2008/10/peri-possum (accessed 22 June 2015).

96 Ibid.

97 Kim Choe, 'Obama rugs up in Untouched World jumper', www.3news.co.nz/world/obama-rugs-up-in-untouched-world-jumper-2014112817#axzz3RDQbT6N3 (accessed 22 June 2015).

98 Gill South, 'Small business: Women entrepreneurs – Peri Drysdale', www.nzherald.co.nz/business/news/article.cfm?c_id=3&objectid=10850215 (accessed 22 June 2015).

99 Ibid.

100 Herd, *Cracks in a Glass Ceiling*, p.39.

101 Tim Barnett, Catherine Healy, Anna Reed and Calum Bennachie, 'Lobbying for Decriminalization', in Gillian Abel, Lisa Fitzgerald and Catherine Healy, *Taking the Crime out of Sex Work*, The Policy Press, Bristol, 2010, p.61.

102 Ibid., p.67.

103 Bridget Kendall, 'Ask NZ Prime Minister Helen Clark', http://news.bbc.co.uk/2/hi/talking_point/3053141.stm (accessed 25 June 2015).

104 Gillian Abel, Lisa Fitzgerald and Cherlyn Brunton, *The Impact of the Prostitution Law Reform Act on the Health and Safety of Sex Workers*, report to the Prostitution Law Review Committee, 2007, p.172, www.

otago.ac.nz/christchurch/otago018607.pdf (accessed 26 June 2015).

105 Catherine Healy, Calum Bennachie and Anna Reed, 'History of the New Zealand Prostitutes' Collective', in Abel, Fitzgerald and Healy, *Taking the Crime out of Sex Work*, p.52. Coney quote p.54.

106 Gillian Abel and Lisa Fitzgerald, 'Introduction', in Abel, Fitzgerald and Healy, *Taking the Crime out of Sex Work*, p.5.

107 Newsweek/The Daily Beast, 'The Best and Worst Places for Women', www.thedailybeast.com/articles/2011/09/18/best-and-worst-countries-for-women-from-iceland-to-the-u-s-to-pakistan-and-afghanistan.html (accessed 29 June 2015).

108 Caitlin Moran, *How to be a Woman*, Ebury Press, London, 2011, p.173.

109 Ministry of Women's Affairs, *CEDAW Report: New Zealand's seventh report on its implementation of the United Nations Convention on the Elimination of all Forms of Discrimination against Women, March 2006–March 2010*, p.42, www.women.govt.nz/sites/public_files/cedaw-2010.pdf (accessed 2 October 2015).

110 Jim Rolfe, 'Armed forces: Non-military tasks', *Te Ara: The Encyclopedia of New Zealand*, www.teara.govt.nz/en/armed-forces/page-5 (accessed 14 October 2015).

111 'Programmes and Activities of the Council of Women World Leaders', www.undp.org/content/undp/en/home/operations/leadership/administrator/biography.html (accessed 5 August 2015).

112 'Programs and Activities of the Council of Women World Leaders', www.unfoundation.org/features/Programs-Activities.html (accessed 5 August 2015).

113 'Helen Clark', www.undp.org/content/undp/en/home/operations/leadership/administrator/biography.html (accessed 6 August 2015).

114 Colin James, 'My politician of the year – Greens' Steel Magnolia', www.nzherald.co.nz/opinion/news/article.cfm?c_id=466&objectid=10482891 (accessed 6 August 2015).

115 *Whānau Ora: Report*, 2.4.2, p.19.

116 *Whānau Ora: Report*, 2.4.4, p.19.

117 *Whānau Ora: Report*, 4.2.2, pp.28–30.

118 'Dr Parmjeet Parmar', www.national.org.nz/team/mps/detail/parmjeet.parmar (accessed 10 August 2015).

119 Emma Howard, 'Bring back our girls: global protests over abduction of Nigerian schoolgirls', www.theguardian.com/world/2014/may/07/bring-back-our-girls-global-protests-abduction-nigerian-schoolgirls (accessed 10 August 2015).

120 Rachel Morton, 'New Zealanders support Bring Back Our Girls campaign', www.3news.co.nz/nznews/new-zealanders-support-bring-back-our-girls-campaign-2014051418 - axzz3RTzxEY51 (accessed 10 August 2015).

121 'Wellington Young Feminists', www.facebook.com/wellingtonyoungfeminists; 'Kiwi Mummy Blogs', www.kiwimummyblogs.co.nz; 'Advocacy Report October 2012' greypower.co.nz/wp-content/uploads/2012/03/Advocacy-full-report-Oct-2012.docx (both accessed 11 August 2015).

122 'About', http://thehandmirror.blogspot.co.nz/p/about.html (accessed 12 August 2015).

123 Moran, *How to be a Woman*, p.254.

124 Andrew Unterberger, 'Lorde "Royals" Lyrics Analysis: Will Becoming "Royal" Come Back to Haunt Her?', http://popdust.com/2013/09/12/lyrics-analysis-will-becoming-a-royal-herself-come-back-to-haunt-lorde (accessed 12 August 2015).

125 Phil Taylor, 'Interview with Eleanor Catton', www.nzherald.co.nz/lifestyle/news/article.cfm?c_id=6&objectid=11127814 (accessed 12 August 2015).

126 Ross Brighton, 'Catton, Criticism and the Great Cringe', http://pantograph-punch.com/post/catton-criticism-and-the-great-cringe (accessed 12 August 2015).

127 Michael Morrissey, 'Review of *The Luminaries*', www.investigatemagazine.co.nz/Investigate/4573/book-review-the-luminaries-by-eleanor-catton (accessed 13 August 2015). *The Times* reviewer also noted her physical qualities. See 'All that Glitters: Gender Politics and the Case for Catton', http://wordsatwerk.com/2013/10/18/all-that-glitters-gender-politics-and-the-case-for-catton (accessed 13 August 2013).

128 Charlotte Higgins. 'Eleanor Catton: "Male writers get asked what they think, women what they feel"', www.theguardian.com/books/2013/oct/16/eleanor-catton-male-writers-female-luminaries-booker-2013

(accessed 14 August 2015).

129 Siobhan Downes, 'Radio host Sean Plunket stands by calling Eleanor Catton a "hua"', www.stuff.co.nz/entertainment/books/65493542/radio-host-sean-plunket-stands-by-calling-eleanor-catton-a-hua (accessed 14 August 2015).

130 'FAQs', www.slutwalktoronto.com/about/faqs (accessed 9 August 2015).

131 Kirsty Johnston and Victoria Robinson, 'Hundreds of Kiwis protest in SlutWalk', www.stuff.co.nz/national/5193174/Hundreds-of-Kiwis-protest-in-SlutWalk (accessed 9 August 2015).

132 Brendan Manning, 'Roast Busters: Protests today aim to "bust rape culture"', www.nzherald.co.nz/nz/news/article.cfm?c_id=1&objectid=11158233 (accessed 9 August 2015).

133 Lynley Bilby, 'Catton criticises CK Stead on Roast Busters comments', www.nzherald.co.nz/lifestyle/news/article.cfm?c_id=6&objectid=11158459 (accessed 13 August 2015).

134 Ibid.

135 Independent Police Conduct Authority, *Report on the Police's handling of the alleged offending by 'Roastbusters'*, p.15, www.ipca.govt.nz/Site/media/2015/2015-Mar-19-Roastbusters-.aspx (accessed 13 August 2015).

136 Andrea O'Neil, 'Beauty pageants great for women – minister', www.stuff.co.nz/national/politics/63676478/beauty-pageants-great-for-women--minister; http://mwa.govt.nz (both accessed 14 August 2015).

137 'Default Calendar', www.breakingboundaries.org.nz/forum/calendar.php (accessed 19 August 2015).

138 'Factsheet # 9: Are there gender differences in achievement rates?', www.nzqa.govt.nz/qualifications-standards/qualifications/ncea/understanding-ncea/the-facts/factsheet-9 (accessed 25 August 2015). Between 2001 and 2006, degree completions by New Zealand women outnumbered those of men by 56%: James Newell and Paul Callister, 'The Gender Transition in Tertiary Education in New Zealand and Australia', paper presented at the Australian Population Conference, Alice Springs, 2008, p.2.

139 Newell and Callister, 'The Gender Transition', p.3.

140 Hannah August, *No Country for Old Maids? Talking about the 'Man Drought'*, BWB, Wellington, 2015, pp.82–84.

141 Michael Cropp, 'Gender wage gap pervasive', www.radionz.co.nz/news/national/266103/gender-wage-gap-pervasive (accessed 9 August 2015).

142 'Gender Pay Gap', http://women.govt.nz/our-work/utilising-womens-skills/income/gender-pay-gap (accessed 9 August 2015).

143 Fraser, 'After the Family Wage', p.134.

144 Marilyn Waring, *Counting for Nothing*, Allen & Unwin, Wellington, 1988.

145 Margaret Wilson, 'The Challenges Facing Women in the 21st Century', Suffrage Lecture, University of Otago, September 2013, p.10.

146 Ibid., p.8. See *Service and Food Workers Union Nga Ringa Tota Inc v Terranova Homes and Care Ltd* [2013], New Zealand Employment Court, p.157.

147 'Gender: How does New Zealand's legal profession compare', www.lawsociety.org.nz/lawtalk/issue-868/gender-how-does-new-zealands-legal-profession-compare (accessed 9 August 2015); in 2008, 3.2% of doctors identified themselves as Māori and only 1.8 as Pacific Island: Allison Kirkman, 'Health practitioners: Māori and Pacific health practitioners', Te Ara: The Encyclopedia of New Zealand, www.teara.govt.nz/en/health-practitioners/page-6 (accessed 9 August 2015).

148 'Women in Engineering: Snapshot 2015', www.ipenz.org.nz/ipenz/forms/pdfs/2013Snapshot-HiRes.pdf (accessed 9 August 2013).

149 Ministry of Women's Affairs, *Women in Trades: Interviews with Employers and Tradeswomen*, Ministry of Women's Affairs, Wellington, 2011, p.3.

150 Jo O'Brien, 'Maori nurses "paid significantly less"', www.radionz.co.nz/news/te-manu-korihi/281009/maori-nurses-suffering-a-pay-gap (accessed 10 August 2015).

151 'Gender: How does New Zealand's legal profession compare'.

152 'Teacher Census 2004', www.educationcounts.govt.nz/publications/schooling/teacher_census (accessed 10 August 2015).

Index